THE HANDBOOK FOR

WORLD ACCESS

CITIZENS OF THE EARTH

KATHRYN & ROSS PETRAS

MAPS BY BEKI

A Fireside Book   Published by Simon & Schuster   New York   London   Toronto   Sydney   Tokyo   Singapore

FIRESIDE
Rockefeller Center
1230 Avenue of the Americas
New York, NY 10020

Copyright © 1996 by Kathryn Petras and Ross Petras

All rights reserved, including the right of reproduction
in whole or in part in any form.

FIRESIDE *and colophon are registered trademarks*
of Simon & Schuster Inc.

EDITORIAL ASSISTANCE PROVIDED BY K&N BOOKWORKS
DESIGNED BY BARBARA MARKS

Manufactured in the United States of America

2 4 6 8 10 9 7 5 3 1

Library of Congress Cataloging-in-Publication Data

Petras, Kathryn.
    World access / Kathryn & Ross Petras.
        p.   cm.
    Includes index.
    1. World history.   I. Petras, Ross.   II. Title
D23.P46   1996
909—dc20   95-42925 CIP

ISBN 0-684-81479-X
ISBN 0-684-81016-6 (pbk.)

Pages 641–42 represent an extension of this copyright page.

CONTENTS

INTRODUCTION

This book is about the culture, history, and politics of the world outside the borders of the United States of America. It includes some of what an educated citizen of the world should or might want to know. The days when the well-educated person needed to know just a bit about Broadway plays, Impressionist paintings, and classical music to sound cultured and knowledgeable are over. In 1995 more than seventeen million Americans traveled overseas—just as a record number of Mexicans, Haitians, Russians, Arabs, and Asians entered our borders. So the nineties are about a global mind-set. At today's gatherings you're more likely to be talking about the Dalai Lama than *Hello, Dolly!*

To use a cliché, the world is truly becoming a global village . . . but just as our interest is increasing, our ignorance is beginning to show. To add to that cliché: if the world is a global village, then many Americans are lost on the outskirts of town with no idea which way to turn.

This is why we've written this book. It provides readers with information about the great thinkers, writers, artists, and politicians of cultures other than our own—the philosophies, revolutions, political and artistic movements that changed the world—that many of us know little (if anything) about. We're forgetting even the basics of European culture, let alone learning anything about Africa, Asia, and Latin America. Today we know more about

trivia than great literature, more about the *Beverly Hillbillies* than the great classics of China—not to mention the classics of Europe.

This book is a blueprint to what's *important* about the world around us, what we need to know and what we should know to read the newspapers, to meet with foreign businesspeople, to understand what is happening elsewhere, to travel abroad, to sound tuned-in or, more important, to begin to *be* tuned-in. In short, it's what we need to understand the world culture of the nineties.

Packed with lists, capsule histories, charts, brief chronologies, and eclectic biographies, *World Access* is a kaleidoscope of world history and culture, a browser's guide that, in a readable format, communicates the essentials as well as, even more important, the connections among us all.

HOW TO USE THIS BOOK

This book is unique. At least we think so. We were inspired to write it because a while back we wanted a sort of world cultural almanac and couldn't find one. For the first time you'll be able to have a broad range of information about history, culture, current events, and political issues in one place. *World Access* covers cultures and countries other than the United States—both the East and the West, from Africa to Europe to the Middle East to the Far East, and, in so doing, it takes you from ancient times to the present.

Frankly, that's a lot of material to cover, but we've made it as easy for you to read as possible by arranging the book in a modular and accessible format.

The book is divided into ten main sections:

- History of the World
- Philosophy of the World
- Religions of the World
- Art and Architecture of the World
- Literature of the World
- Drama and Film of the World
- Music of the World
- Languages of the World
- Political Geography of the World
- Politics of the World.

Each chapter opens with a brief introduction and a table of contents to further help you pinpoint the information you want to read. And in each of the major sections you'll find a wide range of information broken down into smaller, bite-size units that give you the essentials—and, often, a few facts that you don't need to know but might find interesting.

For example, *History of the World* as a whole takes you from ancient cultures to the twentieth century. It is broken down into smaller sections on the major cultures of the past, from the Sumerians to modern-day China, with everything in between. But beyond this, it includes spotlights on some of

the most important events in history—the key people, the key movements, the key wars—that changed the world. It is, in effect, a crash course on the history of the world—everything (well, almost everything) you need to know.

We chose to begin with history and then move on to philosophy and the other sections because this order seemed the most logical and conducive to learning. Each section in many ways springs from the one preceding it. History gives you the groundwork, and philosophy and religion the mind-set, to understand the arts and literatures of the world. With languages, you're ready to see the world as it is today. And so we go on to describe the *current* politics of the world—the stuff of TV news and newspapers. Throughout this book, we've used B.C.E. (before the common era) and C.E. (of the common era).

That said, this book is too long and too packed with information to be read linearly, page by page. Think of it more as a rough guide to world culture, to be picked up when an obscure reference comes on the TV or is found in a paragraph of a book. You can and should flip back and forth to get a better idea of all aspects of the person, idea, or object you are interested in learning about. Our idea is to show the connections among cultures and across time. The world is a very diverse place, but ultimately we all share much more than we sometimes think.

CONTENTS

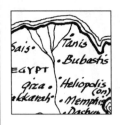

HISTORY OF THE WORLD

 Henry Ford of Ford Motor Co. once said, "History is more or less bunk," which is hardly a good recommendation for this section. Worse yet, many people today would probably agree with him, judging from the woeful state of historic knowledge.

But it is better to listen to the ancient Greek Polybius, who had a better idea of history:

For it is history alone, without involving us in actual danger, that will mature our judgment and prepare us to take right views, whatever may be the crisis or the posture of affairs.

It's easy to overgeneralize in statements like that, but to a degree history does provide guideposts to human conduct. The lessons are often subtle, and the means of applying those lessons are sometimes difficult to find, but history does give us a better understanding of how to live today.

But where to start? With some basic facts, with an overview of the massive sweep of human endeavors. That's what this section is—an *introduction,* a brief overview of the high and low points of human history around the planet. It starts at the beginning of recorded history, with the first cultures that developed a system of writing (even if we can't read what they wrote). And it goes on to give snapshots of the classical Greeks, Romans, Persians, and Indians, and then on to the great medieval cultures and early modern societies. And along the way it stops and goes into detail about a few major wars and seminal movements such as the Renaissance and the Industrial Revolution.

Because world history is such a massive topic, and because the number of pages is so few, it is hard to draw any great lessons that Polybius would like. But there is one that stands out: human history is interconnected.

It is perhaps a cliché to say it—or maybe it sounds politically correct—but human achievement really belongs to everyone, even though one culture or another might seem paramount in a given time. Cultures give and take from one another. When one group does something, another group builds on it. Consider the essential human invention of writing. Writing was probably developed in the ancient Middle East as a picture language. Then a group of people living on the periphery of these Middle Eastern civilizations borrowed two dozen of the symbols and made them represent individual sounds. This was the Ugaritic alphabet. This early alphabet was borrowed and further modified by the ancient Greeks, who added vowel sounds to what was a mostly consonant-based alphabet. It was modified further by the ancient Romans and their successors to the letters we use today. The alphabet was invented not by one culture but by many that borrowed and modified it.

Or take the paper this book is printed on. The idea of paper comes from China (supposedly from a man named Tsai Lun who died in 114 C.E.). It was a closely kept secret until Arab troops took Chinese prisoners in a battle near Samarkand in central Asia. The Arabs learned papermaking, which spread throughout their empire, then on to the West. In turn, the West transmitted to the Chinese and East Asians other ideas written on the paper they had invented.

History is ultimately a recording of the ebb and flow of peoples and ideas—the written story of a heritage we all share.

DEAD (NON-EUROPEAN) WHITE MEN— AND WOMEN: SIX ANCIENT CULTURES THAT PRECEDED GREECE AND ROME

 All right, so what is Western civilization anyway? The story of dead white males?

Not necessarily. Like virtually every other civilization, the West is the product of a tremendous cross-fertilization of peoples and ideas. From the letters and numbers we use every day to the paper we read and the religions we follow, we owe an enormous debt to a great *world* culture. And so we've listed some of the civilizations that preceded the heights of Greece and Rome and were as great—or greater—in their own right. In many cases they helped bring about the later greatness of Greece and Rome . . . and our later greatness.

SUMER

(3200–2300 B.C.E.)
Mesopotamia (modern-day Iraq, along the Tigris and Euphrates rivers)

Who were the Sumerians? Were they the first people to develop a written language? No one will ever know for sure, but the bets are on the Sumerians as the first to put words to paper . . . or, rather, clay.

Much of what we know about the Sumerians comes from their habit of recording economic data and, later, literary and political information on clay tablets in a wedge-shaped writing style called cuneiform. Some archaeologists surmise that Sumerians influenced the ancient Egyptian writing system as well.

But although we can read what they wrote (and if you, too, for some reason want to read Sumerian, the University of Pennsylvania is publishing a giant comprehensive dictionary of Sumerian; the first volume unexpectedly sold out in a day), we don't know as much as we'd like about these people who spoke a language unrelated to any other. In fact, we don't even think they were native to Mesopotamia, today called Iraq.

What we do know is that they built one of the world's first civilizations. They lived in city-states, some of which probably sound familiar: Uruk (the biblical Erech), Ur, Lagash, and Babylon. This culture gave the world a vibrant mythology, including the epic of Gilgamesh, maybe the first epic about the perennial themes of love, friendship, death, and immortality. And tantalizing evidence links the Sumerians to the story of the Great Flood. Unlike the Egyptians, the Sumerians seemed to focus on the here and now rather than an afterlife, and prayed to their gods for favors and fortune.

But no amount of prayers could save them from the Semitic-speaking conquerors from the south (the ancestors of the modern Arabs and Israelis, who

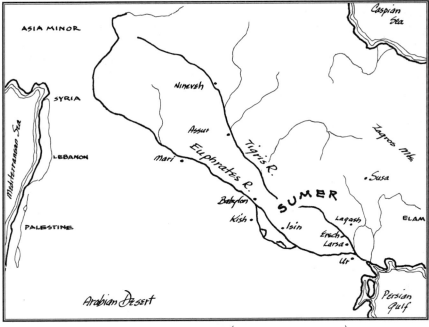

SUMER IN MESOPOTAMIA (MODERN-DAY IRAQ)

speak languages quite similar in structure). Ironically, Sumer was probably unified only in the last days of independence when the last great ruler of the Sumerians, Lugalzaggisi (Ruler of the Lands), conquered most of the city-states. Shortly thereafter, the Sumerians apparently fell to the Semitic-speaking Akkadians. The problem is that this history is still sketchy, and it's hard to be sure how—or even if—the Sumerians were conquered. Some historians prefer to say the Sumerians were *absorbed* by the Akkadian culture, particularly since their language and customs were adopted to a great degree by the new people of the area. The Akkadians and their successors kept on publishing Sumerian dictionaries (in clay, of course) and used the language in formal ritual texts, similar to the Western cultures continuing to use Latin long after the Roman Empire had fallen.

Honors for the first unemployment program go to the Sumerians—who offered support to those temporarily unemployed. They also offered adoption facilities for childless couples.

EGYPT

(3100–343 B.C.E.)
Egypt (along the Nile River and in the Nile delta—expanded into other parts of the Middle East as well)

Egypt is one of the old-timers, an independent kingdom that survived nearly three thousand years with a culture that endured even longer, making virtually any other civilization a young upstart. In ancient Greek and Roman times, Egyptian antiquity was viewed with a mixture of awe and suspicion. Egypt was the land where life and the gods began, where time began.

In fact, the ancient Greek historian Herodotus reported on a somewhat horrible experiment of the day where two young children were kept isolated in a farmhouse away from any spoken language, the idea being to discover their true, natural language. Everyone was sure it would be Egyptian. Unfortunately for the Egyptians, the first word the children uttered was "becos," which was said to be a word from the "Phrygian" language (unknown today but spoken in Asia Minor at the time). So the Egyptians had to concede first place as the birthplace of humanity.

Nevertheless, for generations Egypt was the richest land in the world. Its civilization grew along the banks of the Nile, a relatively beneficent river that each year flooded its banks and brought crop-enhancing silt, making the Nile Valley the richest farmland in the world. This in turn supported the development of a civilization that could afford to bury its rulers in splendor and to erect huge temples to worship its gods. Even today the feeling of awe when confronting Egypt hasn't diminished, perhaps because of the sheer size and majesty of her temples, pyramids, and tombs, and the huge numbers of artifacts.

You can't get near an Egyptian artifact without hearing or reading about dynasties. Egyptian history is divided into manageable portions by them—the period a specific family of pharaohs (kings) ruled the land. Historians count thirty dynasties extending from the first king, Narmer, who unified Egypt somewhere around 3100 B.C.E., to the last independent Egyptian king (or pharaoh), with the tongue-twisting name of Snedjemibre Nectanebo II, who ruled until the Persians conquered in 343 B.C.E.

But to make it easy, historians also divide its history into larger major periods as well. The dates below are of course approximations:

The Old Kingdom (2700–2200 B.C.E.): This is usually considered Egypt's golden age. It is an era of strong rulers and the pyramids, including the Step pyramid of Zoser at Saqqara and the three great pyramids of Giza (of the pharaohs known to the Greeks as Cheops, Chephren, and Mykerinos,

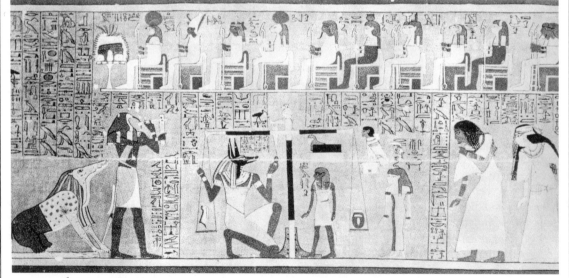

ANCIENT EGYPTIAN WALL PAINTING WITH HIEROGLYPHS—JUDGMENT SCENE IN THE HALL OF OSIRIS (REPRODUCED FROM THE COLLECTIONS OF THE LIBRARY OF CONGRESS)

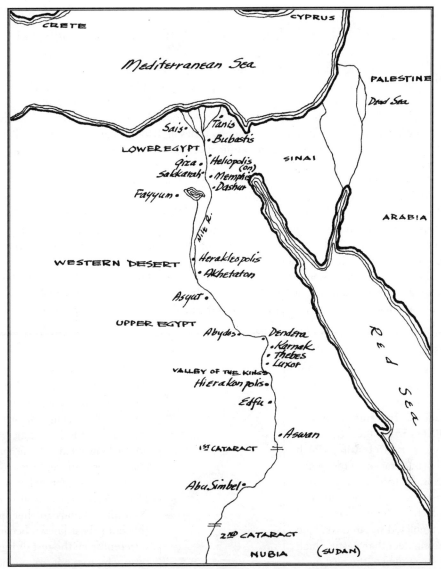

CRETE

CYPRUS

Mediterranean Sea

PALESTINE

Dead Sea

Sais• •*Tanis*
LOWER EGYPT •*Bubastis*
SINAI
Giza• •*Heliopolis*
Sakkarah• (on)
•*Memphis*
•*Dashur*
Fayyum•

ARABIA

Nile R.

WESTERN DESERT •*Herakleopolis*
•*Akhetaton*

Asyut•

UPPER EGYPT

Abydos• *Dendera*
•*Karnak*
•*Thebes*
•*Luxor*

VALLEY OF THE KINGS
Hierakonpolis•

Edfu•

•*Aswan*

1ST CATARACT

R e d   S e a

Abu Simbel•

2ND CATARACT

NUBIA   (SUDAN)

ANCIENT EGYPT—MAJOR CITIES AND TEMPLE AND PYRAMID SITES

and to the Egyptians as Khufu, Khafre, and Menkure). Egyptian literature of the period is confident; the statuary reveals powerful pharaohs with an air of calm control.

The First Intermediate Period (2200–2050 B.C.E.): For various reasons the self-confident Old Kingdom collapsed, and a shadowy period of 150 years of strife and crime ensued.

The Middle Kingdom (2050–1800 B.C.E.): This was a period of reconsolidation. Commoners were promised life after death like the pharaohs, provided they adhered to specific codes of conduct. Pharaohs

The Ultimate Picture Writing: Egyptian Hieroglyphs

The ancient Egyptian writing has fascinated people for centuries. To us it looks complicated and mysterious: a series of small pictures of different kinds of birds, people, and symbols, the ultimate picture writing.

But it's more like our alphabet than it looks. Ancient Egyptian writing involves a system where most of the little pictures actually stand for sounds. It has alphabetic signs (*a, b*, etc.), syllabic signs (*nr, wn*, etc.), as well as other signs called determinative, which are pictures that tell the reader what the other signs refer to.

Hieroglyphs were the formal writing on tombs and temples, but many Egyptian scribes probably had some trouble reading it. Instead, they usually wrote in a cursive script called hieratic that is far removed from the formal hieroglyphics. Hieratic writing looks something like the shorthand systems that were used in many offices. In later times the Egyptians adopted an even more cursive (or scrawling) script called demotic, which is probably one of the most difficult handwriting systems ever invented—at least for modern decipherers. Maybe the Egyptians thought so, too, because not long after the Romans conquered them, they started using modified Greek letters in a new system called Coptic, and hieroglyphs soon died out. In the early 1800s, a Frenchman, Jean-François Champollion, deciphered the ancient system of writing and began the modern science of Egyptology.

lost some of their absolute power; this was a feudal age in which local governors had more power.

The Second Intermediate Period (1800–1550 B.C.E.): Now came another period of strife, which culminated in an invasion of foreigners called Hyksos. In 1552 B.C.E. a young prince named Kamose tried to oust these people from foreign lands; his work was completed by Ahmose, who founded the eighteenth dynasty, which marked the beginning of the next great period of Egyptian history.

The New Kingdom (1550–1200 B.C.E.): This is Egypt's imperial era, packed with names of famous pharaohs, monuments, and royal tombs in the Valley of the Kings and Valley of the Queens. Under the diminutive but great conqueror Thutmose I (an early prototype of Napoleon, only much more successful), much of Palestine and the Levant fell under Egyptian rule.

This is also the era of Akhenaton, who ruled from 1353 to 1335 B.C.E. and who appears in statues and temple reliefs as an odd, elongated-looking man with wide hips, long gawky legs, and a long head. (Some suggest that Akhenaton suffered from some sort of hormonal disorder, which seems quite plausible.) Akhenaton was married to Nefertiti, famous for her beauty. But this era is best known because it is so different from the rest of Egyptian history, which tends to be quite traditional. The art is much freer (a well-known relief shows Akhenaton kissing and playing with his children, something not found anywhere else in Egypt's long history), and the traditional religion was overturned. Instead of the panoply of gods, Akhenaton focused on one—the Sun god, Aton, often represented as a disk. This has led some to claim he was the world's first monotheist. Akhenaton let the temples of the other gods fall into decline, a politically unwise move that didn't last after his death. His successor, Tutankhamen (who ruled from 1364 to 1370), brought back the rest of the Egyptian godly pantheon and reversed Akhenaton's reforms. Tutankhamen is famous for more than this, of course. He was fortunate enough to be entombed in an obscure portion of the Valley of the Kings; his virtually untouched tomb was discovered thousands of years later.

The other key pharaoh of the time was Ramses II, who ruled from 1292 to 1225 B.C.E. and is the bane of the archaeologist. The problem? Tourists and laypeople think more of the man than archaeologists do, mainly because Ramses was an early genius at public relations. He put up hundreds of monuments boasting of his accomplishments, particularly of one famous incident, the battle of Kadesh. Unfortunately for Ramses, the *other* participants in the battle, the Hittites, wrote terse accounts of the battle and the forthcoming treaty. And it turns out that Ramses's great victory was more of a stalemate, and his behavior was probably less than competent. No matter. His name has been immortalized, and his giant monument at Abu Simbel, with four great statues cut into the stone of Upper Egypt, is one of the wonders of the world.

Late Dynastic Period (1150–663 B.C.E.): This is the beginning of Egypt's long decline, as Egyptians increasingly relied on foreign (often Greek) mercenaries and ultimately were conquered by the Persians, then Alexander the Great, then Rome.

The old Egyptian culture entered a final decline with the coming of Chris-

*One of the few words from Ancient Egyptian that we use in English is a word associated with Santa Fe and the southwest—*ADOBE. *The word comes from the Ancient Egyptian word* DJOB'ET, *meaning "sun-dried mud." It passed into Arabic as* TUBA, *or, with a definite article tacked on, as* AL-TUBA. *When the Arabs conquered Spain, the word passed into Spanish as* ADOBE. *And then when the Spanish conquered Mexico, the word came into English, referring to the sun-dried brick houses of the Native Americans.*

tianity, and the Egyptian language entered the Christian liturgy written in Greek characters (with some modifications) and was called Coptic.

THE INDUS CIVILIZATIONS

c. 2500–1500 B.C.E.
Indus Valley, India

On the dusty plains of the Punjab region in India stand the ruins of two very ancient cities of brick, with broad streets, public baths, and an advanced covered sewer system that speaks of a level of comfort and civilization quite advanced for its time. Even the lowliest workmen seemed to live in comfortable two-room brick cottages.

The cities are called Harappa and Mohenjo-Daro (meaning Mound of the Dead), although no one knows what the true names were or who lived there. According to archaeological evidence, this civilization grew wealthy on trade with others as far away as central Asia and Sumer (in fact, some archaeologists speculate that they may have been early Sumerians themselves). But beginning in 2000 B.C.E., it looks as though a dangerous threat to their comfortable way of life was waiting on the horizon, perhaps invaders, with horses and strange new weapons—swords with strengthened midribs and strong copper axes. Could these be the famous Aryan invaders, the speakers of an Indo-European tongue, who swept through India and Europe? It looks that way. Once-spacious houses were subdivided (to accommodate refugees coming in

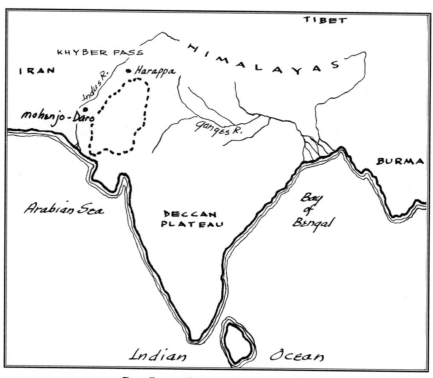

TIBET

KHYBER PASS

IRAN

Indus R.

• Harappa

H I M A L A Y A S

Mohenjo-Daro

Ganges R.

BURMA

Arabian Sea

DECCAN PLATEAU

Bay of Bengal

Indian Ocean

THE EARLY INDUS CIVILIZATIONS

from the hinterlands?), fortress walls were thickened, jewelry was buried, city gates blocked with brick. Finally, it seems that the cities were abandoned, perhaps at the last minute.

A poignant snapshot from the past: in empty Mohenjo-Daro, in the last layer, archaeologists found a small group of huddled skeletons on the steps of a well, possibly stragglers who did not leave in time. Unfortunately for that romantic view, other more prosaic archaeologists believe that the civilization declined gradually, and the last people whose remains were found were squatters rather than the final remnants of a great civilization. But because we can't read their writing (and, more to the point, the surviving inscriptions are very brief) and must rely only on archaeological evidence,

the mystery of the Indus civilizations persists.

AKKAD

(2334 B.C.E.–present)
Mesopotamia (modern-day Iraq, along the Tigris and Euphrates rivers)

When most people think about Iraq, they automatically think about Saddam Hussein and his invasion of Kuwait. But Iraq's history goes far back in time—to the days when it was the site of Akkad and other great Semitic civilizations that were the cradle of Western civilization. Even in the past, though, it has been a battleground

Oil's Long History

The oil industry—and the intrigues and wars surrounding it—is nothing new to the Middle East. As far back as the 'Ubaid people of prehistory natural gas fires, lit by lightning, were worshiped as eternal flames. The Sumerians, Babylonians, and Assyrians used oil and tar by the ton from natural seeps in the ground to line irrigation systems and caulk ships, and as an additive to make bricks more resistant to the elements. But the big oil barons of the day were the Nabateans, who lived in what is today Jordan and Saudi Arabia. They sold their bitumen (an oil substance) to the Egyptians, who used it for various purposes, including mummification, after their supply of resins had run dry. By Cleopatra's time this was a big business, and the intriguing queen managed to pull off a big oil coup of the day when she got the Roman Mark Antony to conquer the oil fields and give them to her. She in turn leased them back to the Nabateans for 200 talents (about $400,000) a year, gaining a guaranteed supply of oil and income for her pursuit of power. Exxon couldn't have done it better.

between numerous different cultures, from the Sumerians to the Akkadians to the Assyrians to the Persians to the Turks and, finally, to the Americans.

Sumer was the first great civilization of the region. But at the height of Sumerian rule, when the great Lugalzaggisi was conquering neighboring city-states, another man rose to conquer him. His name has gone down in history as Sargon, but that means "the true (legitimate) king" and was more of a title. His real name is unknown, but his exploits and perhaps even something of his personality have reverberated through the centuries. There are many stories and folktales of this great king. Some say he was the illegitimate son of a priestess. Another story is similar to that of Moses: he was

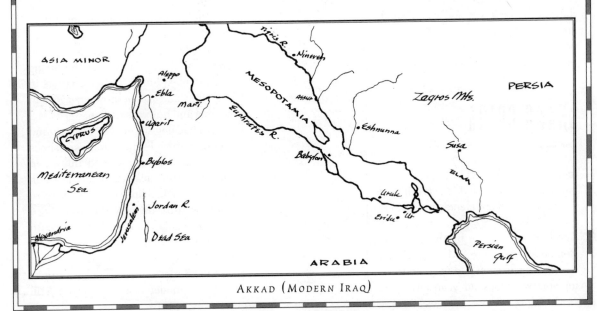

AKKAD (MODERN IRAQ)

found as a baby in a basket among the river rushes. At any rate, in his young adult life he was an ambitious officer of the city of Ur-Zababa. He seized the local throne in a palace revolt and began a long series of conquests and wars, killing the Sumerian ruler Lugalzaggisi and reorganizing society around the capital city of Agade. With his accession to the throne, Semitic-speaking peoples would dominate the Middle East for the next four thousand years, until the present day.

Just who were these Semitic peoples? Their origins are obscure, but they apparently were nomads who immigrated to Sumerian territory and began to adopt the Sumerian sedentary lifestyle. As the Akkadians grew stronger, they agitated and fought to achieve political domination. And when they won, they gradually absorbed the Sumerians into their own culture.

The dynasty Sargon founded ended with his descendant Naram-Sin, and the entire region went through ups and downs of invaders and conquests and reconquests. But the Semitic basis of the Middle East was now established, and today distant relatives of Sargon's people still live and work in Iraq, Israel, and the rest of the Middle East.

SHANG CHINA

(c. 1750–1000 B.C.E.)
Northern China (around the Hwang-he River in northern Henan province)

Another old culture: by the time the Romans ruled the Mediterranean, Chinese civilization had been flourishing for two thousand years. And the

Ancient China, More Ancient Than Ever

While the established view has long been that Chinese civilization began in the Yellow River valley about five thousand to seven thousand years ago, a 1993 discovery may push that date back. The oldest and most completely preserved prehistoric village discovered so far in China was unearthed in Inner Mongolia. Dating back roughly seventy-five hundred years, the village contains pottery fragments, house foundations, funeral objects, jade ornaments, and stone and bone implements that are different from the artifacts previously found.

founders of this long-standing civilization (or at least the *known* founders) were the ancient Shang.

The Shang were unique in their time. Unlike the great hydraulic societies of the Middle East (where people were clustered in great cities and went out to work the fields, which were irrigated in complex systems), Shang society comprised a large group of farming communities dispersed throughout the countryside.

What we know about the history of the Shang state is a bit sketchy. From archaeological evidence discovered from burials, we know that the Shang leaders liked hunting, used chariots in warfare, and apparently engaged in animal and human sacrifice.

Archaeologists have also found many partly burned tortoise shells inscribed with writing and thrown in the fires (the heat cracked the shell, and the cracked lines on the shell were then used for divining the future). So Shang society was one of the first with a developed writing system. They used a writing system that is clearly linked to the Chinese script of today—primitive by modern standards but still clearly well developed. No one has yet discovered how the writing evolved or what it looked like in its earliest stage. (But note that even if the Sumerians were the first to put words to clay, the Chinese most likely *independently* developed writing as well.)

As in Mesopotamia and Egypt, Shang society was hierarchical. At the top were the aristocrats and priests; they lived in royal compounds, supported crafts people and scribes, and maintained stores of food for times of famine. Shang China was probably organized around three hundred separate clans. The clans were ruled by an aristocratic warrior class of leaders who were ruled by a Shang emperor; he had strong control over a central region but much less control over the outlying areas. A list of Shang kings spanning seventeen generations has

been preserved, but interpretations of the list vary.

Religious life centered around ancestor worship. A supreme being, Shang Di, controlled human affairs; human ancestors were intermediaries between God and man, so they were obviously carefully placated.

The Shang dynasty is perhaps best known to art lovers for the beautiful, sometimes frightening, bronze vessels used for sacrifice, often with geometric monster motifs called "ding." Most Shang bronzes were three- or four-legged vessels that could be placed over a fire; the monsters sometimes inscribed on them usually had horns, protruding eyes, and fanged upper jaws. The meaning is unknown: Was it to frighten away evil spirits? Was it symbolic of gluttony? Was it decorative? Or was it used to scare people?

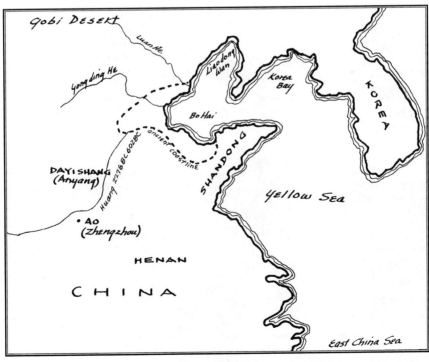

SHANG CHINA

THE HEBREWS

(beginning about 3700 B.C.E. to date)

The Middle East of ancient times was not so different from today in at least one respect: it was a place of violent conflict, competing ethnic groups, and great-power rivalries.

Sandwiched among the larger powerful empires such as Egypt, Babylon, and the Hittite Empire was a small group of people, partly nomadic and apparently known as the Hapiru or Habiru—the Hebrews. Even at their height these people never controlled much land or were feared much by the great empires of the day. Yet their legacy, their ethics, their language, and their religion survive to this day. Among the world's first monotheists, they were a religiously and ethically sophisticated people who worshiped a spiritual God called, among other appellations, Yahweh (written as YHWH). They spawned also two of the world's largest religions—Islam and Christianity—and their thought permeates Western and Middle Eastern culture. Clearly, size and political power are not everything.

Who were the Hebrews, and what do we know of their history? In one sense we know more of them than

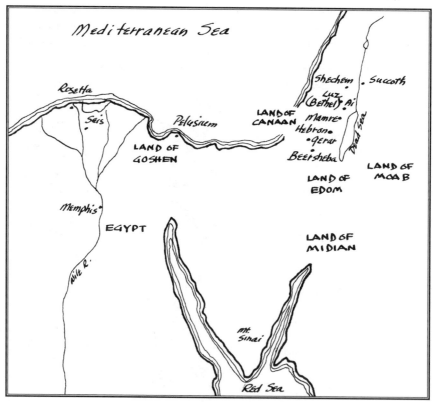

ISRAEL AND NORTHERN EGYPT
DURING THE TIME OF THE ANCIENT HEBREWS

many other early Middle Eastern peoples. We have the Bible, which is a recounting of Hebrew history, beliefs, and literature. The Bible is a good starting point, but it is a religious document and not truly a comprehensive history in the modern sense; for example, it says virtually nothing of the years under Egyptian servitude. And of course historians debate its accuracy, while archaeologists dig in the dry deserts of Israel for verification, and religious scholars debate the meaning and derivations of its words. Learning the history of the Hebrews is very much an ongoing process.

Most people agree on the origins of the Hebrews. They were a nomadic people whose homeland was in northern Mesopotamia (literally, the land between the rivers in what is today Iraq). The Old Testament, the first part of the Bible, speaks of three main phases of early Hebrew history. The first phase is the migration of the Hebrews from this area under the patriarch Abraham to Palestine, said to be the land that God had promised. The second phase is a sojourn in Egypt, which ended in oppression and slavery and the exodus of the Hebrews under Moses. The third phase, according to the Bible, is the journey back to Palestine, during which God revealed himself to Moses and gave him the Law.

In Palestine, the Hebrews adopted a settled existence. Now came a period of centralization. The Hebrews were unified into a kingdom under Saul, whose later successor, David of Bethlehem, established the capital at Jerusalem and whose son Solomon (965–925 B.C.E.) ruled over Israel at its material height. He built the great temple at Jerusalem that became the

focal point of the Hebrew religion. Solomon's kingdom split into two at his death. In the north was Israel, with the capital at Samaria, and in the south was Judah, with Jerusalem the capital. This was the period of the great prophets, of men who lamented the loss of purity of the Hebrew religion in the new overcivilized monarchies. The prophets were right when they spoke of dire consequences for turning away from purity: Samaria soon fell to the rising might of the Assyrian Empire of Sargon. Then came Judah's turn to fall to the Assyrians, of whom the prophet Jeremiah said, "They are cruel and have no mercy; their voice roareth like the sea." Judging from the archaeological evidence, which includes reliefs of impaled captives displayed before the Assyrian king, the prophets were not overstating the case. After the conquest, the Jews were sent to Mesopotamia to prevent them from revolting. This is called the period of Exile and marks the end of independent Israel. Although the Assyrians were in their turn conquered by the Persians, who let the Jews return to Palestine, they were now under greatpower rule except for very brief historical intervals. After the Persians came the Greeks, then the Romans. In a famous revolt, the Jews failed to oust the Romans and instead met a tragic defeat. Many were expelled, and their temple at Jerusalem was destroyed.

But they were not destroyed as a people. Scattered across the world (Jewish groups lived in much of the Middle East and as far east as China and India), the Jews would return once more to Palestine and proclaim another independent Israel two thousand years later, in 1948.

THE GLORY THAT WAS GREECE AND ROME AND PERSIA AND INDIA: A QUICK LOOK AT THE "CLASSICAL" CIVILIZATIONS

 The great English writer George Orwell wrote that when he was a child he learned that four hundred thousand volumes from the great ancient Greek library of Alexandria had been burned centuries before, and he was thrilled that this ancient tragedy had occurred. In his view it saved him from thousands of boring school hours of reading and translating the Greek classics into English.

Orwell was a product of an era in England and America when the Greek and Roman classics formed a large part of a basic education. Students learned Greek and Latin, read and studied the classics from those eras, and often ignored modern and non-Western history. This was classics overkill, but today the pendulum has swung too far in the other direction. Many people know next to nothing of the Greeks and Romans of the classical era. This age began around 400 B.C.E. with the flowering of Greek culture in Athens and ended about the time Rome fell to invaders in 476 C.E. And few Americans have any idea of what was going on in the rest of the world or about the great cultures of Iran and India during that time. Learning a few basics is therefore in order.

ANCIENT GREECE

(c. 1800–30 B.C.E.)

For ours is a constitution which does not imitate those of others but rather sets them as an example. Its name—because power rests not with a few but with the majority—is Democracy; in private disputes all are equal before the law, and in public life, men are honored for conspicuous achievement in any field, and not for sectional reasons. . . . Ours is a free state, both in politics and in social life.

This eloquent portion of the oration of the great Athenian leader Pericles reveals what is best about Greek civilization. The Greeks had many faults, but at their best they produced one of humanity's golden ages. They were among the handful of peoples who actively championed the idea of democracy. They supported, to a great degree, the free inquiry into ideas. They helped begin the great scientific, literary, and humanist trends in Western thought.

When we say the Greeks, though, we're speaking a bit too broadly. Greece was not centralized (except briefly) like the great empires of Persia and Rome. For the most part it was divided into a series of city-states that ranged in size from five thousand to three hundred thousand inhabitants. These states were scattered about the mountainous and jagged peninsula of Greece, as well as among the hundreds of islands in the Aegean Sea and in colonies in Sicily, southern Italy (Naples was a Greek colony called Neapolis, meaning New City), and the Anatolian (Turkish) peninsula. There were great differences in government forms and in levels of culture and philosophy among these states and during different periods, but they all shared the Greek language, though with various dialects; they all met during the great Panhellenic athletic games like the Olympics or others; and they all considered outsiders *barbarou* or barbarians.

The first civilization in the area was centered in the Mediterranean island of Crete and ended around 1450 B.C.E. The Minoans had a highly developed capital, Knossos. They traded with the Egyptians and the Syrians. (In fact, their early statuary looks a lot like that of Egypt, with some variations.) But although they contributed to the rise of Greek culture, they weren't Greek.

The building of the underground Athens subway system has led to the discovery of relics from ancient Athens, including public buildings, plazas, temples, houses, fountains, and graves from as far back as the third century B.C.E. Everything is being left intact so the subway passengers will be able to view these ancient treasures after the metro is done.

In particular, the Minoans influenced, and eventually were absorbed into, the Mycenaean civilization, which flourished until 1100 B.C.E. on the mainland of Greece. Later it was assimilated into Dorian culture. The Dorians were the last of a mass movement of invaders called Indo-Europeans to sweep through the region. They brought Iron Age technology to Greece, and out of their synthesis with the earlier Greeks rose classical Greek civilization. As those who have studied architecture know, their name has been given to the simplest type of column—the Doric variety used in the Parthenon.

Then there were the two greatest city-states of classical Greece: Athens and Sparta.

Athens is the quintessential "democracy" that Pericles praised in the quotation at the beginning of this section. Of course, the reality of Athens didn't quite fit the ideals he extolled. First of all, the ideal of democracy didn't extend to one-third of the Athenian population: slaves or

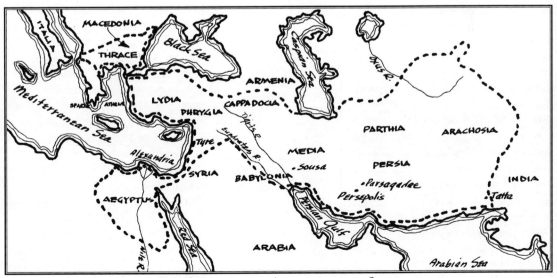

THE CONQUESTS OF ALEXANDER THE GREAT

women. Second, at its height of power, democratic Athens became an imperialist power, subjecting many other city-states and peoples to her rule. In spite of this, Athens was among the first to uphold democratic ideals. Her golden age encouraged some of the world's greatest philosophers, such as Socrates and Plato, who established the foundations of Western thought. The Athenian literary scene, with works by Aeschylus, Aristophanes, Sophocles, and Euripides, helped form the basis of much Western literature.

Sparta was the antithesis and traditional rival of Athens. It was a city-state focused on war. Early in their history the Spartans had conquered their neighboring Greek city-states and forced their inhabitants to work as quasi-slaves called helots. The helots farmed while Spartan citizens trained from youth for war. Life was difficult for everyone in Sparta. After eating a meal of gruel and water at one of their communal dinners, a non-Spartan Greek commented it was no wonder the Spartans loved war so much if the alternative was living and eating in Sparta.

The Greek city-states commonly squabbled and fought one another, but Sparta and Athens were united when the greatest threat to Greek freedom came in the form of a Persian invasion. Together, along with a consortium of Greek allies, they defeated the Persian threat (see pages 34–35). Athens remained the leader of the Greek world. It formed the Delian League of two hundred Greek city-states— something like a Greek N.A.T.O.— against a future Persian threat.

But the Persians never attempted another invasion, and the Delian League became in effect an Athenian empire. Other Greek city-states re-

sented Athenian power, and they coalesced around Sparta. Soon war broke out between the two. These Peloponnesian Wars lasted from 404 to 331 B.C.E. and ended in a Spartan victory. But now an anti-Spartan league of city-states formed under the city-state of Thebes and defeated the Spartans in 371 B.C.E.

All this squabbling was ultimately brought to an end by the Greeks from the north, the Macedonians, under Philip II. With the new military innovation of the phalanx (a corps of sixteen thousand men with spears twice the normal length) Philip unified most of Greece under his rule. His son Alexander III, known to history as Alexander the Great (see pages 39–40), attacked the great Persian Empire and brought much of the Middle East under his rule. This ushered in a new age of Greek civilization called the Hellenistic Age.

Alexander died young. As he was dying he was supposedly asked, "To whom do you leave your empire?" He replied, "To the strongest." And indeed his empire was split among the strongest of the Diodochoi (his successors), the generals who accompanied him on his great conquests. For the most part they set up centralized states; the two most notable Greek states of the Hellenistic era were Ptolemaic Egypt, under (General) Ptolemy I and his successors, and the Seleucid Empire, comprising much of the Middle East, under Seleucus I and his successors.

The Hellenistic age was a great age of commerce. The Egyptian city of Alexandria rose to become one of the greatest world cities, notable particularly for its *museion* (museum) of scholars who contributed to science

(Euclid of geometric fame worked there on his famous textbook) and its library with the ambitious mission of including every known work of literature. During this age, Greek culture spread to the Middle East and India; in turn, Greeks were influenced by new ideas from the East. Ultimately, though, it was the West that was to prove the downfall of the Hellenistic empires. The Romans defeated the last Hellenistic empress, Cleopatra of Egypt, in 30 B.C.E. When she died, supposedly by a snake bite to her breast, Hellenistic rule was over. But Hellenistic culture lasted to influence the Romans and ultimately to survive in a transformed fashion in the Byzantine Empire.

ANCIENT ROME

(753 B.C.E. [traditional date for founding of Rome] to 476 C.E. [end of the Western empire]; 1453 [end of the Eastern Byzantine Empire])

You, Roman, make your task to rule the nations by your government (These shall be your skills), to impose ordered ways upon a state of peace, To spare those who have submitted and to subdue the arrogant.

With these words Roman poet Virgil sums up the guiding principle of the Roman civilization. Their greatness lies

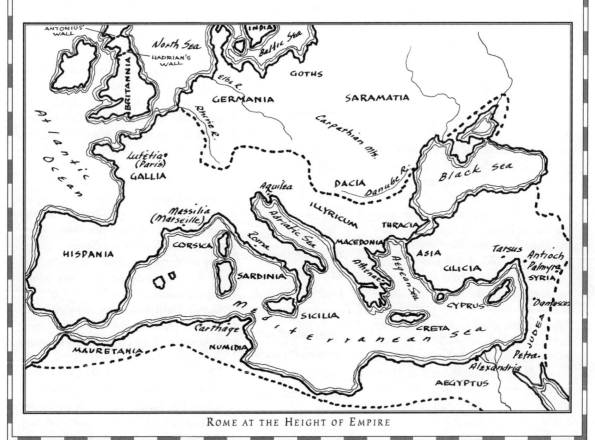

ROME AT THE HEIGHT OF EMPIRE

What's in a Name?

 Roman emperors would not have been content with the simple titles of democratic America. In addition to their names, they were known by their imperial titles:

- *Caesar,* after the great Julius Caesar, who destroyed the old Roman Republic.
- *Augustus,* or "revered one," the title Octavian took when founding the empire.
- *Imperator,* or "commander in chief," emperor.

As the empire continued, emperors often had less security and power but more titles, often celebrating dubious victories or pompous accomplishments.

For example, Emperor Tiberius, who ruled at the beginning of the empire from 14 C.E. to 37 C.E. had this simple title: Tiberius Claudius Nero Caesar Augustus. But Probus, who ruled from 276 C.E. to 282 C.E. when the empire was beginning to crumble, was known by this mouthful: Imperator Caesar Marcus Aurelius Probus Pius Felix Augustus Gothicus Maximus Persicus Germanicus Maximus Medicus Maximus Parthicus Maximus.

not in their arts or sciences (although, obviously, they did make contributions in these areas). Conquering land, imposing order, establishing a centralized government—these are the main legacies of Rome.

Like the Greeks, the Romans were part of an Indo-European–speaking people who conquered the original inhabitants of Italy. For a time, Rome was under the domination of the Etruscans, a mysterious people who are believed to be originally from Asia Minor (see page 496). Around 509 B.C.E. the Latin inhabitants of Rome expelled the last Etruscan king and independent Rome began her rise to world prominence.

The use of purple as a royal color began with the Romans. Their emperors sometimes wore nothing but purple—a purple toga and purple underwear. They sat on purple thrones, were surrounded by purple curtains, and stood to receive guests on a purple marble circle.

Roman history is divided into three great periods: the Republic, or the early years of representative government; the Empire, or the great years under the emperors; and the Byzantine period, after the Western portion of the empire had fallen and the empire was ruled by Greek speakers from Constantinople.

The Republic began as a virtually patrician (rich upper class) monopoly. The government of Rome was centered around the Senate, an elective body not too different from our own Senate—and controlled by the wealthy patrician class. Gradually, the poorer classes (the plebeians) gained some rights. By 470 B.C.E. they were allowed to elect ten tribunes who could veto illegal actions by other officials; by 362 B.C.E. one of the two consuls (who were elected officials with many of the powers of the old kings) was a plebeian. But most power was still in the hands of the rich, and out of their ranks would come the later emperors.

Meanwhile, Republican Rome was expanding externally, first conquering her Latin neighbors, then the Italian Greek colonies to the south, her Carthaginian enemies in Africa (see pages 48–50), and the Greeks to the east. An ambitious aristocrat named Julius Caesar (100–44 B.C.E.) conquered Gaul (modern-day France) and earned the fear of the Senate, which was concerned that he would attempt to seize absolute power. They sponsored another general, Pompey, to fight Caesar, but Caesar was victorious and named Dictator for Life of Rome. (Pompey fled to Egypt and was murdered, his head pickled in an urn.) Ultimately some democratic-minded senators stabbed Caesar to death on the ides of March, or March 15. In the ensuing chaos, Caesar's adopted son

Octavian defeated all rivals (including Marcus Antonus, or Mark Antony, and Cleopatra of Egypt) and became absolute ruler of Rome. He now called himself Augustus Caesar.

The empire began as a fiction: Augustus claimed that he was merely reforming the Republic. But since he controlled the Senate, the army, and the people through his immense wealth, he was really the absolute ruler, and his successor emperors perpetuated this. Under Augustus and his successors the Mediterranean world lived under Pax Romana—a "Roman peace" enforced by the power of Roman legions. Gradually, however, the power of Rome began to fade, as "barbarian" tribes from Asia swept westward and threatened its frontiers. Taxes were raised, inflation increased, and land went out of cultivation. For a while, under the emperor Diocletian, the decline was stayed. Diocletian split the empire into two great regions, west and east, and introduced monetary and social reforms. But Teutonic tribes eventually invaded the Italian peninsula, and the age of the Caesars ended.

Meanwhile, the eastern half of the Roman Empire survived. It was called the Byzantine Empire (330–1453 C.E.), and it was really more Greek than Roman. It was Roman in law and administrative style, but Greek in language, culture, and customs.

Its origins lie with Diocletian's division of the Roman Empire into two, but the Byzantine Empire really began in 330 C.E. when the Roman emperor Constantine (also known as the first Christian emperor) dedicated the new capital of the Eastern Roman Empire. First called Nova Roma, it was soon called Constantinople, and it still survives as Istanbul in modern Turkey.

Rome had far more people living off government handouts than even the most liberal city government of today. Estimates are that 33 percent to 50 percent of the population lived on free grain distributed by the emperors. Under the emperor Claudius 159 days of the year were holidays; 93 of them included games sponsored by the government.

The average taxpayer in ancient Rome wound up paying taxes on a number of strange items—urine, children, slaves, house doors, acts of prostitution, even marital sex (this under Emperor Caligula).

This empire retained the eastern possessions of the Roman Empire, including the rich Middle Eastern provinces. Constantinople became a great trading center as well as the center of Christianity in the East under the Orthodox Church. After a long period of prosperity the Byzantines, too, declined. They lost much of their territory to the dynamic Arab expansion, and more to the new groups of Turkish nomads who succeeded them. Finally, in 1453, the great capital of Constantinople was conquered by the Turkish Ottoman ruler Mehmed II, and the last vestiges of Roman rule ended.

Legends of the Fall

The fall of Constantinople, the great capital city of the Byzantines, to the Turks was filled with drama—and legend. Supposedly, as the Turks were at the gates to the city, the Byzantine emperor was frying some fish for dinner. Told that it was all over, the brave emperor disagreed, saying, "Only when the fish in this pan come to life." And at that moment (of course), the fish leaped from the pan into a nearby well. Another legend says the emperor turned to marble after being struck from his horse by the Turks and waits in a cave to this day for his sword to be delivered by an angel so he can lead the fight against the Turks. If so, he's been waiting a long time: Constantinople has been Turkish since 1453 and is modern Turkey's leading commercial city.

ANCIENT PERSIA (also known as Iran)

*(civilization from 2000 B.C.E.;
Achaemenid Empire, 539–330
B.C.E.; Parthian Empire, 248
B.C.E.–224 C.E.; Sassanian Empire,
224–651 C.E.)*

Iran has taken on the West many times before the Ayatollah Khomeini called the United States the Great Satan. It actually started more than seventeen hundred years ago.

Back in 259 C.E., the Persians were the largest threat to the Roman Empire. They faced a Roman army led by the emperor himself and defeated it completely. The great Roman Caesar Valerian ended his days working as a slave laborer on a dam project in Iran. (To this day the dam is known as Caesar's dam.) Clearly, the Persian Empire was a force to be reckoned with.

The three major Persian empires of ancient times were as follows:

Achaemenid Empire: founded by Cyrus the Great, who united the Persians and conquered the Middle East. His son Cambyses II conquered Egypt. Then came Darius the Great, who extended Persia into part of Greece and triggered the Persian Wars in which he tried to conquer the rest. He failed. And ultimately the man of Greek culture, Alexander the Great, conquered the Persians, and the Persian Empire collapsed. Unfortunately, not much literature survived the defeat. But the Zoroastrian religion that emerged at the time has survived to this day. (See pages 207–8.)

Parthian Empire: founded by a nomadic tribe that swept out of northeastern Iran and beat back the Greek

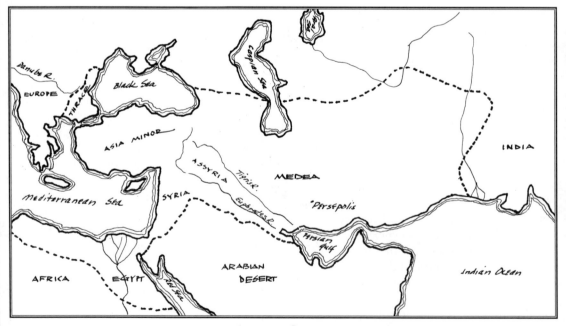

ANCIENT PERSIA

Hellenistic conquerors of the country. Under their great kings Mithradates I and II, they reconquered half of the old Persian Empire. They also managed to give Rome its first scare. Crassus, Rome's richest citizen and ambitious politician, a sort of Ross Perot of the times, financed and led an army against the Parthians. He assumed he'd win an easy victory. He was wrong. The Parthian cavalry killed Crassus and destroyed his Romans at the famous battle of Carrhae.

Sassanian Empire: the Persian Empire that managed to capture the Roman emperor Valerian. The empire rose out of Fars province in Iran, the center of Persian culture (Fars means Persia in the Persian language). It was a great centralized civilization, with a national religion (Zoroastrianism) and a distinctly Persian culture that greatly affected later generations. Its greatest leader was Chosroes I (Khosrow), known as a skillful administrator and warrior and seen as the ideal Persian leader. The Sassanians were often at war with the decaying Roman Empire and its Byzantine successors. Sassanian art and architecture influenced European medieval art. For example, a French church near Orléans was built on the plans of an Iranian Zoroastrian fire temple; pictures of Christ as a king on earth are probably derived from Sassanian models.

For a while it looked as if the Sassanians would defeat the Byzantine Empire and take Constantinople. In a great turnaround, however, the Byzantines attacked the heart of the Sassanian Empire and defeated its army. After this, the empire fell into decay and disunity until it was conquered by Muslim Arabs. But much of Persian culture passed on to the new Muslim Empire and survives in a modified form today.

INDIA, MAURYA EMPIRE

—

(322–184 B.C.E.)

India is home to many different peoples and religions, and for many centuries of its history it has been split. But for a period of several hundred years, much of it was unified by a family of kings who gave their name—Maurya—to one of India's greatest ages.

The greatest ruler of this dynasty was one of the most unusual in all history. His name was Asoka, and after defeating his enemies from the Kalinga state, Asoka had a change of heart. In his own words:

When an unconquered country is conquered, people are killed, they die or are made captive. That the Beloved of the Gods finds very pitiful and grievous.

And for the rest of his rule Asoka sought peace before war. But before going on with this great man, let's go back to the beginning.

The Maurya Empire rose out of the unrest that was the aftermath of Alexander the Great's attempt to conquer the world. While he didn't conquer India, he got close and stirred up trouble. After his death, the outer area of India was ruled by one of his generals, who was now on the verge of taking more territory. Nearby there was a native Indian state called Magadha, which was ruled by a king who was detested by his own people. The king was no match for the Greeks or for his people. Clearly, the entire area was

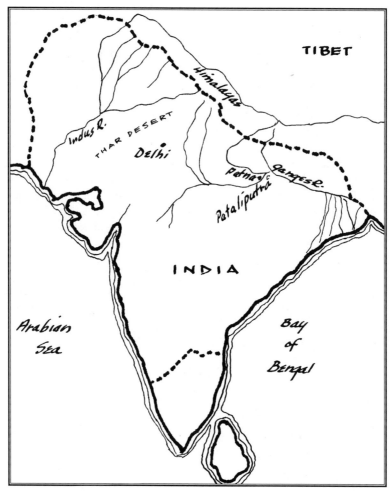

MAURYA EMPIRE

potentially chaotic as well as ripe for the plucking, for the right kind of ambitious prince.

This was where a young and energetic man named Chandragupta Maurya came in. Aided by a shrewd advisor named Kautilya, he seized power in Magadha and soon made himself India's most powerful ruler. He centralized administration, pushed back the Greeks (but then maintained friendly relations with them), monopolized trade, and lived a life of splendor in a great wooden palace.

All this was written up by the advisor Kautilya in one of the world's first political science textbooks, called the *Arthasastra*. In reality, this new centralized state was a primitive police state, and Kautilya has not been called an "Indian Machiavelli" for nothing. Chandragupta's son kept up his father's work and further extended the empire's boundaries until only the Tamil-speaking areas of the far south were free of hard-nosed Maurya control. Then Asoka took the throne, and everything changed.

ENOUGH ABOUT THE REST OF THE WORLD, WHAT WAS HAPPENING IN EUROPE?: THE THREE R'S OF EUROPEAN HISTORY, OR THE MOST MOMENTOUS MOVEMENTS IN EUROPE

 Wars are one thing, momentous social changes are another. The origins of wars are usually easy to trace; it's more difficult to trace the origins of social movements. But for reasons that are still being (hotly) debated today, starting around 1350 medieval Europe society began changing in ways that put it ahead of the rest of the world technologically—with consequences that are still being felt. The first two changes came almost simultaneously: the Renaissance, which brought about a new, humanistic way of looking at things, and the Reformation, which revolutionized and split the dominant Catholic religion. These shake-ups of society and thought are responsible to a degree for the rapid rise of Europe to world power. The final change, the Industrial Revolution, came three hundred years later, but the seeds were planted long before.

But what goes around comes around. Now that Asia is booming economically, artistically, and technologically, maybe a new type of Renaissance is being born as we speak—with untold advantages for the world.

THE RENAISSANCE

c. 1350–1600

In brief: It's difficult to be brief about the Renaissance. It's the great period of transition in Europe: from feudalism and faith to a more free-spirited sense of inquiry and skepticism, leading to new and dynamic trends in art, science, and society. Traditionally, it meant a revival of interest in the old Greek and Roman classics, a revival of urban life, the increased use of technology, the rise of banking and modern commerce, great new art, and a renewed interest in humanity rather than God as the center of things.

Background: Why did the Renaissance begin at all? And why in Europe and not in, say, China, which was technologically much more advanced?

Scholars have debated these questions for years, but of course there is no definitive answer. Maybe it was because Europe was relatively isolated from invasions (unlike the "barbarian" and Manchu invasions that devastated China) and so had the leisure to develop along new lines. Maybe it was because Europeans began to undertake long sea voyages and were now open to new ideas. Or maybe it was due to the synergies created from the rise of small competing city-states in Italy (as in classical Greece). Maybe it was even partly due to the arrival by ship of rats bearing the black plague, which decimated much of Europe but opened up jobs and society for the innovative and ambitious who had managed to survive.

Obviously, there is no clear answer. Probably the Renaissance resulted from a combination of these causes and many others. Whatever the causes, a new spirit was beginning to sweep through Europe in the 1300s, beginning most notably in Italy but present elsewhere as well.

Key events: Rather than go through all the tortured political events of this era (many of which are covered in other parts of this book), it's quicker to take a few key concepts and mention a number of key individuals who literally changed the world.

First of all there was the rise of Humanism, the belief in man as the center of things. The word comes from the Latin, *humanitas*—or, on second thought, from the Greek. The ancient author Cicero used this word to translate the Greek word *"paedeia,"* or education and culture. Those who lived by this word were called humanists, and many were devoted to the literature of ancient Greece and Rome, not only rediscovering the classics (which were often moldering in old libraries) but critically reading them and going beyond them, inspired by the same skeptical and questioning spirit that had animated their authors so many centuries before.

One of the first and greatest of the humanists was Petrarch, a poet famous for his love of the classics (he collected ancient Greek and Roman manuscripts although he couldn't read Greek) and his love sonnets (many devoted to a young married woman by the name of Laura).

Most of these early humanists were patricians, leaders, and diplomats of the Italian city-states in which they lived. They sought to develop all sides of a personality to produce what they called the universal man—we'd probably say very well rounded, maybe even too well rounded. For example, the humanist architect Leon Battista Alberti was famous as a playwright, poet, essayist, mathematician, art critic, singer, organist, and patrician. As a young man he had been a runner, wrestler, and mountain climber. To his contemporaries he symbolized the ideal man, a new Socrates.

As for the fine arts, even merely listing the great artists would take pages. This was truly a revolutionary time for artists. The Renaissance saw the beginning of scientific perspective in painting and drawing, and of humanist attention to the body inside and out, from the muscles and ligaments to the soul inside—the personality. Anyone can see the great changes just by going to a museum. A medieval nude is flabby, almost formless; a Renaissance nude has muscles and curves and fat and sinew—its humanity jumps out at you. A listing of great Renaissance artists is like a history of art in itself: Michelangelo, who painted the Sistine Chapel of Saint Peter's in Rome; Leonardo da Vinci, a painter, sculptor, architect, and inventor best known for his mural *The Last Supper* and his *Mona Lisa;* Raphael, known for his masterpiece portraits of the Madonna; Giotto, Titian, Donatello, Fra Angelico, Botticelli, Correggio, Tintoretto, to name just a few.

The spirit of inquiry also led to great

leaps in science. Instead of accepting things at face value, Renaissance scholars began to question things and learn by observation and experimentation. Nicholas Copernicus (1473–1543) revived the idea that the earth rotates on its axis and revolves around the sun. Galileo Galilei (1564–1642) built a telescope and confirmed that fact, and also developed the science of dynamics, discovering the law of falling bodies by dropping different objects from various heights. Johannes Kepler (1571–1630) discovered that the planets revolve around the sun in ellipses rather than circles, and at the end of the Renaissance, the Englishman Isaac Newton (1642–1727) completed the discoveries of these men in works such as his monumental *Principia Mathematica;* he also discovered general laws of physics and optics, and invented calculus. Modern medicine was born in the Renaissance as well: William Harvey (1578–1657) discovered the circulation of the blood; Andreas Vesalius (1514–1564) founded modern anatomy; and Paracelsus (1493–1541) studied diseases and their causes.

Technology, that great word that transformed the world, got a jump start in the Renaissance as well. In some cases the inventions came from outside, but as with the Japanese so many years later, Renaissance Europeans took foreign ideas and tinkered with them so effectively that the originators were almost forgotten. Cannon and gunpowder, which were probably Chinese inventions, were used in warfare. Printing, probably developed in China, was used extensively and brought about the wide dissemination of learning (by 1500 there were already forty thousand different editions and twenty million books in print).

Urban life became more widespread, and with it came the rise of banking, vital to the expansion of business and commerce. Even time became more definite. Instead of the old inaccurate sundials and hourglasses, the counterpoise clock was developed. At first only the hour hand existed; the minute hand came in 1400 (but was not widely used), and the second hand came in about 1550. If you happen to be in an art museum, take a look at the clocks in a Brueghel painting (a Dutch painter)—chances are you'll see only the hour hand.

Let's end with a Renaissance invention ignored by many scholars: the sidesaddle, invented by Catherine de Medicis. This seemingly minor innovation actually symbolized a great change, as pointed out by historian Hugh Thomas. It got women out of the home and onto the horse—and into the world. It symbolized a new attitude in Europe: the idea that women were important as autonomous individuals. Feminism to some degree was born in the Renaissance.

Significance: Tremendous. The Renaissance triggered the modernization of Europe, which brought about the immense changes of today.

THE REFORMATION

1517–mid- to late 1500s

In brief: The end of the monopoly of religious power in western Europe, brought about by religious reformers including Martin Luther, John Calvin, and Huldrych Zwingli. At the end, a new, far less unified Europe was open to new ideas as well as more conflict.

Background: Until the Reformation, all Western eyes ultimately turned to Rome. There was basically a religious and moral monopoly in western Europe. Anything to do with religion went through the one Church of Rome, headed by the Pope and run by his hierarchy of intermediaries: cardinals, bishops, and priests. The Pope and his men not only controlled the only avenue to salvation for Christians but they controlled huge tracts of land and much wealth, and wielded a great deal of political power. One weapon was particularly potent: excommunication. Disagree with the Pope, and you could be cut off from the Church—and presumably doomed to hell.

But by 1500 the old order was getting creaky. The Church was already losing political power. Princes and kings were seizing power for themselves, and an increasingly independent middle class was questioning the old ways. A number of early reformers also questioned the church; some, like John Hus, were burned at the stake for their troubles. But various kings were more successful in at least influencing the Church by starting at the top and choosing or backing popes for political reasons. At one point there were three rival popes, each backed by a secular power and each busy excommunicating the rivals' followers. Clearly the Church was in trouble. Maybe all this ferment stimulated the arts; at any rate, this was also the period of the greatest Church accomplishment in the arts—the age of the Renaissance and Michelangelo.

Key events: In October 1517 a little-known but very zealous Augustinian friar named Martin Luther nailed

Under the Counter-Reformation, Jews were once again made to wear a yellow badge (they had been ordered to do so originally in 1215 by a Lateran Council) and live in ghettos. The word "ghetto" is derived from a foundry (GETTO, meaning "casting" in Italian) in Venice where Jews were segregated in the 1500s.

ninety-five theses (statements) to the door of the church in Wittenberg, a small town in Saxony, Germany. This act was the spark that ignited a series of reformations that would ultimately split the church.

Luther was protesting the Church practice of selling indulgences, specifically those sold in his neighborhood by a Dominican friar named Tetzel. If you believed in indulgences, they were a wonderful deal. Buy them—and thereby give money to the Church for various projects—and in return the Church would intervene for you and reduce your stay in purgatory after death. Some people thought (and some unscrupulous priests did not disabuse them of the notion) that you could literally buy salvation if you spent enough. Luther argued that salvation lay with God, not via intermediaries such as the Church. He touched a raw nerve among many Germans. Aided by the power of the press—printing presses churned out thousands of his pamphlets—Luther's ideas were heard or read throughout Germany. But as his ideas spread, they changed. Luther now made a basic attack on the structure of the Church, the new idea being that the only really important aspects of religion were God, the Scriptures, and the individual. The huge Church hierarchy was not really that necessary.

Needless to say, the Church did not take this lying down. But Luther was lucky: he had political support from the ruler of Saxony, and political unrest in Germany as a whole made it difficult for the Pope to excommunicate him until 1520. By that time it was too late. Luther had translated the Bible into German, which enhanced his reputation as a theologian, and he had

Trying Times

Out of the Counter-Reformation came the infamous Inquisition, which was the chief agent of the Catholic Church in stamping out heresy. Inquisitors held secret trials of those they suspected of not following Catholic doctrines. Those they convicted were burned at the stake in a public ceremony called the auto-da-fé, or Act of Faith. The excesses were horrifying. The writer Aonio Paleario was accused of heresy because the inquisitors said the omission of the *t* in his name showed he abhorred the sign of the cross. He was hanged, strangled, *and* burned in 1570.

The Inquisition was at its worst in Italy and Spain. Because Spain had long been under the Arabs, it had many people of Muslim or Jewish extraction, and the inquisitors went after those it said had not truly converted to Christianity. The chief agent was a Jesuit named Torquemada (ironically, he had Jewish ancestors). The Inquisition lasted until 1834, but the first years were the worst. Estimates are that four hundred thousand people were tried and about forty thousand were burned alive.

---

thousands of supporters, who now called themselves Protestants. (Ultimately, the church he founded would be called the Lutheran Church.) Luther had unleashed a whirlwind of change, as serfs and soldiers of local princes attacked rich monasteries and lands owned by the Church. In the end, many freedom-seeking peasants were dead (Luther supported their suppression), but the local aristocracy kept most of the Church lands. Lutheranism spread all over northern Germany, Denmark, Sweden, and Norway.

That was the German Reformation. In Switzerland, other reformers, notably Huldrych Zwingli and John Calvin, soon imposed their own brand of reform, the Swiss Reformation.

Rather than go into doctrinal differences (Zwingli and Luther met to iron out their differences but failed to agree on Communion), suffice it to say that by the mid-1500s there were other new churches as well. These were called Reformed and were located in a band across Europe, including parts of France (where their adherents were called Huguenots), Scotland, Switzerland, parts of Austria, Bohemia (Czechoslovakia), Hungary, Poland; later, they would spread to North America.

There was also the English Reformation. Henry VIII, he of the six wives, wasn't taking all this change lying down, either. Predictably, his move to leave the established Church began with his desire for another wife (who would give him a longed-for son). The result was a reformation led partly from above but also with much popular support—and yet another new church, the Anglican Church, or Church of England.

And last but not least, there was the Catholic Reformation, or the Counter-Reformation, the response to all this by the Church of Rome. The Church reaffirmed the basic beliefs that had been challenged by the reformers, and to root out heretics it authorized an Inquisition, along with the Congregation of the Index, which read and banned books deemed detrimental to the faith. (They had learned the lesson of Luther's printing presses.) More important, there was now major administrative reform. And out of it all came Ignatius Loyola and his Society of Jesus, a religious order formed along military lines that was extremely well organized and ultimately ran Catholic education, and its members served as advisors and confessors to Catholic kings. At the end of the Reformation the Catholic Church was smaller but better organized, far less corrupt, and, if anything, more powerful. The self-examination resulted in much brilliant scholarship, from Loyola to Matteo Ricci, the great missionary to Ming China. In all, the Church had proved far more resilient than its detractors had suspected.

Significance: Europe was no longer unified religiously or morally, and this was the recipe for further conflict. The reform churches, lumped together as Protestant churches, and the old Church, the Catholic Church, would now be represented by ambitious princes and kings anxious to use religious differences for political ends. And religious controversy would not end either: Protestant churches would vie with one another for authority and power. Truly the idea of a unified Europe was dead, but in return the new intellectual and political ferment brought fresh ideas and reforms to Europe. Rarely, if ever, does monolithic power bring progress.

The Reformation also highlighted the importance of printing. Without it, Luther would have been isolated and probably a failure. The Catholics, too, turned to the presses. It was thousands of printed Jesuit tracts that inspired and supported the men who converted South America to Catholicism.

Let's end on one important point: don't assume (as many do) that the reforming Protestants automatically supported free-spirited inquiry and that the Catholics automatically supported blind dogma. Copernicus, a Catholic Pole who expounded on the old Greek idea that the earth revolved around the sun, was attacked by Luther (and not initially by the Catholics); another rev-

olutionary thinker, Miguel Serveto, who discovered the pulmonary circulation of blood, was burned to death at the instigation of John Calvin. Both sides had their bad moments.

The working day in earlier times was long. A statute of 1563 in England set hours for day laborers (hired between March and September) as 5 A.M. to begin work, half an hour for dinner, sleep for one hour, drink for half an hour, and quit at 8 P.M. That's a thirteen-hour day. The Industrial Revolution didn't improve things for many—during English Parliamentary hearings in the 1800s, children described work days exceeding twelve hours—with less than an hour's break daily.

REVOLUTION: THE INDUSTRIAL REVOLUTION

roughly 1740–1850, but the effects have continued to this day, with further technological revolutions such as the nuclear and computer revolutions

In brief: The transformation of society into industrial modes of production and the use of steam power. This changed the economy and society of the world, mostly beginning in Britain and then extending to the rest of the world.

Background: The Industrial Revolution separates us from the past like no other historical event. Because we live on the "other side," we can only imagine life before.

Before this far-reaching revolution, we all lived in a world of plants and animals, a world in which we traveled by horse or foot, read by sunlight or firelight, and where most of our clothes, furniture, buildings, and tools were made by hand, slowly, one by one. Our spiritual life, our sense of being, was different before this age of machines. Nature was closer, the pace of life slower and more tied to the seasons and to the daily cycle of light and dark.

Then in Europe, particularly in

Britain, a series of technological innovations changed all this. These innovations and the changes are called the Industrial Revolution, but modern scholars don't particularly like this term. They argue that the changes weren't all that sudden, that they're linked to the past, and that it's difficult to say when this "revolution" began or ended, if it has ended at all. But for better or worse, the term has stuck and is usually applied to the first phase of major industrial transformation.

The beginning was in England in the mid-1700s. Why England? Probably due to an increasing population, a stable government, a geography suited to production, the stimulus of a growing economy, and other factors. Whatever the reasons, the early revolution centered around technical innovations in three areas: the textile industry, the iron industry, and the improvement of the steam engine.

Stop for a second and think about the shirt you're wearing and the amount of work that went into making it. First, raw fibers of wool or cotton had to be taken, "carded," and combed so they're parallel; they must be spun to make yarn or thread, and then they must be woven and "finished" by various complicated methods. Before the Industrial Revolution, this was all extremely time-consuming and labor-intensive. Usually, the job was farmed out to hundreds of individuals who worked at home and then delivered the fabric. Worse yet, because fibers are fragile, it was hard to tighten them and easy to break them or weave them poorly. As a result, fabric was costly and relatively rare. The huge wardrobes of today were not the norm in the pre-industrial world. Only a few could afford to be fashionable.

Underwear was not commonly worn until the Industrial Revolution made mass manufacturing possible. In Europe and China, underclothes were virtually unknown except for the richer classes, who primarily wore linen underneath their outer clothes. The introduction of underwear probably reduced skin diseases drastically; they were quite common, particularly among rarely bathing Europeans.

Then came a dazzling series of innovations that transformed the way textiles are made. They included the spinning machine of Lewis Paul in 1738, the spinning jenny invented by a carpenter, James Hargreaves, in 1764, and the "throstle" developed by a barber named Richard Arkwright in 1769. Together these innovations allowed one operator to simultaneously process up to one hundred spindles of fabric. And then came even more innovations, such as the self-acting "mule" of Richard Roberts (and the improved version by the mechanic Henry Maudslay) that allowed less skilled operators to make fine fabrics. What was the result of all this? One statistic says it all: cotton production was under one million pounds of finished cotton in 1700; just one hundred years later it was over sixty million. Britain had become the textile capital of the world.

In the process, a new class of people had come to the fore: the innovative entrepreneurs. Take a look at the initial occupations of some of the innovators mentioned above: a barber, a carpenter, a mechanic. The Industrial Revolution was an acceleration of a trend in which humble "common folk," the middle class, became increasingly important in society. It is difficult to comprehend that in medieval Europe innovation was sometimes *illegal*; if you invented a new labor-saving device, you might be imprisoned. The established order was seen as best, and anything that threatened it was sometimes seen as wrong. This had now changed, and a new class was building a new society.

Meanwhile, the steam engine was dramatically improved. A primitive steam engine had been built (as a toy) as far back as the Hellenistic Greeks in around 300 B.C.E., but a more modern prototype was developed in 1698, improved in 1712 to help pump water from mines. It was then further improved in the 1760s by a British instrument maker named James Watt. The effects were tremendous: deeper mines could be dug, and industry was freed from reliance on water, human, and animal power.

And then came innovation in the iron industry, particularly improved methods of smelting iron ore. It is hard to realize that the few machines in existence before the Industrial Revolution were made of wood. But with more and better iron, hardier and higher quality metal machines were built, steel production increased, and mass production truly began. One more statistic shows the extent of the change: at the beginning of the revolution in 1740, Britain produced less than twenty thousand tons of pig iron; one hundred years later the number reached two million.

Significance: How did the Industrial Revolution change life and society? Among other things it ushered in the age of the railroad. A map of Britain in 1844 shows a few tentative lines of mechanized transport; just a few years later, iron railways cover the map. Population became more mobile, ideas and production less rooted to a small place. More important, the revolution changed all aspects of society: it brought huge increases in industrial production and wealth, and changed the economy of the world.

More people gravitated to cities; mass transit developed; people wore high-quality mass-produced clothing and used high-quality machine-produced tools and implements. The middle classes grew more important

and powerful, and the acquisition of power, education, and wealth was opened to more people. An industrial working class or proletariat developed, and trade unions to represent their interests formed. New ideologies, such as socialism and Marxism, were created. More people began to *expect* innovation and an increasingly better life.

And despite the well-known horrors of industrialization, life improved for many. For example, at the beginning of the Industrial Revolution the death rate in Sweden was twenty-eight per thousand; one hundred years later it was less than half that rate. Of course, there was a dark side as well. Independent crafts people feared that machines were destroying their livelihood and sometimes tried to destroy the machines themselves. The Luddite movement, relatively short-lived, became famous for this form of anarchism. Children were often employed in factories with horrendous conditions: Charles Dickens made a career writing of their misery in early industrial London.

The pace of change did not stop by the end of the Industrial Revolution but actually increased. Industrial methods spread across the globe. The Industrial Revolution also fostered an increase in the differences among nations. Before the revolution Europe was not much more powerful than other world societies. Even though it had managed to conquer overseas territory, the odds were still relatively even when European armies confronted foreign ones. But now, with new wealth from industrialization, along with iron gunships and better weapons, Europe was able to conquer less industrialized nations easily, helping to usher in a new age of European imperialism.

Highlights of the Ongoing Technological and "Idea" Revolutions

The changes stemming from the Industrial Revolution are by no means the only one revolutionizing our lives. Here is a brief listing of many of the great or notorious ideas that brilliant people have had over the span of the thousands of years of human history. Most of the inventors are anonymous, and virtually all depended on the work of many others from many different cultures and times.

70,000 B.C.E.	The idea of using fire in controlled fashion for cooking, stampeding game, and protection is first developed, probably in Africa
20,000	Oar invented
15,000	Bow and arrow invented, probably in central Asia
15,000–10,000	Dog domesticated
12,000–7000	Organized agriculture begins (recent evidence in Thailand and Burma shows cultivation of peas, beans, and cucumbers as long ago as 9750 B.C.E., and in the Nile, flint blades possibly used in cutting plants were found dating back to 12,000 B.C.E.)
7000	First surgery on humans, trepanning of skulls (bone is cut to relieve pressure or let out spirits), in Iraq. Technique spreads to Africa and China; probably developed independently in South America
7000–6000	Ox domesticated (in Turkey and Greece; domesticated cattle are found in Egypt by 4000 B.C.E., central Africa after 3000 B.C.E., northern Europe 2500 B.C.E., China, 2000 B.C.E.)
6000	Corn cultivated in Mexico (cultivation of beans, squashes, etc., had begun about a thousand years earlier)
4350	Horse domesticated (probably first in central Asia)
4000	Discovery of how to turn vegetable fibers (flax, etc.) into fabric
3500	Wheel developed (apparently in Iraq); camel domesticated
2600	Seagoing ships
2500	Iron technology discovered by the Hittites in Asia Minor (Turkey); for a long time they keep their technology secret, allowing for considerable military and political success
2000	Development of money (near and far East)
1200	Steel first forged by the Chalybes of Asia Minor, a tribe of the Hittites
580	Electricity discovered by Thales of Miletus (Greece), who finds that if amber is rubbed it attracts light substances such as cork
400	Clinical method of medical care developed by Hippocrates
300	Invention of the pump
200	Use of water mill in Europe and China

850 C.E.	Gunpowder developed in China (by 1200 the Chinese were using a gunpowder tube for throwing spears; by 1275 metallic guns were used in China and India; Guns were in general use in Europe in the 1300s)
852	Coal used for heating
900	Widespread use of water mill for grinding grain (Europe)
1000	Chinese discover inoculation against smallpox with a mild form of the disease (seven hundred years later the Englishman Edward Jenner discovers inoculation against smallpox with cowpox)
1100	Stern post rudder invention in China enables helmsmen to steer from the rear, much improving seagoing travel
1200	Rocket invented by Chinese (a paper tube filled with gunpowder)
1250	Water mill now used for making cloth, extracting oil, and sawing wood
1300s	Mechanical clocks in use in Europe (Strasbourg, France, around 1354; Salisbury Cathedral in England, 1386; Rouen, France, 1390)
1350s	Cannon in use in China
1448	Lead-type printing developed, either by Johannes Gutenberg, of Mainz, Germany, or others including Peter Schöffer, a Dutch inventor, or Procope Waldfogel of Prague
1494	The "first modern army" of France's Charles VIII invades Italy; it includes batters of light, mobile, bronze, and field artillery, and can destroy virtually every castle it aims at
1498	First rifled handgun developed in Leipzig, Germany
1600s	Portable clocks and microscopes invented
1606	Primitive steam engine developed in Italy
1608	Telescope invented, probably in Holland
1630	Flintlock rifle, first modern rifle, developed in France
1709	Coal used in iron industry
1712	Steam engine for use in industry developed by Thomas Newcomen in England
1738	Spinning machine patented by John Wyatt and Lewis Paul in England
1740–50	Cast steel smelted for the first time in England, by Benjamin Huntsman, but it took over a hundred years for the age of steel to begin; only after 1877 did the British allow steel to be used in bridges
1745	Leyden jar invented (independently) by Ewald Georg von Kleist of Pomerania (Germany) and Pieter van Musschenbroek in Holland; this jar released a small amount of electricity
1765	Modern steam engine invented by James Watt in England
1770	"Spinning jenny," the first mechanical spinner, patented in England by James Hargreaves

1780s	Gas lighting developed in England by William Murdock
1783	Chlorine bleach is discovered by Claude-Louis Berthollet in France
1787	Steamboat developed in the U.S.A.
1790	Sewing machine invented in England
1800	Electric battery invented in Italy by Alessandro Volta
1803	Power loom invented in France
1804	First steam locomotive built in England by Richard Trevithick (a model one built in England in 1785 traveled at eight miles per hour)
1807	Sir Humphry Davy produces the first arc light
1812	Steam locomotive that worked well invented in England
1813	Joseph-Nicéphore Niepce and Louis Daguerre of France begin collaborating on first camera. The first photograph, a fuzzy photo of Burgundy, took eight hours to expose. In addition, W. H. Fox Talbot of England later began experimenting and is today regarded as a co-founder of photography
1831	Electric current artificially generated in England by Michael Faraday; electric motors were built shortly thereafter, but their use was confined to toys
1833	Electric signals first sent by Carl Friedrich Gauss of Göttingen, Germany
1840s	Samuel Morse of the U.S.A. develops his telegraph
1842	Anesthetics such as ether first used successfully in the U.S.A. by William Clark. Although the Chinese had invented acupuncture and the Arabs used opium, ether was by far the most successful anesthetic and revolutionized medical practice
1852	Passenger elevator developed in the U.S.A. by Elisha Graves Otis
1859	First oil well drilled in U.S.A.
1860s	James Clark Maxwell of Scotland gives a detailed and definitive description of electromagnetic phenomona, unifying all, including light, in four simple equations that revolutionized scientific thought. (One hundred years later, American Nobelist Richard Feynman said this was the single most important achievement of the nineteenth century; by comparison, the U.S. Civil War was of "provincial insignificance")
1862	Dynamite invented in Sweden
1865	Englishman Sir Joseph Lister discovers antiseptics
1864	Machinery for making shoes developed in the U.S.A.
1874	Chain-driven bicycle invented in England
1874	Four-cycle gasoline engine and carburetor invented in Germany
1874	Telephone invented by American Alexander Graham Bell
1877	Phonograph developed by American Thomas Edison (although the first "phonautograph" had been developed by Leon Scott of England in 1859 as a theoretical exercise)

1879	James Clark Maxwell proves that radio waves exist
1880	Light bulb patented in U.S.A.
1880s	Typewriter in general use. The idea seems to have come first from a Marseilles, France, printer in the 1830s with a "machine cryptographique," but the final form was developed by Christopher Sholes of the U.S.A. and sold to Elipahbet Remington, the U.S. arms maker, who brought out the first commercial typewriters in the 1870s.
1880s	Large-scale dynamos provide electric power for customers
1884	Steam turbine developed by Charles Parsons, and the turbo generator developed in England
1887	First gas-powered car developed in Germany
1892	Diesel engine developed in Germany
1895	First moving picture on screen by Louis and Auguste Lumière of France, drawing on the work of such notables in early film as Athanasius Kircher, a German Jesuit mathmetician who thought of a "magic lantern" in 1645; the Belgian physicist Joseph Antoine Plateau, who developed the "phenakistiscope" in 1833; and others
1895	Wilhelm Roentgen discovers unknown (X) rays
1899	Guglielmo Marconi of Italy sends radio waves between two cruisers, develops radio technology
1900	Rigid airship (zeppelin) developed in Germany
1903	Successful airplane flight by Wright brothers in the U.S.A.
1905	Albert Einstein publishes a paper relating his theory that light consists of packets of energy called photons
1919	Robert Goddard pioneers idea of rocket for use in space exploration
1923	Bulldozer developed in the U.S.A.
1924	Television developed in Scotland by John Logie Baird, who sent the first TV image (a Maltese cross) across a room with a makeshift TV made of, among other things, a tea chest and a biscuit tin. In the U.S. Vladimir Zworykin, a Russian immigrant, invented the iconoscope that further improved the TV
1937	Jet engine developed in England
1944	Germans develop modern rocket prototypes, the V1 and V2, for use in terror bombing
1942	First nuclear reactor built in the United States
1945	First nuclear explosion in the United States
1945	First computer using electrical energy developed at the University of Pennsylvania, called ENIAC.

1947	Transistor developed in the United States at Bell Labs by William Shockley, Walter Brattain, and John Bardeen, revolutionizing the computer age and ushering in the booming era of electronics
1954	First nuclear power plant in operation, in the U.S.S.R.
1957	First artificial satellite put into orbit around earth by the U.S.S.R., followed by the U.S.A. in 1958, France in 1965, Great Britain in 1971, and India in 1980
1958	Laser developed in the United States
1969	U.S. astronauts land on moon
1970s	Computer networks linking computers across geographic boundaries begun at the U.S. Department of Defense with ARPANET, the predecessor of the Internet. Within twenty years millions of computers and databases worldwide are linked
1980s	Biotechnology revolution begins

TWO MORE KEY MOVEMENTS IN EUROPEAN HISTORY

 The momentous events described above began with ideas: that man is the center of all things (the Renaissance), that you don't need an intermediary to talk to God (the Reformation), and that you can use other sources of energy to create things (the Industrial Revolution). All are keys to understanding modern Europe.

But we can't forget two other major ideas that also permeated Europe. They're a little less intellectual and in many ways more negative; at least, a lot of the world thinks so. The first is imperialism—the outward extension of European power. Europeans were far from the first or the last of the imperialists, but the age of European imperialism was far-reaching and certainly its effects are being felt today. The second major event is reunification, which is historically linked to nationalism. Medieval Europeans owed their allegiance to a king; modern Europeans owe their allegiance to a nation-state. The story of how this change came about, of how the petty kingdoms, duchies, and states of Germany, for example, became unified into a powerful nation-state, is not an idle exercise in history. It led to the powerful nationalistic movements of this century, the ones that literally tore apart Europe in two world wars.

THE AGES OF EUROPEAN IMPERIALISM

1500–1900s, two major phases: the first beginning in 1500, the second beginning around 1880

In brief: The conquest or influencing of most of the world by European powers

Background: A person looking at a map in the 1930s saw a world very different from today: more than 80 percent of the land surface of the globe was controlled by Europeans or European descendants. Most likely much of the map was colored red, the color that on many maps represented the British Empire, which ruled over one-quarter of the world's population. Europeans were not the first imperialists—as far back as ancient times the Assyrians preyed on the weak—but they were inarguably the most successful.

Today, the age of European imperialism is over, but the legacy remains. English is the language of international commerce, French is spoken in much of Africa, and the roads and industries built (mostly by indigenous labor) because of imperialism are still there. Maybe of more importance are the political aftereffects of domination by outsiders that still scar Africans, Asians, and Native Americans.

Key events: The age of European imperialism, or the outward thrust of European society and the conquest of diverse peoples in America, Asia, and Africa, began in the fifteenth century and is considered *the first phase of imperialism.*

Imperialism Phase 1: First came a series of explorers, men such as Columbus, Magellan, and Balboa. They were searching for new trade routes to India and the Far East. In the process they ushered in an age when Europe would rule the seas. It began somewhat innocuously. The major maritime powers of the day—Spain, Portugal, Britain, the Netherlands, and France—started setting up trading posts in the newly explored regions.

But the Spanish in particular wanted even more: real control over the new territories. Back in 1494 the non-European world had been officially split into two spheres of influence by the two dominant powers, Spain and Portugal. In their zone in the New World, the Spanish began a series of conquests. Hernando Cortés conquered the Aztec Empire in Mexico in 1519–21, Francisco Pizarro and others in 1532–33 toppled the Inca Empire, and others set out for the rest of the Americas to set up new colonies on the ruins of vanquished indigenous empires and civilizations. The Spanish were lucky; their territories were rich in gold and silver, and they grew wealthy from the output of their new mines. This was the age of mercantilism when each great power sought total control over colonies and total economic self-sufficiency, and the Spanish were the greatest mercantilists—for a while.

The other powers of the day—the British, French, and Dutch—

For all the talk about arms budgets today, it was worse several hundred years ago during the height of imperialism. In the late 1500s, Spain was the great imperial power of the day and spent 70 percent of its state revenues on soldiers and weapons. In 1993, the United States spent less than one-tenth that amount proportionately.

expanded their control into North America and set up trading posts and colonies. The French controlled much of what is today Canada; the British and Dutch, the Atlantic colonies of North America. In these cases the colonies themselves became pawns in the great power rivalries in Europe; eventually the Dutch colonies and most of the French colonies went to Britain. (A tiny sliver of land on Canada's Atlantic coast, Saint Pierre and Miquelon, survives to this day as a piece of North American France. It costs the French millions in subsidies, but the government is keeping it for prestige reasons.)

The pattern of imperialism in the Far East was different. Here, trading posts and private interests were paramount, colonists relatively few. At first the Portuguese maintained a monopoly of trade. But by the 1600s, the newly powerful Dutch and British were setting up companies (the Dutch and British East India companies) and sending commercial travelers to various outposts in Asia to trade. The men they sent were called factors, and the outposts, appropriately enough, were called factories. The companies grew rich and powerful. They eventually expelled the Portuguese (who were left with a tiny colony in India called Goa that remained under their rule until 1961, and another outpost in China called Macao, that is only now reverting to Chinese rule). The French also moved into India, but it was the British who eventually controlled (either directly or through treaties with indigenous rulers) most of this subcontinent. The amazing thing about much of this activity is that it was most often controlled by private companies, not the government—similar to General Electric hiring armies, fielding troops, making treaties, and conquering foreign lands. Only in 1858, after Indian troops of the East India Company revolted (the British said they "mutinied"), was power in India transferred to the British government.

By the time the *second phase of imperialism* began in the late 1800s, most of the New World colonies had become independent or were self-governing. But those are relative terms since independence was mostly won by the colonists, not the original inhabitants. And now, with the rise of industrialization, many Europeans questioned the need for any colonies at all. The 1800s was an era of free trade, and colonies were seen by many as a costly hindrance.

Imperialism Phase 2: But very suddenly the next phase of imperialism began. There are probably many reasons. Some Europeans argued that trade was actually better served by a colonial policy—keeping colonies as a source of raw materials and a market for finished products; closed to competitors in a "neo-mercantilist" system. Others became caught up in the

nationalist rivalries of the day and advocated seizing territory for strategic reasons or just to keep one step ahead of rival nations. "Thinkers" of the day expounded the idea that Europeans were superior and had a duty to expand, to take on the "white man's burden" and help the "inferior races." Very often a number of factors converged, sometimes sucking government troops into areas where there was no real desire to go in the first place. The popular press played up all this as well, with illustrations of imperial soldiers in resplendent uniforms and frequent calls to avenge minor wrongs committed by foreigners.

The best example of this new phase of imperialism occurred in Africa, although in this period the Europeans expanded into territories in Asia and the Middle East as well. Most of Africa was virtually unknown to Europeans a few short years before, but as European explorers "opened" the interior of Africa in the 1880s, they were followed by European traders, missionaries . . . and troops.

Most of the action began in the

Technology and Exploration

European exploration began in the 1500s because of a number of technological improvements. Prior to this period, most ships hugged the coastline. But the Vikings and Arabs introduced a number of innovations in the 1100s, including the Arab lateen (triangular) sail, which allowed a ship to sail against the wind. The Chinese developed the stern post rudder (allowing the boat to be steered from the back), and the Arabs introduced the (Chinese) magnetic compass and the (Persian) astrolabe, which allowed sailors to figure out where they were by measuring the height of the sun. Then in 1456 a European invented the sea quadrant, which measured the height of the North Star and allowed nighttime sailing.

The country that used most of these innovations first was Portugal. The Portuguese were among the first to venture out beyond the sight of land in a major way. They rounded Africa by 1497 and (with the Vikings) had probably reached America even earlier.

An Empire Linked by Blimps

 In the 1930s the British had grand, almost bizarre, plans to link their worldwide empire. Using airships (blimps or dirigibles like the German zeppelins), they planned to provide regular passenger service to all the main points of the empire—India, Australia, Canada, and South Africa. They envisioned thousands of travelers, including the king-emperor himself, dropping in by airship on all the imperial outposts. The first official airship was readied for a long voyage in 1930. Called the R101, it was launched amid great publicity and was all set to make a 3,652-mile trip to British India. Unfortunately, it got only as far as France, where it bumped into a low hill and burst into flames. The imperial airship scheme was scrapped, and soon the British Empire would be history, too.

periphery, in the coastal areas along the trade routes in sub-Saharan Africa, and in Arab and Berber North Africa on the Mediterranean.

Back in 1824, France had acquired Algeria (as a result of an expedition against pirates along the coast). Now, as part of a European agreement, it acquired neighboring Tunisia. Then in 1904, it gained "influence" in Morocco, effectively colonizing it (which is why in the film *Casablanca,* set in Morocco's second major city, the people in charge are French, not Arabs or Berbers).

Meanwhile, Britain had already moved into areas of coastal West Africa. In 1875 the government purchased shares of the Suez Canal company (the Suez Canal was vital for sea travel to the crown jewel of the British Empire, India), bringing them into Egypt. After 1882, Britain effectively took over the Egyptian government. Once this was done, British influence began moving down the Nile.

But Britain was already moving in Africa as well. Britain had taken over the old Dutch colonies in South Africa. Now a grand dream arose: a stretch of British colonies across Africa, linking Cairo in Egypt to Capetown in South Africa by a giant new railway.

The other European powers were not idly watching Britain gobble up the continent. France added such a huge amount of territory in West Africa that it soon became the largest colonial power in Africa. In response, Germany took Tanganyika (now Tanzania), South-West Africa (now Namibia), and the Cameroons; Portugal expanded on its old coastal trading posts and controlled the territories of Angola and Mozambique; the king of Belgium personally acquired the giant Congo colony (now Zaire).

The Beginnings of the End of Imperialism: By the early twentieth century there were only two small independent bits of Africa left: Liberia, which had been settled by former American slaves (who behaved as colonialists to the indigenous Africans), and Ethiopia, which was attacked by the fascist Italians in the 1930s in the final gasp for territory. (The Ethiopians resisted the Italians heroically, fielding lightly armed troops against modern bombers. Emperor Haile Selassie appealed to the League of Nations for help, but his requests fell on deaf ears.)

In one sense the height of colonial rule was reached in the 1930s when the British Empire reached its greatest extent. But already the empires were getting creaky. The colonial peoples were beginning to agitate for independence or at least a larger say in their destinies. One of the first incidents of *anti-imperialism* occurred in South Africa in 1900, when the Boers, the white Dutch settlers (also called the Afrikaaners), almost defeated British imperial troops. Paradoxically, anti-colonialists back in London supported the Boers; it was chic at this point to be against the empire. But no one thought much about the black inhabitants at all.

Meanwhile, in India, the reformist Indian Congress was formed (it included enlightened British as well as Indians). The Congress initially agitated for greater autonomy, but after World War I, and particularly as World War II approached, it began to seek independence. Both world wars hastened the end of the imperial colonies. The Europeans were materially and emotionally exhausted. Their colonies in Asia had been conquered by the Japanese, who destroyed the myth of invincible European armies. A new class of Africans, including men such as Kwame Nkrumah in Ghana and Jomo Kenyatta in Kenya, began arguing loudly and effectively for African rights as well.

The end of colonial rule for the most part was marked by some violence but not outright war. The European powers seemed to recognize the writing on the wall. Britain relinquished control of India peacefully in 1948 (but violence among Indians was terrible); the Mau Mau uprising in Kenya was met with force, but here, too, the British left, in 1963. The same occurred with other colonies—the

Europeans mostly left Asia in the 1940s and 1950s, Africa in the 1950s and 1960s. The Portuguese were among the most tenacious colonists; they gave up Mozambique and Angola only in the 1970s, after long and bitter wars. And in South Africa the legacy of European rule ended only in 1994, although Britain had long ago relinquished rule—but instead of giving it to the majority, it gave it to the white minority.

Today, a little over one hundred years after the race for Africa began, Africa is ruled by Africans. Unfortunately, the continent is now ruled all too often by undemocratic and corrupt regimes.

Significance of Imperialism: Colonial government varied considerably. In the Sudan, British rule was relatively benign, colonists were few, and benefits

Imperialism and Language

The well-known Kenyan writer Ngugi wa Thiong'o has argued that Western imperialism's worst influence is on language and culture:

The biggest weapon wielded and actually daily unleashed by imperialism . . . is the cultural bomb. The effect . . . is to annihilate a people's belief in their names, in their languages, in their environment, in their heritage of struggle, in their unity . . . and ultimately in themselves. . . . It makes them want to identify with that which is furthest removed from themselves, for instance, with other people's languages rather than their own.

An example of what Thiong'o is talking about: until the French decolonized Africa and Asia, schoolchildren in both Vietnam and Senegal, for example, read on the first page of their histories, in French, "Our ancestors, the Gauls . . ."

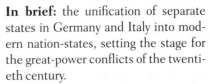

such as the suppression of the slave trade to Arabia were carried out. In Kenya the best land was seized and given to British and European colonists. In South Africa a new white class brought great national prosperity, but relatively little went to the black majority. Usually the colonies were developed economically, but development was primarily designed to benefit the colonial power. Railroads, for example, were often built from mines in the interior to the sea, but a network of transport was not emphasized as it would have been in Europe. The worst excesses were probably in the Belgian-ruled Congo, which was developed almost exclusively for the benefit of the European owners. But many areas received benefits as well. India was helped by an extensive rail network, an increase in industry, new educational centers, and a (forced) introduction into the world economy. Its early leaders in the drive for independence, Mohandas K. Gandhi and Jawaharlal Nehru, were British educated and to some extent promoted British ideals of democracy and rule of law. The unanswered question is: would development have been faster without imperialism?

We don't know the answer, but it's important to remember that there were costs to any benefits that accrued. The colonizing powers ruled by force even though they acted as if they had a divine or moral right to do so. And for every enlightened imperialist there were probably many more like the British governor of the Sudan, Sir Rudolf Slatin, who once said of the people he ruled: "The nigger is a lazy beast and must be compelled to work—compelled by the government." When asked how, he replied, "With a stick." So behind all the flags and

heroic events, imperialism was, at the bottom of things, an ugly episode in European history.

REUNIFICATION IN EUROPE

1848–71

In brief: the unification of separate states in Germany and Italy into modern nation-states, setting the stage for the great-power conflicts of the twentieth century.

Background: Here is almost two thousand years of European history in a nutshell, focusing on one key factor in its politics: the dream of a unified Europe.

Once most of Europe was unified as a single state. Under the Romans, most of the European lands around the Mediterranean and much of what constitutes Britain, France, and Germany today fell under the rule of the Roman emperors. Then a great movement of tribes from Asia swept into Europe; Huns, Vandals, Visigoths, and others helped topple the great empire. But once they had settled down, new attempts at a unified Europe began. Over the course of years it sometimes seemed as if the old Roman Empire would rise again in a different form, but each time a new universal king was crowned, the unified areas got smaller. For example, Charlemagne (742–814) is described as a great European ruler yet he ruled only over northwest Europe, most of Italy, and just a sliver of Spain—a truncated Roman Empire. His successors ruled over even smaller bits of territory, although after 962 one of these smaller semi-unified states was called by the high-sounding name Holy Roman Empire.

By later medieval times, Europe was divided into a hodgepodge of duchies, kingdoms, states, and cities, all separated by language or dialect, ruler, and loyalty, and sometimes paying nominal loyalty to a far-off king. Not that it mattered much to the common folk. They were more concerned with their local rulers anyway and thought of themselves as belonging to their local city rather than, for example, Europe or Germany.

But as Europe moved into the modern age, nationalism—identity with a state that shares the same language and custom—became more prevalent. In effect, now that the idea of a unified, universal Europe was dead, and as nobles began to lose powers to central armies, the idea of powerful centralized nation-states based on people sharing a common language or heritage became more important. France and Britain had made the transition into modern unified states relatively easily; their kings had long ago asserted their centralized power. But Germany and Italy, our major concerns here, were different. As Europe approached the mid-1800s, these two areas were still divided, still odd, anachronistic collections of tiny states. Then two great leaders, Otto von Bismarck and Camillo Benso, Conte di Cavour, smelled opportunity. They succeeded in uniting most of the Germans and Italians, respectively, and in so doing they transformed modern Europe.

Key events: The events outlined below are part of any elementary course in modern European history. Anybody taking the course comes away

with the names of two countries (Italy and Germany), two names (Cavour and Bismarck), and one word (nationalism).

Nationalism is a relatively recent phenonomon. Its power was revealed during the French Revolution and its aftermath when French citizens beheaded their king and decided to pay homage to themselves and to the ideal of their nation and liberty instead of an individual king or queen. By the mid-1800s the idea was everywhere. But Germans and Italians, many of whom were infected with the nationalism virus and wanted their own powerful nation-states, were stuck.

Italian Reunification: Italy had been briefly united after Napoleon conquered it in the early 1800s, but after his defeat in 1814, it was once again divided into twelve major parts, some dominated or controlled by powerful Austria to the north, others by the Pope, and others by hidebound aristocrats. An attempt at a liberal Italian republic by an unfortunately impractical revolutionary named Giuseppe Mazzini failed in 1848. Unification was left to another, an innocuous-looking, somewhat roly-poly man whose looks belied his genius. Camillo Benso, Conte di Cavour, came into the government of the most liberal Italian state, the kingdom of Piedmont-Sardinia, in 1848, and began plotting a way to reunify Italy.

First, he cleverly brought Italy into the Crimean War against Russia—for no other reason but to win powerful friends for his next move: war against the Austrians, who controlled much of Italy. Sure enough, he acquired his friends. Then he picked a fight and got Austria into war. Aided by France, Cavour managed to get some Italian territory from Austria, but not enough. Napoleon III (the nephew of the great Napoleon I), the ruler of France, was afraid of the Austrians. But the die had been cast, and when a popular adventurer by the name of Giuseppe Garibaldi set off with a band of adventurers called the Thousand Red Shirts to liberate the people of the corrupt southern Italian states, Cavour saw opportunity. Garibaldi's small army (probably about twenty thousand) actually succeeded in overrunning the Italian island of Sicily and then crossed the Italian straits to Naples. Cavour moved quickly and sent his army south. Garibaldi was a hero but no politician; he turned over his winnings to Cavour, who declared the kingdom of Italy. A short time later Italy joined yet another war against Austria and received the Austrian-dominated Venice as a reward. Italy was now a nation-state— but a rather backward one. In the balance-of-power games going on in Europe, not many feared this new addition to the roster of major powers, but it set an example for another unification—that of Germany.

German Reunification: While Italy was coalescing, Germany was still a loose collection of states in a weak Confederation dominated mostly by Austria. But the events in Italy did not go unnoticed in some of the German states, particularly in the most powerful, Prussia.

Enter a powerful, enigmatic figure who dominated European history in the latter part of the nineteenth century: Otto von Bismarck was a hale, beer-drinking man fond of boldness and tough talk, but the inner man was often melancholic and moody. He was a late bloomer who entered the diplomatic service and saw what had to be

done to unify Germany. Unlike most people who have a grandiose idea, Bismarck stuck to his plans and accomplished his goal. It was left to later, more politically careless Germans to undo much of his work.

Bismarck became chief minister of Prussia in 1862. Now he had a platform where he could "persuade" the independent or Austrian-dominated states of Germany to accept unity under Prussian rule. Bismarck was no pacifist; persuasion would come by force if necessary. As he said in a famous speech, "Not through speeches and majority resolutions are the great questions of the day decided . . . but through blood and iron."

Bismarck realized, as had the Italians, that Austria was the major problem, but first he *joined* Austria in a war against Denmark for two duchies in the north that Bismarck said should be part of the German Confederation. He won that war and was then ready to pick a fight with Austria, after carefully providing assurances to the other European powers that he wasn't seeking to upset the tenuous balance of power in Europe. This was an era of nervous and competing great powers; all feared unrest and war. Bismarck's Prussians defeated Austria easily. Now Bismarck dissolved the Austrian-dominated German Confederation and instead created a new North German Confederation dominated by Prussia.

The ease with which Prussia's army won her wars was beginning to alarm leaders in other European capitals, particularly Paris. Many feared (rightly, it turned out) a unified Germany. Bismarck realized that he would have to fight the dominant power on the continent if he was to unify Germany. France would not allow reunification to proceed otherwise. But he had to make it look as if France, and not Prussia, sought war. He didn't want other powers intervening on France's side and spoiling his plans. Deviously, he doctored the transcripts of talks between the French ambassador and the Prussian king to make it appear as if the Prussians had been rudely insulting; in this atmosphere of distrust France declared war. Again, Prussia's military machine was invincible, crushing French forces in a matter of weeks. At Versailles in 1871 the Prussian king was crowned the new emperor of Germany, and the French provinces of Alsace and Lorraine were given to Germany. A new power now dominated Europe.

Significance: To at least some degree Bismarck's actions inadvertently set the stage for World War I, which in turn set the stage for World War II.

Bismarck himself was not a lover of war for war's sake. He made efforts to appease Britain and Russia, and was concerned that the balance of power was maintained in Europe. He did not want a large-scale war in Europe. But his successors were not so careful. Bismarck was fired from his job by the king of Germany, Kaiser Wilhelm I, a

bombastic, militaristic man who was not adept at playing the great-power game. Within a matter of years World War I would begin.

But some of the blame does fall on Bismarck. He was probably mistaken in taking Alsace and Lorraine from France. He created a sense of unfinished business in France, a sense that the war of 1870 was not really over. And in one of those ironies of history, the French and Allied victors after World War I had the Germans sign their surrender in the same Versailles where they had so confidently proclaimed their new empire almost fifty years before. And then, of course, in the next act of revenge, Hitler forced the French to sign their surrender to the Germans during World War II in the same area.

Today, the violent nationalisms in western Europe seem to be over. Germany and France are linked together in the European Community, and the significance of national boundaries is fading. But it took decades of fighting and millions of lives to reach this happy conclusion. And meanwhile the power of nationalism is now fragmenting other parts of Europe into small, "ethnically pure" national units. To a great degree politicians who play with nationalism play with fire.

THE FOUR GREATEST CONQUERORS IN HISTORY, PART II:
THE ONE WHO TRIED TO CONQUER EUROPE . . . AND FAILED

 If one man ever dominated Europe, it was Napoleon Bonaparte. He was unafraid of war and killing, but he was no Hitler. He was literally bursting with *ideas*; he accelerated the rate of change on an already rapidly changing continent. He was a revolutionary with a fatal flaw (read the first quotation below), but after the wars were over, his impact remained—even in the most esoteric areas. To take one example, when Napoleon's troops invaded Egypt, he ordered them to bring along scholars and experts (imagine a modern army doing that). One of them found the Rosetta stone, written in ancient Egyptian and Greek. From that stone a French scholar deciphered ancient Egyptian hieroglyphs—clearly an unusual legacy for a conquerer.

NAPOLEON BONAPARTE

(1769–1821)
(original name, Napoleone Buona-
    parte)

Conquests: much of Europe
Background: born in Corsica.

At sixteen he was a second lieutenant in the French army.

At twenty when the French Revolution erupted, he had already proved his mettle in battle.

At twenty-five he was already a brigadier general in the French Revolutionary Army.

At twenty-seven he was in command of the French army in Italy, where he won a series of tactically brilliant victories. From there he went to conquer Egypt, where he succeeded on land but saw the French fleet destroyed by the British. No matter. He dashed back to France where he organized a coup d'état that established a new form of government called the Consulate.

At thirty he was the First Consul, the leader of France.

Many people would have quit there, but not Napoleon. He saw all this as just a *beginning*.

He next led France in a series of campaigns against numerous enemies. After realizing he could never conquer Great Britain (which had won a series of naval battles and now ruled the seas), he focused on the somewhat more modest goal of controlling all of continental Europe.

After crowning himself emperor of the French, a series of famous battles ensued. Napoleon defeated the Austrians at Ulm in 1805, the Russians at Austerlitz in 1805, the Prussians at Jena and Auerstadt in 1806, and the Russians again at Friedland in 1807. So far, so good, but Napoleon had a problem with the British, who still controlled the seas and who were harassing him in battles in Spain and Portugal. And the Russians were not abiding by the deals he had struck with them back in 1810.

So in 1812 he made his fatal mistake. He invaded Russia and actually took Moscow (unlike Hitler 130 years later)—but the Russians simply faded away from Moscow, concentrating on harassing Napoleon's armies' flanks rather than initially confronting him. In the end, the harsh winter and Russian troops destroyed the cream of Napoleon's army. In 1813 at the Battle of the Nations at Leipzig, Napoleon was at last decisively defeated and exiled to the island of Elba off the coast of Italy.

Again, many people would have quit there, but again, Napoleon did not.

He escaped and for a famous hundred days led enthusiastic French troops once more against the other European enemies. He was defeated again, this time at Waterloo. And this time Napoleon was exiled far away, on the lonely island of Saint Helena, off the coast of Chile. He died there, fat and depressed (some say he was slowly poisoned with arsenic, either deliberately or from breathing fumes in the wallpaper), in 1821.

Personal characteristics: As a cadet in French military school, Napoleon was short, spoke with a Corsican accent, and was taunted by his schoolmates. Yet by all accounts he countered all these disadvantages the old-fashioned way—with hard work. He finished school in a record one year, read widely (years later scholars would periodically find books with detailed annotations in the margins in Napoleonic handwriting), and planned carefully. He was a genius tactically, but in terms of grand strategy—the big picture—he was inclined to overdo. Perhaps his wife, Josephine's, description of his lovemaking fits his personality: he *attacked*, swiftly, suddenly . . . and then it was over.

NAPOLEON BONAPARTE (ENGRAVING BY LANGIER, 1835, AFTER A PAINTING BY DAVID, 1812) (REPRODUCED FROM THE COLLECTIONS OF THE LIBRARY OF CONGRESS)

Reality of War

Napoleon's era is famous for its romantic paintings and depictions of war, with Napoleon and his generals in magnificent uniforms in the midst of heroic battles. The reality was much worse.

Soldiers approached battle in open, unprotected battle line formations, exposed to enemy artillery that often ripped through the lines. As two opposing lines of soldiers approached (to a monotonous and deep marching drumbeat), soldiers were faced with prowling cavalrymen who slashed at them with swords and fired guns trying to break their ranks. At a distance of about a football field apart, both sides would open fire into the tight mass of men on the opposite side. Soldiers didn't even have the comfort of a rapidly reloading weapon. They had to go through the laborious process of loading their weapon, then priming it, aiming it, and then firing.

Once the two sides met face-to-face, the bayonets came out for hand-to-hand fighting in the midst of gunpowder smoke, accompanied by the screams of men wounded by bayonets or trampled by the mass of men pushing forward. The basic strategy was to push through the enemy lines and then turn and attack from behind, but by this time the battle was usually a confusing mass of clawing, stabbing, and shooting men so that it was hard to follow classic strategy. Observers talked about bits of human flesh and bone flying about as primitive hand grenades (round iron cases filled with gunpowder) exploded in clouds of iron shards and smoke and the screams of horses filled the air. Then as now, war was hell.

In a nutshell: The following is perhaps Napoleon's most revealing comment:

My power depends on my glory and my glories on the victories I have won. My power will fail if I do not feed it new glories and new victories. Conquest has made me what I am and only conquest can enable me to hold my position.

An outstanding leader and tactician, he said:

A battalion commander should not rest until he has become acquainted

with every detail. After six months of command he should even know the names and the abilities of all the officers and men of his battalion.

Influence on history: In terms of territory, disastrous. France had less territory than she had at the beginning of the French Revolution. In terms of *ideas,* tremendous. Napoleon introduced a code of law (called, appropriately enough, the Code Napoleon) that was based on the revolutionary idea that all were equal before the law. Variants of it are still in effect around the world.

A WORLD STILL AT WAR:
FROM WORLD WARS TO COLD WAR

 "War is the continuation of politics by other means," said the great German military historian Carl von Clausewitz. The death and devastation of war has been an all too common feature of world history, often marking the major transfers of power and rule.

And it's a feature that hasn't disappeared.

As humankind has been waging war for thousands of years, so historians have studied wars. More recently, political scientists have joined in and have discovered some interesting (preliminary) trends that bear repeating (although remember that these results are highly tentative and controversial):

Wars seem to follow twenty-year cycles. Having said that, let's qualify the statement: wars and other international violence seem to follow weak but identifiable twenty-year cycles of higher and lower levels. Interestingly, roughly every twenty years a new generation also comes into power. Do generations alternate warlike behavior, with sons avoiding the sins of their fathers? Or do these war cycles come as part of larger cycles, like the so-called Kondratieff cycles (which postulate that economic upturns and downturns follow regular waves), with economics playing a driving role in war? Or are all of these cycles illusory or coincidental, the product of the imagination of numbers-happy political scientists?

More wars have been fought in Europe and the Far East. You

wouldn't think this today with all the wars raging in the Middle East and Africa, but historically this seems to be the case. Europe has averaged about six wars per decade since 1815. The average number of wars per country has declined in the twentieth century, although the level of destruction has increased dramatically.

Bigger powers are the bigger bullies. Major powers are more prone to warlike behavior than smaller powers. In one study of ninety-seven conflicts since the end of World War II, major powers intervened in 63 percent of them. A study by Ole R. Holsti of eighty-six conflicts since World War I found that 44 percent involved major powers against small states, 18 percent were between major powers only, and 38 percent were among small states only. Those states with military power tend to use it, and they are usually larger and richer than their neighbors.

Nations of the world have attempted to control war for years, with little success. In 1926 war was condemned as a means of policy by the international Kellogg-Briand pact. And not long after, of course, World War II broke out. Even more recently, signatories to the United Nations charter agreed to renounce the use of force except in self-defense. It is obvious that this agreement, too, has not been followed.

In some cases, though, war seems to be losing some of its popularity. Other than the Serbian atrocities in Bosnia, much of western Europe has been quiescent in recent years; even the Arabs and the Israelis, and the Irish and the British, are talking peace instead of war.

Unfortunately, everything is not getting better everywhere. Africa seems to be heading toward increased political violence exacerbated by poverty, and the end of the Cold War has brought violence to eastern Europe and the former Soviet nations.

War, it seems, is not giving up without a fight.

Here, then, to remind us of what brought the entire world (or major parts of it) to nearly total war—and total destruction—is a brief rundown of the three major wars of the modern world: World War I, World War II, and the Cold War.

WORLD WAR I

(1914–18)
A war that exhausted the old European colonial powers of Britain and France, and ultimately destroyed European hegemony in the world.

Adversaries: Germany, Austria-Hungary (which also comprised Bosnia-Hercegovina, Slovenia, Czechoslovakia, etc.), and Turkey. Against them were arrayed the Allies: Russia, France, Britain (along with its huge empire, including India, the dominions, including Canada, South Africa, and Australia), the United States, Japan, and other nations.

MODERN WAR: TWO GERMANS UNDER HEAVY ARTILLERY ATTACK IN TRENCHES BEFORE LENINGRAD, 1941 (REPRODUCED FROM THE COLLECTIONS OF THE LIBRARY OF CONGRESS)

History: By the end of this terrible war, the youth of Europe was decimated. *Half* of all Frenchmen between the ages of twenty and thirty-two were dead. England lost over one million men; 20 percent of the Oxford University students who served died on the battlefield. If anything, Germany and Russia fared worse. For years afterward, sidewalks were filled with the partially destroyed bodies of the "lucky" who survived with missing limbs, poison gas burns, or blindness.

And for what had these people suffered? The victorious Allies justified the war as an act against aggression, a "war to end all wars," and placed the blame squarely on Germany. But many knew better. The blame really belonged to all the participants. All were guilty and all were victims of a European balance-of-power game gone awry.

The problem began with the great-power rivalries that had plagued continental Europe for years. Who would be the dominant power in Europe? For centuries the major European powers fought for dominance or, more often, fought to *prevent* one nation from becoming the leader. Britain was often the deciding factor; by entering the fray it would tip the balance against the one nation challenging the precarious balance. But by the late 1800s the Pax Britannica that had kept the continent relatively quiet was fading; and Germany was clearly on the rise economically as well as militarily. Germany wanted more in the way of great-power perks and was agitating to get them. United in alliance with Austria-Hungary, a creaky empire in central Europe, as well as Italy, Germany faced with some trepidation the Triple Entente, an alliance of Britain, France, and Russia.

The spark that set the alliance dominoes falling occurred in a place recently in the news again: Sarajevo. The liberal-minded Archduke Ferdinand of Austria-Hungary was on a visit to this newly annexed Bosnian domain in the Balkan peninsula when he was assassinated by a Serbian terrorist. The dominoes then began to fall in 1914:

- Austria demanded concessions from Serbia, blaming the government for the assassination. (They had long been harassing independent Serbia anyway, concerned that it was leading unrest in Austria's Serbian territories.)
- Serbia replied and agreed to *almost* all of Austrian demands.
- Austria was not satisfied. In consultation with Germany, Austria declared war on Serbia.
- The Russians backed Serbia and partially mobilized their army to scare the Austrians.
- This set the Germans mobilizing as well, culminating in a declaration of war against Russia.
- France refused to guarantee her neutrality to Germany, so Germany declared war on France, deciding to follow a long-held plan of striking first at France through neutral Belgium, then turning after victory to settle Russia.
- Britain asked Germany to guarantee Belgian neutrality; when Germany said it couldn't, Britain declared war as well.

Only Italy failed to meet its treaty obligations and ended up on the British side in 1915. Ironically, the original architect of the German alliance system, the great German chancellor Otto von Bismarck, had once said that the Balkans were not worth the bones of a single Pomeranian grenadier. Now they had set off one of the bloodiest conflicts in history.

The war itself was a dreary and horrifying round of battles and slaughter on a relatively stationary battlefront. The Germans initially swept into France; German troops were within sight of Paris when they were repelled in the battle of the Marne. By the end of 1914 the war had stabilized: trenches were dug, and most of the battles were fought over a few yards of territory until the end four years later. Turkey entered the war on the side of Germany, and battles were fought in the Middle East (Gallipoli in Turkey was the site of one of the bloodiest Allied defeats) as well as in Africa, but it was on the two fronts in Europe that most of the carnage occurred: France and eastern Europe.

The war decimated the Russian troops in particular and helped trigger the Russian Revolution (see page 586). Revolutionary Russia sued for peace early. By making a separate peace with Russia in 1918 the Germans hoped they could win a decisive victory on the French front. But after a great push, their exhausted troops were repulsed. And now the situation was worse for Germany. The United States had entered the war in 1917 on the Franco-British side, and the impact was now being felt. Fresh U.S. troops and, more important, the immense U.S. industrial machine helped turn the tide. In October 1918 the Germans and the Austrians sued for peace; on November 11 an armistice was signed.

Epilogue: A peace treaty was signed at Versailles seven months after the

armistice. Although President Woodrow Wilson had proposed a liberal agenda of Fourteen Points as the basis of negotiations, by the time the politicians were through, much of the liberalism was gone. The victors Britain and France received more colonial territories while Germany was obligated to pay war reparations, to demilitarize border regions, to lose border territories, and to accept the blame as an aggressor nation. Hitler later used the onerous Versailles terms as a starting point for his Nazi party platform. In a very real sense World War I was simply part one of a twentieth-century world war. After an intermission, Adolf Hitler set part two in motion.

World War I also accelerated revolutionary change and ideas, from the moderate woman's suffrage movement to the successful revolution in Russia and the abortive ones in Germany. And although the British and French empires were larger than ever, the nationalisms the war spawned made it evident that the colonial days were ending.

WORLD WAR II

(1939–45)
War against the aggression of Germany, Japan, and Italy. This war was truly worldwide in scope. Fighting took place in Europe, Asia, Africa, and off the coasts of North America and South America, and involved nations from all areas of the globe. At the end two great powers vied for dominance: the United States and the U.S.S.R.

Adversaries:

The Axis Powers
- Germany (under the Nazi Party of Adolf Hitler)
- Italy (under the Fascist Party of Benito Mussolini)
- Japan (under the war party of General Hideki Tojo)
- minor allies including Hungary, Romania, and Croatia

The Allies
- Great Britain (the only ally to have fought in the war from beginning to end)
- U.S.S.R. (initially a lone advocate of force against Germany, it then decided to cooperate after being rebuffed by the Allies; it later switched sides again after the Germans attacked it)
- United States (at first supported the British financially and materially; joined the war after the Japanese attack at Pearl Harbor)
- France (an initial ally, defeated by the Germans; the Free French, who left after France surrendered, fought with the Allies under Charles de Gaulle)
- numerous minor powers, including governments in exile of Poland, Holland, Norway, etc.

History: On a gray day, September 1, 1939, German war planes screamed over Polish targets while German troops marched across the border into Poland—all because of ostensible Polish "aggression," a lie promulgated by Adolf Hitler, a master of the technique.

So began World War II, a war of conquest by the Axis powers. The bloodiest conflict in history, it cost the lives of at least twenty-two million sol-

diers and about twenty-five million civilians, and included the systematic murder of six million European Jews.

But the war in some ways began much earlier, as Germany, Italy, and Japan launched their territorial expansion with only token protests from the Allied governments.

- In 1931, Japan attacked China. The League of Nations did nothing but express its "regret."
- In 1935, Italy attacked Ethiopia. France and Britain had planned an oil embargo, but nothing was done.
- In 1935, Germany occupied the Rhineland, a border area demilitarized by the Versailles Treaty. German generals later admitted that had the Allies reacted, they would have had to retreat because the army was still so weak. But the Allies did nothing.
- In 1938, Germany forcibly annexed Austria. Britain made a verbal protest, "in the strongest terms," but nothing else. By now Hitler's racist policies were well known; during Kristallnacht, the property of Jews was destroyed, and blame was collectively assigned to them. The world watched and waited and did nothing.
- In 1938, the Russians proposed an international conference to forestall future German aggression. The British prime minister, Neville Chamberlain, said no, that it would be "inimical to the prospects of European peace."
- In 1938, Germany demanded the right to annex the German-

speaking areas of Czechoslovakia. At Munich, British Prime Minister Neville Chamberlain agreed, producing a famous scrap of paper in which Hitler in effect promised no future territorial ambitions. Chamberlain announced to an anxious world that he had produced "peace in our time."

- In early 1939, Hitler annexed the rest of Czechoslovakia. The Allies protested but didn't attack, although at Munich they had agreed to guarantee Czech frontiers. The Allies had now decided, however, that rearmament and new alliances were in order.

Poland finally brought the Allies into open conflict. The war itself had several phases. Hitler conquered Poland in four weeks (splitting it with the Soviets, who attacked from the east). There followed a period of armed waiting, called the "phony war." Then in a series of lightning or "blitzkrieg" attacks Hitler took over Denmark and Norway, smashed through Holland and Belgium, and swept into France. He isolated a British expeditionary force at Dunkirk, which was rescued by a hastily put together fleet of private and British navy ships. Western Europe was now Nazi ruled. Even the initially lukewarm German public was enthralled. It all seemed so easy.

The next phase was the Battle of Britain. Hitler's air force attacked the isolated British Isles in wave after wave of bombing attacks; they were successfully resisted by the British Royal Air Force. A land invasion of Britain never occurred. Instead, Hitler intervened in Greece, where his Italian allies were

When the Japanese launched a surprise attack on Pearl Harbor, the American and British press was full of talk about this "treacherous, outrageous, cowardly act." Yet, interestingly, more than thirty-five years before, during the 1904 Russo-Japanese War, the Japanese had also made a surprise attack on another navy, the Russian fleet anchored at Port Arthur. This time the British were allied to the Japanese, and THE TIMES of London said, "The Japanese Navy has opened the war by an act of daring which is destined to take a place of honor in naval annals."

bogged down in fighting. He rescued them and conquered Greece, but this delayed his next operation, the keystone of his strategy, the invasion of Russia.

On June 22, 1941, the German army activated Operation Barbarossa, the planned conquest of the East. Germans smashed through the surprised Russian lines and advanced to the suburbs of Moscow. This had long been Hitler's primary goal—to seize the lands of the supposedly inferior Slavs of eastern Europe and the Soviet Union for German living space, or *lebensraum*. Although the German advance was initially a success, eventually the Soviets proved better fighters than expected, and at the high tide of his expansion, Hitler's luck began to run out.

It wasn't evident at first. His Japanese allies declared war on the United States on December 7, 1941, after a surprise attack on Pearl Harbor. The raid was successful, as were subsequent Japanese attacks on the British colonies of Hong Kong, Malaya, and Singapore, the U.S. territory of the Philippines, and the Dutch colonies in Indonesia. But the Japanese had brought the largest industrial power of the world into the war, and they and the Germans would pay the consequences. By one economist's appraisal, the measurement of U.S. "war potential" (economic and military capability) was almost equal to that of all of the other war powers combined. Previously, via lending and leasing military supplies to the British, the United States had helped the war effort against Germany, but now U.S. industrial might was fully committed.

Hitler's setbacks began to mount. The Soviet military machine and the harsh Russian winter exhausted a large

The Swastika

When people think of the Nazis, the symbol they automatically think of is the swastika. Adolf Hitler claimed it as a pure Aryan symbol, the perfect means for conveying his vision of a pure Aryan state. But the swastika (or crooked cross or twisted cross) has a long history prior to its usage by the Nazis and, in fact, was most often a symbol of good, of rebirth.

It appears that the swastika was first used by the ancient Aryans in India as a solar wheel that depicted the sun's movement across the sky. The word "swastika" actually means well-being, and the symbol connoted the sun's goodness.

Similarly, many Native American tribes used the swastika as a symbol of peace and also as a compass rose, signifying North, East, South, and West.

In Asia and the Middle East, the swastika continued being used. Often, in line with its meaning of eternal rebirth, it was a symbolic stand-in for the Buddha. It also was a simple decorative design motif, probably symbolizing happiness or prosperity, appearing in such objects as wall paintings, Persian rugs, even ancient Greek and Roman coins. It has been found etched in the walls of the Roman catacombs, where early Christians met to escape prosecution—and used the swastika as a cover-up for the cross.

But it is Hitler's swastika that most people remember, a symbol twisted not only in form but in its meaning—not eternal rebirth but racial superiority.

proportion of German troops, and at Stalingrad, perhaps the most important battle of the war, Soviet troops turned the tide against Nazi expansion. They fought building by building in this now destroyed industrial city and surrounded and annihilated the army of Field Marshal Friedrich Paulus. Thereafter, they gained the offensive. In North Africa, Allied troops ousted German forces, then fought their way to Sicily and up the Italian peninsula. On June 6, 1944, D-day, combined

British and American troops landed in France and drove toward Paris; meanwhile, Russians were pushing hard on the eastern front.

Although the United States had promised the British to give Europe top priority, it committed a large number of men and vast quantities of matériel to the Pacific as well. United States naval forces stemmed the Japanese tide at Midway; following this they pursued a tough island-hopping campaign, winning Japanese-held islands one by one until they reached the last Japanese-held islands before the main islands of Japan.

Despite a desperate German counterattack in Luxembourg (the Battle of the Bulge), Germany was doomed. Anglo-American forces crossed the German frontiers into central Germany, Russian troops entered her capital, Berlin, and in May 1945, Germany surrendered to Allied forces in a little red schoolhouse in Rheims. Hitler was not there: he had shot himself in his underground bunker in Berlin, determined not to be taken alive. Among his last directives was one enjoining "the government and people to uphold the racial laws to the limit and to resist mercilessly the poisoner of all nations, international Jewry." To the end he was unrepentant and unaware of who was the real poisoner of all nations.

Shortly thereafter, on August 6 and 9, 1945, the United States exploded two atomic bombs over the Japanese cities of Hiroshima and Nagasaki. On August 8 the Soviet Union entered the Pacific conflict, late but anxious for the spoils of war. There was not long to wait: on August 14, 1945, Japan surrendered unconditionally, and the guns were finally silent.

Epilogue: Out of the rubble two

great powers remained, the United States and the U.S.S.R. In effect relative outsiders to the great-power game of the Europeans, by now they were the only real players, and in the post-war years their conflict, called the Cold War, would dominate world politics. On the positive side, the United Nations was formed by the end of the war as well, a national assembly of the world that at least tried to keep the peace.

The age of colonialism was truly over. Japanese occupation of European colonies in Asia was a great turning point. Although the Europeans reoccupied the land, newly confident nationalists were now in place to successfully oppose colonial rule.

COLD WAR

(1945–90)
The undeclared war of two super-powers fought around the world, overtly as well as covertly.

Adversaries: The United States and its allies against the Soviet Union and its allies.

History: "From Stettin in the Baltic to Trieste in the Adriatic, an iron curtain has descended across the continent."

With these words the great British Prime Minister Winston Churchill evocatively described the Soviet seizure of power in eastern Europe that marked the beginning of what would be called the Cold War. The Cold War was a conflict between the two super-powers remaining after World War II, the United States and

the Soviet Union, and in some ways between the two different systems each represented: capitalism and communism.

Although it is called the Cold War because there was no formal declaration of war and little direct fighting between the two, there was no lack of bloodshed. From Hungary to the Middle East to Vietnam, Korea, and Afghanistan, the Cold War was an era of sporadic "brush wars" fought by proxies on both sides, and sometimes by troops from one or the other side as well. As with all wars, the battlefield also extended to the cultural and propaganda fronts as well, each side marshaling facts, statistics, writers, and film producers to show the justice of its cause.

The origins of the Cold War began with the mistrust and different ambitions of the victors of World War II. During that war the "big three"—Britain, the United States, and the Soviet Union—had met periodically to discuss war aims and plans. They managed to agree or put off disagreements sufficiently well to win the war. After the war, the alliance agreements began to break down, and the ideological differences began to show. Impelled by its ideology and its dictator, the Soviet Union was a revolutionary power, seeking great changes in the world and supporting revolution, whereas the United States was now a status quo power, preferring gradual change.

The problems began with the arguments over the fate of Germany, which was occupied by British, American, French, and Russian troops. The Allies had agreed that occupied Germany would be treated as one economic unit, but Soviet dictator Joseph Stalin, once the war was over and a substantial chunk of Germany was in his hands, reneged. He separated his section of eastern Germany from the rest of occupied Germany and began to do the same to the rest of eastern Europe, which his troops had liberated from the Nazis. Stalin eventually restricted both the inflow of information and the outflow of emigrants: many Europeans were now prisoners in their own lands, forced to watch as communist governments were imposed on them.

Stalin's motives for all this were probably complex. Like all leaders of Russia he was interested in keeping friendly or quiescent governments on his border, particularly since his nation had suffered the effects of invasion from the West many times. He also probably had imperial desires to expand the boundaries of his rule, and he wanted to keep his powerful ideological capitalist enemies at bay.

And so Churchill's speech described what was happening: Europe was now split into two rival systems. This was the beginning of a long conflict that was fought not only in Europe but around the globe. Rather than go through a year-by-year account of all the diplomatic, social, and military actions, here are some of the highlights of this long war:

Berlin Blockade (*1948*): The capital of Germany was in the Soviet zone of occupation, but by prior agreement Berlin was a special case; it was split into four zones representing the four occupying powers. Stalin tried to drive the Westerners out of Berlin and back into their zones by closing all rail and highway links to the city; the United States responded by airlifting supplies for almost a year until the Soviets backed down.

Marshall Plan (*1948*): For a mix-

ture of humanitarian and pragmatic reasons, U.S. Secretary of State William Marshall announced a cooperative plan for massive economic aid to the nations devastated by war. The United States ultimately contributed $18 billion; the Europeans the rest. Stalin refused to allow the eastern European states to accept U.S. aid. The Marshall Plan is widely credited with reinvigorating the European economies and allowing moderate governments to succeed.

NATO (*1949*) **and the Warsaw Pact** (*1955*): In response to the real and perceived threats from the others, the United States and the Soviets set up rival military alliances. NATO included most of western Europe along with the United States and Canada; the Warsaw Pact included most of eastern Europe.

Containment (*1947*): In a *Foreign Affairs* article a senior State Department official, writing under the mysterious pseudonym "X," outlined a strategy for the United States that called for resistance to Soviet expansionism around the globe. "X" turned out to be a U.S. State Department official named George Kennan, and the policy was termed *containment*. It would be used to justify U.S. protection of democratic Greece, U.S. intervention in Korea, U.S. protection of Taiwan, and, ultimately, U.S. action in Vietnam.

Korean War (*1950–53*): A cold war turned hot in Korea, which had been split into two after World War II. The communist side attacked the southern U.S.–supported side in 1950; U.S. troops entered the conflict under the aegis of the United Nations (as we did much later in Kuwait) and pushed the communist troops north. The war ended in a stalemate.

Hungarian uprising (*1956*): The Soviet-supported government was overthrown by a popular uprising in 1956; Soviet troops crushed the opposition and reimposed a communist government.

Space race (*1957–69*): In 1957 the Soviets orbited the first man-made satellite, *Sputnik.* In 1961, they launched Yuri Gagarin, the first man in space. Both incidents aroused fear in the United States; leaders promised a program to beat the Soviets. Success in space had much propaganda value and implied great military prowess.

Berlin Wall (*1961*): Concerned by the continuing exodus from communist East Berlin to capitalist West Berlin, the Soviets demanded once again that the West leave Berlin. The West refused, and the East German government erected a wall separating the city, supposedly to prevent "contamination" from the West. In many ways, the Berlin Wall came to symbolize the Cold War conflict.

Cuban missile crisis (*1961*): Cuba was an ideological thorn in the side of the United States, a communist power just offshore. The United States had launched an abortive attempt to invade the island and overthrow the leader, Fidel Castro; this was called the Bay of Pigs invasion. The invaders were émigré Cubans backed by the CIA who were shot or captured as they came ashore (ironically, today the beautiful beaches of the Bay of Pigs are a popular resort for Westerners). Cuba's role in the super-power Cold War conflict increased when the Soviets decided to base missiles there. President John F. Kennedy ordered a naval blockade; the Soviets announced they would not back down, and the Soviet Union and the United States

came quite near to war. Compromise was eventually achieved: the Soviets withdrew the missiles, and the United States withdrew missiles from Turkey near the Soviet border.

Czechoslovakian crisis (*1968*): The rise of a liberal communist government under Alexander Dubcek brought about a much freer version of communist rule called the "Prague Spring." This angered the Soviets, who felt their influence was eroding. In 1968 they invaded the country and reimposed a more orthodox communist government. Dubcek was deposed and sent to a new "important" posting in the ministry of forestry.

Vietnam War (*1945–75*): Split into a northern communist half and a southern noncommunist half, Vietnam (and the neighboring states of Laos and Cambodia) became the site of an enormous Cold War conflict. As the northern and southern communists began to challenge the rule of the South Vietnamese government, the United States sent in a limited number of advisors; eventually their presence escalated into 500,000 troops. The Soviets contributed financial and military aid but only a few advisors to their northern comrades. It was a good investment for the Soviets, at least initially. In 1975 the southern half fell to communist rule. But eventually the Soviets could not keep giving aid to their poor but victorious communist allies, and Vietnam gradually reopened itself to Western influence.

Afghan War (*1979–89, Soviet withdrawal complete; 1992 rebels victorious, although fighting continues*): This is called the "Russian Vietnam." Afghanistan borders the Soviet Union but was not communist. In the 1970s, when a Soviet-backed leader gained power and then began to face domestic opposition, the Soviets sent in increasing numbers of advisors and then troops to buttress his pro-Soviet rule. As with the United States in Vietnam, Soviet troops faced a determined opposition backed by the advanced weapons from the opposing superpower; and this time the United States watched as the Soviets withdrew and their proxy government fell.

The incidents above are just a few aspects of the Cold War. The war itself was fought every day: submarines and ships cruised the world's oceans looking for the enemy; jets patrolled the skies; missiles were ready and aimed at each other. Spy planes and satellites monitored the other's activities (and recently it has been learned that many such planes were shot down by both sides). Proxy nations were supported in battles over local territory. Clearly, all this posturing and fighting cost money, and if any factor determined the beginning of the end of the Cold War, it was cost. The United States could better afford the high price of conflict.

The end of the Cold War: By the 1970s many Soviet leaders were secretly aware that the Soviet Union was in big trouble. Not much was done under Premier Leonid Brezhnev. His successor, Yuri Andropov, former head of the KGB, attempted significant reforms, but he died prematurely and was replaced by a dull half-head (literally—he had to be propped up to vote in the election) Konstantin Chernenko. He, too, died and was succeeded by a young Andropov protégé named Mikhail Gorbachev. At last it seemed that the Soviet Union could be reformed. He began a program of

reform and openness (*perestroika* and *glasnost*) in an effort to revive the nation. He put reformers in top positions, loosened the political reins of the press, and curtailed the powers of the KGB. But everything seemed to go wrong. Rising forces of nationalism hastened the breakup of the union, as non-Russians—Latvians, Estonians, and Lithuanians—sought freedom. The economy got worse, not better. Gorbachev backtracked, firing some reformers and putting in more doctrinaire communists. Then, in a bizarre twist, as Gorbachev was on vacation, some of his new cronies seized power, claiming they were doing it in his name. It seemed like the days of old Soviet politics were back. But Boris Yeltsin, one of the prominent reformers who had been elected, led the opposition from the Russian White House, facing down the old Soviets and, by force of personality and events, preventing the army from intervening on the side of the old communists. The aftermath left Yeltsin with much prestige. Although he put Gorbachev back in power, he forced him to relinquish much, and in the next round of elections, Yeltsin won the presidency of Russia. The formal dissolution of Soviet communism had begun.

Epilogue: The missiles are no longer aimed at each other, but the world is still a very tense place. The nations of the former Soviet Union are plagued by economic problems and unrest; both the United States and Russia are still major arms producers, and there are new worries that private arms producers in Russia will now release weapons to terrorist groups for a price. And China, "the third superpower" of the Cold War, is only getting stronger.

YET *MORE* WARS:
A TIME LINE OF HUMAN WARFARE UNTIL 1975

 "Make love, not war" was perhaps a naive slogan in the sixties, but some scientists have discovered there might be more validity to that statement than first appears. Early studies of primate behavior, particularly those of chimpanzees, showed that these animals were prone to violent behavior just like ourselves. War seemed inevitable to man and chimpanzee. But then scientists studied the highly intelligent pygmy chimpanzees of the central African jungle and found that this subspecies is surprisingly nonviolent. These chimpanzees apparently substitute frequent sex for violence. Obviously, humankind has not fol-

lowed suit. The number of wars seems unending.

Here's a brief summary of a few more highly important, historically significant, or interesting wars we have fought while the chimps were doing something more productive. This list serves as a kind of time line of human history; signposts of history that show the important problems of the day. We've put modern and modern revolutionary wars, including those of the French Revolution, in the Political Geography section on page 499 since in most cases the effects are still clearly with us.

Assyrian Wars (*fought around 600 B.C.E*)
> Various wars fought by the Assyrian Empire that resulted in the conquest of much of the Middle East, including ancient Israel.

Peloponnesian War (*431–404 B.C.E.*)
> The major victor of the Persian Wars, Athens tried to create a federal system out of the many independent city-states, but the other cities resented Athens's heavy-handed ways. (When the island of Melos resisted, Athens killed the men and enslaved the women and children.) The militaristic city-state of Sparta, in particular, resisted Athens; in 404 B.C.E. with the help of Persia it captured Athens and won the war. This war exhausted the heartland of Greece, making it ripe for conquest.

Wars of Alexander the Great (*334–323 B.C.E.*)
> The young son of the Macedonian king Philip reestablished hegemony over Greece, then turned to the Persian Empire, sweeping through its outer provinces of Anatolia, the Levant, and Egypt, and eventually conquering its heartland and burning the capital, Persepolis. Alexander finally stopped at India, not because of a lack of nerve but because his troops were tired. His successors, the Diadochoi, ruled much of the East and brought Greek ideas to the East. For more, see pages 39–40.

Conquests of Charlemagne (768–814 C.E.)

Frankish warriors had earlier defeated the last remnants of the Roman Empire in Gaul (modern-day France). After years of squabbling, a succession of strong leaders—Charles Martel, Pépin, and finally, Charlemagne—united western Europe under their rule. Charlemagne conquered the Lombards of northern Italy, the Muslims in the Spanish border regions, the Slavs of Bohemia (modern-day Czechoslovakia), and the Saxons of northwestern Germany.

Crusades (1096–1291)

Over a period of two hundred years, there were seven major and many more minor crusades, or attempts to take back the Holy Land of Palestine and Jerusalem from the Muslims, who had conquered it from the Greek Byzantines years before. The two most important Crusades were the First and Third. The First Crusade in 1096 drove the Muslims from part of Palestine and set up a Christian kingdom there; it was retaken for the Muslims by Saladin one hundred years later. The Third Crusade of 1189 was led by three European kings: Frederick Barbarossa of Germany, Philip Augustus of France, and Richard the Lion-Hearted of England. It failed, but Saladin agreed to allow Christian pilgrims to travel to the holy sites.

Conquests of Genghis Khan (1209–27)

Temüjin was elevated to the leadership of the Mongols in 1206 as Genghis Khan, the supreme ruler of the peoples of central Asia. Shortly thereafter he began his career of conquest, fighting and defeating petty kingdoms in the north of China and much of central Asia. His successors completed the conquest of China, and captured much of Russia, Poland, and Hungary. All of Europe did not fall to the Mongols only because of the death of Genghis's successor, Batu. For more, see pages 41–42.

Conquests of Timur (1360–1405)

Proclaiming himself the leader of the Mongols, Timur (called Timur the Lame or Tamerlane) renewed the Mongol conquests, seizing much of central Asia and defeating the empire of the Khwārizm in Iran, the Ottoman Turks, and with his Golden Horde advancing into India. For more, see pages 42–43.

Hundred Years' War (1337–1453)

English kings were not content with only the English throne; they wanted France's as well. Backed by claims of blood and a powerful army, they engaged in an on-again, off-again war in France, often with French allies. During this period, bands of soldiers rampaged over the countryside along with the black plague (the bubonic plague epidemic). Finally, Jeanne d'Arc (Joan of Arc) helped unite the French. Joan was burned at the stake by the British, but the momentum was now with the French. Charles V was placed on the French throne, and the British were thrown out of France, which now had become a powerful, unified state.

Mughal Conquest of India (1526–1605)

Babur, a descendant of Timur (and possibly Genghis Khan) and the ruler of Kabul, Afghanistan, used artillery to defeat the sultan of Delhi and went on to capture Gujarat. His successor, Akbar, completed the conquests, capturing northern and central India by 1605. A later successor, Shāh Jahān, extended Mogul control south into the southern Deccan portion of India.

Spanish Conquest of Mexico *(1519–22)*

Through a series of daring moves, Hernando Cortés, an ambitious and unscrupulous Spaniard, marched into the Tenochtitlán, the capital of the Aztec Empire. He allied himself with the subjected enemies of the Aztecs and so brought down the great Aztec Empire in central Mexico, remaking Tenochtitlán into Mexico City, the capital of New Spain, and enslaving his Aztec subjects. Meanwhile, Cortés's lieutenant, Pedro de Alvarado, went south to conquer the Maya civilization; eventually the Montejo family would finish the job. A sad consequence of this conquest was the burning of all Maya books (except for three that were overlooked), an irreparable loss to world culture. For more, see pages 52–56.

Spanish Conquest of the Incas *(1531–50s)*

The Incas were a great nation of Native Americans who ruled a long swath of land on the western coast of South America. Encouraged by the success of Cortés, another Spaniard, Francisco Pizarro, marched into the Inca city of Cajamarca with 180 men, twenty-seven horses, and two cannon. It was deserted: the Incas were planning a trap for the Spaniards. But the Inca leader, Atahualpa, accepted an invitation by Pizarro to meet in the deserted city. Once there he was seized and his cohorts were killed. He offered a huge ransom for his release (gold and silver piled seven feet high in a twenty-two-foot room); once Pizarro received it, he killed the king. With the king dead, it was easy for Pizarro to conquer the empire. He reached the capital city of Cuzco and looted it; then he marched to the coast and founded the new capital city of Lima. For more, see pages 56–58.

Thirty Years' War *(1618–48)*

This European war started as a religious conflict but ended as a general power struggle, with Spain seeking to control the Netherlands, Austria trying to unite the Germanic Holy Roman Empire into a modern state, and France and Scandinavia seeking to stop Austria. The war ended with the Treaty of Westphalia, which recognized Switzerland and Holland as independent states. Prussia, a northern Protestant German state, had now become powerful, and religion as a basis of war was recognized as pretty much over. More important, this treaty established the modern nation-state system and established diplomatic norms that are still followed today.

War of the Spanish Succession *(1702–13)*

A sort of mini-world war. The grandson of the great French King Louis XIV inherited the Spanish throne, delighting Louis but angering the other European powers, who saw a vastly more powerful France. The Netherlands, Britain, and the German states of the Holy Roman Empire opposed Louis, who eventually sued for peace. At the Treaty of Utrecht it was agreed that the crowns of Spain and France could never be united, although Louis's grandson could keep the throne. This war was important because it maintained the European agreement on the importance of a relative balance of power.

War of the Austrian Succession *(1740–48)*

A very complex series of campaigns among the European powers: Prussia versus Austria over the province of Silesia; France and Austria over who would succeed to the throne of Austria; Austria and Spain over the control of Italy; Britain against France and Spain over control of the sea and

103

overseas colonies in India and the Americas. At the end of all these conflicts, there were some relatively minor territorial adjustments, the main one being that Prussia kept Silesia.

Seven Years' War (1756–63)

Another power struggle of the European powers, with France and Austria allied against Britain and Prussia. One phase of the war took place in the colonies overseas: in North America, Britain controlled the coastal areas (the thirteen original colonies), and France controlled the interior, including Quebec and the Ohio valley. The British eventually seized the French holdings, also winning the French colonies across the globe in India. Meanwhile, in Europe, Austria had allied itself with France against the ambitions of the increasingly powerful Prussian (north German) state. Britain weighed in with Prussia, but Russia joined the French. Through brilliant tactical maneuvers, the king of Prussia, Frederick II, managed to hold off his enemies. The war ended with the Treaty of Hubertusburg, which essentially ratified the status quo. Prussia now was one of the five great powers of Europe.

Opium Wars (1839–42)

A very black stain on British history, these wars were fought over the "right" of the British to sell opium to the Chinese. Ostensibly the dispute was over legalities; the Chinese government had seized opium belonging to British subjects, an action the British said was illegal. With superior firepower, the British won, extracting territorial gains (including a natural port that they would make into the city of Hong Kong) and indemnities.

Crimean War (1853–56)

War was declared by the Turks against the Russians over the Russian demand that it be allowed to protect Christians within the Turkish Empire. The Christian states of Britain and France intervened on Turkey's side, concerned over Russian expansionism, and attacked Russia's Crimean peninsula in the Black Sea. The war was very ineptly fought by both sides. In one famous incident, the Charge of the Light Brigade, British cavalry advanced against machine guns—the wrong soldiers at the wrong place at the wrong time. This carnage contributed to the fame of the nurse Florence Nightingale, one of the few genuine heroes of the war. Russia accepted the peace terms of the allies in 1856.

Franco-Prussian War of 1870

Basically caused by the rivalry of France and the Prussian-dominated North German Federation for leadership in Europe. (The Prussians were a militaristic north German state.) France was ruled by the overconfident Emperor Napoleon III (who was nothing like his more famous uncle). He declared war on Prussia and managed to lose the war within months. France ceded the provinces of Alsace and Lorraine to Prussia; Prussia crowned its king the German emperor in the Hall of Mirrors at Versailles in France, humiliating French honor. (The French had their revenge after World War I when Germany had to sign its surrender terms in the same room.) The Franco-Prussian War brought about the unification of Germany and heightened Franco-German tensions.

War of the Pacific (1879–83)

You've probably never wondered why Bolivia has a navy but no coastline, but if you ever have, you now have an answer: it stems from this war. It also could easily be called the fertilizer war since it centered on nitrates, a lucrative product mined on the Pacific coast of South America. At that time Bolivia possessed a small coastline rich in these chemicals, and it demanded the right to tax Chilean investors who were mining nitrates there. The Chileans refused. In retaliation, Bolivia seized Chilean-owned property. Chile intervened on behalf of her countrymen. Peru then intervened on Bolivia's side, which was a mistake because Chile then won a stunning military victory over both nations. The war was a disaster for Bolivia, which lost its coastline to Chile and became a landlocked nation. It still maintains a navy, however, in the hope of one day regaining it. Peru was occupied by Chile and disrupted economically.

Sino-Japanese War *(1894–95)*

The Japanese had modernized along Western lines and now wanted the same concessions in the decaying Chinese empire that the Westerners had. (The Westerners had the right to control various ports and railways; they could have their citizens tried in non-Chinese courts, and so forth.) What the Japanese really wanted was Korea; in 1894 they attacked and won soon after. The Treaty of Shimonoseki established Korea's independence, but it was really a sham since Japan dominated the country. Japan also won substantial concessions in China, but Western pressure forced the Chinese to give many of them up. The Western powers didn't like non-Western imperialists.

Russo-Japanese War *(1904–5)*

Russia was moving troops into Chinese Manchuria; Japan wanted them to withdraw and finally launched a surprise attack on the Russian navy at Port Arthur, declaring war. Japan won and received half of Sakhalin Island and Russia's sphere of influence in Manchuria.

Arab-Israeli Wars *(1947–48; 1956; 1967; 1973)*

In the late 1800s, Zionism was born. It called for the Jewish return to their homeland. Jews began settling in Palestine in large numbers. The impetus for *aliyah,* or return, increased during and after World War II. Initially Palestine was under British colonial rule; after World War II, the United Nations agreed that the land would be split between Jews and Arabs, each group establishing an independent state. The Arabs disagreed and attacked the Jewish lands, now called Israel, and were beaten back. An armed peace with border incursions lasted until 1956 when Egypt announced it would nationalize the Suez Canal, and Israel, Britain, and France attacked and seized the canal region. They were ordered to withdraw by the U.N. In 1967, Egyptian president Gamal Abdel Nasser closed the Strait of Tirān to the Israelis, who responded by attacking Egypt. They seized the Sinai peninsula, Jerusalem, and the West Bank, and the Golan Heights of Syria. Another armed peace followed, until 1973 when Anwar al-Sadat of Egypt launched an initially successful surprise attack on Israeli forces in the Sinai. A peace brokered by the United States and the U.S.S.R. ended that war.

Korean War *(1950–53)*

After Korea was liberated from Japanese control in 1945, the United States and the Soviet Union each established zones of occupation, eventually resulting in two separate nations: (communist) North Korea and (capitalist) South Korea. In 1950 the North Koreans attacked the South. The United Nations responded by ordering the defense of South Korea; a U.N. army of mostly U.S.

and South Korean troops counterattacked. After victories got U.S. troops close to the Chinese border (evidently the U.S. General Douglas MacArthur was acting against orders from President Harry Truman to keep well back), Chinese troops entered the conflict. Eventually a truce was reached with an essential return to the status quo, but it had a major difference: U.S. troops stood guard at the border as a trip wire, a guarantee that the United States would fight again if need be.

Vietnam War (*1946–75*)

France had made Vietnam, along with the rest of Indochina, a colony back in the 1800s. In the aftermath of World War II, the Vietnamese had a developed independence movement (which had resisted the Japanese, with U.S. help). Led by Ho Chi Minh, they were the Vietminh. But the French fought these nationalists, finally losing a key battle at Dien Bien Phu. A 1954 international conference in Geneva called for a truce and free elections in 1956; its provisions were never carried out as phase two of the war erupted. North Vietnam now had a communist government under Ho Chi Minh. The South remained pro-Western, but now with more of an American orientation as the United States replaced France in the war. Aid and advisors were few in the early years, but by 1964 a few U.S. troops were on the ground; more important, U.S. destroyers were patrolling the waters off North Vietnam. An attack on these destroyers produced the Gulf of Tonkin Resolution in which Congress supported the president's action in bombing the North in retaliation. The war quickly escalated, with continuing air strikes and a dramatic escalation in U.S. troop presence—over five hundred thousand men on the ground. The tide had turned (possibly) by 1968 when communist guerrillas led the Tet Offensive against the South. By all accounts it was militarily disastrous, but in terms of public relations it was a major success, turning U.S. opinion against the war. By 1972 more than five hundred thousand U.S. troops had been withdrawn. South Vietnam fell to an attack by the North in 1975. In addition, the war had previously spilled over into Laos and Cambodia, spawning indigenous communist movements there. Both nations fell to communist rule—Cambodia's to a bloody regime that sponsored a mass genocide of its own people.

Shaka

(*c. 1787–1828*) *South Africa*

He has annihilated the enemies!
Where shall he now make war?
He has vanquished all the kings!
Where shall he now make war?
—Great Song of Zulu King Shaka's regiments

History has a way of creeping up on you. During the recent elections in 1994 in South Africa, there were constant street battles among the major contending forces. And the divisions between white and black were to some degree less of a worry than the divisions among the blacks themselves, particularly among the Zulu and non-Zulu people of South Africa.

The Zulus are a great people in their own right, the heirs to an empire formed by their first great leader, Shaka. He developed a small tribal group into a powerful fighting machine—the African equivalent of the Greek Spartans. In a few years he had conquered much of South Africa, unified his people, and created a strong identity. Ultimately, Shaka was assassinated, and his successors were later defeated by the British, but not before giving a very good fight. The Zulu identity has survived even though the Zulu nation is part of a larger unit, South Africa. As South African citizens, Zulus share a dual loyalty to their nation and their old kingdom. Their major politician, Chief Mangosothu Buthelezi, is to some degree a "spoiler" in South African politics. The hope is that he, or someone else, will lead his people to full participation in South African politics and away from the frightening prospects of internecine strife.

The story of the rise of the Zulu nation is a fascinating bit of African history. Its founder, Shaka, will be remembered in history as a major innovator of war and a great leader who inspired—and terrified—thousands.

Before Shaka's times, the Zulus were a small petty state of Bantu-speaking people allied to a somewhat larger group. Shaka's father, Senzangakhona, was the chief of this small Zulu nation. Shaka was conceived out of wedlock, and although his father married his mother before he was born, his theoretical illegitimacy bothered Shaka deeply. Even more important, Shaka's beloved mother, Nandi, did not get along well with Senzangakhona, and they left to live with a neighboring group of people called the Mthethwa. This childhood of quasi-exile also scarred Shaka greatly. Shaka was a great man but clearly had his troubles. As a ruler he used terror to keep his subjects in utter subordination. For example, when his mother died, he banned private sex among all his subjects.

But Shaka found his calling under the Mthethwa chief of the North Nguni Bantus. Dingiswayo had expanded his empire and placed Shaka in a high position in his court and in the Mthethwa army. Here Shaka introduced a number of innovations, but he found that the Mthethwa ruler preferred diplomacy to war.

No matter. When Shaka's father died, the Mthethwa clan helped Shaka become the new Zulu leader. Now Shaka began to put his own stamp on the kingdom. He reorganized the army, adopting the innovative stabbing spear in addition to the old throwing spears. He drafted young men from all over the kingdom and put them into his new army. They were housed separately and developed loyalty to the state rather than to their local chiefdoms. With his army in shape, Shaka began an ambitious series of conquests of the surrounding peoples of Natal, South Africa, absorbing them into his kingdom or destroying them.

And now the tables turned even more in Shaka's favor. The Mthethwa king was defeated and killed in battle, and Shaka rallied the kingdom to accept his rule as well. He kept up the military lines of his Zulu state and expanded its functions. He went to war with virtually everyone around him, enlarging his kingdom greatly and conquering or receiving tribute from many other rulers to become the greatest power in southern Africa. Sadly, though, his last battle was his one major defeat. He had sent his army to southern Mozambique, where tropical diseases ravaged them. While his army was away, his half-brothers saw an opportunity; they assassinated him and seized power for themselves.

But Shaka's legacy remains. The Zulus regrouped to inflict several defeats on the best army of the day—the British—until their king Cetuashyo was at last captured. (He was sent to London where he achieved such popularity that the British reinstated him as Zulu king.) Even after this, and after an unsuccessful revolt in 1906, the Zulus have remained a formidable force, although more in the realm of politics than war.

HISTORY APPENDIX I— THE COMPLETE HISTORY OF CHINA IN 17 PAGES: THE WAY THE CHINESE SEE IT

THE GREAT DYNASTIES OF CHINA

In many ways China is a world in and of itself—a *large* world with a history dating back to before 2200 B.C.E.

Physically, it's impressive: 3,691,502 square miles—larger than the United States—occupying most of the habitable space of the huge continent of Asia, and with 1.16 billion people occupying the area. In fact, a full one-quarter of the world's population is Chinese. These people look back on a history stretching back thousands of years, and most of us know next to nothing about it.

Chinese history from the beginning until almost the present has been arranged by dynasties, by great families of emperors who have ruled this huge land. You can't miss encountering these names; for example, Chinese art is usually described by its dynastic period. Who hasn't heard of a Ming vase? Even kung fu films talk of evil emperors and good rebels; in fact, much of Chinese culture is infused with its history. It has provided the stuff of drama, novels, art, and poetry (much as writers from Shakespeare to John Jakes have mined Western history).

But China is not the West, and as you read this section, you'll notice major differences. At the risk of oversimplifying, there are some basic characteristics that make Chinese history very different from that of Europe and America:

- **Chinese history is much more continual:** Unlike the West, there were few great breaks with the past such as the fall of the Roman Empire.

CHINESE COUPLE IN SAMPAN, 1902 (REPRODUCED FROM THE COLLECTIONS OF THE LIBRARY OF CONGRESS)

- **There was less social change:** Although China was a very innovative society (inventing paper, printing, the compass, gunpowder, and developing hydraulics, to name just a few), technological changes produced fewer social changes . . . until recently. Why? Maybe because China was more unified than Europe. Social change tends to come more rapidly when competition is rife, as in disorganized and politically messy Europe. (This isn't necessarily bad. Many Chinese would argue that their more stable society is better poised to survive in the next century.)

- **Scholars and intellectuals were more important:** Probably no other society has respected intellectuals as much as the Chinese. During most of Chinese history you had to be a scholar to make it in government. You had to pass a rigorous civil service exam based on the classics.

- **Chinese history often follows a basic pattern:** The pattern is usually this: a bad emperor is deposed by a heroic rebel who then founds a new dynasty. Time passes. The good emperor's great-grandsons are corrupt and evil. Bad portents such as a flood or civil unrest point to a loss of their divine right to rule, called the Mandate of Heaven. Then a new heroic rebel leads the people against the emperor and wins the throne for himself. Sometimes, of course, this was a self-fulfilling prophecy. If an emperor lost to a rebel, he was by definition declared a bad emperor, and

historians were quick to explain why (just as our modern news commentators are ready with post-election analyses on election victories).

Until very recently most Chinese were much better educated about their history than we are about ours. The names of emperors good and bad were often invoked as metaphors. Now as pop culture and technological culture invade China, the Chinese preoccupation with history and classics is fading.

If you want to understand a Chinese film or a Chinese poem, you should know at least something about China's great rulers and dynasties. Listed below are the major Chinese dynasties along with a traditional history and some of their great accomplishments. The list ends with the fall of the last Chinese dynasty in 1912; Chinese history after that belongs to the realm of modern politics, which is covered on page 589. Note: There are two basic ways of transliterating Chinese names. We've used the modern (pinyin) way first with the more traditional (Wade-Giles) in parentheses in this section. Both styles are used throughout the text.

SAGE KINGS

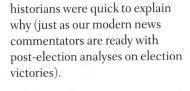

(before 2200 B.C.E.)

The ancient Greeks have their Olympians; the Chinese have their Sage Kings. They were supposedly the rulers of China before her true history began, in the time of such mythical figures as Fu Xi, the inventor of writing, fishing and trapping, and Shen Nung, the inventor of agriculture and business. In reality, pre-dynastic China was probably Neolithic in culture (using stone tools for hunting and farming) along with most of the rest of the world.

XIA (HSIA) DYNASTY

(2200–1500 B.C.E.)

Traditional Chinese history books mark this as the beginning of their history, but there's a major problem. Not a shred of archaeological evidence has been found showing this dynasty actually existed. Yet traditional Chinese history books are usually fairly reliable, if sometimes apt to embellish things a bit. They talk of kings and civilization beginning with the first Xia emperor, Yu the Great, supposedly the last minister to the Sage Kings. Hopefully some future archaeologist will find some tangible evidence of this dynasty.

SHANG DYNASTY

(1766–1122 B.C.E.)

Quick look: The earliest known dynasty in China, centered in northeastern Henan province, in the lower basin of the Yellow (Hwang-he) River.

History: The basics of the Shang dynasty were covered on pages 20–21, but here's a little traditional history. The Shang dynasty began with the spicy ending of the Xia dynasty.

The Chinese imperial color—the equivalent of the royal purple of Western civilization—was yellow.

According to tradition, the last Xia emperor was a depraved man whose greatest pleasure was to sail on a private lake and watch thousands of men and women on the shore eating and making love. This depravity angered a man named T'ang, renowned for his virtue. He overthrew the corrupt emperor and founded the Shang dynasty.

The last Shang emperor has a reputation as a Chinese Nero: an eloquent but decadent collector of horses, dogs, and rare objects who, like his Roman counterpart, loved orgies and raunchy entertainment. He was clearly a classic bad emperor, at least for posterity.

Highlights: The Bronze Age of Chinese art . . . literally. The Shang are known for their magnificent bronze work (known as "li"). These were usually vessels, such as bowls, wine pots, beakers, and cups; they were found in the tombs of rulers and aristocrats after being used for sacrifices to ances-

---

Losing Face

"Face" is a Chinese concept that most people are vaguely aware of, mostly from watching kung fu movies and getting the wrong idea. Face is basically a set of unwritten rules by which the Chinese try to maintain someone else's prestige or self-respect. For example, in a fierce bargaining session, the winner should try to make some sort of concession to save the other's face. In the same way, winning teams are apt to congratulate losing ones and not make much of their win. The "I'm the greatest" attitude of Muhammad Ali wouldn't be tolerated. When a Chinese "loses face," he or she will usually adopt a stony or blank expression, as if the incident didn't occur. But times are changing, and the older generation complains that the young are too brash, too rude, and not as concerned with saving face for others.

tor spirits; they were often decorated with stylized yet naturalistic animals, monsters, and other creatures.

The Shang are also famous for their carved jade, the white or greenish stone often used in Chinese art and also used in Neolithic times. Symbolic of virtue and purity, jade was used in burials in particular, carved into different ritual objects.

ZHOU (CHOU) DYNASTY: WESTERN ZHOU (CHOU)

(1122–221 B.C.E.)

Quick look: The longest dynasty of them all, and the one considered the first golden age

History: Golden ages are usually less golden in reality than in popular perception. For all the accomplishments of this dynasty, the times were very turbulent.

The Zhou reign was a dependent state under the Shang Empire, blessed in the beginning with good (if somewhat austere) rulers. The best known of them was King Wen, father of the first Chou emperor. His name means culture and civilization, and he lived up to his name, building a reputation for piety, concern for his subjects, and diplomatic skill.

His son King Wu was called the Martial Emperor. He was aptly named because he led the revolt against Shang rule and won, founding a new dynasty. Wu advocated impartial justice and set up a fair administrative system. He was also perhaps the first prohibitionist in history: he imposed a

death penalty on all participants of group drinking parties, although he did allow drinking at ritual sacrifices for ancestors. (The ancestors reportedly liked to get drunk.)

The Zhou age was a feudalistic one. Local princes received fiefs and in return paid homage to the emperor. But gradually, the emperor lost power to the local princes.

In 770 B.C.E. the Zhou capital Hao was invaded by nomads called the Jung, and the emperor was killed. The new emperor moved the capital east, to Lo-yang, giving rise to what is called the Eastern Zhou dynasty.

Highlights: Still the Bronze Age, but the more improved version. The Shang-type bronze work continued to be produced during the Chou dynasty, but the decorative motifs were more refined and the overall style more restrained. In later years of the period, the Shang motifs were dropped entirely, replaced with more abstract decorations. A key reason was that bronzes weren't used in traditional ritual as much and were more often intended as decorative pieces only. During this same period, bronze coins also evidently began being produced and used. Jade carving also evolved during this period, becoming more refined, more intricate, and more sophisticated.

ZHOU (CHOU) DYNASTY: EASTERN ZHOU (CHOU)

(770–221 B.C.E.)

Quick look: A period of disunity and warfare but also of the heights of Chi-

111

nese culture (this is the period of Confucius and the great classics).

History: The Zhou dynasty got weaker and weaker, and, typically, others got the idea of taking control away from the emperor. The merchant class grew more important, and wars were decided more by the power of peasant soldiers than by nobles on chariots. Historically, this period is divided into two: The spring and autumn period, and the warring states period, named because of the widespread wars.

Spring and autumn period (770–481 B.C.E): the era of numerous small states, all contending with one another and all paying lip service to the emperor. Just naming all the contenders would take pages, so here's a highly abbreviated look at the top challengers for the imperial throne:

- In the beginning there was Zheng, who ruled numerous small states in the name of the Zhou emperors.
- But he was challenged by Duke Han of the Qi state . . .
- Who in turn was challenged by Duke Xiang of Song.
- Then along came Duke Wen of the Jin state, who challenged him.
- Then Zuang of Chu conquered Zheng.

And so on and so on . . .

At the end of all this confusing competition, two southeastern states, Wu (on the lower Yangzi River) and Yue (in northern Zhejiang) were the most powerful.

Of all the contenders, there's one that most educated Chinese still remember: *Zi Chan of Zheng*. Zheng was a weak state surrounded by strong contenders. But by subtle diplomacy

The Chinese were probably the first to use eating utensils. Chopsticks were used as early as 400 B.C. Europeans stuck with knives; forks were usually used only in the kitchen. In Byzantine times, small two-pronged forks were used in about the tenth century; forks reached Italy in the sixteenth century.

(always admired in China) Zi Chan was able to keep conquerors away. Even the ever skeptical Confucius admired this man. He had a penchant for administration (he ordered different ranks of people to wear different types of clothing) and believed in discipline, saying: "It is not possible to make people happy in a self-indulgent way."

Warring states period (480–221 B.C.E.): like the preceding period only more so. More wars, bigger wars, more people involved, bigger stakes. Basically, seven independent states in China fought to get the big prize: the emperor's throne of a unified China. These states (which frequently crop up in Chinese history books, popular novels, and film) were as follows: Qi in the northeast, Chu in the south, Qin in the northwest, Shu in the west, Wei in the center, Zhao in the north, and Yan in the far north.

Qin was the winner at the end of it all because it had several key advantages, among them top-notch statesmen and diplomats, many of whom were not natives of the state; the strategy of diverting other states and making them quarrel among themselves; a good irrigation system and therefore ample food; and, finally, troops that had learned how to use cavalry from its nomadic neighbors to the north.

But Qin was a tough place to live. The society was organized along totalitarian lines. One Qin minister said, "The people must be organized into groups responsible for each other's behavior. Anyone who does not denounce a culprit will be cut in two at the waist." When King Zheng, hailed as the unifier of China, came to the throne, the rest of China was waiting to fall into his lap.

Highlights: This was a very vigorous intellectual era, a golden age of scholars and philosophers.

It was the period of Confucius K'ung Fu-zi (Kongzi). Other great Confucian thinkers including Mengzi (Mencius) and Xunzi (Hsün-Tzu) followed. Lao Zi (Lao-tzu) (whose title means "Old Master"), Zhuangzi (Chuang-tzu,) and other Taoist masters all lived during this period as well. They believed that tranquillity is derived from not striving, from following the path of nature. Other schools of thought include those of Mo-tzu, who believed in universal love and redistribution of wealth. The most successful school of thought was the Legalist School, which believed that since man's nature was essentially evil, a strong centralized state was necessary to curb man's passions. They critically influenced the successful Qin dynastic rulers.

QIN (CH'IN) DYNASTY

(221–206 B.C.E.)

Quick look: The first dynasty of a unified, imperial China and the beginning of centralized Chinese government.

History: As mentioned above, at the end of all the warfare in the previous dynasty, one state—the state of Qin—looked ready to take the prize of the imperial throne. And so it did—or, more precisely, Emperor Zheng did.

Most of the history of the Qin dynasty is the story of Zheng, who was named its leader at a young age. Following the success of his predecessors, he annexed the remaining independent states of China and unified the nation for the first time.

Among his many accomplishments: establishing a truly centralized state; dividing the country into departments and prefectures; standardizing weights and measures; attacking the Hsiung Nu (Huns); and building the Great Wall—not the much-photographed brick wall of today but heaps of mounded earth. He also is notorious for burning the books of the previous dynasties in order to prevent an uprising based on the past.

Most important, Zheng introduced certain totalitarian concepts of the Legalist School of politics (such as firm centralized control, collective punishment, and presumed guilt before the law) that would remain part of Chinese government in some form for the next thousand years of history.

But as Zheng grew older, his empire began to die with him. Zheng grew preoccupied with immortality, sending couriers out to the far reaches of his empire to find herbs and elixirs that would give him eternal life. Although he took at least one elixir that his sycophantic advisors assured him would do just that, he died in 210. Within a few years of his death, his empire was dead.

Highlights: The Qin were totalitarian rulers, so you can't expect a cultural flowering, particularly when books are being burned and scholars harassed. But one of China's most famous (and very recent) archaeological discoveries dates from this era. This is the royal mausoleum, a huge underground burial chamber with a scale model of the empire and terracotta life-size models of seven thousand soldiers. These are not just department store–style dummies. They are clearly works by artistically accomplished workers; the faces even show different personalities.

HAN DYNASTY

(206 B.C.E.–220 C.E.)

Quick look: The classic dynasty that made China, China—setting basic precedents of Chinese government and culture. (In fact, to this day the Chinese still call themselves "Han.")

History: The founder of the Han dynasty was Liu Bang (Liu Pang), a peasant who had been an official in charge of a group of convicts. When the convicts escaped, Liu faced the death penalty, so he fled and led a group of rebels. At the time, China was in the middle of a civil war. Because of his charisma and humane manner, Liu became the head of one group and ultimately defeated his chief rival, the aristocrat Xiang Yü.

As emperor, Liu Bang took the name Gaozu. He proved to be a wise ruler, lowering taxes and relying on expert advisors rather than personal whim to rule. He selected his advisors on the basis of merit rather than nobility. This marked the origins of the Chinese examination system for civil service, which was noted for being fair. Gaozu never forgot his humble origins and preferred the company of soldiers to the literati of the royal court, at one point asking scholars, "I conquered the empire on horseback! What are your [classics] to me!" (Unfortunately, he hated doctors as well and died when an untreated wound became infected.)

His successor, Wu Di (Wu-ti, Martial Emperor), was more of a cultured sort. The classics that had been burned by the Qin dynasty were now resurrected. Old men with good memories were sought out and asked to

recite what they remembered to copyists.

But Wu Di is remembered for more than this; he is known as the greatest Han emperor. He expanded the size of China by conquering south China, expanding beyond the Great Wall and taking over the huge Tarim basin in central Asia. Confucianism became the state philosophy, and just as Rome had established a Roman Peace, the Chinese now sought to pacify the East in much the same manner.

But "barbarians" were always a threat on the frontiers, and the imperial rule after Wu Di declined, culminating in Wang Mang, possibly one of China's most inept rulers, who tried to reform the country but succeeded only in bollixing up everything.

This was followed by a series of revolts and counter-revolts, which ended in a period of restoration called the Later Han period. But eventually corruption became rampant—powerful landlords seized land making many peasants serfs. After famines and plagues, the peasants formed a revolutionary movement called the Yellow Turbans, which fostered more unrest for some twenty years. You can get an idea of the tenor of the times in this horrifying contemporary poem:

The Western capital lies in sad
   confusion . . .
Whitened bones were strewn across
   the plain.
Upon the road I saw a starving woman
Abandoning her infant in the grass

Highlights: This was the era of the great historian Sima Qian (Ssu-ma Ch'ien), the first to write a comprehensive Chinese history. He and his followers set a pattern that was followed

Traditional Chinese Medicine

Chinese medicine developed for the most part separately from the Western medical tradition. Some of its earlier tenets—such as the postulation that there are as many bones as there are days in the year—are clearly outdated. In fact, in recent years the Chinese themselves have focused on Western techniques. But many aspects of traditional Chinese medicine are only now being appreciated. The Chinese doctors focused on the "whole person" and not the isolated disease, as was often the case in the West. They believed that the body contains energy channels, or meridians, that link the body together. Acupuncture, or the sticking of needles in prescribed places in the body to reduce pain or heal, is based on these meridians. Traditional Chinese doctors often diagnose by feeling the pulse, and many illnesses are healed through elaborate herbal remedies.

for centuries and account for the detailed knowledge we have of China today. The Han was also a scientific age, an era in which the concept of anesthetics was discovered and medical writing reached new heights of sophistication. Zhang Heng (Chang Heng) of this era built the world's first seismograph. Chinese textile works improved, and porcelain production began, an industry that would become a Chinese specialty for centuries.

THE THREE KINGDOMS

(208–264)

AND DISUNITY

(until 581)

Quick look: A period of unrest, with three kingdoms jockeying for dominance. Known to the Chinese as a romantic era—the equivalent of England's days of King Arthur

History: The Han dynasty was collapsing, and three contenders vied for

the imperial throne: Cao (Ts'ao), a general and a scholar who managed to seize the Yellow River basin; Sun Quan (Sun Chü'an), who won much of the South; and, finally, Liu Bei (Liu Pei), a man of noble birth, a prince of the Han dynasty, but so poor that he had to support his ailing mother by making straw sandals, at least according to the more romantic accounts of this era.

The struggles among the three contenders have entered Chinese literature, particularly the exploits of Liu and the three companions who helped him: Kuan Yü, who later become deified in popular religion as the god of war; Zhang Fei (Chang Fei), a former butcher who became famous for his courage; and Chu-ke Liang, a warrior and diplomat.

But at the end of it all was tragedy. China remained divided for virtually all of this period. And then the Xiongnu (Hsiung Niu), or Huns, swept into northern China. For a while it looked as if they might take over the entire country, but they were defeated at the battle of the Fei River in 383.

The upshot of all this was the division of China into two cultural zones, a northern zone dominated by central

Asians, and a southern zone dominated by short-lived Chinese states. Finally, a Chinese warlord named Yang Jian (Yang Chien) usurped the throne of a small kingdom and reunited China under a new dynasty, the Sui.

Highlights: This period was immortalized in the fourteenth-century work called *The Romance of the Three Kingdoms,* which was read and reread until modern times. During this time of strife, Buddhism became quite popular as a religious refuge. Buddhist sculpture of this period is famous for its otherworldliness and mystical sense.

SUI DYNASTY

(581–618)

Quick look: A brief (but important) period of reformation and reunification.

History: This was a yin-yang dynasty, with one classically good emperor and one classically bad one.

The first emperor, Yang Jian (Yang Chien), took the imperial name Wen Di. He was the "good emperor" who did everything right. He distributed land to poor peasants, reduced taxes, reformed the penal code, threw corrupt officials out of office (or executed them), and put soldiers to work farming.

The second emperor, Yang Di (Yang Ti), has gone down in Chinese history as the archvillain among emperors. He was a moody man, prone to paralyzing depression alternating with extreme activity. In his active phase he conceived the building of the Grand Canal that linked the Yellow, Huai, and Yangxi rivers. These great rivers flow west to

east, whereas the canal ran north to south, so with it Yang Di linked a major part of north China to mid-China, a very important accomplishment. But Yang Di had more in mind for his rule. He loved luxury and sought to create the ultimate palace and capital. Unfortunately, his people had to pay the price. He collected taxes ten years in advance, and he forced peasants to work on his grandiose projects. One account speaks of forcing peasants to carry tree trunks on their backs to make columns for his new palace at Lo-yang; half of them died from the tremendous effort.

Yang Di also waged a disastrous war with Korea. Finally, a young officer by the name of Li Yüan (more below) put an end to it all; he routed the Sui leaders and put himself on the throne.

Highlights: Lo-yang was rebuilt as the second capital. There was a Buddhist and Taoist revival under the first emperor, and a Confucianist revival under the second.

T'ANG DYNASTY

(618–907)

Quick look: One of the heights of Chinese history, another golden age. China's borders expanded, her arts reached new levels, and the economy prospered. This dynasty includes three of China's most famous emperors and three of her most famous poets.

History: The rise of the T'ang dynasty under Li Yüan was covered on pages 44–47. Here are some more historical highlights of this dynasty.

The second great T'ang leader was

the empress Wu Tse-t'ien, who came into power as an unscrupulous concubine of another emperor. Ever ambitious, she smothered the empress's baby, then subtly shifted the blame onto the empress. Not surprisingly, she soon wangled her way into the emperor's affections and trust. When he died, she seized power. Despite her lack of scruples, she was a capable ruler but was finally forced out of power (with a dagger held to her neck) at the ripe age of eighty-two.

Her grandson Xuanzong (Hsüantsung) was the last of the great T'ang emperors. He was known as a patron of the arts and not a bad poet himself. But his end was mired in a tragedy that became the basis of a famous poem by the equally famous poet Bai Juyi (Po Chü-i). As an old man, Xuanzong fell in love with his daughter-in-law and married her. But her adopted son, An Lu-shan, a former Turkish slave turned general, revolted and routed the imperial army. His rebellious troops turned against the empress and demanded that she be killed. The emperor was forced to relent, and she was led away and strangled.

Although imperial authority was eventually reasserted, T'ang China never really recovered from the revolt. The golden years were now over.

Other early T'ang emperors were also good rulers; they consolidated the empire and opened the imperial administrative ranks to virtually all who could take the civil service examinations. They excluded only members of degraded classes, which included prostitutes and beggars, as well as actors and merchants.

Highlights: One of the greatest ages of Chinese artistic achievement. As previously noted, this was the era of

great poets like Li Bai (Li Po), Bai Juyi (Po Chü-i), and Du Fu (Tu Fu). Buddhist influence also reached its height under the early T'angs. During this period the famous pilgrim Xuanzong made a round trip to India to gather original Buddhist documents from the homeland of Buddhism. Upon his return the Tayen Pagoda was built to store his treasures for posterity.

SONG DYNASTY— THE NORTHERN SONG

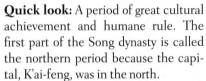

(960–1127)

Quick look: A period of great cultural achievement and humane rule. The first part of the Song dynasty is called the northern period because the capital, K'ai-feng, was in the north.

History: Song history opens with the famous story of the reluctant emperor. For seventy-five years China had been plagued by anarchy, as competing powers fought for control amid the declining power of the T'ang dynasty. Worse yet, on the northern borders a group of Turkish nomads called the Khitans threatened Chinese rule. They eventually seized much of northern China, but they were held back from gaining more through the efforts of the general Zhao Kuangyin (Chao K'uang-yin).

One day, this modest general who had never sought power awoke to find his soldiers gathered around his tent. Before he could do anything, they dressed him in an imperial yellow robe, lifted him onto his horse, and proclaimed him emperor. Supposedly, he called out to his men: "Do you intend to obey me? Because if you are not willing to obey, I will not become your emperor!"

The soldiers stopped and listened as Zhao detailed his conditions on becoming their ruler: the troops were not to pillage, the previous emperor and his mother were not to be harmed, and the government ministers were to be left untouched.

As the Song dynasty began, so it went; it was (usually) a cultured, humane government. Zhao disbanded much of the army after reuniting the south of China; he amnestied most of his enemies and was an able administrator. His successors followed his model. They tended to rule well, and they expanded state granaries to provide for the poor in times of famine.

These reforms reached their culmination under Wang An-shih. Wang was the type of man liberal Democrats would like. He developed a state bank to lend to the populace (unfortunately, with 20 percent loan rates, his well-meaning government often ruined the very peasants it tried to help). Although agriculture advanced considerably, the condition of the peasantry was still very poor and dominated by wealthy land-owners. But Wang really seemed to care about their plight, as illustrated by one of his poems, in which he states:

If anyone is in need of money for a
*   wedding or a funeral,*
I will lend it to him to dispel his
*   anxiety.*
If anyone has a poor harvest,
I will give him all the grain I possess so
*   that he has something to live on.*

But tragedy came after Huizong (Hui-tsung) succeeded to the throne.

He was perhaps the most cultured ruler of China, a painter, art collector, art critic, and religious thinker. Unfortunately, he was ill equipped in the more practical arts of diplomacy and war.

He became embroiled in power politics. He wanted to reestablish Chinese rule over all of China and kick out the "barbarian" Khitans, who had fought the founder of the Songs so many years before. The problem was that Huizong picked the wrong allies, another fierce central Asian people called the Jurchen, who inhabited the dark forests of Manchuria and Siberia. They fought for him but then turned and attacked him, and took over his empire. Huizong ended his days as an exile in a cold clearing of the Manchurian forest, far from the rarefied beauty of his palace.

Fortunately, one of Huizong's sons had escaped the catastrophe and was ultimately proclaimed emperor. But the era of the Northern Song was over.

Highlights: another great era of Chinese art and literature. Some specifics: The art of landscape painting reached a pinnacle, particularly those by the two masters Guoxi (Kuo Hsi) and Mi Fei. Years before landscape art developed in the West, the Song were technical and theoretical masters of this art. As Guoxi wrote:

Every distance causes a difference; the shapes of the mountains vary with every step. A single mountain may combine the shapes and aspects of several hundreds of mountains.

The Song poetry often evokes the same beauty of landscapes, as seen in the work of Ou-yang Xiu in his *Song of the Distant Mountains*. He is also famous for his histories, for pioneering work in archaeology, and for arguing for interpretation rather than blind memorization of the classics. Another famous Song poet, Su Shi, wrote the *Red Cliff*, a masterpiece of Chinese literature. Shao Yung was a well-known hermit poet-philosopher who lived in a hovel, which he called the "Nest of Tranquil Joy."

The Song dynasty is also noted for its porcelain. It was manufactured in subdued shades of green, gray, and blue, with ivory and white glazes, and was treasured throughout Asia and later Europe. The best porcelain came from the Ting area in Hubei province. Pieces are usually a creamy white tinged with brown, often with lively incised decorations—plants, birds, and flowers. Unfortunately, the overly refined emperor Huizong didn't like them; he actually sponsored a new kiln to make different, more restrained pieces.

This was also an era of the Confucian renaissance, a reinterpretation of the classics written by Confucius and his early disciples. Hu Yuan argued that the classics must be brought to life and used to solve modern problems, not just read as dead ancient literature.

Movable type was invented during this period by Pi Sheng, four hundred years before Gutenberg reinvented it in Europe. Soon large numbers of classics and other books were reproduced, expanding literacy and education, a fitting tribute to one of the most literary dynasties of history. Trade increased dramatically, and Chinese junks regularly reached India and Africa. There were new technological breakthroughs in mining, sericulture (silk cultivation and manufacture), and metallurgy. All in all, a great age of China.

SONG DYNASTY— THE SOUTHERN SONG

(1126–1279)

Quick look: A continuation of the Song dynasty, now centered around the new southern capital of Hangzhou (Hangchow).

History: The Jurchen nomads had seized the heartland of the Song dynasty, capturing the capital of K'ai-feng along with the emperor. But as we have said, one of the emperor's sons, Huizong, had escaped. He spent the next several years as a wanderer himself, avoiding the marauding Jurchen. At one point he even had to seek refuge offshore in a boat.

Finally, he settled with his entourage in what was then the small town of Hangzhou. Meanwhile, his remaining Song troops, under the leadership of General Yue Fei, had turned the tide against the Jurchen and was beating them back from southern China. The question was now whether or not to pursue the Jurchen further and liberate the North. General Yue and some others favored action, but the emperor agreed with the other side, and the decision was made to stay put—and Yue was murdered for his political views. Now the Southern Song leaders focused on recreating the luxury and culture of old K'ai-feng in their new southern capital.

In this they succeeded brilliantly. Hangzhou grew into a great city, with single-story buildings giving way to multistory towers. Like Venice, it was filled with canals; barges and boats plied the waters. Just outside the city was the West Lake, studded with pavilions and temples, famed for its beauty. By the end of the century Hangzhou was the largest and most populous city in the world. Years later, Marco Polo visited the city and was awed by its size, wealth, and commerce. This was also an age of commercial expansion and the rise of great fortunes. Unfortunately, some of these fortunes came from corruption, which became an increasing problem in the civil service.

The glittering life of the capital was eventually doomed by the rise of Genghis Khan in the north, the supreme ruler of the newly unified Mongols. At first the Song leaders didn't see a threat but an opportunity. Why not ally themselves with the Mongols and so oust their old enemies, the Jurchen? Sure enough, Genghis Khan's troops did succeed in winning against the Jurchen (Genghis Khan captured Beijing [Peking] and burned it to the ground). And soon after, Genghis concentrated on his westward expansion, giving the Song dynasty something of a reprieve. But eventually Genghis's grandson Kublai Khan marched south and captured the Song capital of Hangzhou. The last Song forces were defeated at Yai-shen (near Canton) in 1279.

Highlights: The neo-Confucian revival begun in the Northern Song years continued, but now the scholars were less apt to get involved in politics and more apt to debate metaphysics. In fact, the greatest scholar of this school, Zhuxi (Chu Hsi), irritated many politicians by his willingness to criticize without being willing to put his ideas into practice. Nevertheless, he is justly famous for introducing Buddhist metaphysics into Confucian thought and providing a more balanced approach to philosophical questions.

Landscape painting also continued. Great painters like Fu Kuan, Guo Xi, and Ma Yuan inspired generations of later artists.

The porcelain manufactories were now reestablished in the south. The Ting ware was now produced in Kiangsi province, where it was made throughout the Ming period and became the imperial porcelain during the last Ching dynasty. Celadon ware, now normally of a jade-green hue, also reached new artistic heights.

Interestingly, this period was one of declining status of women. Foot binding (girls' feet were tightly bound so that they would have tiny, bent-back, crippled feet that supposedly graced them with a mincing walk) became the vogue, proof that the husband of such a wife could afford a nonworking wife. The fashion plagued Chinese women of the upper and middle classes until the early twentieth century.

YÜAN DYNASTY

(1279–1368)

Quick look: The dynasty of the Mongol conquerors of China, the descendants of Genghis Khan.

History: The Mongol leader Kublai Khan took the imperial Chinese throne after defeating the last Song emperor. His grandfather, Genghis Khan, had been prone to nomadic fighting and pillaging, but Kublai was not his grandfather's type. He was a cultured, enlightened ruler, known to his Mongol brethren and subjects as a lover of things Chinese. He proved this when he moved his seat of power from the

traditional Mongol capital of Karoko-
rum to Beijing, which grew dramatically under his rule.

Kublai centralized administration
and divided the country into new large
provinces that survive to this day. As his
rule continued, his Mongol cousins
revolted against him in the Mongol territories, and although he fought against
them, he focused more on China and
Chinese ambitions. Kublai tried to
expand his empire south and east, and
was repulsed twice in his attempt to
invade Japan, once by a disastrous
typhoon. The Japanese called the
typhoon a "divine wind" or "kamikaze"
—a word that has another significance
for Americans.

Mongol forces were also defeated in
attempts to conquer Burma, Champa
(Muslim-dominated Cambodia and
southern Vietnam), and Annam
(northern Vietnam). All these wars
took money, so Kublai reorganized the
tax system and hired foreign finance
ministers. Paper money was introduced under Mongol rule. Unfortunately, inflation soon followed. Kublai's
rule is well known to the West from the
travels of Marco Polo. This Venetian
trader traveled with his uncle to China
twice and served Kublai as an official
of the Mongol dynasty.

Although Kublai spoke Chinese
poorly, he made certain his sons studied the language diligently. His grandson Temur, who eventually succeeded
him, was not a fluent speaker but was
an able ruler. Unfortunately, his successors were not. The Yüan dynasty
became known for ineffective and
debauched rulers, and fell victim to a
revolt by its Chinese subjects, who
founded the last Chinese led dynasty.

Highlights: Kublai had many cultural interests: he founded an observa-

tory, sent expeditions to discover the
source of the Yellow River, and sponsored scholarship. *The Water Margin,* a
book about the adventures of a band of
108 brave outlaws, dates from this
period. (It was supposedly Mao
Zedong's favorite book as a child.) One
of China's great playwrights also dates
from this period, Kuan Han-ch'ing,
who wrote many plays based on social
themes, including one about women
fighting traditional oppression.

MING DYNASTY

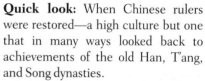

(1368–1644)

Quick look: When Chinese rulers
were restored—a high culture but one
that in many ways looked back to
achievements of the old Han, T'ang,
and Song dynasties.

History: By the end of the Yüan
dynasty, the Mongol rulers were corrupt and soft, and had lost their martial
spirit. Secret societies had formed
among the populace, dedicated to
overthrowing Mongol rule. In the
1350s one group, known as the White
Lotus, fomented a major insurrection.

At this point the engaging Zhu
Yuanzhang (Chu Yüan-chang) enters
into Chinese history. The son of a poor
farm worker and orphaned at seventeen, he had entered a Buddhist
monastery but then decided to join the
rebellion against the Mongol rulers of
China. At first he seemed to be just
one of many quasi-bandit chieftains,
but he stood out. He was an unusually
wise and tolerant leader, and people
recognized this. His band grew larger
and larger; soon he had gained power

over much of southern China. What next but to march on the capital of Beijing? He did, and he easily conquered the divided Mongol rulers. They were too busy quarreling among themselves.

So now a poor farmer's son was the emperor. But Zhu Yuanzhong was no revolutionary. He made it a goal to revive China's past, the glorious period before the Mongol and Turkic rulers. He reinstated the examination system for entry into the civil service, reestablished titles of nobility, and sponsored Confucian scholars.

His grandson Zhu Yunwen moved the capital to Beijing, the first time a purely Chinese dynasty had chosen this northern city as the capital. Zhu Yunwen drew up plans for what was to become the magnificent imperial center called the "Forbidden City." But he also found time to fight the Mongol clans to the north and the Vietnamese to the south, and to sponsor exploratory and trading sea voyages to the west. His

ministers disapproved and ultimately halted exploration; but one can't help but wonder what would have occurred if the Chinese, rather than the Europeans, had taken the lead in exploring and trading in the Pacific.

After Zhu Yunwen the Ming dynasty produced no rulers of distinction. Eunuchs of the royal harems and household gradually assumed real power. They increased taxes, seized land from poor peasants, and watched as peasant uprisings and general unrest paralyzed administration of the countryside. The peasant leader Li Zicheng (Li Tzu-ch'eng) was honest, a true leader, and a real threat to the Mings. He finally marched on Beijing and toppled the Ming dynasty. As Li's troops advanced, the last emperor hanged himself on a locust tree behind the imperial palace, writing:

Poor in virtue and of contemptible personality, I have incurred the wrath of God on high. My ministers have deceived me, I am ashamed to meet my ancestors, and therefore I myself take off my crown . . . and await dismemberment at the hand of the rebels.

Highlights: The Ming dynasty is known as the age of the novel because many classic novels were written in this era. Among them were *Monkey,* about the travels and fantastic adventures of a rebellious monkey with supernatural powers, which is based on the real travels of a Buddhist monk to India, and *The Romance of the Three Kingdoms,* an account of struggles during the third century.

Ming ceramics are also famous. Whereas previous dynasty porcelains were mainly monochromes, Ming porcelain was often polychrome. The

Faux China

Chinese ceramics were brought back in large numbers to Europe in the seventeenth and eighteenth centuries. The blue-and-white and transparent enamels became the fashion item of all the big cities. But they were very expensive, so European chemists got to work trying to copy the Chinese technique. Johann Friedrich Böttger, a chemist employed by the (German) Saxon king Augustus the Strong, was the first (or one of them) to figure out the process, closely followed by French and British counterparts. Soon, cheaper blue-and-white ceramics, with European designs, became the new rage of Europe. Eventually, blue-and-white pottery was brought by the Spaniards to the New World, where it took hold in Mexico. To this day blue-and-white ceramics remain popular all over the world.

famous blue-and-white porcelains (copied by the Dutch) date from this era, as do the "three-color" (green, violet, and yellow) and "five-color" (additionally blue and red) styles.

In keeping with their looking to the past, the Mings compiled all the writings of the neo-Confucian philosophers. But not all philosophy was stale or backward-looking: Wang Yang-ming challenged traditionalist beliefs that were based on reason. He argued that the heart, or intuitive knowledge, was the way to understanding the essence of the universal order.

QING (CH'ING) DYNASTY

(1644–1911)

Quick look: The last Chinese dynasty—founded by Manchu conquerors.

History: Up in the northern reaches of present-day China was yet another nomadic tribal group, not different from the many others who surrounded China's borders. Typically, the Chinese called them barbarians, but they called themselves the Jurchen and later the Manchu.

The Manchus happened to be in the right place at the right time. As the Ming dynasty decayed and unrest increased, they were invited by a Ming general to put down the peasant uprisings. They succeeded. But then they turned on the Mings and won the imperial throne. They were not heavy-handed conquerors. They encouraged and rewarded Ming notables who came over to their side and soon won legitimacy as the new rulers of China.

The greatest Manchu emperor was Kangxi, a contemporary of the great French "Sun King" Louis XIV. His reign lasted almost as long and was as successful. He centralized Manchu power over China under himself and stabilized Chinese borders. He intervened successfully in Mongolia to the north and clashed with the Russians who were expanding south. A settlement was reached with a final treaty that went down in diplomatic history. It was negotiated with the help of a Jesuit father who worked for the emperor and was drawn up in the unusual linguistic combination of Latin, Manchu, Chinese, Mongolian, and Russian.

Kangxi's son and grandson were the last great emperors of China. Together these three great rulers conquered much of Tibet and Mongolia, redistributed land, improved the lot of the peasantry, and completed work on the great Ming project of the imperial "Forbidden City" in Beijing. Their successors now faced a rising new threat. European powers had entered Asia. In a typical pattern, the Europeans first asked for trading rights. Once these were granted they worked to extend their control over the politics and economies of the Asian nations.

The worst abuses were probably committed by the British. They wanted to sell opium from their imperial domains in India to the huge Chinese market, but China banned opium imports. So the British fought two wars, appropriately called the Opium Wars, and forced the Chinese to let the opium in. (It's almost as if Colombia fought a war with us demanding that we legalize cocaine.) The British also

---

Chinese Dragons

Unlike the dragons of Western myth, in China these mythical creatures were considered (and by some still are) benevolent and just, bringers of wealth and good fortune. But because they were so powerful they were feared, too—but more like we'd fear a powerful ruler or boss. Dragons were said to live in lakes, rivers, and the sea, but some lived in the sky, notably the one-quarter of the sky called the Palace of the Green Dragon. Other accounts say that dragons spend half a year in water, the other half in the sky. Dragons were the symbols of the Chinese emperors and are still frequently used in design.

---

forced the Manchu government to grant them various perquisites, including extraterritorial rights for their citizens, trading posts, and business monopolies.

Once the British got their perks, other European powers demanded similar concessions. A spiraling trend toward more and more concessions began. Meanwhile, the Ming dynasty was collapsing. Corruption was up, and the peasants were forced to pay more taxes. China was getting ripe for revolt.

The Taiping Rebellion was the result. It was the largest peasant revolt in world history. It was led by Hong Xiuquan (Hung Hsiu-chüan), a poor peasant scholar who had come into contact with Christianity. During an illness he experienced a number of visions that called upon him to spread the faith and liberate the land. His army of peasants seized parts of southern China and set up a reform state. Surprisingly, the state worked well. This scared the Chinese government no end, as well as more than a few European governments. The Chinese government hired the great British General Charles Gordon to destroy the upstarts. Eventually Manchu troops and Western arms succeeded.

But the Manchu dynasty was

doomed. Ever more concessions granted to foreigners further reduced the prestige of the government. Outsiders sensed Chinese weakness. In 1894, Koreans revolted against Chinese rule, and then the Japanese attacked China, winning Taiwan and the Pescadores islands as well as ports and trading stations on the mainland.

And now a new set of revolutionaries challenged the status quo. They were a secret anti-Manchu, anti-foreigner society that called themselves "The Society of Righteous and Harmonious Fists." They were better known as the Boxers, and they fomented an attack on the foreigners who effectively ruled so much of their land. The Boxer Rebellion was put down by foreign troops, and the Manchu government was forced to pay indemnities to the Western powers and Japan.

But this couldn't go on forever. Finally in 1911, a year of famine and mounting discontent, the Double Ten Revolution (so named because it occurred on the tenth day of the tenth month) broke out, and Manchu rule was finally ended.

Not surprisingly, the revolt started over yet more concessions to foreigners. The Manchu government had seized property belonging to private railroad companies. It was planning to turn them over to the Europeans. This was too much for many people. Popular protests grew, and then the imperial garrison at Wuchang revolted. They were joined by more and more citizens. The navy was called in by the Manchus to attack, but it did not and the end was clearly near. Manchu officials fled the provincial capitals. Finally, the young emperor Pu Yi abdicated.

Over two thousand years of imperial history was over.

Highlights: Chinese porcelain art reached heights with the reconstruction of the imperial porcelain works in Kiangsi. The major styles were peach bloom and sapphire blue monochromes and painted decorative pieces

with green, powder blue, and black backgrounds. Unfortunately, the level of artistry soon declined. The Chinese exported their wares to Europe, and as European demand increased, the quality decreased.

Literature reflected a growing malaise and discontent with government. *The Scholars* by Wu Jingzi satirized the ruling mandarin class by exposing the corruption and ignorance. *The Dream of the Red Chamber* by Cao Xueqi (Tsa'o Hsüeh-ch'in) is superficially a romance but really a study of the decline of a great family amid the corruption of the times. Even more important, by the end of the dynasty new political ideas of democracy were coming into vogue. It was not a good time for royalty.

HISTORY APPENDIX II—
THE KINGS AND QUEENS OF ENGLAND:
A CAPSULE LOOK AT ENGLISH HISTORY THROUGH THE
TRIUMPHS AND SCANDALS OF THE ROYAL RULERS

If you go on a vacation to England, you'll find that the English often view their history through the prism of their royal rulers. As Americans, we don't say, "This building was built during the presidency of James K. Polk," but the English may very well describe a castle as having been built during the reign of Henry I. And they often put their kings and queens into literature. Shakespeare made a creative industry out of it.

English kings and queens are important for more than that, however. We can get a sense of the sweep of English history that gave us our national language and many of our traditions, laws, and customs. By looking at the English ruling families we can see the gradual diminution of royal power and the gradual rise of democracy. The English, for all their faults, helped usher in an age where common people had a real voice

HENRY VIII (PHOTOGRAPH OF A PAINTING, PROBABLY BY LUKE HORNEBOLT) (REPRODUCED FROM THE COLLECTIONS OF THE LIBRARY OF CONGRESS)

in their own affairs, at least in the home country. (The Irish and others can tell different tales.)

One reason is that the English have been blessed with many kings and queens who were fairly competent, or at least were able to see the writing on the wall and give up some of their powers in return for staying on the throne. The English monarchy learned the one lesson many other royal families didn't: how to survive. That may be its greatest single accomplishment. Over the years royal families have had a hard time of it: the last emperor of Byzantium died fighting the Turks, the last shah of Iran spent his final years searching for a refuge, the last king of France was beheaded, the last czar of Russia was shot, the last emperor of China spent the end of his life sweeping up leaves as a brainwashed communist gardener. Yet in the words of the distinguished English diplomat and historian Harold Nicolson, "The British monarchy, being sufficiently elastic to stand the

Democracy Comes to England . . . Gradually

Most nations, including England, feared more democracy and the extension of the vote to the working classes. The great British prime minister Benjamin Disraeli said in 1867 that he hoped "it will never be the fate of this country to live under a democracy." But despite those feelings, the vote was extended to the lower classes, and even Disraeli agreed. Before 1820, less than five hundred men in the House of Lords elected most of the members in the House of Commons. Then came a series of reform bills:

- 1832: extended the vote to 12 percent of adult males
- 1867: extended the vote to 30 percent of adult males
- 1884: extended the vote to 75 percent of adult males
- 1918: all adult males *and females* were given the right to vote

strains and stresses of successive upheavals, has survived them all."

One more point: English history is not just the story of "dead white males." British royalty has included women as some of its greatest (and most notorious) members.

Here is a listing of all the British kings and queens since 1066. That date is not just a random starting point. That's the date of the Norman conquest, the last time someone from outside successfully conquered the British Isles. The Normans brought in their own culture and French language to England, and gradually merged with the Anglo-Saxons and others already living there to produce . . . the English.

We've included a bit of personal detail to humanize these rulers, all but the last one long dead. We've also broken this list down into the different "houses" or ruling dynasties of what is one of the world's most enduring

monarchies. The dates given are for their reigns.

HOUSE OF NORMANDY

WILLIAM I
(1066–87)

The founder of modern England, he was called William the Conqueror and William the Bastard. The latter title is not William's fault—he was the product of an illegitimate union between the Duke of Normandy and a tanner's daughter. But the former title was all William's doing. He was a brilliant man, always striving, always fighting, and finally conquering.

William's original home was not in England but in France—on the Norman peninsula. But William's claim to the English throne wasn't all that illegitimate. If you can follow the genealogy, Edward the Confessor, the English king, was William's cousin, the son of his aunt on his father's side.

Using this claim, William decided upon Edward's death and the accession of Harold as king to cross the English Channel and take England. With a band of fellow Normans and ambitious adventurers, William crossed the Channel in 1066. As he landed on English soil, William tripped and fell forward on his hands. A loud cry went out in fear of this evil omen, but William called out, "See, my Lords, I have by the grace of God taken possession of England with both of my hands."

At the ensuing Battle of Hastings, William's troops battled and killed the cream of the opposing Anglo-Saxon knighthood. King Harold died with an arrow in his eye.

The long-term results of this so-called Norman Conquest were many. It brought England, which had been part of the Danish orbit, back into Latin Europe. It resulted in the present-day duality of the English language, split between Latinate French words (usually longer and more "highbrow") and Anglo-Saxon words.

And in the short term, England now had an absolute ruler. William broke up the powerful semi-independent earldoms and introduced centralized control. His famous *Domesday Book* was a meticulous survey of all England, so detailed that, in the words of a contemporary, "there was not a single hide nor a rood of land, nor . . . was there an ox or a cow or a pig passed by that was not set down on the accounts." With it, William learned virtually every source of revenue in his kingdom and was able to tax and control very effectively. His

rule marked the true beginning of a strong and independent English monarchy.

One interesting note and then a bit of trivia: About the same time as the Norman conquest of England, the Normans sent a fleet south to Sicily and conquered it as well. At the time it was the richer of the two conquests. And now for the trivia: Although majestic in bearing, William the Conqueror suffered from a large round potbelly. King Philip I enjoyed bothering William by pretending that he thought William was expecting a child.

WILLIAM II
(1087–1100)

Also known as William Rufus, he was the son of William the Conqueror and was a tyrannical ruler whose tyrannies were challenged by Anselm of Aosta, the archbishop of Canterbury. This shows another aspect of William the Conqueror's rule: the Church of Rome was now able to intervene and balance the absolute power of English kings. Later English kings would challenge this power and ultimately take England once more out of Rome's orbit.

HENRY I
(1100–35)

The youngest son of William the Conqueror and the brother of William II. He fought his eldest brother, Robert, who had inherited Normandy as his own fief. Henry won it back for England and himself. His daughter Matilda married Geoffrey Plantagenet, Count of Anjou (sprig of a broom, for the device on his helmet). That couple would start a new dynasty with their son, Henry II.

How the French Changed English

Because of William the Conqueror and his French-speaking Normans, English changed radically. Many French words replaced old English ones—for example, we don't use *worts* in our food but *herbs*. The old English word *wort* was replaced with the French word *herbe*, with a slightly modified meaning.

But far more important, because of William, English has a huge number of couplets; in other words, a French word and an Anglo-Saxon word that mean the same thing:

English	French
commence/begin	commence
pardon/forgive	pardon
suspend/hang	suspend
labor/work	labor

HOUSE OF BLOIS

STEPHEN

(1135–54)

Stephen, grandson of William I, failed to follow through on his grandfather's reforms. Instead there was much anarchy, caused in part by his uncle's daughter, as we will see below.

MATILDA

Matilda's father, Henry I, forced the nobility to recognize her right to the throne. In 1139, Matilda landed in England to challenge her cousin Stephen's rule, and she did so successfully. Now her son would succeed to the throne.

HOUSE OF ANJOU— LATER CALLED PLANTAGENET

HENRY II

(1154–89)

The son of Matilda, he repaired the damage of Stephen's rule and centralized administration and justice under the curia regis, a supreme court with judges who went on circuits throughout the country. Juries were chosen by the people, and this was one of the first and most important aspects of English common law. Henry also sought to limit the power of the Church. When one of his counselors, Thoma à Becket, the archbishop of Canterbury, resisted,

Henry had him murdered (and unwittingly provided a source of drama for future writers, poets, and filmmakers). Henry also began the conquest of Ireland, a tragedy with consequences extending to today.

RICHARD I

(1189–99)

The third son of Henry II was called Coeur de Lion, the Lion-Hearted. This is the Richard famed in film, the gallant crusading king, friend of Robin Hood and justice. The reality is a bit different. First of all, as a crusader Richard faced the famous Islamic ruler of Egypt, Saladin (known to his subjects as Salāh ad-Din), but behaved less honorably than his famous opponent. Saladin treated his Christian captives in Jerusalem well while Richard slaughtered several thousand of his captives in cold blood. Nevertheless, he managed to conclude a treaty with the Muslims that ceded the area between Jaffa and Acre (the coast of present-day Israel) to Christians.

When he returned from the wars in the Middle East, Richard quelled the revolt of his brother John (called "the Landless"), but unlike most of the literary or film depictions, the story has an unhappy ending: Richard died at the gates of the castle of Chaluz, and his brother succeeded him.

JOHN

(1199–1216)

John is known to literature as a classic bad king—and he was. The brother of Richard I, he was conceited and moody and prone to childish rages, probably the result of doting parents. He was known as the Landless or Lackland because he was born late, and his father had already willed everything to his other children. As king, John made up for his lack by taking money from the royal treasury for his own use. Unfortunately, he lost most of England's possessions in France and became embroiled in intrigue, even facing excommunication from the Pope. He overtaxed and overrode the local aristocrats.

Ultimately the English barons presented him with a document, the famous Magna Carta. This forced the king to observe "ancient law" and respect the rights of barons to resist abuses of their privileges by the king. In effect, it was the beginning of the long history whereby the English kings gave up some of their royal powers but in return got to remain on the throne. In addition, the Magna Carta guaranteed fair trials, proportionate punishment, and certain feudal rights. It was the basis of democratic liberty that culminated centuries later in the U.S. Constitution and the United Nations Declaration of Human Rights.

As for John, he died of dysentery at the age of forty-eight while seeking revenge against the English barons for forcing him to sign the Magna Carta.

HENRY III

(1216–72)

Henry, son of John, was a devout man (Westminster Abbey was built under his reign) with a blind spot when it came to his subjects. Obsessed with winning Sicily for his young son Edward (perhaps the ultimate Christmas present), he overtaxed and overspent, put French favorites in positions of power, and was finally confronted by the uprising of the English barons, led by Simon de Montfort. They captured him in battle and forced him to grant the Provisions of Oxford, which gave

the English barons the right to advise the king, in effect a crude Parliament.

EDWARD I

(1272–1307)

Edward, the son of Henry III, was a strong and ambitious man, yet a realistic one who let Parliament develop into a regular institution. In 1295, Edward summoned the Model Parliament, which included commoners as well as lords and which ultimately provided that new taxes could not be levied without its approval. This was the beginning of legal parliamentary rule (since technically the first Parliament convened against the king's wishes) and so was the beginning of the long trend to constitutional monarchy and English republicanism. Edward was relatively enlightened, but he was also ambitious. He tried to become king of Scotland but was defeated by the Scottish champion Robert the Bruce.

EDWARD II

(1307–27)

The fourth son of Edward I, he was affable, engaging, but ineffective—and he faced the ultimate penalty: he was murdered.

EDWARD III

(1327–77)

Eldest son of Edward II, he wanted to rule more than England—he wanted the land of his ancestors, France, and he decided to fight to get it. He claimed his right to the French throne on the basis of his being the grandson of French King Philip the Fair on his mother's side.

He began the Hundred Years' War, sporadic fighting in the French countryside among the English, some French allies, and more French enemies. Initially Edward was successful, utilizing his "people's army" of archers and primitive cannon (called bombards) effectively. The famous British victory at Poitiers and Crécy led to the capture of the French port of Calais in 1347; his son Edward, the famous Black Prince, won at Maupertuis. Finally, in 1360, Edward gave up his claim to the French throne in return for gaining sovereignty over a huge chunk of southwestern France, the Aquitaine.

Also during Edward's rule, Parliament divided into two houses and began to take its modern form.

RICHARD II

(1377–99)

Under the rule of this grandson of Edward III and son of the Black Prince, peace with France was maintained. But there was so much social discontent that finally Henry of Lancaster deposed him and sent him to the Tower of London. While rotting in prison, Richard made a famous statement:

A wondrous and fickle land is this, for it hath slain, exiled, or ruined so many kings, rulers, and great men, and is ever tainted and toileth with strife, variance and envy.

Shortly thereafter he was killed.

HOUSE OF LANCASTER

HENRY IV

(1399–1413)

Cheerless, cold-blooded, and tough, Henry IV was the son of John of Gaunt, the fourth son of Edward III and brother of the Black Prince. Henry was worn out by his soldiering in Prussia and Hungary, and had a hard time facing rebellions by the Welsh and fights with the Scots.

HENRY V

(1413–22)

The son of Henry IV and subject of the famous eponymous play by Shakespeare, Henry V was the perfect subject for the playwright. He was young, fiery, and burning with the flaming ambition to take the French throne. He renewed the war with France in 1415 and won a famous victory at Agincourt. At the ensuing treaty of Troyes, Henry won the regency of France and the hand of a French princess, Catherine of Valois, the daughter of the French king. It was agreed that Henry and not the king's son would next take the throne of France. Unfortunately for Henry, he died in the flower of manhood, poisoned, his soldiers said, by the magic verses of his French enemies.

HENRY VI

(1422–61)

The son of Henry V, Henry VI was feeble, overshadowed by a masterful and unpopular French wife. He also had significant mental problems. Worse yet, under his rule Joan of Arc stimulated French resistance to English rule in France. Although she was captured and burned to death, the English lost the impetus in France.

During his rule the War of the Roses began between the great aristocratic houses of Lancaster and York. The basic reason for the war was perhaps habit: the English nobles, so used to fighting in the hills and valleys of

France during the Hundred Years' War, couldn't settle down to peace in England. There were, of course, other more respectable reasons for the war; the house of Lancaster claimed it was basically championing constitutional government and religious orthodoxy. These wars consisted of battling nobles allied to one or another house (with a white rose of York or the red rose of Lancaster as emblems). The common people were barely affected, and business thrived.

Henry's end was unpleasant: he was defeated at Towton, deposed, exiled, and most probably murdered.

HOUSE OF YORK

EDWARD IV

(1461–83)

Edward of the House of York was victorious in this phase of the War of the Roses. He was the probable murderer of Henry, but by most accounts was a handsome, affable middle-class-minded soldier. He married the beautiful Elizabeth Woodville, the daughter of a man who had started life as a lowly knight. In the morals of the day, this was scandalous and shocking. Woodville's father was almost a commoner! Worse yet, Edward had a habit of playing around. He died, supposedly of his debaucheries, at the age of forty-eight, and the Yorkist dynasty died soon after him.

EDWARD V

(1483)

The eldest son of Edward IV—murdered by Richard III.

RICHARD III

(1483–85)

This Richard usurped the throne by having his nephews Edward V and Richard strangled to death in the Tower of London. His end, too, was ignominious: he was defeated by Henry VII, and with his defeat the War of the Roses was over.

HOUSE OF TUDOR

HENRY VII

(1485–1509)

Henry was the first king of the famous Tudor dynasty of English royalty (he was the son of Edmund Tudor, the Earl of Richmond). He was an heir to the house of Lancaster, and when he defeated Richard III at the battle of Bosworth, he began a dynasty that lasted until 1603.

The early years of Henry's rule were difficult. The royal treasury was virtually empty, and English nobles were busy fighting among themselves and barely listening to orders from the throne. To top it off, England was facing interference in her internal affairs from the great powers of the day: Spain, France, and the Holy Roman Empire (the loosely linked German and Austrian states).

Henry resolved to solve these problems by hard work and personal attention to details. As a sort of King Accountant he took personal charge of the treasury, hired tough and expert tax collectors, and brought the treasury back to solvency. Through expert diplomacy he increased English power and prestige abroad and eliminated foreign interference. But his stern, hardworking demeanor and tendency to tax did not win him popularity; he lacked the "common touch." When he died of overwork and tuberculosis, his subjects were not sorry to see him go, although today he is reckoned as a great king.

HENRY VIII
(1509–47)

Henry VIII, son of Henry VII, is one of England's most famous kings, notorious for his six wives and immense girth. But he is far more than a cardboard character. Handsome (his large size came in later years), ruthless, and capable though lazy, Henry is famous for the widespread change he brought to England. He (and, by extension, England) left the Church of Rome and so contributed to the immense changes in Europe during the Reformation (see pages 67–70). Through his chief minister Thomas Wolsey, he followed his father's steps and further smashed the independence of England's unruly aristocrats. But Henry was a spendthrift and overly ambitious. He tried (and failed) three times in three fruitless wars and much exhausting diplomacy to win the throne of France for his royal self.

Henry had a penchant for marriage and then divorce or beheadings—primarily for the purpose of begetting royal sons to succeed him. Henry's six famous wives and their birth and death dates were the following:

1. Catherine of Aragon (1485–1536)

She was the daughter of Ferdinand and Isabella of Castille, an independent kingdom of Spain, and the mother of Mary I, Bloody Mary. She was dour and aloof, and Henry had the

marriage annulled because she provided only daughters (Henry's role apparently didn't count) and because Henry was in love with Anne Boleyn. But the Pope didn't accept Henry's annulment, and this prompted Henry to break with the Catholic Church. Catherine died in England.

2. Anne Boleyn (150[?]–1536)

Anne was young, pretty, and, in the careful words of one historian, "appealed to the less refined part of Henry's nature." Despite this, she was executed for adultery and treason. Her daughter Elizabeth became England's greatest queen.

3. Jane Seymour (1509[?]–1537)

She was the lady-in-waiting to Henry's first two queens and married Henry eleven days after Anne Boleyn's execution. She gave birth to a son who became King Edward VI but died twelve days later.

4. Anne of Cleves (1515–1557)

Her marriage was never consummated; Henry supposedly was attracted to her by a portrait but found her unattractive in reality. He probably married her for political reasons, to ally England to Protestants. The marriage was annulled by the English Parliament six months later.

5. Catherine Howard (1520[?]–1542)

Catherine was executed for treason and adultery. After her marriage she apparently had clandestine meetings with two men: a musician named Henry Mannock and a kinsman named Thomas Culpepper, whom she had known before her marriage. She confessed to the archbishop of Canterbury that she had had premarital intercourse, so on the basis of this the two men were executed and Catherine lost her head. When the execution took place, Henry supposedly burst into tears.

6. *Catherine Parr (1512–1548)*

A very scholarly woman, she was knowledgeable about religion and enjoyed discussing her ideas; in fact, Henry almost beheaded her for her opinions. She persuaded him to restore succession to the throne for his daughters, Elizabeth and Mary. After Henry's death she married a former lover and died in childbirth.

At the end of his reign Henry was grossly overweight and suffered from varicose ulcers; he was carried about in a chair and hauled upstairs in a primitive elevator. Through his spendthrift ways he undid much of the good of his predecessor. He died while planning yet another conquest of France.

EDWARD VI

(1547–53)

Edward, the son of Henry and Jane Seymour, was a sickly boy king. The pressures of state overwhelmed him and led to his early death, but not before Protestantism was firmly established in England. Edward's ministers tried to block his technically Catholic half-sisters, Mary and Elizabeth, from ascending the throne in favor of Lady Jane Grey. This led to royal difficulties that make the 1992 *annus horribilis* of Queen Elizabeth look like nothing, as we'll see below.

MARY I

(1553–58)

Mary, known as Bloody Mary, was the half-sister of Edward, the daughter

of Henry VIII and Catherine of Aragon, and unfortunately she valued her Spanish blood and Roman Catholic religion, which resulted in much unrest. She married King Philip II of Spain and with him tried to reintroduce Roman Catholicism to England. A coup was attempted against her, but she managed to win and execute the ringleaders, along with Lady Jane Grey and her husband. She then began to reduce Protestantism in earnest. Several prominent Protestants and about three hundred humbler ones were burned at the stake; many others fled England just in time. Mary also embroiled England in a war with France as allies of Spain, resulting in popular hatred of Spain, a drain of the treasury, and the loss of Calais, England's last foothold in France.

Mary died broken-hearted, childless, and sick, convinced that she had been a failure as a queen and frustrated because she knew that her half-sister, Elizabeth, whom she hated, would succeed her.

ELIZABETH I

(1558–1603)

One of England's greatest rulers, Elizabeth, the daughter of Henry VIII and Anne Boleyn, was tough, tall, and red-haired; by turns dominating and accommodating, she was at once inscrutable, exasperating, and charming. In the words of the noted British historian Lytton Strachey, she succeeded as a queen by "dissimulation, pliability, indecision, procrastination, and parsimony."

She united a divided England by sponsoring a religious settlement that took moderate aspects of Catholicism and Protestantism and established a middle ground—and defended this compromise against extremists on both sides. By clever diplomacy she maneuvered England away from threats from the Catholic powers of France and Spain. Then when Spain became too threatening, she took to open warfare. She sponsored Sir Francis Drake's and other invasions of the rich Spanish Atlantic empire, ultimately defeating the Spanish fleet (the Spanish Armada) in 1588.

At home she dominated the Parliament by cajolery, by extending and then withholding her hand in marriage, and by other means of clever manipulation. She was a tough queen—she executed Mary, Queen of Scots, the daughter of James V of Scotland, because she feared that as a Catholic, Mary was the natural leader of those who wanted to restore the ties to the Church in Rome that Henry had broken.

Elizabeth enhanced the prestige of the Crown and managed through astute balancing acts to accommodate all major interests. She ruled over an unusually creative period in history; hers was the England of Christopher Marlowe, Edmund Spenser, and William Shakespeare. English music reached new heights, and a new English style, separate from Continental styles, developed.

Toward the end of her rule, when she was in some trouble with Parliament, she made her famous "golden speech" that once more won them over: "Though God hath raised me high, yet this I count the glory of my crown, that I have reigned with your loves. . . ." Sixteen months later she died peacefully in her sleep.

HOUSE OF STUART

JAMES I
(1603–25, also James VI of Scotland)

The son of Mary, Queen of Scots (who had been executed by Elizabeth), James loved theology and had a good sense of humor. But he also had a great number of character defects: he was slovenly (and had, according to one biographer, "a long weedy body, skinny legs . . . and a deep fear of soap and water"), conceited, apt to tell dirty jokes, and managed to irritate most of his English aristocratic subjects. He had a knack for making unpopular statements to the independent-minded Parliament, such as "The state of the monarchy is the supremest thing on earth. . . . Kings . . . even by God himself they are called gods."

His bark was actually worse than his bite; he tended to abide by many of the limitations set by Parliament, but he did try to circumvent them in an effort to raise money (he priced baronetcies for quick sale at 1,095 pounds) and was surrounded by sycophants. Toward the end of his rule he suffered from some sort of disease (probably porphyria, a metabolic disorder)—he slobbered in public over two of his favorite courtiers. But he allowed them and others too much leeway and money. When Parliament attempted to reassert itself, he ripped out the statement of their rights in the House of Commons journal.

To his credit, James attempted to pursue a moderate, peaceful foreign policy, but even here he was unpopular. Parliamentary opponents lectured him on the need for intervention in

Europe, yet they never voted him the money to do so.

CHARLES I

(1625–49)

Charles I was like his father, James, in his ability to misread his subjects. He paid the ultimate price: he lost his head. We'll go into some detail because what happened to Charles—and how he behaved at the end—were seminal moments in English history. Charles died better than he lived, and in dying well, he may have saved English royalty.

The problem began, as always, over money. Parliament had refused to grant Charles the traditional "tunnage and poundage" customs revenues for the royal purse. Charles collected them anyway, and Parliament responded by passing a ruling that anyone paying the tax was an "enemy of England." Many in Parliament thought things were getting out of hand, and there was room for compromise. Unfortunately, Charles had a knack for avoiding compromises. He tended to behave deviously during negotiations. England eventually erupted into a complicated civil war, fought basically between supporters of the king and supporters of Parliament, although alliances shifted. Radicals in Parliament soon demanded control over the army as well as executive power and created the "New Model" Army, which eventually took control of the opposition and Parliament itself.

The army commander was an obscure, tough-minded country gentleman by the name of Oliver Cromwell. In 1646 he defeated Charles for the last time. Cromwell and his allies wanted to negotiate concessions with Charles and keep him on the throne,

but the king by his deviousness managed to elude compromise. Finally, Cromwell decided the king must die, and on Tuesday, January 30, at about 9 A.M. on an unusually cold day, Charles took his last walk, to the executioner's block. He behaved nobly and unflinchingly, and some said that in dying he did far more for the Crown than he did by living. He created a wonderful myth of an unselfish monarchy above the common fray. Some of his last noble words:

If I would have given way to an arbitrary way, for to have all laws changed according to the power of the sword, I need not have come here. And therefore I tell you, and I pray God it be not laid to your charge, that I am a martyr of the people.

Soon after, the king stretched his head and the ax fell, his head severed by one strong stroke. When the executioner held up the bleeding head, the happy shouts of soldiers were drowned by a loud groan from the assembled people. The legend had begun.

INTERREGNUM

No King on the Throne: Period under the Republican rule of Oliver Cromwell, called the Lord Protector (1649–60). Cromwell by many accounts was a decent ruler, but his allies were ineffective and Cromwell was almost a one-man government. After his death, his government fell apart.

HOUSE OF STUART

CHARLES II

(1660–85)

Oliver Cromwell's son Richard succeeded him as Lord Protector of England (Cromwell had refused the Crown for himself or his heirs). But England wanted the Crown back, and, in an act known as the Restoration, Parliament invited Charles's son back as king. Charles II was tall, dark, and handsome, an athletic, pleasure-loving man who was clever enough to know how to play off the different parliamentary factions. He radiated a sense of excitement and fun (he had many mistresses, fourteen illegitimate children and no legitimate ones). To many of his subjects he seemed a welcome change from the rather grim though successful years of Cromwell's rule. During the last years of his rule, the king managed to dissolve Parliament and rule directly.

Yet because of his efforts at independence, Parliament pushed to get the Habeas Corpus Act onto the statute books in 1679; it required the government to issue a writ stating why a person was arrested. This law against arbitrary arrest was a significant milestone in human rights, though it is still not respected in many other nations today.

JAMES II

(1685–88)

James, son of Charles I, was bigoted and not very bright. As an open convert to Catholicism, he appointed Catholic supporters to key posts and tried to weaken the power of Parliament, to the

dismay of his subjects. Parliament hoped his "reforms" would die with him, but when his long childless second wife, Mary of Modena, had a son in 1688, there were fears that England would now have a Catholic dynasty. This led to the Glorious Revolution of 1688 in which Parliament supported William III of Orange (Holland) "for the Protestant Faith and a Free Parliament." James fled to France.

HOUSE OF ORANGE AND STUART

WILLIAM III AND MARY

(1689–1702)

Summoned by the English, William's role in the Glorious Revolution of 1688 was to defeat the Catholic (pro-James) forces in Ireland, at the famous battle of the Boyne still lamented in Ireland and among Irish-Catholics in the United States.

In England he was celebrated for his Declaration of Rights in 1689, which granted free speech and no taxation without approval from Parliament. This was truly the beginning of a real constitutional monarchy in England since it officially ceded a significant portion of power to Parliament and since Parliament was by now powerful enough to keep the momentum in its favor. Under William, England was unified with Holland and became the paramount sea power. William married Mary (she was James II's daughter by his first, Protestant wife) for political reasons, but fortunately it became a love match.

HOUSE OF STUART

ANNE
(1702–14)

Anne was James's other daughter and Mary's sister. Under her rule England fought in the War of the Spanish Succession (quite naturally, over who would succeed to the Spanish throne), the first "world war." At the end, England gained Gibraltar, a large part of Canada, Minorca, and a monopoly on the slave trade in Latin America. Anne died childless.

HOUSE OF HANOVER

GEORGE I
(1714–27)

George, the elector (ruler) of the German state of Hanover, was declared a successor to the throne of England because his mother was the granddaughter of King James I. After Anne's death he arrived in England accompanied by two mistresses (one thin and one fat), two German advisors, and a knack for annoying the English. Irritable, lazy, brave, and stubborn, George was no fool. He was well served by one of England's greatest (and first) prime ministers, Robert Walpole, who by astute diplomacy kept England strong, and by frugal internal policies kept taxes low and helped business prosper.

GEORGE II
(1727–69)

The constitutional monarchy—that

is, control of the monarchy by the people—was firmly established in George's reign, although he tried to resist the trend. He had a habit, as did his father, George I, of running back to his other domain, the German state of Hanover, where he could rule absolutely.

George's reign included the War of Austrian Succession, a series of wars about who would rule over much of Europe. Under his great prime minister William Pitt the Elder, England managed to preserve its power and prestige, and expand her role in the Americas.

George also fought and won against the famous Bonnie Prince Charlie, a claimant to the English throne as the last member of the Stuart dynasty. The charming Bonnie Prince won the support of the Scottish highland clans (who still talk about him to this day), but he was defeated at Culloden Moor by the Duke of Cumberland, called the "Butcher" because of the reign of terror he unleashed in the Scottish highlands.

GEORGE III
(1769–1820)

George was a conscientious fellow but was not particularly bright or talented. He began his rule by trying to take as much power as he could from Parliament. He ended by having very little, suffering from periodic mental derangement caused by porphyria, a metabolic disorder.

But much happened under George: victories against the French in the Seven Years' War (which gave Canada to England), the loss of North America in the Revolutionary War; and the victory against Napoleon in the Napoleonic Wars. Under Prime Minister William Pitt the Younger, England achieved political stability and international power. Meanwhile, the Industrial Revolution was in full swing, and the rising power of independent businessmen and manufacturers further reduced George's power.

GEORGE IV

(1820–30)

The oldest son of George III, with whom he was on very bad terms, George IV was a hedonist who was much disliked by the public, partly because of his first marriage to a Catholic (declared invalid) and his efforts to divorce his second wife. Fortunately, he had artistic taste: under his rule the Pavilion at Brighton and the West End of London were developed.

WILLIAM IV

(1830–37)

Described by some as "fatuous," William, the third son of George III, had the political wisdom to help shepherd the Reform Bill of 1832 through the House of Lords, just as opposition was hardening among the aristocrats. This important bill extended the vote to many more citizens (although still only one in five citizens could vote), opened up the vote in the cities, gave Jews the vote, and extended the momentum for further reform. England, unlike much of the world, was changing gradually, legally, and relatively nonviolently.

VICTORIA

(1837–1901, and empress of India from 1876)

The only child of George III's third son, Edward, Duke of Kent, Victoria was a constitutional monarch, but she was an opinionated one who let her

feelings be known to her ministers. She began her rule when the British Empire was barely an idea. By the end of her reign, British power extended over India, much of Africa, parts of southeast Asia, treaty ports in China, parts of the Middle East—indeed, over almost one-quarter of the peoples on earth. India became the crown jewel of the empire. British industry ruled the world of business. Victoria's navy ruled the waves, and she was the paramount power on earth.

The queen reigned as her capable ministers, including the great Benjamin Disraeli and William Gladstone, eventually extended voter franchises, negotiated settlements in Europe that kept the peace, and extended the empire and kept the manufactories humming.

The "Victorian Age" symbolized relative peace and progress, both in England, her empire, and in the world in general. She died as her empire was beginning to fade. South African Boers had challenged British rule in South Africa, and for the first time in memory, British imperial troops faced significant defeats, although they won the famed Boer War.

HOUSE OF SAXE-COBURG-GOTHA

EDWARD VII

(1901–10, and emperor of India)

Victoria thought her son Edward indiscreet and denied him access to state papers until he was over fifty. So Edward, born in 1841, lived for a considerable part of his life as an over-grown playboy, surrounded by mistresses, sycophants, and all the pomp of the British Empire at its height. Oddly enough, many Europeans overestimated his role as a ruler when he finally succeeded to the Crown in 1901. He was little more than a fun-loving constitutional monarch, but the Germans in particular read into his travels to France an insidious policy of attempting to gain the French as allies and thereby encircling Germany. In reality, Edward was there to have fun as only a king can.

HOUSE OF WINDSOR

GEORGE V

(1910–36, and emperor of India)

The ultimate constitutional monarch, he intervened only when his constitutional advisors suggested he do so. Unlike his father, he reigned under difficult times. World War I saw the slaughter of a million of England's finest young men, and the postwar years were marked by political unrest, economic downturns, and the waning years of empire. Yet under George's reign there was strong and growing affection for the Crown among common people, helped by George's annual Christmas messages and his happy family life, highlighted by the Silver Jubilee Celebrations of 1935.

EDWARD VIII

(1936, and emperor of India)

He is better known as the Duke of Windsor, the man who gave up his crown for love. The oldest son of George V, he succeeded to the Crown but was immediately faced with a problem: he wanted to marry an American commoner and divorcée, Mrs. Wallis Simpson. His advisors felt that her two previous divorces would weaken Edward's role as "supreme governor" of the Church of England. A morganatic marriage (where Simpson would be allowed to marry the king but would not receive the title of Queen) was considered, but the dominion governments (Canada, Australia, and South Africa) rejected this idea.

Faced with the choice of the Crown or his love, the king chose love and abdicated the throne, giving an eloquent speech over the radio that some said was written by Winston Churchill, ever a romantic. Edward then left for France with Mrs. Simpson. He later visited Hitler's Germany where he was a bit too chummy with Hitler for British taste (although some suggestions that he was plotting with the Nazis to overthrow his brother George VI are purely conjectural and most probably false). During World War II he sought a responsible role in the wartime government; instead he was given the governor-generalship of Bermuda. He died an enigmatic, sad-faced perpetual exile.

GEORGE VI

(1936–52, and emperor of India until 1947)

Succeeded after his brother's abdication and, like his father, was a consummate constitutional monarch. He stuttered, and was admired for his persistent efforts to overcome this disability, as well as for his calm, inspiring presence during World War II. His reign saw victory in war, under the dynamic leadership of Winston

Churchill, and significant social reform at home, under the Labour government of Clement Attlee. The British Empire was rapidly waning: India won her independence in 1947 and soon many of England's African colonies would leave the empire as well.

ELIZABETH II

(1952–)

Young and ambitious, Elizabeth, daughter of George VI, succeeded to the throne in 1952 and was crowned at a glorious coronation in 1953. She sought to become a truly international queen, visiting as many of the newly independent British colonies over

whom she was still the constitutional sovereign. In doing so she helped increase the prestige of her royal house, only to see much of her work undone in recent years as scandals among her children and their wives hurt the prestige of the Crown. In particular, there has been growing resentment over the tax-free status of members of the royal family and their large allowances.

Characteristically, the queen has given up some of her monetary perquisites, including some tax advantages, illustrating once more that the British Crown will yield with the times.

CONTENTS

—

PHILOSOPHY OF THE WORLD

A VERY BRIEF LOOK AT A MAJOR PHILOSOPHICAL QUESTION: JUST WHAT IS PHILOSOPHY, ANYWAY?

 "The philosopher's aim in his theoretical studies is to ascertain the truth," wrote the Arab philosopher al-Kindi.

What is truth, anyway? What is reality? Philosophy attempts to answer these ultimate questions.

But first, let's look at an even more *general* question: What, really, is philosophy?

It sounds basic, even a little flip, but take a second to think about it. It's tougher to answer than you might expect. In fact, most philosophers themselves couldn't answer it succinctly. And there's a good chance that those who could probably wouldn't agree with each other's definitions.

But for all the differences, there is a central core to philosophy. The word *philosophy* means "love of wisdom"—and, in line with that, philosophy at its most basic is thought trying to get to the bottom of reality. It tries to answer the big questions: What is real? What are we doing here? Is there a God? What is knowledge? More important, it tries to find *rational* reasons for the answers it does come up with. (In the process, it takes a look at the reasons that don't cut it as well.) It's this focus on the rational that makes philosophy different from other disciplines that try to answer questions—like art, literature, and especially religion.

Of course, the answers to the questions and, for that matter, the systems of thought that lead to the answers differ from philosopher to philosopher, and from philosophical school to philosophical school. Just because they're all trying to answer the same questions doesn't mean they come up with the same answers—or even the same *ways* of coming up with the answers.

So this section covers the many different approaches to answering the ultimate questions about existence and the many great philosophers who bent their minds towards finding the answers—from the ancient philosophers like Socrates and Chuang Tzu, whose work shaped the way people think, to modern political and economic philosophers like Karl Marx and John Maynard Keynes, whose work changed the way the world runs.

It covers the people behind the philosophies, their claims to fame and their key thoughts. It also covers the concrete results of philosophic thought—the documents and books that started political movements, and sometimes, wars. All in all, it's a look at philosophy in theory and philosophy in action—and the role philosophy still plays in the world at large.

WHAT IT ALL BOILS DOWN TO:
THE DIFFERENT AREAS OF PHILOSOPHY

THE FOUR CLASSIC FIELDS OF PHILOSOPHY

Philosophy is a broad-based discipline. To be frank, you can think philosophically about virtually anything. But, of course, most philosophers throughout history have worked within specific philosophical disciplines. The following are the four classic divisions of philosophy, the traditional areas that stretch back to ancient Greece—and that still dominate philosophical thought:

Logic, the backbone of philosophical thought. When you boil it down, logic is concerned with the principles of reasoning and arguing, the ways philosophers are able to arrive at the answers to their questions. (To be precise, logic is actually split into two main parts, *formal logic* and *philosophical logic,* plus there are two different types of logic—deductive and inductive—but unless you're planning to be a philosopher, you really don't need to know the differences between them.) The bottom line: Logic sets forth a formal way of reasoning based upon premises (leading statements) and a conclusion (what the premises lead to).

Metaphysics is concerned with the most basic subject of all: reality. It gets a little more complicated, though. Technically, metaphysics examines the basic *categories* of reality—fundamental divisions of everything that the world (or, more broadly, *any* world) contains. What's the point? In examining categories, we can understand the world in general and so get at the role humankind plays in it. For example, a metaphysical philosopher asks questions like How can we classify everything that exists? What are the relationships between everything? Are some things dependent upon others? And, the most general question of all, What is the universe?

Epistemology focuses on human knowledge, what it is, what its limits are, and how valid it is. In other words, epistemology asks, What can we know and how can we know it? But, of course, it's not always that simple. This field has been changing over the years, and is focused more on language—language as the transmitter of knowledge and the means of expressing knowledge—than on knowledge itself.

Ethics focuses on how people should live. The most prevalent type of ethics asks, How should people act *in general,* not as a means to an end? It looks at such concepts as obligation and duty, right and wrong, and, most basically, good and evil. But, again, it's not always that simple. There's another (less popular) view of what ethics is, focusing on value and asking what is valuable, desirable, or good in itself. Plus, there's a split in ethical beliefs between the deontologists, who hold that some obligations or duties come before values, and are completely independent of values; and the teleologists, who hold that duties are completely tied to ends. But in spite of the split, at bottom, they're still both dealing with morality.

EIGHT OTHER PHILOSOPHICAL DISCIPLINES

These are the more modern philosophic subject areas—the sexier, less dry divisions that arose after the four classic areas. Some of these are actually subdivisions of the classic areas, others overlap into different areas.

Aesthetics (also called the philosophy of art) focuses on art appreciation and essentially tries to get at what makes something a work of art. It can get pretty rarefied: How can you analyze aesthetic judgment? Can aesthetic judgments be true or false? And what about art and morality? And so on.

History of philosophy, as you'd expect, looks at philosophy through history (the major philosophical movements, etc.) and examines how it developed, and the impact it had.

Philosophy of language looks at the structure of language and how it affects the world, society, and how we think.

Philosophy of mind focuses on the human mind, more specifically the nature of thought and consciousness.

Philosophy of natural science pulls together metaphysics (the study of reality) and epistemology (the study of knowledge) and explores what scientific reality is and what methods should be used to establish scientific knowledge.

Philosophy of religion, obviously, focuses on religion, basic religious theory and practices. The big question: Is there a god?

Philosophy of social science breaks down social-scientific theories into categories and analyzes methods for establishing knowledge in the field.

Social and political philosophy looks at the basics of society and government, trying to determine, for example, what the best type of government is and why.

Yes, it begins to sound complicated—and, frankly, it is. But, remember, for all the divisions, the splits and specialities and schools of thought, there's one key point to philosophy: to find the answers to the questions about the universe, about reality—to search for the truth behind everything.

WORLD-CLASS BRAINS:
TWENTY-ONE THINKERS OF ALL CULTURES, ALL TIMES

These are some of the leading philosophers of the world—from Eastern and Western traditions—arranged chronologically. As you read through their lives and theories, you may notice a number of differences between them, particularly between the philosophers of the East and the West. And for good reason. Eastern and Western philosophy are often seen as being at odds with one another. It's the classic division—one stemming from the differences between the cultures that spawned them. Because of different

SOCRATES
(ENGRAVING BY
L. P. BOITARD IN
COOPER, "THE
LIFE OF
SOCRATES,"
LONDON, 1750)
(REPRODUCED
FROM THE
COLLECTIONS OF
THE LIBRARY OF
CONGRESS)

emphases in the general cultures, philosophical approaches to truth are often different as well. For example, in many cases, Western philosophy appears more concerned with process, while Eastern philosophy appears more mystical.

But for all of the differences (and there are many), there are also more similarities than you may initially think. For example, Jewish philosopher Moses ben Maimon (Maimonides is his Westernized name), Islamic philosopher Ibn Rushd (Averroës is the Latin form of his name), and Christian

philosopher Saint Augustine all tried to reconcile their specific religions with philosophy. In addition, you'll notice that there was cross-fertilization between the philosophies of East and West. The best example: Ibn Rushd actually had a greater impact on medieval Christian thinkers than on his own culture.

You'll also notice that, for all the supposed rifts between East and West, there have been larger rifts between schools of thought within one culture. For example, the Chinese philosophers take up points of view almost diametrically opposed: The Confucianists, who spread the teachings of religious founder Confucius, taught that humankind needs to follow a strict ethical system of behavior, while the Taoists took an opposite tack, and focused on the need for humankind to get in touch with the natural flow of things. (Note: We've used the names these philosophers are most commonly known by but we have included modern transliterations as well.)

SOCRATES

(c. 469–399 B.C.E.)
(Greek)

Claim to fame: The pivotal influence on ancient Western philosophy—everything before him is called "pre-Socratic" philosophy.

Gist of philosophy: As Roman orator Cicero put it, he was "the first to call philosophy down from the heavens"—instead of analyzing the cosmos and the natural world, he focused on the ethics of human life and conduct.

It's no wonder ancient Greece spawned three of the most influential Western philosophers: Socrates, Plato, and Aristotle. The Greek way of life revolved, to a great degree, around the intellect. In fact, the word SCHOOL actually comes from the Greek word for leisure. The reason? Ancient Greeks thought a person with leisure time wouldn't sit around and do nothing, but would spend the free time thinking and learning about the world.

And he did this via the "Socratic method"—asking questions of others about their definitions of basic concepts and using their answers to demonstrate the need for further analysis. For example, a student would ask Socrates: "Is love more powerful than hate?" "What do you mean by love? And what do you mean by hate?" would be Socrates' response. It would be up to the student to explore the ideas. In effect, Socrates wouldn't give answers to the questions put to him, but would give his students even *more* to think about—and, in this way, would give them the means to form their own conclusions.

Major works: None—Socrates didn't write anything, but is known primarily through Plato's works quoting him, especially the *Apology, Crito,* and *Phaedo* (Plato's later dialogues purport to quote Socrates, but are generally accepted as Plato's words and thoughts, not Socrates').

In his own words (or, more precisely, in the words of the Delphic motto, which Socrates advocated): "Know thyself."

Socrates left no written work, founded no school, had no distinct sect of disciples, left no actual historical evidence of his life but there are accounts of his life and writings about his philosophy by others, including the playwright Aristophanes, who ridiculed him in his play *The Clouds;* Xenophon, a soldier and admirer; memoirist Ion of Chios; and, most compellingly, his student Plato, who wrote about his life, trial, death, and teachings. Piecing together the different sources, we come up with an interesting combination of bare facts and personal details about him.

His early life is sketchy but straightforward: He was born to a stonemason (or sculptor, depending on the source) who was a friend of the son of Aristides the Just, founder of the Delian League (an alliance of Greek city-states formed to conduct war on Persia). By all accounts, his family status was quite high; as a youth, Socrates is said to have been friendly with the leading Athenians who formed the Periclean circle. He was married late in life to a woman named Xanthippe (described as a woman with a temper by Xenophon, and in later, probably exaggerated accounts, a shrew) and had three sons—none of whom distinguished himself.

His fairly high social status apparently gave him enough money to serve as a hoplite in the Peloponnesian War, where he fought bravely and impressed many with his powers of endurance, especially his ability to withstand fatigue, climate, and alcohol. These powers of endurance worked to his advantage as he aged as well. He was so involved with his philosophizing that he ignored his private affairs and wound up quite poor. But this poverty actually dovetailed with his philosophical belief that material goods were relatively unimportant.

He is described as unattractive, with a paunch, a snub nose, a wide mouth, and broad nostrils, but with an apparently magnetic personality. Plato talks about his wit, sense of humor, and social grace, and Socrates inspired his students and listeners with his ideas and his enthusiasm. His key point: that happiness isn't a question of material comfort or externalities, but a matter of delving within and mastering one's psyche.

But this ran counter to popular belief, and eventually passion brought

Plato may be considered one of the greatest Western philosophers nowadays, but in his time, he met with a great deal of criticism. Among his detractors, historian Theopompus accused him of lying; writer Athenaeus of envy; Roman writer Aulus Gellius of robbery; playwright Aristophanes of impiety; and philosopher Porphyry of incontinence.

him trouble. At age seventy, Socrates was condemned to death for "not believing in the gods the state believes in . . . and also for corrupting the young." Although he could have paid a fine to gain his release and later had the opportunity to escape from prison, he stuck by his ideals and did neither. Instead, willing to die for his beliefs, he drank hemlock as sentenced and died.

PLATO

(c. 427–347 B.C.E.)
(Greek)

Claim to fame: Right in the middle of the Big Three Ancient Philosophers—student of Socrates, teacher of Aristotle—and founder of Platonism, a philosophy that revolves, to a great degree, around the following concept: What we see in the world are just copies of eternal ideas; these ideas are the ultimate reality, and thus should be the object of philosophical inquiry and true knowledge.

Gist of philosophy: No real system, but a lot of ideas: His most important and lasting idea was the Theory of Forms, which held that the material world, which consists of "particulars" (i.e., objects of perception, opinion, and belief) is only a reflection of the timeless world of "forms" (concepts or ideas), which are the realities we seek behind appearances—sometimes called Platonic ideas. Other key concepts include: Humankind, by nature, has a tendency to seek what is good or virtuous; the soul is immortal; the main virtues of the soul are wisdom, justice, courage, and temperance.

Major works: The twenty-four *Dialogues,* including the *Euthyphro, Hippias Minor,* the *Phaedo,* the *Republic,* the *Symposium,* the *Meno,* the *Phaedrus,* the *Parmenides,* the *Sophist,* and the *Theatetus.*

In his own words: "The law is not concerned to make any one class specially happy, but to ensure the welfare of the commonwealth as a whole. By persuasion or constraint it will unite the citizens in harmony, making them share whatever benefits each class can contribute to the common good."

The name *Plato* means "broad." Whether this nickname was applied to his shoulders, as some have said, his forehead, or his girth, no one is sure. But it certainly can be applied to his influence. As twentieth-century philosopher Alfred North Whitehead said, Western philosophy is "a series of footnotes to Plato."

Details about his life are sketchy. Plato, whose real name was Aristocles, was born into a wealthy, aristocratic family. He apparently harbored political ambitions. But two members of his family were heavily involved in antidemocratic politics, which quashed any political prospects for Plato when the democratic cause won. Add to this the fact that he was tied to Socrates, who was killed for his political views, and it is clear that Plato had no chance politically.

After Socrates' death, Plato apparently traveled first to Megara, where he stayed with philosopher Euclides, then through Greece, Egypt (according to some), and Syracuse in Sicily. He returned to Athens in roughly 387, at some point after which he first began teaching young men, then later (some say as early as 385 B.C.E.) actually

We all know Socrates, Plato, and Aristotle, but who was the first ancient Greek philosopher? According to tradition, the first philosopher was Thales of the Ionian city Miletus (c. 636–c. 546 B.C.E.). Among his major teachings: The earth is made of water. In fact, everything is—condensed water is earth; thin water is air, and the substance that stars, sun, and plants are made of. While he had no proof for this theory and possibly took this idea from the ancient Mesopotamian religions that held that everything came from the primeval ocean, his idea was groundbreaking primarily because he DIDN'T ascribe creation to a miracle or a god. Instead, creation was a PROCESS that followed a pattern; in other words, it was the result of natural law.

started the school known as the Academy, probably named after its site—a park and gymnasium in Athens' outskirts sacred to the hero Academus. The school grew in importance, attracting students and disciples. It became a center of mathematical, scientific, and philosophical research.

In 367 he went back to Syracuse when Dion, the brother-in-law of the tyrant there, Dionysus the Younger, invited him to teach the new ruler how to be a philosopher-statesman. But it turned out to be a disaster—the young tyrant eventually banished Dion, and Plato returned to Athens. He returned once again in 361, hoping to effect a reconciliation, but it didn't work. He nearly lost his life in the process and finally returned to Athens. He spent the remainder of his life overseeing matters at the Academy, teaching, writing, and lecturing. He died at the age of eighty-one, leaving a prodigious amount of writing behind him, and a wealth of doctrines that still represent the core of Western philosophy.

ARISTOTLE

(384–322 B.C.E.)
(Greek)

Claim to fame: A student of Plato's who broke with Platonic philosophy and developed his own systematic approach to understanding life, reality, and knowledge—subsequently called Aristotelianism—that was the flip side of Platonism, since it focuses on objects, concrete realities, instead of abstract ideas. In doing this, he created a new science, logic. He devel-

Aristotle: A Non-PC Philosopher

Aristotle might have been one of the world's greatest philosophers, but like many other Greek men of his time he was also a male chauvinist. He tried to prove scientifically that males were superior to females, and that the female had no role in creating children beyond nurturing the fetus. The genetic contribution came totally from the male; scars, for example, were passed from father to child but not from mother to child. He conceded that occasionally some of the mother's features were visible in a child, but decided this was due to a defective father. He concluded that a female was a male without genitals—a maimed male. The fact that females don't get bald as frequently as males he saw as further proof of male superiority: Females were more "childlike," even though they aged faster. Aristotle also thought women had fewer teeth than men. This supposedly prompted English philosopher Bertrand Russell to comment, "Aristotle would never have made this mistake if he had let his wife open her mouth once in a while."

the Ideas (none of which have survived in full), and the scientific, including *On Coming into Being and Passing Away*, *On the Soul*, the *Organon* (logical works).

In his own words: "Virtue . . . is a state of character concerned with choice, lying in a mean, i.e., the mean relative to us, this being determined by a rational principle by which the man of practical wisdom would determine it."

Maybe we should thank a man named Speusippus for the development of Aristotelian philosophy. He was the man who, instead of Aristotle, was asked to succeed Plato as the leader of Plato's Academy. That is why a peeved Aristotle left the Academy and began working on his own interpretation of Platonism, which evolved into a new philosophy entirely.

The son of the court physician to King Amyntas II of Macedonia (the grandfather of Alexander the Great), Aristotle was orphaned at an early age. He was brought up by a guardian who eventually sent to him to Athens to study at Plato's Academy. Once there, Aristotle stayed for twenty years, first as a student, then as a teacher. And he may very well have stayed on as a purveyor of Platonism if it hadn't been for the afore-mentioned Speusippus. Instead, when he wasn't named Plato's successor, Aristotle left Athens and joined a Platonic group that Hermias, the ruler of Assos (a city in Asia Minor) had formed. A few years later, Philip of Macedonia asked Aristotle to tutor his son, Alexander (then thirteen). When Alexander became king, Aristotle left and finally returned to Athens, where he formed his own school, called the Lyceum. Here he taught and evolved his philosophy.

oped the syllogism—a type of deductive reasoning that consists of a major premise, a minor premise, and a conclusion (if A, the major premise, is true, and B, the minor premise, is true, then C, the conclusion that follows, is irrefutably true.)

Gist of philosophy: Philosophy with a scientific bent—emphasizing observation and analysis of the world instead of metaphysics, and putting forth two key (and, at the time, groundbreaking) ideas: that humankind is, by nature, seeking *"eudaimonia"*—happiness—and that in doing so one should follow the middle ground, "the Golden Mean."

Major works: Divided into two major groups—the popular works, including the *Eudemus*, the *Protrepticus*, *On Philosophy*, *On the Good*, *On*

For all of his orderliness and attention to detail in his works, he was apparently quite restless. In fact, tradition has it that because he used to pace up and down in front of his classes while lecturing, his students became known as the "Peripatetics." But this restlessness didn't get in the way of his work. He produced an enormous number of writings on a very wide range of subjects—from biology to zoology, from physics to poetry—most of them during the twelve years he headed his school.

But his tie with Macedonia ended up causing problems for him. After Alexander the Great died, anti-Macedonian sentiment was prevalent

The Other Greek Philosophers: Cynics, Epicureans, and Stoics

Cynics, Epicureans, and Stoics. We've all heard about them. A Cynic, of course, is a person who figures that other people are acting virtuous but have hidden agendas; an Epicurean is a sensualist, someone who loves the good life; and a Stoic is the ultimate stiff-upper-lip type, someone oblivious to both pain and pleasure.

But back in ancient times, the terms meant something a bit different. These three terms applied to adherents of popular philosophical schools that captured the imagination of the common people. If you look at the different philosophies, you can see how the terms evolved into their present-day meanings.

Cynics thought that virtue should be the supreme goal in life, and the path to a virtuous life was simplification. Their key belief? If people did away with traditions, customs, social conventions, and materialism, they'd become free—and nature would provide everything they needed. Cynics took materialism very literally and would often go without adequate food, clothing, or housing in their efforts to go back to nature. They also held that people didn't owe allegiance to any particular government because everyone was a citizen of the world at large, a "cosmopolitan." The school of Cynicism was founded by Antisthenes (c. 445–c. 360 B.C.E.), but the Cynic who really spread the word was Diogenes (c. 412–323 B.C.E.).

Epicureans weren't as ascetic as the Cynics, but they weren't quite as fun-loving as the name sounds to modern ears. Yes, they held that pleasure is the principal good in human existence, so all people should strive for it. But their idea of pleasure wasn't running around having a great time. Instead, they believed that pleasure was simply the absence of pain. Founded by Epicurus (c. 340–270 B.C.E.), the Epicurean philosophy is pretty simple: People should take the middle path, avoid extreme emotions, ignore the world around them (especially such emotion-provoking areas as politics), and look inward for peace.

Stoics took still a different tack. They thought Epicureans were too passive and Cynics too ascetic—so they taught a philosophy that was more active and less stringent. The school was founded by Zeno (335–263 B.C.E.), who first was interested in the Cynics' point of view, then decided to form his own school—the Stoa, or porch, which was where the Stoics conducted their teachings. The key belief of the Stoics? One law governs everything. This law is the natural law. If people submit to the natural law, i.e., live in harmony with nature and with one another, they will be happy. Stoicism was the most popular Hellenistic philosophy and later became popular in Rome as well. In fact, the concept of natural law was a key factor in the building of the Roman Empire.

in Athens. Worried that his school was in danger of being attacked by the anti-Macedonian party, possibly worried about his fate being the same as fellow philosopher Socrates, and publicly accused of impiety, Aristotle fled to Chalcis on the island of Euboea, where he died a year later.

MENCIUS (MENG-TZU, MENGZI)

(c. 390–c. 305 B.C.E.)
(Chinese)

Claim to fame: A popularizer of Confucianism (a philosophical/religious system that revolves around ethics, moral code, and behavior) and, in many ways, a cofounder. To put his relationship with the founder of Confucianism, Confucius, in a Western context, Mencius was Plato to Confucius' Socrates. (For more on Confucianism, see page 195; on Confucius, see pages 213–14.)

Gist of philosophy: Confucianism with a twist. Earlier Confucianism held that human beings needed to follow a strict ethical code to ensure social and political order. Mencius agreed, but added his own emphasis: He stressed the innate goodness of humankind and the need for benevolence, especially on the part of rulers. In other words, Mencius taught that human beings are innately good, but they need the right conditions and support to help them to realize this goodness and to grow morally. His Confucianism wasn't only theoretical; it was very practical—he recom-

mended social and political reform, and brought his philosophy down to earth, even relating it to such mundane things as road maintenance and taxes.

Major works: *Works of Mencius.* Pithy sayings, ranging from sentence to paragraph length, written as conversation between Mencius and his pupils.

In his own words: "Whoever is devoid of the heart of compassion is not human, whoever is devoid of the heart of shame is not human, whoever is devoid of the heart of courtesy and modesty is not human, and whoever is devoid of the heart of right and wrong is not human."

Mencius (Chinese name Meng Ko, but called Meng-tzu—Master Meng—by his students) was born a century after the death of Confucius in Tsou, a small principality close to Confucius' birthplace of Lu. Like Confucius, he was an aristocrat and a teacher who believed that man should strive for goodness through moral and ethical conduct. But what Confucius considered an attribute of the saints (*ren*), Mencius considered "humane goodness"—something anyone could cultivate, because human nature was innately good. Central to Mencius' Confucianism was *hsiao,* serving one's parents and other family members according to their seniority. Mencius also believed in fate (*ming*), a subject Confucius never addressed, and taught that while people can determine their conduct, and so achieve the goodness they are capable of, they can't determine their fate, for ultimately heaven, or the supreme being, determines this.

And Mencius' fate turned out to be similar to Confucius': He hoped to find a prince to back his ideas and "put his

Way into practice," and, like Confucius, he failed. Instead, he put in a brief stint as a minister in the state of Chi, then retired from public life and turned to full-time teaching. Shortly after his death in 305 B.C.E., his pupils pulled together his teachings and sayings and used these to spread their master's word.

CHUANG-TZU (ZHUANGZI)

(c. 369–c. 286 B.C.E.)
(Chinese)

Claim to fame: The second most famous and influential Taoist (Daoist)—one of the leading Chinese religion/philosophies—after Lao-tzu, the legendary founder of this mystical system of thought that was the opposite of Confucianism. (For more on Taoism [Daoism], see pages 206–7. For more on Lao-tzu, see pages 214–15).

Gist of philosophy: Very mystical and transcendental. It's essentially an individual Taoism, based on the fact that everything is continually changing, going through self-transformation; this means everything is part of the same cycle of change, which leads to his famous doctrine of "the equality of all things." In other words, everything and everyone is one.

Major works: The *Chuang-tzu* (written by him and his students), parables written in the form of dialogues between Chuang-tzu and his students and critics.

In his own words: "Life and death are one, right and wrong are the same."

The Book of Changes

There's an ancient book of Chinese wisdom that is still popular today—both in the East and here in the United States—the *I Ching* (The Book of Changes). Part ethics, part philosophy, and part common sense, it's based on ancient oral traditions dating back possibly seven thousand years, and first emerged in written form over three thousand years ago. It's a book of no particular religion or philosophical school (some of it is Taoist, some of it Confucianist, and some neither), but one that was heavily used by the common people in China in the past and is still in use. It all developed from the oracular tradition: People believed that the best way to get advice or guidance on how to live was through oracles. And the *I Ching* is a collection of oracles. The book is arranged around eight trigrams, each of which is composed of combinations of three divided or undivided lines. By combining two of the trigrams, you get sixty-four hexagrams. And each of these sixty-four hexagrams has a written description, explaining its symbolic meanings. These are supposed to help readers live an ethical life in harmony with the universe by answering questions based on the pattern left by randomly thrown coins or rods. It's a simple process: You ask a question, throw the coins, then read the passage relating to the pattern the coins make. An example of the type of advice you can get if you want guidance on how to be in harmony with the universe: "If one is to be in touch with the cosmic flow, he must develop a consciousness that will permit communication. Through the wide gate of his spirit's awareness, the sage receives the earth-intended force and humbly puts it to use for all men. Through this attitude of serving, he builds cooperation so that men may learn to work together in the shaping of their destinies."

Unlike Lao-tzu, the legendary founder of Taoism, Chuang-tzu was definitely a historical figure. Unfortunately, little is known about his life but the bare basics. He was born in the state of Meng, became a minor government official, and was offered a prime ministership in the small Chinese state of

Chu but turned it down, preferring to remain a reclusive hermit.

His hermit's lifestyle was the focal point of Chuang-tzu's philosophy. Believing that the universe (and everything in it) is in a constant state of flux, he felt that humans should go with the flow, following the way of nature instead of trying to impose the "way of man." While he didn't expect everyone to become a hermit like himself, he did believe that the path to happiness was through discarding attachment to material things and knowledge. Most important, he believed that by "fasting in the mind," as he put it, people could forget the hypocritical strictures and

rules of society. This is the way they could eventually be in accord with the Tao—the underlying One of the universe—and so find true peace and happiness.

HSUN-TZU (XUNZI)

(c. 298–238 B.C.E.)
(Chinese)

Claim to fame: Third member of the three founding fathers of Confucianism (with Confucius and Mencius). Like Mencius, he added his own thoughts to Confucianism and helped spread it across China.

Gist of philosophy: A rationalistic and materialist Confucianism emphasizing social control. Only through education and moral training can human beings become good.

Major works: The *Hsun-tzu,* a thirty-two-chapter selection of essays.

In his own words: "If there is no dull and determined effort, there will be no brilliant achievement." "The nature of man is evil; what is good in him is artificial."

Hsun-tzu's life mirrors the times in which he lived: near the end of the period called "the Age of a Hundred Philosophers," a time filled with intellectual, social, and political change. His brand of Confucianism bears the marks of many other thinkers that preceded him and was able to withstand the onslaughts of dozens of other competing philosophies.

According to early writings, his real name was Hsun Kuang or Hsun

---

Legalism:
Another Chinese School of Thought

Confucianism and Taoism weren't the only theories competing with one another. There was another school of thought that tried to compete with both of them—and failed to last. This was Legalism, a superauthoritarian, none-too-uplifting school that wasn't a religion or a philosophy as much as it was a political system. It emerged during the late Chou period, in about 250 B.C.E., founded by two former Confucians who were also influenced by Taoism. At its core was the belief that human nature is essentially evil. So there has to be an ultrastrong state or ruler, who should quash all dissent and competing ideas and keep people disciplined, even suppressed if need be. The people should work and produce for the ruler, not waste time learning or having fun. And in return, the ruler should treat the people well (unless, of course, they were dissidents, in which case they could be eliminated). Not a particularly enlightening system, but it worked for a while—chiefly because it helped leaders rule during the sometimes tumultuous Chou dynasty. But it faded out, probably because it was so tough.

Ching, but in respect for his teachings, he was called Hsun-tzu (Master Hsun). He lived in an era when China was divided into many small competing states. Hsun was born in the Chinese state of Chao, but for most of his life he worked and taught in two other states, Chi and Chu. And in both places, he held influential positions. At Chi, he was a member of the famous group of scholars, the Chi-hsia group, who served as royal counselors, and eventually became its leader. Later, he went to Chu, where the prince became his patron and made him magistrate of the city of Lan-ling. When the prince was killed, Hsun-tzu resigned as magistrate but stayed in Lan-ling, writing and teaching.

And he lived long enough to see a dramatic shift in the world in which he lived. Toward the end of his life, the Age of a Hundred Philosophers and the small states came to a crashing close, resulting in the rise of the Chin empire, the first time China was unified. Two of Hsun-tzu's students were prime players in the Chin state, and were not noted for their tolerance. They fell in with the prevailing Legalist school of thought, a very rigid, virtually totalitarian system. In fact, one of Hsun-tzu's students advised that 460 Confucian scholars who opposed him be buried alive.

But although Hsun-tzu held that human nature was inherently evil, it appears that he didn't subscribe to the ruthless practices of the Legalists in the new empire. According to one record, when he heard that his student Li Ssu had become premier of Chin, he went on a fast. His philosophy wound up lasting longer than the Legalist school and still influences Chinese thought and culture.

SAINT AUGUSTINE

(354–430 C.E.)
(North African)

Claim to fame: Considered the most influential Christian thinker after Saint Paul.

Gist of philosophy: Both philosophy and religion seek wisdom and, ultimately, supreme happiness or blessedness. But the only way to succeed in this quest is through Christianity. His system is based on the work of the followers of Plato, the Neoplatonists.

Major works: *Confessions,* a largely autobiographical work written in the form of a long prayer to God; *The City of God,* a history of humankind from a Christian perspective.

In his own words: "Believe in order that you may understand; unless you shall believe, you shall not understand."

Called the "Doctor of Grace" and "the first modern man," even "God's own busy bee" (by the bishop of Milevis), Saint Augustine was more than just a religious philosopher. He is also credited with writing the first self-analytic autobiography (his *Confessions*); he is considered a major father of theology, a key formulator of the philosophy of history, and more. But this important Christian philosopher led a life far from what one would expect: He was born a pagan; had, as was common at the time, a mistress at the age of eighteen and had a son by her (but did remain faithful to her for twelve years); initially found the Bible somewhat simplistic; didn't convert to Christianity until he was thirty-two; and, unlike many other

Christians, considered philosophy, particularly Neoplatonism, a preparation for belief in Christianity.

He was born Aurelius Augustinus in the Roman city of Tagaste in North Africa to a lower-middle-class Roman father and a Christian mother who focused more on his worldly education than on his religious. As such, he was a typical young man of his times—prone to love affairs and a somewhat dissipated lifestyle while a student, even while he led his class in rhetoric. But when he was eighteen (some say nineteen), his life took a crucial turn. He read a dialogue of the Roman scholar Cicero, the *Hortensius,* which Augustine himself said in his *Confessions* and elsewhere switched his interests to a new path, searching for wisdom. After Cicero he tried the Bible, which he dismissed as crude. Then he followed the popular Manichaean religion, which based its beliefs on scientific proof; but Augustine wound up dismissing it as unscientific. Next came a move to Milan, his discovery of Neoplatonism, which eventually led to his rediscovery of Christianity, and finally, his conversion to Christianity in 386.

Once he became a Christian, Augustine kept up with his search for wisdom and developed his philosophy, focusing on the relationship between faith and reason (or understanding) and stressing that man needed God's grace. He eventually became bishop of Hippo, a major seaport city in Africa, and his influence and teachings spread. He died when the enemies of Rome, the Vandals, were invading Hippo. Possibly in deference to his fame or his scholarship, the only buildings the Vandals didn't burn were the cathedral and Augustine's library.

SHANKARA (SANKARA, SAMKARA, SANKARACHARYA)

(generally accepted as c. 788–c. 820 C.E. but others say he lived 686–718 C.E. or c. 700–c. 750 C.E.)
(Indian)

Claim to fame: Considered the leading Hindu religious philosopher; founder of nondualistic (Advaita) Vedanta, an offshoot of Hinduism.

Gist of philosophy: *Vedanta* literally means "end of the Veda." The Vedas were the ancient sacred texts of Hinduism, and Shankara intepreted these texts differently than they had been interpreted before. His philosophy teaches that there is no real difference, no separation, between the self and God (or *Brahman,* the major force underlying the entire cosmos). People are another aspect of God; we're all part of the same stuff. The trick, of course, is getting to the point where you really understand this. So first, you have to accept that thought and matter are not real. The only thing unchanging and real is our deep consciousness, our Self (called *Atman*). Again, this isn't distinct from God or the divine. It's just one aspect of the one force that underlies the cosmos (called *Brahman*). By realizing that the world is illusion, we can be released and become one with the Divine.

Major works: The *Brahmasutrabhasya* (a commentary on the *Brahma Sutra* of Badarayana), commentaries on the Upanishads and on the *Bhagavadgita,* and (attributed to him) the

Vivekachudamani (The Crest-Jewel of Discrimination), the *Prasnottara Malika* (Garland of Questions and Answers), among others.

In his own words: "*Brahman*—the absolute existence, knowledge and bliss—is real. The universe is not real. *Brahman* and *Atman* [man's inner Self] are one."

Sometimes called the Thomas Aquinas of Hinduism, Shankara led a very short but very busy life. He was born into an orthodox Brahmin family and at age ten was an intellectual prodigy who relished religious study, wrote commentaries on what he read, and met with traveling scholars.

But even at this young age, he believed that his teachers weren't practicing what they preached, and he grew dissatisfied with book knowledge. When his father died, he began puzzling over the meaning of life and death and, with his mother's reluctant consent, left home in search of a teacher who would help him in his quest for knowledge. He became a disciple of Govindapada, a yogic philosopher, who initiated him and instructed him in yoga and meditation. Eventually, he went to Benares, where he began teaching and acquired his first important disciple, Samandana (later called Padmapada).

From then on, he continued traveling, teaching, and spreading his philosophy. First he went to Badari, a city in the Himalayas, where he wrote his famous commentary on the *Brahma Sutra* of Badarayana, a major Hindu sacred text; then he went on to a number of other cities. In these places, he established four or five important monasteries, set up a network of teachers of his Advaita Vedanta philosophy,

established ten monastic orders, and continued defending his views against opponents. He died in Kedarnath, in the Himalayas, at a young age—thirty-two—but his words continued living, fueled by the network he left behind.

ABU HAMID MUHAMMAD AL-GHAZALI

(1058–1111 C.E.)
(Iranian)

Claim to fame: Given the honorific title "the proof of Islam" and considered one of the leading spiritual philosophers of Islam; in particular, known for his attempts to develop an orthodox Sufism (the mystical sect of Islam) and credited with giving Islamic theology a philosophical base.

Gist of philosophy: Actually, al-Ghazali was a critic of philosophers, so much of his writing was devoted to refuting contemporary philosophical thought. His most ardent desire was to show that there was no such thing as causality. At the same time that he was using reason to disprove the teachings of others, he held that reason can't explain everything. The thinking soul comprehends reality without the need for knowledge or reasoning because it is reflecting the universal Soul—God. The bottom line, then? Much of al-Ghazali's writing is ultimately paradoxical. But his most lasting teaching was a basic one, and one that enabled many Muslims to pursue a more moderate form of Sufism than before: A spiritual inner life can and should coexist with strict adherence to

Shariah—Islamic law—and traditional Islamic doctrine. In other words, a person could be a mystic, a Sufi, while still observing the basic Islamic tenets.

Major works: His most famous, *Ihya Ulum al-Din* (The Revival of the Religious Sciences); as well as numerous others (by some accounts, over four hundred), including the *Tahafut*.

In his own words: "Remember it is the heart and not the body which strives to draw near to God. By 'heart' I do not mean the flesh perceived by the senses, but that secret thing which is sometimes expressed by spirit, and sometimes by soul."

According to legend, when al-Ghazali was traveling home from a break in his studies, robbers stole his notebooks. He asked for them back, but the robbers jeered at him, saying that while he claimed to be knowledgeable, what he knew was only in his notebooks, not in his mind. Upset by this because he recognized its truth, al-Ghazali spent three years memorizing what he had learned.

This type of application epitomizes al-Ghazali. He was born in Tus (near the modern Mashad in eastern Iran), and eventually went to study at the Nizamiyah college in Nishapur. He eventually joined the court of the vizier of the ruling Seljuk sultans, Nizam al-Mulk. Then, at age thirty-three, he became the chief professor of philosophy at the Nizamiyah college in Baghdad—one of the top positions in the Sunni Muslim intellectual world. But only three years later, he went through a massive spiritual crisis. According to his own autobiographical work, he first became skeptical of ever finding truth, then got over his skepticism and began searching for truth in four different

areas—through studying rational theologians (called the Ashari); Neoplatonic philosophers; the Ismailiyah, a Shiite group who held that knowledge could only be gotten from an infallible imam; and the Islamic mystics (the Sufis). Ultimately, his delving into Sufism led him to hate the material life he had been living in Baghdad and made him fear that he would go to hell. He suffered a nervous breakdown and psychosomatic illness—his mouth grew so dry that he couldn't lecture anymore and couldn't even eat. His solution: to opt for the life of a Sufi mendicant. He spent time traveling, then eventually settled back in his native Tus, where he founded a hostel for Sufis.

But when the Muslim year 500 began, it was the beginning of a new century, and friends told al-Ghazali that he was the "renewer" Muhammad prophesied that God would send at the start of each new century. So al-Ghazali began teaching again, becoming main professor at the Nizamiyah college he had attended in Nishapur. There he stayed for about three years, until he returned home, ill. To the end, he was highly spiritual. According to his brother, himself a scholar, al-Ghazali awoke, said his dawn prayer, lay back on his bed facing Mecca, kissed his shroud, said, "Obediently I enter into the presence of the King," and died before the sun arose.

IBN RUSHD (ALSO KNOWN BY HIS LATIN NAME, AVERROËS)

(1126–1198 C.E.)
(Spanish Arab)

Claim to fame: Considered the foremost Islamic medieval philosopher; had a great deal of influence on Latin thought for about five centuries after his death.

Gist of philosophy: One of his key points: Reason and faith can coexist harmoniously. More specifically, Aristotelian philosophy (which Ibn Rushd followed) can and should be reconciled with Islamic traditions (which he also followed). So his philosophy is based on Aristotelianism, but also fits in with Islamic theology. At its core is the belief that nature and reality are one structure that has hierarchical levels leading up from lower levels of being to greater levels of being. God is at the top, and human souls seek to, eventually, meld with God. In this sense, immortality is possible, but it's not individual immortality, it's impersonal. It's similar to a Buddhist point of view: Your soul doesn't live on after death as you, an individual, but as part of God.

Major works: *Commentaries on Aristotle, The Incoherence of Incoherence* (a refutation of al-Ghazali); and (a medical work) *Kulliyat* (meaning "generalities," and Latinized to *Colliget*).

In his own words: "Philosophy is the friend and milk-sister of religion; thus injuries from people related to

philosophy are the severest injuries [to religion] apart from the enmity, hatred, and quarrels which such [injuries] stir up between the two, which are companions by nature and lovers by essence and instinct."

Ibn Rushd was a quadruple threat, known for his work in law, medicine, science, and philosophy. Throughout his life, in spite of his busy schedule as a judge and court physician, he managed to put out a large body of work in all the different fields that interested him, from jurisprudence to medicine, from divine law to philosophy. He was a Renaissance man, but one who lived in medieval times. And while he became, perhaps, the top Islamic philosopher of his time, his influence was actually stronger in Western Latin philosophy.

Born in Arab-ruled Córdoba, Spain, to a family of jurists, he started by following the family tradition, becoming a judge (*qadi*) in Córdoba. Details about much of his life are somewhat sketchy, but according to most accounts, he became a favorite of the caliph of Marrakesh, who was known for his interest in scholarship. In fact, the caliph possibly was the person who encouraged Ibn Rushd to begin his famous commentaries on Aristotle, which Ibn Rushd apparently began working on after he was appointed *qadi* of Seville in 1169. Next was a move back to Córdoba, again holding the post of *qadi*. Then he switched over to medicine as his primary occupation, becoming court physician to Caliph Abu Yusuf in 1182.

But a little over ten years later, he went from being a court favorite to being exiled. No one is sure exactly what happened, beyond the fact that his teaching of Aristotelian philosophy and his repudiation of strict Islamic philosophy (particularly as put forth by al-Ghazali in his *The Incoherence of the Philosophers*—a work refuted point by point by Ibn Rushd in his *The Incoherence of the Incoherence*) put him at odds with many strict Islamic thinkers and religious leaders. Some scholars believe he, with a group of other scientists, was indicted for being irreligious. Others say he was exiled as a way of protecting him from conservative theologians who opposed him. But while the reasons are still somewhat unclear, the upshot wasn't: The caliph's son (and successor) banished him to a village outside of Seville.

With his banishment, his work fell into disfavor, and much of it was burnt. But a few years later, his reputation was restored and his work reexamined. He died in Marrakesh shortly thereafter.

CHU HSI (ZHUXI)

(1130–1200 C.E.)
(Chinese)

Claim to fame: Key formulator of neo-Confucian theory and largely responsible for preserving Confucian tradition in spite of the spread of competing religions and philosophies Buddhism and Taoism.

Gist of philosophy: Traditional Confucianism with a bit of a hedge—people are good, but they may have evil in them. So they should strive to be good and vanquish that evil. More specifically, there is a supreme principle (*li,* or reason) underlying the universe, and everything in the universe

(each object, action, or relationship) *also* has a principle that is a manifestation of this supreme principle. In other words, everything also has *li.* It's the reason everything exists, and it's also the rule to which everything should conform. The problem is, everything in the physical universe also has *chi* (material force). And depending upon the amount of *chi,* people can be evil or immoral. So people must cultivate their higher nature to be in harmony with the *li,* the supreme principle.

Major works: *The Collected Commentaries on the Four Books* (the major Confucian texts—*The Great Learning, The Analects, The Book of Mencius, The Doctrine of the Mean*); and (not by him, but collected by his students) *Chu Hsi yulei,* The Conversations of Master Zhu in Categories).

In his own words: "When one is angry, if one can directly forget his anger and examine the right and wrong according to principle, then right and wrong will be clearly seen and desires will naturally be unable to persist."

"There has never been any *Chi* [that which composes the entire universe and all things, including thoughts and activities of the mind] without *li* [principle] nor any principle without *chi.*"

Chu Hsi is, to a great degree, the reason that Confucianism didn't die out in the face of the spread of Buddhism and Taoism. And his ability to rebut these two popular religions is possibly based on his early years spent studying both Buddhism and Taoism.

He was born in the Chinese province of Fujian to a family of officials. His father, the subprefectal sheriff, was forced out of office due to his criticism of the Song dynasty, and began teaching Chu Hsi at home,

chiefly focusing on neo-Confucianist theory and the Confucianist texts *The Great Learning* and *The Doctrine of the Mean*. Upon his father's death in 1143, Chu switched to studies at different Buddhist and Taoist schools, and he continued studying their teachings until about the age of twenty-six, when he fell back into Confucianism.

One reason he was able to continue in his pursuit of philosophical and religious knowledge was that he passed the extremely difficult civil service exam at eighteen, an early age compared to most. So the years most people spent preparing for the exam he was able to spend on more scholarly pursuits. This focus on learning is one that he held throughout his life: He strongly believed that people should learn for learning's sake, not for the sake of passing exams. Even after he was appointed to a government position (subprefectal registrar of Tongan, a post he held from 1153 to 1158), he still focused more on his studies and less on official positions. From 1158 to 1179, he held mainly sinecurial positions, and spent much of his time writing, developing theories, and meeting with leading philosophers and scholars. After this, he held several more important official positions (such as prefect), but still was more a scholar than an official. In fact, over the course of his life, he actually served in office for a total of only nine years.

Up until the end, the prime goal of his life was spreading Confucianism. To this end, he focused on ways to update it and make it more accessible to the people of the times, and in so doing, fight against the appeal of Buddhism and Taoism. And for this reason, he is still thought of as a great synthesizer, combining the different theories of different philosophers from the Confucian Mencius to non-Confucians and coming up with a new, strong version of Confucianism that enabled it to survive into the twentieth century.

MAIMONIDES (ALSO KNOWN BY HIS HEBREW NAME, MOSES BEN MAIMON)

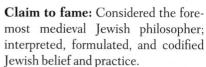

(1135–1204 C.E.)
(Spanish Jew)

Claim to fame: Considered the foremost medieval Jewish philosopher; interpreted, formulated, and codified Jewish belief and practice.

Gist of philosophy: Like Ibn Rushd, the Islamic philosopher, Maimonides holds that religious faith and tradition (specifically Judaism) and philosophic reasoning (specifically Aristotelianism) can coexist compatibly and, in fact, are interrelated aspects of wisdom. People should seek perfection by being reflective and by being truly pious; in other words, by seeking knowledge and spirituality—again, blending the philosophic and the religious. One of the key ways of seeking perfection? Sticking with the Golden Mean. People should follow the middle ground and avoid extremism.

Major works: *Mishneh Torah* (Second Law; also called *Yad ha-Chazakah*, The Strong Hand); *Moreh Nebuhim* (Guide of the Perplexed).

In his own words: "The great sickness and the grievous evil consist in this: that all the things that man finds written in books, he presumes to think of as true—and all the more so if the books are old."

"Every ignoramus imagines that all that exists exists with a view to his individual sake; it is as if there were nothing that exists except him. And if something happens to him that is contrary to what he wishes, he makes the trenchant judgment that all that exists is an evil."

Moses ben Maimon was his proper name; Maimonides the name under which he is better known. These two names, one Hebrew, one Greek, also signify the two traditions he sought to reconcile. And just as his philosophical work revolved around two different elements, so his life revolved around two different areas: on the one hand, the intellectual, exhibited by his love for philosophic contemplation and study; and on the other, the active, required by the demands of his job as a court physician and his standing as leader of the Jewish community in Egypt.

To a great degree, he was a product of his times. Maimonides was born in Arab-ruled Córdoba, Spain, to a family with a legacy of scholarship in both the Talmud and Greek science and philosophy. When an Islamic sect, the Almohads, conquered Córdoba and required all inhabitants to convert to Islam, Maimonides and his family were forced to flee their home. They wandered through Spain and North Africa, finally settling in Fez, Morocco. In line with family tradition, Maimonides was educated in a wide range of disciplines, including rabbinical lore, the Talmud, mathematics, philosophy, astronomy, and medicine.

He began wandering himself in 1165, traveling to Palestine. Unable to settle there due to the Crusades, he moved on, passing through Acre, Jerusalem, Hebron, and eventually settling in Fustat (now Old Cairo). Here he started practicing medicine and met with great success, eventually working his way into a post as court physician. His reputation as a physician was widespread; he wrote numerous medical works and was known for his medical knowledge. In fact, according to certain records, Richard the Lionhearted asked him to join his court as physician, an offer that Maimonides declined.

His life wasn't only medicine, however. He also became the untitled, unpaid leader of the Jewish community in Egypt, acting simultaneously as rabbi, judge (on the local, appellate and administrative levels), and government and philanthropic administrator. (He felt very strongly about being unpaid for his duties, and actually wrote passionately against an institutionalized, paid rabbinate, although this system did eventually come to pass).

Yet with all the time he had to spend in both his official medical position and unofficial community position, he managed to find time to follow his scholarly bent and wrote both rabbinical and philosophic works. Most of these were written in Arabic and later translated into Hebrew. His earlier works, the *Commentary on the Mishnah* and the *Book of Commandments,* revolve around Talmudic tradition, but even these foreshadow his later focus on harmonizing Torah study with philosophy. His two major works reflect the dichotomy that was his life. His *Mishneh Torah* (1178) is considered a major Jewish work, codifying Jewish law and philosophy. And his philosophical masterpiece, *Guide of the Perplexed*, expands upon his belief that Talmudic study and Greek philosophy, faith and reasoning, could coexist.

Maimonides died in 1204 in Fustat, his ideas still not widely accepted (in fact, at one point his works were actually ordered to be burned). But with time, both his rabbinical and philosophic views caught on. The articles of faith laid out in his commentary now form the basis of orthodox Jewish faith; his *Mishneh Torah* is considered the primary code of Jewish law; and his philosophy has influenced a number of philosophers, Jews and non-Jews alike.

IBN ARABI (ABU BAKR MUHAMMAD IBN AL-ARABI AL-HATAMI AL-TAI)

(1165–1240 C.E.)
(Spanish Arab)

Claim to fame: Considered one of the leading mystic Islamic philosophers; although he was a Sunni, his beliefs were (and are) highly influential in Iranian and Shia Islam.

Gist of philosophy: Mystical experience is the key to spiritual knowledge. Called *whadat al-wujud* (the "unity of existence"), it centers around *tawil*—literally meaning "to bring something back to its ultimate point." People should seek the inner meaning of reality (whether in religious texts or in existence itself) through visions.

Major works: *Fusus al-hikam* (The Bezels of Wisdom); *Al-futuhat al-makkiyah* (The Meccan Revelations), sometimes called the "Bible of esoteric Islam."

In his own words: "The whole of existence is imagination within imagination, while true Being is God alone."

From the beginning, Ibn Arabi was attracted to the mystical side of life and knowledge. Born in Arab-ruled Murcia in southeastern Spain, he moved to Seville, the intellectual center, at age eight to begin studying. There he received an education in traditional Muslim subjects, became exposed to Sufi teachings, and eventually chose the Sufi way of life as his mission.

In some ways, the Sufi way of life seems to have chosen him: He met the aged Sufi Saint Fatima of Córdoba, but, as Ibn Arabi tells it, she appeared beautiful to him, like a girl in her teens. In fact, legend has it that whenever he was with her, he couldn't keep from blushing. Fatima considered him her spiritual son, made him one of her favorite disciples, and initiated him into Sufi ways. When he reached his twenties, Ibn Arabi began traveling, meeting Sufi masters and scholars, maturing as a philosopher, and even matching wits (and winning) with Ibn Rushd. He eventually decided to leave Spain, spurred by a vision that told him to go to the eastern part of the Islamic world; he spent the next twenty-three years traveling in the Middle East.

When he first visited Mecca at age thirty-six, his host was an Iranian sheik with a beautiful daughter. Dazzled by her beauty, intelligence, and spirituality, he fell in love and wrote a love poem, the *Tarjuman al-ashwaq* (The

Interpreter of Ardent Longings). But it was more than simply a love poem; it was meant to be read on a different level, that of its inner meaning. This idea of a hidden meaning beneath the surface text (called *tawil*) became central to his philosophy. Ibn Arabi spent the latter half of his life applying *tawil* to the Quran and *hadith,* using his own visions to supply the hidden meanings for which to search.

He died in Damascus, having written more than two hundred works, and while he is considered controversial, even heretical, by many, particularly orthodox Muslims, he is considered *al-Shaykh al-Akbar*—greatest of all spiritual leaders—by others, particularly Iranian Muslims.

SAINT THOMAS AQUINAS

(1225–1274 C.E.)
(Italian)

Claim to fame: Christian theologian; the systematizer of much Roman Catholic dogma still followed today.

Gist of philosophy: A metaphysical Christian philosophy based on Aristotle that supplanted Augustinianism and relies on scientific analysis rather than blind faith. Like Augustine, Thomas holds that humankind's goodness comes from God's nature, not from human will. But he uses Aristotelianism to explain Christianity—in other words, sets forth a proposition, then lists proofs (from the Bible, from tradition, from reasoning) backing it up. He answers more than ten thou-

sand objections to Christianity in this way. In effect, he's trying to reconcile the Christian doctrines of faith with scientific rationalism.

Major works: *Summa Theologica; Summa Contra Gentiles.*

In his own words: "Truth follows the existence of the thing."

Thomas Aquinas, son of the lord of Roccasecca and Montesangiovanni, was groomed to be a monk from the very beginning. In fact, when he was five or six, his parents gave him to the Benedictine abbey of Monte Cassino for training. But when he was eighteen or nineteen, Thomas rebelled against his family wishes—a bit. He decided that the Dominican order, known for its simplicity and poverty, was more to his taste. His mother fought back. She had her older son, a soldier in the army of Frederick the Great, intercept Thomas and force him to return home, where he was imprisoned in the family castle for over a year. But force didn't work. Even the local prostitute they hired to seduce Thomas couldn't sway him from his chosen order.

This kind of singlemindedness served him well throughout his life. As a teacher and writer, he was known for his scholarly, clear-cut arguments, and his emphasis on order, beginning with his differentiation between philosophy (in his case, Aristotleanism reworked to fit a Christian framework) and theology (based upon the divine gift of faith). And his works were attempts to impose order on the whole of the Christian religion. His major work, the unfinished *Summa Theologica,* was intended "to set forth briefly and clearly the things which pertain to sacred doctrine" and included his famous "five ways" or proofs of the existence of God.

But for all his comprehensiveness, Thomas had little influence in his own day. When he died in 1274, scholars and theologians were his key admirers. The religiously orthodox preferred to stick with Augustinianism; contemporary philosophers were opting for heterodoxy. Even after he was canonized in 1323, Thomas's teachings were largely taught only in the Dominican order. It wasn't until the sixteenth century that his ideas truly took off, establishing him as the primary supplier of Christian doctrine, even today.

RENÉ DESCARTES

(1596–1650 C.E.)
(French)

Claim to fame: Called "the father of modern philosophy." Introduced the method of systematic doubt; the one indubitable truth, "I think therefore I am"; and the dualism of mind and matter.

Gist of philosophy: Above all, a method; its key goal to reconcile the spiritual and the physical, science and religion. The bottom line to this method? Start with doubt and work systematically toward knowledge. Thought, or reason, is the basis of knowledge; through thought we can have absolutely certain knowledge of certain topics in the world around us. To attain this knowledge, we follow a rational, five-stage approach that takes us from skepticism to knowledge. His key points: We can know that we exist because we think. (*"Cogito, ergo sum"*—I think, therefore I am.) In addition, an all-powerful and all-good God

Descartes's work wasn't universally appreciated by any means. In 1926, all of his philosophical works were banned by the Soviet government—which termed them too "subversive." And more than twenty years later than that, his MEDITATIONS *and six other works were put on the papal* INDEX— *banned for heresy.*

exists, who has created us and the external world. Since God made us, we have the capability of understanding things if we use all our faculties. Finally, based on the previous conclusions and following systematic reasoning, we can know that external material things cause our sensory ideas; because the universe is made up of both mind and matter, we know that our ideas are caused by something and not created in our own mind.

Major works: *Discours de la Méthode* (Discourse on Method); *Meditationes de Prima Philosophia* (Meditations on First Philosophy); *Principia Philsophiae* (Principles of Philosophy), among others.

In his own words: "I think, therefore I am." "[Outside things] are not perceived because they are seen and touched, but only because they are understood."

According to some accounts, on November 10, 1619, when he was serving in the army of Maurice of Nassau, the duke of Bavaria, Descartes had some dreams that changed his life—and the face of philosophy.

He had spent the day reflecting about his life and his quest for truth. That night, he had dreams that he believed charged him with a divine mission: to devise a unified system of truth and nature based on mathematics. Whether or not this story is apocryphal, the bottom line remains the same: Thereafter, Descartes did indeed pursue just that . . . but not until he had traveled and theorized some more.

Details about his early life are sketchy. He was born to a family of lesser nobility; his father was a government official. At the age of eight, he entered a Jesuit school where, after eight years, he grew dissatisfied. While he admired the teachers, he later held that the course of education offered little of substance; only mathematics seemed to have any value. So he left, believing that the best way to pursue knowledge would be to seek it on his own, outside of traditional authority. He received a law degree from the University of Poitiers; traveled to Paris, where he joined the army; then continued traveling, to Holland, Germany, France, and Italy. He finally returned to Holland in 1628, where he stayed for twenty-one years, working on developing his system of establishing that absolute certainty was the basis for human knowledge.

While he was willing to break new ground with his theories, he was a cautious man. In fact, he abandoned his first book, *Le Monde,* which espoused the Copernican theory (that planets revolve around the sun) that Galileo taught, when he heard that Galileo was being condemned for heresy. His next book, a complete work called *Discours de la Méthode,* came out in 1637, and thereafter his reputation was set. He continued writing until 1649, when Queen Christina of Sweden asked him to come to her court and tutor her in philosophy. This he did reluctantly—and his decision led to his death. Cautious in his lifestyle as well as his academics, he had always preferred waking late and working in overheated rooms. But in Sweden he was confronted with an extremely cold climate and a royal student—a queen who summoned him often and at odd hours. This combination weakened him, and he caught pneumonia and died.

BARUCH SPINOZA

(1632–1677 C.E.)
(Dutch)

Claim to fame: One of the greatest rationalist metaphysical philosophers of the eighteenth century; also considered to be the founder of scientific psychology because he was the first to try to come up with a scientific, objective study of human behavior—and a key figure in the development of a rationalist approach to the Bible and Christian theology.

Gist of philosophy: A rejection of Cartesian dualism in favor of monism. His philosophy is a combination of systematic thinking and almost Buddhist mysticism. It's based on mathematics (particularly geometry) in that he tries to deduce his theorems from a set of supposedly self-evident axioms, so it's very systematic and rational. But at the same time, it has a (given the traditional Western beliefs) groundbreaking take on God: God isn't a personal creator, but the ultimate, infinite, and eternal force and being of the world. In other words, God is the reason why things exist and the reason why everything happens as it does.

Major works: The *Ethics,* the *Tractatus de Intellectus Emendatione* (Tractate on the Correction of the Intellect), *Tractatus Theologico-Politicus.*

In his own words: "I have striven not to laugh at human actions, not to weep at them, nor to hate them, but to understand them."

Spinoza is often referred to as the only major Western philosopher who didn't found a school. Yet, even so, he is considered one of the great minds of his time and his ideas have appealed to a wide range of people, from Goethe and Coleridge (who were among the first to recognize him) to the American transcendentalists to Albert Einstein. But it took about a century after his death for his work to be appreciated. During his lifetime, it was considered subversive and heretical.

Spinoza led a difficult life. Born in Amsterdam to Jewish émigrés who had fled Portugal to escape Catholic persecution, Spinoza was apparently formally schooled only until he reached age 13 or 14. He then worked in his father's merchant business and became its manager (with his brother) after his father's death. But after only two years managing the business, he dispossessed himself of his father's estate. And two months later, in 1656, Spinoza was excommunicated for heresy by the board of the Amsterdam Jewish community. Central among his heretical views was that there is no God save for a philosophical one. The anthropomorphic God of revealed religion doesn't exist.

After the excommunication, Spinoza lived in Rijnsburg, became the center of a small philosophical circle, and made his living in optics, grinding and polishing lenses. He wrote his first philosophical essay, the *Short Treatise on God, Man, and His Well-Being*, in which he began to expound his philosophical system, and other works. He then moved to Voorburg, where he wrote the only book published in his lifetime under his own name—a Euclidean geometrical account of Descartes's *Principia philosophiae*, published with his *Cogitata Metaphys-*

Oliver Wendell Holmes was also a Spinoza fan, and was especially influenced by his ETHICS. *In fact, one of his most famous statements—that freedom of thought reaches a limit only when it poses a "clear and present danger"—appears to derive from Spinoza's teachings.*

ica (Metaphysical Thoughts). Then, in 1670, he wrote the *Tractatus Theologico-Politicus,* which was published anonymously, and he was in trouble again for his controversial views on theology. The Reformed Church Council of Amsterdam condemned the book; other groups followed suit. But work remained the most important part of his life, so he continued writing and theorizing, turning down a professorship at Heidelberg (for "mere love of quietness," he said in his rejection). In 1675, he finished his major work, the *Ethics,* but while arranging for its publication learned that there was a rumor going around saying that he had written the book to prove there was no God. He withdrew the book.

Spinoza was beginning to have an impact on other thinkers. In 1676, the rationalist philosopher Gottfried Leibniz came to see him. By this point, though, Spinoza was in the advanced stages of consumption, aggravated by glass dust in his lungs. He died the following year, with no heirs and very few possessions. But in the same year, his *Ethics* was finally published posthumously.

IMMANUEL KANT

(1724–1804 C.E.)
(Prussian)

Claim to fame: Leading Western philosopher, proponent of critical philosophy or critical idealism (also known as Kantianism).

Gist of philosophy: A philosophy that evolved out of rationalism and empiricism—and that revolves around three key areas (each explored in one of his *Critiques*): reason, ethics, and aesthetics. Here's a quick look at crucial points in each. (1) Reason: Reason has an active role in the process of knowing the world. Why? Because the human mind structures the world, using such things as space, time, number, substance, and cause and effect, both in thinking and perceiving. When we perceive something, some of what we are perceiving is not due to the object itself but to our own minds. (2) Ethics: Humans are innately aware of moral law, and, through reason, are given the autonomy to follow it. This is exhibited in what he called the Categorical Imperative—"Act only on that maxim which you can will to become a universal law." (3) Aesthetics: We can recognize "purposiveness" in nature. This forms an objective basis for taste.

Major works: *Critique of Pure Reason, Critique of Practical Reason, Critique of Judgment.*

In his own words: "The mere, but empirically determined, consciousness of my own existence proves the existence of objects in space outside me."

Kant's life was, by all accounts, a quiet, uneventful, orderly one. In fact, his life was so regular that townspeople said they set their watches by the time of his daily walk.

He was born in Königsberg, East Prussia, the son of a saddler (according to his own writings, his grandfather was an emigrant from Scotland), and spent his entire life there. Both his mother and father were devout Pietists, adherents of a religious movement that emphasized personal devotion from the heart rather than external

observances (like the Lutherans); and the school in which Kant spent his early years, the Collegium Fridericianum, was also involved in Pietism.

In 1740, Kant studied science and philosophy at the University of Königsberg. Upon graduation, he became a private tutor while pursuing his master's degree; when he received his master's, he began lecturing at the university as a *privatdocent* or private lecturer who received fees from students, but no pay from the university. Fifteen years later, he was finally appointed professor of logic and metaphysics.

His life revolved around teaching and writing. He never married; in fact, he never left East Prussia, but instead devoted all his time to work. He first wrote primarily about the natural sciences or natural philosophy. It wasn't until 1760 that he became more interested in modern philosophy and began producing his masterpieces, especially his *Critique of Pure Reason* (on philosophy in general), *Critique of Practical Reason* (on ethics), and *Critique of Judgment* (on aesthetics), which taken together are a three-volume explanation of his philosophy. His ideas had great impact on contemporary scholars and on later ones such as Fichte, Hegel, and Schelling. He continued writing and teaching, but, aged and ailing, was unable to complete what he meant to have been his masterpiece on metaphysics and died in 1804 in Königsberg.

GEORG HEGEL

(1770–1831)
(German)

Claim to fame: The last—and by some accounts, the most influential—German speculative idealist philosopher; especially famous for his mode of argument or reasoning called the dialectical method. Briefly, it works like this: First, a *thesis* emerges; then comes the opposing point of view, the *antithesis*. From the conflict of these two warring ideas, a new idea or entity arises—the *synthesis*.

Gist of philosophy: A neat, organized philosophy that takes Kant one step further: Everything in the universe is completely rational, so reality can be rationally understood. More specifically, past, present, and future experience as well as thought are all a part of a dialetic process. So everything is moving toward a higher synthesis, a supreme reality.

Major works: *Phänomenologie des Geistes* (Phenomenology of Mind); *Wissenschaft der Logik* (Science of Logic); *Encyklopädie der philosophischen Wissenschaften im Grundrisse* (Encyclopedia of the Philosophical Sciences in Outline); *Grundlinien der Philosophie des Rechts* (Philosophy of Right).

In his own words: "Whatever is rational is real, and whatever is real is rational."

Hegel's philosophy has influenced many disciplines—metaphysics, aesthetics, political theory, social theory, and theology, to name a few. It has had major impact on movements from Marxism to Positivism to Existential-

ism. Hegelians themselves fall into right-wing and left-wing camps, each emphasizing different aspects of his thinking and methodology.

This is, in many ways, a fitting legacy for a philosopher who based his work on the dialectic method—wherein thesis gives birth to antithesis, after which both meld into a higher synthesis—and an interesting, if ironic, one for a man who had hoped through his teaching and writing to help pull German culture together.

He was born in Stuttgart, and schooled extensively in the humanities, with an emphasis on history and literature. Believing that Western Europe was going through a cultural disintegration, he felt he should work to reintegrate the culture of his native Germany. In the beginning, he intended to do so through religion, and entered the Lutheran seminary at Tübingen in 1788, where he studied theology and philosophy. He then shifted his focus to political philosophy, and finally, in 1800, to philosophy in general as a means to engender a cultural reintegration in the religious, social, and political spheres.

He worked as a tutor, then became a lecturer at the university in Jena. Here he wrote his first important work, the *Phenomenology of Mind,* in which he laid out his philosophic system. But just before the book was published, the Napoleonic wars forced the closing of the university. He worked for a brief time as a newspaper editor, then became headmaster of the Royal Gymnasium at Nürnberg until 1816. The *Phenomenology* was published in 1807; his second important work, the two-volume *Science of Logic,* came out in 1812 and 1816. The *Logic,* which explained his dialectical theory, resulted in his becoming professor of philosophy at the university in Heidelberg. In 1817, he wrote his huge compendium, the *Encyclopedia of the Philosophical Sciences,* and one year later won the chair of philosophy at the University of Berlin. Here he stayed, winning more attention, accolades, and students; his philosophy became the more-or-less official one of the Prussian state. Here he finally died in 1831 during a cholera epidemic.

ARTHUR SCHOPENHAUER

(1788–1860)
(German)

Claim to fame: Known for his philosophy of pessimism; influenced Nietzsche and Freud.

Gist of philosophy: Will is more important than knowledge or reason. Will, or more specifically, the will to live, is the key force in human nature, and in fact, in *all* of nature. The rub? While it's the strongest force in human nature, it's also inherently evil. So humankind has to constantly fight a losing battle against will by renouncing desire. The only respite from the constant pain of being human? Contemplating or creating art—because only art (or creative expression) isn't subservient to will.

Major works: *Die Welt als Wille und Vorstellung* (The World as Will and Idea); *Über den Willen in der Natur* (On the Will in Nature), *Die beiden Grundprobleme der Ethik* (The Two Main Problems of Ethics), *Parerga und Paralipomena.*

In his own words: "The nature of

Most Western philosophers have been influenced by Plato or Aristotle. Schopenhauer was one of these as well, but he also drew inspiration from an Eastern source: Buddhism. "All life is suffering" is one of the Noble Truths of Buddhism, and a point Schopenhauer espoused. Unlike Buddhists, he tried to find a logical explanation for the evil in the world. But like them, he tried to figure out a way for humans to get past the pain of worldly desires. In fact, Schopenhauer's solution is very much like that of Buddha himself: The only way to achieve salvation is to negate the will, and deny the self and its desires through living an ascetic, passion-free life.

things before and beyond the world, and consequently beyond the will, is open to no investigation."

Schopenhauer's philosophy of pessimism is one that mirrors the man's life—a life shadowed by a variety of negative events and influences, including the apparent suicide of his father, an estrangement with his mother, few friends or roots, and little recognition for his work for much of his career. He slept with a loaded pistol beside him, was prone to brooding and depression, and was generally cynical and truculent.

Schopenhauer was born in Danzig, Germany. His childhood was marked by the poor relationship between his parents. His father was a banker, his mother a novelist (who had received more education than the average for a woman of the time). The family moved to Hamburg in 1793, after the Prussians took over Danzig. During this time, Schopenhauer's education was unconventional, to say the least: two years of study in France in the care of a friend of his father's, and sporadic studies during a long tour of Europe with his family. After his father's death, he received private tutoring, then entered the University of Göttingen. Beginning as a medical student, he became interested in philosophy, inspired in particular by Plato and Kant. He moved to Berlin, then a philosophical center, where he began working on his doctoral thesis. When the university was closed due to uprisings against Napoleon, he moved yet again, to Rudolstadt, where he finally completed and published his thesis. In 1813, he moved to his mother's house in Weimar. This was his last permanent home for twenty years. After only one year, he and his mother realized they couldn't live together, so he moved out and never saw his mother again. He traveled, moved from place to place, wrote, and tried to make a name for himself, unsuccessfully. His chief work, *The World as Will and Idea,* came out in 1818, but it didn't win him the attention he expected. It did result in his taking a lecturing position at the University of Berlin. But even there he was disappointed and ignored. He taught in Berlin at the same time as Hegel, and his lectures and ideas received little respect or acclaim. Bitter and resentful, he moved on, opting out of the academic life. Instead, he settled down in 1833 to a lonely life in Frankfurt, where he had few friends and little company, save for his poodle.

But he kept writing, crystalizing his ideas and putting them forth in such works as *On the Will in Nature, The Two Main Problems of Ethics,* and a second edition of his *The World as Will and Idea.* In 1851, he finally began to have an impact with his collection of essays and aphorisms, *Parerga and Paralipomena.* And for the last years of his life, he was able to see his work widely read, both in Germany and abroad; his system taught in universities; and, ultimately, his influence spreading.

ALFRED NORTH WHITEHEAD

(1861–1947)
(English)

Claim to fame: Leading mathematician and metaphysical philosopher; developed what is called a metaphysics of process.

Gist of philosophy: Modern metaphysics that incorporates psychological as well as physical experience, philosophy of nature, and of organism. Complicated? You bet. A key thrust of his philosophy of nature: There should be no distinction between apparent nature (the world we experience through our senses, by hearing sound, seeing color, etc.) and causal nature (the world that science explains). What we observe in perception through the senses is nature—nothing more, nothing less. As for his philosophy of organism, it gets even tougher. To put it as succinctly as possible, its aim is to come up with new, specific categories to express the interlinking relationship among matter, time, and space—and to incorporate metaphysics. So here's a quick idea of its thrust: Reality is made up of elements, "actual entities," which aren't things but processes—processes of self-development and self-creation. And these processes, once complete, become the material for the next phase of actual entities. To oversimplify a bit, but to try to make it understandable, events are the key basic elements of reality.

Major works: *Treatise on Universal Algebra; Principia Mathematica* (with Bertrand Russell, his former student); *Process and Reality, Adventures of Ideas, Modes of Thought.*

In his own words: "I find myself as essentially a unity of emotions, enjoyments, hopes, fears, regrets, valuations of alternatives, decisions—all of them subjective reactions to the environment as active in my nature. My unity—which is Descartes's 'I am'—is my process of shaping this welter of material into a consistent pattern of feelings."

Echoes of Whitehead's childhood—spent in a country vicarage in a closely knit community—are evident in the philosophy he later developed. Among them, an interest in nature, in history, and an especially strong interest in religion and natural theology.

Whitehead was born in Ramsgate on the Isle of Thanet. His father was an Honorary Canon of Canterbury; family members were both teachers and ministers. He studied at an ancient public school, Sherbourne, where he was taught history as a living tradition—i.e., historical concepts were illustrated by finding the contemporary analogy. This combination of history at school, tradition in the community, and religion at home wound up having a profound impact on his philosophy. But before he developed his philosophy, he was primarily interested in mathematics.

In 1880, he received a scholarship in mathematics at Trinity College, Cambridge, where, four years later, he became senior lecturer in mathematics. While here, he wrote the *Treatise on Universal Algebra,* which became the basis for his 1903 election to the Royal Society. He also married (in 1890) and, in another important union, began teaching a young student named Bertrand Russell. Some years later, in 1910, he and Russell collaborated on what was to be the first of three volumes in the *Principia Mathematica*—considered by many to be one of the greatest works of logic since Aristotle. This work wound up spanning ten years of collaboration.

During this time, Whitehead continued winning acclaim and notice. In 1910, he became professor of applied mathematics at the University of London. For the next decade or so, he did

most of his work in the philosophy of science. But then, in 1924, when he became professor of philosophy at Harvard, he began evolving his philosophy of science into a broader metaphysical philosophy—called "the philosophy of organism"—which broke with the popular Newtonian conception of nature and with the notion that mind and matter were dualistic. This philosophy was explained in three popular works: *Science and the Modern World* (1925), *Process and Reality* (1929), and *Adventures of Ideas* (1933). On the basis of his theories, he came to be regarded as the leading metaphysician of the time.

Interestingly, in spite of his impact on philosophy at large, Whitehead founded no distinct school and had no distinct group of disciples. Even so, he was highly regarded—he was elected to the British Academy in 1931, and awarded the Order of Merit in 1945. Two years later, he died in Cambridge, Massachusetts.

LUDWIG WITTGENSTEIN

(1889–1951)
(German)

Claim to fame: Founder of linguistic analysis, which made him one of the leading twentieth-century philosophers, influencing both language philosophy and logical positivism.

Gist of philosophy: Two different philosophies—the second one refuting much of the first but both dealing with language. Philosophy number one: Logical atomism tries to set up a completely logically foolproof language, a meaningful language that consists of literal "pictures" of reality. Much of regular language isn't this at all; it's meaningless. Therefore, many value judgments and philosophies are also meaningless. Philosophy number two: Language philosophy drops the picture theory and focuses instead on studying language to understand reality. By better understanding language and how people use—and misuse—it, we can get to the bottom of many philosophical problems. The reason? The problems only seem to exist because muddled use of language causes misunderstanding.

Major works: *Tractatus Logico-Philosophicus* and (posthumously) *Philosophical Investigations; Remarks on the Foundations of Mathematics; The Blue and Brown Books; Philosophische Bemerkungen* (Philosophical Notes); *On Certainty.*

In his own words: "A thought is a sentence with a sense." "Whereof one cannot speak, thereof one must be silent."

By all accounts, Wittgenstein was a brilliant, multifaceted, and complex man—a math scholar who evolved a philosophy of language, dabbled in architecture and sculpture, loved music, thought philosophy should be approached like a business, and developed two philosophical systems—the second in response to (and as a criticism of) his first.

He was born to a wealthy steel industrialist and a banker's daughter who loved music. One of eight artistically and intellectually talented children, Wittgenstein began as a mediocre student. He was educated at home until the age of fourteen, where

he showed little interest in anything but machines. So he entered a school specializing in mathematics and physical science instead of classics. Upon graduation, he studied mechanical engineering in Berlin, then at the University of Manchester, where he did aeronautical research and designed both a jet-reaction engine and propeller. But he became more interested in math than in engineering, and after reading Bertrand Russell's *Principles of Mathematics,* moved to Cambridge to study with Russell. He called this his salvation—confiding to a friend that until that point he had been considering suicide as a possibility almost every day. And he threw himself into his studies. His research at the time wound up being the basis for his famous *Tractatus.*

In 1913, he decided to move to Norway for a life of seclusion where he could devote his time solely to problems in logic. Then World War I broke out, and Wittgenstein served in the Austrian army. Even during this time, he continued taking notes for his book. He wound up in an Italian P.O.W. camp, where he finished the book and through diplomatic channels sent it to Russell.

The work was eventually published after his release, and it made his reputation. It was considered groundbreaking, a short work written in numbered remarks about the nature of language and thought. But in spite of its impact, Wittgenstein decided to drop out of the mainstream philosophical eye. He had received a large inheritance upon his father's death in 1913 but chose to give it away. Some went anonymously to needy Austrian poets and artists; the rest he gave to two of his sisters. Now he opted for a simple life as a village elementary schoolteacher. Then, in 1926, he quit teaching and thought about becoming a monk but was talked out of it by the father superior of a monastery. Instead he became a gardener's assistant at another monastery for one summer, worked on designing and building a house for one of his sisters with his friend the architect Paul Engelmann, and even did some sculpting. But even though he wasn't actively involved in philosophy, his *Tractatus* continued to have great impact on other philosophers, particularly Moritz Schlick, who convinced him to visit with the small group of Viennese philosophers known as the Vienna circle.

By January of 1929 he was back in the philosophical swing of things, returning to Cambridge as a research

fellow and winding up ten years later as a professor of philosophy. He held this position from 1939 to 1947; during the war, however, he served as a hospital porter and lab assistant. During this period he wrote about his second philosophic system, one that criticized his own earlier work. But he became dissatisfied with academic life and once again decided to go back to a simpler life.

He moved to Ireland, settling in a cottage on the west coast, where he spent most of his time (health permitting) on the *Investigations*. In 1949, upon returning from a three-month trip to the United States, he learned that he had cancer. By this point, he said he was ready to die. And two years later he did. His last words: "Tell them I've had a wonderful life."

BOOKS AND WRITINGS THAT CHANGED THE WORLD: POLITICAL AND ECONOMIC PHILOSOPHY IN ACTION

 The pen is mightier than the sword. Maybe that's a cliché, but it has a lot of truth in it. The American Revolution didn't come out of nowhere; it came out of the minds of the Founding Fathers, who wrote reasoned and stirring words that moved a nation to revolt.

MAGNA CARTA (LINCOLN CATHEDRAL MS. COPY) (REPRODUCED FROM THE COLLECTIONS OF THE LIBRARY OF CONGRESS)

The books and writings below are a collection of *other* important words, words that lie behind many of the political and economic movements of today. More often than not, they're not easy reading—in fact, if there were an award for "world's most boring book," one or two of these might be in the running.

But they're important books that carry the weight of a lot of thought, which we've summarized and simplified. These books and writings are representative of *practical philosophy,* if you will. They're not ivory-tower dreams of the meaning of life, but some hardheaded looks at what's wrong with the world, along with some solutions.

THE CODE OF HAMMURAPI

HAMMURAPI
(c. 2100 B.C.E.)
(Babylonian king)

In 1901 a French expedition to the Middle East discovered an eight-foot-high pillar of black basalt inscribed with about eight thousand words in cuneiform writing in the Old Babylonian language. Deciphering the writing, scholars read:

These are the laws of justice which Hammurapi the able king has established. . . . That the strong may not oppress the weak, to give justice to the orphan and the widow, I have inscribed my precious words on my stela and established it in Babylon. . . .

Hammurapi was a great Babylonian king, ruler of an ancient Semitic people who lived in what is today Iraq. The inscription goes on to list 282 laws, carved in 49 columns, covering a wide variety of civil subjects (religion is barely mentioned), all in a conditional, if-then, pattern:

- If a man has broken into a house, he shall be killed before the breach and buried there.
- If a woman has brought about the death of her husband because of another man, they shall impale the woman on stakes.

As you can see, the penalties are harsh; in fact, the code is famous for setting forth the principle of *lex talionis,* an eye for an eye. But is Hammurapi's code a true legal code at all, in the sense that its provisions were the law of the land? Modern archaeolo-

Ancient Double Standard

"An eye for an eye" seems straightforward, but it actually wasn't as straightforward as you may think. Yes, Hammurapi's code clearly explains the punishment a person would get for any committed offense. But there was a double (actually a triple) standard at work—the punishment varied according to a person's social status. There was one punishment for aristocrats, another, more severe, for commoners, and another, yet more severe, for slaves. Furthermore, the "eye for an eye" punishment only applied to social equals. An aristocrat who put out the eye of a slave or a commoner didn't necessarily lose an eye. He could get off with a fine instead. But if an aristocrat put out the eye of another aristocrat, then it could be a matter of exact payment.

gists are not so sure. Some speculate it might be more of a justification or a précis of Hammurapi's past deeds, a stela erected for the gods to show what a just ruler he was. The fact remains that of the large number of other Babylonian legal texts discovered, only one mentions this specific code as law. Nonetheless, the code was evidently admired as a work of legal literature by the ancients: copies have been found in the library at Nineveh of the Assyrian ruler Assurbanipal, who ruled more than one thousand years later.

The long-term influence of Hammurapi's code is difficult to assess but was most probably great. With other Babylonian legal works, it greatly affected the development of Jewish and Roman legal thought, which in turn greatly influenced modern law. A tantalizing bit of etymologic history traces a microscopic bit of Babylonian law to the present day: Babylonian law mentions people known as *mushkenum,* people who do not own property. The word has survived to this day in the French *mesquin,* and the Italian *meschino,* meaning pauper.

KITAB AL-KHARAJ

ABU-YUSUF
(798, recording the ideas of Abu Hanifah al-Numan ibn Thabit, d. 767)
(Persian-Arab)

Here's a legal problem that confronted early Muslims: How do you deal with social or political problems in accordance with Islam? This question was vital because Islam didn't recognize the separation of "church and state"—

Islam was the state. So when an Islamic judge or politician was confronted with a problem or a question, he should quite naturally look to the Islamic holy book, the Quran, or the collected sayings of the Prophet Muhammed. But what if they didn't deal with a certain problem? What then?

One answer came from philosopher-jurist Abu Hanifah. In answering the question, he founded the largest and what is called by some the most tolerant judicial school in Islam, adhered to by over half of all Muslims in the world. When you remember that law, religion, and society were all mixed together in the Islamic state, you can see that Abu Hanifah's thoughts directly affected the daily lives of countless millions.

Abu Hanifah advocated juridical speculation, in contrast to schools that advocated a strict reading of the Quran. So (in some ways like the judges who interpret our Constitution today) Abu Hanifah derived Islamic rules via logical reasoning. For example, the Quran forbids wine to believers because it produces intoxication. By analogy, it can be assumed that it forbids other intoxicating substances as well, even though they are not specifically mentioned. Naturally, this sort of informed speculation produced much dissent, as jurists wrangled over the correct avenues toward decisions.

The classical Islamic legal tradition includes three other major schools of judicial thought: the stricter Maliki school, the Shafii school (in between the two), and finally the Hanbali school, which was very conservative. Together the founders and commentators of these schools produced some of the world's foremost early legal scholars, and established the rules of law that dominated the Middle East and Central Asia up to the twentieth century.

MAGNA CARTA

1215
(signed by King John of England, probably written by Stephen Langton, Archbishop of Canterbury)

King John was one of England's worst kings. The great constitutional historian William Stubbs described him as "a man whom no oaths could bind, no pressure of conscience, no consideration of policy restrain from evil; to his people, a hated tyrant. Polluted with every crime that could disgrace a man, false to every obligation that should bind a king, he had lost half his inheritance by sloth, and ruined and desolated the rest."

Clearly not an ideal king. But because of his tyrannical rule, England—and the world—benefited. The English nobility forced him to sign Magna Carta, a document that guaranteed them certain political liberties, and which became the basis for the freedoms we enjoy today. Magna Carta is the mother of such documents as the U.S. Constitution.

How did a tyrant like John become associated with a medieval human-rights movement? Not deliberately. Besides being a tyrant, John was not blessed with political genius. He taxed the local nobility heavily and at the same time kept cutting back their traditional feudal privileges. They eventu-

To be technical, Magna Carta was not actually signed by King John. Instead, he validated it with his royal seal. Reason: Like many rulers during this period, King John could not write.

ally had enough. Heavily armed barons and knights occupied London while John fled to Windsor. Finally, he met them at a meadow called Runnymede by the River Thames. After a few days of negotiations, John caved in to their demands and signed the document they gave him: *Magna Carta Libertatum*, which a later great politician described as the "Bible of the Constitution."

At first glance, Magna Carta doesn't seem all that revolutionary. Its intent is to reassert the feudal rights of the nobility; it doesn't establish a parliament; it doesn't formulate a policy of taxation by consent. So what *does* it do? The key is that it limits the role of absolute kings like John and it sets forth the basis of constitutional liberties. It establishes the idea that individuals have natural rights; it establishes the rule of law. It doesn't give too much to the common folk, but it began a trend which ultimately would. The most famous provision is the thirty-ninth article, which states:

No free-man shall be seized, or imprisoned, or dispossessed, or outlawed, or in any way destroyed; nor will we condemn him, nor will we commit him to prison, excepting by the legal judgement of his peers, or by the laws of the land.

Even today, no like provision exists in the law of many countries. So the real importance of Magna Carta lies in its being first, a beginning. It was copied, studied, and added to over the years, and it culminated in the liberties many enjoy today. As for John, he died trying to overturn what he had signed, a bad king to the end.

THE PRINCE

NICCOLÒ MACHIAVELLI
(1459–1517)
(Italian)

Machiavelli didn't get what he wanted from writing *The Prince*. He dedicated it to the new ruler of the Italian city of Florence hoping to win his way into the favor (and the employment) of Lorenzo de' Medici.

Unfortunately, Machiavelli remained at the small country estate to which he had been banished when the republic that he had served was overthrown by the returning Medici, and where he would die. His book was ignored by the prince it was intended for; it circulated in manuscript and was published only after his death. But it lived on, and so does its author's name as an adjective. *Machiavellian* means the unscrupulous, wily, amoral pursuit of power.

That's what this notorious book is

about: *power. The Prince* explains how governments really work—not the ideal, but the real. And the reality is that power permeates government. This isn't necessarily bad. When many separate groups pursue power within a state, they often limit the power of any one group and so contribute to the liberty of all. Machiavelli himself was a democrat—he admired the Swiss republics most of all—but he saw that in his native Italy power politics was the order of the day. So *The Prince* is full of advice for leaders (or the state government as an entity) to rise above ordinary morality:

Where the very safety of the country depends on the resolution to be taken, no considerations of justice, humanity, or cruelty, nor of glory or of shame should be allowed to prevail.

Machiavelli also advocated propaganda. He viewed people as inherently gullible and thought princes should not hesitate to deceive them when

India's Machiavelli

India had a Machiavelli long before the Italians produced their famous writer who argued that a prince can—and should—basically do *anything* to get and keep power. The Indian version of Machiavelli was a fourth century B.C.E. government minister named Kautilya (also known as Canakya), and he's gone down in Indian history as an infamous master of intrigue and wile. Supposedly, *he* was the real mover and shaker behind the throne, killing off the competition and putting an extraordinarily spineless and simpering fool named Chandragupta Maurya in power while he ruled behind the scenes.

Historians aren't sure this is all true, but they are fairly certain that Kautilya existed, and that he wrote a book that later became known as the *Arthashastra*. The version known today was clearly revised so much that Kautilya can't be considered the author, but he's clearly behind all the advice, including the use of murder, poison, assassination, false accusations, and extremely severe penalties and harsh laws to run a government. Kautilya's favorite mode of operation was the "sting"—using spies to ferret out any potential wrongdoers or complainers.

necessary. But Machiavelli did not advocate deceit and cruelty when unnecessary. It is better for a prince to be feared than loved, but there is no need for unnecessary cruelty.

The impact of this little book was enormous. Among some of its most avid readers were Emperor Charles V, Catherine de Médicis, Oliver Cromwell, Henry III and Henry IV of France, Frederick the Great, Napoleon I, and Napoleon III—as well as Adolf Hitler and Benito Mussolini (who ignored fundamental tenets of Machiavellian thought). Machiavelli is credited with founding the modern sciences of political science and sociology.

TREATISES OF CIVIL GOVERNMENT LETTERS ON TOLERATION

JOHN LOCKE
(1632–1704)
(English)

Forget George Washington. The author of the two works above, the Englishman John Locke, is a better candidate for the title of father of the American Republic. For that matter, he's the true parent of most modern democracies. He was among the first and was certainly the most influential modern liberal thinker. He gave the world a concise rationale for liberalism, political tolerance, and limited government—ideals that permeate the

freest modern governments today from Japan to Britain to the U.S.

At the time Locke was writing, most of the world was still in the thrall of absolute rulers who ruled by divine right; that is, they were kings and queens because God had supposedly given them their thrones. But Locke's homeland was changing. In England, people (at least the nobility and rich gentry) felt that *they* had certain rights in choosing their rulers, as well as God or fate. Locke approved of this trend. Instead of absolute monarchies, he advocated constitutional governments that rule with the consent of the people they represent. Governments should not trample the *natural rights* of humans, that is, rights that all humans should enjoy regardless of the form of government. These "inalienable rights" include the right to life, freedom, property. If those last words sound vaguely familiar, they should—Thomas Jefferson read Locke and incorporated his ideas and some of his words in the U.S. Declaration of Independence.

Philosophers on Philosophy

There is nothing so strange or so unbelievable that it has not been said by one philosopher or another.
—René Descartes

The philosophers have only interpreted the world in various ways; the point is to change it.
—Karl Marx

Philosophy is the product of wonder.
—Alfred North Whitehead

Philosophy is not a theory but an activity.
—Ludwig Wittgenstein

THE WEALTH OF NATIONS (Inquiry into the Nature and Causes of the Wealth of Nations)

ADAM SMITH
(1723–1790)
(Scots)

Modern economics began inauspiciously. A Scottish university professor from Glasgow, hired as a private tutor to the Duke of Buccleuch, was bored with life in Europe. As he wrote: "The life which I led at Glasgow was a pleasurable dissipated life in comparison of that which I live at present. I have begun to write a book in order to pass away the time."

That book was *The Wealth of Nations,* and it became the basis for modern economic thought—all the way from laissez-faire capitalism to Marxism (Karl Marx was a fervent admirer). But what did Adam Smith say?

First of all, he said a lot. Adam Smith's book is not easy reading; it's filled with meandering asides and examples that can stretch on so long you miss the point. In fact, one of Smith's earliest proponents later confessed he had never read the book, and you can't blame him. Nor is the book completely original. It draws upon the work of other thinkers of the day; in fact, *many* others. This leads to its strength. It is comprehensive. It takes isolated ideas and links them into a

coherent whole: an entire philosophical system that explains the workings of the economy.

Smith's basic idea seems to be an unusual one: Economic selfishness leads to public good. In his words, the "private interests and passions of men" lead in a direction "which is most agreeable to the interest of the whole of society." How does this happen? Through competition, which regulates human greed and pushes results to the optimum. Smith explains how competition forces a manufacturer to set prices in keeping with consumer demand (if prices are too high, no one will buy, forcing the manufacturer to lower them). So consumers benefit. In the same way, competition forces wages to a "fair" level: If a manufacturer pays his laborers too little, they'll leave and go somewhere else. So employees benefit, too. The key to all this is that the economy is self-regulating—Smith called this the "invisible hand." No government intervention is needed; competition works to increase wealth and prosperity for society as a whole.

Smith was also fascinated with the specialization of labor. In a famous passage, he describes how by dividing the labor of manufacturing a pin, many more could be made than if each individual worker made an entire pin. This may seem obvious, even silly, today, but Adam Smith was not far removed from an era when innovation was actually *banned*, since it threatened the established order. Finally, Smith realized that innovation came from accumulation—earning and keeping wealth to plow back into the business. All this sounds familiar to us today. But not all of Adam Smith's ideas have lasted; much has been much modified, or even discarded. And Smith was not always prescient. While he (correctly) saw that the American colonies would become great economic powers, he didn't see much hope in machinery.

It's not surprising that Smith was championed by the entrepreneurial capitalists of his day. His book was translated into numerous languages, and his ideas were used to champion the free-trade policies of England and later of other nations as well.

One final note: Don't make the mistake of thinking that Smith was cold-blooded toward the plight of those less fortunate; in fact, he was an advocate of public education and was wary of the power of the specialized factory: "The man whose whole life is spent in performing a few simple operations . . . generally becomes as stupid and ignorant as it is possible for a man to become."

But all in all, Smith was an optimist: The economy, under the guiding influence of the Invisible Hand, would get better and better for all. A happy philosophy for an optimistic age; but then, economics had not yet been nicknamed "the dismal science."

DAS KAPITAL (CAPITAL)

KARL MARX
(1818–1883)
(German writing in England)

"The day the manuscript goes to press I shall get gloriously drunk," said Karl Marx to his friend and sponsor, Friederich Engels, talking about his monumental book which attempted to "lay bare the economic law of modern society."

Did he succeed in discovering the key to society? Given the failure of modern Marxism in Russia, Vietnam, Cuba, and Eastern Europe, many would say no—but *Das Kapital* succeeded in stimulating thought and revolutions across the globe. Marx's hard sixteen-hour days spent toiling and studying in the British Museum paid off in later influence. Sadly for Marx, only the first volume of this massive work was published in his lifetime—the other two volumes came out after his death, in 1885 and 1894.

Everyone knows about Marx, but what does his book actually say? Not for nothing is Marxism called a materialistic philosophy: His book focuses on the economics of life as a central aspect of society. Productive forces arise and increase in efficiency as humankind better masters nature, and society evolves as well. But not without conflict. In fact, borrowing the idea of the dialectic from the philosopher Hegel (see pages 171–72), Marx sees historical evolution as the clash between groups and ideas, which produces a new synthesis of the competing ideas, and then a new set of conflicts. "The history of all existing society is the history of class struggles," said Marx. As these struggles develop, society moves from primitive communism to slavery to feudalism to capitalism and then to socialism. Ultimately, the long series of class struggles culminates in a classless society where humans are at last truly free, a true communist society. And in such a society the state withers away, there being no need for coercive government.

Of course, the theory is far more

complex than this, but there is one other key aspect that's central to Marxist theory: surplus value. Marx accepted the idea that the value of a product is measured by the labor put into making it. This is called the labor theory of value. But, as Marx explained, a capitalist sells a product made by a worker for more than he paid the worker for making the product. Thus by definition capitalism is exploitative. No matter, says Marx. Capitalists will ultimately be unable to harness the ever-increasing productive forces of society, wealth will grow more concentrated, markets more competitive, and just as feudalists were doomed by the increasing productive forces, so too will be the capitalists. Revolution is the inevitable answer, followed by a dictatorship of the proletariat (workers) and the final stage of communism. Modern economists sharply disagree with Marx's theory of value. For example, Marx seems to deny the role of ideas in his definition of value; why can't, for example, a capitalist argue that his or her *ideas* on marketing, sales, or distribution add value to the product? But to be fair, modern economists have had some troubles of their own explaining how to value goods.

Like most economics texts, *Capital* is not an easy book to read; many critics and readers complain that it is dull. But this is no mere college text. It is also chock full of long digressions, passion, satire, bitter attacks against enemies—as well as a host of speculative and brilliant ideas.

Marx and his partner Engels also wrote the *Communist Manifesto,* a stirring call to arms for workers that includes the immortal lines "Workers of the World Unite! You have nothing to lose but your chains." That rhetoric

and Marx's sometimes obtuse, sometimes compelling writings inspired the rise of communist political societies, then revolutionary groups that seized power in Russia, China, and various nations in Africa, Asia, and Latin America. The heyday of communism is clearly over: very few governments that attempted to use Marx's ideas as a whole have survived. But Marx's ideas were so diluted by practicalities that no true Marxist state ever really existed—many would add that a true Marxist state is probably impossible. Reality is always a difficult testing ground for *all* theories.

THE GENERAL THEORY OF EMPLOYMENT, INTEREST, AND MONEY

JOHN MAYNARD KEYNES
(1883–1946)
(English)

Keynes was yet another economist with something important to say. But don't dismiss him as another pie-in-the-sky theorist: Keynes put his money where his mouth was. He devoted a half hour or so after waking up each morning to making his own personal fortune. By quickly reading the financial papers, performing a few calculations, and phoning in orders to his brokers, he ultimately earned about two and a half million dollars—and had the rest of the day to do other things, including writing one of the most monumental books of modern economics.

Keynes's book is initially depressing.

Unlike Adam Smith, Keynes did not believe that the economy, left to itself, would necessarily lead to the common good. Let's take a look at unemployment, a key concern of the time. Classical economics held that the workings of the invisible hand of capitalist economics would solve most, if not all, economic crises. High unemployment, for example, would cause a reduction of salaries, which in turn would restimulate employment. Keynes was not so sure. In fact, he found that wage decreases would lead to a fall in prices (don't bother asking why) and to a new equilibrium of high unemployment. In other words, if an economy were in a depression, the market forces that Adam Smith had been so confident about might not do anything at all. The economy could stay stuck. The problem was due to investment, upon which economic progress depended. If businesses during a depression got worried about the future and started decreasing investments, a worsening spiral could begin—less investment leading to a worse economy, more concerns about the future, and even less investment.

So what could be done? Keynes was not one to state a problem and

leave it there. He advocated government intervention, but as a friend of capitalism, not as an enemy. (In fact, he hated Marx's book, calling it "without interest or application to the modern world . . . [advocating] a creed which [prefers] mud to fish.") Increased investment, this time from the government rather than from individual businesses, could restart the economic spiral and move it upward. All of this is familiar today—the government intervenes during economic or unemployment crises with public works spending and maintains budget deficits or surpluses to keep certain levels of employment or economic activity. But at the time it was revolutionary, a rethinking of classical economic theory.

And so Keynes's influence was immense. His ideas were to some degree incorporated by Franklin Roosevelt and his New Deal planners in their attempt to get the U.S. out of its disastrous depression. Later his ideas were adopted (and adapted) by liberal economists across the globe. Keynesian economics in fact reigned over most of the free world, until challenged by another school of economics, a conservative school from our side of the Atlantic. But that's another story.

CONTENTS

RELIGIONS OF THE WORLD

ANSWERING THE UNANSWERABLE—
THE EVER-PRESENT ROLE OF RELIGION

 Religion is the spiritual brother of philosophy—designed to fill in the blanks, to explain the inexplicable. Both are attempts to answer questions beyond human experience or knowledge, questions like Why are we here? What is the point of our lives? What happens after we die?

But there's a decisive difference between religion and philosophy. Philosophy is limited by the burden of proof—the answers have to be logically or reasonably arrived at. Religion, on the other hand, is limited only by the human capacity to believe—the ability to have faith in the unprovable.

And this capacity has been with the human race for millennia, back to prehistoric times. There are archaeological indications that religion in some form or another existed in the cultures of the Old Stone Age, dating back to about 500,000 B.C.E. Most of these center around burial of the dead (skulls made into drinking cups, possibly for ritual use; skeletons laid out with tools and weapons around them, and more). And for good reason. Death is the one aspect of human life that is the most incomprehensible, the most puzzling, and, in fact, the most disturbing. What happens after one dies? No one can be sure. So religion supplies an answer to the unanswerable.

In earlier times, before science stepped in with provable answers, religion answered other unanswerable questions: Why does the lightening flash and the thunder roll? Why does the earth move, the volcano erupt, the tidal wave devastate? Why does it rain? It's Zeus hurling his thunderbolts, or Neptune expressing his anger, or Tlaloc, the rain god, allowing the crops to grow.

The answers the ancients came up with may seem farfetched, or even quaint, to modern ears. But at the time, they were just as believable as modern belief in different aspects of religion. Religion, after all, is a way of seeking answers according to the knowledge and insight available at the time.

Of course, as time has moved on, religions have developed and changed with the times.

But at the core, religion remains the same. In the world of genetic engineering and space travel, our questions still persist. And for all the questions we answer by other means, the unanswerable still remain. Religion fills in the answers for those who want them and who believe. As it has for centuries, it gives people a way to seek the truth about their own existence, about that of the human race in general and the universe that surrounds us.

This chapter offers some of the answers religion has come up with, filtered through the different minds of different cultures across the globe. As you read, you'll be struck by the similarities and the differences of these faiths. Similarly, when you look at the lives of the founders of many of the world's major religions, you'll notice many surprising parallels.

The key lesson: At bottom, for all the differences, religions seek answers to the same questions. As the Tibetan *Book of Golden Precepts* puts it:

The Path is one for all; the means to reach the Goal must vary with the Pilgrims.

GOD, THE MEANING OF LIFE, AND WHAT HAPPENS AFTER DEATH FROM A (AFRICAN RELIGIONS) TO Z (ZOROASTRIANISM): TWELVE RELIGIONS OF THE WORLD

Most religions share common features, the key one, of course, the belief in *something*—something bigger than humankind, something eternal, a creative force or being. What the *something* is, though, varies; rituals vary and specific beliefs vary, though often there are surprising similarities. And logically so, for religions are all seeking the same thing: truth. In the words of Sri Ramakrishna, the Hindu teacher: "So many religions, so many paths to reach the one and the same goal."

In reading about the following world religions, then, you'll be struck more by the similarities than by the differences and realize that, for all the wars waged under the name of religion, we wind up fighting ourselves.

AFRICAN (SUB-SAHARAN)

Traditional beliefs that evolved long before Christianity and Islam and still coexist with them, and that, to a great degree, determined the culture and still rule the daily life of believers.

Beliefs: First, the problem: Even when you look only at sub-Saharan Africa, there really isn't one basic tradi-tional African religion. In fact, there probably are something more like seven hundred—that's the rough number of ethnic language groups, most of which have their own specific religions. But all of these highly specific religions *do* share common bonds, themes, and beliefs. And these, in turn, have influenced African culture and lifestyles. While Islam eventually trickled down from North Africa and Christianity was imported by missionaries, the traditional beliefs have persisted. In some cases, they have become secularized, more of a cultural identity than a spiritual calling; in others, they still remain a distinct religion.

Traditional African beliefs are a mixture of the accessible and the remote. For example, there is a supreme being (this concept existed *before* Christianity or Islam, and wound up helping the traditional religions assimilate into one or the other), but there also are other, lesser, gods (usually representing an aspect of nature) more easily approachable by humans, as well as ancestor spirits. The supreme god is a remote being who represents the ultimate force, fate or destiny. There are usually no cults, shrines, or priesthoods connected with him but are with the lesser gods and ancestor spirits. They act as intermediaries between the gods and humans and are directly involved in day-to-day living. There's quite a bit of interaction between the spiritual and the actual worlds. Priests, diviners, prophets, and the like communicate with the spiritual world, telling the gods what the people need or want through prayer or ritual—and telling the people what the gods want.

As with many other religions, African religions hold that humankind is doomed to suffer through disease, hard labor, death, and so on. But there's a way around this, or at least a way to turn the bad into good for a while—ritual. Unlike other religions, which count on an afterlife to make up for any suffering on earth, traditional African religions give believers a

chance to stop the suffering in the here and now by following the proper ritual actions.

In fact, to a great degree, ritual is the heart of African religion. It's the means by which people can communicate with the gods, the way children become adults, and, ultimately, the way that people can control their own world. In fact, some describe African religion as a pyramid: supreme being at the top; gods and ancestor spirits at the side; and ritual belief and practice as the bottom or foundation. Perhaps this is why, even as the traditional religions have been assimilated by Christianity and Islam, the strong magical or ritual beliefs have persisted.

Divisions: Hundreds—possibly as many religions as there are ethnic language groups (seven hundred plus).

Founded: Difficult to pinpoint, but recent archaeological evidence points to the presence of a very basic form of the traditional African religion back in the Paleolithic period; a more developed religion can be dated back to around 1500 B.C.E.

Followers: Estimated at more than seventy million.

Sacred texts: None widely known, probably because of the focus on oral tradition.

BUDDHISM

Often considered as much a philosophy as a religion—instead of relying on a god, people must rely on themselves to reach enlightenment.

Beliefs: To the uninitiated, Buddhism can sound extremely cut and dried,

Who's Worshiping What? A Percentage Breakdown of the World's Religions

Religion	Percent of the World Population
Christianity	32.4
Islam	17.1
Nonreligious	16.9
Hinduism	13.5
Buddhism	6.2
Confucianism/Taoism/Chinese Folk Religions	5.0
Atheist	4.4
New Asian religions (combined local tradition with Hinduism, Buddhism, Islam or Western thought)	2.2
Tribal religions (African and other animistic religions)	1.9
Judaism	0.4
Sikhism	0.34
Spiritism	0.14
Bahaism	0.09
Jainism	0.07
Shintoism	0.07
Zoroastrianism	0.01

with its core beliefs neatly falling under numbered descriptions. For example, it revolves around the Four Noble Truths and the Eightfold Path that keeps a person on the Middle Way. Not to mention the five basic moral observances and the eight precepts . . .

But while Buddhism can be boiled down into these neat numbered beliefs or practices, it is complex even in its simplicity. The typical rule of thumb: To understand Buddhism, you must practice Buddhism.

For those who don't practice it, though, here's a quick explanation. Briefly, at the center of the religion are the Four Noble Truths: (1) All life is suffering; (2) this suffering is the result of selfish desire; (3) this desire can be destroyed; (4) specifically, it can be destroyed by following the Eightfold Path.

And what is the Eightfold Path? Right Understanding (or Right Views), Right Thought (or Right Resolve), Right Speech, Right Conduct, Right Livelihood, Right Effort, Right Mindfulness, and Right Concentration. These all fit into the simpler *three*fold path, consisting of morality, meditation, and wisdom—all of which are to be adhered to simultaneously.

People who follow the Eightfold Path will eventually acquire wisdom, understanding that everything is in constant flux and, most important, that because of this, there is no permanent unchanging "soul" (or *atman*) in a person. At this point, they break through their desires and attachments to the world. They can move beyond this earthly life of suffering and decay into the desire-free life, *nirvana*.

Founded: In roughly 525 B.C.E., near Benares, India, by Prince Gau-

The Tripitaka, a sacred Buddhist text, is one of the longest books in the world. According to some estimations, it would take the average person 450 days of reading eight hours a day to read the entire Tripitaka.

And the book isn't only one of the world's longest books; one copy of it is also the largest—engraved on 729 marble pages three and half feet wide and five feet long. It was carved under the orders of King Mindon of Burma in 1861, who wanted the sacred words to last forever, and took fifty stone masons seven and a half years to complete.

tama Siddhartha, renamed the Buddha, or enlightened one.

Followers: Currently more than 334 million, making it number four worldwide; most followers are in Asia, although the U.S. has a growing Buddhist population.

Divisions: For all the neatly numbered core beliefs of Buddhism, there are a number of ways to *be* a Buddhist. In other words, this religion has a range of sects, each with its own practices (some of which seem fairly removed from the original doctrine). The common thread? Belief in the Buddha, the founder and first to realize the true path. Beyond that, it's a very mixed bag, ranging from the Theravadin school, dominant in Sri Lanka and Southeast Asia and the only survivor of the ancient Hinayana school, which adheres strictly to the central teachings of Buddha; to Zen (or Chan, in Chinese), widely practiced in Japan, which holds that enlightenment can come through intuition, not intellect; to Reiyukai (Soul-Friend Association), which emphasizes ancestor worship and allows followers to also follow other Buddhist or even Shinto groups.

Sacred texts: The Tripitaka, a collection of Buddha's teachings, monastic rules, philosophical commentaries on the teaching, etc.; as well as a vast body of *sutras* (or teachings), which number as many as 84,000.

CHRISTIANITY

A religion of redemption. Through faith, humankind can be redeemed—this, because of the resurrection of Jesus Christ, the Son of God.

Beliefs: The heart of Christianity isn't the teachings of Jesus as much as it is the resurrection of Jesus. It is this that makes Christianity completely distinct from Judaism, and is the event that marks the birth of a new religion.

Christianity evolved out of Judaism. Like Judaism, it holds that there is one God—the God of the Jewish Bible and of the Christian Old Testament, who spoke to Moses and declared Himself the God of Abraham, Isaac, and Jacob. But while Christianity shares the one God, God the Creator, with Judaism as described in the Jewish Bible and Christian Old Testament, it also holds that God is actually a trinity, subsisting in three divine persons: the Father, who is the Creator; the Son, who is the Redeemer; and, finally, the Holy Spirit, the Sustainer.

A key focus of Christianity is on the second person in the trinity—Jesus Christ, the Son and the Redeemer, anointed by God to deliver believers. Traditional Christian beliefs hold that since Adam and Eve's expulsion from the Garden of Eden, humankind has been born with original sin. It is Christ who serves as the means of reconciling humankind, which has fallen into sin, with the holiness of God.

In addition, Christ's resurrection and ascension act as a pledge to humankind: Believers have the possibility of eternal life. According to Christian doctrine, the "day of the Lord" promised by God in numerous Bible chapters, when humankind will be redeemed, the righteous rewarded, and the wicked punished, and when everyone would, automatically, love his or her neighbor, is already coming to pass because of Christ. So, upon Christ's death and resurrection, believers were pressed to spread the word,

Puns are amusing today, but to many ancient peoples, they had a deep religious meaning. For example, in the Book of Genesis, God takes some earth and makes a man; the words EARTH and MAN (via the name Adam) are similar in Hebrew. A more famous biblical pun occurs in Matthew 16:18, when Jesus says: "Thou art Peter [in Greek: Petros] and upon this rock [Greek: petra] I will build this church." The wordplay translates in Greek. Obviously, it does not work in English, but does work in French, with PIERRE, the name, and PIERRE, the rock.

the good news—*euangelion* in Greek—that humankind was saved from sin and from death. Evangelism has always been a key mission of the Christian church. Christians are charged with letting others know that they can be saved through Christ.

Although the dogma of Christ as both divine and human in nature is a central tenet of the Christian belief, it

Cities of Vice

The book of Genesis in the Old Testament speaks of the cities of Sodom and Gomorrah and the Lord's retribution for their promiscuous lifestyles, raining "fire and brimstone" down upon them and destroying them. Some scholars think they have located the whereabouts of these cities near the southern end of the Dead Sea in Israel. In this shallow portion of the otherwise deep lake, remains of ancient trees have been seen; in addition, many have noted the presence of salt pillars—shades of Lot's wife. As for fire and brimstone, the area is prone to earthquakes, which may have thrown up bitumen and natural petroleum; their ignition would account for the fires and destruction mentioned in the Bible. Archaeologists wishing to excavate the dead cities underwater would face formidable problems: The Dead Sea has five times the salt of normal seawater, so divers would have to wear heavy lead weights, and face unusually long decompression times.

The Bible: Translations Through Time

 Translating the Bible, written in Hebrew, Aramaic, and Greek into English, to try to capture the power and force of its words in a completely different language, has been a formidable task. Here are a few of the many attempts made over the years, from a passage of the Gospel of Matthew (25:14).

1380: Wycliffe translation:

Sothely as a man goynge fer in pilgrimage, clepide his seruantis, and bitoke to hem his goodis.

1611: King James version:

For the kingdome of heauen is as a man trauailing into a far countrey, who called his owne seruants and deliuered vnto them hys goodes.

1941: Basic English version:

For it is as when a man, about to take a journey, got his servants together and gave them his property.

1989: The Revised English Bible:

It is like a man going abroad, who called his servants and entrusted his capital to them.

The Bible is more than a religious document; it has dramatically influenced literature. Its stories, parables, and characters have been a part of Western literature for centuries, ranging from John Milton (PARADISE LOST, 1667) to Lord Byron (CAIN, 1821) and Thomas Hardy (FAR FROM THE MADDING CROWD, 1874). In more popular genres, there was slew of biblical movies of the 1950s and 1960s, and the works of such best-selling authors as Thomas Costain and Jeffery Archer (CAIN AND ABEL).

has caused great rifts in the past. Early on, in the fourth century, the Christian church split into two when the Alexandrian presbyter Arius preached that Jesus was created, not eternal, so He was subordinate to God. A few decades later, there were debates about the humanity of Christ versus His divinity, and about calling Mary the mother of God. The debates raged, often resulting in great schisms. And like many other religions, Christianity continues to have rifts within it—differences in worship, in interpretation of the Bible or of traditional dogma.

Founded: C. 33 C.E., after the resurrection of Christ, although it really caught on in a big way in the fourth century, when Emperor Constantine made Christianity legal, then later converted to it himself and created the Christian Roman Empire.

Followers: More than 1.8 billion, more than any other religion (although Islam is gaining ground), chiefly in Europe, North and South America, and Oceania, as well as in parts of South Asia and sub-Saharan Africa.

Divisions: While all Christians believe in the divinity of Christ, their way of following him differs according to the denomination they adhere to. And there are many, including the following major ones: Baptists, Anglicans, Lutherans, Methodists, Orthodox, Pentecostal, Presbyterian, Roman Catholic, and Congregationalists. And within all of these different denominations are varying degrees of strictness, etc.

Sacred texts: The Bible (consisting of the Old Testament—Judaism's scriptures—and the New Testament), written over a span of time from roughly 1000 B.C.E. to 100 C.E.; the canonical form was set in 325 C.E. at the Council of Nicea.

CONFUCIANISM

A religion of ethics, morals, and social behavior more than spirituality. Humankind's goal should be to live a virtuous life, following the code of ethics laid out by Confucius and his followers.

Beliefs: You can't serve the spirits unless you serve your fellowman first—this is the heart of Confucianism. As founder Confucius himself put it: "The gods should certainly be revered, but kept at a distance. . . . The way is not beyond man; he who creates a way outside of man cannot make it a true way. A good man is content with changing man, and that is enough for him. . . ."

This makes Confucianism a very here-and-now system, with emphasis on daily conduct. To a great degree, to be a Confucian means focusing on the relationships between yourself and your fellow human beings, and especially your family, both dead and alive. In this way, you can become a *chun-tzu,* or superior man. Confucius spelled it all out to his followers, giving many examples about how the superior man behaves in contrast to the inferior man. All his teachings boil down to a crucial point: To be a superior man, you must always think of virtue.

The key element of virtue is *jen* (in modern transliteration *ren*), a term Confucius never fully explained except by example. Someone of *jen* is a paragon of virtue, respectful, truthful, benevolent, diligent, generous, and so forth. The bottom line is being true to your own moral nature and treating others as you would want to be treated yourself.

But Confucianism doesn't leave it

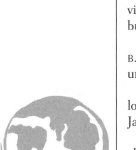

up to you to figure out how to do this. It's very big on advice, with rule after rule about just how you should behave. There are rituals to follow to show respect for ancestors; ways to act with your children or parents; guidelines for rulers. As such, Confucianism has become more than a strict religion. It has become intrinsically tied to Chinese culture and life. Even under communist rule, Confucianism remained a vital force in China—secularized, yes, but still true to the original concepts.

Founded: Circa late sixth century B.C.E., although it didn't really catch on until over a century later.

Followers: About 160 million followers, chiefly in China, but also Japan, Korea, and other parts of Asia.

Divisions: Perhaps because it was always more practical than spiritual, Confucianism doesn't really have any distinct divisions. While there are different ways of being a Confucian, from a strictly secular (sticking with the philosophical) to a traditional (going to Confucian temples), and while throughout history there were different schools, there are no specific sects.

Sacred texts: Four key works: the *Lun Yu* (called the Analects in the West), a collection of Confucius' sayings and teachings, collected by his students and compiled over about seventy years following Confucius' death in 479 B.C.E.; the *Meng-tzu,* a compilation of teachings by the Confucian philosopher Mencius (see pages 154–55); and the *Ta Hsüeh* (the Great Learning) and *Chung Yung* (Doctrine of the Mean), both Confucian commentaries on one chapter in the classic *Li Ching* (or Book of Rites), written by numerous Confucian authors, and said to have been written anywhere between 500 and 200 B.C.E.

HINDUISM

A diverse religion that was (and still is) formed by the people, centering around the notion of reincarnation and the caste system. Your actions in this lifetime determine your caste and status in the next—until finally your soul is released from this world.

Beliefs: One of the best ways to begin understanding Hinduism is to understand what it *isn't*. It isn't straightforward or neatly organized. It has no central hierarchy, no group of exclusive adherents, no defining doctrine. In fact, if you look in the dictionary, the first definition of "Hindu" isn't an adherent of Hinduism, but a native of India who speaks an Indic language.

So then what is it? Essentially, it is a loose collection of cults and sects that are aligned with a high tradition, one that is itself an amalgamation of tribal religions, most with different gods, rituals, and philosophies.

It sounds confusing, but in this jumble you can find a pattern of beliefs and practices that embody classical Hinduism: Life is a series of births and rebirths (called *samsara*); your lot in life is determined by your past deeds (*karma*); and through good acts, thought, and devotion, you can finally break out of the cycle of rebirth and escape (*moksha*). To achieve *moksha*, you must recognize the *Vedas* (the oldest Indian religious text) and the sages who made them (or, in some cases, other religious texts) available, worship the gods who created the universe, show regard for your ancestors

A major Hindu holiday is Dipavali, the Festival of Lights. It celebrates the triumph of good and light over evil and dark. According to one legend, it commemorates the killing of a demon king, Narakasura, who was the son of Mother Earth, and abused his divine powers. A good king, Indra, appealed to Krishna, who was victorious over the demon. Dipavali is celebrated for five days. On the eve of the holiday, incense is burned and statues of Lakshmi, the goddess of beauty and love, are adorned with ornaments and jasmine. During Dipavali, Hindus put on their best clothes, visit friends and family, eat delicacies, and go to temples and pray.

(through having children, as well as through offerings and prayers), and exhibit asceticism through fasts and vows.

Beyond this most basic common thread, it gets complicated. Hinduism has numerous guises and rituals, and thousands of gods, with the key ones being Vishnu, Shiva, and the goddess Shakti, and the lesser ones being their various incarnations, aspects, offspring, and spouses. In addition, like the belief in perpetual rebirth that is central to the religion, Hinduism itself is constantly being reborn—or, more precisely, being renewed and expanded—by incorporating current events and heroes into the religion. For example, since Prime Minister Indira Gandhi's assassination in 1984, busts of her have begun appearing in village and town crossroads. She is wearing garlands of flowers like a goddess and has a fresh red dot on her forehead. There is no Indira cult yet, but one could very well develop and become another part of the diverse Hindu religion.

Founded: By Aryan invaders of India c. 1500 B.C.E., when their Vedic religion (so called because of the hymns they wrote, making up the *Rig Veda*, the oldest religious text in the world) mixed with the religions of the natives.

Followers: Number three worldwide, with more than 751 million people, which includes more than 70 percent of India's population.

Divisions: As mentioned before, there are hundreds, ranging from academic philosophical schools to ones based on folklore. Among the more famous are Yoga, which emphasizes meditation; Tantra, which emphasizes special rituals involving mantras (chants) and mandalas (mystical diagrams) for enlightenment; and Bhakti, which emphasizes love for different dieties.

Sacred texts: The *Vedas;* the *Upanishads,* which summarize the philosophy and ethical code of the *Vedas* and traditional Hinduism in general; the *Laws of Manu,* classical Hindu law; the *Mahabharata,* a religious epic poem that includes the *Bhagavad Gita,* which is a dialogue between the god Krishna and the warrior Arjuna.

ISLAM

The fastest growing religion today, teaching that humans should submit to God's will, and in so doing, will fulfill their purpose in life on earth and will eventually be rewarded in the afterlife.

Beliefs: Islam is a back-to-the-basics religion and it is relatively easy to understand, particularly for people familiar with the Judeo-Christian tradition.

In many ways, Islam holds a middle

Hinduism and the Caste System

Hindu Indian society, like most others, is divided into numerous groups which are ranked according to prestige. But the Hindu social system is probably among the most rigid, particularly because it is codified by the Hindu religion. It's almost as if the major religion in the U.S., Christianity, sanctified the existing class differences. Among Hindus, there are five major castes. At the top are the Brahmins, the priestly caste. Next is the Ksatriya, or warrior caste, followed by the Vaisya, or merchant caste, and Sudra, or laborers, peasants, and servants. Below all of them are the "untouchables," or to use the name Mahatma Gandhi (see page 597) gave them, the Harijans, the children of God.

These major castes are divided and subdivided into numerous smaller subcastes, called *jati.* No one is sure of how many there are—some say more than twenty-three hundred. The *jatis* are further subdivided into local units, and all enforce certain codes of behavior among members governing what may be eaten and advising on how to avoid "contamination" through contact with a person of a lower caste. Interestingly, even those at the bottom, the outcastes, Harijans, or untouchables, also have distinctions. Higher-status Harijans try to avoid contact with lower-status harijans.

As you may have guessed, the Harijans or untouchables have the worst of things. In some areas, they may not come within twenty feet of contact with a Brahmin; until fairly recently, Harijans were not allowed to build brick houses or wear clothes similar to that of higher castes, or even travel on the same roads or enter the same temples. Harijans often do the dirty work in society: collecting garbage, cleaning out drains, and doing agricultural labor.

The Indian government has tried to rectify the problem by outlawing the caste system (although the law is ignored by many) and by guaranteeing untouchables places in schools and jobs in the government. In fact, recently members of higher castes protested that *they* were now being discriminated against. But in the villages, the untouchables still feel the brunt of prejudice.

position between Christianity and Judaism. According to Islam, Jews made the mistake of denying the mission of Christ; but on the other hand, Christians made the mistake of overvaluing Christ and deifying him. This is why Islam makes it very clear that its founder, Muhammad, was a man with a divine mission to accomplish, but not divine himself. His mission? To share the revelations that God gave him, steering people back to the fundamentals of religion.

At the heart of these revelations is the concept of submission, from which the name of Muhammad's religion comes: "Islam" means *submission*.

The Holy Month of Ramadan

 The Muslim holy month of Ramadan is one of the pillars of Islam. All adult Muslims of good health (with exceptions made for pregnant women, travelers, and the sick) are expected to fast from daybreak to dusk each day for the entire month. All drink, food, smoking, even the swallowing of saliva, are forbidden. Because the Muslim calendar is lunar, Ramadan falls on different periods over the years; it can be particularly difficult to follow the fast during the height of hot summers. At the end of the month comes the great feast called the *Id al-Fitr,* a high point of the year, with special services—and mounds of food, including many sweets.

The largest Muslim country in the world is located not in the Middle East but in Southeast Asia: Indonesia. Over 90 percent of this huge nation is Muslim. In Indonesia, a rapidly modernizing nation, Islam tends to be more moderate than it is in many parts of the Middle East. It's also often linked with earlier, pre-Islamic rites. But fundamentalism is rising along with modernization. The famous Muslim preacher Zainuddin says that Indonesian managers should ideally have their brains in America and their hearts in Mecca.

Human beings have a choice: to submit to God's law or not. Those who don't submit run the risk of going to hell, because they aren't fulfilling the purpose for which they were created. Those who do submit are *Muslims,* literally those who submit.

And, in keeping with its clear-cut core, Islam has clear-cut ways by which to submit. It isn't left to personal choice. There is a distinct method to being a Muslim, centering around the five basic elements of worship, called the Five Pillars of Islam.

First, and most important, is the *shahadah,* or confession of faith: "There is no God but God and Muhammad is his messenger." In addition to believing in the one God and prophecy, Muslims must also believe in angels, in revealed books, in God's messengers, and in the Last Day. The second pillar is prayer (*salat*), to be said five times a day (sunrise, midday, midafternoon, sunset, and before retiring). The third pillar is the *zakat,* the annual payment of one-fortieth of a person's moveable possessions for the year to help the needy. Fourth is *sawm,* a fast during the daylight hours of the month of Ramadan every year. The fifth is a pilgrimage or *haj* to Mecca at least once in a person's lifetime, if possible.

Islam doesn't stop with the Five Pillars. It is equally clear cut about the way believers should conduct their lives in general, giving specific directions and laws according to the *shariah* (literally "Path," which is God's pattern for the universe) that governs everything from how to pray to what to eat to what to wear to how to behave socially. (One interesting side note: Islamic law and ritual share a number of elements with Judaism. Muhammad incorporated Jewish elements into Islam—like

Mystical Islam

 The whirling dervishes are one of the most interesting groups of Muslims—the Sufis. The Sufis are Islamic mystics. They feel that to achieve true peace individuality must be subsumed; the soul must be "swallowed up" by God in a mystical union that reveals the underlying truth of life. There are many different kinds of Sufis, but all believe that the path to mystical oneness must be guided by a Sufi director or master, and that the initiate must pass through "way stations" of repentance, abstinence, poverty, trust, and patience. At last, in a blinding flash, the Sufi initiate receives the long-sought union with God and perceives the reality of divine love. Although dervishes and the like are the best-known Sufis, whirling themselves into ecstatic union with the universe, many other orders follow quieter paths of meditation to the same end.

not eating pork, the laws concerning circumcision, fasting regulations, and more. But in other ways, Muhammad went his own way completely. (For example, Sabbath is on Friday; when people pray they pray toward Mecca, and so forth.)

Founded: C. 610 C.E., by Muhammad.

Followers: Number two worldwide, with more than 1 billion followers, chiefly based in the Middle East, Central and Southeast Asia, and Africa.

The Shia or Shiites, one of the two major Islamic sects, today form a majority in only one Middle Eastern nation, Iran, but there are substantial numbers in Lebanon, Saudi Arabia, Bahrain, Iraq, and Yemen. The Shia are sometimes second-class citizens in these areas. They complain that power and money goes to the Sunni Muslim majority. Some have reacted by becoming militant radicals. Shiite terrorist groups, aided (according to Western intelligence services) by Iran, have attacked Western and secular targets in the Middle East and elsewhere.

Divisions: Yes, the beliefs are basic, and yes, there are specific rules a Muslim must follow to be a believer, but there are different ways to follow the rules. There are two major sects: the orthodox Sunni, which believes in determinism, and tends to have a simpler practice, and the Shia, a more ecstatic branch, which stems from a breech in early Islam. The Shia follow the teachings of 'Ali, the cousin and son-in-law of Muhammad, believes in human free will and mostly follows twelve *imams* (or teachers) who will ultimately lead people to Paradise. In addition, there's the mystical tradition called Sufism, which holds that people can receive direct revelations from God.

Sacred texts: The key sacred book of Islam is the Quran (also known as the Koran), the text of which was revealed

The Islamic Difference

A few other crucial distinctions between Islam and both Christianity and Judaism: While Islam holds that the soul is immortal and that humans must account for their actions in another existence, they don't accept the notion of original sin, which Christians do. Moreover, while souls can be redeemed, redemption isn't guaranteed through faith. Each soul has to work out its own salvation. And salvation isn't reserved for followers of Islam alone. Those who are righteous and God-fearing of all religions are eligible for salvation.

by God to Muhammad beginning in 610; the *hadith* are collections of the sayings of Muhammad and stories of his acts as related by his companions.

JAINISM

Best summed up by the practice of its monks sweeping insects from the path before they walk, epitomizing the core belief that the path to salvation is through nonviolence.

Beliefs: Jainism comes across as a very orderly religion. While it holds that the universe is timeless, with no beginning or end, it splits up this infinite amount of time into cosmic cycles. The universe passes through an endless number of these cycles, each divided into two phases, ascent and descent, which correspond to the rise and fall of human civilization during that cycle. And in each of these phases, twenty-four religious leaders, *tirthamkaras*

("ford-makers"), appear. Their job? To teach the path of salvation so people can be freed from the cycle of reincarnation that binds them to earth.

It sounds somewhat like Hinduism or other Indian philosophies and religions. But there are very important differences. Jains believe that there are no absolutes, that reality is neither eternal nor momentary. Also, while Jains believe in the law of *karma* (that actions will affect a person's life even after death), they hold that *karma* is physical—that people are bound to earth, and so stuck in a cycle of reincarnation, because of *ajiva,* or karmic matter that gets stuck in the soul when passions and evil actions are present.

This is why people must follow the right path to break the cycle and keep karmic matter from being absorbed into the soul. It isn't easy. Because the founder was ascetic, Jains must be quite ascetic themselves to "cross the ford," that is, break free from bondage. There are very strict vows to follow: one extremely tough set for monks; another, less stringent but still strict,

The Six Blind Men—Jain Logic

One of the most important contributions Jains have made to Indian thought is Jainist logic. The key belief underlying Jainist logic is that all human knowledge is relative and transient. Given this, nothing is either absolutely true or absolutely false. Everything the human mind concludes is both true and false simultaneously—so all questions can be answered both yes and no at the same time. All human thought is always logically incomplete or logically fallacious. The only time humans attain perfect knowledge is when their free, purified souls make it to Jainist heaven.

The best example of Jainist logic is the famous ancient story of six blind men who run into an elephant and try to conclude what the elephant is like. The first man put his hands on the ears of the elephant. An elephant is exactly like a fan, he decided. The second put his hands on the side of the elephant and concluded that the elephant was like a wall. Like a snake, said the fourth, whose hands were on the elephant's trunk. . . . And so on. The moral of the story? Each of the blind men is being logical based upon his experience, so each of them is right and each of them is wrong.

for everyone else, involving rules for fasting, begging, meditation, giving charity, and more. At the center of these vows is the belief that all life is sacred. This is why Jains are strict vegetarians (some more advanced spiritually are even forbidden from eating fruits with seeds and fermented milk products) and also why Jainism, while a relatively small religion in terms of number of followers, has had such impact. Mahatma Gandhi himself, one of the most famous proponents of nonviolence, was said to have been greatly influenced by Jainism.

Founded: Traditionally, 527 B.C.E. —the date when founder Vardhamana Mahavira, a prophet also called the Jina ("the Victor") died—although many scholars say it started one century later.

Followers: A smaller number than many other major religions, with about 3.9 million, primarily in India; many of these followers are in influential positions and so have quite an impact on the country.

Divisions: Early on (c. late 200s B.C.E.) two sects emerged: the Digambaras, or the sky-clad, so called because they held that monks should hold to a vow of nudity to exemplify total renunciation; and the Svetambaras, or the white-clad, who thought nudity should be optional. Both sects still exist, although the Digambaras have few monks (perhaps due to the extremely strict rules) and instead have their followers chiefly governed by lay people advanced in spiritual discipline. The Svetambaras, on the other hand, have many monks. But because of their not-too-ascetic worship practices, they've also spawned a reform branch, called the Sthanakavasis.

Sacred texts: Numerous texts,

including the Svetambara canon (called the *agama* or *siddhanta*) and the Digambara canon—the *Tattvartha-dhigama Sutra,* which outlines Jain doctrine in aphorisms; the *Karma-granthas,* canonical texts outlining Jain views of *karma;* and more.

JUDAISM

Tied inextricably to the history of the Jewish people, Judaism holds that there is one God, and that people should live their lives according to his divine will, which is detailed in the Torah.

Beliefs: As with many other religions, Judaism is difficult to summarize briefly because there are different interpretations, different practices, and different branches.

However, traditional Judaism does have certain basic tenets: There is one God, the Creator, who is absolute ruler of the universe. He created humans and gives them the option of choosing between good and evil. God has given humankind the divine law in the form of the Torah, the first five books of the Hebrew Bible, and, because he revealed the Torah to Moses, he has chosen the Jewish people to be his people. And by following the law as set forth in the Torah, people can hasten the time when God sets up his kingdom on earth after a human messiah, descended from the house of David, has come to spread the word.

In Judaism, the focus is on life *today,* even given this future to look forward to. In this sense, it is similar to Confucianism: the crucial task for followers is to live a moral life, following the commandments in the Torah. Instead of waiting for the afterlife for salvation, you seek salvation now, in this world.

Many contemporary Jewish scholars and religious thinkers hold strongly differing opinions on what exactly Judaism is—ranging from the ultra-conservative to the superliberal. For example, Orthodox Jews hold completely to the traditions and beliefs set forth in the Torah and the Talmud—living their daily lives according to the divine law; Conservative Jews hold strictly to the religious rules but have adapted the day-to-day rules to suit modern times; and Reform Jews

emphasize the ethical aspects, but followers don't have to follow the other aspects of Judaism, such as abiding by dietary laws. Then there are those for whom Judaism isn't a religion but a secular code of behavior or a cultural identity. Judaism actually is all of these, but they all stem from a central core: the history of the Jewish people.

You can't separate Judaism from this history for a simple reason: From its beginning, the religion defined the people. And, in turn, the culture and history of the people influenced the development of the religion.

For example, when the Temple of Jerusalem was destroyed by the Romans in 70 C.E., much of the basis for modern Judaism emerged. The local synagogue became the focal point of worship; as knowledge became more important than lineage, members of the priestly class (the *cohanim*), while still important, were no longer the only religious leaders. And the sacrificial system of worship that revolved around the temple died with the temple, replaced with rabbinical teachings stressing charity and ethics as the way to worship. The medieval diaspora, when Jews were persecuted and dispersed around the world, is another case where history affected the religion. Jews often had limited relationships with non-Jews, were often forced to live in certain prescribed areas, had to attend separate schools, and so on. As a result, many Jews became more focused on their differences with the rest of the world, more inward-directed, and more concerned with their faith. This time saw the birth of the conservative Hasidic movement and mystical Kabbalaism as well as Jewish philosophy. Similarly, in the nineteenth century, when liberalization broke down many of the barriers

Mystical Judaism

The mysticism of Jewish Kaballah arose during the Middle Ages, and it's still tantalizing some lovers of the esoteric today. The word *Kaballah* comes from the Hebrew *qabbalah,* meaning "something received." It refers to the idea that the follower of Kaballah can achieve a personal union with God, understanding his inner life and the deeper meaning of religious observances by receiving his divine secrets through meditation, study, and contemplation. One key belief of the Kaballah: Language in general, and biblical language in particular, contains hidden codes and secrets about the world and God. By assigning numerical values to the letters in these texts, these codes could supposedly be deciphered. And in so doing, the mystic could receive insight into the meaning of God and his relationship with the world, and even possibly influence God in his dealings with humankind, thus hastening the coming of the messiah. Kabbalistic thought influenced Christian thinkers but declined during the 1700s; today, a few mystics still search texts for hidden meanings.

The ultimate goal of Kabballaists is a personal union with God achieved through meditation, study of the Kaballah, and contemplation of messages received.

The Significance of the Synagogue

According to Talmudic tradition, the synagogue—the place where Jews worship—began not as a place but as a group of people. While scholars now believe the synagogue originated in the Maccabean period, the traditional belief was that it began when exiled Jews were in Babylon or shortly thereafter and was intended to keep their religion intact and their hope alive. At the weekly synagogue, people read from the Torah, discussed what they had read, explained to one another the meanings of the different readings, and reaffirmed their faith. The synagogue could be established wherever Jews lived. As time went on, the synagogue changed somewhat: a legal minimum of at least ten adult men was set; in addition, because it was difficult for everyone to be a scriptures expert, eventually each synagogue had one specially trained person in charge, a teacher or rabbi, who could settle questions about meaning. But the importance of the synagogue was clear: by enabling them to worship in small groups away from Palestine or Jerusalem, in virtually any country and amidst believers and non-believers alike, the synagogue preserved Jewish identity. It sounds obvious now, but back before 600 B.C.E., this was a revolutionary idea, because most religions were tied to specific places and temples.

separating Jews from non-Jews, the Reform movement started in Germany, allowing Jews to live more like Gentiles while maintaining their faith. Finally, the growth of Zionism, which advocated return to the land of Israel and the eventual foundation of the state of Israel, added to the secular form of Judaism, shifting the focus from spirituality to nationalism.

Founded: Generally thought to have been founded by Abraham, circa 1700 B.C.E., although it wasn't until Moses, in roughly 1300 B.C.E., that the religion became organized.

Followers: About 18.1 million

believers, spread over the world, with chief concentrations in Israel and the United States.

Divisions: There is a wide range of Judaic beliefs, falling into three major groups, Orthodox, Conservative, and Reform (as well as the nonreligious, humanistic, and political schools of Judaism, which see it as an ethnic culture, ethical system, or a folk culture).

Sacred texts: The Torah, consisting of the five books of Moses; other writings of the Hebrew Bible—that is, the other thirty-four books in the Old Testament of the Christian Bible; the Talmuds, books of canonical law consisting of the Jerusalem Talmud, written in the late fourth century C.E., and the Babylonian Talmud, written in the early sixth century; and the Midrash, recording the oral tradition of interpretation of the Hebrew scriptures, written between the fourth and fourteenth centuries C.E.

SHINTO

Evolved from ancient Japanese ancestor and nature worship; focuses on ritual and custom instead of philosophy, and as such is in many ways as much a cultural identity as a religion.

Beliefs: The key to Shinto is *kami*. In fact, *Shinto* means "way of the *kami*." But it gets complicated because *kami* is so difficult to explain. As James Clavell wrote in *Shōgun*, "To speak Japanese, you must think Japanese." Well, to understand *kami*, you must also think Japanese—although even the Japanese have only a vague idea of what *kami* is. But let's try anyway.

Kami, basically, is that which inspires awe. It can be a phenomenon of nature, a wave, the wind, mountains, or oceans; it can be an animal, a plant, a bird. It is a vague concept, one that Shinto followers can intuitively understand through faith alone. But it's not just a concept. *Kami* are also beings who create life, bestow blessings, and embody virtue. And because humans receive life from the *kami,* they have the essence of *kami* themselves, hidden inside. (In fact, the goal of a Shinto follower is to become a *kami* upon death.) The key, of course, is to live life properly—to follow the way of the *kami.* And you do this by purifying the heart and mind.

Purification is a matter of being aware of and worshiping the divine through specific rituals and prayer, at both town and home shrines, and of living with the right attitude: being truthful, doing the best possible job at work, and treating others fairly.

It's a very "here and now" approach to religion. There's no speculation about an end to the world, a judgment day, or a battle between good and evil. Instead, Shinto requires being obedient and following the correct customs. And since it evolved from ancestor

worship, it's also not overly concerned about individuals. Yes, people are individuals, but they aren't *independent* individuals. They're part of a continuing tradition—a midpoint between ancestors in the past and descendants in the future; a member of social groups today.

It's this team-oriented approach that epitomizes Japanese society and is a perfect example of how Shinto is inextricably tied to the Japanese culture and lifestyle. Shinto is more than an indigenous religion; rather it is an ethos that has influenced other religions in Japan as well as the nonreligious side of Japanese life.

Founded: Difficult to pinpoint, because there was no founder, but most experts agree that Shinto evolved out of existing ancestor and nature worship around 660 to 700 B.C.E.

Followers: Roughly 3.3 million, chiefly in Japan; but many millions more follow Shinto rituals in marriage ceremonies and other rites.

Divisions: There are three basic types of Shinto: Jinja (Shrine) Shinto, the main Shinto tradition, consisting of worship at local shrines; Kyoha or Shuha (Sect) Shinto, which emerged in the nineteenth century, when thir-

Shintoism in Decline

Traditional Shinto, in which people worship the sun goddess and the descendant of the goddess, the emperor, is on the decline. The reason? World War II and Japan's defeat at the hands of the allies. This failure discredited the emperor and his so-called divinity; he was required to appear in public and deny his divinity. Adding to the new nondivinity of the Japanese rulers was his son, who married a commoner rather than a member of the nobility. So now traditional Shinto is falling by the wayside. While shrines and temples are still used and old rituals still persist, more people are following different forms of religion, including folk religions. And now different forms of Buddhism have replaced Shinto.

teen sects were formed, and in which followers usually worship in churches, not shrines; Minzoku (Folk) Shinto, the folk religion generally practiced by the lower classes, with no real doctrine or organization. All three are interrelated, with spillover between them.

Sacred texts: Technically none, but there are ancient texts that are highly respected and that explain the myths and beliefs of the ancient Japanese from which Shinto evolved: the *Kojiki* (Record of Ancient Matters), written around 712 C.E., and the *Nihonshoki* (or *Nihongi*; Chronicles of Japan), written circa 720 C.E.

SIKHISM

God is the only reality, so people must completely submit to God's will. And the best way to find out what God's will is is by following one of the gurus.

Beliefs: Sikhs don't call it Sikhism; they call it *Gurmat*. But in the West, the religion is called Sikhism, and the word itself describes the religion succinctly. The word *Sikh* is derived from Sanskrit and Pali words meaning "disciple"—which sums up the most crucial aspect of Sikhism: Believers are disciples of spiritual mentors or gurus.

More specifically, Sikhs follow the teachings of ten specific gurus, beginning with Guru Nanak, the founder, and ending with Guru Gobind Singh, who died in the early eighteenth century. These gurus aren't worshiped as divine. God is the only divinity. But they *are* the teachers who can show followers the path to salvation.

Troubles in India

For the past ten years, some Sikhs have been engaged in a bloody conflict with the Indian government for greater control of their own affairs. The Sikh homeland is in the Punjab region of India, where Sikhs make up more than 60 percent of the total population of 20 million. Some Sikhs, under the *Khalsa Dal* (Society of the Pure), have agitated for complete independence from India, and conflict between this group and the Indian government has been violent. In 1984 the Indian government raided the main *Khalsa Dal* base in the Golden Temple of Amritsar; the Sikhs retaliated and assassinated Prime Minister Indira Gandhi. More than twenty thousand people have died in the course of the conflict. Recently, tensions have eased somewhat, and the economy, shattered by terrorism and counterterrorism, has improved. But the Indian government still refuses to allow Amnesty International to report on the status of Sikh prisoners, and the Sikhs still complain of government intolerance. Meanwhile, the Indian government justifies its actions as preventing what it sees as a dangerous attempt to split its nation apart.

The Sikh path to salvation isn't as tough as some other religions'. Nanak preached against asceticism and penance, and the religion doesn't call for restrictive vows or practices. (In fact, this is one of the reasons Sikhism is such an influential religion today—Sikhs have had the room to advance materially and to emigrate.) What it *does* require is devotional discipline, called *nam simran* (remembrance of the divine Name). Sikhism holds that people are stuck in the cycle of reincarnation because they are loyal to the world and its values, instead of the true reality of God. But people can recognize God and truth through following what the gurus said; they then can begin to understand the physical and spiritual order of the universe, and, eventually, achieve perfect harmony with the universe and so break free of bondage to the earth.

To do this, Sikhs are supposed to worship God through three practices: first, reciting passages from the chief holy text, the *Guru Granth Sahib,* from memory after getting up and bathing; second, daily family observance (which sometimes consists of a random reading from the *Guru Granth Sahib*); third, attending temple.

Followers can't be saved by just going through the motions. Nanak preached that true devotion came from worship in the heart, not in the temple. People are supposed to use their hearts to focus on God and truth, to inwardly "see" and so understand. And by meditating in this way, a person gets enlightenment on the installment plan, bit by bit, winding up in the final revelation that saves him or her.

Founded: In the sixteenth century C.E. by Nanak, who synthesized elements of Hindu and Muslim devotion.

Followers: More than 13 million in India (primarily in the Punjab region); 19.8 million total worldwide.

Divisions: There are no real sects, but there is a group called the Khalsa that operates somewhat like a brotherhood or sisterhood of believers, combining religious, military, and social duties and holding more strictures than basic Sikhism.

Sacred texts: The *Guru Granth Sahib* (also called the *Adi Granth*), a collection of writings (chiefly hymns used by different gurus) put together about 1603; the *Dasam Granth* (which isn't read too much today), a collection of writings attributed to Guru Gobind Singh, compiled in the 1700s.

Taoists were somewhat like modern-day libertarians, teaching that the fewer laws and rules, the better. In fact, founder Lao-tzu laid out his reasoning for this: public works and services, including such things as building roads, holding legal court, and so forth, lead to higher taxes, which then lead to public dissatisfaction, the possibility of civil unrest, and general unhappiness.

TAOISM (DAOISM)

By cultivating nonaction and living a life in tune with nature, people will lose their desires, and so find happiness by flowing with the underlying force in the universe, the Tao.

Beliefs: *Tao* means "way," and Taoism originally developed as the philosophy/religion that was the *other* way. That is, it emerged as the antithesis to the strict doctrines of Confucianism. Where Confucianism emphasized duty and discipline, Taoism emphasized spontaneity and spirituality. Instead of focusing on rigid rules, Taoism focused on the fluid.

And for good reason. At the core of Taoism is the metaphysical belief that there is a Oneness underlying the universe—a power that has no attributes. Everything emanates from this One, so everything is related. As Taoist Chuang-tzu (see pages 155–56) put it: "Heaven and Earth came into being together with me, and with me all things are one."

Given this, opposites like good and evil, right and wrong, beauty and ugliness are actually part of each other. The key to finding happiness isn't trying to impose rules, government, or human will on life. Instead, it is following your own destiny and letting everything around you do the same, and in so doing, being in accord with the Tao. The ultimate goal of a Taoist follower, then, is to live in symbiosis with nature and so become a part of the infinity of the universe. In effect, you can meld with the Tao once you recognize that you are part of it. And the only way to do this is to penetrate the veils with which civilization has shrouded the Tao.

It isn't necessarily easy to find the rhythm of nature. Taoism goes into great detail about the contemplative exercises to follow, including meditation, visualization, and breathing control. All these are also means of attaining longevity—another focus of Taoist writing and teaching. Not that death is to be feared or avoided. Taoism teaches that while there is no afterlife like those described by other religions, no heaven or paradise or judgment, death isn't the end of life. Instead, since everything is one, death is merely another form of existence.

In keeping with the whole notion of going with the flow, Taoism itself has gone through some transformations. The basic philosophical tradition spawned a religious offspring in the second and third centuries C.E., called *Tao-chiao* in Chinese. While many of the major concepts are the same, many others were transformed under religious Taoism. For example, the idea of striving for longevity (even immortality) is a key element in the Taoist church. Rites and services evolved; a religious hierarchy of monks, priests, and laity emerged; ties to folk religions strengthened.

But, to look at it in typical Taoist fashion, both Taoisms—the philosophical and the religious—are part of the same initial force. Both can coexist because, after all, both are of the Tao.

Founded: In the third or fourth century B.C.E. by the possibly legendary sage Lao-tzu.

Followers: More than 36 million, chiefly in China, but also in Japan and other areas of Asia.

Divisions: As mentioned, the two chief divisions are strict philosophical Taoism and religious Taoism (*Tao-chiao* in Chinese, *Dokyo* in Japanese), which in turn has different schools, ranging from magic-based folk religion to the more scholarly and scientific.

Sacred texts: The *Tao-te-ching*, traditionally said to have been written by Lao-tzu but perhaps instead a written collection of the Taoist oral tradition compiled in about the third century B.C.E.; the *Chuang-tzu*, initially written by Taoist sage Zhuangzi in about 340 B.C.E., and later completed by his students in about 742.

ZOROASTRIANISM

Revolves around the battle between good and evil, with humankind having the choice as to which side to support.

Beliefs: When many people think of Zoroastrianism, they immediately think of an ancient religion that has something to do with fire worship. Yes, it is ancient, dating back to the fifth century B.C.E. And, yes, fire worship (or, more correctly, a fire ritual) is part of the religion. But Zoroastrianism is far from being a simple tribal religion. It's actually a well-developed ethical system, similar in many ways to Christianity and Islam, with a battle between God and the devil, humans judged at death according to the good or evil they have done in life. And it's still alive in the modern world—for example, several members of the Iranian parliament were Zoroastrians.

"Environmentally Sound" Burials

 Because Zoroastrianism is a religion that developed among agricultural peoples, it holds that its followers must be careful not to contaminate the earth or the water. This has led to a unique ritual surrounding death still practiced by Parsis, those following Zoroastrianism in India. Instead of burying dead bodies and so contaminating nature, they use structures called *dakhmas*, or "towers of silence." These are open-air towers, essentially a stone floor surrounded by a circular wall with no roof. The floor is built in three levels—the highest level for men, the middle level for women, and the lowest for children—with a pit in the center. When a person dies, the body is brought to the *dakhma*. After mourners have viewed the body for the last time, it is taken inside and put in a pit on the appropriate level. The shroud is slit so as to partially uncover the body. Then vultures swoop down to dispose of the body. A few days later, the pallbearers return to throw the bones into the central pit. Most *dakhmas* are located out of town, on hilltops so no one can look inside. But recently in the Bombay area, a new high-rise went up and had to be closed because it was tall enough to overlook a *dakhma*.

So what is this ancient-modern religion? At its most basic, Zoroastrianism worships only one God as creator, Ahura Mazda. And it focuses on the *finite* battle between good (Spenta Mainyu) and evil (Argra Mainyu). The battle is split into four three-thousand-year segments. Good and evil prepare their forces (the Amahraspands and the Yazatas—similar to archangels and angels—on God's side; demons and evil spirits on evil's) in the first and second segments, in the third they fight, and in the fourth, God vanquishes evil.

It's this happy ending that makes Zoroastrianism such a hopeful religion. Followers are urged to follow God through worship and ethical actions, and through avoiding such evils as anarchy, disobedience, and lying. Right action in Zoroastrianism is somewhat Epicurean: People are supposed to avoid both overindulgence and asceticism. Such humble basics as good health, marriage, and work are revered as good. Most important, people are supposed to be joyful; they are urged to enjoy life and help others to do so.

Hope permeates Zoroastrianism. Even the damned don't have to abandon hope. While those who have done more evil than good go to hell, it's not eternal damnation. Hell is actually more a reform school than death row—people are punished so that they will reform. And ultimately, when all have reformed, the devil and his works are destroyed, heaven and earth become one, and everyone can live with God.

Founded: Around 628 to 551 B.C.E. in ancient Iran by Zoroaster (also known as Zarathustra).

Followers: Relatively few—estimates generally fall between two hundred thousand and five hundred thousand (this low number is largely due to the fact that Zoroastrians don't actively seek converts and marry only among themselves); most in Bombay, India, but also in Iran.

Divisions: None.

Sacred texts: The *Avesta*, written around the fifth century B.C.E., which contains the older *Gathas*—hymns attributed to Zoroaster—as well as other hymns, liturgical texts, and prayers.

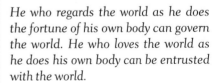

THE GOLDEN RULE IN DIFFERENT RELIGIONS

Differences in religion are always apparent, often easy to identify and (unfortunately) frequently the cause of enmity, dissension, even hatred. Wars are fought over holy matters, over beliefs not shared, over the meaning of "God."

Often we focus so much on the differences that we lose touch with the similarities. And it is the common bonds that are often more interesting—and often the reminder that, for all the arguing and fighting and killing over religion, the essentials are, very often, the same.

One essential: the Golden Rule. It's expressed differently in each religion, but the thought is the same: Do unto others . . . Some examples:

Tsze-kung asked, saying, "Is there one word which may serve as a rule of practice for all one's life?" The Master said, "Is not Reciprocity such a word? What you do not want done to yourself, do not to others."
—Confucius (K'ung Fu-tzu) (551–479 B.C.E.), Chinese philosopher, founder of Confucianism, in the *Analects*

No man is a true believer unless he desireth for his brother that which he desireth for himself.
—Muhammad (570–632 C.E.), prophet of Islam

I will cease to live as a self, and will take as my self my fellow-creatures.
—Santideva (c. 7th century C.E.), Buddhist guru

He who regards the world as he does the fortune of his own body can govern the world. He who loves the world as he does his own body can be entrusted with the world.
—*Tao-te-ching*, XIII

He who hath compassion upon others receives compassion from Heaven.
—Talmud, *Shabbat* 151

Deal with others as thou wouldst thyself be dealt by. Do nothing to thy neighbor which thou wouldst not have him do to thee hereafter.
—*Mahabharata*, c. 400 B.C.E., Hindu sacred text

Nature only is good when it shall not do unto another whatever is not good for its own self.
—*Dadastan-I dinik, Zend-Avesta*, c. 800 C.E., Zoroastrian sacred text

Ponder well the maxim: Never do to other persons what would pain yourself.
—*Panchatantra*, c. 300 B.C.E.

Whatsoever you would that men should not do to you, do not do that to them. This is the whole law. The rest is only explanation.
—Hillel Ha-Babli, in the Talmud, c. 50 B.C.E., *Shabbat*

As ye would that men should do to you, do ye also to them likewise.
—Luke 6:31, c. 75 C.E.

RELIGIOUS FOUNDERS:
THE BIRTH OF SOME LEADING RELIGIONS

Following is a look at the founders of the world's major religions, arranged in chronological order.

But first, a basic story about rebellion: Once there was a young man who, when he reached age thirty, began questioning the very basics of life: Why are we here? Why does humankind have to suffer? He then entered on a quest for self-perfection and on the way received an epiphany that unlocked the mysteries of life. To receive this revelation he had to conquer compelling temptations. Then, secure in his belief, he took to the road, teaching others. Along the way, he faced extreme opposition from the establishment. He was forced to flee his homeland with his followers, but once relocated, became even more popular.

Fill in a different name for the young man, be it Gautama Siddhartha or Jesus or Zoroaster, and you've got the bare bones of the story of the founding of many leading religions.

Yes, there are variations on the theme. Some religious founders stay in their homes to answer the questions, others hit the road in their quest. Confucius was a failure in his own time, Buddha a success when it came to drawing followers and setting up the framework of a religion. And Lao-tzu may not have been a real person at all, while Muhammad most definitely was. And so on.

But the basics remain the same: The young man, often from a comfort-

The second largest religious bloc in the world is actually formed of people who call themselves agnostics (nonreligious) or atheists (antireligious). Over a billion of the world's inhabitants consider themselves one or the other, according to THE WORLD CHRISTIAN ENCYCLOPEDIA, *making this group the second largest in the world after Christianity.*

able background, seeking answers to the big questions. (Thirty or thereabouts seems to be the crucial age—the age when most religious founders have their revelation or learn the mission they are charged with.) The battle with temptation. The dispute with the religious establishment of the time. The migration. And finally, the spreading of the word and the growth of a new religion.

ZOROASTER

(c. 628–c. 551 B.C.E.)

Who he was: Prophet of the ancient Iranians; considered to be either the founder of Zoroastrianism or the reformer of the ancient Parsi religion to Zoroastrianism.

What he taught: A ritualistic monotheistic religion preaching peace and truth, with one God, Ahura Mazda, the Creator, centering around the battle between Good (Truth, represented by Spenta Mainyu) and Evil (the Lie and Pride, represented by Argra Mainyu).

What he wrote: The *Gathas,* seventeen hymns noted for their zeal and love for God.

Key words: "In doubt if an action is just, abstain."

According to tradition, Zoroaster was born laughing. He also is said to have radiated light; three days before he was born, his village shone so brightly that people abandoned it, thinking it was on fire. An apt legend, since Zoroaster and the religion he promoted use fire worship as a way of pleasing the gods.

Fire worship was a holdover from preexisting traditions, but as with much of his religious philosophy, Zoroaster put his own spin on it. He changed the old fire ritual to symbolize the cosmic law of God and took the belief in personal judgment at death to further his preachings on social justice.

The specifics of Zoroaster's life, chiefly based upon the one record of him in the sacred book of Zoroastrianism, the *Avesta,* are fairly sketchy: His family name was Spitama; he was poor; he was known for his compassionate nature; and when he turned twenty, he left his father, his mother, and the wife they had chosen for him to wander in search of answers to his questions about the nature of life. The answers didn't come to him until he hit age thirty (as with so many other religious leaders), when he received a revelation. On the banks of the Daitya river, the archangel Vohu Manah (Good Thought) came to him and took him to visit the Supreme Being, Ahura Mazda, who taught Zoroaster the doctrine and duties of the "true religion," which came to be called (logically) Zoroastrianism.

Once converted, Zoroaster did what many other believers have done—confronted the religious establishment

ZOROASTER

with his new religious philosophy and was forced to flee when they proved less than eager to change their ways. He wound up taking refuge with Vishtapa, chief of the Fryana tribe and, eventually, convert to Zoroastrianism. He married, had two children, and spent the next years spreading his religion throughout ancient Iran and fighting invading nomads. And, according to tradition, he was eventually killed by the second invasion of nomads, murdered at age seventy-seven in a fire temple by murderers disguised as wolves.

BUDDHA

(c. 563–c. 483 B.C.E.)

Who he was: The founder of Buddhism (although some instead call him the reformer of previously existing Brahmanism into Buddhism).

What he taught: The path or way—broadly consisting of belief, morality, and meditation—by which anyone (regardless of class or caste) can transcend human desires and reach the purest state of being.

What he wrote: Nothing, but his sermons or discourses were collected and written as the *Sutras,* and his sayings written in Pali as the *Dhammapada.*

Key words: "There are two ends not be served as a wanderer. What are these two? The pursuit of desires and of the pleasure which springs from desire . . . and the pursuit of pain and

biography are cloudy—some sources put his birth at c. 624 B.C.E.; others at c. 563; still others c. 448. According to tradition, he was married and had a young son; but many scholars dispute this as legend.

In any case, tradition has it that, as with so many other religious leaders, age thirty was an auspicious year. It was then that Siddhartha became concerned with the perennial questions about life: Why are people born only to suffer, age, and die? He renounced court life and, hoping to find answers to his questions, became an ascetic. But after six years begging and wandering, he felt he was no closer to the truth. So he left the band of ascetics he was traveling with, sat beneath a banyan (bodhi or bo) tree near Buddh Gaya in Bihar and began meditating, planning to continue until he reached the enlightenment he sought. While meditating, he was tempted by Mara (the Evil One) and his three daughters, but stayed the course, overcame the evils which tie humans to mortal existence, and became Buddha—"the enlightened one." He could have stayed in the transcendental state he had entered but, because he was compassionate, chose instead to return to the mortal world and teach the Dharma, the truth he had gained through his awakening. And for the next forty years he taught what he had learned: that existence is suffering; that enlightenment comes from following the Buddhist path of contemplation and from recognizing the underlying unity of life.

According to one of the *sutras,* Mara returned to him years later, again trying to get him to put behind him his mortal existence, and this time Buddha apparently agreed, saying he would die in

hardship. . . . The Middle Way of the Tathagata avoids both these ends. It is enlightened, it brings clear vision, it makes for wisdom, and leads to peace, insight, enlightenment, and *nirvana.* What is the Middle Way? . . . It is the Noble Eightfold Path."

Buddha was born Prince Gautama Siddhartha, the son of a rajah in a region north of Benares. Specifics about his

CHINESE
WARRIOR BESIDE
A HORSE PRAYING
BEFORE BUDDHA
(REPRODUCED
FROM THE
COLLECTIONS OF
THE LIBRARY OF
CONGRESS)

three months. Even so, evil did not win, because the Buddha had done his work, establishing a missionary community that could teach the Dharma and instruct converts.

CONFUCIUS

(551–479 B.C.E.)

Who he was: Considered China's first philosopher, as well as the father of the eponymous Chinese religion still practiced today in various forms (see also Mencius [pages 154–55] and Hsuntzu [pages 156–57]).

What he taught: An ethical code of behavior (called Confucianism) chiefly aimed at the ruling class; under this code, the chief goal of humankind is to live a moral life.

What he wrote: *Lun-yu* (Analects)—pithy, easy-to-read sayings, maxims, and anecdotes, collected in twenty books by Confucius' students.

Key words: "Five things constitute perfect virtue: gravity, magnanimity, earnestness, sincerity, kindness."

"If you don't know how to serve men, why worry about serving the gods?"

Born in the city-state of Lu, Kung Futzu (romanized to Confucius) was an aristocrat who tutored the offspring of others of his class. He believed that China should return to the values and practices of the earlier Chou dynasty, the priest-kings who ruled from 1027 to 771 B.C.E. So he developed a system of ethics and morals based on the Chou religion, focusing on the behavior of royalty. He taught that they should follow the "Way of the Former

CONFUCIUS (WOODCUT BY KANO TAN'YU) (COURTESY MUSEUM OF FINE ARTS, BOSTON)

Kings" who ruled by being *jen*—having the ideal attributes such as loyalty, unselfishness, deference, and courtesy, as well as boldness to do right. In so striving, a prince must cultivate his virtue, or *te,* and must live his life according to *li,* a code of conduct that includes dress, manners, demeanor, and—a key point—filial piety.

Confucius spent years trying to find a prince in Lu who would support his theories and put them into practice. When he couldn't find this sponsor, he left Lu and became an itinerant

Bahai: A World Religion

There's one religion that could truly be called a world religion—Bahai. Bahai is an independent religion that holds that all of the religions of the world are actually in agreement. The prophets and founders of each of the religions were indeed revealing the word of God and were right for their particular time and place. Bahai was founded in Iran by Bahaullah ("Glory of God") in 1844 and has since spread, with about 5.7 million members worldwide. A famous American member was Dizzy Gillespie. Many Bahais from Iran have suffered in recent years; the fundamentalist government there considers them heretics and has imprisoned many.

LAO-TZU RIDING ON A WATER BUFFALO (CHINESE TAOISTIC PAINTING; PEN AND INK AND WATERCOLOR ON CARDBOARD, 21 X 61 CM) ("RELIGIOUS" COLLECTION, MARBURG CASTLE, GERMANY; FOTO MARBURG/ART RESOURCE, N.Y.)

teacher. But the neighboring states were as unimpressed by his teachings as the leaders of Lu were. Faced with indifference and often hostility, he died disappointed—and, except for a small band of loyal followers, largely ignored in his own time.

LAO-TZU

(c. 300 B.C.E.—or [traditionally] c. 580–c. 500 B.C.E.)

Who he was: Considered the chief exponent of Taoism (also called Daoism).

What he taught: The "Way" (or the Tao), an alternative to Confucianism, holds that the universe has no morality. Therefore, instead of trying to live by rigid codes of ethical behavior, humans should try to return to the simple life of nature.

What he wrote: The *Tao-te-ching*, the chief Taoist spiritual text, a brief philosophical treatise written chiefly in verse.

Key words: "Act nonaction; undertake no undertaking; taste the tasteless."

The first question: Was there a *real* Lao-tzu? The jury is out. Some think he was a legendary figure; others that he was historical—usually a man born Li Erh Dan, later called Duan-gan, who was given the courtesy title Lao-tzu (meaning the "venerable viscount") when his son was made viscount of Duan-gan. There is also a debate about his birth date—some data point to c.

300 B.C.E. as his probable lifetime, while tradition has it that he lived at the same time as Confucius (c. 500 B.C.E.). According to popular belief, Confucius came to Lao-tzu, then an archivist or imperial tutor in the court of Chou, seeking instruction on ritual. The other traditional belief about Lao-tzu's life is that he left the Chou domain when he believed the regime was going to fail. He traveled west and was stopped at the Han-ku Pass by a gatekeeper named Yin Hsi, who asked him to write a text on the concepts of Tao and Te, which became the *Tao-te-ching*.

Beyond this, little is known or surmised about the (theoretical) life of Lao-tzu. Some scholars held that he lived the life of a recluse; legend has it that he lived to be between 160 and 200 years old. Some legends elevate Lao-tzu to god status: He existed *before* the universe did, went through some cosmic metamorphoses, and finally descended to earth to save humankind and counsel numerous generations of Chinese sage-kings.

But there is no debate about the importance of Lao-tzu and the work he (allegedly) wrote, the *Tao-te-ching*.

JESUS

(c. 6 B.C.E.–c. 30 C.E.)

Who he was: Founder of Christianity; considered by believers to be the Son of God, an aspect of the Holy Trinity of God.

What he taught: Redemption and eternal life are possible for those who believe.

What he wrote: Nothing, but his sermons, parables, and other teachings are gathered in the Gospels in the New Testament.

Key words: "And ye shall know the truth, and the truth shall make you free."

Jesus probably wasn't born on December 25. This day was chosen as his birthday by later Christians trying to push their religion because it was a pagan holiday, the winter solstice celebrated as the Nativity of the Sun on the Julian calendar.

In fact, no one is sure about Jesus' actual birthday. As with the other religious founders, his biography is scant. Most of what we know about the historical Jesus is based not only upon the four gospels of the New Testament (Matthew, Mark, Luke, and John), but also upon mentions made of him in the writings of Tacitus, Suetonius, and Josephus. But the information is sparse: According to tradition, Jesus was the son of Joseph, a carpenter, and Mary (of the tribe of Judah, a descendent of David) and was born in a stable in Nazareth. His childhood and early adulthood are a blank.

But all accounts begin going into detail when Jesus reached age thirty. This is when his cousin, John the Baptist, baptized him, and when he first realized the divine nature of his mission on earth. He spent forty days in the wilderness, facing a range of temptations, and emerged successful. Then, knowing that he was to spread the word of God, he gathered twelve disciples and began preaching throughout Galilee and Judea, still practicing Judaism. But his some of his practices (which included performing miracles on the Sabbath, driving moneylenders from the Temple, and associating with

JESUS
(PANTOCRATOR
MOSAIC,
DAPHNE,
GREECE)
(REPRODUCED
FROM THE
COLLECTIONS OF
THE LIBRARY OF
CONGRESS)

"publicans and sinners") angered the Jewish establishment.

He didn't identify himself to his followers as the Messiah until he fled for a while to Tyre and Sidon. He then returned to Jerusalem; at a Passover seder (the Last Supper) he was betrayed by one of his disciples, Judas Iscariot, by a kiss, stood trial and was condemned to death. He was most probably crucified by the Romans in Jerusalem sometime between 29 and 33 C.E. Contemporary witnesses said that he rose from the dead after three days and showed himself to his disciples at different times in the next forty days, after which he ascended to heaven—which is the cornerstone of Christian belief today.

MUHAMMAD

(c. 570–632 C.E.)

Who he was: The founder of Islam; more strictly, the Messenger of God or the "Seal of the Prophets" to Muslims; that is, the receiver of the final and perfect revelation from God; also known (to non-Muslims) as the Prophet of Islam.

What he taught: A reaction to Judaism and Christianity that brought religion back to the fundamentals; emphasizing the power of the one God who reveals himself through prophets and messengers.

What he wrote: Nothing, but the Quran was revealed to Muhammad by God and dictated by Muhammad; and the *hadith* includes the sayings of Muhammad.

Key words: "Actions will be judged according to intentions." And "No man is a true believer unless he desireth for his brother that which he desireth for himself."

Muhammad never saw himself as the founder of a religion, but as a man with a mission to return the earlier religions to their purity. This mission began when he was forty years old.

Until that point, he had lived a fairly straightforward life, marked to some degree by hardship: He was born on August 20 in Mecca to a poor family of the tribe of Quraysh, hereditary guardians of the shrine in Mecca; his father died before his birth, his mother when he was six, so he was raised by his uncle Abu Talib, a trader. Like his uncle, Muhammad worked as a trader; at age twenty-five, he worked as steward for a wealthy widow (said to be about forty) who made him an offer of marriage which he accepted. She bore him two sons (who died as infants) and four daughters. All in all, he seems to have led the typical life of a trader.

Then it all changed. Tradition has it that, about 610 C.E., he began receiving revelations from God—the key ones commanding that idols of the shrine be

destroyed and that the rich give to the poor. At first, he told only his family and a few friends, but slowly his words spread and more people accepted them as true. When he had about fifty followers—chiefly young men—he began preaching publicly and did so for about ten years. But more and more opponents began harassing him and his followers. When his wife and then his uncle died, he faced even more troubles when one of his most bitter opponents, another uncle, named Abu Lahab, became clan leader. It was time for Muhammad to leave, and leave he did, emigrating with his followers to Yathrib in 622.

This migration (called the *Hegira*) became the starting point for the Islamic calendar; it marked a turning point for Muhammad and his fortunes. Yathrib's name was changed to Medina, city of the prophet, a sign of his growing importance. He continued preaching and extending his influence. By 629 he was leader of Mecca and recognized as the "Messenger of God"; by 630 he controlled most of Arabia due to a combination of skillful diplomacy and armed might. But he had little time to continue the growth of his ideas or set plans for the future. Only two years later, he died unexpectedly; he led one final great pilgrimage to Mecca, and two months after his return to Medina, died on June 8, 632.

BEAUTIFUL THOUGHTS FROM SACRED TEXTS: QUOTATIONS FROM THE WORLD'S HOLY BOOKS

 Each of the world's great religions expresses its beliefs about the divine in words. Spurred by faith, these words often reach heights of beauty unsurpassed in other forms of literature. In other cases, it's not the words themselves that soar, but the thoughts. But whether it's the beauty of the words or the beauty of the thought, you can feel the power of the ideas conveyed.

Here are a few examples:

In the beginning God created the heaven and the earth. And the earth was without form, and void; and darkness was upon the face of the deep. And the Spirit of God swept over the face of the waters. Then God said, Let there be light: and there was light. And God saw the light, and it was good: and God divided the light from the darkness. And God called the light Day, and the darkness he called Night. And the evening and morning were the first day.
—Genesis, the Bible, Jewish and Christian sacred text

*Before heaven and earth were
    produced,
There was Something, without form
    and yet all complete,
Silent! Empty!
Sufficient unto itself! Unchanging!
Moving everywhere but never
    exhausted!
This indeed might well be the mother
    of all below heaven.*
—*Tao-te-ching*, sacred text of Taoism

Some fools declare that God created the universe. If God created the universe, where was he before creation?

Did God create the universe out of something? If he did, who created the material out of which he created the universe? . . .

. . . Know therefore, that the universe is not created; it is like time itself without beginning or end. Uncreated and indestructible, the universe is self-sustaining, working by its own inherent power.
—*Mahapurana*, sacred text of Jainism

Wherefrom has this world come? He who is in the highest heaven has made it; perhaps, He too hasn't made it. He alone knows; maybe even He doesn't know.
—*Rig Veda* (c. 1000 B.C.E.), sacred Hindu literature

There is a Light that shines beyond all things on earth, beyond us all, beyond the heavens, beyond the highest, the very highest heavens. This is the Light that shines in our heart.
—the *Chandogya Upanishad*, 3.13.7, translated by Juan Mascaro; from *The Upanishads* (Penguin Classics, 1965)

God is the Light of the Heavens and of the Earth. The similitude of His light is as it were a niche wherein is a lamp, the lamp within a glass, the glass as though it were a pearly star. It is lit from a blessed Tree, an olive-tree neither of the East nor of the West, the oil whereof were like to shine even though no fire were applied to it; Light upon Light; God guideth to His Light whom He will.

—Quran, sacred book of Islam, sura xxiv, v. 35

Every moon, every year, every day,
Every wind comes and goes
And all blood reaches its final
resting place.

—*Chilam Balam*, Mayan prophecies

Free thyself from the past, free thyself from the future, free thyself from the present. Crossing to the farther shore of existence, with mind released everywhere, no more shalt thou come to birth and decay.

—the *Dhammapada*, 348; sacred text of Buddhism

Death is uncertain for anyone born, and birth is certain for the dead; since the cycle is inevitable, you have no cause to grieve!

—the *Bhagavadgita*, sacred text of Hinduism

Once upon a time, I, Chuang-tzu, dreamt I was a butterfly, fluttering happily like a butterfly. I was conscious only of my happiness as a butterfly, unaware that I was Chuang-tzu. Suddenly, I awakened, and there I lay, myself again. Now I do not know whether I was then a man dreaming I was a butterfly, or whether I am now a butterfly dreaming I am a man.

—*Chuang-tzu*, a sacred text of Taoism

The more we say, the more there remains to be said.

—attributed to Nanak, founder of the Sikh religion

The mind that is occupied leaves no room to accept anything else. A guest room can be used to receive guests only

Some religions are not that enthusiastic about translating their sacred books, preferring they be read in their original language. Judaism, Hinduism, and Islam fall into this catagory. In fact, Islam does not consider a translation of the Quran as the Quran at all—it is merely an imperfect rendering of the true Arabic words of God. On the other hand, Buddhism and particularly Christianity welcome translations. The Christian Bible has currently been translated into about two thousand languages.

when it is empty. If occupied, where is there room for guests? Everything which appeals to the mind is like the guests, and our mind is like the guest room. When the guest room is cleared, only then can the guests be received and entertained in a desired manner. . . . When the clouds do not appear, the sky is clear of objects and remains serene. The clouds come and float in the sky, but the space the clouds occupy is not prepared in advance. After the clouds move away, there remains no trace in the sky.

—*Takuan Osho zenshu*, Vol. V, *Tokai yawn*, p. 19, pp. 84–85, Zen text

God—there is no god but He, the Living, the Self-subsistent. Slumber seizeth Him not, neither sleep. To Him belongeth whatsoever is in the Heavens and whatsoever is in the Earth. Who is there that shall intercede with Him save by His Will? He knoweth what is present with men and what shall befall them, and nought of His knowledge do they comprehend, save what He willeth. His Throne is wide as the Heavens and the Earth, and the keeping of them wearieth Him not. And He is the High, the Mighty One.

—Quran, sacred book of Islam, sura ii, v. 256

Believe nothing, O monks, merely because you have been told it . . . or because it is traditional, or because you yourselves have imagined it. Do not believe what your teacher tells you merely out of respect for the teacher. But whatsoever, after due examination and analysis, you find to be conducive to the good, the benefit, the welfare of all beings—that doctrine believe and cling to, and take it as your guide.

—attributed to Buddha

He who dreams . . . does not know he is dreaming . . . only when he awakens does he know he has dreamt. But there is also the great awakening (ta-chiao), and then we see that [everything] here is nothing but a great dream. Of course, the fools believe that they are already awaked. . . . What foolishness! Confucius and you, both of you are dreams, and I, who tell you this, am also a dream.

—*Chuang-tzu*, a sacred text of Taoism

The material things which ye are given are but the conveniences of this life and the glitter thereof; but that which is with God is better and more enduring: Will ye not then be wise?

—Quran, sacred book of Islam, sura 28, v. 60

The highest good is like that of the water. The goodness of water is that it benefits the ten thousand creatures; yet itself does not scramble, but is content with the places that all men disdain.

—*Tao-te-ching*, sacred book of Taoism

Absolute truth is indestructible. Being indestructible, it is eternal. Being eternal, it is self-existent. Being self-existent, it is infinite. Being infinite, it is vast and deep. Being vast and deep, it is transcendental and intelligent.

—*Analects*, sacred text of Confucianism

This is the Spirit that is in my heart, smaller than a grain of rice, or a grain of barley, or a grain of mustard-seed, or a grain of canary-seed, or the kernel of a grain of canary-seed. This is the Spirit that is in my heart, greater than the earth, greater than the sky, greater than heaven itself, greater than all these worlds.

—the *Chandogya Upanishad*, 3.14, sacred text of Hinduism

The kingdom of heaven is like to a grain of mustard seed, which a man took, and sowed in his field: Which indeed is the least of all seeds: but when it is grown, it is the greatest among herbs, and becometh a tree, so that the birds of the air come and lodge in the branches thereof.

—St. Matthew, 13:31, the New Testament of the Bible, sacred text of Christianity

When our senses of sight and hearing are distracted by the things outside, without the participation of thought, then the material things act upon the material senses and lead them astray. That is the explanation. The function of the mind is thinking: when you think, you keep your mind, and when you don't think, you lose your mind. This is what heaven has given to us. One who cultivates his higher self will find that his lower self follows in accord. That is how a man becomes a great man.

—*Meng-tzu*, a sacred text of Confucianism

The Buddhas do but tell the Way, it is for you to swelter at the task.

—*Dhammapada*, collection of ancient Buddhist poems/aphorisms, XX.276

Grasping without eyes, hasting without feet, he sees without eyes, he hears without ears. He knows what can be known, but no one knows him.

—*Upanishads*, sacred text of Hinduism

To God belong the East and West; wherever you turn, there is the face of God—for God is All pervading, All knowing.

—Quran, sacred book of Islam, famous lines cited by Muslim mystics as example of mystical intent in the Quran

The Lord is my shepherd; I shall not
  want.
He maketh me to lie down in green
  pastures: He leadeth me beside the
  still waters.
He restoreth my soul: He leadeth me
  in the paths of righteousness for his
  name's sake.
Yea, though I walk through the valley
  of the shadow of death, I will fear
  no evil: for thou art with me; Thy
  rod and thy staff they comfort me.
Thou preparest a table before me in
  the presence of mine enemies: Thou
  anointest my head with oil; my cup
  runneth over.
Surely goodness and mercy shall follow
  me all the days of my life: And I will
  dwell in the house of the Lord forever.
—Psalm 23, the Bible, sacred text of Judaism
and Christianity

"Be humble, and you will remain
  entire."
Be bent, and you will remain straight.
Be vacant, and you will remain full.
Be worn, and you will remain new.
He who has little will receive.
He who has much will be embar-
  rassed.
Therefore the sage keeps to One and
  becomes the standard for the world.
—Tao-te-ching, XXII, sacred text of Taoism

Blessed are the poor in spirit: for theirs
  is the kingdom of heaven.
Blessed are they that mourn: for they
  shall be comforted.
Blessed are the meek: for they shall
  inherit the earth.
Blessed are they which do hunger and
  thirst after righteousness: for they
  shall be filled.
Blessed are the merciful: for they shall
  obtain mercy.

Blessed are the pure in heart: for they
  shall see God.
Blessed are the peacemakers: for they
  shall be called the children of God.
—St. Matthew, 5:3, the Bible (New Testament),
sacred text of Christianity

According as a man acts and walks in
the path of life, so he becomes. He that
does good becomes good; he that does
evil becomes evil. By pure actions he
becomes pure; by evil actions he
becomes evil.
—Brihad-aranyaka Upanishad, sacred text of
Hinduism

Do not say, that if people do good to us,
we will do good to them; and if people
oppress us, we will oppress them; but
determine, that if people do you good,
you will do good to them; and if they
oppress you, you will not oppress them.
—The Sunnah of the Prophet (The Sayings of
Muhammad), 195; sacred text of Islam

If a man foolishly does me wrong, I will
return to him the protection of my
ungrudging love; the more evil comes
from him, the more good shall go from
me.
—The Sutra of 42 Sections, sacred text of
Buddhism

You have said to me when I was still
young and could hope, that in difficulty I could send a voice four times,
once for each quarter of the earth, and
you would hear me.
  Today I send a voice for a people in
despair.
  You have given me a sacred pipe,
and through this I should make my
offering. You see it now!
  From the west you have given me
the cup of living water and the sacred
bow, the power to make life and to

destroy it . . . and from the south the nation's sacred hoop and the tree that was to bloom . . . At the center of the sacred hoop you have said that I should make the tree to bloom.

With tears running, O Great Spirit, my Grandfather—with running eyes I must say now that the tree has never bloomed. A pitiful old man, you see me here, and I have fallen away and done nothing. Here at the center of the world, where you took me when I was young and taught me; here, old I stand, and the tree is withered, my Grandfather.

—*The Sacred Pipe, Black Elk's Account of the Seven Rites of the Oglala Sioux,* Black Elk (Hehaka Sapa), Oglala holy man

Walk on!
—last words of Buddha to his disciples

ART & ARCHITECTURE OF THE WORLD

CONTENTS

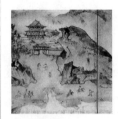

ART AND ARCHITECTURE OF THE WORLD

When we talk about art, we immediately classify it by time or place. We talk about different artistic styles, different movements, different periods. We speak of Eastern art and of Western art, or, more specifically, of Chinese art or European art or African art, or, even *more* specifically, of the art of the Tang dynasty, or the art of the impressionists, and so on.

Clearly we view art in the context of culture and history. By classifying art this way, we see the similarities between different works within the same time period and the same culture—the characteristics they share, the cultural signposts they include, and so forth.

But art, of course, doesn't exist in a cultural vacuum. No culture is hermetically sealed from the rest of the world—and so, the art produced by any culture is inextricably tied to the rest of the world.

In this sense, then, there is a world art—because all art is world art. Yes, there are cultural styles, just as there are historical styles. And naturally, any piece of art is to a great degree the conception of an individual, his or her own unique vision. But there is also cultural cross-fertilization that forges links between the art of different cultures and periods.

Take, for example, printing. The ancient Sumerians invented a form of printing using carved stone seals to make impressions on clay. This technique spread to India, then to China, where it continued to evolve. By the ninth century, the Chinese were using woodblocks to print on paper. Then, finally, in the Middle Ages, artisans in Europe began doing their own woodblock prints.

Japanese woodcut prints of the 1800s had a more direct effect on Western art. When trade between France and Japan opened in 1854, these woodcuts were imported into Paris and became a hot item, winning the appreciation of such noted European artists as Manet, van Gogh, and Toulouse-Lautrec.

Of course, the flow of ideas goes from West to East as well. The Hellenistic empire of Alexander the Great left its marks on a large part of the Eastern world—for example, Buddha statues from Gandhara (now Afghanistan and part of Pakistan) exhibit definite elements of Hellenistic sculptural style.

So to a degree, art is the result of the rise and fall of empires, the onslaught of conquerors, the flow of commerce, even the emergence of new science and technology. In fact, virtually anything and everything that affects a culture affects the art that culture produces. As Mexican writer Octavio Paz said:

An artistic style is a living entity, a continuous process of invention. It can never be imposed from without; born of the profoundest tendencies within a society, its direction is to a certain extent unpredictable, in much the same way as the eventual configuration of a tree's branches.

So you could say that the art of all cultures is interrelated but separate—branches on the same tree. The following chapter, then, gives you examples from the family tree of world art and architecture—different styles, different artistic movements, different forms—all representing different moments in world history.

It covers the West and the East—the most famous artists of the European tradition and the different artistic movements, the art of the ancient civilizations that influenced later art styles, master-pieces from cultures outside of the West, and architectural masterpieces from ancient times to the present.

From the wall paintings in Egyptian tombs to Michelangelo's *David* to the Great Mosque of Córdoba, these different artistic samples are visual manifestations of the thoughts, emotions, and beliefs of different cultures—and of the inevitable links between these different cultures.

A WALK THROUGH THE WORLD MUSEUM OF ART: MASTERPIECES FROM AROUND THE WORLD AND ACROSS THE YEARS

 Picture a huge museum with a number of different wings, each holding masterpieces from a range of artistic traditions—from ancient Egypt to Africa, from ancient Greece to India. That's what we've put together here. We've collected some of the top artistic treasures from around the world and from across the years; we've taken them from the museums of many countries; we've uprooted carvings from temples and statues from churches. Under one roof (or actually, on a few pages), we've exhibited the artwork of centuries, the designs of millions—masterpieces of world art. These masterpieces say more than a textbook could about the

hearts, minds, and sensibilities of people living years ago and continents away from us.

You'll be able to see how specific styles evolved over time, what characteristics were refined as the cultures themselves became more advanced, what elements remained important to a culture over hundreds (even thousands) of years, and so forth.

And, since the art a culture produces mirrors the times and thoughts of the culture itself, by understanding the art these different cultures created, you'll be able to better understand the culture itself. So let's start the tour through the World Museum of Art.

ANCIENT EGYPTIAN WING

THE STYLE

Plato once said that Egyptian art hadn't changed in ten thousand years. Well, Plato was exaggerating—but he wasn't that far off the mark.

Egyptian art isn't the most flexible or spontaneous of styles. From 3000 to 500 B.C.E., ancient Egyptian art did go through changes and adaptations, but the central artistic sensibility and ideas stayed roughly the same. One key concept that ties together many different forms of *existing* ancient Egyptian art: *a connection with death.* From paintings to sculpture, many art forms were chiefly used to honor or serve the dead and were left in necropolises and tombs. Among the art forms found in tombs: tomb wall paintings of scenes from everyday life; sculpted portrait busts of the dead person; small carved figures of servants to serve the ka (an aspect of the soul); painted coffins; the carved stone sarcophagus; sculptures of the deceased that could serve as a home for the ka should the mummy be destroyed or damaged.

The bottom line? Most Egyptian artists and architects were charged with a simple, yet daunting, task: their work had to last not only a lifetime, but an eternity.

MASTERPIECES OF EGYPTIAN ART

Mycerinus and His Queen. Here we see two figures—the king who built the third pyramid at Giza, and his wife. They're immobile, solid, caught in

MYCERINUS AND HIS QUEEN, EGYPT (DYNASTY IV, 2599–1571 B.C.E.), SCHIST, 54½" (HARVARD M.F.A. EXPEDITION. COURTESY MUSEUM OF FINE ARTS, BOSTON)

227

stone for all time. These are typical characteristics of ancient Egyptian statuary. Egyptian sculptors apparently saw the human figure from a "cubist" point of view—which means that figures wind up looking not all that natural. Imposing, yes. Lifelike? Not exactly. Look at how Mycerinus and the queen are standing. Both straight on, shoulders squared, perfect posture, and with the left foot forward—but no one would ever think that they're walking, or that they would ever move at all. Their eyes are blank, their faces devoid of individualism. The king's arms are rigid at his side. His wife has one arm around him, one across her body holding his arm—it's all kind of stiff-looking. But there's a power to the figures that's undeniable. And there certainly was an effort at naturalism. The sheer gown of the queen clings to her body, showing the shape beneath it (something the ancient Greeks weren't able to master for years). Plus, there's a good chance these statues were originally painted, which would make them more lifelike. But ultimately naturalism wasn't the point for these figures. What mattered was the feeling of

HUNTING SCENE (LEFT): FRAGMENT FROM A PAINTING FROM THE TOMB OF NEBAMUN, THEBES, EGYPT (NEW KINGDOM, c. 1390 B.C.E.), PAINT ON PLASTER WALL (BRITISH MUSEUM, LONDON)

POND IN A GARDEN (RIGHT): FRAGMENT FROM A PAINTING FROM THE TOMB OF NEBAMUN, THEBES, EGYPT (NEW KINGDOM, c. 1390 B.C.E.), PAINT ON PLASTER WALL (BRITISH MUSEUM, LONDON)

strength, of power, of almost supernatural serenity, and, yes, of eternity. And in this, the sculptor clearly succeeds.

Pond in a Garden and Hunting Scene. One of the main things you'll notice in these two paintings? Perspective—or rather the *lack* of it.

Found on the walls of the tomb of Nebamun, these two wall paintings are typical of the tomb decorations common to ancient Egypt. In *Pond in a Garden*, the pond is shown from above; fish swimming in the pond are shown in profile; the trees on the side of the pond are painted sideways, but the ones on the bottom of the pond are right side up; and so on. And in *Hunting Scene*, the water is shown in a cross section, so you can see the fish swimming in it; and the boat looks as though it's balanced on top.

It seems confusing and haphazard, but it's actually very logical: Tomb paintings weren't intended as decoration, but as a sort of catalog of supplies for use in the afterlife. In other words, the ka, or soul, would be able to use the objects included in the tomb painting. So artists had to be careful to include virtually anything a person might want, and to be extremely clear in its representation. More often than not, objects are shown in the most easily recognized view possible—and the Renaissance idea of perspective simply doesn't matter.

It's the same with the people in the painting. Nebamun, standing in the middle of his boat, is painted in the typical ancient Egyptian way: head in profile, torso facing front, feet in profile. Clearly not realistic at all, but the easiest way for the artist to get his point across, which is the key in much of ancient Egyptian art. Plus, there's the matter of scale. Nebamun is much larger than his wife (a few steps behind him), who is larger than his daughter (crouched in the boat). This is all a tip-off to the subjects' status. In paintings and bas-reliefs (a form of raised sculpture where the figures protrude from a flat piece of stone), an artist used scale not to reproduce reality, but to indicate relative *importance*. This is called hierarchical scale. So a ruler or noble like Nebamun will tower over everyone else in a bas-relief or painting. (Which may be only fair—after all, it *is* his tomb.)

OTHER MASTERPIECES, OTHER ARTISTS

Imhotep, first recorded artist of Egyptian history, designer of the funerary complex of Sakkara, which includes a step pyramid and a walled necropolis. Imhotep was not only known for his design work, he eventually even reached divine status—becoming the god of learning and medicine.

Most other Egyptian artists remain nameless, but their masterpieces are known: the portrait statue of Chefren

KROISOS (KOUROS FROM ANAVYSOS), GREEK (C. 520 B.C.E.), MARBLE, 72" (NATIONAL ARCHAEOLOGICAL MUSEUM, ATHENS; FOTO MARBURG/ ART RESOURCE, N.Y.)

(Khafre) and the bust of Prince Ankhhaf, both in the Giza necropolis (c. 2500 B.C.E.); the famous limestone bust of Queen Nefertiti (c. 1360 B.C.E.); and the contents of Tutankhamen's tomb (c. 1340 B.C.E.), to name a few.

ANCIENT GREEK WING

THE STYLE

Greek art is progressive art—literally—an evolutionary style that picked up where Egyptian art left off and continued moving toward greater naturalism.

It's difficult to reduce the subject of Greek art to a few lines. So much of what the Greeks did formed the basis for following centuries of art and design. However, there are key concepts that the Greeks either introduced or developed that form the core of the Western tradition. These concepts evolved over time. It's possible to see the development of the different elements in the three distinct styles that span the five-hundred-year Greek period: Archaic, Classical, and the not-so-catchily-named Fourth Century style. (Plus, some scholars also refer to the Severe style, which bridged Archaic and Classical and is really an early Classical style.)

MASTERPIECES OF ANCIENT GREECE

Kroisos. At first glance, you might think this statue is a lot like an ancient Egyptian one—same stance, one foot in front of the other, arms at the figure's side, clenched fists, and rather impersonal facial features. But look again.

You can see muscles. Curves. There's a tension in his stance. It's as if his muscles were tightened and ready to move. Unlike the solid immobility of the Egyptian statues, there is an energy to this piece.

This is a funerary statue of a young man named Kroisos who, according to the inscription on the base, died a hero's death in battle. It is an example of a kouros (youth), common throughout Greece in the Archaic era. (The female counterpart is called a kore—maiden.) These statues were set up at shrines, used as grave monuments and offerings.

And they're great examples of how far the Greeks progressed beyond the Egyptians in terms of representing the human body. The key? Using nature as an artistic model. It sounds obvious, but back in ancient times, it was a real breakthrough. The Greeks realized that to make a statue lifelike they had to understand anatomy, how the bones and muscles worked, and how they would appear in a statue of a person. They also moved past that "block of rock" look of ancient Egyptian statues. This kouros is free of the stone. The space between the legs and between the arms and torso has been cut out. And even though the figures are still a bit primitive, they look less locked in time, and more ready to move. The final touch—a smile, called "the Archaic smile," that was apparently supposed to make them look more lifelike. It actually didn't—it's a kind of strange, otherworldly touch. But it was an effort at making faces look human, and the smile eventually died out after 500 B.C.E., when facial expressions became more truly lifelike.

DORYPHOROS (SPEAR BEARER), ROMAN COPY OF A BRONZE ORIGINAL BY POLYKLEITOS (c. 450 B.C.E.), MARBLE, 6'6" (NATIONAL MUSEUM, NAPLES; ALINARI/ ART RESOURCE, N.Y.)

Doryphoros. Here's the perfect human figure, Classical-style. An ideal of human beauty. In a way, it's the Classical Greek equivalent of a Barbie doll (or, actually, Ken).

The *Doryphoros* is a prime example of Classical-style sculpture and helps illustrate how Greek naturalism evolved. The *Doryphoros* is less than one hundred years younger than the kouros, but in that short time, art moved ahead in leaps and bounds. Notice how he's standing—not that rigid eyes-front, shoulders-back look of the past. Instead, he looks relaxed, his weight resting on the right leg. The muscles in that leg are taut, while those of the left are relaxed. His right arm is relaxed, and his left holds the spear. And maybe you can't tell just by looking at the photograph, but he's perfectly proportioned.

Classical sculptor Polykleitos set forth a system of ideal proportions for the human figure called the Canon, and then constructed this statue, in which the proportions of the figure are fractions of the total height. It all adds up to perfection.

Of course, this attention to proportion wasn't limited to statues. It's a crucial aspect of all Greek arts—from music to architecture. In the visual arts, the goal was to create visual harmony—and (again, involving nature in design) this by following a system of proportions based on the proportions found in nature. The rule of thumb: The size of the smaller part relates to the greater part, just as the greater part relates to the whole. The Greeks called this "the division of a line in extreme and mean proportions," but it's more widely known as the golden section. It gets quite technical, but it typically boiled down to one ratio that sets the relationship between each of the parts of a design, and between the parts to the whole. This one ratio? Five to eight. It's this ratio that the Parthenon is based on, and very possibly the *Doryphoros* as well.

Hermes with the Child Dionysus.

The next leap forward, sculpturally speaking. Praxiteles was the master of Fourth Century (B.C.E.) sculpture—and it shows.

Look how Hermes is standing. Not completely erect, but leaning slightly, his body forming an S-curve (which came to be called the curve of Praxiteles). He's muscular like the *Doryphoros,* but Hermes' muscles look much more real—they're less defined, less like the Incredible Hulk and more like the well-built man next door. His facial expression is also more lifelike than that of earlier statues. He's smiling slightly, a sort of teasing smile. (Art historians think he's smiling because he's dangling grapes just out of the baby's reach, perhaps the act of a teasing father). In fact, the entire statue gives this impression. Yes, it's a statue of a god, but it's a very relaxed, very *human* god. It's all part of the evolution in Greek art from ideal to natural (but still sort of ideal).

HERMES WITH THE CHILD DIONYSUS, GREEK (4TH CENTURY B.C.E.), MARBLE, 7'1" (NATIONAL MUSEUM, NAPLES; ALINARI/ART RESOURCE, N.Y.)

OTHER MASTERPIECES, OTHER ARTISTS

Unfortunately, a huge number of ancient Greek artists remain unidentified, with only their work as evidence of their artistry. But there are those whose names survived. Among them: Exekias (sixth century B.C.E.), known for his black-figure vases (pottery with black figures on a red background), such as *Achilles and Ajax Playing Draughts*; the team of Euphronios (painter) and Euxitheos (potter), who produced red-figure vases, like *Death of Sarpedon During the Trojan War* (c. 515 B.C.E.); Kallikrates and Iktinos (fifth century B.C.E.), architects of the Parthenon; Phideas (and his workshop), sculptors of the pediment and other sculpture for the Parthenon; Lysippus (c. 370), sculptor known for works such as the *Apoxyomenos* (Scraper).

ANCIENT ROMAN WING

THE STYLE

Roman art is really Classical Greek art with a Roman purpose: to glorify the empire.

A quick explanation: First, most of the artists in Rome weren't Romans, but Greeks, imported from Greece from as early as 500 B.C.E. Second, in addition to importing artists, Romans also imported thousands of Greek artworks from earlier periods, and made even more copies of these. Third, often Romans commissioned works from contemporary Greek artists who were also producing works in Greece. In spite of this, there are certain features that distinguish Roman design (even when it was produced by Greeks)—

THE GARDEN (C. 1ST CENTURY B.C.E.), WALL PAINTING IN THE VILLA OF LIVIA, PRIMA PORTA, FRESCO, HEIGHT OF WALL 10' (ALINARI/ART RESOURCE, N.Y.)

and certain works that epitomize the Roman look.

MASTERPIECES OF ANCIENT ROMAN ART

The Garden. Sit in the room that this wall is in and you may feel as though you're really sitting in a garden. Or so the artist intended. This is an example of Roman "illusionism," the style that, logically, is intended to create an illusion—in this case, of a garden. It's refreshing in this case, but over time the style got a bit worky. By the time it evolved into the so-called Fourth Style (which was the hot style in the year Vesuvius erupted—79 C.E.), walls were covered with everything from faux-marble paneling to fake windows; there even were ornate make-believe frames painted around different scenes.

Equestrian Statue of the Emperor Marcus Aurelius. This is the kind of statue you often see in the center of a park—the all-conquering hero on his horse. In this case, it's Roman emperor Marcus Aurelius who has been frozen in time, the image of a victorious ruler. It's not the style that's important about this piece (which is similar to classical Greek statues—possibly because Marcus Aurelius himself was an admirer of the Greeks); it's the subject matter. Unlike the Greeks, who used idealistic subjects in their friezes, reliefs, and statues, the Romans were much more prone to toot their own (or their leaders') horns in their artwork.

This is quite an imposing piece. It's literally larger than life. Marcus Aurelius is shown controlling his lively mount. According to scholars, to really send home the image of victory, there probably originally was a bound barbar-

EQUESTRIAN STATUE OF MARCUS AURELIUS, PIAZZA DEL CAMPIDOGLIO, ROME (c. 160–180 C.E.), BRONZE, OVER LIFE SIZE (ALINARI/ART RESOURCE, N.Y.)

ian under the raised hoof of the horse. But because Marcus Aurelius saw himself not as a conqueror but as a keeper (and bringer) of peace, he's not wearing armor, not carrying weapons, and his face is actually pretty detached. It's a fine example of the bronze equestrian statues that were the vogue for years in imperial Rome—and, in fact, is the only one still existing. But there are other types of commemorative monuments intact, among them: altars, usually covered with friezes (like the Ara Pacis [Altar of Peace], built to honor Augustus), and freestanding columns, sometimes topped with statues and usually covered with reliefs (such as the 125-foot Column of Trajan, c. 106–113). Finally, an extremely popular mode—the *arcus triumphalis,* or triumphal arch (an arch within a rectangle) built to memorialize a particularly important victory (like the Arch of Titus, built to commemorate Titus's conquest of Jerusalem in 70–71). These were so popular that at one time there were over fifty standing in Rome—and many can still be seen in the modern city.

The guiding thought behind all these pieces: Instead of creating art for art's sake, why not let the world (and posterity) know what the Romans had achieved?

Colossal Head of Constantine.

When this statue was whole, it stood in the ancient Roman Basilica of Constantine—or rather *towered.* These marble fragments are from what clearly was a huge statue—probably about thirty feet tall. The head alone is eight and a half feet tall. Because so much of Roman art and design was intended to exalt the empire and/or the emperor, the general rule of thumb seems to have been "The bigger the better." Modesty wasn't an issue; grandeur was.

But there's more to these fragments than size. Look closely at the face. It's not the typical superrealistic portrait you might expect. It's much more impressionistic, even abstract. Yes, some of the features are clearly realistic depictions of Constantine's face (judging by comparisons to other portraits of him)—his nose, for example, and his thick neck. But the hair, the huge eyes, the immobility of expression are abstract. And for all the abstraction, the statue comes closer to giving the viewer a real feel for Constantine, the first

COLOSSAL HEAD OF CONSTANTINE (EARLY 4TH CENTURY), MARBLE, 8' (CAPITOLINE MUSEUMS, ROME; SCALA/ART RESOURCE, N.Y.)

Christian emperor of Rome, than a technically realistic sculpture. By not sculpting Constantine as he actually looked, the unknown artist is portraying him as he actually was *seen*: as an exalted leader, with both absolute spiritual and political power, almost like a Roman Superman.

OTHER MASTERPIECES, OTHER ARTISTS

As with the ancient Greeks, many of the names of Roman (or Greek) artists have been lost over time; here, then, is a brief rundown of some of the masterpieces these nameless artists produced: *The Bacchic Mysteries,* wall fresco in the so-called Villa of the Mysteries, Pompeii (c. 30 B.C.E.) as well as numerous other wall paintings in Pompeii and Herculaneum; *Aulus Metellus,* bronze statue (early 1st century); *Augustus of Prima Porta,* marble statue of the emperor Augustus in the Vatican Museums (c. 20 B.C.E.); numerous life-size marble portrait heads including *Portrait of a Lady* (c. 90 C.E.), *Vespasian* (c. 75 C.E.), *Trajan* (c. 100 C.E.), *Phillipus the Arab* (c. 244 C.E.)

CHINESE WING

THE STYLE

Chinese art in a nutshell? It's usually a depiction of nature or the Buddha, or decorative work—with a distinctly philosophical undertone.

Actually, when you talk about Chinese art, you're talking about many different arts—the art of the Tang dynasty or the art of the Ming dynasty, for example. Remember, the culture that produced what is considered traditional Chinese art spans hundreds of centuries. Moreover, there are many different types of Chinese art, from lacquerware to landscape paintings, Buddha sculptures to

STANDING BUDDHA, CHINESE (NORTHERN WEI DYNASTY, 5TH CENTURY C.E.), GILT BRONZE, 55¼" (THE METROPOLITAN MUSEUM OF ART, NEW YORK CITY, KENNEDY FUND, 1926 [26.123])

porcelain vases. But these different media share certain uniquely Chinese characteristics of artistic expression.

MASTERPIECES OF CHINESE ART

Standing Buddha. This Buddha is like many others from the late fifth and early sixth centuries. He's tall and slim, elongated in somewhat the manner of an El Greco figure. His face wears an ethereal, otherworldly expression. The effect is one of calm serenity.

This image is a good example of how depictions of the Buddha evolved in China. The artwork mirrored the spread of the religion itself. Later Buddhas are superaesthetic and less spiritual—often highly colored, covered in gilt, essentially baroque ornaments. But this Buddha and others like it represent Buddhism when it was a strong spiritual force. Created when the emperors of the Wei dynasty, who were active Buddhists, reigned, it represents a pure, spiritual vision of the Buddha. The characteristic serene smile, the appearance of inner thought—it all adds up to the force of Buddhism at the time.

A Solitary Temple Amid Clearing Peaks. First notice the color—or the lack of it. All the better to show off each line. Next, pay attention to the details. You'll notice that we see not only trees as they appear, but also the parts we can't normally see—the roots, the inner skeleton, buds that aren't ready to bloom, and so forth. This isn't your average

A SOLITARY TEMPLE AMID CLEARING PEAKS, ATTRIBUTED TO
LI CHENG, CHINESE (NORTHERN SUNG DYNASTY, 919–967
C.E.), HANGING SCROLL, INK AND COLOR ON SILK, 44" X
22" (THE NELSON-ATKINS MUSEUM OF ART, KANSAS CITY,
MISSOURI [PURCHASE: NELSON TRUST 47–71])

landscape by Western standards. Li Cheng, like so many other Chinese artists, is painting not simply nature as it appears, but the essence of nature—which requires getting to the force underlying nature, the *chi*.

Yes, there is realism here—you can see the detail in all the buildings, the peasants eating in the inn, people in the pavilions. But it's not a naturalistic representation; it's the inner reality of nature that's expressed.

This is part of the whole intellectual or spiritual approach to art that makes Chinese painting so different from Western. It's not specific to a religion, but rather part of all of the Chinese religions—from Buddhism to Taoism to Confucianism. It was spelled out in the different guidelines to painting that were passed down. In the late fifth century, painter Xie He wrote the six principles that constituted a good painting: (1) spirit consonance and life movement—that is, recognizing and attuning oneself to the natural energy underlying the universe; (2) structural power in use of brush—transmitting natural energy through dynamic brushwork; (3), (4), and (5) upholding the visual truth of nature—through fidelity to the object, correct color, and proper placement and disposition; and, finally (6) transmission of the ancient masters, through copying or imitating their works. And in the late sixth century, painter Ching Hao laid out his six essentials: spirit, rhythm, thought, scenery, brush, ink.

The other key difference between a landscape like this and a Western one is the shifting perspective. With this and other scroll paintings, as the scroll is unrolled, your perspective shifts. You can look at this painting from different perspectives—in fact, you're encour-

沿谿四十九迴折
搜書秦淮六
代奇雪霽峯
山誰著

硯屏
雜自戲
詩憲儀

阿誰長吞伴
其剩樣手只幾
鈇滿地藤花春
未勺酸心如豆耐人思
仲賓毛生以字紙八幅寧

平真州命画圈憶苦時秦
淮探梅飛有三地寫傳就教
清湘石濤濟道人

Boat Descending the Rapids. Here is a cross between expressionism and calligraphy. Notice the Chinese characters in the upper left corner. This is an example of "literary painting," in which the poem or words are as much a part of the work as the painting itself. But aside from the characters, the painting itself reminds the viewer of calligraphy. The black shapes and strong brushstrokes are similar in spirit to Chinese characters on a scroll. It's a strong, simple style that broke away from the growing refinement and academic quality of Chinese painting at the time. As the artist Shih-tao once said, "The best method is that which has never been a method." He and two other painters, Chu Ta and Shih-chi, were considered the Individualists, artists who broke with tradition and made their own rules. And, while they founded no school, theirs was the last major development in Chinese painting until the twentieth century.

OTHER MASTERPIECES, OTHER ARTISTS

Wang Wei (699–759), a poet and artist known for his monochromatic landscapes (called the master of the Southern School); Chang Hsüan and Chou Fang (c. 700–800), known for their

aged to by the artist. Your eyes start at the lower left corner, and they keep moving—across the bridge, down at the rooftops, up to the temple, beyond to the peaks. You're visually walking through the scene Li Cheng painted. You're there, a participant rather than an observer. The bottom line: the Chinese artist assumes the viewer is in the picture, part of nature; the Western assumes the viewer is outside, looking in.

REMINISCENCES OF THE QIN-HUAI RIVER BY DAOJI (1642–1707), CHINESE, QING DYNASTY, INK AND LIGHT COLOR ON PAPER, 25.5 x 20.2 CM (© THE CLEVELAND MUSEUM OF ART, JOHN L. SEVERANCE FUND, 66.31) court paintings; Huang Ch'üan (c. 1000–1100), known for animal paintings; Huang Kung-wang (1269–1354), Wu Chen (1280–1354), Ni Tsan (1301–74), Wang Meng (1309–85), the four great Yuan masters known for their landscapes; Hsüan Te (c. 1400–1500), Ming ceramics (especially known for work in blue and white), as was Ch'eng Hua period (1400–1500); Guo Xi (c. 1000–1100), a student of Li Cheng's and a scroll painter in a similar style, known for works such as *Early Spring*.

JAPANESE WING

THE STYLE

Japanese art was born of foreign parents—namely the Chinese (and, to a lesser degree, the Koreans), who set-

FIRST ILLUSTRATION TO THE "AZUMAYA" CHAPTER OF "THE TALE OF GENJI," ATTRIBUTED TO TAKAYOSHI, JAPANESE (LATE HEIAN PERIOD, c. 1000–1100), HAND SCROLL, INK AND COLOR ON PAPER, 8 1/2" (TOKUGAWA ART MUSEAM, NAGOYA, JAPAN)

tled in the Japanese islands at the end of the fifth century. They brought with them certain cultural techniques, such as metal casting, silkworm production, and calligraphy, which were picked up by the indigenous Japanese and became the foundation of Japanese art and design.

So, yes, the Japanese got much of their arts and design ideas from the Chinese. But it's not a case of the Romans and the Greeks again. Instead of just copying the Chinese style, the Japanese took it and changed it, ending up with something *yamoto-e,* quintessentially Japanese.

MASTERPIECES OF JAPANESE ART

***First Illustration to the "Azumaya" Chapter of* The Tale of Genji.** Here you have a bird's-eye view, literally. You're in the air, looking down into the interiors of roofless houses and buildings.

"Landscape of the Four Seasons," by Sesson Shūkei, Japanese (Muromachi Period, 2nd Half of 16th Century), Ink and Light Color on Paper, 156.8 x 337.8 cm (Photograph © 1995, The Art Institute of Chicago, All Rights Reserved, Gift of the Joseph and Helen Regenstein Foundation, 1958, 1958.168)

This is just one example of how the Japanese opted for subjectivism, instead of strict realism. You could almost call it an Eastern form of impressionism. Instead of going the hyperrealistic route of the Chinese, Japanese paintings are more idealistic, more imaginative. This style (called *yamato-e*) emerged in roughly 1000 and is both the first purely secular art and the style most recognizably Japanese. The subjects vary, but often they're narratives of someone's life, scenes of court life, historical epics, or the like. And unlike the Chinese, who usually focused on the immensity of nature, a lot of Japanese paintings focus on people; the natural landscape is just the backdrop. But the key isn't the subject matter as much as the style. It's atmospheric work, often with bright colors and always with clean lines—vigorous, stripped down, and extremely evocative. The artist wants

to get his or her point across, and reality takes a backseat.

Landscape of the Four Seasons. A monochromatic landscape, with very simple lines, lots of blank space, asymmetrical composition, and washes used to blur certain lines or to suggest subject matter.

This is an example of artist Sesson Shūkei at the top of his form. Known for his masterful suiboku technique (india ink wash, such as this), he uses detailed brushwork to show pine needles, yet leaves much of the rest of the landscape very simple—just hints of what is there. (Later, his work became even simpler—what he called the haboku, or "flung ink," technique looks a lot like modern abstract art.) So *Landscape of the Four Seasons* is actually a boiled-down version of a scene—the basics, if you will. And the viewer has to fill in the missing elements.

It's a lot like being in a Japanese Zen garden—with its rocks, raked sand, perhaps some water. Stillness. Serenity. The goal—harmony of the spirits and the senses. This feeling comes through in this painting and in other examples of Japanese art and design of this period. Unlike other Japanese paintings, paintings such as this one and other Zen-inspired works inspire contemplation. They're not intended to show the viewer a scene as much as to evoke something in you. The Zen influence on the arts grew with the spread of Zen philosophy through Japan, beginning in the late 1300s. Zen teaches that truth is reached through an intuitive leap, a flash of enlightenment—and the art produced in line with Zen thought mirrors this concept.

Women at Koto Practice, from the series "Eight Parlor Views," and Waterfall at Ono. Think of these as Japanese posters. Strong, clean images, forceful graphics, and uncomplicated subjects. In fact, at the beginning, the subjects were theatrical in nature—theater people, scenes from plays and Kabuki drama, courtesans, and the like.

Both are examples of woodblock prints, the hottest Japanese art form from the seventeenth to the nineteenth centuries. They were called ukiyo-e—pictures of the floating world—and were art for (and often by) the common people. As such, they weren't considered "real" art—until Europeans discovered them in the late 1800s.

Women at Koto Practice is an example of this extremely popular type of print. The scene itself is graceful and appealing. In addition, soft pastel colors were used. They're not only appeal-

WOMEN AT KOTO PRACTICE BY SUZUKI HARUNOBU (18TH CENTURY), JAPANESE FULL-COLOR PRINT (PHOTOGRAPH © 1995, THE ART INSTITUTE OF CHICAGO, ALL RIGHTS RESERVED)

ing and enhance the graceful qualities of the scene; they also mark a breakthrough in woodblock printmaking. Harunobu invented a polychrome process that made sophisticated full-color prints (nishiki-e) possible. Before them, it was black-and-white, or, a bit later, three-color prints (benizuri-e).

Artist Katsushika Hokusai is responsible for another type of breakthrough in prints. Instead of sticking with the dramatic, he focused on landscapes, and made them every bit as sophisticated and graphically appealing as the previously popular portraits and city scenes, if not more so. *Water-*

fall at Ono is sort of like pop art of the time. It's graphically strong, with bold images and clear, high-contrast outlines.

OTHER MASTERPIECES, OTHER ARTISTS

Scrolls of *Animal Caricatures,* satirical cartoons, attributed to the priest Toba Sōjō, portrait artist Takanobu Fujiwara (1142–1205), known for vivid character studies such as the portrait *Minamoto no Yoritomo;* the great painters of the Muromachi period (fifteenth century)

included Noami Shūbun (1397–1471), his son Geriami (1431–85), and *his* son Sōami (1472–1506); *Irises,* by Ōgata Korin (1639–1716); Yosa Buson (also a poet) (1716–1783); Kitagawa Utamaro (1753–1806), famous for his portraits of women, such as *Melancholy Love.*

INDIAN WING

THE STYLE

Religious expression first, artistic impression second.

Much of Indian traditional art focuses on the religious more than the artistic. In other words, the goal of the artist isn't to create a work of art as much as to pay homage to a god or a religion or to shed light on the spiritual world. The religion varies—it may be Buddhism, Jainism, or Hinduism. But the emphasis on veneration tends to remain the same. The works, then, speak of the spiritual more than the physical, the realm of the ideal more than the actual. It's as if they're mutely speaking a sacred language in which abstract forms are the words, and the complete piece is a statement about the religion.

The bottom line? Spiritual expression takes precedence over strict realism, and religion takes precedence over simple observation.

MASTERPIECES OF INDIAN ART

Lion Capital from the Pillar of Asoka. This relic from ancient India was erected under the rule of King Asoka, the first Buddhist ruler of India,

LION CAPITAL FROM THE PILLAR OF ASOKA (242–232 B.C.E.),
7', ORIGINALLY STOOD IN THE DEER PARK AT SARNATH,
INDIA (ARCHEOLOGICAL MUSEUM, SARNATH, INDIA;
LAUROS-GIRAUDON/ART RESOURCE, N.Y.)

and is a good example of the intertwining of art and religion. The large pillar on which this capital rested stood in the Deer Park at Sarnath, where the Buddha first preached the Eightfold Path to Salvation. An ardent Buddhist, Asoka was eager to show his support for the religion, educate his people about it, and encourage them to follow the Way of the Buddha, so he built monuments at various historical sites important to the life of Buddha. Of course, not only the sites were connected to Buddhism. The capital itself is heavy on Buddhist images. One you can't see, since it's now missing: the huge wheel that was originally on top of the four lions and that symbolized the notion of dharma, Buddha's law.

Interestingly, though, this piece speaks of Asoka himself—or more precisely, his imperial leanings—not just his religious bent. When you look at this piece, you may be reminded somewhat of Persian artifacts, and for good reason, as King Asoka was big on things Persian. But since it's combined with specific Buddhist iconography, it winds up being a visual example of the imperial style of Asoka: a blend of the foreign and the indigenous, the outer world and the inner.

Standing Buddha from Sultanganji, Bihar.
The immediate impression of this piece? A Buddha who isn't a man, but a god. All aspects have been stylized. His physique has no visible muscles; his posture is completely static; his face is a serene, smiling mask. He appears to be caught in time, caught in copper, in an eternity of reflection.

The overwhelming characteristic of this piece is its lack of naturalism. According to some sources, the artists

STANDING
BUDDHA FROM
SULTANGANJI,
BIHAR, INDIA,
GUPTA (c. 500),
COPPER, 7'6"
(CITY MUSEUM
AND ART
GALLERY,
BIRMINGHAM,
ENGLAND)

of this period followed specific rules when portraying something sacred. In fact, instead of copying the human form, they were supposed to take their inspiration from more perfect shapes. For example, eyes were supposed to be the shape of a lotus petal, the head of an egg, and so forth. So even while this Buddha is human in shape, he's really not. He's perfect, a composite of perfect objects on earth. The outcome, then, is a powerful religious statement conveying the spiritual teachings of the Buddha.

Siva Nataraja (Lord of the Dance). One of the most famous Indian images, this is one representation of the Brahmanic god Siva dancing the eternal dance—that is, God's endless destruction and reconstruction of the world. The entire sculpture is ripe with symbols: Siva's hands are in different positions, signifying different aspects of his power; the skins of the tiger and the cobra cover his body, signifying his victory over the rishis; and, signifying the river Ganges that he gave to humanity, the goddess Ganga is in his hair.

This is one of many dancing Siva figures, most of them similar, or at least with similar elements (the wheel, the symbols, etc.). And, yet again, it's easy to see that this is more a religious reminder than a work of art—a sacred symbol that is meant to serve as a focusing point for the viewer.

The Child Krishna Crying for the Moon. Clear bright colors. Clean sharp lines. And a story being told. This is yet another religious piece, and it's representative of many Hindu paintings. In contrast to the supernatural air of the Buddhist style, this

NATARAJA: SIVA AS KING OF DANCE, SOUTH INDIA (11TH CENTURY), BRONZE (© THE CLEVELAND MUSEUM OF ART, PURCHASE FROM THE J. H. WADE FUND, 30.331)

painting is romantic in tone. It's more an illustration of an event than a timeless image. Notice the details: the woman holding young Krishna, the reflection of the moon in the pool, the other women bending toward the child. Without knowing the exact story, you can figure out what's going on. The emphasis, clearly, is on communicating an instant in Krishna's life. Even while Krishna is a god, you're not seeing him as Krishna the never-changing, you're seeing him as Krishna the child. It's a snapshot of a god's life—and the culmination of different styles of Indian painting.

OTHER MASTERPIECES, OTHER ARTISTS

Though we don't know the artists, there are many masterpieces of Indian art existing—among them: *Seated Buddha* from Gandhara (c. 200–300 C.E.), a thirty-six-inch figure; *Descent of the*

Ganges (c. 600–700), a huge bas-relief on the east coast of India, marked by life-size figures all supposedly emerging from Maya (the force underlying the universe); *The Beautiful Bodhisattva Padmapani* (c. 600–642), a wall painting in Cave No. 1, Ajanta, India.

THE CHILD KRISHNA REACHING FOR THE MOON, INDIAN (THE GULER-KANGRA SCHOOL, c. 1820), PAINTING (© THE CLEVELAND MUSEUM OF ART, ARTHUR R. AND MARTHA HOLDEN JENNINGS FUND)

ISLAMIC WING

THE STYLE

You might think a specific Islamic art style would be difficult to pinpoint. After all, the Islamic empire lasted thirteen centuries and spanned several countries, including Egypt, Spain, the Middle East, India, and areas of North Africa. There were different dynasties, such as the Umayyads, the Abbasids, and different empires such as the Seljuk and the Ottoman. So, on one hand, someone could argue that there isn't one single Islamic art style, but many styles gathered under an umbrella term—Persian and Indo-Persian art, Arabic and Turkish and Spanish Moorish, and so on.

Yet a singular Islamic style *does* exist, for all the slight differences, an art that springs from one civilization. The unifying factor? The religion of Islam, of course. For all the differences in time and style, each of these individual art forms has belief in Islam—and thus, a centralized system of beliefs, both religious and political—at its center.

MASTERPIECES OF ISLAMIC ART

Carved wooden doors inside the Great Mosque, Kairouan, Tunisia. Intricate carvings, almost like wooden lace, cover the doors. It's a masterpiece of craftsmanship, with a rich variety of complex designs playing off of one another. Because the Islamic faith of the time didn't allow figurative representations of God or his prophets, the designs show no people, no important religious moments, no icons, no images

CARVED WOODEN DOORS INSIDE THE GREAT MOSQUE, KAIROUAN, TUNISIA (c. 862) (COURTESY THE TUNISIAN INFORMATION OFFICE)

fruits from different plants, different leaves, even different trees all growing from the same main tree. Branches grow into sharp, geometric shapes. Images change in the middle of the panel into something completely different. There's an energy in this sometimes confusing but always eye-gripping, imaginative mix, and it sets the stage for later carvings found in such places as the Great Mosque of Córdoba, Spain.

Illuminated Page from a Quran. The holy book of Islam, the Quran, was the perfect canvas for a calligrapher's disciplined imagination. Look at the mazelike lines intertwining, surrounding different geometric and floral designs. Even the painted edges of the page are part of the overall design. Calligraphy was the only art form allowed in the Quran. Islam prohibits illustrations in the book itself. So calligraphers had to take Arabic script and raise it to an art form. In this case, Ibn al-Bawwab, a master of calligraphy, took the traditional illumination a step forward from where it had been in the past. Earlier, designs were usually smaller, a central pattern on a page. But in this example, he covers the entire page, and gives it an energy through the composition. Layout makes the work almost three-dimensional; the designs seem to leap off the page. The result: it's almost like modern abstract art—design for design's sake—but in this case it's actually design for the glory of the word of God.

The Ascension of Muhammad. A scene of an important moment in Islam—yet there's a distinct Chinese flavor to it. Examine the faces of the

comparable to those of the Buddhist or Christian traditions. Instead, it's pure design—abstract florals and geometrics. This is a newly developed style that emerged during the Arab Abbasid dynasty. Until this point, most mosque carvings were based on somewhat lifelike designs of nature—that is, they showed flowers, leaves, and the like. But when these panels were carved, artisans were developing a new style—abstract, not naturalistic. It's almost like a fantasy. On one panel, you'll see

angels, their costumes. There's a definite Chinese look to them. And other less obvious elements look Chinese as well, like the flames behind Muhammad's head.

Why the Chinese influence? Because it was produced after the Mongol invasion of Persia. When the Mongols converted to Islam, they brought to it their own sensibilities and ideas, fostered by association with China. Thus, much of the art of this period (considered the point when the golden age of Persian painting began) is heavily colored with Chinese technique.

But it's not only in the design that you can see the Chinese influence, but also in the subject matter. Until this time, Islamic rulers stuck with the rule that artists couldn't represent religious figures in their work. But the Mongol rulers were used to the Buddhist tradition, in which the art is filled with depictions of Buddha. The upshot? Persian artists were free under Mongol rule to paint Muhammad and other religious figures.

Since there had been no tradition of this before in Islamic art, artists borrowed from Buddhist and Christian

ILLUMINATED PAGE FROM A QURAN, COPIED BY IBN AL-BAWWAB (c. 1000), ISLAMIC, BAGHDAD, IRAQ (REPRODUCED BY KIND PERMISSION OF THE TRUSTEES OF THE CHESTER BEATTY LIBRARY, DURHAM, ENGLAND)

THE ASCENSION OF MUHAMMAD (1539–43, OR 2265 F. 195R), ILLUMINATION IN A PERSIAN MANUSCRIPT (BY PERMISSION OF THE BRITISH LIBRARY, LONDON)

art. In this piece, you can see the touch of Christian medieval art in the composition—it's reminiscent of contemporary Christian pieces, with the host of angels filling the page, the energy in their movements, and other familiar features. So this piece, as definitely Islamic as it is in content, is also a blend of the techniques of two *other* religions: Buddhism and Christianity.

OTHER MASTERPIECES, OTHER ARTISTS

The interiors of most of the great mosques are examples of Islamic art at its finest—among them: the Great Mosque of Córdoba, Spain (see page 288 for more); the Mosque of Ahmed I in Istanbul, Turkey; the Great Mosque in Damascus, Syria; and more. Illuminated manuscripts are another form of Islamic art, and include the Arabic translation of Dioscorides's *De Materia Medica* and illustrations in the *Maqamat* of Hariri; also illuminations of the Quran—in all cases, the specific artists are unknown.

AFRICAN WING

THE STYLE

Ceremonial, ritualistic, and political art, to a great extent—that is, art with a purpose.

African art is yet another case where a range of different styles exist, but with common threads. First, it's important to note the many different peoples and cultures that have existed in Africa, thus the many different types of creative output. For example, there are wide differences between the

HEAD OF QUEEN OLOKUN, IFE, NIGERIA (11TH–15TH CENTURIES), CLAY AND BRASS SCULPTURE, 36" (BRITISH MUSEUM, LONDON)

sophisticated art of Ife or Benin, and that of the Congo or the Dogon.

Nevertheless, there are common characteristics. Chief among these is the *intention* of the artwork. As with that of India and other cultures, much of traditional African art is linked with religion. Along these lines, you'll find a great number of pieces specifically intended for use in ceremony or ritual: masks, effigies, and the like. In addition, a large number of works were created to honor rulers (as in Roman art)—which means a high number of portrait busts, thrones and chairs, decorated cloths, and other items.

So, for all the differences, much of traditional African art revolves around paying homage—to gods and ancestors, and to rulers. The methods and the materials vary, but the message is often the same.

MASTERPIECES OF AFRICAN ART

Head of Queen Olokun. A regal head, with a face at once idealized and realistic. This is a prime example of portrait sculpture from an area in what is now southwestern Nigeria. While the facial features are somewhat regular and so give you the impression of an ideal face, there's an undeniable realism to this head. You feel as though you are seeing an actual person—one who has been idealized, but one who retains her individuality. In fact, other sculptures from this area and time were equally realistic; some even had holes around the chin and mouth where a beard and mustache were probably attached.

Interestingly, the naturalism of this and other Ife pieces seems unique both to the time and place. Most scholars date these works roughly from

ALTAR HEAD, BENIN; EDO (c. 1600–1700), COPPER AND IRON SCULPTURE, 8³/₄" (NATIONAL MUSEUM OF AFRICAN ART, SMITHSONIAN INSTITUTION, WASHINGTON, D.C.)

the eleventh to the fifteenth century, leaning to the middle of the period. And during this time, in most other areas, even in Europe, naturalistic representations were rare, if not nonexistent. The upshot—Ife heads like this are considered not only the height of African metal sculpture, but also among the first examples of artistic naturalism in sculpture.

Altar Head. This head is from a later date than the one on the previous page and is a direct descendant of the Ife sculptures. In the late thirteenth century, a king of Benin (which was southeast of Ife) had Ife-style sculpture

Benin: An African Florence

Details are sketchy about how Benin began and, for that matter, how exactly it declined. But there's no doubt that in its heyday it was one of the most sophisticated and influential African kingdoms. It emerged in the fifteenth century and was apparently the site of numerous power struggles between the king, or oba, and the nobility of the area, such as village chiefs. Eventually, the position of oba became an exalted one, evolving from a warrior kingship to a spiritual one, and the region stabilized and grew. During its golden years, in the late sixteenth century, Benin appears to have been an extremely sophisticated and well-developed society. European visitors to its capital, Benin City, commented on how well run it was (the cleanliness of the streets, the lack of beggars, and the nonexistence of theft, due to good public security) and on its physical beauty (an elaborate palace, large well-designed houses with verandas and balustrades, and wide avenues).

introduced to his people. And from then until the nineteenth century, artists in Benin followed the edict and produced numerous metal sculptures in the Ife style—meant to be court art, or art designed in honor of the rulers.

When you look at this head, which is representative of so many works from Benin, you can see the resemblance to the Ife head—but you can also see the difference. The key one? This head is not nearly as realistic. Somewhere along the line, the naturalism that characterizes the Ife sculpture fell by the wayside. Look at the facial features. They are regular, smooth, almost abstract. The eyes, the lips, even the nose, are reduced to clean, geometric, nonnaturalistic forms. Then look at the necklace and hair. They're also regular

and geometric, but much more detailed than the face. You can see each coil in the bead necklace, the intricate braids in the hair. The result of this juxtaposition of abstract and detailed? This is probably intended to be the head of an individual king, yet by virtue of the idealized features, it is more an image of all kings—the office, rather than the individual, is emphasized. In effect, it's a portrait not of a specific ruler as much as a portrait of *all* rulers.

OTHER MASTERPIECES, OTHER ARTISTS

Most African art isn't attributed to an individual artist. This is the case largely because artistic styles are broad—that is, styles are specific to a group, a people, more than to an individual.

THE GREAT MOVEMENTS IN WESTERN ART:
THE STYLES, THE INSPIRATIONS, AND THE LEADING ARTISTS

 Instead of looking at major themes and design elements of Western art through individual masterpieces, it's easier to look at it through *time*. Different movements in Western art spawned specific styles—for a period of time. Then it was on to a *new* style, which either built upon the last or emerged as a reaction to it. Within these different movements, you can see distinct artistic styles, elements, and motifs. Often these disappear for hundreds of years, only to resurface when a new movement starts.

So the simplest way of getting a handle on Western art is to understand the great movements in art. This chart runs through the major movements, what the movement was intended to do, and who the greatest artists of these movements were.

It starts with the Renaissance for a very simple reason: until this point, most artworks weren't signed, so it's almost impossible to name specific artists. Moreover, pre-Renaissance art tends to be church-related. But with the coming of the Renaissance there arose a new artistic mood in which art *wasn't* tied to religion. And since the Renaissance, a number of different art movements have emerged, peaked, and, yes, died—as tastes have changed, problems of technique have been overcome, and culture has moved ahead. The more famous distinct styles have emerged, then, as a response to what was happening in the world.

This chart isn't intended to cover

every artist or every artistic movement. That would take many pages—and even then it would probably be incomplete. Instead, it's intended to give you a quick thumbnail sketch of the major art movements in Europe and the artists who best represent those movements.

A few explanatory notes: You'll see that there is a great deal of overlapping in time. That's because few artistic styles existed in isolation. Usually, different styles would coexist, with different artists following one style or another. You'll also note that some of the greatest artists in the world aren't included in this chart—and for good reason. Several artists were such individualists that their style defies classification. Yes, they painted or sculpted in the *time* that the realist school dominated, or the romantic. But their work stood apart. One of the best examples? Francisco Goya, who is discussed on page 263. He painted during the romantic and realist periods—but his work can't be pigeonholed in either style. Instead it is, well, just Goya. You'll also see that some artists are listed under a movement that just doesn't seem right. The best example of this is Manet. Most people automatically think of him as an impressionist. And, yes, he *inspired* the impressionists, but he wasn't really one; he was more of a realist. On the flip side, you'll find Edgar Degas listed as an impressionist, even though he considered himself an independent or, if pushed to classify himself, a realist. But his work embodies so much of the impressionist style that we've decided to include him among the other impressionists. Finally, you'll notice that some art movements (particularly some of the twentieth century) aren't listed. In some cases, this is because the movement was tiny—like Dada, which really involved only Hans Arp and one or two other artists and lasted only a short time. In other cases, it's because the key proponents of the styles (such as abstract expressionism or pop art) are American, so they aren't covered in this book. In addition, in recent years artistic movements are less of a force among artists. It seems that, lately, individualism has become the most popular artistic movement of all.

EARLY RENAISSANCE

(14th and 15th centuries)

WHAT IT WAS ABOUT:

The beginning of the "rebirth" of the arts and sciences—rediscovering the classical and uniting it with the natural. A focus on techniques, in particular. Using natural observation to understand the world and the principles underlying nature, then translating this to art. A key concern: figuring out how to re-create three-dimensional reality in two dimensions.

LEADING ARTISTS:

Giotto di Bondone (1266–1337), Italian painter and architect (see page 258)

Lorenzo Ghiberti (1378–1455), Italian sculptor

Donatello (Donato di Niccolò di Betto Bardi) (c. 1382–1466), Italian sculptor

Jan van Eyck (c. 1385–1441), Flemish painter

Fra Angelico (Giovanni da Fiesole) (1387–1455), Italian Dominican monk and painter

Rogier van der Weyden (1399–1464), Flemish painter

Petrus Christus (c. 1395–1472), Flemish painter

Piero della Francesca (c. 1420–1492), Italian painter

Fra Filippo Lippi (1406–1469), Italian painter

Sandro Botticelli (1447–1510), Italian painter

Masaccio (Tomasso di Giovanni di Simone Guidi) (1401–1428), Florentine fresco painter

HIGH RENAISSANCE

(early 16th century)

WHAT IT WAS ABOUT:

The main goal? The harmony of all parts, instead of focusing on technical problems, as in the past.

LEADING ARTISTS:

Giovanni Bellini (c. 1430–1516), Venetian painter

Leonardo da Vinci (1452–1519), Italian painter, sculptor, and architect (see page 259)

Hieronymus Bosch (also known as Jerome van Aken) (c. 1450–1516, Dutch painter

Albrecht Dürer (1471–1528), German painter and engraver

Giorgione (Giorgio da Castelfranco) (1478–1511), Venetian painter

Titian (Tiziano Vecellio) (1477–1576), Venetian painter

Raphael (Raffaello Sanzio) (1483–1520), Italian painter

Michelangelo (Michelangelo di Lodovico Buonarroti Simoni) (1475–1564), Florentine painter, architect, and sculptor (see page 260)

Matthias Grünewald (Mathis Gothardt Nithardt) (c. 1480–1528), German painter

Hans Holbein the Younger (1497–1543), German painter

MANNERISM

(16th and early 17th centuries)

WHAT IT WAS ABOUT:

The name came from the Italian *maniera*, meaning "sophisticated, refined style," and the art produced in this period was in just such a style. The emphasis on complexity instead of simplicity, an artificial sophistication instead of naturalism. The artist's goal? To impress the viewer (or the patron) with technique, and to engage both the eye and the mind.

LEADING ARTISTS:

Tintoretto (Jacopo Robusti) (1518–1594), Venetian painter

El Greco (Doménikos Theotokópoulos) (1541–1614), Greek-born painter who lived in Spain (see page 261)

Antonio Allegri da Correggio (1489?–1534), Italian painter

Il Bronzino (Agnolo di Cosimo) (1502–1572), Florentine painter

Paolo Veronese (Paolo Caliari) (c. 1528–1588), Venetian painter

Pieter Brueghel the Elder (c. 1520–1569), Flemish painter

BAROQUE

(17th and 18th centuries)

WHAT IT WAS ABOUT:

A reaction to mannerism, studied art, and austerity. Focus on decorative flourishes, heavy ornamentation, and general exuberance in style.

LEADING ARTISTS:

Gianlorenzo Bernini (1598–1680), Italian sculptor, architect, and painter

Michelangelo Merisi da Caravaggio (c. 1565–1610), Italian painter

Peter Paul Rubens (1577–1640), Flemish painter

Frans Hals (c. 1580–1666), Dutch painter

Rembrandt van Rijn (1606–1669), Dutch painter (see page 250)

Jan Vermeer (1632–1675), Dutch painter

Anthony Van Dyck (1599–1641), Flemish painter

Diego Velázquez (1599–1660), Spanish painter

ROCOCO

(18th century)

WHAT IT WAS ABOUT:

Baroque taken to the nth degree. Originated in France, where aristocratic tastes and values were the rule of the day. Marked by superrefinement, lightness, ornamentation. The goal—to produce elegant, aristocratic art.

LEADING ARTISTS:

Jean-Antoine Watteau (1684–1721),
    French painter (see page 263)

François Boucher (1703–1770),
    French painter

Étienne Falconet (1716–1791),
    French sculptor

Clodion (Claude Michel)
    (1738–1814),
    French sculptor

Thomas Gainsborough (1727–1788),
    English painter (founder of the
    English school of painting)

Sir Joshua Reynolds (1723–1792),
    English painter

NEOCLASSICISM

(mainly 18th century)

WHAT IT WAS ABOUT:

Classicism existed alongside baroque, but neoclassicism didn't really hit its stride until the period from roughly 1774 to 1793. A reaction to baroque and, especially, rococo—and a return to simpler, classic styles—emerged

with the new interest in classical antiquity (brought about, in part, by the rediscovery of Pompeii and Herculaneum in the mid-1700s). The goal—perfection through attention to rules and order.

LEADING ARTISTS:

Nicolas Poussin (1594–1665),
    French painter

Claude Lorrain (Claude Gellée)
    (1600–1682),
    French painter

William Hogarth (1697–1764),
    English painter

Jacques-Louis David (1748–1825),
    French painter

Antonio Canova (1757–1822),
    Italian sculptor

Jean-Antoine Houdon (1741–1828),
    French sculptor

Théodore Géricault (1791–1824),
    French painter

ROMANTICISM

(early 19th century)

WHAT IT WAS ABOUT:

Brought about, in part, by the spirit evoked in the American and French revolutions, as well as other uprisings. The underlying idea—the common man mattered, not just aristocrats. A guiding principle for many: the power of nature to heal, to restore the spirit.

LEADING ARTISTS:

Caspar David Friedrich (1744–1840),
    German painter

John Constable (1776–1837),
 English painter

J.M.W. Turner (1775–1851),
 English painter

Eugène Delacroix (1798–1863),
 French painter (see page 264)

REALISM

(mid-19th century)

WHAT IT WAS ABOUT:

A reaction against the extreme emotionalism of the romantic style. Emphasis on life as it really was, instead of the idealized, romanticized version of the romantics.

LEADING ARTISTS:

Honoré Daumier (1808–1879),
 French lithographer and painter

Gustave Courbet (1819–1877),
 French painter (see page 265)

Édouard Manet (1832–1883),
 French painter (see page 265)

IMPRESSIONISM

(late 19th century)

WHAT IT WAS ABOUT:

A move to take realism one step further. The goal of the artist: to capture reality exactly as it appeared to him at the moment; to make, in effect, a snapshot of an image without a camera; to create, literally, an impression of a subject. Key design elements include capturing the play of light and color, use of expressive brushstrokes.

LEADING ARTISTS:

Claude Monet (1840–1926),
 French painter (see page 266)

Auguste Renoir (1841–1919),
 French painter

Edgar Degas (1834–1917),
 French painter

Camille Pissarro (1830–1903),
 French painter

POSTIMPRESSIONISM

(late 19th century)

WHAT IT WAS ABOUT:

Nothing really, but some impressionists and those inspired by impressionism evolved individual styles that moved away from the impressionist style. An umbrella term for a wide range of styles, then, each as individual as the artist who produced it.

LEADING ARTISTS:

Paul Cézanne (1839–1906),
 French painter (see page 267)

Paul Gauguin (1848–1903),
 French painter

Vincent van Gogh (1853–1890),
 Dutch painter (see page 267)

Georges Seurat (1859–1891),
 French painter

Wilhelm Lehmbruck (1881–1919),
 German sculptor

Aristide Maillol (1861–1944),
 French sculptor

FAUVISM

(early 20th century)

WHAT IT WAS ABOUT:

Color, color, color—an exuberant, sensual style that aimed to represent harmony between humankind and nature.

LEADING ARTISTS:

Henri Matisse (1869–1954),
    French painter (see page 268)

André Derain (1880–1954),
    French painter

Maurice de Vlaminck (1876–1958),
    French painter

EXPRESSIONISM

(late 19th and early 20th centuries)

WHAT IT WAS ABOUT:

Emerged just before the turn of the twentieth century—partially inspired by the Machine Age. Started in Germany with two groups of painters, Die Brücke (the Bridge) and Der Blaue Reiter (the Blue Rider), who were rebelling against the dull German academic painting school. Guiding principle—moving past rational concepts to nonrational, emotional ones. In the 1920s and 1930s, the thrust of expressionism came from Mexico.

LEADING ARTISTS:

Emil Nolde (1867–1956),
    German painter

Ernst Ludwig Kirchner (1880–1938),
    German painter

Oskar Kokoschka (1886–1980),
    Austrian painter

Franz Marc (1880–1916),
    German artist

José Clemente Orozco (1883–1949),
    Mexican painter and muralist

Diego Rivera (1886–1957),
    Mexican painter and muralist

ABSTRACTIONISM

(also known as nonobjectivism)
(20th century)

WHAT IT WAS ABOUT:

A move away from representationalism. Images in works of art created in this movement don't look like actual forms in the visual world.

LEADING ARTISTS:

Wassily Kandinsky (1866–1944),
    Russian painter (who founded one
    of the first expressionist groups,
    but moved toward a more
    nonobjective style) (see page 270)

Piet Mondrian (1872–1944),
    Dutch painter

Constantin Brancusi (1876–1957),
    Romanian sculptor in France
    (see page 270)

Kasimir Malevich (1878–1935),
    Russian painter

CUBISM

(early 20th century)

WHAT IT WAS ABOUT:

A form of abstraction that reduces objects to simple cubes, then goes one step further by flattening the images into a two-dimensional shape.

LEADING ARTISTS:

Georges Braque (1882–1963),
    French artist
Pablo Picasso (1881–1973),
    Spanish painter (see page 269)
Juan Gris (1887–1927),
    Spanish painter
Fernand Léger (1881–1955),
    French painter

SURREALISM

(20th century)

WHAT IT WAS ABOUT:

Inspired to a great degree by Freudian psychoanalysis. An attempt to capture the subconscious on canvas, usually expressed in symbolic form.

LEADING ARTISTS:

Joan Miró (1893–1983),
    Spanish painter (whose work
    later tended more toward
    abstractionism) (see page 271)
Max Ernst (1891–1976),
    German painter and sculptor
Salvador Dalí (1904–1989),
    Spanish painter (see page 272)

Frida Kahlo (1907–1954),
    Mexican painter (while not overtly
    surrealistic, work is usually
    considered as such—especially by
    other surrealists)

FANTASY

(20th century)

WHAT IT WAS ABOUT:

An offshoot of surrealism, which explores the fantastic behind the realistic. The goal—for the artist to reveal other realities he or she believed existed apart from what the eye could see.

LEADING ARTISTS:

Giorgio de Chirico (1888–1978),
    Italian painter
Paul Klee (1879–1940),
    Swiss painter (a founder of
    expressionism; moved toward this
    style in later years)
Marc Chagall (1887–1985),
    Russian painter in France
    (see page 271)

IF A PICTURE PAINTS A THOUSAND WORDS . . .
EUROPEAN ARTISTS WHO SPOKE VOLUMES

Yes, the history of European art is filled with famous names, many of which you know. But among the great (and not-so-great) artists, there are those that stand out. Their work is unique—often they were the founders of an artistic movement, or their work epitomizes a certain school of art or a time. What-ever the reason, the following artists are those that are undeniably masters, people who shared their unique vision and, via paint and canvas or chisel and sculpture, created something greater than the sum of its parts.

(You'll note that, as in the preceding chart, we stopped at surrealism. It's not that there hasn't been great art or great masters since then, but much of the top modern art is American—and our book is designed to tell you about the *rest* of the world, not our own backyard.)

MASTERS OF WESTERN ART
FROM THE RENAISSANCE TO SURREALISM

GIOTTO DI BONDONE

(1266–1337)

The period: Renaissance, specifically the Early Renaissance or the late Mid-dle Ages, depending on how you look at it.

Claim to fame: The revolutionary artist who sparked the Renaissance with his innovative style—which broke away from the rigid Byzantine style that was heavy on symbols and short on realism.

Style: Came up with the concept of a "painting as a window"—the viewer is looking in on a scene, a moment from a narrative tale. And the people in his scenes look lifelike, natural, *human*. Not that his work is perfect. To be frank, he was prone to errors of per-spective. Then again, since he was the first to paint this way, he didn't have any guidelines from the past. And who really cares? The effect of his work was (and is) so strong that you don't notice picky perspective problems.

Thumbnail sketch: Not a starving artist by any means—Giotto was widely acclaimed in his day, and won money, fame, powerful friends (like the poet Dante), and political position (he was appointed master of works for the cathedral and city of Florence). He was supposedly discovered when he was only ten by artist Cimabue (the leading Italian artist of the time), who found him drawing a lamb on a stone while he was tending sheep. Cimabue may have wished he had never taken

Giotto under his wing—a year later, his student had surpassed him and was winning all the kudos.

Major works: Frescoes on the walls of the Arena Chapel, Padua (such as the

Old Masters, Old Mummies

 When you're admiring a painting by a Renaissance old master, you may be also appreciating an old mummy—literally. Mummies in ancient Egypt were embalmed in asphaltum, a preservative used as a base for paint, and especially good if aged. The premise was simple; since embalming substances kept a mummy well preserved, it would also keep paintings from cracking with age. So centuries after the days of ancient Egypt, money-minded Egyptians would unearth mummies and grind them up to make paint.

There were other uses for mummy as well. As early as the twelfth century, mummy powder was a cure-all element showing up in medicines. It was so popular that a fake mummy trade emerged with unscrupulous salespersons taking pieces of fresh corpses, packing them in asphalt, then pickling them. In nineteenth-century America, mummy bandages were used to make paper. But the practice faded out when a cholera epidemic was traced back to infected mummy wrappings from one paper producer.

Just as there are art masterpieces, there are also the blunders of the art world—pieces that by their sheer badness deserve attention. Some choice examples: a painting of the Madonna and Child by a German painter that shows the two subjects being serenaded—not by a heavenly host, but by a violinist! An anonymous Dutch painter chose to immortalize Abraham's sacrifice of Isaac—and painted Abraham holding a loaded blunderbuss to Isaac's head. Finally, in the dubious-subject category, there's the drawing La Remède by Jean-Antoine Watteau that shows a Venus reclining—about to be given an enema.

Flight into Egypt and *The Lamentation*); *St. Francis Blessing the Birds*, fresco in the Upper Church of Assisi.

Impact: For the fifty years following his death, no other painter challenged his position. His work influenced many other painters, including Michelangelo, who studied Giotto's compositions. In fact, his approach to painting was the rule of thumb until the late nineteenth century, when Cézanne and the cubists started their own revolution.

LEONARDO DA VINCI

(1452–1519)

The period: High Renaissance

Claim to fame: The true Renaissance man—artist, architect, scientist, engineer, scholar, and more. Ushered in the High Renaissance.

Style: Based on painstaking observation of nature, particularly of light and shade. Developed new form of unified composition in which groups of figures are arranged in a geometrical form—usually a pyramid, which on one hand represents the Christian trinity, and on the other fits in with the Renaissance idea that everything in the universe is based on the order of geometry. But his work isn't cut-and-dried: There's an emotional, expressive reality to the people in his works. As he put it, "Painted figures ought to be done in such a way that those who see them will be able to easily recognize from their attitudes the thoughts of their minds."

Thumbnail sketch: According to da Vinci, art was "an unrivaled opportunity given to man to continue what God has begun." And his life was spent pushing the envelope, not only in art but in other facets. The illegitimate son of a Florentine notary, he designed and built models which were so good that his father sent him to study under the then top Florentine artist, Verrocchio. He was a lifelong student of nature; his notebooks—written in mirror writing (backwards writing that can be read in a mirror)—included studies of everything from plants to military machines, cloud formations to hydraulic machines, even the properties of sound. But he didn't just study a range of topics, he actually participated in a variety of projects—from developing a system of hydraulic irrigation for Lombardy to directing court pageants. In fact, he did so much that he didn't complete many of his paintings. He *did*, however, accept money for paintings that he never even started.

Major works: *Mona Lisa; The Last Supper; Virgin and Child with St. Anne; Vitruvian Man* (pen and ink); *The Virgin of the Rocks.*

Impact: Enormous—his notebooks contain designs and ideas that are still being explored; his *Mona Lisa* became a model of Renaissance portraits and, more generally, his pyramidal composition was widely copied by other painters.

MICHELANGELO

(1475–1564)
(*Michelangelo di Lodovico Buonarroti Simoni*)

The period: Actually three—High Renaissance, Mannerism, and early Baroque

Claim to fame: A triple threat throughout the three artistic periods—sculptor, painter, and architect. Considered the leading figure of the Italian Renaissance.

Style: Felt that art was "the making of men"—which can be taken literally since so much of his work (especially

Big Money in Old Art

The old image of the starving artist didn't apply to many of the artists of the Renaissance. The successful artists of the time had economic security and good reputations—all in all, a pretty cushy lifestyle. The reason? The Renaissance signified not only a rebirth in art, but also a change in the status of the artists producing the work. Until the Renaissance, artists weren't that highly considered by the public. They were laborers, similar to mechanics or other lower-level workers. But with the Renaissance, their status skyrocketed. Artists were usually sponsored by wealthy princes or other rulers, for whom they would produce commissioned works. To paint or sculpt uncommissioned works for the general public was a no-no, and would result in a quick drop in status. Instead, artists could count on steady work, a good reputation, and a healthy amount of money by sticking with their powerful patrons. In fact, it could pay off very well. For example, Leonardo da Vinci made about two thousand ducats a year—at a time when a very comfortable living was provided by an income of three hundred ducats a year.

the sculpture) is of the nude human figure. More interested in form than color, even as a painter. His work has a startlingly lifelike appearance. His stated goal: to produce works that were sublime and grand, rather than beautiful—and he succeeded—although most are beautiful too.

Thumbnail sketch: The consummate artist from day one—in fact, as a child, he wasn't the greatest student, preferring drawing to studying. And art was his life until the last day of his eighty-nine years. He wasn't the easiest person to work with; he was known for his mood swings, his feeling that he wasn't quite in sync with the world. But when forced, he toed the line. Like when he received an offer he couldn't refuse—from Pope Julius II, who commissioned him to do his tomb. The tomb was never finished, though, because the pope then wanted him to decorate the Sistine Chapel ceiling, a job Michelangelo didn't want. (In fact, he begged the pope to get Raphael to do it instead. After taking the job, he wrote a sonnet about how physically demanding it was to do.) He ran into a similar situation with the next pope (Leo X), who ordered him to take a job rebuilding the façade of the Church of San Lorenzo in Florence and doing statues for it. Years later, he wound up as architect of St. Peter's, a commission he apparently liked, and worked on until his death.

Major works: Paintings: Sistine Chapel ceiling; *Holy Family.* Sculpture: *David; Pietà* (Rome).

Impact: He led the way artistically in his time—first with his statue *David,* which elevated statuary to new heights; then with his Sistine Chapel ceiling, and finally with his work in the Medici Chapel (sculpture and archi-

tectural design) in San Lorenzo, where he sowed the seeds for mannerist art and design.

EL GRECO

(Doménikos Theotokópoulos)
(1541–1614)

The period: Mannerism

Claim to fame: The last and greatest mannerist painter.

Style: Very distinctive—and very distorted. Lots of long thin bodies with small heads and a halo of light surrounding the entire figure. Some say this wasn't a deliberate style, but that El Greco was painting what he actually saw since he had an astigmatism. His work has an active, energetic look to it, with almost impressionistic touches in his later paintings. Even the drapery on the figures he painted looks like it's moving. The bottom line—it's highly charged, dramatic stuff that looks like no one else's at the time.

Thumbnail sketch: Called El Greco (logically) because he was a Greek—a Cretan, actually, who moved to Spain at age thirty-five and lived the rest of his life there. But he stuck with his Greek roots, signing all of his works in Greek. For all of his success, his reputation as a painter was somewhat precarious—regularly fluctuating. The reason? He was primarily a portrait artist, but his distorted style made people wonder if he was really that good.

Major works: *Burial of Count Orgaz; Assumption of the Virgin; Self-Portrait; View of Toledo; Purification of the Temple; Christ's Agony in Gethsemane.*

Supporting the Arts

Corporate patronage of the arts—like Exxon funding a *Masterpiece Theater* presentation or IBM backing an art exhibition—isn't a recent development born in the twentieth century. In fact, in the early days of the Renaissance, such patronage was one of the most popular ways of showing how powerful a particular organization was. Guilds and religious groups would commission works of art to prove their power and financial health. For example, to show the community how influential they were, the cloth merchants of Florence commissioned Brunelleschi to build the dome on Florence's cathedral and Ghiberti to design the bronze doors of the baptistery. By the later fifteenth century, corporations were replaced by individuals as patrons of the arts. It still was a way of showing the community at large how influential, powerful, or simply rich you were. Princes and other political leaders, popes and other religious leaders, and bankers, merchants, and other business leaders would spend fortunes commissioning fine artwork to glorify their business, their own name, or their family name. One of the most famous of these patrons, of course, is the Florentine oligarch Lorenzo de' Medici, who in about 1470 proudly noted that he and his family had spent 666,755 gold florins over the previous thirty-five years on art and architectural commissions. As a way of putting this amount into perspective, at roughly the same time the head of Florence's city government earned about five hundred florins a year—considered a princely sum at the time.

Impact: To a great degree, his work put Spain on the map artistically in his time period.

REMBRANDT VAN RIJN

(1606–1669)

The period: Baroque

Claim to fame: Considered the greatest genius of Dutch art and, by some, the first true "modern" artist.

Style: The obvious element in his work—strong light and dark shadow (especially in his later works). But there's much more to it. It's highly naturalistic and emotionally rich. Unlike most other Dutch artists, his works capture an essential humanity in his subjects and often their dark side, literally and figuratively. That is, the sub-

jects are usually shown surrounded by shadow, and often are shown as people who are suffering. In fact, in his early and late years, he often painted the poor and outcast. He offers a sympathetic yet unflinchingly honest look at people, including himself. His self-portraits are revealing psychological studies.

Thumbnail sketch: Uncompromising, stubborn, and convinced of his own artistic worth. Initially known as a master of group portraits of Dutch burghers, he became quite famous, especially after painting *The Night Watch*. But he started going downhill financially. Rumor has it that the culprit was his artistic integrity and his growing experimentation with light and shadow—the people who paid for their portraits wanted to see themselves, not search for themselves among the shadows. But it was probably due to something much more prosaic—poor money management. Whatever the reason, in spite of his reputation as a master, he died penniless.

Major works: *The Night Watch; Aristotle Contemplating the Bust of Homer; Bathsheba with King David's Letter; Return of the Prodigal Son.*

Impact: His work with chiaroscuro, the use of light and shade in a painting to create a modeled effect, influenced many contemporary and later artists; while his reputation plummeted shortly after his death, it rebounded in the nineteenth century, when realists discovered his work and were influenced by it.

JEAN-ANTOINE WATTEAU

(1684–1721)

The period: Rococo

Claim to fame: The top rococo painter; captured the elegant sensibilities of prerevolutionary France.

Style: Known for his *fêtes galantes*—paintings of aristocratic people in court dress at play in a natural setting. As such, the style is poetic and dreamy. Heavy use of soft colors and light brushstrokes. Captured natural gestures as a way of conveying mood or character of the people. The sum of the parts: the creation of an idyllic, not-quite-real world.

Thumbnail sketch: Lived a somewhat romantic life—at eighteen he ran away to Paris, where he worked as a scene painter at the Opéra, among other things. But after he painted *The Embarkation for Cythera*, he became a

member of the Academy—more properly, the French Academy of Painting and Sculpture, which helped students in their studies and also basically set the standards for artists. (It became a bit of a pejorative, in more modern times, to label someone's work "academic"—this, because the Academy was known for its conservatism and traditionalism.) Watteau then switched over to the type of painting he's best known for: idyllic pastorals of people in court dress. He became a friend of his upper-class patrons, and often stayed with them to paint their parties and such, but really didn't get much of a chance to enjoy the high life. Suffering from tuberculosis most of his life, and perceived as somewhat remote, he died at thirty-six.

Major works: *The Embarkation for Cythera; fêtes galantes.*

Impact: His reputation suffered during the French Revolution since his work featured idle aristocrats, but rose again at the end of the nineteenth century; now considered one of the precursors of impressionism.

FRANCISCO GOYA

(Francisco José de Goya y Lucientes)
(1746–1828)

The period: While he painted during the neoclassic and neobaroque periods, Goya's work is individualistic and thus really unattached to any greater school.

Claim to fame: The genius of his time, known for his highly individual style.

Style: Unflinchingly realistic—

both his portraits, which reveal his subjects as he saw them, and his other paintings, such as those on war. The chief elements in his work: Power. Energy. Drama. His work hits the viewer, through both the subject matter and the technique, which is marked by strong colors, dramatic lighting, and fluid brushwork.

Thumbnail sketch: Started as a typical rococo painter of court pastorals, but slowly switched over to realism. True to his artistic integrity and convictions, he was uncompromisingly realistic and honest. As a court painter to three kings, he turned out less-than-flattering portraits (unlike so many other court painters) that exposed his true feelings about his subjects. Nevertheless, his work was extremely popular, even among the subjects he exposed on canvas. He later did a series of etchings satirizing the court, and still later, after the Napoleonic occupation, a series on the horrors of war. Sadly, at the peak of his career, he became seriously ill and became blind, deaf, and paralyzed. While he recovered everything but his hearing, he retained a fear of death. This dark side of him became especially apparent after the death of his wife and four of his five children—he retired to a house outside Madrid (called the House of the Deaf Man) and painted the walls with his visions of horror.

Major works: *King Charles IV and His Family; The Third of May, 1808; Los Caprichos* (etchings); *The Disasters of War* (etchings); *The Lunatic Asylum.*

Impact: Huge—virtually every painter after him was influenced by his powerful originality. The expressionists, in particular, followed his later techniques.

EUGÈNE DELACROIX

(1799–1863)

The period: Romanticism

Claim to fame: Considered the leading romantic painter; one of the first to break away from the more rigid, dry classical style.

Style: Brilliant colors (in fact, he rarely used black or earth tones), fluid brushwork, and dramatic subjects, typically drawn from history or literature. Work marked by emotion, light, and energy. His extensive experimentation with color led to the development of many new techniques, used by most artists after him. Among them: used complementary colors next to one another to heighten their effect; painted flesh outdoors or in sunlight, not in a studio, to get its true color.

Thumbnail sketch: A rebel of the art world, he was both acclaimed and criticized in his time. A perfect example: his *Massacre at Chios* was called by critics *Massacre of Painting,* yet it was bought by the government. His breakthrough techniques also pushed him out of the art mainstream. Yet he was a popular figure in French artistic circles. He was a friend of Frédéric Chopin and George Sand (both of whom he painted), and had a lifelong interest in literature.

Major works: *The Massacre at Chios; Frédéric Chopin; Odalisque; Dante and Virgil in Hell; Liberty Guiding the People.*

Impact: A precursor of much of modern art; particularly influential as a result of his experimentation with color.

GUSTAVE COURBET

(1819–1877)

The period: Realism

Claim to fame: Founder of realism.

Style: Strong, vigorous, simple, the antithesis of romanticism. Noted particularly for his subjects, which were considered outrageous in his time—literal, objective views of everyday nineteenth-century life (funerals, people working, etc.). Style is usually straightforward. His famous later work *The Painter's Studio* breaks from his usual subject matter. A triptych of him in his studio surrounded by people, it's a comment on society and the role of the artist.

Thumbnail sketch: His credo was "I cannot paint an angel because I cannot see one." An ardent realist who rebelled against romanticism and academic art, and an artist with little formal training, Courbet ran into trouble periodically because of his strong convictions. One example: He was denied entry in the Paris World Exhibition of 1855, so he set up a show in a shed outside and distributed a "Manifesto of Realism." Friends like novelist Émile Zola and poet Charles-Pierre Baudelaire frequently had to defend him against criticism. Yet he became the most famous living artist of his time, chiefly because of his habit of lecturing about the glories of realism whenever he had a show. In fact, he sold over a hundred paintings at the Paris World Exhibition of 1867. But he ran into political trouble as a result of his radical leanings during the political turmoil surrounding the Franco-

Prussian War of 1870–71. He was imprisoned, his possessions and paintings were confiscated, and he went into exile in Switzerland.

Major works: *The Stone Breakers; Funeral at Ornans; Peasants of Flagey; L'Atelier* (The Painter's Studio).

Impact: Had special influence on French artists younger than he; paved the way for the impressionists by painting commonplace subjects.

ÉDOUARD MANET

(1832–1883)

The period: Realism (Many erroneously consider him an impressionist.)

Claim to fame: An avant-garde revolutionary who broke many of the standard rules of painting; hero (even father figure) to the impressionists.

Style: Devoted to what he called "pure painting"—viewers should not look through a painting, but at it. Work is fresh, clean, stark. A key reason (and a major breakthrough)—the flat areas of color. This makes most subjects almost two-dimensional—a complete break from all painting done since Giotto. The work is also temperamentally reserved. Subjects often appear emotionless, cold, even blank. And the subject matter was often provocative by the standards of the times: a nude woman lunching al fresco with clothed men; an unembarrassedly naked prostitute. For all the innovation, though, most of Manet's work is clearly modeled on other painters, such as Titian, Raphael, and Velázquez.

Thumbnail sketch: Manet always

wanted official recognition, but it took most of his life to get it. One of his first important works, *Le Déjeuner sur l'herbe,* wasn't accepted in the official 1863 Salon, and his next attempt, *Olympia,* was accepted, but met with public outcry. He kept on painting and fighting against the hidebound conventions of the day. It wasn't until the year before he died that he finally got the official recognition he craved—he was appointed a Chevalier de la Légion d'honneur. Yet he clearly had always had the support of his peers: When he died, novelist Zola and painters Degas and Monet were pallbearers; people like Renoir, Pissarro, and Cézanne came to pay their respects.

Major works: *Le Déjeuner sur l'herbe* (Luncheon on the Grass, or The Picnic); *Olympia; Le Buveur d'absinthe* (The Absinthe Drinker); *A Bar at the Folies-Bergères.*

Impact: Influenced the impres-

Thank the Industrial Revolution for the emergence of impressionism. With the Industrial Revolution came the invention of the collapsible, resealable tube of paint. This enabled impressionists to paint outdoors—and to capture on canvas the elusive play of light. In addition, synthetic pigments were invented, which gave artists a cheaper version of intense colors.

sionists (and, for that matter, was influenced by them in his later years) through his efforts to break away from the conventions of the past.

CLAUDE MONET

(1840–1926)

The period: Impressionism

Claim to fame: One of the founders of impressionism.

Style: Light, color, and atmosphere—the three key elements in all of Monet's work. His goal was to capture reality as he saw it at the moment—and his style shows this. There's a transitory nature to his work—light playing on water, color shifts due to atmosphere or light, and so on—and an energy, a result of his colors, his depiction of light, and his bold brushwork.

Thumbnail sketch: The impressionists named themselves after Monet's painting *Impression-Sunrise.* This is probably fitting, since Monet was one of the most fervent exponents of impressionism. His life was devoted to exploring the nuances of impressionism, studying light and color, how things affected them, and trying to translate on canvas the reality he saw. It obviously worked: Critics of his painting *The River* complained that the sunlight he painted was so bright it blinded them.

Major works: *Impression-Sunrise; Gare Saint-Lazare; Paris; Haystacks* (series); *Rouen Cathedral; Water Lilies* (series).

Impact: As a founder of impressionism, had enormous impact and set the stage for modern art.

Manet and the Critics

Manet's painting *Déjeuner sur l'herbe* is considered by many to mark the end of traditional art and the beginning of modern art. But while it's now considered a masterpiece, in its time it met with strong criticism: "Is this drawing? Is this painting?"—Jules Castagnary, "Salons." Some critics thought it must be a joke: "This is a young man's practical joke, a shameful open sore not worth exhibiting this way."—Louis Étienne, "Le Jury et les exposants." Others just vilified it: "Unfortunately the nude hasn't a decent figure and one can't think of anything uglier than the man stretched out next to her, who hasn't even thought of taking off, out of doors, his horrid padded cap."—Thoré, "L'Indépendance belge." In fact, even after Manet's death, public criticism of the painting continued, and the government had to be persuaded to buy it.

PAUL CÉZANNE

(1839–1906)

The period: At first, impressionism, but broke away into his own postimpressionist style

Claim to fame: Called the Father of Modern Painting.

Style: Above all, marked by solidity and color. Takes impressionistic qualities of light and color and grounds them with three-dimensional representation of objects and strong composition. Color is pure, rich, often startlingly brilliant; objects depicted seem to have real weight and mass. Much of his work revolves around the three forms he said were the basis of all nature: the cone, the sphere, and the cylinder. A key to his painting? He ignores "correct drawing"—that is, he doesn't pay attention to accurate draftsmanship. Oddly enough, it's this that makes his work appear more realistic. He's painting objects as the eye sees them, not scientifically.

Thumbnail sketch: Cézanne strove for a balance between color, composition, and solidity until he died. His aim: "To make impressionism something solid and durable like the art of the old masters." And his life was dominated by this. He broke away from the impressionists because he felt they weren't interested enough in painting objects that appeared three-dimensional and because he thought their work wasn't compositionally strong. He was so into his work that his wife (whom he married after a reputed secret affair) had to go find his canvases when they were completed—he would leave them wherever he was

Cézanne was an archetypal bohemian with a capital B. He considered himself an artistic genius unbound by the usual social considerations—such as cleanliness, manners, etc.—and tended to go for shock value. When asked the subject of a painting he was going to submit to the Salon, he said, "A pot of shit."

when he finished. For all his attention to work, though, he wasn't hugely successful in his time. In fact, he broke with his good friend Émile Zola when Zola's novel *L'Oeuvre* had as a central character an unbalanced and unsuccessful impressionist painter—namely, Cézanne. He finally was recognized in the last few years of his life, although he still felt he hadn't achieved what he wanted.

Major works: *Still Life with Basket of Apples; Mont Sainte-Victoire; Fruit Bowl, Glass, and Apples; Self-Portrait.*

Impact: Huge, which is why he's earned the title of Father of Modern Painting; he set the stage for cubism.

VINCENT VAN GOGH

(1853–1890)

The period: Postimpressionism, but his style is actually more in tune with expressionism.

Claim to fame: Known as much for his tortured life as for his tortured, brilliant paintings, in which van Gogh broke away from impressionism and developed a distinctive expressionistic style.

Style: A mirror of the man—emotional, turbulent, even violent. The hallmarks of his work are thick paint, heavy textures, twisted forms, and strong color. Influenced by Japanese woodcuts, van Gogh uses some of their attributes, such as intricate patterns of lines, unique viewpoints, bright colors. His work has odd perspectives (some say he suffered from epilepsy, others that he used the narcotic drink absinthe, which distorted his vision).

Thumbnail sketch: Far from the happiest of lives, as most people know. The son of a Lutheran pastor, he first worked in art, beginning as an assistant to an art dealer at age sixteen. But an unrequited love affair with an English schoolmistress threw him into an attempt at a religious life—he tried unsuccessfully to become a Methodist preacher, then became an evangelist. When he finally went to study art in Brussels, he went through another disastrous love affair (this time with a cousin), after which he went to the Hague and lived with his model. His brother, an art dealer, made it possible for him to study in Paris. Here van Gogh fell in with artists like Toulouse-Lautrec and Gauguin, and at Toulouse-Lautrec's urging, moved to Arles to paint. This was a high point of his creative output, but this too ended tragically: He invited Gauguin to come and help him found a colony of artists, but the two had a huge argument that culminated in van Gogh's threatening Gauguin with a razor, then, in remorse, cutting off part of his own ear. He was placed in an asylum for this act. When released, he stayed under a doctor's care and was beginning to win some recognition. But the black cloud of depression apparently hadn't lifted. He shot himself in the field where he had painted his last work, *Wheatfields with Flight of Birds,* and two days later, died.

Major works: *The Potato Eaters; Self-Portrait; The Starry Night; The Night Café; Sunflowers; Vincent's Chair; Wheatfields with Flight of Birds.*

Impact: Heavy influence on the Fauves and others.

HENRI MATISSE

(1869–1954)

The period: Fauvism

Claim to fame: The oldest founding father of twentieth-century painting.

Style: Bright colors, curving shapes, and an ineffable joy flooding the canvas. Usually two-dimensional designs, consisting of rhythmic lines and the bold use of color. For all the color and movement, though, it's a very simple style. Matisse boils everything down to the essentials, reducing the number of colors he uses, the shapes, the lines, everything, in fact, to the bare minimum. The result: a sensuous style that is expressive rather than descriptive. As he put it: "What I am after, above all, is expression. . . . Expression does not consist of the passion mirrored upon a human face. . . . The whole arrangement of my picture is expressive."

Thumbnail sketch: First a law student and a law clerk, Matisse switched over to painting—and in a big way. He first came under the influence of the impressionists and neoimpressionists, particularly the divisionist school of Seurat and Signac. Then he was caught up by Cézanne's work, to the point where, though extremely poor, he managed to save up enough money to buy Cézanne's *Bathers* from a dealer. Then he switched back to divisionism and put his own spin on it, by using his now characteristic bold, bright colors. The style met with a healthy dose of criticism. In fact, the fauve movement got its name when his and other artists' works were displayed in a room with a classical sculpture,

and critic Louis Cauzcelles said, "*Donatello au milieu des fauves!*" (Donatello among the wild beasts). It wasn't only the critics who weren't in love with Matisse. When his famous *Joy of Life* came out, the painter whom Matisse had earlier followed, Paul Signac, claimed that Matisse had "gone to the dogs." Matisse had the last laugh though. The fauve movement may not have been long-lasting, but Matisse worked throughout his life— on ballet sets, stained glass, and more.

Major works: *Woman with the Hat; The Joy of Life; Harmony in Red.*

Impact: Still being felt, even though the fauve movement only lasted a few years; his experimentation with color spawned the abstractionist movement.

PABLO PICASSO

(1881–1973)

The period: Cubism

Claim to fame: One of the greatest artistic innovators; founder of cubism (with Georges Braque).

Style: Varies depending upon the period. For example, the Blue period was lyrical, with sad studies of the poor; the Rose or Harlequin period was life-affirming, with cheerful studies of the circus; the Iberian-African period was based on African masks and art. But Picasso's most famous and influential style was cubism. The goal: to represent three-dimensional objects on a flat surface without using perspective. The look: Objects are broken down to simple geometric forms, sometimes fragmented; it's as if you're

seeing the object from many angles at once (called "simultaneity of vision"). Picasso himself once said about his *Girl Before a Mirror* that he showed the girl "simultaneously clothed, nude, and x-rayed." The result: sometimes discordant, sometimes confusing, sometimes grotesque, but always active and filled with energy.

Thumbnail sketch: A long creative life. Picasso began studying art at age fourteen at the academy in Barcelona; two years later he was in advanced training in Madrid; one year after that he won a gold medal for his painting; and two years later he set up his own studio in Montmartre. All in all, it was a swift beginning, followed by years of artistic exploration. He switched from a traditional style to neoimpressionism, then began developing his own unique style. One main source of inspiration: African art. He joined with artist Georges Braque in 1909 and developed cubism, pushing it through a number of different incarnations: analytic, synthetic, hermetic, even rococo. The two split in 1914, but Picasso kept exploring different aspects of art. He designed for Diaghilev's Russian Ballet, which made cubism accessible (and acceptable) to a wider public. One of his chief works after this, *Guernica,* gripped public attention with its expression of the horrors of war (evoked by Picasso's feelings about the bombing of the Basque town during the Spanish civil war). After this, he continued in his artistic explorations, producing everything from ceramics to sculpture to lithographs, even writing a play. One problem with this immense output: His work is very uneven. In fact, some say that, except for *Guernica,* his work lacks insight and emotion. But the criticism certainly didn't affect his success. He turned out numerous copies of his work (in fact, one reason for his popularity was that his work reproduced so well), and made quite a bit of money. He died, still an active artist, still pushing the boundaries of his creativity.

Major works: *Les Demoiselles d'Avignon*; *Three Musicians*; *Girl Before a Mirror*; *Guernica*; the Picasso peace dove, abstract paper cutout series including "Jazz."

Impact: Immense; he's probably one of the most influential artists of the twentieth century

WASSILY KANDINSKY

(1866–1944)

The period: Nonobjectivism, or abstractionism

Claim to fame: Originator of nonobjective painting; forerunner of much truly modern art; broke away totally from representationalism.

Style: The most important element in his work is what *isn't* there—a subject, in the traditional sense. The work is completely nonrepresentational. It's about nothing—or, rather, it shows nothing concrete, but is about emotion and feeling. Shape and color say it all. As he put it, summing up his work, "Depiction of objects in my paintings was not only unnecessary, but indeed harmful."

Thumbnail sketch: Kandinsky started as a law professor and wound up as one of the most influential theoreticians in modern art. Of course, quite a bit happened in the middle too.

A late bloomer, he didn't become a painter until he was thirty. At the beginning he was heavily influenced by impressionism, expressionism, and fauvism. But he took those styles one step further and developed theories about nonobjectivism that he put down in his book *On the Spiritual in Art* (1911). In it he talked about how art was supposed to reveal an internal truth. During the same year, he and other expressionists formed an artists' group in Munich called Der Blaue Reiter (The Blue Rider). A lot of his work later on shows his importance in the world of modern art: He was head of the Museum of Modern Art in Russia, founded the Russian Academy, and taught at the Bauhaus.

Major works: *Sketch 1 for "Composition VII"*; *First Abstract Watercolor.*

Impact: Paved the way for other modern nonobjective artists.

CONSTANTIN BRANCUSI

(1876–1957)

The period: Abstractionism

Claim to fame: Pioneer of abstract sculpture.

Style: Simple, smooth, egglike shapes; soaring lines; abstract images. His stated goal: to get to the essence of things. The work shows this, evolving from more representational work through a series of reductions, winding up with his famous geometric forms. There are actually two styles at work in his sculptures: stone and wood statues are in his "primevalist" style, visual throwbacks that evoke ancient statues or monoliths; marble and metal pieces

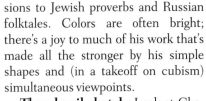

are in a simple nonrepresentational style, usually either egg shapes or vertical "bird" shapes that seem to embody the energy of flight.

Thumbnail sketch: His first job wasn't the typical one for a sculptor—he was a shepherd in the Carpathian Mountains. But at an early age he won a scholarship to the Bucharest Academy, then went from there to Paris, where he began developing his style. Two chief influences: Romanian folk art and African art. Both spurred him to seek a simple elemental truth in his work. He was prone to aphorisms describing his abstract style. One of the more famous explains his theories about abstraction: "Simplicity is not an end in art, but one arrives at simplicity in spite of oneself in drawing near to the reality of things."

Major works: *The Kiss; Sleeping Muse; The Prodigal Son; Mademoiselle Pogany; Bird in Space; The Sea-Lions.*

Impact: Essentially broke through old traditions of sculpture—his work was the launching pad for the modern sculpture that followed.

MARC CHAGALL

(1887–1985)

The period: Fantasy

Claim to fame: One of the fathers of surrealism, in fact, it's said that the French poet Apollinaire came up with the word "surrealism" to describe Chagall's work, and it became the name for an entire movement.

Style: Fantastic dreamlike scenes populated with flying people, horses, folkloric touches, including visual allu-

sions to Jewish proverbs and Russian folktales. Colors are often bright; there's a joy to much of his work that's made all the stronger by his simple shapes and (in a takeoff on cubism) simultaneous viewpoints.

Thumbnail sketch: Look at Chagall's work and you can see what's behind the man himself: a zest for, indeed an almost giddy take on, life, an abiding love for his wife, Bella (in several of his paintings, he painted the two of them together in loving dreams), and a child's ability to imagine the fantastic. A Russian Jew, he came to Paris in 1910. He had a one-man show in Berlin and was commissar of fine arts at Vitebsk, but after this he left Russia and settled in France, where he lived the rest of his life save for a few years in the United States. He illustrated books as well, such as Gogol's *Dead Souls* and La Fontaine's *Fables.*

Major works: *Bouquet of Flying Lovers; The Bride and Groom of the Eiffel Tower; Birthday.*

Impact: The breadth of his work—paintings, stained-glass windows, ceramics, etchings, set designs for *Firebird*—and his dreamy fantasies have made his works among the most recognizable of twentieth-century art.

JOAN MIRÓ

(1893–1983)

The period: Surrealism

Claim to fame: A modern innovator who took surrealism down a new path.

Style: Called "bimorphic abstraction," which, in plain English, means fluid, curved odd shapes that look like amoebas. Earlier works were less purely abstract and, instead, were surrealistic, whimsical compositions that captured a certain absurdity about the world or about the human condition. But his later work is totally abstract, compositions of those curving shapes that often seem to move, dividing and subdividing, in front of your eyes.

Thumbnail sketch: In the beginning, he was influenced by primitive Spanish art and the art nouveau look of the work of Spanish architect Antoni Gaudí, both of which are evident in his later work. Add to this the fact that he began as a Cézannist and fauvist, and you wind up with an interesting combination of influences. He studied in Paris and Barcelona and, after World War I, settled in Paris, where he met Picasso and Juan Gris. He started getting interested in surrealism, switched his painting style to the form for which

he is now famous, and began exhibiting with the surrealists in 1925.

Major works: *Composition; Person Throwing a Stone at a Bird; Dog Barking at the Moon.*

Impact: Had particular influence on American abstract expressionists.

SALVADOR DALÍ

(1904–1989)

The period: Surrealism

Claim to fame: One of the principal members of the surrealist movement.

Style: Hyperrealistic style coupled with an almost paranoid, nightmarish vision of a dreamlike world. Heavy on symbolism; work filled with images pulled from the subconscious. Like a

Critics Dishing the Masters

 Some of the painters we now consider the great masters were considered much less than that in their time. Some examples of criticism:

On Manet's painting *The Absinthe Drinker* (NOTE: Absinthe is a narcotic drink): "There is only one absinthe drinker, and that's the man who painted this idiotic picture." —critic Thomas Couture, 1860

On Matisse: "Matisse is an unmitigated bore. Surely the vogue of those twisted and contorted human figures must be as short as it is artificial." —*Chicago Tribune* critic Harriet Monroe, 1913

On Michelangelo: "He was a good man, but he did not know how to paint." —fellow artist El Greco

On Picasso: "If I met Picasso in the street I would kick him in the pants." —British Royal Academy member Sir Alfred Munnings, 1949

On da Vinci: "He bores me. He ought to have stuck to his flying machines." —artist Auguste Renoir

On the flip side, there's painter Paul Cézanne, who decided to take critical matters into his own hands and taught his parrot to repeat only one phrase again and again. The phrase? "Cézanne is a great painter!"

dream, landscapes usually have a cold, flat, eerie quality to them. And objects are represented very realistically, but they're manipulated into new, surprising forms—like the limp watches in his famous painting *The Persistence of Memory.* The result? Disturbing images that are like hallucinations.

Thumbnail sketch: Dalí's odd vision of the world is partially based on his studies; intrigued by abnormal psychology and the symbology of dreams, he studied both, and translated what he had learned to the canvas. He also tapped into his own childhood fears and fantasies as a basis for his work. His surrealistic vision wasn't confined to canvas though. He also worked with

film director Luis Buñuel on the films *Un Chien Andalou* and *L'Âge d'Or.* From his often disturbing paintings of the subconscious, he switched over to religious subjects, this after he moved to the United States and became a Catholic. Aside from his work, he was also known as a character, with his extravagant waxed mustache, his propensity for outrageous statements and actions, and his love of promotion.

Major works: *The Persistence of Memory; The Christ of St. John of the Cross.*

Impact: Debatable—on one hand, he set the stage for a clean surrealistic style; on the other, many have considered his work overrated.

SEVEN (PLUS SIX) MAN-MADE WONDERS OF THE WORLD: ARCHITECTURAL MASTERPIECES

 Certain buildings are more than buildings; they're silent testimony to the design skill, engineering wizardry, and artistic vision of architects and designers (many nameless) of different times. Often these architectural master-pieces are religious buildings or shrines, and logically so. Spurred by spiritual belief, eager to show rever-ence to a god or gods, architects often reached the highest peak of their crafts. The building, then, is mute tes-tament to the faith that created it.

Of course, other masterpieces have less lofty purposes—they're tombs or, in the case of the Roman Colosseum, an arena for public entertainment. But in these cases as well, architects and designers created more than a simple structure, more than a roof covering an interior space. In the act of building, they've transcended utility and come up with art. Here, then, are some of the world's greatest architectural trea-sures—wonders of the world created by humankind.

THE GREAT PYRAMIDS

When: c. 2530–2470 B.C.E.

Where: Giza, Egypt

What: Tombs for three kings; respectively, by date and size, Myceri-nus (Menekure) (built in 2470 B.C.E.), Chefren (Khafre) (c. 2500 B.C.E.), and Cheops (Khufu) (c. 2530 B.C.E.).

Henry David Thoreau on the Great Pyramids, c. 1854: As for the pyramids, there is nothing to wonder at in them so much as the fact that so many men could be found degraded enough to spend their lives constructing a tomb for some ambitious booby, whom it would have been wiser and manlier to have drowned in the Nile, and then given his body to the dogs.

At a glance: Three huge shapes against a blue sky in the desert—prob-ably among the most recognizable buildings in the world. Even in their time, they were considered architec-tural wonders.

Blueprint: Each pyramid took about twenty years or so to build; lime-stone was quarried on the site, granite shipped down the Nile. For siting, sur-veyors would take exact readings from the stars to determine directions, so each side of the base of a pyramid faces in the direction of a cardinal point of the compass. Blocks of lime-stone were slid up ramps to construct the pyramids, and as a final touch, a polished capstone was placed on the top to capture the rays of the sun. One final note: While the pyramids look like lonely sentinels in the barren desert, they were far from them in their time. Instead, they were part of an entire funerary complex—with tem-ples, other grave sites, and other build-ings surrounding them—which was used for religious celebrations. And, of course, crouched in part of this necropolis was the *Colossal Statue of Chefren as the God Hu*—or, as it's more popularly known, the *Great Sphinx*.

Distinctive feature: Size. It's ob-vious, but there's no getting around the impact of the pyramids' sheer mass. Interestingly, with each pyramid, the builders went one step down in size, making the oldest of the three, the pyramid of Cheops, also the largest; 480 feet high, and 755 feet long on each side of the base. The reason for

the vastness of these and so many other Egyptian structures and statues? Aggrandizement of the ruler. Anyone seeing these structures would know that the ruler had been someone to reckon with.

Architectural notes: Why a pyramid? Why not a simple square building that would have been easier to build? According to popular theory, pyramids are physical representations of the sun-god Ra, and symbolize the rays of the sun. The shape would help the buried ruler slide up to heaven. One thing we're sure of: Pyramids such as these evolved from a cruder structure called mastabas (from the word meaning "bench")—mud-brick structures

THE GREAT
PYRAMIDS AND
SPHINX, GIZA,
EGYPT

with flat tops and sloped walls, built on top of underground chambers holding the body, statues, and other accoutrements.

THE PARTHENON

When: 447–438 B.C.E.

Where: On top of a hill, the Acropolis, overlooking Athens, Greece

What: A temple to the patron goddess of Athens, Athena; built after the Persian Wars (in fact, the name Parthenon means "maiden," since Athena was the maiden goddess).

At a glance: A perfect blend of design elements set on top of a huge hill overlooking Athens. Rows of columns supporting a simple gable roof. And above the columns, beautifully detailed sculpture, showing battle scenes, scenes from Athena's life, and more.

Blueprint: Designed by architects Kallikrates and Iktinos, the Parthenon took about nine years to build. It had two inner chambers, a small treasure chamber and a larger room, the naos, where a forty-foot ivory-and-gold statue of Athena in full military dress stood. The sculptures on the pediment and friezes (areas above the columns) were completed in about twelve years

THE PARTHENON, GREECE

by the sculptor Phidias and his assistants. Although all you can see is the marble now, originally they were probably decorated with metal; some may have been gilded; and most probably were painted. So the image that most of us have of the Parthenon—white, pure, pristine—is probably far from the image the ancient Greeks actually saw.

Distinctive features: *Proportion.* The entire Parthenon is built according to the golden section: the size of the smaller part relates to the greater part as the greater part relates to the whole. The general ratio that it's built on? Five to eight. Plus, the design elements are carefully proportioned to

achieve visual harmony. Take the columns, for example. The general rule: The proportion of the capital to the column is the same as that of the human head to the human body.

Little tricks you probably wouldn't notice that enhance visual appeal. These architects knew what they were doing. All horizontal lines in the structure—from steps to entablature (the area above the columns)—aren't perfectly straight, but raised slightly in the middle. Why? Because the eye usually sees a long straight horizontal line incorrectly, as if it was sagging. The columns bulge slightly about one-third of the way up. This practice of "fattening" the column, called entasis, makes it look more organic, and prevents the illusion of concavity. And the columns aren't perfectly upright, either, but tilt slightly inward, which makes the Parthenon look more compact and increases its structural stability. Finally, the stylobite (top of the platform base) tilts up at the southwest corner—to make the building look more imposing from the entrance to the Acropolis and from Athens below.

Architectural notes: The Parthenon is an example of Doric architecture, the first of the three architectural orders devised by the ancient Greeks. (Actually, to be strictly technical, there are only two orders, Doric and Ionic, with Corinthian being a variation on Ionic.) At its simplest, the parts of an order include column, capital (top of the column), and entablature (everything on top of the columns, including the cornice, the frieze, and architrave, the part resting directly on the capital). The Doric order (seventh century B.C.E.) is simple and muscular in appearance. The Ionic (sixth century B.C.E.) is more del-

Greek architecture was the most popular building style in the United States by the early nineteenth century. And to make it workable for the do-it-yourselfers, publishers put out how-to design and construction books filled with plans for Greek-style houses, complete with Doric porticos, columns, and other Greek features.

One reason for the popularity of the Greek Revival look? Since ancient Athens was the first known democracy, its ideals mirrored those of young America. The American love affair with Greece didn't stop at buildings. Place names show the fascination with ancient Greece—cities such as Troy, New York; Demopolis, Alabama; Olympia, Washington; Athens and Sparta, Michigan.

icate and more detailed; finally, the Corinthian (fifth century B.C.E.) goes one step further in terms of decorative elements and slenderness. In fact, there was an old mnemonic device for remembering the different styles of columns: Doric columns, thicker and relatively unadorned, were men; Ionic columns, thinner and with a carved capital, were women; Corinthian columns, the slenderest and fussiest of the three, were maidens. It's not as far-fetched a metaphor as one might think. Remember, the Greeks were big on the human figure, so even architecture was designed with the human figure in mind.

THE GREAT STUPA AT SANCHI

When: Begun c. 200 B.C.E. by Indian king Asoka; enlarged in the second and first centuries B.C.E.

Where: Sanchi, India (near Bhopal)

What: Buddhist religious monument—in fact, probably the oldest surviving sacred Buddhist building, built by the first Buddhist ruler of India.

At a glance: A massive dome surrounded by tall railings punctuated by high carved gateways. The entire structure looms on top of a hill. The impression: solidity, permanence, serenity.

Blueprint: First, a quick explanation of what a stupa is: a hemispherical dome set on a circular or square base. The oldest form of Buddhist architecture, the stupa is generally the focal point of a religious complex, a monastery with kitchens, meeting

halls, and the like. The Great Stupa is built like all other stupas—a mound of stone-faced brick and rubble covered with white stucco that is partially gilded—all of which forms a dome. The dome eventually reached a height of fifty-four feet. (When it was enlarged, the original building was covered with earth and stone—because it was sacrilegious to destroy the original.) On top of the dome is a mast on which are three tiers of umbrellas—all of which is surrounded by a railing. The base around the dome is surrounded by a path, and there's a second path at ground level around the entire structure, with a railing around it. Four thirty-two-foot gateways at the cardinal points of the compass allow

THE GREAT STUPA FROM THE SOUTH, SANCHI, INDIA (SHUNGA AND EARLY ANDHVA, 3RD CENTURY B.C.E. TO EARLY 1ST CENTURY C.E.) (BORROMEO/ART RESOURCE, N.Y.)

access to this path. It sounds somewhat complicated, but it isn't at all—it's a simple, powerful structure.

Distinctive features: *Symbolic structure:* The Great Stupa, like other stupas, is built to symbolize different aspects of Buddhism. First, the entire structure itself symbolizes nirvana—that is, the state of enlightenment that all Buddhists seek. It's set off from the rest of the world by the high railings that surround the grounds. The base of the stupa is earth, the dome the sky. The mast of the umbrella shape at the top is the axis around which the universe revolves. The three umbrellas represent the Buddha, his law, and the monastic order or (a different theory) different heavens or gods. And the railing around the top structure probably is a throwback to the railings the Indians put around sacred trees, setting off sanctified ground. That's not all, though. Even the paths have religious significance: The path on the base was intended for processions; the path at ground level represents the Path of Life Around the World Mountain and allows pilgrims to walk clockwise around the Stupa (an offshoot of an old ritual in which religious participants retrace the path of the sun).

Ornate relief sculpture: The gates to the Great Stupa are covered with detailed sculptures, a dizzying interwoven mass of scenes from the Buddha's life. These sculptures are among the first in the style that was used in Indian carving for the next thousand years—they're cut very deeply, so figures stand out against shadows. And the figures themselves are very alive-looking; there's an energy to them, enhanced by their almost sensuous forms—fluid, graceful, and full.

Architectural notes: The stupa at its most basic—a simple burial mound—actually dates back to prehistoric times. But the Great Stupa (and for that matter, other lesser stupas) is clearly a more developed version than just a basic mound. It was built on the orders of Asoka, the first Buddhist king of India, who was so religious he is said to have had eighty-four thousand stupas erected around the empire—all at sites of religious significance. One interesting point: Coincidentally (or perhaps not so coincidentally), these sites often corresponded with the trade routes of the day. So stupas were crossroads of sorts for traders and monks. (In fact, this is probably one of the reasons that Buddhism spread as rapidly as it did.)

Another example of the modernity of ancient Roman architecture: The Western world's first apartment buildings, or, more technically, high-density dwellings, were built in Rome—which counted about 1 million residents in 100 C.E.

THE FLAVIAN AMPHITHEATER

(or, more commonly, the Roman Colosseum)

When: 72–96 C.E.

Where: Rome, Italy

What: A site for games—initially fights between gladiators or between gladiators and animals, and also (after gladiatorial events were banned in the fifth century) between animals. (One quick note: It's unlikely that many Christians were persecuted here. This type of "entertainment" was usually held in the circuses.)

At a glance: A huge round amphitheater near the center of present-day Rome. Arches upon arches upon arches encircling an open oval. It looks a lot like a (ruined) modern sports stadium, and for good reason: Most modern stadiums are modeled after this.

Blueprint: In the Colosseum we can get a good look at the most important innovations in Roman architecture—the introduction of the arch and the vault, and the development of concrete, all of which enabled the Romans to create huge interior spaces (a central aspect to Roman architecture, in general). The arena was built on the site of the emperor Nero's Golden House, a palace complete with lake and pleasure gardens. One reason: the emperor Vespasian wanted to show his citizens that the days of Nero's excesses were over; he was making amends to the people. Made of travertine (a type of limestone), brick, concrete, and volcanic rock (tufa), the Colosseum is four levels high, roughly 615 feet long and 510

A Gladiator's Lot

 The Colosseum was the premier stadium of gladiatorial contests in a land that was peppered with amphitheaters.

Romans flocked to see gladiators hack each other to death. This was *the* most popular form of entertainment. As far back as 168 B.C.E., Romans in one instance deserted the theater where the great playwright Terence's *Hecyra* was being performed in order to go see a bloody gladiatorial show.

The name of the game was blood. Sometimes wild animals were let loose in the arena, to be met with a hail of arrows, or hunting spears, or fire. In one day in 80 C.E., five thousand animals were killed at the Colosseum (which is why lions are now extinct in Europe and the Middle East, and elephants are no longer found in North Africa).

But the worst were the human contests. The night before, the gladiators (who were usually slaves specially trained for fighting, or convicted criminals) were wined and dined in a lavish banquet. The public was invited to view the feast and see the attitude of the gladiators. Some of the gladiators took the attitude of "eat, drink, and be merry"; others nervously made out their wills.

The next day they all paraded to the Colosseum, saluted the emperor if he was there, and got ready for combat. Arms were distributed according to the category of gladiator: Samnites carried a shield and sword, Thracians got a round buckler and a dagger, mirmillones wore a helmet, and the retiarii carried a net and a trident.

The gladiators were now paired off. Sometimes gladiators were pitted against others of the same category; other times different categories went against each other. Sometimes bizarre combinations were entered, like a dwarf against a woman.

To the sound of trumpets and horns, the first pair began fighting. They were sometimes whipped from the sidelines to increase their fighting ardor. As the blood flowed, the audiences screamed like people at a modern football game, particularly as their favorites got in good cuts. When one of the gladiators finally fell, attendants (dressed in costumes) came running from the sidelines and made sure the man was dead by striking his head with a mallet. If he was, their assistants carried him out of the arena on a stretcher. And at other times a stunned loser, down but not dead, lying on the ground, appealed for mercy. Sometimes the winning gladiator left the decision to the emperor, who often turned to the crowd for advice. Supposedly, thumbs up meant the loser could live. But it may have meant the opposite.

The victorious gladiator was awarded on the spot with silver and gold. But underneath the joy of victory was the knowledge that soon he would have to fight again. The real prize was the wooden sword, usually won after numerous victories. It meant the most precious thing of all—freedom from the arena.

---

feet wide, and was originally faced with travertine held in place by iron clamps. The exterior was a simple design: arches flanked by engaged half columns. The interior had banked seats reached by interior stairs.

Distinctive features: *Size.* Simply

immense. It's one of the largest buildings in the world, in terms of mass, and so, a perfect symbol of the grandeur of ancient Rome. To put it in simple perspective: It was able to seat fifty thousand people, only seventy-five hundred fewer than Yankee Stadium today.

Balance: For all the size, the design is an example of Roman attention to order and organization. The best example: The columns are arranged in terms of architectural order, and so, weight. At the bottom, the heavier Doric columns, next level up, Ionic, and finally at the top, Corinthian. (Granted, you can't really tell that much difference between the three orders. Unlike the Greeks, who had clear distinctions, these faded out a bit by Roman times. So the different orders of columns aren't immediately obvious—but the idea is brilliant.)

Engineering expertise: This structure shows Roman engineering and ingenuity at its best. The biggest obstacle to surmount: the problem of crowd congestion. The solution: a network of

THE FLAVIAN AMPHITHEATER (THE ROMAN COLOSSEUM), ROME, ITALY

passageways and stairs at the core of the amphitheater. More specifically, arched passageways on the ground level led to a double row of tunnel vaults that encircled the arena, which, in turn, led to stairs that took you to the upper levels. A smaller but no less pesky problem: how to shelter patrons from sun and rain. The solution: an awning that could extend over the arena, supported by poles anchored in the top section, sort of a primitive Astrodome. Engineering was even applied to showmanship. To make the games exciting, animals were raised on simple elevators from their underground chambers to the arena floor. The floor could even be flooded if the day's games were to be naval battles.

Architectural notes: The answer

to the obvious question: If the Romans called it the Flavian Amphitheater after the imperial dynasty that built it, why do most people today call it the Colosseum? Simple. Until the mid fourth century or so, a huge statue (about one hundred feet tall) of Nero as the sun-god stood next to the amphitheater. A popular eighth-century Roman guidebook took the term for the statue (colossal, or, right, colosseum) and applied it to the amphitheater itself. And since then, that's what it's usually called.

THE PYRAMID OF THE SUN

When: c. 100 B.C.E.

Where: Teotihuacán, Mexico

What: Religious shrine used for ritual worship.

At a glance: A massive step pyramid with gently sloping sides. In the middle of a valley that held the ancient city of Teotihuacán, it vies for attention with the mountains in the distant background.

Blueprint: Built over a sacred cave, the Pyramid of the Sun is just one of the structures still standing in the ancient city of Teotihuacán, and was the central building of the entire city, which included apartment buildings, smaller temples, theaters, markets, a smaller pyramid, the Pyramid of the Moon, and even steam baths. The city was built in a valley and was laid out in a remarkably precise and accurate way. The Pyramid of the Sun lines up with the exact spot that the sun sets over Teotihuacán when it reaches its

Teotihuacán was the first planned city in the world. In its heyday—about 1500 B.C.E.—over 200,000 people lived there. (Compare this to Athens, which in Greece's Golden Age housed only about 150,000.) It was a very class-conscious city: The upper class lived in a separate neighborhood of large, luxurious houses. The working class, including tradespeople, artisans, and craftspeople, lived on the outskirts of the city in apartment compounds housing about one hundred people each, and agricultural laborers lived outside the city. But the apartments for the working class were far from housing projects. In fact, when they were first excavated, some of them appeared so spacious and comfortable that the archaeologists thought they may have been small palaces.

highest point during the summer solstice. The main street, the Avenue of the Dead (built later), is exactly parallel to the main façade of the Pyramid of the Sun and is aligned with the axis of the Pyramid of the Moon and the Plaza of the Moon. When it was built, the Pyramid of the Sun had a temple on the upper platform, used to worship a god (probably the rain god Tlaloc).

Distinctive features: *Size.* Another massive monument built by an ancient civilization. The Pyramid of the Sun is 738 feet on each side, and 215 feet high, and was about 246 feet high when the temple on the top still stood. The sheer mass, plus the shallow slope of the sides, adds up to an immense structure both in actual size and in impact.

Shape. If you think about it, it's actually not one, but *five* pyramids—each with the top chopped off, each with the same slope—stacked on top of one another. This style, echoed by the smaller Pyramid of the Moon in Teotihuacán, was the chief style of the preclassic period in Mexico.

Architectural notes: Teotihuacán means "birthplace of the gods." And according to myth, when the end of an era came, the sun "died." So the gods collected in this valley to create a new city to mark the beginning of a new era. And so this city, revolving around the huge Pyramid of the Sun, was built. According to most theories, the Pyramid of the Sun (and the Pyramid of the Moon) were built before the rest of the once bustling surrounding city. The Pyramid of the Sun was probably built in about 100 C.E., the Pyramid of the Moon a bit later, and the main avenue, the Avenue of the Dead, sometime during this period. Then, about two hundred years later, the rest of the city now remaining was built—possibly fol-

lowing the original plan. In terms of size, function, and physical placement, however, the Pyramid of the Sun, remained the central focus of the city.

PYRAMID OF THE SUN, TEOTIHUACÁN, MEXICO

HAGIA SOPHIA (CHURCH OF HOLY WISDOM)

When: 532–37 C.E.

Where: Istanbul (then Constantinople), Turkey

What: Built as a Christian church of the Greek Byzantine empire, it was adapted to become an Islamic mosque after the Ottoman Turks captured the city in 1453.

At a glance: A large central dome flanked by two smaller half domes, with four minarets at the corners. An impressive structure, but actually, the most impressive feature isn't on the outside, but on the inside—a huge space punctuated by rays of bright light that make the central dome seem as if it's floating.

Blueprint: Anthemius of Tralles, artist and scientist, and Isidorus of Miletus, architect and engineer, came up with a groundbreaking design. But for all the unique qualities of the design, it took only six weeks to formulate—and it took an extremely short five years to complete. All this speed because the Byzantine emperor Justinian was hot to have it finished. Initially, there were ornate mosaics inside. These were whitewashed over by the Ottomans, and in their place, eight large discs with sayings from the Quran and names of prophets added. Also added at this time were the four minarets on the four corners of the building.

Distinctive features: *Size—espe-*

cially the large interior space: The Hagia Sophia is a biggie—it covers about one and a half acres, is 270 feet in length, and the 108-foot-diameter dome reaches a height of 184 feet. Step inside, and the space really hits you. The two half domes lead up to the central dome, soaring above. It's a masterpiece of vaulted architecture, with the domes billowing upward—even the support systems are part of this billowing design, all contributing to the feeling of expanding space.

Windows: There were more of them in the past (earthquakes forced the rebuilding of the dome three times, and some windows were lost), but they're still plentiful and are placed in such a way that rays of light filter in and bounce off the immense space. The designers were able to have more

HAGIA SOPHIA
(CHURCH OF THE
HOLY WISDOM),
ISTANBUL,
TURKEY

windows than usual because of their design: The dome is supported by four arches (pendentives, curved triangular segments) that sit on four supporting piers that form a square. This way the walls under the arches don't have to support much, and so can be broken up with more windows than were possible in the past; and the dome itself can be taller and have more windows as well.

Architectural notes: The design of the Hagia Sophia is actually a blend of Eastern and Western design elements. To put it simply, it's as if a huge dome was plunked down in the middle of a typical early Christian basilica. There's a typical church structure, but with a huge dome over the nave, two half domes on either side of it, and half-circle niches with open arcades attached to each of the half domes. The combination of vaulted architecture (from the Romans), the dome on pendentives (later a central element of Byzantine architecture), the early Christian longitudinal axis, and the later additions of minarets makes this an interesting pastiche of the best of both East and West.

THE HORYU-JI MONASTERY COMPLEX

When: c. 600–700
   Where: Nara, Japan
   What: A Buddhist monastery and temples.

THE HORYU-JI MONASTERY COMPLEX, NARA, JAPAN (JAPAN AIRLINES; PHOTOGRAPH BY MORRIS SIMONCELLI)

At a glance: A collection of wooden buildings with low curving roofs, their shapes echoing those of the trees around them—cedars, pines, ancient maple trees. The overwhelming mood is one of peace, harmony with nature, and serenity.

Blueprint: Although they're in Japan, these buildings appear very Chinese in design; in fact, the style was imported into Japan by Buddhist monks from Korea. They're the oldest wooden structures in the world, built in about 607 to serve monks and pilgrims who wished to worship. Initially, there were more buildings, but those that survived are the main ones: the Hall of Dreams (the yumedono, or pagoda), the Golden Hall (the kondo, or prayer hall), and the Lecture Hall (the kodo).

Distinctive features: *Unique broad roofs.* One of the key elements in these buildings—large, heavy roofs with flaring upturned corners. This type of design is possible because of the construction method used—the Chinese system of timber framing (which is called wa-yo, or the Japanese system, in Japan). It's a post-and-beam system that gives the builder flexibility and allows roofs to have unique shapes. In effect, the roofs are the capital on a column—a *huge* capital that's supported by beams that are, in turn, supported by brackets. A bit technical. But the upshot—roofs could be wide, curved, cantilevered to amazing depth. And the brackets themselves are decorative elements as well.

Religious iconography. It's a Buddhist complex, so Buddhist images and symbols abound. The kondo is the main building of the complex, so it in particular is heavily decorated. The ceiling is shaped in the form of a canopy, signifying heaven. Inside is a trio of Buddha statues. On the walls are paintings of Buddha and the different paradises that lie in each cardinal direction. The result: The kondo is a physical representation of Buddha's otherworldly realm; it's set up in the form of a mandala, with a seated Buddha in the center of the temple, and in the center, then, of the universe. The central statue is a larger-than-life bronze of Buddha sitting in the lotus position on a huge throne.

Architectural notes: While the buildings are pure Chinese, the layout of the monastery complex is more Japanese—or rather, a Japanese refinement of Chinese theory. Monasteries were built on a symmetrical square plan, a gridiron, actually. Often they had two pagodas with relics, a main

hall that held the statue of the Buddha, lecture halls, a library, and a bell tower. But while in China a person would pass through a succession of buildings to get to the spiritual core, the kondo, in Japan buildings are laid out more laterally. The result is an interesting spatial arrangement that evolved over time to be less rigid and symmetrical and more free-form, with buildings arranged to work with nature rather than imposing order on it.

KAILASANATHA TEMPLE

When: c. 760–800
  Where: Ellora, India
  What: A Hindu cave temple.

  At a glance: An enormous temple—a multilayered structure with doors, arches, columns, and windows—carved completely from a natural outcropping of rock. It's as if an ornate building grew organically from a natural stone foundation, surrounded on all sides by mountains.

  Blueprint: Building (or rather carving) this temple was similar to carving a statue: The first task, getting a block of stone, or isolating it from the rest of the cliff. In this case, craftsmen cut three trenches into the cliff face, in effect creating a block of stone separated from the cliff, but still attached on one side. Then they carved the temple directly from the block of stone they had created, cutting away unnecessary chunks. They worked from the top down, starting above the highest point and carving down. The chief danger of this method—having the

temple wind up at the bottom of a pit. To avoid this, the temple was placed on a high base, covered with a frieze of elephants and lions, who look as though they're carrying the temple on their backs. The result is a huge, free-standing temple in a court 276 feet long and 154 feet wide, with a tower that is 96 feet high.

Distinctive features: *Light*—or rather shadow. Since the temple is carved from a mountain, deep shadows from the surrounding mountain shade the reliefs and passageways. The result is an interplay of bright sunlight and dark shadows, throwing the carved sculptures into high relief and making them look even more three-dimensional, almost animated.

Ornate sculpture and reliefs. In some ways, the temple is more a sculpture

KAILASANATHA TEMPLE, CAVE 16, ELLORA, INDIA (MID 8TH CENTURY) (VANNI/ART RESOURCE, N.Y.)

than a building—a dizzying conglomeration of detailed carved reliefs and statuary. Since the temple is supposed to represent Mount Kailasa, the mountain where Siva and his consort live, most of the sculptures and reliefs show the legend of Siva, a visual episode from the Hindu epic the *Ramayana*.

Architectural notes: The Kailasanatha Temple is one of many temples carved out of the rock at Ellora. In fact, there are thirty-four different temples at the site—Buddhist, Jainist, and Hindu. The first wave of building was devoted to the Hindu god Siva; these shrines focus more on fertility (in fact, the Kailasanatha Temple has buried in its main shrine a box filled with different symbolic items, such as soil, roots, and herbs, that are supposed to tie it to these older fertility beliefs). Next, in about 600 C.E. the caves around Ellora became a focal point for Buddhist worship. Finally, under the rule of Krishna II of the Rastrakuta dynasty, came a resurgence in Hinduism, specifically Siva worship, and thus the building of the Kailasanatha Temple.

THE GREAT MOSQUE OF CÓRDOBA

When: 786–987

    Where: Córdoba, Spain

    What: An Islamic house of worship.

    At a glance: Outside, a courtyard with orange trees surrounded by a portico, in front of a large domed mosque. And inside, a fantasy forest of columns and arches amid a soaring space. The overall result: a decorative vision that could have been pulled from the pages of *The Thousand and One Nights*.

    Blueprint: The Great Mosque is the pinnacle of the Arab Umayyad empire architecture—and the result of years of design, restoration, and additions. The first mosque was built in about 784 under the auspices of the first Muslim ruler of Spain, Abd al-Rahman, and was a simpler, smaller structure—nine (or eleven) twelve-bay naves—built on the site of an old Christian church. This initial design used the marble pillars that were already there, but topped them with a double row of arches. Next came the first enlargement, needed to accommodate the growing Islamic population. In the second enlargement, done between 961 and 976, more bays were added to the mosque and, more dramatically,

Problems in Designing a Mosque

Like other religious buildings, many mosques are among the architectural masterpieces of the world. Yet in many ways the architects and designers of these buildings faced a more difficult task than those of other religions. The reason? Islam forbade any representations or symbols that could be considered idolatrous. (The only symbol allowed in a mosque was an indication in one wall of the direction of Mecca. This usually took the form of a niche in the wall, the mihrab.) So, unlike the Christian artists and designers who had full rein to fill their churches with icons, religious statues, and sculptures, their Islamic counterparts had to come up with different ways of decorating the space. Add to this the fact that the commandment against idolatry actually grew more stringent as time went on, and the end result is the evolution of highly decorative qualities we now associate with Islamic art. Instead of naturalistic representation, artists developed a sophisticated style that included abstract designs, interlacing geometrics, stylized representations, and the decorative use of lettering.

four domes were erected. The third addition, done in 987, widened the mosque. There were other later, but lesser, additions as well. The end result of this ongoing construction and design: a huge mosque, larger than any Christian church, with an interior space of 584 feet by 410 feet—covering 240,000 square feet—that is considered one of the finest examples of medieval architecture.

    Distinctive features: *A forest of columns.* The interior of the mosque is filled with columns—twelve hundred of them—supporting double-tiered arches. The effect is one of infinitude. In all directions, there are columns under arches, all alike, one after another, seemingly stretching on forever.

Double-tiered arches. These arches actually grew out of necessity: Because the original builders didn't have access to tall columns and because the columns that were already on the site were short, the architects had to come up with a way of raising the roof height while still using the relatively short columns. The solution? Building one set of arches that were supported by the columns, and a second set supported by a system of long piers resting on the columns and rising between the other arches. The result—a very intricate, very impressive network of arches. And emphasizing the shape of

THE GREAT
MOSQUE,
CÓRDOBA, SPAIN
(ALINARI/ART
RESOURCE, N.Y.)

this multitude of arches is color. They're made of alternating marble and brick; and the resulting color pattern keeps the eyes moving along the lines of the arches.

Intricate decorative work. Carvings and mosaics cover much of the ceiling and walls in the mihrab (the niche set in the back wall of the prayer hall) and the gates. For example, the central dome that marks the entrance to the mihrab is paved in detailed tile, stucco, and glass mosaic. The mihrab walls have filigreed carved marble panels covered in arabesques and geometric forms. Also on the walls are numerous inscriptions

from the Quran. As for the area outside of the mihrab, columns and brackets in the main mosque area are carved, but here the effect is merely to heighten the impact of the architectural details. The end result, then, is a harmonious use of decorative elements.

Architectural notes: The mosque at Córdoba contains the same basic elements as other great mosques. Briefly, there's a wall surrounding a court, which has porticos on three sides and the prayer hall on the fourth. The hall's rear wall faces in the direction (the qibla) of Mecca and is the focal point for prayers. A mihrab—an empty niche—is set in the qibla wall. As mentioned above, the mihrab is usually the most heavily ornamented spot in a mosque, containing carved panels, mosaics, and the like, while the surrounding wall is generally much simpler. There's typically a carved minbar—a lectern reached by a stair—by the mihrab. And in front of the mihrab, there's an area separated from the rest of the mosque by a screen; this, the maqsura, is used for dignitaries. So, yes, the mosque at Córdoba contains the "typical" features of a mosque, but the architectural and design elements in it transcend the typical, making the mosque at Córdoba a breathtaking architectural gem.

ANGKOR WAT

When: c. 1100–1150

Where: Ancient city of Angkor, Cambodia

What: Both a temple to the Hindu god Vishnu and a monument to King Suryavarman II, its builder.

ANGKOR WAT, CAMBODIA

At a glance: Across a moat, at the end of a long paved boulevard, one sees towers against the sky, rising above the jungle trees. The complex is a set of tiered terraces, topped by towers. It's almost like a walled step pyramid in the middle of a large clear space, anchored by towers and surrounded by trees—massive yet graceful.

Blueprint: In a space 5,000 by 4,000 feet, Angkor Wat, the largest

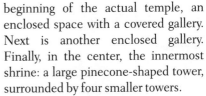

temple in Indochina, was erected. In many ways, Angkor Wat is similar to an ancient Egyptian pyramid—intended to allow a king and his world to live after death. Since a king had both religious and political power, he was divine. His birthright, then, was a continued life, and a complex like Angkor Wat was a physical symbol of both his secular and spiritual power. So the innermost shrine probably held a god statue of King Suryavarman as Vishnu; in this way, he would live on after his death.

Distinctive features: *Symbolism.* The complex in general represents Mount Meru, the World Mountain that was the dwelling place of the gods. Its layout is based on the mandala (the Buddhist symbolic representation of the cosmos), making the temple in harmony with cosmic order and with the forces underlying the universe. But that's not all. Actually, virtually every part of the complex has religious significance. Starting from the outside: The moat represents the outer ocean of Hindu mythology; the walls, the mountains; the balustrades lining the boulevard leading to the temple represent the cosmic serpent. Finally, the central tower is the world's axis—as well as the home of the god (or, actually god-king).

Simple symmetrical design. The walled complex is based on a very symmetrical pattern. At its most basic, it's simply three concentric terraces with covered galleries, separated by paved courtyards, rising toward the center to the crowning point—a large tower. More specifically: A paved roadway, lined with carved balustrades, crosses a moat and leads to the main entrance, a gateway of three pavilions topped by towers. The road continues to the

beginning of the actual temple, an enclosed space with a covered gallery. Next is another enclosed gallery. Finally, in the center, the innermost shrine: a large pinecone-shaped tower, surrounded by four smaller towers.

Ornate sculpture. Angkor Wat is as notable for its sculpture as for its architectural design. Almost the entire temple is covered in carvings, from purely ornamental scrollwork, flowers, fruits, and the like that twine around the pillars to the narrative carvings that line the galleries. Of special note: the kilometer-long relief carvings on the walls of the open gallery. The narrative carvings are chiefly of Vishnu, scenes from his life and other religious myths; but there are representations of both Siva and Buddha as well, a sign of the different religions also prevalent at the time. And since it's also a monument to King Suryavarman, there are scenes of his moments of triumph. For all the carvings, though, there's a restraint to their design. They enhance the structure rather than dominating it.

Architectural notes: Until recently, the world that was supposed to live forever was almost forgotten: After the thirteenth century and the fall of the Khmer kingdom, Angkor Wat, like many other Khmer buildings, fell into decay. Slowly the jungle reclaimed the land, swallowing up the entire complex. Eventually the natural growth was cleared, revealing the once magnificent buildings. But signs of the more recent past, and the communist domination of Cambodia, remain. Bullet scars mark some walls. Rows of gods stand headless, decapitated by the communist revolutionaries, the Khmer Rouge. And above it all, on a wall carving, the god Vishnu oversees the battle between good and evil.

THE TAJ MAHAL

When: 1632–52

Where: Agra, India

What: The tomb of Shah Jahan's wife, Mumtaz Mahal (thus the name —Crown of the Queen).

At a glance: One of the most recognizable buildings in the world—a gracefully curving dome atop a white marble building, surrounded by four delicate towers, all reflected in a long rectangle of water before it. The effect? A picture out of a fairy-tale romance.

Blueprint: The principal designers of the Taj Mahal were Turkish brothers, Ustad Hamid and Ustad Ahmad Mamar Nadir ul-Asar, who oversaw a team of thirty-seven workers, including architects, inlayers, metalworkers, sculptors, calligraphers, and mosaicists from different parts of Asia and Persia, plus an additional general labor force of about twenty thousand. Even with all these people, the Taj Mahal took about twenty years to complete. One reason: the elaborate mosaics, carvings, and calligraphic inscriptions. These are particularly evident in the main chamber, where the decorated marble sarcophagi of both the emperor and the empress are located. (Their actual bodies are buried in a vault beneath the chamber.)

Distinctive features: *Symmetry and proportion.* This is Mogul (Mughal)—the Indian Muslim rulers from 1526 to 1857—design at its best and most harmonious. Everything is geometrically laid out, from the garden, to the placement of the mausoleum, to the shape of the mausoleum itself. One example of how important balance was

to the designers: The Taj Mahal is flanked by two red sandstone buildings; one, a mosque with three domes. The other is the duplicate of the mosque, but it's not facing Mecca so it couldn't be used for worship. The reason it's there, then? Probably just to act as an architectural balance for the real mosque.

The surrounding Persian formal garden. Another example of symmetrical design, and one of the most notable features of the Taj Mahal. The garden that surrounds the Taj Mahal is divided into four equal parts by two marble canals, and right in the center, between the gate and the tomb, is a marble reflecting pool. Both the layout and the use of water is deliberate—the garden isn't just simple decoration; it's supposed to represent both the universe and paradise. As such, it has to have both water and earth. And the layout is supposed to reflect humankind's role in nature—by imposing order.

Architectural notes: The Taj Mahal is an example of a blend of two design styles: Islamic Persian and Indian. First, the Persian. The design is basically one of many Islamic Persian domed mausoleums: a large central dome with a bulbous, curving shape (it's actually a double-shelled dome—there's a smaller dome inside the outside dome that serves as the ceiling), surrounded by four smaller cupolas. The entrance looks like a mosque or other Islamic structure: a large central arch (a liwan), which is flanked by smaller arches stacked on top of one another. And, of course, the four minarets at the corners of the terrace on which the Taj sits are Islamic. As for the interior, rooms are laid out in a popular Mogul-period plan— an interlaced square and cross. The

rooms surrounding the main chamber are octagonal (and, incidentally, are supposed to have amazing acoustics). But one specifically Indian touch—the different rooms are surrounded by the

THE TAJ MAHAL, AGRA, INDIA

equivalent amount of exterior wall. Another Indian touch—for all the size of the dome, the soaring space isn't exploited as it would be in a mosque; instead, it's a distinct, discrete unit.

CHARTRES CATHEDRAL

When: 1194–1220

Where: Chartres, France

What: Prime example of High Gothic style.

At a glance: A cathedral marked by a huge rose window and two towers of different heights, but both slender, pointed, and reaching into the sky. Religious statues and reliefs cover the portals; filigreed carvings richly embellish the towers. The overall effect is one of soaring spirituality.

Blueprint: Around 1145 the bishop of Chartres decided he wanted the cathedral rebuilt in the new Gothic style, but the resulting efforts were largely obliterated just fifty years later when a fire destroyed everything but the west façade. So the rebuilding began again in 1194 and by 1220 had produced the first masterpiece of the High Gothic style. The floor plan is that of most Gothic cathedrals—a large cross consisting of the nave (the large central hall), with narrow galleries on either side, and the intersecting transept. The nave, arching up to 120 feet, is testimony to the extraordinary engineering abilities of the architects and builders.

Distinctive features: *Height, height, and more height.* Actually, it's not only height; it's verticals in general. Nearly everything about the cathedral focuses on "up"—pointing to heaven, if you will. This was a major element in the High Gothic style, and it's brilliantly realized in the cathedral. The narrow vaults form pointed arches; thin columns (colonettes) and narrow ribs on the vaults draw the eyes along with them to the heights of the arch;

WEST FRONT CHARTRES CATHEDRAL, CHARTRES, FRANCE (12TH CENTURY) (COURTESY FRENCH GOVERNMENT TOURIST OFFICE)

finally, stained-glass windows placed high on the wall, above other stained-glass windows, let light in at the top of the vault.

The magic quality of stained glass. The stained-glass windows in the cathedral don't let in a great deal of light, but what they let in is transformed in the high-arched space. Because there are so many windows and so little wall—and because the little wall area there is generally covered by ribs and colonettes, the windows actually make the walls seem translucent. They're not windows, but an integral part of a shimmering wall. When the sun shines through them, the interior of the cathedral is awash in soft colors, creating a spiritual, otherworldly effect.

Unmatching towers. Not a major design statement, but definitely a unique feature of Chartres Cathedral. The two towers are of different heights, different design, and actually, different styles. The smaller tower is the older one, built before 1194, and one of the parts of the cathedral not destroyed in the fire. Since it was built when the Romanesque style was first giving way to the Gothic, it's an example of the transitional style—thicker, shorter, less fine, less detailed than the style to come. The taller tower is pure High Gothic—lofty, thin, covered with ornate decoration.

Architectural notes: High Gothic design, of which the cathedral at Chartres is a prime example, used a combination of several key features: pointed arches, flying buttresses (open half arches), and ribbed groin vaults. Other styles used these elements, but in Gothic architecture they were used in a rational system, actually a philosophical system (called scholasticism) that held that every design element had to be interrelated. So cathedral interiors are actually intricate skeletal constructions, with parts on display. Yes, it sounds technical, but the outcome isn't. The visually harmonious sum of all the parts adds up to a breathtaking design.

ST. PETER'S BASILICA

When: 1505/6–1626

Where: Vatican City, Rome, Italy

What: Catholic church—and the religious center of the papacy.

At a glance: A broad piazza flanked on either side by a semicircle of columns. In the center of the piazza, a tall red granite obelisk. And behind it, a huge church, with a row of tall columns surrounding massive portals, all of this topped by an immense dome.

Blueprint: The world's largest Christian church, St. Peter's is built in the shape of a cross—almost 700 feet long and 450 feet across at the widest point. It was the product of some of the finest artists and architects of the time—from Donato Bramante, who took the design job in 1505/6, charged with rebuilding *old* St. Peter's; to Michelangelo, who became chief architect in 1546 and designed its dome; to Carlo Maderno, who took over in the 1600s and designed the façade, and Gianlorenzo Bernini, the architect-sculptor who not only planned the setting with the colonnades, but also sculpted many of the works in the interior.

Distinctive features: *Soaring dome.* This is possibly one of the most distinctive features of St. Peter's, and one which, while initially conceived by Bramante, was altered by Michelangelo, and given more power. The key? There's a drum—a ring—at the base of the dome, which makes it look almost as though the dome is being squeezed. This, plus the ribbings down the sides of the dome, give it an energy. The dome is springing out of the center of the church; like a balloon, it looks like

it's tugging at its moorings, trying to reach heaven.

Baroque sculptures. Since the interior of St. Peter's can hold fifty thousand people, it could be a cold and barren-looking place. Why isn't it, then? The profusion of statues and sculptures that make the church seem filled, lived-in, somehow accessible. There's a huge bronze canopy atop the altar beneath the high dome, supported by ornate columns and punctuated by carved angels and scrolls. The Chair of St. Peter is a bronze throne covering the wooden chair that was said to have belonged to St. Peter. These and other sculpted elements fill the church—and delight the eye.

ST. PETER'S
BASILICA, ROME

Architectural notes: The planning and construction of the church was a long, drawn-out process spanning 120 years. Over this time, the different architects had to work with the initial plan, plus whatever construction had already been done. The basic floor plan evolved from a Greek-cross (four arms of equal length) to a Latin cross (three short arms and one long one); the interior wall design changed to let the skeleton show; and there were other changes. But the end result realized Bramante's original idea, if not his design: to create a structure that would dominate Rome.

THE SEVEN LEADING MODERN ARCHITECTS OUTSIDE THE UNITED STATES: MASTERS OF TWENTIETH-CENTURY DESIGN

Architecture has always revolved around a very simple problem: How to enclose this space (or house those people, etc.) with the materials and expertise at hand?

And, frankly, while design styles changed through the ages, one thing didn't change all that much—raw materials. Buildings were made of stone, brick, or wood. Simple.

But then came the Industrial Revolution. And with it, new materials, and new techniques for manipulating and building with those materials. Structural metals (made popular with the improvements in metallurgy). Concrete (developed in 1824 when artificial portland cement was invented, then improved when reinforced concrete with iron bars came into use). Not to mention glass and fabricated materials. Add to this the change in business—the evolving need for larger structures to house businesspeople involved in the same enterprise. Then the invention of the elevator, which made skyscrapers feasible. In addition, there was a new design ethos emerging. Artists were exploring new innovative styles. Old-fashioned representationalism was falling by the wayside.

The new questions facing architects: What can we do with the new materials? How can we create a *new* way of enclosing that space or housing those people given these breakthroughs? What can we design that is truly modern, that isn't dependent on the styles of the past?

The answers, of course, are in the works of the seven architects below. These are the masters of modern architecture, the people who took the new materials, took the new techniques, and created the new styles that still grace urban skylines today.

MASTERS OF MODERN ARCHITECTURE

ANTONI GAUDÍ

(1852–1926), Spain

THE MOVEMENT

Catalan "modernism," an offshoot of Art Nouveau.

GUIDING THEORY

An attempt to recapture Spain's romantic medieval past.

DESIGN FEATURES

Similar to abstract sculpture—flowing lines, outrageous curves, waves. In fact, often no straight lines at all. Buildings look like they've been molded out of clay, not built out of concrete. The end effect? Wholly original and pure fantasy.

THE MASTERPIECES

The Palacio Güell; the Casa Batlló and Casa Milá apartment houses, Barcelona, Spain; the Church of the Sagrada Familia, Barcelona, Spain.

GERRIT RIETVELD

(1888–1964), The Netherlands

THE MOVEMENT

De Stijl (The Style), a movement of Dutch artists (like painter Mondrian) and architects.

GUIDING THEORY

Based on modern philosophical movements, like theosophical mysticism and neopositivism. De Stijl's goal: to carry abstraction to "its ultimate goal," as members put it. In this way, they'd create the design equivalent of philosophical and spiritual purity.

DESIGN FEATURES

Marked by contrasts between horizontal and vertical lines, open space and closed; also shows strong use of color. The ultimate impression? Simple, severe, clean-looking, but actually complex in design and the interrelation of forms when you really look at what Rietveld built.

THE MASTERPIECES

The Schröder House, Utrecht, The Netherlands; the Van Gogh Museum, Amsterdam.

WALTER GROPIUS

(1883–1969), Germany

THE MOVEMENT

Bauhaus (this was his very specific movement, but he's often called the first proponent of the International Style, the first original style of architecture since the Gothic).

GUIDING THEORY

Took the name from the word

bauhutte, where the medieval German masters and craftspeople who built the cathedrals of the late Middle Ages lived, and took inspiration for the movement from the notion of a collective of craftspeople. Aimed for the unity of the arts—or, as Gropius wrote, "The arts exist in isolation, from which they can be rescued only through the conscious, co-operative effort of all craftsmen. . . ."

DESIGN FEATURES

Design stripped down to its basics—very stark, very clean lines, with glass walls, cantilevered construction, concrete floors and columns. The essence of modernity.

THE MASTERPIECES

Bauhaus, Dessau, Germany; Harvard Graduate Center, Cambridge, Massachusetts.

MIES VAN DER ROHE

(1886–1969)

THE MOVEMENT

International Style—the first truly innovative architectural style since the Gothic.

GUIDING THEORY

"Less is more" was his credo, and his design style followed this belief to the nth degree.

DESIGN FEATURES

Glass, glass, glass—especially soaring glass skyscrapers. Other common elements he used: slender columns, slab roofs, and heavy use of rich materials

like marble, colored glass, ebony, onyx, chrome, travertine. All this plus expert exploitation of space. Everything looks precise, almost mathematically planned and superdetailed. Picture a modern glass skyscraper and you've got the gist of his designs.

THE MASTERPIECES

The German Pavilion for the 1929 Barcelona Exposition, Barcelona, Spain; Tugendhat House, Brno, the Czech Republic; Seagram Building, New York; Crown Hall, Illinois Institute of Technology, Chicago.

LE CORBUSIER

(Charles-Édouard Jeanneret) *(1887–1965), France (Swiss-born)*

THE MOVEMENT

International Style (at first); later his own "sculptural" style.

GUIDING THEORY

First, the interrelation between machine forms and architectural techniques. Later, espoused "totally free architecture"—modern design that moved away from simple geometry into shapes that echoed nature, were dramatic, unexpected, even mysterious.

DESIGN FEATURES

Depends on when he built. His early style is pure Internationalism—thin walls and shapes, lots of glass, strong horizontals and verticals, very Mondrian-like, strict attention to open spaces. His later style uses thicker walls and more fluid shapes. Marked by soaring lines. Almost sculpturelike.

The Masterpieces

Savoye House, Poissy-sur-Seine, France; U.N. Secretariat, New York; Convent at La Tourette, France; Chapel of Notre-Dame-du-Haut, Ronchamp, France.

PIER LUIGI NERVI

(1891–1979), Italy

The Movement

No name, but he himself is called "the poet in concrete."

Guiding Theory

Concrete can be used in bold, even unexpected, ways.

Design Features

Heavy use of concrete. Huge spaces roofed in dramatic manner.

The Masterpieces

Exhibition Hall, Turin, Italy; Berta Stadium, Florence, Italy; UNESCO Headquarters, Paris; Olympic Sports Palace, Rome; George Washington Bridge Bus Terminal, New York; Port of New York Authority Bus Terminal, New York.

ALVAR AALTO

(1896–1976), Finland

The Movement

Modernism; Aalto was called the father of Scandinavian modernism.

Guiding Theory

Organic modernism—modernity far removed from geometric rigidity, incorporating instead irregular shapes and forms and natural materials.

Design Features

Some elements of the International Style—glass, open spaces, columns, cantilevered roofs, etc.—but with emphasis on the natural and sensual—contrasting textures, rounded shapes, and heavy use of wood, as well as asymmetric forms and irregularity. The end result: a modern yet tactile style.

The Masterpieces

Municipal Library, Viipuri, Finland; Tuberculosis Sanitorium, Paimio, Finland; Town Hall, Säynätsalo, Finland; Nordic Center, Reykjavík, Iceland; Sunila Pulp Mill, Kotka, Finland; Finlandia Concert Hall, Helsinki, Finland; Baker House, Massachusetts Institute of Technology, Cambridge, Massachusetts.

LITERATURE OF THE WORLD

CONTENTS

LITERATURE OF THE WORLD

In all ages, literature aims at an interpretation of the universe and a deep perception of humanity by means of language.

 These are the words of Japanese writer Yukio Mishima—and a perfect summary of the role of literature across culture and across time.

Literature by its very nature is, of course, communication—communication of ideas and ideals, of the real or the imaginary, and, perhaps most simply, of the state of being human in a universe beyond comprehension. And literature is a way of attempting comprehension. In that sense, it's very similar to philosophy. In the act of writing, the writer is seeking *truth*—and the words he or she puts on paper seek to convey the truth the writer has found.

Writers, then, have to be triple threats: observers, interpreters, and transmitters all at once. They must see what is going on around them, interpret it according to their own experiences or views, then communicate to others what they have seen and understood. Because there's the human ingredient—interpretation—writers can give us a snapshot of a culture, a time period, and a way of thinking.

The problem is, many people don't get the chance to read much outside of their own culture or time period. Because of this, they're missing one of the best ways to get an insight into the rest of the world. For example, when you read in the newspaper about the prodemocracy movement in China, it's a rundown of facts and events. But if you read a poem written by a prodemocracy activist, the movement comes alive—it's no longer something that's happening "over there"; it's something *real* happening to real people.

That's why this section covers the voices of the writers you may not know—from the past to the present. You can read about the classic authors from other cultures, like Japanese haiku poet Basho and Persian Sufi mystic Rabi'a, to get an idea of the great masters of other poetic traditions—and about the European masters, like Virgil and John Milton, to get a handle on our *own* poetic roots.

For insight into the world of today, we cover the great voices of the present: poets of revolution or social protest who can give you the human feel of current events, like Yehuda Amichai from Israel or Nizar Qabbani of Lebanon; novelists who capture the turmoil in their countries, like Ding Ling of China or Chinua Achebe of Nigeria.

We've included a rundown of the poetic traditions of other cultures and a quick look at the trends in modern literature across the world to put the works of these people into a greater historical context. This will help you better understand where these writers fit in, the traditions they came from, and the direction in which they're moving.

Literature doesn't exist in a vacuum . . . because writers don't. When you read, you're not only getting information filtered by culture and time; you're reading someone's individual *idea* of something—facts filtered by imagination. As South African writer Lewis Nkosi once said, "Every writer has a vision. Otherwise I do not see what he is doing writing."

The following, then, offers you different visions of different writers, cultures, and times.

POETIC VOICES YOU (PROBABLY) HAVE HEARD . . . OR AT LEAST SHOULD KNOW: THE GREATEST POETS OF THE WESTERN TRADITION

 These are some of the leading poets of the West, the ones who are taught in college literature classes—or who wind up as answers in a *Jeopardy* game. For good reason: These are the poets that the well-educated person should have a nodding acquaintance with, at the least. The poets' names should be familiar, if not their works. So, without further introduction, here's a quick rundown of the poetic voices you've probably heard.

HOMER

(Eighth century B.C.E.)
(Ancient Greek)

The big question: Was there really a Homer, a man who wrote two of the greatest epic poems of the West, the *Iliad* and the *Odyssey?*

No one is quite sure. Some scholars say he never existed and that the epics attributed to him are actually a compilation of shorter works written by anonymous poets. Others say that two or more poets writing under the name Homer were the real writers of the works attributed to him. To make matters more confusing, the only records of Homer are from ancient Greek writers who lived centuries *after* Homer—and they're pretty sketchy themselves.

According to these ancient accounts, he lived across from mainland Greece in Ionia—either on the island of Chios or in Smyrna (although Colophon and Ephesus also get votes as his birthplace). As to *when* he lived, there's another debate—some said the twelfth century B.C.E., others the seventh. Herodotus, the famous Greek historian, said the ninth century B.C.E. Again, no one is sure at all, but most commonly, he is presumed to have lived in the second half of the eighth century. Tradition has it that he was blind, a wandering minstrel who composed his works while traveling to the different city-states of ancient Greece. More recent assumptions have sprung up, fleshing out Homer's life, including one that centers on "the stone of Homer," an open-air sanctuary on Chios. The legend holds that he used to sit here and recite his poems to his pupils, the "Homeridae," who were themselves professional reciters and who would then travel and recite his poems across the country. Is it true? Possibly not, since the sanctuary used to be dedicated to the goddess Cybele, but then again, no one is sure.

However, there is one thing that is not debatable: the strength of his works. Whether Homer *did* exist or not, whether his works were actually an amalgamation of many poets' works or the work of one genius, the works stand alone. The *Iliad*, about the Trojan War, and the *Odyssey,* about the wanderings of hero Odysseus before his return to Ithaca, aren't only the oldest existing examples of Western literature; they've also inspired a wealth of other works. They launched an entire tradition of epic poetry—from Virgil to Dante and after. So whether or not there was a real Homer, there certainly are real poems—poems that, while ancient, continue to have an impact on the modern world.

Sing, muse, the anger of Achilles, son
    of Peleus,
the destructive anger that sent
    countless Achaeans to grief,
that hurled the stronghearted to Hades,
heroes now carrion, a feast for dogs
    and vultures
—for this is the will of Zeus.
    —from *The Illiad*

PINDAR

(518–438 B.C.E.)
(Ancient Greek)

A professional poet who started his career at age twenty composing choral odes, Pindar became one of the greatest Greek lyric poets of the time. In fact, he evolved a particular form of poetry, now referred to, logically, as the Pindaric ode (comprising strophe, antistrophe, and epode—three movements of the dramatic chorus).

But there's one problem (and probably one reason why many have heard of Pindar but haven't read him): his work isn't the easiest to read . . . and it's even more difficult to translate. And for all that, it is lyrical but its subject matter is often less than lyrical. For

example, his *Epinikia* (Triumphal, or Victory, Odes) were written to celebrate the victories won at the top athletic games. But instead of focusing on the athlete's performance, he often focuses on the athlete's family, praising his lineage and emphasizing the need to bring continued honor to Greece. One reason for this: he was an aristocrat himself, who wrote chiefly for aristocratic audiences. Consequently, his work stresses ethical and physical excellence.

In his time, Pindar was considered the master of his craft—his language, insight and choice of themes were highly praised, his popularity virtually unchallenged.

Golden lyre, held by Apollo in common
    possession
with the violet-haired Muses: the
    dance steps, leaders of festival,
    heed you;
the singers obey your measures
when, shaken with music, you cast the
    best to lead choirs of dancers.
You have the power to quench the
    speared thunderbolt
of flowing fire.
    —from *Pythia 1, The Odes of Pindar,* translated
    by Richmond Lattimore. The University of
    Chicago Press, Chicago. Copyright © 1976
    by Richmond Lattimore.

VIRGIL

(70–19 B.C.E.)
(Ancient Roman)

Virgil (Publius Vergilius Maro) was supposed to be headed for the typical Roman career of public service. But his personality changed all that. Awkward, shy, and sensitive, lacking in self-confidence—and prone to ill health to boot—Virgil opted out of the public career when his schooling was over. Instead, he went back to his father's farm and began writing poetry.

But this idyllic pastoral life didn't last long. In 41 B.C.E. the farm was confiscated—which may have turned out to be a lucky thing after all. Tradition has it that Virgil then pleaded his case to Octavian (later the emperor Augustus). As compensation he received an estate in southern Italy, and possibly more important, he became one of a circle of endowed court poets. His first commissioned work? A poem supporting the emperor's agrarian policy—the *Georgics* (Art of Husbandry, or Poem on Agriculture). However less than gripping it sounds, it won him recognition and the status of leading poet of his time. From there he went on to his most famous task, commissioned by Augustus—a national epic based on the story of Aeneas of Troy, founder of the Roman nation. This epic, the *Aeneid*, took eleven years to write—and was the masterpiece everyone expected it would be. But sadly, in the year it was completed (and before planned revisions), Virgil died.

I sing of warfare and a man at war.
From the sea-coast of Troy in early
    days
He came to Italy by destiny,
To our Lavinian western shore,
A fugitive, this captain, buffeted
Cruelly on land as on the sea
By blows from powers of the air—
    behind them
Baleful Juno in her sleepless rage.
And cruel losses were his lot in war,

Till he could found a city and bring
    home
His gods to Latium, land of the Latin
    race,
The Alban lords, and the high walls of
    Rome.
Tell me the causes now, O Muse, how
    galled
In her divine pride, and how sore at
    heart
From her old wound, the queen of gods
    compelled him—
A man apart, devoted to his mission—
To undergo so many perilous days
And enter on so many trials.
    —from *The Aeneid*

HORACE

(65–8 B.C.E.)
(Ancient Roman)

While Virgil is called the greatest Roman poet, Horace (Quintus Horatius Flaccus) is the one more people read and quote. In fact, he's one of the most popular poets not only of his time, but of all time.

Witty, brilliant, and an excellent observer, Horace rose to fame to be second only to Virgil in his time. And he rose from unlikely beginnings. He was the son of a freed slave who sacrificed to give his son the benefits he never had—chief among them a good education in Rome and later in Athens. When Julius Caesar was murdered, Horace was still in Athens, where he joined the republican forces of Brutus, which were fighting against the heir of Julius Caesar. After the defeat of the republican forces, he wound up back in Italy, to find his land had been confiscated. He opted then for the life of a lowly civil servant and soon began writing poetry as a way out of extreme poverty.

It worked. Virgil himself, already a noted poet, noticed his work and introduced him to emperor Augustus's chief minister of state, Maecenas, who eventually became Horace's patron and even gave him an estate in the posh Sabine Hills. Here Horace was able to devote all of his time to poetry, and he became not only the chief lyric poet of his time, but also poet laureate.

To a great degree, his work shows the fruits of his humble beginnings—and especially the impact of his father's moral instruction. Heavy on philosophy but never dull, he talks of the need to seize the moment. Death is near, he tells us, but we still can enjoy the present day.

*Believe each day that has dawned is
  your last.
Some hour to which you have not been
  looking forward will prove lovely.*
—from *Epistles,* I, iv

DANTE ALIGHIERI

(1265–1321)
(Italian)

A Renaissance man long before the Renaissance began, Dante was a soldier, a politician, a philosopher, a poet, a businessman, and an idealistic lover. He was born to a wealthy family, served in a range of minor public offices, and eventually, when political problems arose in Florence, supported the losing side against the pope and was banished.

But it was his role as a lover that was probably the most important in Dante's life. He met the love of his life, Beatrice, when he was only nine and she was eight. It was love at first sight, even though he didn't see her again for nine years—and, more to the point, even though she married another man at an early age and he, too, married. It didn't make any difference to Dante. He even named a daughter after her. Beatrice was the guiding force in his life, the personification of spiritual beauty. He was so wrapped up in her that when she died, he decided to stop writing. But then she appeared to him in a vision and told him that a relationship that is wholly spiritual can't be destroyed by death. His job was to teach the world that love, specifically the kind of pure love he had for her, was the center of the spiritual universe. Loyal to the end, Dante took her at her visionary word and wrote his most famous work, the *Divine Comedy (Divina Commedia),* in which Beatrice eventually leads him to heaven and, finally, God.

Dante's visions didn't stop even at his death. When he died, the last thirteen cantos of his *Divine Comedy* were missing. His son, according to tradition, then had a dream: Dante took his son into the room in which he had died and put his hand on the wall. The next day, his son went to that room with Dante's disciple, Piero Guardino. In the room, hidden behind some matting, was a hole . . . and in the hole, the missing cantos. (For more on Dante's *Divine Comedy,* see page 344.)

Consider your origins: you were not made that you might live as brutes, but so as to follow virtue and knowledge.
—from *Inferno,* Book xxvi, line 118

You shall find out how salt is the taste of another man's bread, and how diffi-cult is the way up and down another man's stairs.

—from *Paradise*, Book xvii, line 58

GEOFFREY CHAUCER

(c. 1340–1400)

(English)

He's considered the father of literary English—but other than the work he left behind, there's little contemporary note of his work. The first thing written about his output? "A good translator." Or so said a French contemporary. Englishman Thomas Usk referred to his "manly speech," and John Gower to his "glad songs." Not the best record of his talents—but few nowadays dispute Chaucer's merit.

The son of a tavern keeper (or vint-ner, depending upon the source), Chaucer apparently was given enough education to have a strong backing in Latin and other languages. In fact, Chaucer appears in general to have had a somewhat privileged life. He was a member of Edward III's daughter-in-law's household. When he was cap-tured by the French in 1360, the king paid a ransom for his release. He became a member of the king's house-hold seven years later, and after that served the king in a number of differ-ent ways—including traveling to France, Spain, and Italy in a range of capacities and serving as controller of customs and wools. For his troubles, he was granted a pension—as well as a daily pitcher of wine—and was eventu-ally elected a member of Parliament.

A pleasant lifestyle . . . and one that enabled Chaucer to write, for which he is now known best. His work for the king probably wound up enhancing his work as a writer. He was clearly influ-enced by other people's—and other culture's—works, especially French and Italian literature. Chaucer man-aged to take aspects of the literature of other countries and create his own unique synthesis, work that moved beyond the bounds of country or cul-ture. His *Canterbury Tales*, in particu-lar, has been and is still seen as a work beyond place and time. While set in his contemporary England with a real-istic setting, it's more a statement about the human condition in general than that of English people in the four-teenth century. (For more on Chaucer's *Canterbury Tales*, see page 341.)

*Whan that Aprill with his shoures
    soote
The droghte of March hat perced to
    the roote,
And bathed every veyne in swich
    licour,
Of which vertue engendred is the flour;
When Zephirus eek with his sweete
    breeth
Inspired hath in every holt and heeth
The tendre croppes, and the yonge
    sonne
Hath in the Ram his halfe cours
    yronne,
And smale floweles maken melodye,
That slepen al the nyght with open
    eye—
So priketh hem nature in hir corages—
Thanne longen folk to goon on
    pilgramages. . . .*

—from *Canterbury Tales*, General Prologue

JOHN MILTON

(1608–1674)
(English)

Above all, Milton was a man of contradictions and convictions. A Puritan, he also was a humanist. A man who preferred solitude, he was a staunch political fighter. A classicist in his poetry, he tended toward down-and-dirty attacks in his political writings. A poet who dreamed of writing one great work, he spent much of his middle age—twenty years of his life—writing not poetry but political and religious tracts.

To a great degree, though, his early life seemed like a typical one for a man of his status. He was schooled at Cambridge, spent several years in self-study at his father's country house, where he wrote three of his most famous poems (*L'Allegro, Il Penseroso,* and the pastoral elegy *Lycidas*), then went abroad to continue his education. But then civil war in England between the Puritans and the Royalists seemed to be brewing, so he returned home. He still had dreams of spending time writing that one great poem, but got embroiled in the politics of the day—and the poem had to wait. Instead, he threw himself into political writing and turned out pamphlets—a series supporting the revolution, another seeking more liberal divorce laws, and still another, perhaps the most famous, seeking freedom of the press, *Areopagitica.* His political stances (especially those holding that the people have a right to pass judgments on the acts of their ruler—and so supporting the Puritan execution of Charles I), wound up securing him an official

position as Latin secretary to the Council of State (and an unofficial one as apologist for the Puritan Commonwealth). So poetry continued to take a backseat to his other work.

Not that he had forgotten his dream. Even while involved in politics, he managed to come up with the general theme of his great poem—the fall of man, based on Adam. (He had initially toyed with the thought of writing it about King Arthur.) And finally, when the political situation in England began calming down, he was able to begin writing. In 1660, after the Restoration, he was completely relieved of his duties—and the time finally had come for him to complete his great work, *Paradise Lost . . .* over twenty years after he had had his initial idea.

> A mind is not changed by place or
>   time.
> The mind is its own place, and in itself
> Can make a heav'n of hell, a hell of
>   heav'n.
> What matter where, if I be still the
>   same,
> And what I should be, all but less than
>   he
> Whom thunder hath made greater?
>   Here at least
> We shall be free; th'Almighty hath not
>   built
> Here for his envy, will not drive us
>   hence:
> Here we may reign secure, and in my
>   choice
> To reign is worth ambition though in
>   hell:
> Better to reign in hell, than serve in
>   heav'n.
>
> —from *Paradise Lost,* Book I

WILLIAM BLAKE

(1757–1827)
(English)

An eccentric with a reputation for being mad, a nonconformist, a religious seer, a family man, an entrepreneur of sorts, and a mystic—just a few of the ways Blake has been described. And frankly, he was all of these and more.

But first and foremost, Blake was an individualist—both in his lifestyle and his work. Trained as an engraver, he supported his family by engraving books and magazines, and he published his own poetry. Had it not been for the engravings, his family may well have starved. Blake's work wasn't appreciated at all; in fact, it was roundly criticized, seen as the meanderings of a madman. The reason: he went completely against the thoughts of the time. In a materialistic, rationalist age, he wrote antimaterialist, antirationalist works. His poetry urges the reader to free the imagination, trust in intuition, and seek the divine that is within.

O Rose thou art sick.
The invisible worm,
That flies in the night
In the howling storm:
Has found out thy bed
Of crimson joy:
And his dark secret love
Does thy life destroy.
　　—from "The Sick Rose," *Songs of Experience*

GEORGE GORDON, LORD BYRON

(1788–1824)
(English)

The quintessential Romantic—dashing, handsome, aristocratic, and rebellious—Byron sounds like the stuff of literature, and he was . . . thanks, especially, to himself. He made himself (or his type) the hero of his poetry—the Byronic hero.

Both as writer and hero, Byron leaped into the public eye with his *Childe Harold's Pilgrimage,* a poem based upon his grand tour through Europe. Thereafter, he was the darling of society and lived the romantic life people expected of him: he became the lover of Lady Caroline Lamb, married, and was said to have had an affair with his half sister. The latter was too much, though, for polite society, even from a Romantic hero, so he became a social outcast. He then moved overseas, where he continued both to write and to live the life of his heroic ideal. He died in a manner befitting a Romantic hero—fighting the Turks to help Greeks secure their freedom.

His work is as romantic as his life. As many have said, he loved mankind and hated injustice. This comes through in his poetry, which has a viewpoint that is as cynical, proud, and arrogant, yet as idealistic as the man. It is also lyrical and passionate, ironic and tender, with a vitality and energy that matches the near myth of the poet.

She walks in beauty, like the night
Of cloudless climes and starry skies,
And all that's best of dark and bright
Meet in her aspect and her eyes;
Thus mellow'd to that tender light
Which heaven to gaudy day denies.

—from *She Walks in Beauty*

JOHN KEATS

(1795–1821)
(English)

"Beauty is truth, truth beauty" wrote Keats in his *Ode on a Grecian Urn*. And this more than anything sums up the poet. His life—and so his poetry—revolved around the worship of beauty.

There's a strongly sensuous quality to his work. In many ways, his work is a full-body experience—he alludes to scents, colors, sounds, and touch. In this way, he conveys the beauty he has seen and felt. The reader is invited to taste, smell, even feel the touch of what he has experienced.

A medical student and apprentice to a surgeon-apothecary, Keats discovered literature when he was in school (and was particularly impressed with Spenser's *Fairie Queene*). He passed his medical examinations at age twenty-one and turned away from medicine, choosing literature instead. And literature remained his focus for the rest of his life—which lasted only five more years.

They weren't an easy five years. Although he began producing a strong body of work, he didn't meet with critical success. His first book of poetry, *Poems*, was largely ignored. And his second, *Endymion*, was reviewed viciously.

An example of the scathing reviews Keats had to face was this opinion expressed in a letter of fellow Romantic poet Lord Byron to John Murray, October 12, 1820: "Here are Jonny Keats' piss a bed poetry. . . . No more Keats, I entreat: flay him alive; if some of you don't, I must skin him myself: there is no bearing the drivelling idiotism of the Mankin."

To make matters worse, his brother was dying of consumption (tuberculosis) and his love affair with Fanny Brawne was (to judge by his letters) a source more of problems than of joy. Yet in the middle of this less than perfect situation, he published his third book of poetry, *Lamia, Isabella, The Eve of St. Agnes, and Other Poems*—which contains his best work. But by this time he had contracted tuberculosis himself, and a trip to warmer Italy didn't help—he died in Rome and was buried under a gravestone bearing his self-written epitaph: "Here lies one whose name was writ in water."

This living hand, now warm and
*   capable*
Of earnest grasping, would, if it were
*   cold*
And in the icy silence of the tomb,
So haunt thy days and chill thy
*   dreaming nights*
That thou wouldst wish thine own
*   heart dry of blood*
So in my veins red life might stream
*   again,*
And thou be conscience-calmed—see
*   here it is—*
I hold it towards you.

—from *This Living Hand*

CHARLES-PIERRE BAUDELAIRE

(1821–1867)
(French)

A Symbolist poet who was fascinated with the perverse, the macabre, and the dark side of life in general, Baudelaire lived the life that so intrigued him—and wound up dying penniless and insane.

While expressing ideas and emotions through symbolic objects and words, as Symbolists did, Baudelaire was also the archetypal Bohemian from the beginning. He deliberately tried not to fit in at the military school he was sent to. At odds with his soldier-diplomat stepfather, he was sent on a tour to India, but he jumped ship in Mauritania and spent three weeks enjoying his freedom—and hooking up with half-caste Jeanne Duval, who became his longtime mistress. They moved to the Latin Quarter in Paris and he took up a life dedicated to pleasure and to art.

In his work, as well as his life, he avoided the commonplace, the typical, and the bourgeois. His subjects were drawn from what he saw around him—prostitutes, drunks, the poor. His goal: to find the beauty in the squalor, without covering it up in Romantic idealism.

In his later years, he was the image of the self-destructive poet: a rebel who flouted family ties, drank excessively, was fond of hashish and opium. The self-destruction worked. At age forty, he hit bottom; poverty stricken, he was frightened of insanity and considered suicide. An unsuccessful lecture tour was his last act as a literary figure. He died a few years later, paralyzed and unable to recognize his face in the mirror or remember his name.

WILLIAM BUTLER YEATS

(1865–1939)
(Irish)

Yeats lived a dichotomy—he was a recluse who craved action; he looked back at his youth nostalgically and eagerly looked forward to old age; he was fascinated with mystical Irish folklore and French Symbolism, yet considered himself a realist; he fought for Irish independence, yet in later years became a Fascist. And his work reflects this dichotomy.

Initially, he was fascinated by mysticism and delved into Irish mythology—which is the source of much of his poetry. He founded the Abbey Theatre and made a name for himself through his plays, his political and cultural activities, and, of course, his poetry.

By 1906 Yeats appeared to have reached the top of his career: He had already kicked off the Irish Renaissance. He was Ireland's best-known poet and dramatist. His eight-volume *Collected Works in Prose and Verse* had just been published. But, workwise, he hadn't peaked. The best was yet to come.

In the following years, he changed poetry styles several times and wrote what is considered his best work. Some people say it was because he met poet Ezra Pound (in 1908), who had come to London to learn from Yeats, but it was Pound who influenced Yeats in certain ways. Others say it was simple evolution. Whatever the specific reason, Yeats shifted styles—moving away from his mythological, Romantic poetry and starting to write in a modern style. After his marriage in 1917, he shifted gears again, incorporating a different mythology that he learned through his wife—which revolved around moon phases and their relationship with personality and history. Finally, in about 1928, his poetry evolved yet again—into a simpler, more colloquial style using a form based on ballads and folk songs.

For all the stylistic changes, though, there are common threads throughout Yeats's poetry. Even when he moved away from mythological topics, there's often an undertone of mythology in his works. His main themes are ones dealt with in ancient mythology: the passing of time; the permanence of the mind and the spirit versus the transitory nature of human life; and especially, the ultimate tie between creation and destruction.

T. S. ELIOT

(1888–1965)
(English)

Thomas Stearns Eliot is a bit of a paradox: a self-considered classicist in literature who was one of the leaders in modern poetry, a rationalist who chose to be baptized and confirmed at age thirty-nine, a traditionalist who was a literary innovator.

The paradox even spills into his work: it's clean, sharp, and direct on the one hand, written in modern idioms; but on the other hand, it's often filled with classical and religious allusions and quotations from other languages.

But ultimately the paradox works—

making Eliot probably the most influential twentieth-century poet.

American-born, Eliot spent most of his life in England, moving there at age twenty-three (most say at Ezra Pound's urging) and becoming a British citizen at age thirty-nine. With Pound and T. E. Hulme, he was one of the founders of the "new" poetry—free verse about modern life written in modern language. Eliot followed through on their manifesto—turning out works using the language of the time that were pessimistic observations of the emptiness of modern life.

But his poetry is actually more than this. In his work, time and typical linear thought don't exist. He writes as the mind thinks—unrelated thoughts and observations spilling out one after another, yet somehow linking into a greater whole. His work conjures up surrealistic images that are somehow more real than a straight, naturalistic depiction. By using voices and words from the past, whether from other religions or from classical mythology, he creates a world where time doesn't exist . . . or rather, all times exist at once. Eliot has created a universe on paper, the universe of the human mind.

Let us go then, you and I.
When the evening is spread out
*   against the sky*
Like a patient etherised upon a table;
Let us go, through certain half-
*   deserted streets,*
The muttering retreats
Of restless nights in one-night cheap
*   hotels*
And sawdust restaurants with oyster
*   shells . . .*
—from "The Love Song of J. Alfred Prufrock"

FEDERICO GARCÍA LORCA

(1898–1936)
(Spanish)

Lorca's work is much like the man himself—emotional, strong, passionate, and above all, Spanish through and through.

From the beginning, his work resonated with Spanish tradition. He met with success early. His first book of poems was published when he was only twenty-two, and others quickly followed—named after the traditional Spanish forms that were influencing his work: *Canciones* (songs), *Poema del Cante Jondo* (an Andalusian lyric), *Romancero Gitano* (Gypsy romances).

Andalusian folk music and lyrics, Gypsy ballads, Spanish romances (traditional epic-lyric poems)—these all inspired Lorca. In his hands, the traditional forms became modern. Within the strict boundaries of the forms, he used startlingly unique metaphors, new interpretations, and fresh images, and created something new based on tradition. Yet the old still lives in the rhythms, the songlike quality of much of his work. The result: poetry to be read aloud, poetry that is built upon the older oral traditions of the country.

And Lorca met with great success by reinterpreting the traditions of his culture. This was his greatest strength. In fact, his weakest collection of poems, *Poet in New York,* was written during a yearlong trip to the United States, where he was faced with culture shock brought on by the highly industrialized society he found. So he returned to the country he loved, and continued doing what he did best.

And the country he loved ultimately caused his death. The Spanish Civil War was escalating, a vicious war between Fascists and the legal Republican government. Lorca was captured in Granada by members of the Fascist Falange and executed—and his body thrown into an unmarked grave.

Who Are the Most Prolific Writers— or Readers—in the World?

Probably Danes.

According to the German Federal Statistics Office, as of 1994 Denmark published more than 200 books each year per 100,000 people. One reason for this high number: Danish isn't spoken in great numbers elsewhere, so the Danes can't import books from other countries but must produce all their reading material themselves. Numbers two and three in terms of books published per capita, Spain and Great Britain, rank high because of the high number of exports to Spanish and English readers in other countries.

Here's the number of new books published per 100,000 inhabitants per year in the top eight book-publishing countries around the world:

Denmark	214.9
Spain	92.7
Great Britain	91.7
Netherlands	90.3
Germany	84.3
France	73
Belgium	68.2
Japan	29.4

POETIC VOICES YOU MAY NOT HAVE HEARD, PART 1: VOICES OF THE PAST

 Certain poets are alchemists of a sort. By choosing the right words and images, they create more than an individual statement. They make a leap beyond the few words on their page and convey not only their own experience, but that of others. They're the voices of their generation sometimes, the voices of their people or culture at others. Such widely read poets as Geoffrey Chaucer, John Milton, T. S. Eliot, and Robert Frost fall into this category.

Yet there are voices we haven't heard as often—or at all. These voices are not only from other times, but also from other lands and cultures. The poets who follow are among these. If you know their names and their work, you know complete genres of poetry and, often, the moods and thoughts of a country and a time—which usually turn out to be much the same as where we are, here and now. So their voices reach across time and place—reminding us that no matter when or where we live, we are the same.

SAPPHO

(c. 612–580 B.C.E.)
(Ancient Greek)

The Tenth Muse, the Pierian Bee—two of the names given Sappho, and both indicative of her reputation as one of the first lyric poets and the greatest female poet of ancient times. According to contemporary records, she was known for her wedding songs, as well as for other poems written for specific people and events. She was at the center of a group of women and girls, probably their teacher.

This, of course, leads to the other thing she's known for—her lifestyle. She was married and had a daughter; but she also appears to have been attracted to women, judging by the work she left behind. Not that there's much of that work. Her nine books of poetry didn't even make it through the Middle Ages. All that exists is some poem fragments on papyrus and two odes. But these two untitled odes seem to be a tip-off as to her sexual preference. One (below) reveals her feelings upon seeing the woman she loves sitting with a man. The other asks the goddess Aphrodite's help in securing the love of a maiden—which caused quite an uproar in the past. Until 1883, the English translation changed the young girl to a young man.

Like the very gods in my sight is he who
sits where he can look in your eyes,
   who listens
close to you, to hear the soft voice, its
   sweetness
murmur in love and

laughter, all for him. But it breaks my
   spirit;
underneath my breast all the heart is
   shaken.

*Let me only glance where you are, the
voice dies,
I can say nothing,*

*but my lips are stricken to silence,
under-
neath my skin the tenuous flame
suffuses;
nothing shows in front of my eyes, my
ears are
muted in thunder.*

*And the sweat breaks running upon
me, fever
shakes my body, paler I turn than grass
is;
I can feel that I have been changed, I
feel that
death has come near me.*

—from *Greek Lyrics,* translated by Richmond
Lattimore. The University of Chicago Press,
Chicago. Copyright 1949, 1955, and 1960
by Richmond Lattimore.

WANG WEI
~

(699–759)
(Chinese)

A triple threat—painter, musician, and
poet. He's known for his masterful
monochrome landscapes—and for his
nature poems. As writer Su Shih said
of him: "In his poetry there is painting,
in his painting, poetry."

And his life was as peaceful as one
of his landscapes: he worked for years
as a government official during a relatively uneventful time (only one brief
rebellion during his tenure) and retired
to the country (some say to a Buddhist
monastery), where he spent quiet years

reading Buddhist works and discussing
metaphysics with monks. Known especially for his "cut short" (*chueh-chu*)
quatrains, he wrote throughout this
peaceful life. And his work reflects the
life he led and the things he cared
about—his love of nature, hermit's
bent, and Buddhist beliefs.

*City on Wei
the morning rain
wet
on light dust*

*Around the inn
green willows
fresh
I summon you:
Drink one more cup
No old friends, my friend
When you start westward
for Yang Kuan.*

—from *Seeing Master Yuan off on His Mission to
Kucha*

LI PO (LI BO)
~

(701–762)
(Chinese)

He could have stepped from the pages
of an existential novel: Li Po, the
stereotypical romantic image of an
artist. A heavy drinker. Volatile, impa-
tient, mercurial, self-centered, even
irresponsible. A rule breaker. One
example: instead of following the usual
path, taking the civil service examination and landing a government post, Li
Po wandered, took government jobs on
a temporary basis, and wrote. He didn't
become famous until he hit his forties,

when he became a member of the Han-Lin Academy (for top scholars) and was part of court life—but his court days were short-lived. After three years, he was back on the road, traveling throughout China and writing.

His personality traits spilled over into his writing. Instead of the super-regimented forms, Li Po went for the more flexible forms. And instead of the typical historical or social themes, he opted for the personal. And it worked—along with Tu Fu (see next entry), Li Po was a top poet of the T'ang dynasty, considered the golden age of *shih* (see page 331) poetry.

With a pot of wine among the flowers,
All alone I drink—no dear ones at my
*   side.*
Raising my cup, I invite the bright
*   moon*
To make with my shadow a group of
*   three.*
But the moon does not know how to
*   drink*
And the shadow vainly follows me
*   around.*
For a while, with moon and shadow as
*   companions,*
I would seek pleasure while it is spring.
I sing and the moon rambles;
I dance and the shadow runs helter-
*   skelter.*
While sober, we enjoy ourselves
*   together;*
After drinking, we part with each
*   other.*
Forever, we'll pledge a non-sentimental
*   journey,*
Awaiting each other at the distant
*   Milky Way.*
        —from *Drinking Alone Under the Moon*

TU FU (DU FU)

(712–770)
(*Chinese*)

"To send forth one's feelings nothing is better than poetry."

Tu Fu said this once—and in so doing may have summed up his motivation. His work is noted for its deep emotions, whether he writes on personal topics or on social conditions. In fact, he was a man of great empathy, and is considered by many to be the perfect spokesman for the first Buddhist tenet, that "All life is suffering."

A friend of Li Po's, he was yin to Li Po's yang—disciplined, selfless, humble. And his work is in keeping with his personality. He usually wrote in the more stringently regulated forms. His poems are carefully crafted, heavy on allusion and form. As he said in one of his poems, "An odd weakness I have, for I dote on good verse / I shall not die in peace until I have found words that will startle the readers." He was a perfectionist, avidly seeking the perfect words and the perfect images. And it paid off: while Li Po may be the best-known Chinese poet, Tu Fu was (and is) the favorite of critics.

The wind keen, the sky high, the
*   gibbons wailing,*
Blue islands, white sand and sea-birds
*   flying,*
And everywhere the leaves falling,
Then the immeasurable great river in
*   torrent.*
Ten thousand li from home, in such an
*   autumn,*
Wasted by sickness and years, along,
*   climbing the heights:*

Sorrows and griefs and sufferings have
given me new gray hairs.
Utterly cast down, I have just drunk a
glass of wine.

——from *On Climbing the Heights on the Ninth*
Day of the Ninth Moon

AL-MUTANABBI

(915–965)
(Arab)

Abu't-Tayyib al-Mutanabbi is often
called the last great Arab poet. A peer-
less talent. But while his work is now
revered, in his time it (and the poet
himself) met with a healthy dose of
criticism. One reason? Frankly, he
probably wasn't all that easy to like.
Certainly many of his contemporaries
felt this. He was considered arrogant
(which his friends and supporters said
was a function of sensitivity and
pride)—and he often comes across as
boastful and overbearing in his poems.
And this legacy lived on after he died.
Later critics were just as inclined to
color their opinions of his work on the
basis of his personality rather than the
merit of the poems themselves. But
separate the work from the man and no
one can deny its power.

One of the best *qasida* (ode) writers,
he raised the form to new heights. (For
more on *qasida*, see page 329.) Instead
of writing on unrelated topics, as most
others did, he composes his odes
around a series of related themes
neatly segueing into one another.
They're technical gems in their careful
construction and lyrical jewels in their
choice of words and images. He's also
known for his turns of phrase, many of

which were (and are) widely quoted:
"Whoso desires the ocean makes light
of streams." "I consider nothing more
shameful than for a man to give up
when he is capable of running the
course."

Tradition has it that at the end, his
words influenced even him. When he
was attacked by brigands one day, he
began to flee. But one of his slaves
recited his own words to him: "I am
known to the horse-troop, the night
and the desert's expanse, / Not more to
the paper and pen than the sword and
lance!" And swayed by the power of his
poetry, al-Mutanabbi turned back and
fought . . . to his death.

We make ready swords and lances,
and death slays us without a battle;
and we station the swift steeds near
our tents, and they do not deliver
from the ambling of the nights.
Who has not loved this world from of
old? But there is no way to union.
Your portion during your lifetime of a
beloved is as your portion during
your sleep of a phantom.
Time has shot me with misfortunes
until my heart is in an envelope of
shafts
so that I have reached the point that
when arrows strike me, the points
are broken upon the points,
and it has come to be of no account,
and I trouble not about misfortunes
because I have been profited
nothing by being troubled.

——from *Elegy on the death of the mother of Saif*
al-Daula

HAFIZ

(c. 1325–1389)
(Persian)

Shems ud Din Muhammad, known as Hafiz, has some of the nicknames you'd expect for someone considered the leading lyrical poet of Persia: the prince of Persian poets, the Persian Anacreon, Sugar Lips (yes, Sugar Lips—or *Chagarlab,* in Persian). This last was the nickname given him by his contemporaries because of the sensuality of his poetry. He chiefly wrote *ghazals,* the short lyric form. His favorite topics? Love, wine, and roses. But his work isn't always what it appears to be. Hafiz wrote in the tradition of Sufism, the mystical branch of Islam. His work has hidden spiritual meanings—which is why he had yet another nickname, the Tongue of the Hidden (*Lisan-al-ghaib*). Immensely popular in his time, with a reputation extending throughout much of the Islamic empire, he's remained popular ever since—one of the Islamic poets whose fame has spread in the West as well as the East. And he's especially revered in his own country, with his tomb the object of pilgrimages.

> A rose blooms within me, wine is in my
>   hand,
>   And my beloved embraced.
>   This day the world's king is my
>   slave.
>   Bring us no candle-light at dark
>   Because the moon-face of love
>   is full.
>   We worship wine and pour our
>   vows, and it is

> Against my law to be without
>   your face.
> . . . .
> As long as my grief for you is in
>   my heart's ruins,
> My place is in the tavern alley.
> You speak of shame? Shame is
>   my renown.
> You speak of fame? My renown
>   is in my shame.
> We are rakes, wine-drinkers and
>   spinning heads,
> And that person who is not like
>   us—who is he?
> Do not betray his faults to the
>   censor,
> He is like us in always asking
>   luxury.
> Hafiz, do not sit one moment
>   without your love or wine,
> For these are days of rose,
>   jasmine and celebration.
> —untitled, trans. R. M. Rehder

BASHO (MATSUO BASHO)

(1644–1694)
(Japanese)

Beside a small hut in Japan, a banana tree was planted, a gift from a student to his poetry teacher. Before long, the hut was called the Basho (Banana Tree) Hut—and the resident of the hut, the Master of the Basho Hut, and eventually just Master Basho. According to tradition, Basho liked his nickname, believing that he was something like his banana tree—somewhat out of place, not particularly practical, sometimes sensitive, even lonely. It was these characteristics that spurred him in his work and his life in general. A wanderer at heart, often prone to melancholy, he journeyed around Japan, sometimes alone, sometimes with students or friends. And throughout this, he wrote—of the things he saw, the people he met, the nature that surrounded him, and, underlying this, his search for religious truth. He continued evolving his style, trying always to simplify. Perhaps this is why his haiku are particularly memorable. While he was skilled in a number of writing forms, including *renku* (long, linked stanzas), *haibun* (prose essays), and travel journals, he is probably remembered most for his haiku. And justly. Until Basho, haiku was a dilettante's pastime, to a great degree, something to do when there was nothing else to do. He changed it into a serious art form—three short lines of simple images and language that speak volumes. (For more on haiku, see page 327.)

The old pond—
A frog leaps in,
And a splash.

Book Burnings Through History

Book burnings and censorship are common ways dictators and oppressive people and societies destroy freedom. There's something intrinsically horrible about destroying knowledge. History's famous book burnings include:

Ancient China. The emperor Shih Huang Ti burned all the books in his kingdom in 212 B.C.E., his idea being that history would begin anew with him. He supposedly kept one copy of each book—with the plan that these would be burned at his death. Fortunately, some scholars hid some books, otherwise our knowledge of early Chinese history and philosophy would be much more limited.

Library of Alexandria. This famous library contained upwards of four hundred thousand scrolls—the largest library in the world. Who burned all of them is still a matter of controversy. Some say that the Islamic soldiers of the Arab caliph Umar burned them when they captured Alexandria in 640 C.E., using them as fuel to heat the city baths. But other scholars say that Alexandrian Christians had already burned most of them a few hundred years earlier, since they saw them as pagan. And some others say many of the books were burned when Julius Caesar fought a small battle on the city wharfs. At any rate, the books are gone, and history has lost countless classics, including Aristotle's work on comedy.

The Bonfire of the Vanities. This name of a popular book (and not so popular movie) comes from the 1497 burning, in Florence, Italy, of "lascivious and indecent books," as well as countless works of art, inspired by the fanatical ascetic leader Savonarola. Ironically, when the people of Florence ultimately reacted against Savonarola, they burned *him* in a bonfire even larger than the one that destroyed their books.

The Burning of the Mayan Books. The Spaniards destroyed the written records of this great Central American civilization—countless books of astronomy, history, and mythology. According to a Spanish contemporary, "they contained nothing in which there was not to be seen superstition and lies of the devil." Only three or four (one may be fake) Mayan books have survived.

The Library of Beijing. During the Boxer Rebellion, Chinese rebels tried to kick out Westerners, who controlled much of the country. In retaliation, the Western powers sent in troops, and in the fighting that followed, this major library of countless Chinese classics erupted into flames.

The Nazi Book Burnings. The Nazis attempted to destroy all records of Jews' and liberals' achievements by burning books. The largest book bonfire was held in front of the University of Berlin in 1933, in which the works of such notable authors and thinkers as Albert Einstein, Ernest Hemingway, Alfred Adler, Erich Maria Remarque, and Heinrich Heine were consigned to the flames. The Nazis were unable to claim divine approval—during the bonfire, it started to rain.

Bosnia. Serb gunners in 1992 destroyed much of the five-hundred-thousand-volume library at Sarajevo, which included countless rare editions and manuscripts detailing the history of the Serbian, Croatian, Muslim, and Jewish culture of the region.

THE GREATEST STORIES EVER TOLD: EPIC LITERATURE OF THE WORLD

 Epics are poems—long poems—that in a few thousand lines illuminate a culture and a people. In some senses they're like stories of superheros today: they all include a larger than life hero who has a great share of human virtues. But there's a difference, of course: epics deal with very human questions of love, honor, and mortality in an earnest and serious fashion. Usually they're *national* epics, that is, the hero is a representative of the nation or people as a whole. Like Superman, these heroes stand for truth, justice, and the Sumerian/Roman/Indian/German/English way. Here are the ones you should know, in chronological order:

GILGAMESH

The grandfather of epics, probably first told almost four thousand years ago by the ancient Sumerians, who lived in what is today Iraq. It's about King Gilgamesh of Uruk, one part human, two parts god, who sets out to find the secret of immortality. He finds the plant of eternal youth, only to have it stolen by a snake. (If you catch a biblical allusion, you shouldn't be surprised, because in several versions the biblical flood is mentioned as well.) Putting together this epic was a job of detective work for modern archaeologists. No original Sumerian version

exists, nor does any single later version: archaeologists had to synthesize the story from thirty thousand fragments written on tablets.

ILIAD AND ODYSSEY

These epics are the earliest examples of European literature to have survived, and they've influenced European literature ever since they were first told, probably about 850 B.C.E., probably (but no one really knows) by the poet Homer (see page 304). The *Iliad* is primarily about a Greek hero, Achilles, set against the background of the Greek siege of the enemy city Troy. The *Odyssey* is primarily about the travels of another hero, Odysseus, back to his home after the war. Interestingly, these are not the only Greek epics about the siege of Troy, but they're the only ones to have survived. And even in ancient times, these were recognized as masterpieces; in simple but brilliant language Homer gives us a feeling for the times and for the very timeless emotions of hate, revenge, and joy.

THE AENEID

This epic was written to order by the Roman poet Virgil at the request of the emperor Augustus Caesar, beginning in 20 B.C.E. Sadly, Virgil died before completing his revisions, and the work as a whole is uneven. But it's still considered by many the greatest work of Latin literature. *The Aeneid* is about the many trials and tribulations of Aeneas, the legendary founder of Rome, a prince of Troy who fled after it was captured by the Greeks. Along the way to Rome, he meets and woos Dido, queen of Carthage, but his love affair ends in tragedy, as does anything else that interferes with Aeneas's main goal: Rome.

MAHABHARATA

This is the longest poem in the world—eight times longer than the *Iliad* and *Odyssey* combined—whose attribution is unknown. It's the great epic of India, about the struggle between good and evil, filled with numerous digressions, moral tales, and religious poetry. Primarily, it is about the struggle for the throne by the five sons of King Pandu, and most particularly, his son Arjuna. In one of the greatest scenes in world literature (often published separately as the *Bhagavadgita*), Arjuna hesitates before a great battle, afraid to commit men to death and pain. Krishna appears, and explains that no one really dies anyway, and that besides, the disinterested performance of duty, in this case war, is the right path to follow. Unlike Western epics, this epic does not end with riches and wives for the victors, but with a realization that true peace lies with a renunciation of worldly pleasure.

BEOWULF

Composed about 725 by an unknown English person (or Dane, depending upon whom you talk to), *Beowulf* is about the eponymous hero's exploits in fighting the monster Grendel, killing a water hag, and in the last section, fighting as an older man to save his people from a fire-breathing dragon. Interestingly, some scholars have speculated that the composer of this poem was aware of Vergil's *Aeneid;* it is a mature and sophisticated look at a folktale hero.

NIBELUNGENLIED

This is a Germanic epic transcribed sometime around 1200 and written by unknown authors, but it's based on legends and true incidents that occurred sometime around 437 C.E. The epic as a whole is a complex mixture of pagan and Christian. The hero is a prince named Siegfried, who kills a dragon and wins the great treasure hoard of the Nibelung—a treasure so great that one hundred wagons couldn't carry it all. Siegfried bathes in the dragon's blood and is invulnerable, except for a spot on his shoulder where a linden leaf fell. Of course, he is murdered, and the second half of the epic is concerned with the revenge taken by his wife. The poem as a whole betrays its oral origins—with a loose composition and frequent repetitions.

THE FAERIE QUEENE

This is a highly symbolic epic by Edmund Spenser, who lived from about 1552 until 1599. The faerie queene is named Gloriana but is an idealized portrait of Queen Elizabeth. Although the poem was unfinished, it was designed to set forth, in twelve sections, the twelve virtues as represented by twelve knights of King Arthur's court. The knights themselves are allegorical, representing chastity, temperance, and other virtues, and the plot is filled with heroic quests by heroic knights.

PARADISE LOST

Considered the greatest epic of modern times, this work was written by English poet John Milton (1608–1674) and is about the fall of man, from the Garden of Eden to the expulsion from Paradise to the vision of a redeemer who will one day bring salvation to humankind. This is an immensely learned and serious poem—Milton wanted to write something that rivaled Homer and Virgil, and he drew on his readings of most of the great Latin, Greek, Renaissance, and English authors.

Comics—More Than the Funny Pages

One of the most popular ways to convey information or entertainment today is the comic strip. In many countries, comics are used to disseminate health or political information—and in many lands comics are a growing and extremely popular form of entertainment.

Often, comics are ridiculed as a relatively modern invention that symbolizes the decline of literacy—but if we define them a little loosely, as side-by-side pictures that tell a story, we can see the idea of comics as far back as 3000 B.C.E.: in the use of pictures with words nearby to tell a story on Egyptian tombs (but *not* in Egyptian hieroglyphs themselves, which are a complex system of true writing); in the 230-foot-long Bayeaux Tapestry of 1066, which uses pictures to tell the story of the Norman Conquest of England; and in a thirty-six-foot-long picture manuscript discovered by Cortes in Mexico in 1519. In a more gory way, the 1460 *Tortures of St. Erasmus,* a sequence of pictures that shows tongue branding, entrails coiling, boiling, and other assorted horrors, is one of the first *printed* comics. But the founder of the modern comic was probably Rodolphe Töpffer, who wrote and drew satiric comics in the mid-1800s. Even back then, comics were seen as, well, less than intellectual. The great German scholar Goethe said of the inventor of the comic book: "If . . . he would choose a less frivolous subject and restrict himself a little, he would produce things beyond conception." And Töppfer himself said, "The picture story appeals mainly to children and the lower classes."

Today, many would beg to differ.

TUS, FUS, AND HAIKUS: AN ALPHABETICAL GUIDE TO CLASSIC NON-WESTERN POETRY FORMS

Poetry is one of the toughest types of literature to write—and sometimes, to read—for a very simple reason: it's not regular writing. A poet isn't dashing off a few lines the same way he or she would spout off a few lines in conversation. The language used in poetry is artificial, distanced from the type of language we'd use in regular conversation.

Yes, the first poetry was spoken, not written, but even back in those days people weren't chatting. They were choosing words for a reason, fitting them into a special rhythm or meter or time frame. And as poetry evolved into a form of written literature, people still had to choose their words to fit a particular set scheme.

It's this that makes writing traditional poetry such a difficult task. Not only is a poet picking the words that will distill an image or evoke a specific emotion; he or she also must choose the words that will fit a set form. When we read poetry from the Western tradition, we run across a number of these set forms, like sonnets, or dactyls (lines of verse made up of metrical feet—one long or unaccented syllable followed by two short or accented syllables), or whatever—and we're aware of the fact that the poet is deliberately expressing him- or herself within a stringent framework. But often when we read the work of other cultures, we're unaware of this. And for a very simple reason: we usually don't know the other types of poetry from these

cultures. But poets from other cultures are faced with the same tough situation that Shakespeare writing a sonnet was: they've got to communicate something while following certain rules of expression.

So here's a quick rundown on classic poetry forms of other cultures—the sonnets, if you will, of the East—to help you better appreciate the work of poets from other cultures.

CHANGGA

(Korean)
The Korean equivalent of troubadours'
*   ballads; poetry for the masses.*

Changga means "long poem." And that's just what it is: long—generally ten or more lines or stanzas marked by the use of a recurring refrain, typically of drum sounds or nonsense words, which usually appear at the end of a stanza. *Changga,* which emerged during the Koryo dynasty (918–1392), were the people's poetry—literally. More often than not, those who wrote *changga* weren't poets by profession, but regular people. The *changga* they wrote were typically spin-offs of folk songs or ballads, frequently developed for different annual festivals. And in keeping with the common touch of these poems, they generally were passed on orally, not in writing.

The sleet falls thick and fast;
Do you come, false love, who made me
Lie awake for half the night?
Are you crossing the pass
Where the wind cries in the bushes?

Fires of hell or thunderbolts
Will soon consume my body.
Fires of hell or thunderbolts
Will soon consume my body.

On what wild mountain shall I seek
*   you?*
I will do anything, anything you say.
This or that, whatever you ask of me.
I will follow you anywhere, I swear.

—from *Winter Night*

CH'U (OR SAN CH'U)

(*Chinese*)
New-wave lyric songs of the fourteenth
*   century.*

When the old style was becoming
stodgy and stale, *ch'u* poems came
along to shake things up. And it shows:
ch'u poems are relatively gutsy; they
use colloquialisms and conversational
language instead of the more stylized
written language of the past; they're
big on self-expression, giving the
reader (or, in their original time, the listener) a window on the writer's emotions, observations, and insights. And
for the preceding reasons, they seem
spontaneous and fresh. Not that
they're free form. Like other writing
styles of the times, *ch'u* poems followed distinct rules. Because *ch'u*
poems were written to be sung out
loud, many of the rules are ones of

rhythm, rhyme scheme, and tonality.
Even so, these rules were relatively
flexible, especially in contrast with
other forms of writing. This is one of
the reasons *ch'u* were so popular with
writers—they were written by virtually
every class of writer and every school
of writer. Some of the most famous
ones? Dramatists Kuan Han-ch'ing
and Ma Chih-yüan.

A hundred years are no more than the
*   dream of a butterfly.*
Looking back, how one sighs for the
*   things of the past!*
Yesterday spring came;
This morning the flowers wither.
Let us hasten with the forfeit cup
Before the night is spent and the lamp
*   goes out.*

—from *Autumn Thoughts*, Ma-Chih-yüan

FU (OR PHU)

(*Chinese*)
Prose-poetry chants that fit well into a
*   strict Confucianist tradition.*

Even though it usually rhymes and has
a definite metrical structure, *fu* wasn't
considered real poetry by the Chinese,
because it was designed to be recited,
not sung (or nearly sung), as other
poetic styles were. And the subject
matter tended to be less the stuff of
lyrical fancy or personal exploration
and more along the lines of social critiques, political commentary, and
philosophic arguments—and it contained lengthy (often *extremely* so)
descriptions. At its peak during the
Han dynasty, much of it was court
poetry, backed by the emperor Wu and

later emperors, and had little to do with the common people. But this form had real staying power. Although it developed in the second and first centuries B.C.E., it remained in use into the twentieth century—and loosened up, subjectwise, along the way. Leading *fu* poets include Ssu-ma Hsiang-ju, Yu Hsin, Hsi K'ang, and Lu Chi.

All things are a flux, with never any
*   rest,*
Whirling, rising, advancing, retreating;
Body and breath do a turn together—
*   change form and slough off,*
Infinitely subtle, beyond words to
*   express.*
From disaster fortune comes, in
*   fortune lurks disaster,*
Grief and joy gather at the same gate,
*   good luck and bad share the same*
*   abode.*

—from *The Owl*, Chia Yi

GHAZAL

(Persian)
Love, wine, and a touch of mysticism—all presented through use of imagery and symbolism in a lyrical form.

This sums up the traditional *ghazal* at its most basic. The *ghazal* is one of the most popular and most pervasive forms of Eastern poetry. It's a simple form, consisting of couplets—at least five, usually only up to twelve, but sometimes going on and on. Each couplet usually contains a complete thought and is sometimes disconnected from the rest, making many *ghazals* essen-

tially a collection of couplets linked together by rhyme and meter. Typically about love (either profane or—in the hands of Sufis—sacred), *ghazals* are often heavy on introspection in their exploration of human emotion and experience. Arabic, Persian, Turkish, and Urdu poets all used the *ghazal*, starting in the eighth century. Sufis (the mystical sect of Islam) latched onto the *ghazal* as a way of expressing their mystical love of God. And Western poets, most notably the German Goethe, brought the form into the nineteenth century.

Ah for the throes of a heart sorely
*   wounded!*
Ah for the eyes that have smit me with
*   madness!*
Gently she moved in the calmness of
*   beauty,*
Moved as the bough to the light breeze
*   of morning.*
Dazzled my eyes as they gazed, till
*   before me*
All was a mist and confusion of figures.
Ne'er had I sought her, and ne'er had
*   she sought me;*
Fated the hour, and the love, and the
*   meeting.*

—Untitled, 'Omar ibn Abi Rabi'a (c. 644–719)

HAIKU

(Japanese)
Three lines say it all.

Haiku (or hokku) initially *wasn't* the simple verse we think of today. It actually was the first stanza of a *renku* (see page 330)—a longer poem made up of linked stanzas written by two or more poets trading off with one another. And writing haiku was more a pastime than an art form. But with time, haiku became recognized as a distinct art form—especially because of master poet Matsuo Basho. The rules of haiku are fairly basic: it's three lines of seventeen syllables (usually in a 5-7-5 pattern). But haiku themselves cover a wide range of themes and styles. There are playful haiku, ones revolving around puns and other forms of wordplay, serious ones—even haiku parodies (called *senryu*). But whatever the tone and subject, haiku always are image driven. They're heavy on sensory description, quick images, and atmosphere. In effect, a haiku is a verbal snapshot. But for all this, often they say more than they appear to. In describing what appears to be a simple nature scene, the poet may be commenting on the infinite, or on humankind's role in the universe. This is one of the reasons why haiku writing is such a specialized art—in just a few words, the poet must convey a mood or idea without spelling it out. Among the masters at this were Matsuo Basho (1644–1694), Taniguchi Buson (1716–1783), and Masaoka Shiki (1867–1902).

What piercing cold I feel!
My dead wife's comb, in our
bedroom,
under my heel.
—Taniguchi Buson

KASA

(Korean)
A midway point between prose and poetry and the closest thing to the confessional school of poetry in classic Korean form.

A *kasa* is a long string of lines (sometimes up to a thousand) with no stanzas. Not that it's completely free form. There is usually a pattern in the words chosen. To be a bit technical, a *kasa* typically contains lines of eight syllables each, each of which is divided into two phrases of four syllables each—but there are variations on this. The *kasa* form emerged in the fifteenth century and continued on strong. By the eighteenth century, it had evolved to become the poetry of the lower and middle classes—with subjects often about day-to-day life and language based on conversation and colloquialisms. Tops in this form? Chong Ch'ol and Ho Nansorhou (one of Korea's leading women poets).

Yesterday I fancied I was young;
But already, alas, I am aging.
What use is there in recalling
The joyful days of my youth?
Now I am old, recollections are vain.
Sorrow chokes me; words fail me.

. . . .

Dewdrops glitter on the young grass,
Evening clouds pass by; birds sing sadly
In the thickets of green bamboos.
Numberless are the sorrowful;
But none can be as wretched as I.
Think, love, you caused me this grief;
I know not whether I shall live or die.
—from *A Woman's Sorrow*, Ho Nansorho
(1563–1589)

MUWASHSHAH

(Arab)
Love, Spanish-Arabic style.

Muwashshah means "the girdled"—which well refers to the structure of this type of poem, since its form is as constraining as the tightest foundation garment around. One of the first forms of Andalusian poetry, the *muwashshah* consists of four-, five-, or six-line stanzas that can be a number of different constructs or rhyme patterns. That's the flexible part of *muwashshahs*. As for other rules: the lines are broken up in different lengths and rhyme internally. While the entire poem is written in typically ornamental literary language, the final two lines usually are sharp, earthy, and slangy. And the subject is almost always love—although some *muwashshahs* were written on religious topics. With so many rigid guidelines, it's no wonder many critics thought *muwashshahs* were very artificial poems.

QASIDA

(Arab, Persian, Urdu, Turkish)
A sophisticated and intricate version of today's rap songs—poetry chanted out loud by the writer, typically very vigorous, filled with larger than life images and (often) boasts.

The key to a *qasida*? Length. *Qasida* are long odes consisting of couplets—and can easily run to more than one hundred couplets. And they're not only long; they're quite complex, using flexible metrical schemes and, often, rhyme patterns. In addition, they can cover any range of themes, all interwoven. And they're flexible in terms of tone: they can be satirical or elegiac; mystical or profane; filled with laments or boasts—or even all of the above. Often they open with a nostalgic introduction to set a mood, move on to a "disengagement" (usually a camel journey), and only then get to the main body of the poem. They're always in the first person; in effect, the poet is speaking directly to his listeners. Developed by pre-Islamic Arab poets in the sixth century, the *qasida* was picked up by Persian, Urdu, and Turkish poets as well and became the most important poetic form used for years. In fact, for over one hundred years, people would judge a poet's worth by his or her ability to write *qasida*. Often considered the best of this genre: the seven *qasida* known as the *Mu'allaqat* (the suspended ones) and written by pre-Islamic writers Amru al-Qays, Tarafah, Zuhayr, Labid, Antarah, Amr, and al-Harith. Other hot *qasida* writers: Arabs al-Mutanabbi (d. 965) and Ibn al-Farid (d. 1235), Persians Anvari (d. 1190) and Khaqani (d. c. 1185), Persian Sufi poet Rumi (d. 1273). And the form even passed over to the West in later years, with writers such as Tennyson trying their hands at it.

Beyond that reef of sand, recalling a
house
And a lady, dismount where the winds
cross
Cleaning the still extant traces of
colony between
Four famous dunes. Like pepper-seeds
in the distance

The dung of white stags in courtyards
and cisterns,
Resin blew, hard on the eyes, one
morning
Beside the acacia watching the camels
going.
And now, for all remonstrance and talk
of patience
I will grieve, somewhere in this
comfortless ruin
And make a place and my peace with
the past.

—from *The Ode of Amru al-Qays,* Ode in the
Mu'allaqat

RENKU

(Japanese)
A chain-letter style of poetry writing—
a string of linked stanzas written by
two or more poets trading off.

Renku writing sounds sort of like a
game for poets to play on their down-
time—and at the beginning, that's
what it was. After sweating it out writing more regulated forms of poetry, like
tanka (see page 332), Japanese court
poets would get together and write
renku to relax. Not that *renku* sounds
all that relaxing to the layperson: there
are very specific and very elaborate
rules to follow (one of the reasons
renku is the Japanese poetic form studied—and understood—the least). And
with time, *renku* became considered
an art form, and the rules codified.
Among them: Typically, a *renku* is
thirty-six, fifty, or one hundred stanzas.
Certain words can't be repeated within
two, three, or more verses. There's a
specific syllable- and stanza-length
pattern—three lines with a 5-7-5 sylla-

ble pattern, alternating with a couplet
with 7-7. The *renku* has to start with a
triplet and end with a couplet. It has to
show progression in its imagery and
rhythm—so there are parts to the
renku serving as an introduction, main
body, and finale. There are even rules
as to when traditional images like the
moon or cherry blossoms should
appear in the verse. For all the rules,
though, *renku* caught on—and became
one of the most important Japanese
poetic forms through the 1800s.
Among leading *renku* writers: Arakida
Moritake, Matsunaga Teitoku, Matsuo
Basho, and Taniguchi Buson (both also
known for their haiku).

Above a town
Filled with the odors of things,
The summer moon.

"It's hot!" "It's hot!"
Murmurs are heard in the frontyards.

Though the second weeding
Is not yet over, rice plants
Shoot out their ears.

Ashes are brushed off a dried sardine
Just taken from the fire.

Those who live in this area
Have never seen a silver coin.
What a wretched place!

—from "The Summer Moon," Basho, Kyorai,
and Boncho (written in 1690), from *Matsuo
Basho* by Makoto Ueda. Published by
Kodansha International Ltd. Copyright ©
1983 by Kodansha International Ltd.
Reprinted by permission. All rights reserved.

SHIH

(Chinese)
The generic Chinese poetry form,
marked by rhythm, rhyme, and
brevity.

Shih (meaning literally "song") is really an umbrella term for a number of different Chinese poetic forms, starting with the earliest forms of poetry—folk songs, hymns, and so forth, collected in the fifth century B.C.E. in what is called the *Shih Ching* (Classic of Songs)—and evolving into one of the most famous types of *shih*, the *lu shih*, or "regulated poem." The *lu shih* is regulated indeed, with a number of standards to conform to in terms of length, tonalities (remember, these were intended to be heard, not read), rhyme schemes, and more. Then there was the subgenre of *lu shih* called a *chueh-chu* ("cut short") poem, which was even shorter—kind of like a Chinese haiku. And there were other forms as well.

During the so-called golden age of *shih*, the T'ang dynasty years (618–906), *shih* became more standardized. The common form? Five- or seven-word lines only, and usually eight or twelve lines per poem. And there it stayed into the twentieth century. But this description saps the blood of the *shih*, which is, while technically bound, also very melodic (a logical attribute since *shih are*, technically, songs). And the brevity of *shih* forces the poet to find the right words and the perfect images to convey a mood. It's not easy, but when it works, it works well. Perhaps this is why some of the top *shih* writers, among them Li Po, Tu Fu, Wang Wei, and Po Chu-i, are also

among the top Chinese poets of any form.

In late years I desire only peace;
For worldly affairs my heart has no
*   concern.*
I have no long range plans for my own
*   care;*
All I know is to return to the old woods,
Where the pine wind blows on my
*   loosened belt*
And the mountain moon shines on the
*   strung zither.*
You ask the law of failure and
*   success—*
"The fisherman's song enters the river
*   bank deep."*
*   —To Sub-prefect Chang, Wang Wei*

SIJO

(Korean)
Could be called the Korean equivalent
of haiku.

It's short, sweet, and to the point. Three lines, four beats per line, and two pauses—boil down the *sijo* and it's that simple. Well, sort of. . . . More precisely, a *sijo* consists of three lines, each line having four rhythmic groups; there's a short pause (in effect, a comma) at the end of the second line, a long one (in effect, a semicolon or period) at the end of the fourth. *Sijo* means "melody of the times"—referring to the time when *sijo* were sung or chanted with popular tunes—so there's a definite songlike air to them. Most *sijo* deliberately use repeated words for emphasis and, because they're so short, often use stock lines, descriptions, or phrases to quickly clue in the reader as to the mood or image the writer wants to convey. This is one of the reasons *sijo* serve almost as a collective unconscious of Korea, tipping off the reader as to the cultural mood and thoughts of the times. It also makes them easy to remember and quote—possibly why they're the most popular poetic form in Korea.

The green hills—how can it be
that they are green eternally?
Flowing streams—how can it be;
night and day they do never stand
still?
We also, we can never stop,
we shall grow green eternally.
—Untitled, Yi Hwang (1501–1571)

TANKA

(Japanese)
As carefully constructed as a haiku,
but longer.

Tanka (also called *waka* or *waga*, and *uta*) sounds pretty constraining—it's five lines of five syllables or seven syllables each, set in a 5-7-5-7-7 pattern. But for all the clear-cut boundaries, tankas are far from predictable. Styles range from the lyrical to the didactic, subjects from the public to the personal. Tanka emerged during the so-called court period, in the late seventh century, and remained one of the leading Japanese verse forms for centuries—fading a bit during the haiku craze, but bouncing back and remaining popular even into the twentieth century. There have been distinct fads in tanka—for example, during the

twelfth century, most tankas were about blighted courtly love, melancholy riffs on longing. But oddly enough, in spite of the strict confines of the style, many tanka writers through the ages have been experimenters with the form, trying unique imagery or different subjective styles. And in particularly sharp contrast to the regulated form, a number of tankas—both among the earlier ones and more recent—are frankly erotic or passionate. It's possibly this combination of regularity and flexibility that have made tankas so popular.

On such a night as this
When the lack of moonlight shades
your way to me,
I wake from sleep my passion blazing,
My breast a fire raging, exploding flame
While within me my heart chars.
—Ono no Komachi (d. c. 850), in the first
imperial anthology, the *Kokinshu* (c. 905)

TZ'U

(Chinese)
Catchy impressionistic poetry for the
people.

Tz'u means "words"—which is exactly what it is: words written to accompany a tune. In fact, most *tz'u* have no title of their own, just the name of the song they were written to accompany. *T'zu* began as words written for songs sung in brothels and teahouses—an offspring of the older *yüeh-fu* form—and by the end of the T'ang dynasty grew into a legitimate art form. Some people claim that famous Chinese poet Li Po

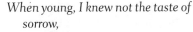

developed the art of *t'zu* writing, but it's unlikely, especially since some of the *t'zu* attributed to him were written to accompany songs written well after his time. It's more probable that *tz'u* writing just evolved organically, especially because the older poetry styles were so sophisticated and formal. With *tz'u,* anyone could write—and many did: from commoners to royalty, ordinary people to writers. Given this, *tz'u* are usually pretty flexible in terms of subject and grammar. A good *tz'u* writer isn't as constrained by rules as writers of other forms; his goal is more an impressionistic than a technical one.

When young, I knew not the taste of sorrow,
But loved to mount the high towers;
I loved to mount the high towers
To compose a new song, urging myself to talk about sorrow.

Now that I have known all the taste of sorrow,
I would like to talk about it, but refrain;
I would like to talk about it, but refrain,
And say merely: "It is chilly; what a fine autumn!"

—Untitled, Hsin Ch'i-chi (1140–1207), to the tune of "The Ugly Slave"

POETIC VOICES YOU MAY NOT HAVE HEARD, PART 2: MODERN VOICES

Modern poets, unfortunately, aren't as well known as those of past centuries. By virtue of being writers of the twentieth century, they haven't had the same time for their work to become widely recognized. And more important, poetry isn't what it was in the past. It has lost its wide appeal. Where once poetry was a major form of entertainment, now it must compete with other forms of communication, like television and film, for the hearts and minds of an audience. And of course, poetry loses.

Most of the time.

There are those modern poets who still manage to seize the imagination of their readers, who (to use an overused phrase) make a difference, who manage to speak to—and for—people. Many of them are revolutionaries of a sort, speaking for the disenfranchised, for the people of their country who have no voice or for people around the world who are similarly oppressed. But all of them are poets able to capture a moment and share an experience with their readers.

AI QING (JIANG HAICHENG)

(1910–)
(Chinese)

"Often my creative life has seemed like a long tunnel, dark and damp. And sometimes I wondered whether I could live through it.

"But I did."

Ai Qing had a lot to live through. His experiences are a mirror of what was happening in China at the time— from the early days of the revolution through later purges. An early admirer of the nationalistic May Fourth Movement, he went to Paris to study painting—and he discovered both literature and radicalism. He became a political activist and was imprisoned for his activities. This was when he began writing socially conscious works about the suffering of the common people and took his pen name. Years later, after his support of Mao Zedong and Zhou Enlai and the communist takeover of China, his work was used as propaganda, it was so strongly partisan and glowing about the so-called war of liberation.

But ultimately his support of the Communist Party wasn't returned in kind. Like many other artists and writers, he fell victim to Mao's antirightist campaign. He was accused of being a revisionist and sent to state farms for reeducation. According to Ai Qing, he was silenced for twenty-one years—his earlier works were denounced, his later works unpublished. But in 1978 his voice began being heard again.

To the right of that perpendicular
A black uniform, part of, in tatters,
Three brass buttons in line with the
*   vertical*
Glow with the pale yellow flame of
*   lamps.*
—But the oil is almost dry.
Copper colored cheeks with antique
*   gleam,*
A few withered palms of
*   unstraightening hands.*
He grips life's tail as it jerks away
—An eel wriggling into the mud.
He shakes his ancient coppery head,
Curses flower from the foam of his
*   spittle;*
And all his words
Are dyed with the tint of hunger.
*   —Old Man* (Lao-jen)

YEHUDA AMICHAI

(1924–)
(Israeli)

"Poetry for me is a release, because it helps me locate my pain and transform it into words. . . . It is my instinctive way of touching a wound."

Yehuda Amichai metaphorically put his finger on it: his work explores the pain in life. But it also explores the joys. Part of the so-called new-wave movement in Israeli poetry, he is known for capturing the Israeli experience. This kind of orientation makes sense: the Hebrew name he adopted after he and

his family emigrated to Israel from Germany means "My people lives." And it is this kind of spirit that his poetry contains. A great deal of it specifically focuses on life in Jerusalem, the people, the tensions, even the buildings. And just as the city itself lives both in the present and in history, his work explores both the past and the present, history and current events. Yet in many ways it's very private poetry. Instead of polemical preachings or political observations, his work highlights the individual experience within the larger picture. And it is this that makes his poetry accessible. Even when Amichai directly talks about the fighting in Israel, he talks about his resignation about it, his fatigue, even alienation.

On a roof in the Old City
laundry hanging in the late afternoon
*   sunlight:*
the white sheet of a woman who is my
*   enemy,*
the towel of a man who is my enemy,
to wipe off the sweat of his brow.

In the sky of the Old City
a kite.
At the other end of the string,
a child
I can't see
because of the wall.

We have put up many flags
they have put up many flags.
To make us think that they're happy.
To make them think that we're happy.

*   —Jerusalem*

KOFI AWOONOR

(1935–)
(Ghanaian)

As George Awoonor-Williams put it in his book *Guardians,* in traditional Ewe culture, a *heno* is "the guiding spirit, the voice and expression of the . . . word which is still a sacred phenomenon."

And Awoonor is that *heno,* that guardian—of the traditional African poetic voice. He is a poet in quest of roots—roots that have been lost or destroyed as Africans move away from a traditional to a Westernized culture. Awoonor is a leading voice of African writers who now are trying to rediscover their past, their heritage, their culture.

To a great degree, his life mirrors the African condition. He spent his early life in the coastal town of Keta, a fishing and trading post, where he was brought up with the name George Awoonor-Williams. He wrote under this name until the late sixties, about the time he also began delving into the traditional culture and poetry of the Ewe people, while he was a lecturer of African literature at the University of Ghana. And the tone and lyricism of this traditional poetry is evident in his work. Unlike many other contemporary African poets who use Western poets (such as Eliot or Yeats) as inspiration and model, he uses the traditional poetry and music of the Ewe. So in his work, rhythm, theme, and mood are all intrinsically African. There's a dirgelike quality to many of his poems, a throwback to the oral tradition of Africa that is sustained on paper.

Go and tell them that I crossed the
   river
While the canoes were still empty
And the boatmen had gone away.
My god of songs was ill
And I was taking him to be cured.
   —from *My God of Songs Was Ill*

CONSTANTINE P. CAVAFY (KONSTANTINOS PETROU KABAPHES)

(1863–1933)
(Greek)

Cavafy's life appears to be an unremarkable one—in fact, somewhat dull. A native of Alexandria, Egypt, he spent most of his adult life—thirty years—working for the irrigation service of the Ministry of Public Works in Alexandria. A homosexual, he never married—but didn't have an active love life, either. (According to him, he had only two love affairs, both brief.) But Cavafy was far from the little gray man this bald recitation of facts might lead one to expect.

Looking at his work proves this: there's a certain life to his poetry. One reason: its clarity. He shunned literary devices and ornate language, preferring instead to rely on factual observation and clean communication. His poetry usually falls into two camps: erotic love poems that, while moving, are unsentimental, and history poems (usually anecdotes and character studies from the past) that are far from dry.

In fact, acquaintances said he had the ability to gossip about historical figures as if they were alive and still in the middle of committing whatever outrageous act he was talking about.

But he was largely unrecognized in his time—becoming somewhat famous in Alexandria, and in Greece only late in his life. For good reason: he just wasn't much of a salesman where his poetry was concerned. Instead of selling his poetry, he would print pamphlets of them and give them to friends and relatives. (In fact, his collected poems weren't published until after his death.) But he did become friendly with the English writer E. M. Forster, who got him the little attention during his life that he did get—and after his death introduced Cavafy's work to the West.

And now, years later, even more people are discovering Cavafy—and he is now considered the leading Greek poet of the twentieth century.

The Alexandrians of course were
aware
that these were just words and
theatrics.
But the day was hot and poetic,
the sky was bright blue,
the Alexandrian stadium
a triumphant feat of art,
the exquisite resplendence of the
courtiers,
Caesarion full of grace and beauty
(Cleopatra's son, blood of the Lagidae)
and the Alexandrians rushed to the
festival,
and they were elated and cheered
—in Greek, in Egyptian, some in
Hebrew—
charmed by the wonderful spectacle,
with all that, of course, they knew
what it was worth

what empty words were these,
words in praise of kings.
—from "Alexandrian Kings"

NAZIM HIKMET

(1902–1963)
(Turkish)

"We can only reach our goal / amid bloodletting."

The words of a revolutionary—which is just what Nazim Hikmet was, both in his writing and in his politics. Educated in Moscow, he was an avowed communist who felt that his country needed social change. And this was what he addressed in his poems—poems he wrote to stir his fellow countrymen and to fellow revolutionaries. He did write lyrical love poems as well, but he's best known for his poems about social injustice, the problems of the masses, the need for revolution.

And he thought this revolution should apply to poetry as well. He was the main popularizer of free verse in Turkey, believing that the traditional poetic forms should cede to the new order. For all his modernization of traditional forms, some critics now think his work sometimes sounds a little old-fashioned. One reason—like many poets of the past, Hikmet wrote to be read aloud, so his work is heavy on rhythm and repetitions. But in spite of this (even possibly because of this), his work is still strong, filled with spirit and passion that captures his revolutionary zeal.

If the half of my heart is here, doctor,
The other half is in China

With the army going down towards the
    Yellow River.
And then every morning, doctor,
Every morning at dawn
My heart is shot in Greece.
And then when the prisoners fall
    asleep,
When the last steps go away from the
    infirmary
My heart goes off, doctor,
It goes off to a little wooden house in,
    in Istanbul.
And then for ten years, doctor,
I have had nothing in my hands to
    offer my people,
Nothing else but an apple,
A red apple, my heart.

    —from *Angina Pectoris*, written when Hikmet
    was in prison

ORHAN VELI KANIK

(1915–1950)
(Turkish)

"The people who fill the modern world are winning the right to live, after a ceaseless struggle. They have a right to poetry, as to everything else, and poetry will address itself to their tastes."

Kanik wrote these words in an introduction to a book of poems. And this sums up his work better than anything else could. With two other poets (Oktay Rifat and Melih Cevdat Anday), he started a poetic-realism movement that broke away from the old traditional forms, from reliance on meter, rhyme, and literary devices. Kanik wrote about the common people and, moreover, wrote for them—not for the literati or the intellectuals. And the people responded. (In fact, the

three-line poem below has virtually reached proverb status in Turkey.) His aim: to help the common people flex their political muscle under democracy. To this end, much of his work was about the living conditions in Turkey, the need for social change, and the like. Some of his work was considered shocking at the time—especially when he spoke badly about his lifestyle.

And his life wasn't all that pretty. He was a heavy drinker and prone both to accidents (he was once in a coma for several weeks after a car accident) and to ill health (often alcohol induced). And his death was a sudden one: he fell in a hole that some workmen had dug and, a few months later, while being treated for alcohol poisoning, died of a cerebral hemorrhage. But his poetry still lives, quoted by the common people he wrote for.

What have we not done for this land!
Some of us have died,
Some of us have made speeches.

    —For the Motherland (Vatan Ici)

PABLO NERUDA

(1904–1973)
(Chilean)

"This is a life made up of other lives, for a poet has many lives."

Neftalí Ricardo Reyes y Basoalto (Neruda) was right when he wrote these words: he was a politician, a diplomat, and of course, a poet. And it is as a poet, especially, that he had many lives. His work is virtually unclassifiable. Throughout his life, it continually changed and evolved. He started as a modernist, moved on to rueful love poems (which made him his name), then on to his *Residencia en la tierra* (Residence on Earth) series, which was less lyrical. Next was his highly political mode, then a simpler, lyrical style. (And of course, during this time, he was also serving first as a diplomat, then as a politician—who was forced to flee Chile at one point because of his subversive activities). His subjects and tone ranged from the political or the public to the introspective and personal.

Yet for all the different voices, at the core Neruda was still simply Neruda—and the styles were just ways to search for the truth. His work was controversial sometimes because of his staunch Marxist ideals, sometimes because of his surrealism and deliberate lack of logic, but ultimately admired—to the point where he won a Nobel Prize in 1971 and is still considered one of the leading Latin American poets of the twentieth century.

*I made my contact with the truth
to restore light to the earth.*

*I wished to be like bread.
The struggle never found me wanting.*

*But here I am with what I loved,
with the solitude I lost.
In the shadow of that stone, I do not
   rest.*

*The sea is working, working in my
   silence.*

—Nothing More (Nada Mas)

OCTAVIO PAZ

(1914–)
(Mexican)

"Enamored of silence, the poet's only recourse is to speak."

And Paz has never been afraid to speak. Part of Mexico's literary avant-garde that emerged in the 1940s, he and the other members of the group believed that poetry should be an active participant in history and politics. Through his long career, Paz has held to this seminal belief.

It makes sense: Paz himself has been an active participant in history (fighting for the Republicans in the Spanish Civil War, holding an ambassadorship and quitting in protest in response to the Mexican government's harsh crackdown during student riots, and more) even as he writes. Often his poetry is a melding of literary experimentation and social commentary. His common themes—Mexico and its roots, and the human condition of alienation in the face of cultural and political ties. And his style often changes. It's part of his (sometimes excessive) love of the avant-garde. This is sometimes a drawback—at times, his attempts at new forms of writing (like his concrete poems in which type is arranged to create an image) frankly fail. But even his critics can't ignore him. Whether his poems work or not, they're never dull.

NIZAR QABBANI

(1932–)
(Syrian/Lebanese)

"Sweep away thousands of synonyms /
Sweep away maxims and ancient wisdom."

In one of his poems (*A Personal Letter to the Month of June*) Qabbani
addresses these lines to the month of
June. He may just as well have been
talking about himself. His work is very
clean and modern—strong, straightforward free verse that doesn't hide
behind musty literary devices or allusions. He hits his subjects straight on.
And when he is criticizing the government, which is often, he doesn't mince
words. Frankly, it's probably easy for
him to get an inside line of the workings of the government and to be a just
(if harsh) critic: he used to be a diplomat—serving in Beirut, Cairo, London, Beijing, and Madrid. He quit to
start a publishing house in Beirut and
to write. Initially, most of his work was

romantic love poems, but with increasing problems in the Middle East, he
began writing poems of social protest
on politics and other social issues.
Clearly these poems strike a chord.
He's considered by some to be the
greatest writer of his generation, is possibly the most widely read Arab poet
among women, and has turned out
twenty-five poetry books as well as an
autobiography.

6
Our shouting is louder than our
*   actions,*
Our swords are taller than us,
This is our tragedy.

7
In short
We wear the cape of civilization
But our souls live in the stone age.

8
You don't win a war
With a reed and a flute.

—from *Footnotes to the Book of the Setback*

GREAT BOOKS 101:
THE LEADING BOOKS OF THE WORLD

 Great Books 101 is a standard course at many colleges and universities—and for good reason. Certain books stand out across time. Sometimes they are masterpieces of writing; other times masterpieces of insight. Sometimes they're a window into humankind in general; other times humankind in a specific culture.

Here is a quick look at some of these great books, books from different cultures and eras that have withstood the passage of time, books that still pack a punch and either comment on the universal human condition or give some fascinating insight into what a certain place or time was really like.

Some of these books you'll probably know; others will be less familiar. But each of them holds a special place in the pantheon of world literature . . . and each is well worth having at least a passing knowledge of.

THE CANTERBURY TALES

GEOFFREY CHAUCER

(late fourteenth century)
(English)

In one line: *On the Road* meets Scheherazade in fourteenth-century England.

Abridged version: A group of trav-elers—thirty different people represent-ing a cross section of fourteenth-century English society—is on a religious pil-grimage to Canterbury Cathedral, shrine of Thomas à Becket. They meet at the Tabard Inn, where the innkeeper (the host of the group) suggests that each of the pilgrims tells stories during the trip to keep everyone entertained. The result? A series of tales, complete with interruptions, interjections, and insights into human nature.

Theme: A double one: 1) Human-kind is often ridiculous, often irra-tional, so best viewed with laughter, and 2) one should value dignity and integrity more than anything else.

Why it's great: Artistic merit plus timelessness. Strong characterization and technical brilliance in the inter-weaving of the tales, the characters, and the general framework. A timeless and universal look at human behavior. Comically realistic and surprisingly readable (once you get past the Middle English).

Technicalities: Written mostly in verse—Middle English verse, to be exact. Since the innkeeper suggests that each of the thirty pilgrims tells four stories (two on the way to the shrine and two on the trip back), there should be 120 stories in all. But the work consists only of a prologue fol-lowed by twenty complete stories, two incomplete ones, and two others that were deliberately interrupted by other pilgrims. Contains every type of medieval story—from romances of courtly love to fairy tales to bawdy fabliaux, cynical, humorous tales usually revolving around sex and typically directed against marriage, the clergy, or women.

CHIN P'ING MEI (GOLDEN LOTUS)

Author Unknown

(c. 1590s)
(Chinese)

In one line: The rise and fall of a man addicted to sex and women.

Abridged version: The wealthy, crude merchant and pawnbroker Hsi-men Ch'ing enjoys the baser things in life—particularly sleeping with a variety of women and partying with his friends. A polygamist, he decides he wants to marry his current lover, P'an Chin-lien. The only obstacle—her husband—is easily removed. They poison him. Wedded bliss doesn't last long. The easily bored Hsi-men is ready for another new lover, so he steals another man's wife, Li P'ing-er, who becomes his favorite over P'an.

Ever the sensualist, Hsi-men keeps looking for ways to keep himself satisfied. Wanting more (and better) sex, he gets his hands on an aphrodisiac from a Buddhist monk. In the meantime, Li P'ing-er becomes pregnant and gives birth to a son, which moves her up a notch in the household. She's the one with status now, even though she was a later wife. This is too much for the jealous P'an, who can't stand seeing her position eroding in the face of this interloper. So she puts an end to the

problem—by arranging the death of both Li P'ing-er and the new son.

Hsi-men is devastated and slowly lets both his wealth and his sexual ability fade away. P'an won't let this happen. She's still an avid lover, still interested in having the good old days of wild sex return now that the other wife is out of the picture. So, in an effort to bring Hsi-men back to his old sensual ways, she gets her hands on his aphrodisiac. But it's a disaster—she accidentally gives him an overdose. And in the middle of sex, he dies—with her on top of him.

The decay of the household doesn't stop with his death. The money Hsi-men leaves behind begins dwindling and the members of his household begin dying off. First, P'an dies; her maid Ch'un-mei also dies (during a sexual act); and at the end, only Hsi-men's main wife is still alive, as is her son, Hsiao-ko (Hsi-men's reincarnation), who—to hammer home the moral—becomes a monk.

Theme: Life is a battle (in this case, played out on the sexual battlefield).

Why it's great: To be frank, there are a number of flaws with this work—namely, different writing styles, problems with plot sequence, and inconsistent characterization. But it's still considered one of the masterpieces of Chinese literature. Why? It was one of the first novels of contemporary social life—plus one of the first Chinese novels written by a single author. It's also technically strong in many ways—particularly in use of imagery. It operates on a number of levels (key one—sex represents social struggles); it's a great example of a number of Chinese fiction techniques.

Technicalities: No one is sure of the author, but some think that he was a well-known writer who didn't want his name attached to the work because of its eroticism. Interestingly, for all the sex, it usually isn't presented as all that great—in fact, a few characters die during sex, or in positions that look a lot like sex.

CRIME AND PUNISHMENT

FEODOR DOSTOYEVSKY

(1866)
(Russian)

In one line: Columbo meets Freud— a sort of murder mystery revolving not around who done it, but what happens to the person who done it *after* he done it!

Abridged version: Raskolnikov, a poor student, plans the perfect crime and murders a pawnbroker and her stepsister. Or maybe not so perfect . . . He receives a summons right after his nefarious deed and panics.

But the summons is a false alarm. Raskolnikov is so overcome with relief that he faints dead away. A bad move, because his overreaction raises the police's suspicions. So do the answers he gives to their questions. Something seems to be up, the police believe, but they can't be sure. Yet.

The crime isn't turning out the way Raskolnikov planned. He buries the jewelry he's stolen under a rock without even examining it, gets a high fever for four days, and takes to bed. But when he recovers, he's sick to discover that he was questioned by the police while he was feverish—and in his delirium, he's said even *more* to the police.

Things get even worse. He continues incriminating himself through his strange, guilty behavior. Even his family and friends begin wondering what's wrong with him. As for the police, they're pretty sure he's guilty, but they have no hard evidence.

Porfiry, the chief of the murder investigation, is determined to get Raskolnikov to break down and confess. He begins playing a cat-and-mouse game with Raskolnikov, asking pointed questions, trying to draw him out. Raskolnikov is slowly being pulled in. To defend himself, he spouts his theory that the superior man is above the law and morality.

But it's clearly only a theory. Even Raskolnikov doesn't completely believe it. He's tortured by guilt—and after a number of events (including his overheard confession to Sonya, the virtuous prostitute), is confronted by Porfiry yet again. Porfiry tries to get him to confess; Raskolnikov holds out until his mother and sister (who now know he's guilty) assure him that they still love him. He turns himself into the police, serves eight years in Siberia, and begins his moral regeneration with the help of Sonya.

Theme: You ultimately pay for your crimes against your fellow man through suffering . . . which is the only path to salvation and purification.

Why it's great: Brilliant psychological characterization and exploration; especially strong in its lack of oversimplification of moral issues and reasoning, its handling of Raskolnikov's ambivalence about his motive to murder. Forces readers to think about the various issues raised; has tremendous impact.

Technicalities: This is Dostoyevsky's first popular novel after his imprisonment and exile for alleged crimes against the czar; it reflects his point of view after a firsthand knowledge of the legal system. Initially Dostoyevsky considered having it end with Raskolnikov's suicide.

THE DIVINE COMEDY

DANTE ALIGHIERI

(1321)
(Italian)

In one line: A straightforward Christian allegory showing the journey through hell, purgatory, and paradise—and showing God's design for the universe.

Abridged version: It's the day before Easter, and Dante, the author of the work, is lost in a forest, where he meets Roman poet Virgil, representing Human Reason. Virgil, sent by Dante's beloved, Beatrice, who now is in heaven, escorts him through hell and purgatory. First, they visit hell—a cone of concentric circles—and meet different souls. As the circles grow narrower, Dante meets souls who have committed more heinous crimes—and at the bottom and center he meets Lucifer, frozen in ice.

On Easter, they emerge and climb the Mountain of Purgatory. Here, too, there are concentric circles, where they meet the souls of repentant sinners. At the top is Earthly Paradise, where the souls who died before the coming of Christ live. Here Virgil (a pagan) leaves Dante. Dante then meets Beatrice (representing revelation), who takes him up through the circles of heaven—and at the top, the Virgin Mary, St. Bernard, and the Empyrean, where God lives.

Theme: Humankind should turn away from evil and, through self-discipline, seek salvation and the path of good. Love and righteousness (with God's help) will ultimately prevail.

Why it's great: Sheer technical and artistic brilliance—on many levels. It's heavy on intricate symbolism, especially numerical. Some examples: The number three (as in the Holy Trinity) is widely used; the work is three poems in one; it uses terza rima (three-line stanzas of eleven syllables). In the exact center of the poem is one fourteen-syllable line. As one critic put it, at this point Dante, who has been pointing down, now points up. The number one, as in the oneness of God, comes through in the one hundred cantos that the entire poem is divided into. There are seven levels of purgatory (as in the seven deadly sins and the seven virtues) . . . plus much more. Add to this the feat of having created an extremely unified, logical, and believable world; the multileveled allegory; and the simple yet lyrical style.

Technicalities: Dante's original title was simply *Commedia* (the Comedy)—*Divine* was added much later. Three parts of thirty-three cantos each—the most famous is *Inferno* (Hell), then there's *Purgatorio* (Purgatory) and *Paradiso* (Heaven).

DON QUIXOTE

Miguel de Cervantes Saavedra

(1605, 1615)
(Spanish)

In one line: The idealistic search for truth, justice, and reality—at first in a comic vein, then in a serious.

Abridged version: Lower-level nobleman Alonso Quijano has spent too much time reading chivalric tales. His head is filled with the deeds of dashing knights—their battles, their wooing of fair maidens, their heroics. So he changes his name to Don Quixote and, riding his broken-down nag Rocinante, sets out as a knight-errant to right wrongs, rescue damsels, and fight for justice. After one trip out alone, he decides he needs to have someone with him. So he asks the farmer Sancho Panza to serve as his squire and help him in his fight against evil.

Thereafter he runs into various misadventures—fighting a giant that turns out to be a windmill, chasing an army that turns out to be sheep. At the end of part one, he decides he's been enchanted, is put in a cage and taken home.

In the less comic part two, Don Quixote sets out again, this time not on a comic quest but on a serious search for the reality behind appearances. He's again accompanied by the talkative rationalist Sancho Panza, and again he fails at his quest. Deciding that he's indeed mad, he returns home and, his spirit broken, dies.

Theme: Part one: the relationship

Don Quixote has been translated into more languages than any other book except the Bible.

between the ideal and everyday existence. Part two: the paradox of life—those who are considered wise are often foolish and morally inferior; those who seek only to be good are considered mad; idealists often do more than realists.

Why it's great: Considered by most to be one of the all-time greatest pieces of literature, it's an eminently readable exploration of what morality is. Part one is marked by good-natured humor, strong elements of parody, and strong characterization; part two features even stronger characterization, examination of social problems, tight structure, and attention to details.

Technicalities: Never planned as a whole unit (even though it works as one)—which works in its favor. Initially intended to be just a burlesque, it wound up with a more serious tone, primarily because as Cervantes wrote, his take on the characters and the theme changed, and he started (as does the reader) respecting Don Quixote; part two, written ten years after part one, is even more serious.

THE DREAM OF THE RED CHAMBER

Ts'ao Hsüeh-ch'in

(eighteenth century)
(Chinese)

In one line: A Chinese *War and Peace* of sorts, with an overlay of naturalism—the slow fall of an aristocratic family during the Ch'ing dynasty.

Abridged version: This is the

story of the Chia family from wealth and high position to a fall from imperial favor and the loss of their estate, wealth, and status—and is filled with subplots, minor characters, and the like. The key story: the story of Pao-yü, who was born with a piece of magic jade in his mouth—thus his name, meaning Precious Jade. He loves his cousin, the orphan Lin Tai-yü, who has a sharp tongue, poor health, and is a bit of a loner. Because Tai-yü is poor, frail and sensitive, Pao-yü's family doesn't want him to marry her—but what they do is *trick* him into thinking he's doing just that. (In classic B-movie Hollywood fashion, the bride is heavily veiled on the wedding day so Pao-yü can't recognize whom he's marrying.) Meanwhile, Tai-yü is off alone dying of consumption. Pao-yü marries the girl the family has chosen—another cousin who is Tai-yü's opposite, Hsüeh Pao-ch'ai—at the moment Tai-yü is dying. Depressed about her death and having lost his magic jade, Pao-yü sinks into illness and has a dream (yes, the dream of the title) about love. The combination of his grief and his disillusionment lead him to suddenly leave his family for the life of a Buddhist mendicant. His family then has no wealth, no status, and no heir.

Theme: Human longing for such things as beauty, riches, status, and honor leads to loss and dissolution.

Why it's great: One of the first books to employ the narrator's point of view, rather than use a detached narrative; also one of the first to examine moral decay and explore human emotions and motivations, all against a detailed backdrop of Ch'ing dynasty China.

Technicalities: Probably only eighty chapters of the novel were writ-

ten by the author; the other forty were revised, edited, or written by others. In fact, the first eighty chapters were circulated first under the title *The Story of the Stone*—the other forty chapters were added by the time the first printed edition came out, in 1792. Interestingly, while the book was received well in its time, the author was apparently worried about criticism: he spends much of the first chapter defending himself, in particular over his choice of a novel instead of a poem, and explains that the point of his book was to tell a story, not recite impressions, as in a poem.

GULISTAN

SA'DI
(1258)
(Persian)

In one line: A Persian *Poor Richard's Almanack* crossed with *Aesop's Fables*—filled with aphorisms on every aspect of public and private life.

Abridged version: There's no plot, so you can't really summarize the *Gulistan*. Essentially, it's a series of prose tales—some historical, others fictional or legendary, mixed with short verses that underscore the action or moral. In some cases, it's written as a partial travelogue—what author Sa'di saw, whom he met, and what happened during his many travels. The upshot? A compendium of parables, moral tales, and snappy proverbs.

Theme: As Ralph Waldo Emerson put it, the *Gulistan* reflects "the universality of moral law."

Why it's great: A fascinating, timeless collection of ethics—in spite of its age, it's very cosmopolitan and not all that preachy. It's a shrewd look at human behavior and motivation; and the writing style (the most famous version was translated by explorer Sir Richard Burton) isn't overly flowerly, but is instead succinct, to the point, and easy to read.

Technicalities: It made its impact in Europe in 1651 when it appeared in a Latin translation, and was extolled by Voltaire and other Enlightenment scholars. When the British colonized India, their civil servants used it as a means of better understanding Muslim India. Sa'di himself became a famous near legend—tradition has it that he lived over one hundred years and traveled from India to Tripoli in North Africa

MADAME BOVARY

GUSTAVE FLAUBERT

(1857)
(French)

In one line: The female *Don Quixote*—with egoism rather than idealism as the driving force behind the quest.

Abridged version: The well-meaning but dull Charles Bovary meets farmer's daughter Emma and falls in love with her. When his nagging, older first wife, Heloise, dies, he marries Emma and everything is fine—for a very short time.

The sentimental, romance-loving Emma realizes she's bored, that she's not in love with her doctor husband, and that her marriage is nothing like the romantic novels she's read. After giving birth to a daughter, she first has a platonic love affair, then it's on to real affairs, which Emma rationalizes away by identifying herself with a fictional romantic heroine. She plunges her husband into debt, buying herself clothes and jewelry; neglects her child; and involves herself in dubious business transactions to raise more money. She finally involves herself in an affair only to get money—which she doesn't get. Caught up with by moneylenders and determined to die a heroine's death, she commits suicide. Her husband dies of grief after learning of his wife's infidelity, and their impoverished child winds up working at a cotton factory.

Theme: The irony (and tragedy) of human life—people have aspirations that they are ultimately unable to achieve.

Why it's great: One of the first realistic novels, and one of the most famous French novels. Noted for its detailed descriptions, its believable characterizations, its convincing plot —all presented in a restrained, technically polished, yet vivid style.

Technicalities: When the book first came out, a number of people and critics weren't thrilled with it, thinking that the heroine was too vulgar, the subject—adultery—immoral. Some modern critics agree, thinking that the style far exceeds the banal subject matter.

THE MAGIC MOUNTAIN

THOMAS MANN
(1924)
(German)

In one line: A series of lectures on history, philosophy, and psychology—delivered in a timeless world.

Abridged version: An unambitious middle-class man, Hans Castorp, goes to a tuberculosis sanitorium to get a rest and to visit his cousin—planning to stay only three weeks. But finding out that he too has the disease, he stays seven years. During this time, he seeks not only a cure, but also an awareness of his own psyche.

To these ends, he winds up engaged in numerous deep conversations and debates with the other patients and the staff at the sanitorium—such wide-ranging characters as Ludovico Settembrini, an Italian scholar; Leo Naphta, a Catholic Jew; Clavdia Chauchat, a Russian adventuress; Joachim Ziemssen, Hans's cousin; and Dr. Krokowski, a psychoanalyst.

These people and others give Hans the sense of other worlds, other lives, other thoughts outside his own. And he grows as he stays in this self-contained world.

For all the time he spends, it feels as if none has passed. Life at the sanitorium is far removed from the rest of the world. Yes, there are the day-to-day realities of health-care routines, petty arguments among people, and the like, as well as the larger changes, including deaths of some patients (Hans's cousin among them) and the arrival of new patients. But on the whole, Hans is liv-

ing in a timeless world, one in which he can afford to explore the big questions about life.

And then he is ready to reenter the world. Time starts again when Archduke Ferdinand is assassinated. The world below becomes real again. And Hans leaves to go back to Germany and fight . . . and is last seen dodging bullets in a mist-covered landscape.

Theme: Through suffering, self-awareness, and confronting reality, people can develop and grow—becoming stronger, wiser, and able to truly love.

Why it's great: An intellectual achievement more than an artistic one (not that it's artistically lacking, although some think it's a bit dull), it explores virtually every aspect of contemporary European culture. Heavily symbolistic on one hand, yet also marked by attention to minute detail.

Technicalities: Initially planned as a novella, it was inspired by Mann's stay in a Swiss sanitorium. Begun in 1912, but finished after World War I—which mirrors the passage of time in the novel. Follows the traditional German development novel (bildungsroman), in which a young, unformed person, through exposure to different aspects of life, becomes educated and finds his calling.

PÈRE GORIOT

HONORÉ DE BALZAC
(1819)
(French)

In one line: *King Lear*, French style (but more pathetic than tragic).

Abridged version: Père Goriot, a rooming-house lodger, is a father who loves his daughters so much he would do virtually anything for them. And gradually, they milk him of every penny he has.

He starts out with a choice suite of rooms on the first floor of the rooming house owned by Madame Vauquer. But his daughters, Countess Anastasie de Restaud and Baroness Delphine de Nucingen, both social climbers, need more—money for clothes, money to enable them to meet the right people, to move up in the world. And they begin doing just that—moving up and becoming wealthy society matrons.

And Père Goriot begins moving down. First into a smaller suite of rooms, then a cheaper room, then even more cheap.

It doesn't matter to his daughters— still spending too much money keeping up with the Joneses, they continue to ask for more help. And it doesn't really matter to Père Goriot. He continues scraping together whatever he can for them.

Finally it's too much. He sells his last possessions to give money to one of the daughters for a ball gown. Utterly destitute and utterly drained, he suffers a stroke. Still ungrateful, the daughters go to the ball instead of staying by his side.

He dies and is buried in a pauper's grave. The only mourners are a law student, Eugène de Rastignac, who respected Goriot, and another poor medical student. Instead of attending themselves, the two daughters send empty carriages to follow their father's coffin—a final tribute.

Theme: Corruption is universal— obsessive love is as corrupt as greed.

Why it's great: A wonderful exam-

ple of realism at its best. Although Balzac doesn't paint individuals so much as character types, he's great at character analysis. Naturalistic details capture life in nineteenth-century Paris—the poor, the social-climbing bourgeoisie, and the aristocracy. Fast-paced, highly energetic style; all in all, a good read.

Technicalities: Initially began as a short story about the obsession of a parent and the ingratitude of his offspring, and grew into a novel. Was part of Balzac's unfinished magnum opus—a series of works using overlapping characters, called *La Comédie Humaine* (The Human Comedy) to contrast with Dante's *Divine Comedy*. By the time he died, he had finished ninety-five novels and had planned to write forty more.

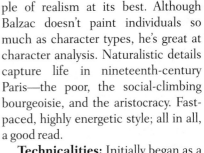

THE TALE OF GENJI

LADY SHIKIBU MURASAKI
(c. 1001–1015)
(Japanese)

In one line: A Japanese soap opera of sorts—the life and loves of Prince Genji.

Abridged version: Before her death, the emperor's concubine Kiritsubo gives birth to a son who grows up to be Genji, a popular, well-placed court figure. He's given in marriage to Princess Aoi when he's only twelve, becomes captain of the guard, and, unhappy with his wife, begins having affairs. After the death of one of his lovers, a poor woman named Yugao, he meets an orphan, Murasaki (the name of the author), and takes her under his care. Princess Aoi gets pregnant and dies—and Genji truly mourns her as he has learned to love her. But a year later, he marries Murasaki, who has now grown up, and resolves to truly settle down.

Theme: The romantic education of innocent lovers.

Why it's great: One of the world's first novels, and a prime example of Japanese court storytelling. Marked by a subtle, sensitive style, witty irony, and elegance. Actually more modern in style than later Japanese fiction. Detailed descriptions of Japanese court life as well as psychologically rich characterizations.

Technicalities: Written by a lady-in-waiting to the Empress Akiko, which explains the rich details about court life. Over eleven hundred pages, divided into six parts—the style improves as the book goes on (and probably as the writer grew more assured); it starts out much more like an adolescent imitation of a court romance, but winds up stylistically mature.

ULYSSES

JAMES JOYCE
(1922)
(Irish)

In one line: The Greek epic the *Odyssey* moved to twentieth-century Dublin—heroic wanderers become unheroic . . . but still wanderers.

Abridged version: A day in the life of writer and teacher Stephen Dedalus (Telemachus), Jewish ad salesman Leopold Bloom (Ulysses), and his wife, Molly (Penelope), among others. Dedalus has been in Dublin a year, having returned from Paris to be at his mother's deathbed. Today he has breakfast, teaches a history lesson, and walks along the beach—all the while dealing with his guilt, his spurning of Catholicism, and his resulting inability to fulfill his mother's dying wish that he pray for her.

Next, it's Leopold Bloom who has the main action (and the main voice)—

The First Book

It's one thing to identify the first novel, another thing to trace the first book. Books began in ancient times looking very different from the bound books of today. In ancient Babylon and Assyria, a book consisted of numbered clay tablets, which were kept in a container. With the discovery of papyrus in ancient Egypt (in about 3000 B.C.E.), books evolved into scrolls—papyrus sheets rolled around wooden cylinders, stored in a box or pot. The ancient Egyptians also came up with their version of a pocket-sized paperback—in this case, mini rolls of papyrus that could be wound up and easily carried. The ancient Greeks also used papyrus, and in addition to rolling up sheets, also came up with the idea of folding the papyrus into leaflets and binding them by hand. In the Middle East, people wrote on thin lamb- or calfskin—which developed into parchment paper, a development brought about by a lag in papyrus supply. And from the development of parchment (or vellum), came the more recognizable book form. Parchment sheets were folded vertically into pages, creating what's called a codex.

he has breakfast, goes to a funeral, takes care of some business, goes to a pub, and more, crossing paths with Dedalus (the son of his old friend), bothered by thoughts of his wife with her lover, and eventually hooking up with Dedalus, whom he sees with a group of rowdy friends and finally takes home with him. He encourages Dedalus to leave his friends and move in with him and Molly, but Dedalus refuses and leaves. Bloom goes to bed, telling his wife to be sure to fix his breakfast. Next, it's Molly's thoughts—she's thinking about her lover, thinking about her life, the loves she's had, her courtship with Bloom, her marriage—while her husband snores beside her.

Theme: Life consists of cycles that constantly recur through eternity.

Why it's great: A breakthrough novel that tries to capture a day in the life of normal people as they would actually live it—complete with their inner thoughts and dreams, their memories, and so on—not presented neatly, but rather as the mind works: with juxtaposed thoughts, jumps, non sequiturs, and the like. Uses a mélange of different techniques and styles—most notably, stream of consciousness.

Technicalities: Joyce chose Ulysses because he was his favorite childhood hero. Initially planned as a short story for the collection *Dubliners*—but it grew into the 767-page novel. For all of its free-seeming technique, it's actually carefully structured. Joyce prepared two charts ("schemas" he called them) to explain the book—each of the eighteen episodes has a title that corresponds to an episode in the Odyssey; they explain the time of day, the style of each episode ("technics" he called it), dominant symbols, and more.

Soon coming to bookstores in Russia: a sequel to Tolstoy's War and Peace. *So far titled a not-so-snappy* War and Peace II, *it's a way for Russian publishers to jump on the sequels bandwagon. But publishers say they're not planning to release the name of the author and will instead publish it under a pseudonym. "We have to keep it a secret," said senior editor Gleb Uspensky of the publishing house Vargius. "To Russians Tolstoy is a god. People would burn the author's house down."*

(Alessandra Stanley, "Frankly My Dear, Russians Do Give a Damn," NEW YORK TIMES, August 29, 1994.)

WAR AND PEACE

LEO TOLSTOY
(1864–1869)
(Russian)

In one line: Four families in Russia during the early nineteenth century, as the country goes through, right, war and peace.

Abridged version: Because it's so long and so detailed, it's virtually impossible to outline the plot of *War and Peace*. So here's a very quick overview, omitting a great deal but hitting the high points:

Russia, 1805—and war with Napoleon seems inevitable. Yet Russian society continues on its merry way, unconvinced that the imminent war will really affect them. Nikolai Rostov joins the army. His friend, Pierre Bezukhov, is the illegitimate son of a count. But he finally gets his father's inheritance and, after years of ridicule, is accepted into society and marries Princess Hélène at her father's pushing—but the marriage is a flop. His good friend Prince Andrei also has a bad marriage, so he goes off to war, during which time his wife dies—but he's not as pleased to be free as he expected. Pierre had joined the Freemasons, thought he had the answer to life, but loses a lot of money and winds up joining Prince Andrei at his family estate. Nikolai Rostov has been in the thick of the war. Prince Andrei falls in love with Nikolai's sister Natasha, and she with him, but his father forces him to wait a year for the wedding. Andrei goes back to war, and Natasha goes to Moscow, where she's tempted by the disreputable Anatol, who arranges an elopement. Her hostess finds out about it, locks Natasha in her room, and it's a huge scandal, especially since Natasha has written a letter asking for her betrothal to Andrei to be broken. Pierre is Natasha's only solace. Prince Andrei is hurt, but busy with the war, then gravely wounded. Natasha nurses him, they fall in love again, but he dies. In the meantime, Nikolai (Natasha's brother) becomes interested in Andrei's sister, Marya; Pierre becomes a prisoner of war; Napoleon's army retreats. Pierre falls

The Fifteen Most Frequently Translated Authors Around the World

1. Agatha Christie, U.K.
2. Disney Productions, U.S.A.
3. V. I. Lenin, Russia
4. Jules Verne, France
5. Mikhail S. Gorbachev, Russia
6. Enid Blyton, U.K.
7. Barbara Cartland, U.K.
8. Isaac Asimov, U.S.A.
9. Alistair MacLean, U.K.
10. R. Goscinny, France
11. Georges Simenon, France
12. Stephen King, U.S.A.
13. Hans Christian Andersen, Denmark
14. Arthur Conan Doyle, U.K.
15. Victoria Holt, U.K.

(Source of data: 1994 U.N. figures)

According to a recent article in THE NEW YORK TIMES, the hottest books in Russia are spin-offs of Margaret Mitchell's GONE WITH THE WIND. With titles like WE CALL HER SCARLETT, THE SECRET OF SCARLETT O'HARA, RHETT BUTLER, THE SECRET OF RHETT BUTLER, and THE LAST LOVE OF SCARLETT, these books are favorites of Russian readers. Most are attributed to one author—Yuliya Hilpatrik, actually a pseudonym for about thirty Russian and Belorussian writers in Minsk who collaborate on these East-West blends. The names of the characters may be the same, but there's a difference between these new creations and the characters who inspired them. For one, they're a bit gloomier—at the end of THE LAST LOVE OF SCARLETT, most people are dead, including Scarlett herself.

in love with Natasha; they marry; Nikolai and Marya marry, even though he's not sure he wants to—but they wind up very happy. And Pierre and Natasha have four children, she's incredibly devoted to her family, and they're extremely happy. (Got that?)

Theme: Two, actually—age and youth, war and peace.

Why it's great: Its immense scope, engaging and believable characters, tight organization for all of the length. Tolstoy uses groups of characters as blocks, elements within the larger structure. Characters, events, and episodes are deftly interwoven. Virtually uncategorizable because of its breadth and depth. The downside—war passages are sometimes stultifyingly detailed, as Tolstoy tries hard to present every action of Napoleon's army.

Technicalities: Based on Tolstoy's theory of history—that free will is an illusion, and events shape the man, not vice versa. In other words, historical events aren't attributable to the efforts of men, great or otherwise.

WHAT YOU DIDN'T LEARN IN AMERICAN OR ENGLISH LIT: THE GREATEST WRITERS OF THE *REST* OF THE WORLD AND THE LITERARY TRADITIONS OF THEIR CULTURES

 These are the great writers you didn't learn about in English literature—and possibly didn't learn in other literature classes either. Some are better known than others; some are still, unfortunately, not known nearly as well as they should be—at least not in the United States. They're writers from the rest of the world—from Africa, China, India, Japan, Latin America, and the Middle East. They're writers outside of the traditions we're most familiar with.

Their work, though, can't be classified simply as non-European writing. And even though these writers are part of a specific literary tradition in their country or area, you can't classify them that way. What they write isn't just non-European writing, or writing of any specific culture. It's too strong for that, too universal. While working within a cultural tradition, these writers actually write works for all of the world. Their words speak to all of us, whatever country or culture we're from.

These are works of one ethos, written in one language: the human language, a language we all speak.

MODERN AFRICAN LITERATURE

 In many ways, modern African literature is designed to be heard as well as read. This is because it's a literature with oral roots—extending back to the oral tradition that's existed in Africa for thousands of years and still rich today.

Experts say that there are over a quarter of a million myths, legends, and folktales still being told by professional storytellers to eager audiences today. Even urban dwellers still pass on the oral tradition.

So it's no wonder that modern African literature clearly springs from this rich past. Even though the words are written rather than spoken, the reader can *hear* the words spoken in his or her head.

It's not just the notion of the oral tradition. Modern African literature shows other ties to a distinct past—which make much of it very different from the literature of the West. The feeling of group living, of respect for ancestors, and of other traditions comes through even in the most modern of novels. In fact, a lot of modern literature is actually based on old folktales and revolves around the traditional story line of a departure, initiation, and return.

But it has been brought into the modern world. Much of modern African literature is concerned with the present, even the future—what happened when the West intruded upon Africa and her people . . . and what *will* happen now that the inevitable culture clash has occurred?

As noted scholar Professor O. R. Dalthorne put it: "The African writer has both the worst and the best of three possible worlds—the new, the old, and his own."

Following is a look at four of the literary giants of Africa—people who are largely responsible for the incredible growth of the African literary movement. These are the acknowledged masters, the writers who made the rest of the world sit up and take notice and, more to the point, start listening.

Other great African writers:

Peter Abrahams (1919–), South Africa (his novel, *Mine Boy,* was the first black South African novel written in English to receive worldwide attention)

Ama Ata Aidoo (1942–), Ghana

Ayi Kwei Armah (1938–), Ghana

Cyprian Ekwensi (1921–), Nigeria

Rachel Emecheta (1944–), Nigeria

Nuruddin Farah (1945–), Somalia

Es'kia Mphahlele (1919–1982), South Africa

Lewis Nkosi (1936–), South Africa

Gabriel Okara (1921–), Nigeria

Ben Okri (1959–), Nigeria

Kole Omotoso (1943–), Nigeria

Ousmane Sembene (1923–), Senegal

Ngugi wa Thiong'o (1938–), Kenya (known as one of East Africa's first major modern novelists)

CHINUA ACHEBE (ALBERT CHINUALMOGO)

(1930–)
(Nigerian)

Achebe calls himself a political writer, "concerned with universal human communication across racist and cultural boundaries."

And he succeeds in breaking through these boundaries. One of Africa's leading writers, Achebe burst onto the scene with a distinctive voice . . . and a lot to say. His first novel, *Things Fall Apart* (1958), spearheaded the influence of modern black African novels in English. One reason for its impact? Its subject matter—the effect of another way of life on an Ibo village, and its eventual disintegration . . . something that was happening across Africa.

Actually his life mirrors much of the development of Africa—he was born during the colonial period, grew older as the different nationalist movements emerged, and finally watched as the different African countries won independence from the colonial powers. And what he saw is the basis for most of his work: the consequences of the European presence in—and domination of—Africa. But while it's clearly spawned of Africa, his work is more universal. Ultimately, it speaks of the impact one culture has on another, the lost traditions supplanted by newer, nonindigenous ones, the changes upon changes upon changes that a culture—and the individuals living in it—must cope with.

His writing is a means of coping with this change. He actually put it best: "Literature . . . gives us a second handle on reality; enabling us to encounter in the safe, manageable dimensions of make-believe the very same threats to integrity that may assail the psyche in real life. . . . What better preparation can a people desire as they begin their journey into the strange revolutionary world of modernization?" (From *Hopes and Impediments* [New York: Doubleday, 1990].)

Reading list: *Things Fall Apart, No Longer at Ease, Arrow of God, A Man of the People* (novels); *Christmas in Biafra and Other Poems; Girls at War* (short stories); *Hopes and Impediments, Morning Yet on Creation Day* (essays).

ELECHI AMADI

(1934–)
(Nigerian)

"The novelist should depict life as he sees it without consciously attempting to persuade the reader to take a particular viewpoint. Propaganda should be left to journalists."

With these words, Amadi clearly states his case—and his works follow through on this stance. He is concerned with painting the day-to-day life of African villagers, but without the intrusion of politics.

This makes Amadi unique among most of Africa's leading writers. While he too writes about traditional African society, he doesn't focus on the changes brought about by colonialism. Most of his novels are set before colonial rule, and whether it's five years or

fifty, it doesn't matter. Time isn't the issue. There's no contrast between the before and after of life. Instead, these works are more concerned with the effects the indigenous African culture has on itself. The events that affect the characters in his novels come from the inside, not the outside. It's a self-contained world he writes about, one that is African to the core.

Amadi once said that "an African writer who really wants to interpret the African scene has to write in three dimensions at once. There is the private life, the social life, and what you may call the supernatural." And in his three novels that form his popular, loosely tied village trilogy—*The Concubine, The Great Ponds,* and *The Slave*—he weaves these three dimensions together, creating a complete vision of the traditional Ikweore world. Even when he breaks away from writing about village life, the elemental traditions still underscore the action.

Some critics have said he is part anthropologist in his ability to present traditional Ikweore beliefs and customs; others have said it's as though the tales are told by a villager himself. But the bottom line is the same: Amadi boils down the traditional elements of Africa and, in setting forth these elements in a clear, strong, modern way, makes them universal, in a sense—germane to those of us who aren't members of the same culture.

Reading list: *The Concubine, The Great Ponds, The Slave, Estrangement* (novels); *Sunset in Biafra: A Civil War Diary, Ethics in Nigerian Culture* (essays); *Isiburu, Pepper Soup, The Road to Ibadan, Dancer of Johannesburg* (plays).

NADINE GORDIMER

(1923–)
(South African)

"The tension between standing apart and being fully involved; that is what makes a writer," Gordimer wrote in the introduction to her *Selected Stories.*

Gordimer, then, is certainly a writer. To a great degree, she stands apart by virtue of her circumstances: Born and bred in Springs, South Africa, not only was she a member of the white minority, she also was isolated as a child—kept home by a mother who believed she had a bad heart. Books were her outlet; she began reading and writing at an early age. Then, as an intellectual, she became a member of another minority. So her perspective is that of an outsider looking in.

Yet through her work—and through her political stance—she is most definitely involved. She's a member of the African National Congress and a founder of the Congress of South African Writers, and has a history of commitment to South African black writers. She usually incorporates political underpinnings in her work, especially apartheid and its effects on the characters, although the focus of her books is usually squarely on her characters, not on issues at large.

Gordimer herself has pointed out that her books aren't formally political—however, as she added, in South Africa, society *is* the political situation. So by focusing on society, especially on different individuals, she's making a political statement. Apartheid and its effects, race relations, and more generally, the effect the African and Euro-

pean cultures have on one another—these all find way into her work, chiefly because these are central to the South African experience.

Her later works have shifted into what critics call her "radical phase"—that is, there's more emphasis on political critique, more attention paid to revolution. However, at bottom, they're still rich, character-driven works, exploring politics as it affects people.

Reading list: *My Son's Story, Something Out There, July's People, Burger's Daughter, The Conservationist, A Guest of Honor, The Late Bourgeois World, Occasion for Loving, A World of Strangers, The Lying Days* (novels); *Selected Stories, Jump and Other Stories, Crimes of Conscience, A Soldier's Embrace, No Place Like, Livingstone's Companions, Some Monday for Sure, Friday's Footprint, Six Feet of Country, The Soft Voice of the Serpent* (short stories); *The Essential Gesture: Writing, Politics and Places* (essays).

WOLE SOYINKA (AKINWANDE OLUWOLE SOYINKA)

(1934–)
(Nigerian)

Soyinka—a dramatist, poet, and novelist—is one of the leading figures in African literature. But he's also known as a champion of human rights. "I have one abiding religion—human liberty," he said in a 1975 autobiographical statement.

And this comes through in his work.

Politics are an underlying current in his work. However, he's not polemical or theoretical. As he sees it, an artist in Africa must think politically. So the political content in his work is a natural offshoot of his circumstances. A common theme in all of his work is the contrast and, in fact, struggle between old Africa and new, between the traditional African ways and the modern ones borne of postcolonialism.

He first emerged on the literary scene as a playwright, winning attention for his verse tragedy *The Swamp Dwellers* and the comedy *The Lion and the Jewel*. He then founded a theater company, the Orisun Repertory, and focused on his goal of creating a new Nigerian drama—a synthesis of traditional and modern. Plays are written in English, but the language used is a pastiche, ranging from superscholastic English of the scholars to pidgin English to the words and expressions used in the slums. And he also incorporates the traditional elements of African festivals, such as drumming, dance, pantomime. The outcome is an image of modern Nigeria, a country that still has its traditions alive but is changing and modernizing.

And as he created a new Nigerian drama, he did the same with fiction. His novel *The Interpreters* is called the first truly modern African novel. Again, the focus of the book is the tensions between the past and the present or future—the old tribal society confronted with the West, the problems of political corruption on the one hand, religious complacency on the other.

Soyinka doesn't confront these issues only in his written work. He speaks out against what he perceives as rights abuses and corruption—and

was, in fact, arrested and imprisoned for openly criticizing the government.

"The man dies in all who keep silent in the face of tyranny," he wrote while he was imprisoned. So Soyinka refuses to keep silent, but lets his voice—and his pen—be heard.

Reading list: *The Swamp Dwellers, The Lion and the Jewel, A Dance of the Forests, The Road, Kongi's Harvest, Madmen and Other Specialists, Death and the King's Horseman, A Play of Giants* (plays); *The Interpreters, Season of Anomy* (novels); *Idanre and Other Poems, A Shuttle in the Crypt* (poetry); *Myth, Literature and the African World* (essays).

MODERN CHINESE LITERATURE

 You could say that modern Chinese literature was born out of politics. In 1917, Hu Shih—often called the Father of the Chinese Renaissance—wrote an article called "A Modest Proposal for Literary Reform." His battle cry? The country was being freed from its old, traditional feudal past. So it was time for a new literature, one written in the people's voice. It was time to move past the old classical style. Time for literature to represent what was happening in the country at large.

And writers and intellectuals agreed.

Since then, modern Chinese literature has continued speaking in the people's voice. In fact, to a great degree, it has remained the literature of social protest, or at least of social realism. It's gone through several changes, echoing the political environment. From its initial social fervor, it evolved into supercommunist propaganda (to coincide with the rise of Mao). Then with time, the lapse of the communist stranglehold on culture, and the rise of prodemocracy activism, Chinese literature remained the voice of social protest, but this time *against* strict communism. But the crackdown in Tiananmen Square and the resulting crackdown on nonparty thought brought about new restrictions on writers. The result? Many writers fled China or toned down their politically incorrect inclinations. But yet again, the climate is changing—and so too the writers who capture the voice of their people.

The two writers we take a look at in depth, Ding Ling and Lu Xun, represent the first modern movement in China. There are, of course, other writers who are acknowledged as leaders in Chinese literature. Some of these are younger and so have a different voice and thrust—they're the writers of post–Tiananmen Square China, and often reflect the prodemocracy ideals that emerged in China. Others are older and capture more of the revolutionary fervor felt at Mao's height. But they're all part of the continually evolving Chinese tradition of literature.

Other great modern Chinese writers include

A Cheng (1949–) (now living in the United States because of the post–Tiananmen Square crackdown on artists)
Ch'en Ying-chen (1937–)
Gao Xiao-shang (1928–)
Lao She (1899–1966)
Mo Yan (1956–)

Wang Anyi (1954–)
Wang Meng (1934–)
Xiao Jun (1907–1988)
Zhang Jie (1937–)

DING LING (JIANG BINGZHI)

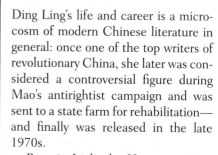

(1904–1986)

Ding Ling's life and career is a microcosm of modern Chinese literature in general: once one of the top writers of revolutionary China, she later was considered a controversial figure during Mao's antirightist campaign and was sent to a state farm for rehabilitation—and finally was released in the late 1970s.

Born in Linli, the Hunan province that was home to many of China's revolutionary leaders, she became an activist because of the influence of the May Fourth Movement of 1919. She began writing, broke off (with her mother's support) an arranged marriage, and moved to Shanghai, then Beijing, where she became the live-in lover of activist poet Hu Yepin. As a writer, she broke new ground with her psychological portraits of women—and with her own independent lifestyle. (Incidentally, she credited her mother—a widow who became an educational pioneer and founded a number of elementary schools—as a major influence and often said her mother was greater than she.) Her writing was as revolutionary as her politics: *Miss Sophie's Diary*, perhaps her most famous story, included the sexual fantasies of the young woman, and most of her other stories focused on the modern woman and her struggle for independence—and dealt frankly with such issues as sex, love, and identity.

Then the Kuomintang government began persecuting radical writers. And Ding Ling became an even more confirmed leftist when her lover, now father of her son, was executed. Her writing shifted to more distinctly radical subjects, focusing on the oppressed peasants, the upcoming socialist revolution, and the like; she joined the Communist Party; and after escaping from the Kuomintang, who had detained her, she married fellow writer Chen Ming, and became editor of the literary page of the *Liberation Daily*—writing chiefly critical essays and trying to stick with party dictates where writing was concerned.

"Happiness is to take up the struggle in the midst of the raging storm and not to pluck the lute in the moonlight or recite poetry among the blossoms," she wrote in her essay, "Thoughts on March 8" (1942), mirroring the revolutionary zeal of the times.

Even so, her independent spirit continued to assert itself even now—for example, in the same essay, she commented on the discrimination of women under communism. But shortly thereafter Mao stressed that literature and art had to promulgate strict party ideology. So she adjusted her writing and stuck with social realism, even winning the Stalin prize for her novel about land reform, *The Sun Shines over the Sanggan River*.

It wasn't enough. While she was one of the top members of the cultural hierarchy in Communist China for a while, she soon fell victim to Mao's antirightist purge of intellectuals. She was accused of immorality, traitorous conspiracy against the party, and ideological shortcomings. Her books were banned. She was expelled from the party. She and her husband were sent to a state farm, then she was in solitary confinement in Beijing for five years.

It wasn't until after Mao's death, when his excesses were corrected, that Ding Ling became a public personage again. In 1979, the ban on her books was lifted and she was able to resume her career. Twenty-three years had passed . . . and she could be a writer again.

Reading list: *I Myself Am a Woman: Selected Writings of Ding Ling* (collection); *Miss Sophie's Diary and Other Stories* (short stories); *Birth of an Individual, A Woman, The Sun Shines over the Sanggan River, Comrade Du Wanxiang* (novels).

LU XUN (CHOU SHU-JEN)

(1881–1936)

Lu Xun is called the father of modern Chinese literature. He was exalted by communist critics, idolized by the Chinese literary left, and imitated by later writers.

But above all, Lu Xun was an individualist and an innovator. He broke new ground with his style—clean, free from old traditional clichés and, for that matter, modern ones. But his subject matter was especially groundbreaking. To a great degree, he is the writer who introduced the art of social protest to Chinese literature.

His scathing attacks on the dark side

of traditional Chinese society stemmed from his own background: his family was one of businessmen and government officials that sank into poverty. When the New Culture Movement of 1917 swept the country, Lu Xun agreed with the view that literary realism should replace the classical style.

His most notable early break away from traditional styles, values, and subject matter was with the story "The Diary of a Madman" (after a piece by Russian author Gogol), about a man who thinks that everyone wants to kill and eat him—and that this cannibalistic drive stems from the traditional moral teachings of China. But he's probably most famous for his *The True Story of Ah Q*, a novella that was a satirical, mock biography of a "typical" Chinese peasant—a composite of the Chinese national character as Lu Xun saw it—who is so ignorant and lacking in self-awareness that he puts up with virtually any abasement, abases himself as well, and is killed during the republican revolution of 1911.

In addition to other stories, he also wrote essays, particularly in the second half of his career. These are similarly satirical, attacking wrongs, seeking exposure of social problems, and pushing for modernization of China. This point of view is one of the reasons he became closely linked with the revolutionaries who formed the Communist Party. They too advocated modernization and a move away from Chinese traditions—and considered Lu Xun a senior representative of revolutionary literature.

However, for all of his high reputation with the Communist Party, he was never a party member. He did take directives from them and generally fell

in with their point of view, but later in life wrote to a friend of how he disliked the regimentation of the party. As he put it: "I only feel that I am fettered by an iron chain, that there is a foreman standing in back of me and whipping me, whipping me no matter how strenuously and vigorously I work. But when I turn around to ask him about my errors he bows politely and says I have done well indeed and that he and I are the best of friends."

He died before the Communist Party rose to power—and many believe, had he lived, he may have been part of the antirightist purge that Mao eventually undertook. But his work still lives—unattached to any party or any specific ideology—completely individual.

Reading list: "The Diary of a Madman" (short story); *Call to Arms, Wandering* (collected as *The Complete Stories of Lu Xun*) (short stories); *The True Story of Ah Q* (novella); *Wild Grass* (poetry).

India is the third largest publisher of books in the world and the third largest publisher of English-language books.

MODERN INDIAN LITERATURE

It's tough to really focus on Indian literature as an entity in and of itself. Indian literature isn't just Indian literature. It's actually Tamil literature, or Bengali literature, or Punjabi literature, or the literature of one of the many other major languages spoken in India (not to mention the large amount of writing being done in English). To be frank, many Indians don't necessarily know the top writers outside of their region, just as many Americans don't know the top writers of, say, Canada.

But modern Indian literature actually began with a nationalistic thrust. Because the twentieth century was also the time of India's fight for independence, a lot of what was being written was patriotic—and for that matter, very mystical. By basing their writings on Indian mystical tradition, writers were reaffirming their patriotism and turning their backs on the West. But then came independence—and with it nationalism faded, to be replaced by more specific cultural identification . . . which is where it stands now, to a great degree.

The two writers we take an in-depth look at are internationally known—Rabindranath Tagore was the first non-Westerner to win a Nobel Prize in literature; R. K. Narayan is probably one of the most widely read Indian writers in the West. But they don't represent the whole of modern Indian literature by any means. Below we've listed other great Indian writers, some of whom are older, others younger and more representative of the most modern of Indian writing.

Other great Indian writers include
Anita Desai (1937–)
Mahasweta Devi (1926–)
Vikram Seth (1952–)
Khushwant Singh (1915–)

R. K. NARAYAN (RASIPURAM KRISHNASWAMI NARAYANSWAMI)

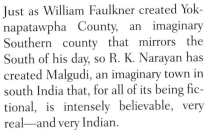

(1906–)

Just as William Faulkner created Yoknapatawpha County, an imaginary Southern county that mirrors the South of his day, so R. K. Narayan has created Malgudi, an imaginary town in south India that, for all of its being fictional, is intensely believable, very real—and very Indian.

Many Indian writers who write in English are criticized for losing their Indian flavor—for somehow watering down their distinctive voices by being overinfluenced by their Western models.

But not Narayan.

While he's probably one of the best-known Indian novelists in the West (in fact, writer Graham Greene once said that "since the death of Evelyn Waugh, Narayan is the novelist I most admire in the English language"), his work remains very Indian in focus and tone. He manages to capture the ebb and flow of daily life in India from a variety of perspectives, from the upper castes to the middle-class merchants down to the beggars on the streets. And just as modern-day India is a contrast between modernity and traditionalism, with the great religious traditions still flourishing in the modern secular world, so his work often focuses on what happens when the sacred and the profane meet.

Yet for all of his regional emphasis, Narayan isn't just an Indian writer. At the root of it, his work focuses on the human condition. As BBC interviewer William Walsh once said, "Whatever happens in India happens in Malgudi, and whatever happens in Malgudi happens everywhere."

Reading list: *Swami and Friends, The Dark Room, Waiting for the Mahatma, The Guide, The Man-Eater of Malgudi, The English Teacher* (American title, *Grateful to Life and Death*), *The Financial Expert, The Vendor of Sweets, The World of Nagaraj* (novels); *An Astrologer's Day and Other Stories, A Horse and Two Goats, Malgudi Days, Under the Banyan Tree.*

RABINDRANATH TAGORE

(1861–1941)

More than just a writer, Tagore is considered one of the three most influential modern Indian thinkers, with Gandhi and Nehru. So his writing is actually more than literature, it's philosophy . . . even religion to some.

His work is a blend of the mystical and the poetic; his themes are usually the major questions or ideas in life: divine and human love, cosmic philosophy, the connection between humanity and God, the meaning of the self. And his writing reflects his own philosophy, one that reflects his life. The son of a Hindu religious reformer and a collector himself of Hindu legends and stories and a student of Hindu reli-

Tagore's Nobel

Tagore was the first non-European to receive the Nobel Prize in literature (in 1913)—and he almost didn't win it at all. The award was going to go to French literary historian Émile Faguet, but one Nobel judge (and poet), Verner von Heidenstam, read Tagore's lyric poems in English and was so enthusiastic he urged his fellow committee members to read them. Problem—Tagore's work (written in his native Bengali) wasn't translated into Swedish, only English. A Swedish professor who could read Bengali was called into service. And he was so thrilled with Tagore's work that, while he was translating them, he wanted the committee members to take a crash course in Bengali so they could read it in its original state and not lose any of its nuances. In spite of his wishes, Bengali proved too tough for the committee members to learn quickly, so on the basis of the Swedish translations, Tagore won his prize.

gious texts, Tagore bases his philosophy partly on traditional Hindu beliefs. But he also incorporates Western thought and literature, which he was exposed to when he went to England to study. Finally, there's the touch of his own strong belief—that there is a divinity in all things. The result is an intriguing blend of the East and the West, plus a personal touch that is purely Tagore—adding up to a cosmic humanism, if you will.

One of his goals throughout his life was to bridge Eastern and Western cultures. To this end, he founded Santiniketan (Abode of Peace), which later became the international university Visva-Bharati (Universal Voice)—with the motto "Where the whole world forms its single nest."

Tagore was possibly best known for his poetry—in fact, he was called the

Bengal Shelley, but he was also a play-wright and a novelist. His novel *Binodini* is considered the first modern Indian novel. And his later works focus on the emerging India, the struggles for independence, the tension between modernization and traditions, and the problems of social injustices.

Throughout his career, he maintained an active interest in politics, and was unafraid to speak up for his beliefs. He received the Nobel Prize for literature in 1913 and was knighted by the British in 1915—but he resigned his knighthood shortly thereafter in protest of British policy in India. And while he supported Gandhi's efforts, he disagreed with his policy of noncooperation.

Reading list: *Binodini, Gora, The Home and the World, Chokkar Bali, Karuna* (novels); *Hungry Stones and Other Stories* (short stories); *Chitra, Chitrangada, Dakghar, The King of the Dark Chamber, The Cycle of Spring, Red Oleanders, The Tragedy of Radachandra* (plays); *Gitanjali, The Crescent Moon, A Flight of Wild Cranes* (poetry); *Sadhana: The Realization of Life, Nationalism, Personality, Creative Unity, The Religion of Man, Crisis in Civilization* (essays).

MODERN JAPANESE LITERATURE

 As the old saying goes, to speak Japanese, you must think Japanese. Well, to understand Japanese literature, you must think Japanese . . . history.

Just as Japanese history is usually broken down by referring to the emperors reigning at the time, so is modern Japanese literature. And aside from making things easier, this actually makes some sense. First of all, with the change in emperors came a corresponding change in the mood of the country—which, of course, is mirrored by the writers of the times. Furthermore, even if the changes in writing are minor, the key point is that the *writers* themselves felt part of a more major change. They represented the new, the modern, the hot style that broke away from the past . . . even if the past was really quite similar.

That said, there are three major periods in modern Japanese literature. First, there's the Meiji (1868–1912), in which most modern writers broke from romantic traditionalism and opted for a more vigorous naturalistic style. Next, the Taisho (1912–1926), in which many writers did an about-face and reacted *against* excessive naturalism. Many scholars consider this a weak time for innovation, with many writers sticking with the tried and true and, in particular, getting back into a feudal or nationalist frame of mind. Next, there's the Showa (1926–1989), which is marked by a great deal of innovation. In this era, we've seen a number of different schools—some big on avant-garde European ideals like expressionism and even dadaism, others espousing leftist literature, still others focusing on the individual.

And in the past few years, an even newer style of Japanese writing is emerging. It's more pop than traditional, less academic and more accessible. This writing mirrors the Japan of the eighties and nineties—a Japan of crowded cities, megabusinesses, and, most important, a Japan that is increasingly influenced by American pop culture. Of course, it's difficult to tell which of the newer writers will last and which will be remembered in the years to come as masters of their art.

The three writers we look at below have already achieved that status. Even though they represent the older modern tradition, they're still read in Japan today—and represent the finest of the twentieth century. Yukio Mishima represents the patriotic past and the more traditional style; Kenzaburo Oe, the postwar progressivism; and Natsume Soseki, the first strong wave of naturalism.

Other leading Japanese writers of the twentieth century include

Abe Kobo (1924–)

Shusaku Endo (1923–)

Osamu Hashimoto (1948–)

Yoshiyuki Junnosake (1924–)

Kawabata Yasunari (1899–1972) (the first Japanese writer to win the Nobel prize for literature)

Kyojo Kobayashi (1957–)

Haruki Murakami (1949–) (one of the first modern writers to move past the more traditional style of modern Japanese novel writing)

Shiga Naoya (1883–1971)

Dazai Osamu (1909–1948)

Masahiko Shimada (1961–)

Gen'ichiro Takahashi (1951–)

Tanizaki Jun'ichiro (1886–1965)

Amy Yamada (1959–)

YUKIO MISHIMA (KIMITAKE HIRAOKA)

(1925–1970)

It's virtually impossible to separate Mishima the writer from Mishima the ultrapatriot, the founder and leader of the Shield Society—a group devoted to reviving the samurai code of honor. The man who, on November 25, 1970, forced his way into the headquarters of the Self-Defense Forces, harangued the troops from a balcony about how they had to preserve Japan's true image by following the samurai way, and who, with the jeers of the soldiers filling the air, went back inside and committed ritual seppuku—disembowelment— and was then, as tradition dictated, beheaded by one of his followers.

This was a literal enactment of his complete devotion to the traditions of samurai Japan—his hope was that, by committing seppuku, he would force the Japanese to realize how much of their traditional heritage they had let slip away. But it's also an example of how he evolved his own personal philosophy, which governed everything in his life, including his writing.

A frail child who was rejected by the army during World War II, Mishima early on decided to mold himself into the man he thought he should be. He changed his name and threw himself into a program of mental and physical self-discipline. Over time, he became a martial arts expert, sang, acted, modeled, organized his own army (he even designed the uniforms himself), and, of course, wrote—and what he wrote supported the extreme lifestyle he had chosen for himself.

The overriding theme in his work: the samurai ideals—belief in a heroic destiny, ideal beauty, and glory . . . or perhaps more simply, the need for honor in the modern world. Several of his novels deal literally with the samurai code; those that don't still have the notion of loyalty and honor underscoring the subject matter. It wasn't only a personal matter. Mishima believed that Japan's prosperity was undermining the traditional ways, eroding the core of values that, to him, were the spirit of Japan. So his work often depicted the new Japan as a moral vacuum, needing a resurgence of the old ways.

His first major work (*Confessions of a Mask*) is about the discovery of his homosexuality and his attempts to conceal it. This, and the subtle sadomasochistic undertones and eroticism in much of his work, led some critics to call his work decadent. However, even they admitted his brilliance. And while some of Mishima's prolific output is admittedly less strong than the rest, at his best, his work is notable. Clean, spare, and quintessentially Japanese in mood, tone, and subject, he examined the problems facing a society as it shifted from feudalism to the modern world—and so captured the spirit of Japan as he intended.

Reading list: *The Sea of Fertility, The Sailor Who Fell from Grace with the Sea, After the Banquet, Temple of the Golden Pavilion, The Sound of Waves, Forbidden Colors, Thirst for Love, Confessions of a Mask, The Forest in Bloom* (novels); *Death in Mid Summer and Other Stories* (short stories); *Five Modern No Plays, Madame de Sade* (plays).

KENZABURO OE

(1935–)

"All I want is to stop being a man who continually runs away from responsibility." So says Bird, the protagonist in Oe's *A Personal Matter*. And these words also sum up the philosophy of writer Kenzaburo Oe.

Oe is a writer who deals head-on with responsibility—political and personal. He is known for his interest in and staunch backing of a variety of progressive issues and causes (although he has never joined a political group).

Most of all, he is a writer who has been irrevocably marked by events outside his ability to control, two events in particular: the end of World War II and the birth of a handicapped child. World War II had a strong effect on him as a child. Only ten when the war ended, he saw a Japan that was overrun by occupying forces and dealing with national guilt and humiliation. In addition, he suffered from shyness and a feeling of inferiority, in part brought about by his thick country accent and stutter—both of which made him feel out of place when he moved from the country to cosmopolitan Tokyo. The combination of his postwar outlook and his outsider identification found its way into his early work as a writer. His stories and essays were often dark and pessimistic; even his more upbeat works typically revolved around antiheroes rather than around the traditional heroes of emperor-centered Japan. More often than not, these antiheroes are a depressing lot, prone to ennui, alcoholism, paranoia, and depression.

Next came a key event that changed Oe's life—and his career. He and his wife had a son who was born brain-damaged. From this point on, his writing changed on a number of levels. It became much more personal, often autobiographical. Instead of revolving around the dark side of the human tragedy, his works centered around redemption and hope. More specifically, a character based on his own life continually appears—a child who is either helpless, deformed, or re-tarded—and serves as a symbol both of fate . . . and of hope.

His work began attracting a great deal of attention and his reputation grew steadily. Reviewers aware of his personal story realized he was playing out his own life through fiction, and applauded him. And his work kept evolving as he synthesized his symbolic child imagery with his political postimperial Japan themes. In lyrical and biting words, he described the aftermath of the atomic bomb and laid out his disaffection for the authoritarian rule of the emperors.

Finally, in 1983, he returned to the heart of his creative message with his first attempt at an "I novel"—Japanese autobiographical fiction—and wrote simply and concisely about life with his handicapped son. The book, *Rouse Up, O Young Men of the New Age,* was a huge hit in Japan, earning him the prestigious Osaragi Jiro Prize.

Yet for all of Oe's reputation in Japan—and in spite of the glowing reviews of his work by American and other critics—he did not have the international recognition many critics and reviewers felt he deserved. But this is changing. In 1994, Oe received the Nobel Prize for Literature, and readers around the world have discov-

ered both the man who faces responsibility and the writer who is unafraid to expose himself and his life in his work.

One final example of Oe's continual efforts to remain responsible, true to himself: After winning the Nobel Prize, his name was added to a list of people who were to receive Japan's Imperial Order of Culture, the highest cultural award in the country. When he received the call telling him the news, Oe followed his own dictates. Because he considers imperial Japan outdated and responsible for the horrors he saw as a child living in the shadows of World War II, he refused the honor.

Reading list: *A Personal Matter, The Silent Cry, Teach Us to Outgrow Our Madness, The Crazy Iris and Other Stories of the Atomic Aftermath, Nip the Buds, Shoot the Kids* (fiction), *Hiroshima Notes, Japan's Dual Identity: A Writer's Dilemma* (nonfiction).

NATSUME SOSEKI

(1867–1916)

Soseki is, first and foremost, a writer of the mind. A true intellectual who approached his art like a philosopher—and one who theorized about the nature of literature and, for that matter, life in general. He's also one of the most famous twentieth-century Japanese novelists, and certainly one of the greatest in the Meiji period.

He began as a professor of English, specifically one involved in Western literary theory. When he began writing, some of his earliest works were haiku—simple poems about a specific beautiful object—and his earliest novel was similar, filled with beautiful language, striking effects. The focus was on the ideal.

But he shifted gears and became more interested in focusing on the real, on expressing truth. His approach was analytical; his concern, expressing universal laws of nature in very particular, very specific terms. In other words, he tried to boil down the universal into individual events, subjects, and acts. As he saw it, "Nature abhors a vacuum. Either love or hatred! Nature likes compensation. Tit for tat! Nature likes a fight. Death or independence!"

These were the types of universal laws that dominated his work. He often wrote about alienation, loneliness, the pain of existence in general. In this, his work has a Buddhist undertone. He agrees with the primary Buddhist tenet that all life is suffering. In his *Kusa Makura*, he said that the only relief from this suffering is spending time on art and literature. As he aged, his view was even more somber. In fact, in *Kokoro*, man was faced with three choices in life: death, insanity, or religion.

This strong subject matter plus his naturalistic style, marked by a crispness and use of conversational language, influenced many younger writers. For these reasons, his work still is popular in modern Japan. His analytical approach, his unshirking look at natural law in nonabstract terms, and his style give his work a timeless appeal—one that speaks of no time in particular, but of the human condition in general.

Reading list: *Kokoro, Kusa Makura, Mon, Grass on the Wayside, I Am a Cat* (novels).

The boom in Latin American literature began as a "five seat movement"—according to Chilean writer José Donoso—with four figurative "seats" being filled by Gabriel García Márquez of Colombia, Julio Cortázar from Argentina, Carlos Fuentes of Mexico, and Mario Vargas Llosa of Peru, and the fifth "chair" filled by different writers (not poets, though) at different times.

MODERN LATIN AMERICAN LITERATURE

 Until about 1970, most Americans didn't really think about Latin American literature. Yes, it was out there . . . but the attitude was, who really cares?

Then came 1970 and the beginning of the so-called boom in Latin American literature—and "boom" is the right word for it. A translation of Gabriel García Márquez's novel *One Hundred Years of Solitude* was published in the United States and became a bestseller, and since then Latin American fiction has been hot.

It took a long time to happen in the United States—and for that matter, even in Latin America. Many writers had trouble getting noticed or even published. The key problem? Traditionally, literature—writing it and reading it—was a mostly upper-class activity, because the bulk of the population was rural . . . and illiterate.

But slowly this changed. A new experimental school, called *modernismo*, emerged at the beginning of the twentieth century and began attracting international notice. This school clashed with the other leading literary group—the so-called regionalists, who focused on the lifestyles of people living in their regions, usually the rural poor, and who wound up writing literature of social protest.

Then came the introduction of the ingredient that enabled the modernists to effectively win the debate and, more important, made Latin American fiction the intrinsically individualistic writing it is today. The ingredient?

Magic realism. Realistic elements are blended with magic and metaphysics, creating a world that initially appears to be our own but one in which the unexpected can, and does, happen.

Even though novels of social protest continue to be written (more often about the urban poor than the rural, nowadays) and even though many writers continue to be political, most Latin American fiction is concerned with the individual—and most of it has an intriguing element of unreality.

It's the element of fantasy that makes Latin American literature so special, so unique—and so, well, Latin American.

Following is a look at four great writers who epitomize Latin American literature—Isabel Allende, whose *The House of the Spirits* won international acclaim and who is one of the foremost female authors of Latin America; Jorge Luis Borges, who spearheaded the early movement in literary innovation; Julio Cortázar, whose work is among the most fantastic of Latin American writing; and of course, Gabriel García Márquez, the master of magic realism who was largely responsible for U.S. recognition of the richness of Latin American literature.

Other leading Latin American writers include

María Luisa Bombal (1910–1980), Chile

Carlos Fuentes (1928–), Mexico

Mario Vargas Llosa (1936–), Peru

ISABEL ALLENDE

(1942–)
(Chilean)

Isabel Allende's life reads like a novel: She was a member of one of Chile's leading families, as the niece of Chilean president Salvatore Allende. But the years of peace and comfort were shattered when Allende's government was overthrown in a coup led by General Ugarte. Forced with her family to flee the country, she went into exile in Venezuela. Yet some members of her family stayed behind in the new Chile—among them, her maternal grandfather.

And she wrote him a long letter once, about her views of what was happening in her country. This letter became the basis for her first—and most famous—novel, *La Casa de los espiritus* (*The House of the Spirits*). But while her work often has politics as a backdrop, the emphasis is on her characters, how they think, how they react, how they evolve in the face of change. Credited with revitalizing the Latin American novel, Allende is known also as one of the foremost women writers in an area dominated by male writers. Her work tends to focus on women and their development in the macho Latin American society; she speaks through their voices, exploring their moves toward empowerment.

In the tradition of other Latin American writers, she often uses magic, or a touch of surrealism, in the worlds she creates on paper. But importantly, there's always the reality of the world in which the characters live—complete with the problems Allende has seen firsthand.

"How can one not speak about war, poverty, and inequality when people who suffer from these afflictions don't have a voice to speak?" she said in an interview. So she continues to speak, giving voice to those who cannot.

Reading list: *The House of the Spirits, Of Love and Shadows, Eva Luna.*

JORGE LUIS BORGES

(1899–1986)
(Argentinian)

"Time is a river which sweeps me along, but I am the river; it is a tiger which mangles me, but I am the tiger; it is a fire which consumes me, but I am the fire. The world, unfortunately, is real; I, unfortunately, am Borges."

In these words, Borges underscores one of the recurring themes in his work—we are bound by the inevitability of time passing, yet we try vainly to create eternities.

In fact, in most of his work, Borges himself tries to break through the chains of time. He creates his own universe in his works, one based on intellectual premises that explore such metaphysical themes as the nature of destiny and time and the meaning of the self. And, in the self-contained world of his written universe, humanity persists in trying to find truth—and fails. As he wrote in *Other Inquisitions*, "Reality is impenetrable and we will never know what is the universe." The world he paints winds up being a world of hallucinations, easily as chaotic as

Borges is one of the most popular international authors worldwide. One example of his popularity: a multivolume collection of his works topped a 1994 nonfiction best-seller list compiled by the RUSSIAN BOOK REVIEW.

the world outside—and certainly as incomprehensible. Reality and dream are often the same; there is no reality behind appearances; humanity is stuck, it seems.

This stems from Borges's own thoughts. He suffered from failing vision at an early age, and became nearly totally blind by 1970. For him, literature was a way of ordering life, indeed justifying life. As he put it, "Through the years, a man peoples a space with images of provinces, kingdoms, mountains, bays, ships, islands. . . . Shortly before his death he discovers that the patient labyrinth of lines traces the image of his own face."

So perhaps the universe Borges created in his works, based on an unreal logic, on metaphysical problems and intellectual enigmas, traced his own image.

Reading list: *Labyrinths, A Universal History of Infamy, Fictions, The Garden of Forking Paths, The Aleph, The Report of Brodie* (short stories); *Poetic Works, Fervor of Buenos Aires, Moon Across the Way, In Praise of Darkness* (poetry); *Other Inquisitions, History of Eternity, Discussions* (essays).

JULIO CORTÁZAR

(1914–1984)
(Argentinian)

The world, as Cortázar usually depicts it, seems completely normal, filled with average people living everyday lives filled with insignificant events. Then something happens. One person vomits a small rabbit. Another is imprisoned inside an amphibian in the aquarium he's visiting. A traffic jam lasts over a year.

Welcome to Cortázar's world now—one that appears normal at the outset, but is invaded by the strange, the fantastic, and the unknown. One of his short stories was used by film director Antonioni as the basis for the film *Blow Up.* He has also written realistic fiction, as well as works that expose his concern about Latin American politics, but even then, there's often the touch of the unexpected.

In his most famous novel, *Hopscotch,* the central character tries to break with conventional reality and the normal order of things. And Cortázar takes it another step: when a reader is done with the book, he gives the reader a pattern by which he can read the book again, following a different chapter sequence—for example, instead of reading chapters 1 through 5 sequentially, the first five chapters become 73, 1, 2, 116, 3. The reason? Cortázar is trying to establish a new metaphysical order on his work. Confusing, yes. Pretentious, possibly. But intriguing . . . again, yes.

This is one of the reasons Cortázar was considered one of the leading revolutionary writers in Latin America in his time. Not that his work is hyperintellectual in and of itself. He writes in a relaxed, humorous style, uses plays on words, even invents his own language in one of his books. In Cortázar's fictional world, anything is possible.

Reading list: *Hopscotch; The Winners; The End of the Game; 62, A Model Kit; Book of Manuel* (novels); *All Fires the Fire, Round the Day in Eighty Worlds* (short stories).

GABRIEL GARCÍA MÁRQUEZ

(1928–)
(Colombian)

"In good literature I always find the tendency to destroy that which is established, that which is already imposed, and to contribute to the creation of new forms of living."

With these words, García Márquez could well be describing his own work. Much of what he writes is magic realism. He creates an inverted world in

Fame

Gabriel García Márquez has learned firsthand the two sides to fame: "Fame is a stupendous thing. [It] offers the possibilities of serving your country, your friends, your continent, and everything better . . . [but fame] has an infinite misfortune that almost annuls all the advantages, and that is that fame lasts twenty-four hours a day. . . . If you could raise and lower the volume or turn it off, as one can do with the radio, fame would be marvelous. But . . . the unfortunate fact [is] that it is not controllable."

He and his books have become so famous that he can't afford the very things he made famous—like the house in Cartagena that was identified as a home featured in his book *Love in the Time of Cholera.* In fact, when he tried to buy the house in Mexico City where he had written his first best-seller, *One Hundred Years of Solitude,* the realtor told him it was far too expensive. The reason? Because García Márquez had written there.

But he hasn't let fame go to his head. As he once said, "I have never permitted pride to blind me to the fact that I am simply one of the sixteen children born to a telegraph operator from Aracataca."

which that which is possible seems impossible, and the fantastic seems commonplace.

He was born in a sleepy town called Aracataca and raised in the huge memory-filled house of his grandparents. The steamy Aracataca bears many similarities to the fictional site of many of his works, Macondo. But there's one big difference—Macondo is home to many surrealistic events: in *One Hundred Years of Solitude*, his best-known work, the entire town is afflicted by insomnia at one point; one character is followed by yellow butterflies; while hanging sheets on the line, one woman ascends to heaven.

It's not all fantasy by any means, however. García Márquez uses the fantastic as a counterpoint to the real. Drab reality and fantastic unreality coexist in his world. And by juxtaposing the two, he creates an almost hyperreal environment—depicting the real struggles of the emerging Latin American countries on the one hand, but also incorporating, on the other, the myths, legends, dreams, and exaggerations of the people. The end result: we see the characters struggling to explain, understand, and ultimately control their world.

"He who expects much can expect little," García Márquez once wrote. And this is perhaps a key to survival in his fictional world. Expecting little is the only way to live in the world he's created—a world that is beyond comprehension to its occupants, beyond domination . . . and given this, perhaps a world much like the one in which we all live.

Reading list: *One Hundred Years of Solitude, The Autumn of the Patriarch, Evil Hour, Love in the Time of Cholera* (novels); *No One Writes to the Colonel*

Gabriel García Márquez's ONE HUNDRED YEARS OF SOLITUDE *is the most famous novel written in Spanish except for Don Quixote. Since its initial publication in 1967, it has never been out of print and has been translated into twenty-seven different languages. When it had been out fifteen years (in 1982), it had already sold more than four million copies in Spanish alone. It's considered the book responsible for the so-called boom of Latin American literature.*

and Other Stories, Leaf Storm, Innocent Erendira and Other Stories (short stories).

MODERN MIDDLE EASTERN LITERATURE

 The Middle East is well known as a land of conflict, of warring factions: Arabs versus Jews, reformers versus fundamentalists, capitalists versus socialists. Whether it's two different cultures clashing or two different groups within a culture, the result is a clash of ideas and emotions.

And the literature of the region reflects the ongoing conflict. Much of it is political in nature; much of it concerns the clashes between different factions—if not as a focal point, then as a backdrop against which modern life plays out. In this sense, of course, Middle Eastern literature isn't a literature of politics only. It's also a literature of place—and of people.

The easiest way to look at Middle Eastern literature is to look at the two major divisions: modern Arab, a literature with a tradition extending back to the rise of Islam; and modern Israeli, a literature that was born of European roots. But in spite of the traditions backing both literatures, both have been changing rapidly in the twentieth century—evolving into distinct modern entities that reflect today's world and concerns at the same time as they draw upon the past.

At the beginning of the twentieth century, Arabic literature split into two camps—the modernists and the classicists, or the old guard and the rebels. This happened when the more innovative writers began pulling away from the traditional Arabic literature and infusing their work with more Western ideas and styles. The result, though, wasn't Western literature, but an Arabic literature with an infusion of modern thought. Naturalism, social commentary, and the contact between Eastern and Western thought and culture became the hallmarks of this modern Arabic literature.

And for all the pull from the classicists, the modern literature caught on and kept evolving—to such a degree that the so-called modernists of the early twentieth century are often now seen as conservatives. Some of the newer generation of writers are opting for even more innovation and experimentation. Others are pursuing the paths forged by the earlier modernists. Yet even with the divergent styles, themes are often similar. As you might expect in an area known for political turmoil, much of what is being written focuses on current issues and their effect on the people of the region—political issues, such as the plight of the Palestinians; social issues, such as urban life in Egypt; or simply human issues, such as love or death. And through it all, even in the more experimental writing, there's still an Arabic flavor—a hint of the traditions long past.

Unlike Arabic literature, Israeli literature began as a transplant. Modern Israeli literature has its roots in Eastern Europe, since the country was first settled primarily by Europeans. But since then, Israel has become a distinct entity—not an Eastern European outpost but a country with an ethos all

its own. So too its literature has evolved into a distinctly Israeli voice.

So modern Israeli literature is actually two different literatures. Literature of the early modern period was written during the early *aliyot,* or emigration from Eastern Europe to Israel. This literature is European literature transplanted. It's the literature of settlers, and so reflects the concerns of the people—the need to keep the traditional Jewish culture alive in the new land; the hardships of settling; the feeling of exile . . . and of hope; and above all the new feeling of nationalism.

But as Israel has matured, so its writers changed. The settler-writers of earlier years have been replaced by writers who are Israeli born, or who moved to Israel as young children. And what they write is no longer the literature of settlers, but the literature of survivors written in the language of today . . . about the concerns of today.

We take a look at two giants of Middle Eastern literature—Naguib Mahfouz of Egypt, one of the most well-known Arabic writers and an early modernist, and Amos Oz of Israel, one of the most widely read Israeli writers.

Other leading Middle Eastern writers include

S. Y. Agnon (1888–1970), Israel
Mohammed Dib (1920–), Algeria
Taha Husayn (1889–1973), Egypt
Abd al-Rahman al-Munit (1933–),
    Jordan-born/Saudi citizen
Yusuf Idris (1927–), Egypt
Nawal al-Sadawi (1931–), Egypt
Ghada Samman (1942–), Syria
Moshe Shamir (1921–), Israel
S. Yizhar (1916–), Israel

NAGUIB MAHFOUZ

(1911–)
(Egyptian)

He's called by some the Dickens of the Cairo cafés—and like Dickens, his output is prodigious (and his work is sometimes criticized as being too light, aimed too much at a popular audience). He's also called the Balzac of Egypt—and like Balzac's, much of his work (especially his earlier writings) is naturalistic and realistic, painting a true-to-life picture of contemporary Egypt.

But Mahfouz is, first and foremost, simply Mahfouz: one of the first great modern Arab writers, winner of the Nobel Prize for Literature—and a master at capturing the political underpinnings to modern society in Egypt . . . and, thus, in the world at large.

He initially intended to be a philosopher, and switched to writing only after writing articles for his master's degree program in Sufism and Islamic philosophy. From then on, writing was his main focus. He worked as a civil servant, chiefly in cultural positions, but writing was the key to his life. As he put it: "When I chose writing as my career, the decision was irrevocable. . . . I saw writing as a responsibility not unlike marriage, where a man produces children who impose upon him an indissoluble bond, from which he cannot back out or retreat. A man cannot abandon or disown his own children."

But the philosopher he once studied to be is still evident in his works.

While much of his work is realistic, he doesn't just put down the details that he's seen. He adds an intellectual dimension and underlying philosophical themes that make his work more than just a depiction of Egyptian life. A common focus: politics—more specifically, the role politics plays in modern life.

Mahfouz once said in an interview that "politics, faith, and sex are the three poles around which my works revolve, and of the three, politics is by all odds the most essential." In his works, he shows that it is politics, not religion, that defines morality. And it is politics, not religion or sex, that reflects the human psyche.

This point of view was first evident in the series of novels that brought him national—and international—attention: the Cairo Trilogy, three novels following one Cairene family from 1918 to 1944. It was an immediate success, lauded for its realism, its ability to capture all facets of Cairo life. Since then, he has written more allegorical and symbolic novels, but the elements of realism—and the subject matter of Egyptian contemporary life, politics, and historical events—have remained. His style is sometimes surrealistic, sometimes simply naturalistic, but it's always essentially Mediterranean. And, after having written over twenty-seven novels, plus numerous short stories and novellas, he remains Mahfouz, not the Arab Dickens or Balzac, but the writer who is single-mindedly painting his philosophical view of the world.

Reading list: *Palace Walk, Palace of Desire, Sugar Street* (the Cairo trilogy), *Wedding Song, The Thief and the Dogs, The Beginning and the End,*

Autumn Quail, Midaq Alley, Mirrors, Miramar, Children of Gebelawi (novels); *God's World* (short stories).

AMOS OZ

(1939–)
(Israeli)

Oz, both in his work and in his lifestyle, epitomizes the modern Israeli spirit.

Born Amos Klausner to a professor father who wanted him to be "the archetype of the new Israeli: simple, blond, cleansed of Jewish neurosis, tough, gentile-looking," as he said in a *New Republic* interview, he rebelled against his family at age fifteen, left home, joined a kibbutz and changed his name. Today, in spite of his income, he still lives on the kibbutz—signing over his (sizable) royalty checks to the kibbutz treasurer.

And as his lifestyle is uniquely Israeli, so too is his work.

Oz once said that a kibbutz was an example of the "perpetual paradox of magnanimous dream and unhappy reality." And this runs through his

work. It uncovers the dichotomy that is Israel—both tough and frightened, uncomplicated and complex. As he put it in a *Partisan Review* interview: "Daytime Israel makes a tremendous effort to create the impression of the determined, tough, simple, uncomplicated society ready to fight back, ready to hit back twice as hard. . . . Nocturnal Israel is a refugee camp with more nightmares per square mile . . . than any other place in the world. Almost everyone has seen the devil."

Much of his writing revolves around guilt and persecution, feelings of besiegement and isolation. While he usually addresses these themes on a personal level—that is, his characters suffer these feelings—they reflect the national level, the feeling many people have that Israel is both a nation under siege and a small outpost of Western thought surrounded by alien cultures. And underscoring most of his work is the basic idea that through suffering comes redemption.

Reading list: *Elsewhere, Perhaps, A Perfect Peace, My Michael, Black Box* (novels); *Where the Jackals Howl, Unto Death: Crusade and Last Love, The Hill of Evil Counsel* (short stories and novellas); *Under the Blazing Light* (essays); *In the Land of Israel* (interviews).

WRITERS ON WRITING:
WORDS ON THE ACT OF CREATING

 Writers are, of course, people of words. On paper, with only words as tools, they paint a picture, create a mood, establish an atmosphere, evoke emotions. And as people of words, they often have a great deal to say about the act of writing itself. Following are a few of these words, quotes on writing by writers.

People create stories create people; or rather stories create people create stories.

—Chinua Achebe, Nigerian writer

I like to think of myself as a painter or composer using words in the place of pictures and musical symbols. . . . In my ideal novel, the reader should feel a sense of aesthetic satisfaction that he cannot quite explain—the same feeling he gets when he listens to a beautiful symphony.

—Elechi Amadi, Nigerian writer

A story is not only meaning, it's music as well.

—Aharon Appelfeld, Israeli writer

Learn about a pine tree from a pine tree, and about a bamboo plant from a bamboo plant.

—Matsuo Basho, Japanese poet

The poet is like the prince of the clouds, who rides the tempest and scorns the archer. Exiled on the ground, amidst boos and insults, his giant's wings prevent his walking.

—Charles Baudelaire, French poet

A writer needs loneliness, and he gets his share of it. He needs love, and he gets shared and also unshared love. In fact, he needs the universe. To be a writer is, in a sense, to be a day-dreamer—to be living a kind of double life.

—Jorge Luis Borges, Argentine writer

The poet . . . gives a gallery of ghosts shaken by fire and the darkness of his times. Perhaps I did not live in myself; perhaps I lived the life of others. . . . This is a life made up of other lives, for a poet has many lives.

—Pablo Neruda, Chilean poet

As for writing, I sometimes feel that it would not be much of a loss if we gave it up entirely. We write, some people read, time passes, and there is no effect whatsoever. What is the meaning of it, then, except we've gotten paid for it?

—Ding Ling, Chinese writer

The poem or the story or the novel must follow a certain line—it is a kind of party line even though what is in question is not a political party, but it is, in the true sense of the word, a party line.

—Nadine Gordimer, South African writer

The secret of all good writing is sound judgment.

—Horace, Roman poet

When a man feels the pangs of loneliness, he is able to create. As soon as he

reaches detachment, he ceases to create, for he loves no more.

Every creation originates in love.

—Lu Xun, Chinese writer

It seems to me that the spoken and
written word are signs of failure. Whoever is truly measuring himself against
fate has no time for such things. As to
those who are strong and winning,
most of the time they keep silent. Consider, for instance, the eagle when it
swoops upon a rabbit: it is the rabbit
that squeals, not the eagle.

—Lu Xun, Chinese writer

If poetry comes not as naturally as
leaves to a tree it had better not come
at all.

—John Keats, English poet

Art is a criticism of society and life,
and I believe that if life became perfect
art would be meaningless and cease to
exist.

—Naguib Mahfouz, Egyptian writer

In all ages, literature aims at an interpretation of the universe and a deep
perception of humanity by means of
language.

—Yukio Mishima, Japanese writer

Twentieth-century poetry has become
garrulous. We are drowning not in a
sea but in a swamp of words. We have
forgotten that poetry is not in what
words say but in what is said between
them, that which appears fleetingly in
pauses and silences. In the poetry
workshops of universities there should
be a required course for young poets:
learning to be silent.

—Octavio Paz, Mexican poet

... the artist, even when he imitates
nature, always feels himself to be not a
slave but a demigod.

—Natsume Soseki, Japanese novelist/essayist

The profundity of a creative work lies
in the degree to which its contents can
be summarized in one sentence—a
sentence that penetrates human reality.

—Natsume Soseki, Japanese writer

[The poets' role is that of] capturing on
their instruments the secret stir of life
in the air and giving it voice in the
music of prophecy.

—Rabindranath Tagore, Indian Bengali writer

A writer needs people around him. He
needs live struggles of active life. Contrary to popular mythology, a novel is
not a product of the imaginative feats
of a single individual but the work of
many hands and tongues. A writer just
takes down notes dictated to him by
life among the people. . . . I love to
hear the voices of the people working
on the land, forging metal in a factory,
telling anecdotes in crowded matatus
and buses, gyrating their hips in a
crowded bar before a jukebox or a live
band. . . . I need the vibrant voices of
beautiful women: their touch, their
sighs, their tears, their laughter. I like
the presence of children prancing
about, fighting, laughing, crying. I
need life to write about life.

—Ngugi wa Thiong'o, Kenyan writer

[Poetry] was invented by primitive man
to make it easy to remember the second line; then he found a certain
beauty in it.

—Orhan Veli Kanik, Turkish poet

CONTENTS

DRAMA & FILM OF THE WORLD

*In order to find reality, each
must search for his own universe,
look for the details that contribute to
this reality that one feels under the surface of
things. To be an artist means to search, to find and
look at these realities. To be an artist means never
to look away.*

 These are the words of Japanese film director Akira Kurosawa and, with them, he sums up the role of the dramatic artist . . . the playwright, the performer in traditional dramas, and the film director.

Drama, whether written by the ancient Greeks or seen in a modern movie theater, is yet another way to see the reality of the world, the reality "under the surface of things." As such, it is a lens through which we can see the reality of other cultures and other times. It's a way to better understand the world that preceded us and the world we live in today.

One key reason is because drama is so often entertainment for the people. Unlike a political document or a religious text, most drama is by the people and for the people, which means it gives us an idea of what these other people are really like— what they enjoy, and what touches their emotions.

We know what Americans watch—sitcoms, and action-adventure movies—and it reflects our national psyche. What do other people watch around the world? What did other people watch in the distant past?

This chapter answers these questions and, in doing so, gives you the flavor of other cultures. It explores different facets of world dramatic arts— from the ancient past right on to the present, from the world's greatest playwrights (besides Shakespeare) to the world's greatest film directors (besides Hollywood's). For insight into other cultural traditions, it looks at dying dramatic arts like Kabuki and No (or Noh) that have existed for years, but that are falling by the wayside because of the onslaught of VCRs and the Hollywoodization of the dramatic arts. To give you insight into our own dramatic traditions, it also jumps back to ancient times with a look at the greatest Greek dramatists. A rundown of the greatest playwrights in the world gives you an idea of the incredible scope of drama. Finally, because film is fast becoming the lingua franca of the modern world, we cover filmmakers outside of Hollywood—the people who create the images for audiences of other cultures, from film pioneers to the hottest current directors of China and India—and brief rundowns of their best films, giving you different views and realities of the world.

NOH, NOH, NANETTE: TRADITIONAL WORLD DRAMA

There are certain forms of drama you wouldn't ordinarily see on Broadway . . . or rather, maybe Broadway will soon be the only place to see some of the following. Between film, television, and the general Westernization of much of the world, cultural traditions have been diluted. In these cases, once-popular indigenous entertainment is now often popular only with tourists.

In other cases, though, the tradi-

NATIONAL CHINESE OPERA THEATER (COURTESY TAIWAN COORDINATION COUNCIL FOR NORTH AMERICAN AFFAIRS; INFORMATION AND COMMUNICATION DIVISION IN NEW YORK)

tional forms not only live, but flourish, attracting modern audiences with their classic styles.

Whether they are still major attractions or merely shadows of the past, the traditional forms persist in spite of the homogenization of the world—or perhaps even because of it. These forms represent the soul of a culture, one that existed centuries ago and evolved into the culture of today. As such, even as lines between different cultures overlap, the traditional forms of drama remind us of where we came from. Each is a mirror, reflecting what was—and, underneath all the similarities, what still is.

JORURI (OR BUNRAKU)

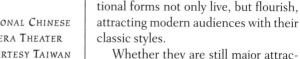

(Japanese Puppet Theater)

Take complicated, lifelike dolls about four and a half feet tall with movable eyebrows, mouths, eyes, hands, and feet. Add three puppeteers per puppet—one in full view of the audience, the other two often hooded in black—and you have *joruri*, Japan's most realistic form of traditional drama.

Yes, realistic. And yes, it sounds like a paradox. The other two main forms of traditional drama, Noh and Kabuki, are performed by people, but are highly stylized; joruri is performed by puppets, but is supposed to be as realistic as possible.

Joruri (popularly called Bunraku, after master puppet chanter Bunrakuken) began as a very simple form of puppetry that probably first emerged in the seventh century. Back then it was a cruder theater—handheld dolls manipulated by hidden puppeteers who also told a simple story. But the puppets grew more sophisticated; a new instrument (the samisen) emerged; a vogue started for love stories; and puppeteers, samisen players, and narrative storytellers joined together to produce joruri.

Joruri quickly became as popular as Kabuki, catching the imagination of the growing merchant class in particular. And no wonder. To fit the new life-like puppets (theoretically), realistic plays were written—history plays and domestic dramas showing merchants' lives with emotionally charged climaxes. These crowd pleasers were the soap operas of the time, offering such exciting scenes as human disembowelment, joint suicides of lovers, and severed heads. The scenery and special effects were as complex as the puppets themselves. In fact, many of the innovations, such as revolving stages or trap doors, that energized Kabuki first originated in joruri.

Just as the innovations moved to Kabuki, so did the crowds. After its heyday in the nineteenth century, joruri began losing popularity. As for today? In Japan, joruri has become more a remnant of tradition than a contemporary entertainment. Only one joruri theater remains, the government-sponsored National Bunraku Theater (the Bunraku-za) in Osaka. Even so, it's recognized as a national art form. Joruri troupes are sent on international tours to expose the rest of the world to a piece of traditional Japanese culture. Joruri players often

One form of traditional drama that has actually been helped by television is Thai "likay"— slapstick comedy that has been performed for the masses for years, usually at provincial fairs. Television has latched on to likay and is spreading it to even more people in Thailand. It's a simple form of theater, with extremely predictable plots, heavy use of bawdy humor, sexual innuendos, and obvious comedy.

become Living National Treasures or Intangible Cultural Assets and receive government stipends. But joruri itself, while theoretically a Living National Treasure, is more a dead national treasure—a drama form caught in time, offering us a view of Japan that no longer exists.

KABUKI

(Japanese Music-Dance Drama)

Kabuki has stuck to its roots: it started out as a highly commercial drama form and remains that today. It didn't have to change much to stay popular and keep up with the times. In many ways, the Kabuki of today is very much the Kabuki of yesterday.

To put it simply, Kabuki is drama with music and dance. Plays generally fall into one of three main groups—historical plays, domestic (usually urban) dramas or comedies, and dance pieces. A Kabuki program usually consists of scenes from different plays, balancing the tone and subject matter. It is performed by actors (men only) in elaborate costumes, using highly stylized gestures. Yes, this does sound somewhat stiff, but Kabuki is far from this. It has always been popular entertainment, aimed squarely at the middle class. In fact, its roots are slightly sordid—which possibly added to its allure in the past.

Kabuki emerged in the very early seventeenth century, an offspring of popular entertainment performed by vagabond troupes for the growing merchant class in the cities. The first Kabuki was performed in the then-capital Kyoto by Okuni, a woman who said she was a priestess of the Grand Shrine in Izumo. But her performances, sketches about contemporary urban life, were quite secular—depictions of her at the time show her in costume as a young male warrior meeting with a coy prostitute—and the urban audiences loved it. Her success drew others, mostly women, to perform Kabuki; but many of her imitators weren't primarily dancers, and the entertainment they offered went far beyond performing on a stage. Kabuki became a way for prostitutes to show off their wares, advertise, and solicit customers.

Then the authorities cracked down. In 1629, the shogunate banned women from performing Kabuki. Next to be banned, in 1652, the young men or boys, called *tobiko* or traveling boys, who replaced the women both onstage . . . and off. Finally, the authorities required the adult men, the only legal Kabuki performers remaining, to add plot development to their performances.

This is the point at which Kabuki became the art form it is considered today. Certain standard elements emerged—stylized poses, choreographed battles and dances, and wooden-clapper sound effects. Distinct families dominated Kabuki, and acting styles and techniques were passed down from father to son. Kabuki plays evolved to a definite format—yet did not become static. In keeping with its commercialism, theater companies added any attraction they could that drew applause: trapdoors into which actors could suddenly disappear, or revolving stages. Playwrights wrote to appeal to the audiences in different cities. Different

The traditional Japanese form of drama, Kabuki, lives in modern film—by way of a Polish director adapting a Russian novel. In 1993, Polish director Andrzej Wajda directed a Japanese version of Dostoyevky's THE IDIOT, and chose to have male Kabuki actor Tamasaburo Bando play the lead female role.

acting styles arose, such as the gentle style called *wagoto* and the swashbuckling style called *aragoto*. Whatever the audience wanted, they got.

Today's Kabuki is much the same. There have been sporadic attempts at reform—sometimes for political reasons, other times for purely artistic. In the late 1800s, for example, the Western-oriented Meiji government's Society for Theatre Reform wanted to make Kabuki less erotic and less violent, and more like European realism. Even Danjuro (one of the line of Kabuki actors named Danjuro) agreed with the reformers, advocating such moves as replacing the male actors in female roles (*onnagata* or *oyama*) with women, and getting rid of the traditional music. In the twentieth century, modern playwrights (including Yukio Mishima) have tried their hands at updating Kabuki, changing the traditional form, eliminating certain elements, and trying for a contemporary touch. But it hasn't always worked. The audiences—both in Japan and abroad—have spoken and what they seem to want is a traditional modern Kabuki.

That's where Kabuki is today. There are new plays, incorporating new subjects or modern psychological themes; but the old traditions—all-male casts (some of whom are descendants of the acting families of the seventeenth century), exaggerated poses and costumes—largely hold sway. True to its roots, Kabuki goes for the crowd-pleasers . . . and it seems to be working. Modern Japanese still are Kabuki goers. (It's a largely middle-class entertainment, with ticket prices the equivalent of forty dollars to sixty dollars). Kabuki actors often also appear on television or in film. Like so many other traditional drama forms, Kabuki hasn't died out as popular entertainment. It has become both classic and contemporary—but always commercial.

NO (OR NOH)

~

(Japanese Music-Dance Epic Drama)

No means skill or accomplishment—which is precisely what No actors need—and, frankly, what many audience members need to truly understand and appreciate this traditional drama form.

At its most basic, No drama is classical epic drama incorporating music and dance. Casts are all male; the orchestra supplying the music is limited to three or four instruments, consisting only of drums and flute. The singing style is reminiscent of Buddhist chanting; the general pacing slow and deliberate. No plots revolve around tragic or noble events, which makes sense, since No drama was originally the dramatic choice of the samurai, the aristocratic warrior class of Japan.

In fact, it was developed specifically for a samurai audience by two *sarugaku* players (essentially performers in variety shows often watched by samurai), Kwanami Kiyotsugu and his son Zeami. Kwanami combined the traditional rhythmic dance (*mai*) with a narrative song (*kuse*) and began using this combination narrative song-dance (*kuse mai*) as the central point in the plays he wrote. He was, in effect, the creator of a form of dance drama. His son further evolved his father's innovation. The future of No became assured when the ruler of Japan, the shogun

Ashikaga Yoshimitsu, impressed by Zeami's performing, invited him to become his companion at the palace. This was Zeami's home for the next fifty years, the place in which he learned Zen Buddhism—the tenets of which are largely reflected in No drama—and the place where No as we now know it was largely developed.

Among the guidelines Zeami laid down: In keeping with the samurai roots, the subject must always be noble; the storyline is generally taken from classical literature, including lyric poetry, novels and diaries of court life, love stories, and history or legends. Plays should follow a distinct three-part structure—*jo-ha-kyu,* with *ha* holding the kuse dance; plus, there should be five plays in a program—opening with a god play. In keeping with Zen philosophy, the stage must be kept essentially bare, props to a minimum, costumes (except those worn by the chief character, the Doer) nonelaborate, masks worn by the players subtle, the actors restrained, and the overall tone simple. Zeami summed up the No acting style best in one of his treatises on No acting: "Move seven if the heart feels ten."

Tied to shogunate patronage as it was, No suffered during the civil wars of the sixteenth century. For a while, No companies survived chiefly by teaching amateurs, and selling plays and instructions. With the rise of the samurai again at the end of the century, No also resurged. Now it became more and more rarefied. Common people were banned from No performances. They weren't even supposed to know any No plays. No actors were made samurai, which meant the imposition of strict codes of behavior and rules of conduct, and a lifestyle that mirrored that of their patrons. Becoming a No actor became a matter of heredity: The head of a No troupe had absolute authority, much like a shogun over his court; he was also responsible for anything his troupe did. As samurais, No performers were assured a high place in Japanese society.

The samurai connection led to hard times for No actors when feudalism was abolished in 1868. The unemployed samurai often had to sell masks and costumes and work in menial jobs. While some actors began charging admission for people to watch them perform in their homes, others formed companies with other actors, and slowly No emerged as an elite art form that few could really understand . . . but many, apparently, could love. The government supported No for a while, but the bulk of the financial and moral support came from the public, which is where it stands today.

The strict traditionalism of samurai society still lives in today's No theater. There are five No schools, each with its own theater. Performances are limited. In fact, most of the income for No companies is through teaching amateurs, not performing. When No theater is performed, it's strictly the classics. No innovative acting methods, no modern plays—nothing but No.

SANSKRIT DRAMA

(Indian Plays)

India is one of the major film centers of the East, with film studios in most major cities. So it's no wonder there are few commercial theater companies—

most actors opt for a film career. Yet in the face of this, old-fashioned Sanskrit drama—a traditional form that had virtually died out—has suddenly become more popular again. Some Sanskrit plays have been translated into modern Indian languages; others are produced in the original Sanskrit, the traditional language of much of India (like Latin in the West). Still others are produced on or adapted for television shows. The appeal could be the elaborate costumes, the well-known stories, or a desire to return to the religious values promoted in the traditional plays.

Perhaps it's a simple matter of venerability. Sanskrit drama is among the oldest in the world. No one is completely sure exactly when Sanskrit drama was born, but if you consider that by the third century C.E. playwright Bhasa was writing fairly sophisticated plays, it's a fair guess that the drama had evolved even before then.

Traditional Sanskrit plays are very circumscribed. According to a comprehensive treatise written about Sanskrit theater, the *Natyasastra* of Bharata (dated anywhere from 200 B.C.E. to 200 C.E., depending upon the source), there are ten types of drama—some merely distinguishable by the caste of the hero. In effect, they are all morality plays showing ideal characters acting with ideal behavior. The story is often a simple one, in which the hero reaches a goal (usually either duty, pleasure, or wealth) after overcoming obstacles. Many of the plays revolve around the Hindu epics, the *Mahabharata* (see page 323) or the *Ramayana*, or historical events, although other plots are completely original.

Like Everyman plays of the West, or more recently, the old silent movies, characters are usually broad types rather than individualistic personalities. Among the main players are the always handsome and brave *nayaka,* or hero, usually a king or other nobleman; the always beautiful *nayika,* or heroine; the wicked, violent, yet courageous villain, the *pratindykaka.* There's also the second banana, the hero's best friend (the *pithamarda*); the clown (*vidushaka*), who is usually gluttonous, bald, and ugly; and the faithful servant (the *ceta*). In the newer Sanskrit plays (developed in about the fifteenth century), characters are also broadly drawn, and generally fall into three types—godly, worldly, or evil-minded. Other elements are very carefully chosen as well. Costumes must show the audience the caste, station in life, and occupation of the character, as must accessories such as jewelry or garlands—even makeup.

It's all extremely deliberate. Bharata, in his *Natyasastra,* explains the aesthetic theory of Sanskrit drama. There are eight types of sentiments connected to human experience, ranging from comic to erotic to terrified. To evoke these sentiments, the actors must convey the corresponding emotions. To do this, the actors must use the "twelve transitory feelings" and the "eight states of emotion." It goes on in considerable detail, but it can be summed up: While a play may include a number of emotions, one must be dominant. This, in turn, will evoke different sentiments in the audience, but the one corresponding to the dominant emotion will be strongest. In this way, the audience can enjoy a perfectly balanced entertainment.

Whether modern audiences are overtly aware of this careful balance is debatable. But Sanskrit drama must be doing something right. It's seeing a rebirth in India, and, like ancient Greek drama and other forms, is considered a classic in the West. One of the most famous Sanskrit plays, with the not-so-compelling title of *The Little Clay Cart (Mrcchakatika),* popularly attributed to King Sudraka (who lived in the fifth century C.E.), has been translated into English, was produced in New York in 1924, and in London in 1964. Kalidasa, one of India's greatest playwrights, has also been widely translated and produced in modern times. Not bad for a drama form that is over a thousand years old. Apparently, where Sanskrit drama is concerned, there's no questioning its staying power or its timeless appeal.

WAYANG KULIT PURWA

(Indonesian Shadow Puppet Theater)

Indonesia is known for having some of the most highly developed dramas in the world. And *wayang kulit purwa*—shadow puppet theater—is perhaps both the most famous and the oldest dramatic form. It's still a highly visible form, but nowadays, much of it is aimed at tourists. The name itself explains what it is: *Wayang* means that it uses a puppet master (*dalang*), and gong chime orchestra (*gamelan*); *kulit* means leather puppet; and *purwa* means original, signaling that the stories performed are based on the Hindu epics, the *Mahabharata* and the *Ramayana.* Put it together and you have a fairly basic idea of what it's all about.

Shadow puppet theater, as well as the other main traditional drama forms of masked dance and female dance dramas, emerged in the seventh century after Hindu Buddhism became the religion of the ruling class. By the ninth century, performers were members of both courts and temples, and the plays usually performed in rituals or festivals. These same plays—or similar ones—are still being performed today in much the same way.

The shadow plays of Bali are generally thought to be more like those of the past while those of Java are more modern, primarily because Java became a Muslim state in the thirteenth century and so diverged from strict Hindu heritage. So there are some variations, chiefly depending on region. For example, Balinese shadow plays are strictly Hindu epics, while those in Java feature the main characters of the Hindu epics in new stories, but not in the legendary epic tales.

Generally, the Balinese style is considered an older form; it is more primitive and less refined that the Javanese. But the basics are the same: The puppets are usually one to two feet high;

their shadows are cast onto a screen by backlighting (often just an oil lamp held by the dalang, or puppeteer). About fifty puppets can be used to tell the story, accompanied by musicians, even (a modern touch added in Java) female singers. Typically, the beginning of the play is also the beginning of the world—while the puppet master chants, the puppet called the "tree of life" dances the creation of the world. Thereafter, the puppets act out a complicated heroic tale—usually the story of a knight (Arjuna more often than not) faced with a world thrust into cosmic imbalance, fighting ogres to right things (there are usually three battles per play). The hero's servants act as comic relief as well as provide satirical views on current events.

This all takes quite awhile—performances often last four or more hours. It's a highly popular form of entertainment, as in the past, to mark rituals such as weddings. Dalangs are highly respected. In Bali, it's a largely hereditary profession, with over three hundred dalangs. Those who are deemed

Don't Switch That Channel: American TV Overseas

For all the traditional drama seen around the world, American drama still packs them in— and, in many cases, the less cultural, the better. Here's a quick sampling of hot American TV exports: The syndicated television show *Dark Justice* (retitled *Justica Final*) is a prime-time hit in Rio de Janeiro, Brazil—especially with Rio's police. The soap opera *The Bold and the Beautiful* has many viewers worldwide—from Egypt to Lebanon to Italy. *Beverly Hills 90210* is another hit around the world—from Mexico to Japan to the Czech Republic (where it was number one in January 1994; number two was the miniseries *North and South* about the American Civil War). In Southeast Asia, the television show *MacGyver,* which wasn't a huge hit here, is the top foreign program across the region. And in Germany, audiences watch a wide range of U.S. television shows, from old sitcoms like *Mr. Ed* and *I Dream of Jeannie* to soaps like *General Hospital* and programs like *Bonanza, Hawaii Five-O, Murphy Brown,* and, of course, *Beavis and Butthead,* which is translated into Spanish and aired throughout Latin America.

highly spiritual also can bless holy water. In Java, it's similarly revered, with the more famous dalangs becoming the equivalent of rock stars, selling cassettes of their finest work in record stores.

Not only do the traditional shadow puppet theater forms remain in Indonesia, there have also been newer ones depicting modern rulers and Javanese kings. In fact, there is even a distinct type of shadow puppet theater called *wayang suluh,* which focuses on very modern events. Developed in 1947, it focuses on modern history, telling tales about Sukarno (founder of the Republic of Indonesia) and others. But when the chips are down, most people still prefer their wayang the traditional way—kalit purwa.

A NIGHT AT THE (BEIJING) OPERA

A typical night at the opera? Some operatic singing, some moving music, some acrobatics, ornate costumes—all performed by a huge cast and backed by a full orchestra.

It sounds a bit like a Busby Berkeley extravaganza . . . except that, until recently, you'd probably be sitting through the not-all-that-entertaining-sounding *Taking Tiger Mountain by Strategy* or the (then) very popular dance-drama *Red Detachment of Women.*

Neither sounds particularly catchy, but this type of politically correct militaristic show was the common attraction at the Beijing Opera under Mao, which is testimony to the resilience of

The hottest operas in China nowadays aren't the traditional ones produced at the Beijing Opera, but the ones they can watch at home: television soap operas. According to Beijing's progovernment CHINA DAILY, *China "has gone crazy over soap operas." Not bad for a country where just a few years ago, soaps were almost unheard of. Some of the most popular: the twenty-five-part series* STORIES FROM A NEWSROOM, *about the lives and loves of journalists; a suspense series,* CLOSE TO THE IMPERIAL WALL; *and the purely romantic* I LOVE YOU, DEFINITELY.

this popular form of Chinese traditional theater. Back then, propaganda and revolutionary history were added to the mixture of music, dance, acrobatics, and singing. Traditional costumes and gestures were often banned because they were said to symbolize the feudal class. The stories acted on the stage were tales of the glory of the Party, not romances or tragedy. The opera still drew audiences and still held on, however tenuously, to its roots. Now, times have changed. With the easing of many ideological restrictions brought about by the death of Mao and the fall of the Gang of Four, the Beijing Opera has loosened up and gone back to its roots.

The Beijing Opera (also known as *jingxi*) style emerged in the early nineteenth century, a blend of two musical styles, the *xipi* and *erhuang,* that replaced the classical Chinese drama style called *kunqu.*

To some degree, the Beijing Opera of today is a lot like the Beijing Opera of years past. As with many other forms of traditional drama, there are certain unchangeable elements that distinguish it. There are usually four main characters: the *sheng,* or lead male (often a statesman or scholar); the *tan,* or lead female (played only by men in the past, but now by women as well, thanks to a great degree to pressures from the Chinese Communist Party), who can be one of two types, the flirtatious female or the proper lady; the *ching,* or male character with the painted face (usually a warrior, bandit, or evil minister); and the *chou,* or clown.

As you might guess, spontaneity or individualism isn't encouraged when it comes to tackling a role in the Beijing Opera. In fact, saying it's a stylized form of drama is putting it mildly. The different stock characters wear standardized, yet ornate, makeup and costumes, tipping the audience off as to their character traits. A character wearing red is brave; gold, divine. Someone with black makeup making furrows on his face is a warrior; red, a jester. Like regular opera, the different characters have a different musical theme that plays when they're coming on to the stage. Even gestures are set in stone: There are twenty types of beards a character can wear and thirty-nine ways the bearded character can touch or manipulate that beard; there are twenty-six specific ways to laugh. One reason gestures and costumes are so important is that there are few, if any, props and no sets. It's up to the actors and the music to set the mood and tell the story.

IT'S GREEK TO ME:
A QUICK LOOK AT CLASSICAL GREEK DRAMA

From Oedipus complexes to sitcom plots, Greek drama has a strong foothold in modern life and terminology. It's one of those ancient art forms that, instead of existing only in a college classroom or in books that no one really reads, has survived. Even though the plays aren't read any more, they're still revived, and they still inspire playwrights, screenwriters, and television producers—in other words, they still live.

No one is quite sure exactly how and where ancient Greek drama developed. On the whole, when we talk about classical Greek drama, we're usually talking about the drama that existed in the fourth and fifth centuries B.C.E. For the most part, we're actually talking about classical Athenian drama. Even though other cities had theaters and dramatists, what has survived through time is Athenian. Its main proponents were Athenian, many times the plays were about specifically Athenian concerns or themes, and the intended audience was, right, Athenian.

The simplest way to quickly understand the growth and development of classical Greek drama is to take a look at the growth and development of Athens. *Tragedy* ran parallel to the Athenian democracy—it emerged at the same time, reached a high point when Athenians had successfully fought off the Persians, and started faltering during the Peloponnesian War and the growing critical nature of Athenian society. The subject matter of tragedy also went through an evolution—from focusing on large groups, generations, or dynasties to the individual.

As for *comedy,* it emerged about fifty years after drama, in roughly 435 B.C.E., with what is now called (logically) Old Comedy. Old Comedy was a broad kind of art, heavy on satire, with references to contemporary celebrities, politicians, and movements. Next, Middle Comedy emerged, which was actually Old Comedy toned down a notch—still satirical, but more social than political. Finally, New Comedy appeared, a nonpolitical, non-acid form of comedy, more a comedy of manners than a satire.

That's the quick background to ancient Greek drama—but perhaps the best (or simplest) way of understanding it is to look at the five key ancient Greek playwrights who embody it: Aeschylus, Sophocles, and Euripides on the dramatic side, and Aristophanes and Menander on the comedic.

EURIPIDES (ENGRAVING OF A SCULPTED BUST; REPRODUCED FROM THE COLLECTIONS OF THE LIBRARY OF CONGRESS)

389

AESCHYLUS

(c. 525–c. 456 B.C.E.)
The father of Greek tragedy.

Called the first great tragedian, Aeschylus gave Greek tragedy much of the basic form that it followed for years. He was the one who introduced a second actor to plays. Until Aeschylus, tragedies consisted of a chorus and one actor . . . a somewhat limiting arrangement.

With the addition of a second actor, Aeschylus was able to broaden tragedy, and broaden it he did. His work was (and is) known for its scope. His main focus was the suffering that sin brings to people, generation after generation, until at last justice is served. His poetry is powerful and passionate; his plotting uses strong, even shocking, events; and scenery and props are equally striking. He wasn't afraid to use anything to get a reaction from the audience—mechanical devices, paintings, and great numbers of extras for crowd scenes. For all of these crowd-pleasers, it took him a while to catch on. He didn't win a prize until 484 B.C.E., but once his genius was recognized, he stayed popular and influential.

He is supposed to have written ninety plays (seventy-nine titles known), but only seven plays are extant today: *Persians; Seven Against Thebes; Prometheus Bound; Suppliants;* and his most famous, the trilogy the *Oresteia,* consisting of *Agamemnon* (considered his masterpiece), *Choephoroi* (or *Libation-Bearers*), and *Eumenides.*

Ancient Greek drama posed a number of surprising (to us) moral questions for Greek philosophers and sages. Among the questions that plagued them: Was it morally right for an actor to represent someone evil? In fact, was it morally sound for an actor to pretend to be someone he wasn't? *Plato in particular had real problems with all this. He proposed in his book* REPUBLIC *that visiting actors be sent away from the ideal state of the future. So it's no surprise that the ancient Greek word for actor—hypokrites—has evolved into our word "hypocrite."*

SOPHOCLES

(c. 496–406 B.C.E.)
The second of the great Greek tragedians.

Sophocles beat Aeschylus in a dramatic contest in 468 and went on to become one of the most popular playwrights (and public figures) in ancient Greece. He won first prize eighteen times at the Great Dionysia—equivalent to the Tonys, the Academy Awards, and the Golden Palm rolled into one.

Not only did he beat Aeschylus, but he also moved beyond him by introducing key innovations to Greek tragedy that made it even more powerful and flexible. Two of the most influential: the introduction of a third speaking actor to Greek tragedy, which led to more flexibility; and the writing of three plays on different subjects for dramatic contests, instead of the Aeschylean tradition of writing three plays that told a continuing story. This shifted focus from the impact of flouting divine law on different generations to its impact on one person. To a great degree, it led to the development of the "tragic flaw"—a minor personality defect, such as pride—which, in combination with personal destiny and the gods, winds up leading a character to tragedy. It also forced the writer to tell the story in less time, which required a strong prologue to kick off the story, quick plot development, and concentrated dramatic action, all of which Sophocles was known for.

He was also known for his involvement in city affairs, but he still found time to write a high number of plays—

as many as 123. Most haven't survived; those that did include *Oedipus at Colonus, Antigone, Electra,* and his masterpiece, *Oedipus Tyrannus* (or *Oedipus the King*), possibly the best known. It even inspired Freud to coin the phrase "Oedipus complex," referring to a son's erotic love for his mother.

EURIPIDES

(480 or 484–406 B.C.E.)
The last of the famous Greek tragedians.

Euripides was known as the most realistic ancient Greek dramatist, even by his fellow writers. It was said that Sophocles' work represented men as they *should* be while Euripides represented men as they *were.* He was also said to be a misogynist, although you couldn't tell from his writing. Most of his main characters are women—strong, passionate ones, at that. His plays are marked by vivid characters, touches of comedy mixed in with tragedy, and gripping plots. But modern critics complain about his too-quick entries into his plots. Instead of letting the story unfold, he uses a prologue to explain the back story, then plunges right into the thick of the action. They also complain about his too-neat exits—he usually uses a deus ex machina to get characters out of the main sticky situation he has gotten them into.

Critics in his time seem to have been equally critical of his work, but probably for different reasons. He was considered shocking, immoral, and

Greek drama often relied upon the miraculous intervention of a god at some point or another. This interfering god was later called deus ex machina, the god in the machine (in Latin). No real mystery about this phrase. In ancient Greece, the god literally was in a machine. A crane on the roof above the proscenium arch would lower the actor playing the god into the midst of the action.

overly experimental. He won only five dramatic prizes (compared to Aeschylus, who won thirteen, and Sophocles, who won at least eighteen). Aristophanes used to parody his work and Aristotle criticized it. But people did pay attention to his work, and he grew very popular after his death. His plays were revived more often than other leading ancient Greek playwrights. He wrote about ninety-two plays, only eighteen of which exist in full today. Among the most famous are *Orestes, Medea, Hippolytus, Electra, Iphigenia in Aulis, Iphigenia in Tauris, Bacchae,* and *Trojan Women.*

ARISTOPHANES

(c. 448–c. 380 B.C.E.)
The leading Greek comic dramatist of social satires.

Aristophanes is the prime example of Greek Old Comedy—the bawdy, raucous style that ridiculed politicians and political movements—possibly because his is the only work existing from that period. He is said to have written over forty plays, of which eleven still exist. Among the most acclaimed: his early masterpieces *Acharnians, Clouds, Knights, Wasps,* and *Peace,* and some of his later works—*Birds, Lysistrata,* and *Frogs.* Most of his work is marked by puns, music and dance, political satire, and pointed observation about different aspects of Athenian life. It also includes Aristophanes's own personal commentary. He would have actors speak on his behalf, chiding the audience for not appreciating his work and criticizing other playwrights. Sometimes his brazenness got him into trouble. He entered into a lifelong feud with political leader Cleon because of his satiric and acid observations of him. But audiences apparently loved it. Save for *Clouds,* his first real failure, his work was definitely appreciated—he won more awards at dramatic contests than his competitors.

MENANDER

(c. 342–293 B.C.E.)
The last of the famous Greek comic playwrights.

A poet as well as a playwright, Menander wrote in the later period, called New Comedy. He is known for ironic comedies, usually about mundane subjects—the stuff of daily life—and is also famous for his pithy quotable lines: "Whom the gods love, die young." "Every accident has a meaning." "In marriage, there are no known survivors."

Considered by many ancients to be one of the greatest comedians, and certainly the greatest New Comedian. Menander's work tends not to be as admired today as that of Aristophanes, his more ancient counterpart of the Old Comedy. But after Menander's death, his plays became the most popular in the Greco-Roman world. To many modern readers, he seems prone to overly light writing and his use of stock characters and improbable plot devices can be annoying. But this is exactly what characterized the New Comedy, which is usually about the average person rather than the great heroes. New Comedy plays were designed to illuminate contemporary life and amuse audiences with light stories about love. And in clear simple writing, Menander does just that.

Roman teacher and rhetoritician Quintilian praised his work; later Roman comic playwright Terence based many of his plays on Menander's works; even Shakespeare and Molière took ideas and plots from him. But the only full text play remaining of Menander's is *Dyskolos* (*The Bad-Tempered Man*); the rest is just fragments.

ALL THE WORLD'S A STAGE: WORLD DRAMATISTS (BESIDES SHAKESPEARE)

Think of drama and Shakespeare is one of the names that automatically comes to mind. And for good reason: the Bard of Avon is possibly the most recognizable playwright in the world (at least the Western world). Of course, drama didn't begin and end with Shake-

speare. Other dramatists are masters of the craft and occupy exalted positions in the world of the stage.

Here, then, is a brief rundown of some of these dramatists who are tops in their craft, from the fourth century B.C.E. to the twentieth century, from Africa to Europe.

Top World Playwrights

KALIDASA (C. 4–5TH CENTURY C.E.): Ancient Indian writer considered India's greatest playwright. He is particularly famous for following the rules of traditional Sanskrit poetry at the same time as expressing his own artistic voice.

LOPE FÉLIX DE VEGA CARPIO (LOPE DE VEGA) (1562–1635): With Calderon, he is considered one of Spain's greatest playwrights of the Golden Age. Highly prolific, he claimed to have written 1,500 plays (but only about 500 plays attributed to him exist). He is best known for developing the 3-act Spanish *comedia.*

Their Most Famous Works (and Why)

Kalidasa's *Sakuntala* (*The Recovered Ring,* or *The Ring of Recognition*) has been called a Sanskrit masterpiece—a love story based loosely on a story in the *Mahabarata,* but known for its originality as well as its lyricism. The English translation of this inspired European writers (particularly Goethe) to become interested in Sanskrit drama. Since then it has been translated many times into English as well as other languages. Other famous works include *Malavikagnimitra* and *Vikramorvasiya.*

Among comedies, the most famous include the "cloak and sword comedy" *La dama boba* (*The Idiot Lady*) and the court comedy *El perro del hortelano* (*The Dog in the Manger*). Of his more serious plays, he is best known for "peasant-honor" plays, which explore the lot of peasants. His most famous: *Fuenteovejuna* (*The Sheep-Well*), about a village revolting against its lord (with a subplot of the lord revolting against his king). As for the numerous plays he wrote about honor in general, the tragedy *El castigo sin venganza* (*Punishment Without Revenge*), about adultery, is considered one of his best.

Top World Playwrights

PEDRO CALDERÓN DE LA BARCA (1600–1681): With Lope de Vega, considered the greatest playwright of Spain's Golden Age. And like Lope de Vega, he was prolific, with 110 comedies and 70 "autos sacramentales" (religious plays) and other works to his credit. His work later influenced German romantics, including Goethe and Wagner, and English Restoration dramatists.

PIERRE CORNEILLE (1606–1684): French playwright, one of the most influential writers in neoclassical drama. Called the father of French tragedy. For a time, was one of Richelieu's "Five Poets" who wrote plays on topics chosen by Richelieu. Wound up being overshadowed by Racine (who had actually written less).

MOLIÈRE (JEAN–BAPTISTE POQUELIN) (1622–1673): French dramatic triple threat—playwright, actor, and theater manager. Although he is especially famous for the comedies he wrote which made French comedy as high an art as tragedy, at the time he was equally known for his acting. Influenced numerous later playwrights, especially during the Restoration period of English drama (many of whom weren't only influenced by Moliere, but completely lifted his stories). Moliere died, ironically enough, after his fourth performance as a hypochondriac in his *Le Malade imaginaire* (*The Imaginary Invalid*).

Their Most Famous Works (and Why)

La vida es sueño (*Life Is a Dream*) is considered the masterpiece of Calderón's nonreligious plays. A dramatic play, it revolves around the themes of free will and predestination. Among his finest religious works are *El divino Orfeo* (*The Divine Orpheus*); *El mágico prodigioso* (*The Wonder-Working Magician*), about St. Cyprian (which was partially translated by Shelley); and a series of "honor plays," tragedies which revolve around the conflicts between honor and religion: *El médico de su honra* (*The Doctor of His Honor*), *A secreto agravio secreta venganza* (*Secret Vengeance for Secret Insult*), and *El pintor de su deshonra* (*The Painter of His Dishonor*).

His tragicomedy *Le Cid*, based on Spanish literature, and the play that made his name in France (as well as earning him the hatred of some of his fellow playwrights), is credited with kicking off the great age of French drama. Other famous works of his include his series of "Roman" plays—*Horace, Cinna,* and *Polyeucte.*

He is known for many famous works, including *Le Bourgeois gentilhomme* (*The Would-be Gentleman*). Interestingly, some of his most famous or most appreciated plays caused Molière a lot of trouble in his time—*Tartuffe* (about religious hypocrisy, which upset the religious establishment); *Don Juan* (about famous lover Don Juan, who was portrayed favorably, which upset a number of people). *Le Misanthrope* (*The Misanthrope*), famous now, was not considered successful then; and *L'Avare* (*The Miser*) was a complete flop.

Top World Playwrights

JEAN RACINE (1639–1699): The French playwright and poet considered the successor to Corneille and one of the—if not *the*—greatest French tragedians. Also known for his ruthless ambition and lack of loyalty to friends, he had public feuds with his former teacher, Pierre Nicole, as well as former friends and fellow dramatists Molière and Corneille. His unlikability wound up hurting him: While he was working on *Phèdre* (his finest play), his enemies got rival playwright Pradon to write on the same topic. This play was produced two days earlier than Racine's and was the greater success, causing a wounded Racine to retire from theatre for a while.

JOHANN WOLFGANG VON GOETHE (1749–1832): More than just a playwright (and director), Goethe is a literary giant, known for his poetry, novels, and essays, not to mention work in science, philosophy, and other fields. His main accomplishments in drama were: he greatly influenced the *Strum und Drang* movement; he later became leader of the New Romantics in Germany; as a director, he developed the so-called Weimar School of acting (which affected German acting through the 19th century), under which actors were to live a model life; and finally, he tried to create "perfect theater" both as a writer and director. All in all, he was one of the more influential dramatists of his time.

Their Most Famous Works (and Why)

He is most famous for a series of works written in one single decade: *Britannicus* (1669), *Bérénice* (1670), *Bajazet* (1672), *Mithridate* (1673), *Iphigénie en Aulide* (1674), and especially *Phèdre* (1677)—all revolving around classical subjects, and all marked by their poeticism. Instead of making the characters (usually great rulers) heroic, Racine focuses on their human passions. The female role in *Phèdre*, Rachel, is one of the most coveted roles in French drama—the equivalent of Hamlet.

Faust is probably the high point of Goethe's career, both in drama and in poetry. He worked on this beginning in 1775 and finally completed Part I (considered one of the masterpieces of world literature in general) in 1808, and Part II in 1832. The play incorporates a number of different dramatic styles and covers the entire range of human experience, including politics, economics, eroticism, and love—all in an attempt to explore the role of human life. For all of its fame, many think it reads better than it plays. In fact, it is said that he didn't write it with performance in mind. This leads to another interesting point: For all of Goethe's fame as a playwright, relatively little of his work has been seen on the stage.

Top World Playwrights

ALEKSANDR SERGEYEVICH PUSHKIN (1799–1837): Known more for his poetry than his plays, Pushkin is considered the Russian Shakespeare. (In fact, he himself considered Shakespeare one of his greatest influences.) He didn't write much drama, but is still considered one of the most influential world playwrights. The little he wrote had great impact—he created a uniquely Russian style of drama (which replaced the French neoclassical one in use) based on folklore, contemporary language and slang, and Russian themes. He died in a duel just after finishing some one-act tragedies (about Mozart and Salieri, and Don Juan), and it appears that he was planning to write more dramatic works.

HENRIK IBSEN (1828–1906): Norwegian playwright and poet, considered one of the most influential dramatists of all time and the founder of modern prose dramas. Especially famous for existentialist plays about social and political issues, he actually began by writing very conventional romantic dramas. He later shifted gears—some say when Norway didn't support Denmark in its fight with Bismarck—and began writing first the social reform plays, then the darker psychological works he's known for.

Their Most Famous Works (and Why)

Called the Russian *Macbeth, Boris Godunov* is Pushkin's greatest drama (actually, one of his few). It's famous for several reasons: It's the first Russian tragedy written about politics, it uses colloquial speech, and it's episodic (divided into scenes). For all this, it isn't produced that often; the opera based on it (by Mussorgsky) is probably much more widely seen.

Ibsen's work is so influential, it's difficult to point to one key work. *Ghosts* (ostensibly about venereal disease, but also about other social diseases unmasked by VD) was the work which truly made his mark outside of Scandinavia, and created a buzz in most major European cultural capitals. Other plays, written before *Ghosts,* wound up being equally famous. Among them are *Peer Gynt* (his first existential play) and *A Doll's House* (about women's rights). *Hedda Gabler* is the most famous of his later works, in which he moved beyond social issues and tackled the notion of individual destiny.

Top World Playwrights

GEORGE BERNARD SHAW (1856–1950):

Irish-born playwright, essayist, critic, and social commentator, he was known for his strong views. He was a vehement vegetarian, pamphleteer, avid letter-to-the-editor writer, and member and officer of the socialist Fabian society. His plays usually mirror his strongly held views—his aim was to reach the intellect of his audiences, not the emotions. He wrote chiefly about intellectual subjects (war, religion, economics, love), or social issues (prostitution, slum landlords, women's rights). This type of strong subject matter (especially when coupled with his equally strong personality) sometimes caused him problems. In fact, many of his plays initially weren't produced, but reached an audience through readings and private productions. After 1904, his plays became very popular, and his work became known around the world.

ANTON PAVLOVICH CHEKHOV (1860–1904):

Perhaps the most well-known Russian playwright in the West, Chekhov, who trained as a physician, actually considered himself more a doctor than writer. Founder of the "theater of the mood" (which breaks from traditional exposition and action in favor of hidden or partially stated meanings and inaction). His work combines impressionistic style with psychological realism. This new style initially hampered him; when his first three plays were produced, they were flops, and the actors had problems with his writing. But once his work caught on, he was a success; when he died after a long bout of TB, he was still a hit.

Their Most Famous Works (and Why)

Shaw wrote many works that are famous, influential, and critical masterpieces. Among his best are *Candida, Man and Superman, Major Barbara, Caesar and Cleopatra, Androcles and the Lion,* and *Pygmalion.* As with most of his work, these plays all represent Shaw's strong social viewpoints, usually with a comedic touch. Later plays, such as *Heartbreak House* and *Saint Joan,* are equally famous and more serious. In his later years, he was evolving a new, experimental dramatic style.

Another playwright with more than one masterpiece, Chekhov wrote a number of plays that were not only great successes in their time, but also still successfully (and often) revived. These include *The Seagull, Uncle Vanya, The Cherry Orchard, Three Sisters,* and *Ivanov.* While the plots differ, most of his work shares common bonds. One main theme is the price one must pay for material success, with the loss of humanity. One of the reasons for both Chekhov's popularity and longevity is that his plays usually revolved around the average middle-class person.

Top World Playwrights	*Their Most Famous Works (and Why)*

BERTOLT BRECHT (EUGEN BERTHOLD FRIEDRICH) (1898–1956): Considered by some to be Germany's greatest dramatist, Brecht is one of the most important voices in Western drama since World War II; others call him pretentious and overly Marxist. But there's no question that he was an innovator who revamped German drama, and Western drama in general. An ardent Marxist, he applied Marxist theory to his work. His key point was that drama should be a social experiment presenting abstract political issues (like revolution, exploitation); so audiences should be distanced or detached from the work, not emotionally involved. His own life was definitely affected by politics. When Hitler came into power, he fled and wound up in Hollywood for a while, but returned to Berlin in 1948 (where, in spite of his Marxist leanings, his work was accused by Marxists of being "formalistic").

The Threepenny Opera, Brecht's first success and one of his best known works, is, along with *The Rise and Fall of the City of Mahagonny,* an example of his "anti-Wagner" operas. They're also early examples of his groundbreaking "epic" theater, in which the audience had to be aware of the stage as a stage, the actors as actors, the scenery, the props, even the orchestra, instead of suspending their disbelief and losing themselves in the play. His Later plays are considered by most to be his major works. The most famous is *Mother Courage and her Children* (in which an actress deliberately flubs her lines to distance the audience).

LAO SHE (PSUEDONYM OF SHU CH'ING-CH'UN OR SHU SHE-YÜ) (1899–1966): Chinese playwright and novelist. Considered one of China's leading writers, he is best known for his novels, although one of his plays (*Longu gou*) wound up earning him the title People's Artist. He is known for his use of colloquial language and examination of social issues, particularly the impact of politics and change on underprivileged people. Politics ended up greatly affecting him: He committed suicide in the early days of the Cultural Revolution.

Best known for *Longu gou* (*Dragon Beard Ditch*), with its political plot about the rehabilitation of a Beijing slum. He is also known for *Chaguan* (*Tea House*), also focusing on social issues—in this case, how people survive in a changing society.

Top World Playwrights

TAWFIQ AL-HAKIM (1902–): Called the father of modern Egyptian drama. The prolific and influential al-Hakim has written over 70 literary works, at least 40 of which are plays. Plays generally fall into two categories: the "plays of the intellect," which usually take a historical or religious subject and popularize it (often designed to be read, not dramatized); and his "modern plays," which typically are social critiques, sometimes written classically, other times using theater of the absurd.

CAO YU (PSUEDONYM OF WAN JIABAO) (1910–): Considered the most influential and important Chinese playwright of the 20th century, Yu credits Ibsen and Shaw as his chief influences. Like them, his works often focus on social corruption and decadence. He held numerous government posts, but ran into problems with the Communists for his "bourgeois thinking." Eventually he was sent for reeducation, and now is not only acceptable, but revered as a key founder of modern theater. Yu is currently director of Beijing People's Art Theater.

JEAN ANOUILH (1910–1987): French playwright, he is considered one of the leading figures in contemporary theater. He started as a copywriter and gagman in films. His first play, *L'Hermine,* was a critical flop, but he kept writing regularly, and perseverance paid off. Heavily influenced by neoclassicism, his work isn't at all stodgy. Instead, he takes a fresh, contemporary approach to the classics, bringing them into the 20th century.

Their Most Famous Works (and Why)

Of his "plays of the intellect," the two most famous are *Ahl al-Khaf* (*People of the Cave*) (1933), based on a Qu'ranic legend, which is somewhat like a religious Rip van Winkle—three Christians sleep for 300 years and awaken to an Islamic world; and *Muhammad,* about the life of the prophet Muhammad, called the longest Arabic-written play. Of his plays of social criticism, two key ones are *Ya Tali' al-Shajara* (*The Tree Climbers*) (1962) and *Al-Sultan al-Ha'ir* (*The Sultan who Could Not Make Up His Mind*).

Leiyu (*Thunderstorm*) is his best-known work and the one that initially won him fame. Two other plays written soon after form a trilogy with this—*Dichu* (*Sunrise*) and *Yuanye* (*Wilderness*)—all focus on prewar decadence in China. His later works are less known and usually are about Chinese history (a safer topic given his reeducation).

Works are generally a blend of the comic and the intensely pessimistic, representing his world view. He divides his plays into two main categories depending on the overriding mood he conveys, not subject: "black plays," which generally have a cynical view of the world, exposing such things as greed and hypocrisy; and "rose plays," his less pessimistic works (while also often satirical and even cynical). Among his best known are *Le Bal des voleurs* (*Thieves' Carnival*), *Le Valse des toréadors* (*Waltz of the Toreadors*), *Antigone*, *Le Voyageur sans bagage* (*Traveller without Luggage*), *L'Alouette* (*The Lark*), and *Becket*.

Top World Playwrights

ATHOL FUGARD (1932–): Playwright, actor, and director, Fugard is called one of the leading figures in South African literature. Although Anglo-Irish and Afrikaner in background, he is perhaps best known for presenting the voice of black South Africans in dramas, figuratively (in terms of plot) and literally (in the usage of colloquialisms and dialects).

Their Most Famous Works (and Why)

He is known for a number of plays, most focusing on the problems of life under apartheid, which is why they've sometimes been censored by government authorities. Among the most famous and acclaimed is *Blood Knot* (about two brothers—one light and one dark— and the attempt to pass for white in an apartheid world). Two of his "workshop plays," written while working with an improvisation group of actors (two of whom were credited as coauthors), are *Sizwe Bansi is Dead* (about pass laws), and *The Island* (about prisoners). Later plays especially popular in Great Britain and the United States include *Master Harold and the Boys, The Road to Mecca,* and *A Lesson from Aloes.*

TEN GREAT WORLD FILM DIRECTORS YOU SHOULD KNOW— AND THE GREAT FILMS THEY MADE

 There's a great big world of celluloid out there. But many of us show little interest and less knowledge of the contributions made outside of Hollywood—and we're not talking about boring obscure films with cryptic subtitles. Many foreign films are great films, many are influential films, and many are entertaining films. Many of them have influenced filmmakers here. *Star Wars, The Magnificent Seven,* detective films, science-fiction films, kung-fu films, *Bonnie and Clyde, Drugstore Cowboy, Down and Out in Beverly Hills* . . . all of these are in some degree intellectual imports, dependent on German, French, Japanese, Chinese, and Italian filmmakers.

Of course, it goes the other way, too. Many foreign filmmakers have been tremendously influenced by Hollywood (it's hard to ignore). The bottom line is simple: film is truly an international medium. The power of the image, even more so than the word, transcends political, cultural, linguistic, and social boundaries. Virtually all the great world directors we've listed below have connections with cultures other than their own. The Russian director Sergei Eisenstein, for example, was influenced by Japan; he then, in turn, influenced British, French, and American filmmakers. The renowned Indian director Satyajit Ray was inspired by the film of an Italian director and encouraged in his first venture by a French director.

So here they are: ten of the greatest film directors in the world along with some of their best films. To show their influence, we've also mentioned some of the American films they've inspired.

FRITZ LANG

(1890–1976)
(Austrian)

When you watch virtually any horror or sci-fi film, from *Frankenstein* and the *Star Trek* films to classics like *2001,* "film noir," or any film with a dark stylistic sense, you owe a debt to Fritz Lang, the Austro/German pioneer of expressionism in film.

Expressionism was an art movement that represented reality through distorted, harsh angles and contrasts, the use of light, and bold strokes to convey usually negative emotion. Lang translated it brilliantly from the canvas to the screen.

Appropriately enough, Lang was trained as an architect and painter, but while convalescing from war wounds during World War I, he began writing film scripts. He began directing in Berlin, where his career took off with the classics *M* and *Metropolis.* He was reportedly one of Hitler's favorite directors (Hitler didn't know he was partly Jewish) and was offered a position heading the Nazi film industry. He refused; eventually director Leni Riefenstahl would take it and become

401

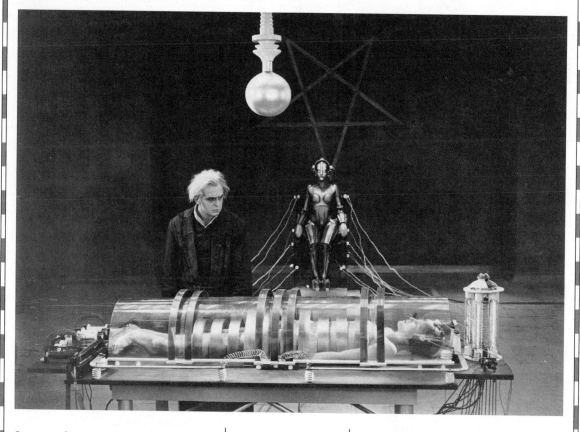

famous for her Nazi propaganda. When Lang's next film, *The Last Will of Dr. Mabuse,* was banned by the Nazis, Lang fled to France (and was divorced by his wife, a member of the Nazi party), then went on to Hollywood, with an MGM contract. There he directed a number of successful Westerns, including *Rancho Notorious,* and the critically acclaimed film noir *The Big Heat.* Later, he returned to Europe, refusing offers to remake his silent classics. It was left to the East Germans to recut *Metropolis* and add a driving rock score that isn't that inappropriate.

METROPOLIS (1927)

Comment: This science-fiction film was supposedly inspired by the New

FRITZ LANG—
METROPOLIS
(THE MUSEUM OF
MODERN
ART/FILM STILLS
ARCHIVE)

York skyline, and maybe like New York's skyline, it looks somewhat better than it actually is. Yet its visual images are so world famous it must be included in any listing of major works of art; famous for haunting sets of an angular, harsh, yet beautiful German Expressionist style, it represents a futuristic super-industrial world of steel and machines.

Plot: *Metropolis* is about a divided world of capitalists and workers. The setting: Above, in soaring skyscrapers, live the bosses; far below them on the ground are their machines and the workers who slave with them; underground are the workers' homes. Even further below the earth are the tunnels and catacombs of an ancient, long-deserted city.

Inevitably (of course) someone from above falls in love with someone from below: the boss's son Freder falls in love with Maria, the worker's daughter (for *Star Trek* fans, this theme was partly repeated in an original *Star Trek* television story). Maria is saintly; she preaches a Christian type of gospel to the oppressed workers in those deserted catacombs. Naturally, Freder's father is furious over her love affair with his son. So he enlists the aid of a mad scientist (one of the first mad scientists in film) named Rotwang, who creates a robot in the form of Maria. (Incidentally, this scene inspired a later film, *The Bride of Frankenstein*). The robot Maria is a sensual-looking, metallic, yet somehow very feminine version of the original, who goes about spouting Marxist ideas to the workers, along with a hefty (and very believable) amount of sexuality. The film ends happily—workers and bosses are reconciled; the future looks to be better than the present.

Meaning: This is one of the first films to cinematically explore the dehumanization brought about by industrialization; it was produced at the height of the post-World War I German depression, which pitted workers against capitalist factory owners.

M (1931)

Comment: A masterwork thriller about a serial killer that manages to convey horror without modern Hollywood gore. In fact, although all the murders take place off camera (for all the problems of life back then, it was in many senses a gentler age in the arts), the tension and horror is unbearable. Incidentally, this was famous actor Peter Lorre's film debut.

Plot: Peter Lorre (for those few who don't know who he was, he's the cringing Ugarte in *Casablanca,* a small man with buggy eyes and a huge film presence) brilliantly plays Beckert, a pitiful, pudgy man with glasses, who is compelled, again and again, to kill children. The plot is what mystery fans call a "police procedural," concerned with the mechanisms of crime and detection. And so we watch as Beckert is inexorably drawn to murder, inexorably discovered, and then trapped like a rat in the warrens of a crowded city. The impact of Beckert's murders is poignantly shown in such images as a child's empty place setting at a dinner table, or a stray balloon drifting in the wind. Beckert has terrorized a city; yet it is not the police who first catch him but his fellow criminals, who hold a mock trial, which in turn is broken up by the police.

Meaning: We are all victims, Lang seems to be saying, including the pitiable criminal compelled to kill children. The original title, *The Murderer Among Us,* points to this idea, the power of those dark forces within us as individuals and as part of collective societies. Lang directed this film in the dying days of the Weimer Republic, two years before a serial killer on a mass scale by the name of Adolf Hitler would seize power. This is a dark, paranoid film. It inspired the film noir style which Hollywood would later produce in great numbers.

SERGEI EISENSTEIN

(1898–1948)
(Russian)

Cabaret, Saturday Night Fever, Flash-dance, and *Natural Born Killers* are modern American films that use a montage of image, sound, and movement to create a mood, a feeling that defines the film and makes it memorable and powerful. So it's not stretching things too much to say that the man who made John Travolta a star in *Saturday Night Fever* is the man who was one of the pioneers of this film technique so many years before: the Russian director Sergei Eisenstein, one of the greatest directors of all time.

Eisenstein grew up in a comfortable bourgeois household, but he came of age in revolutionary Russia. While serving in the Red Army on the Eastern Front, Eisenstein came into contact with Japanese culture, which fascinated him and influenced his later films. After the revolution, he actually planned to study Japanese, but in order to get a ration card he took a job as a set designer. From there, he began directing plays, then turned to film. His first film, *Strike,* was boldly experimental—it shocked the Soviets but delighted the world; due to this acclaim he was chosen to direct a film about the 1905 revolution. That film, *Potemkin,* was a critical and popular hit,

SERGEI EISENSTEIN (THE MUSEUM OF MODERN ART/FILM STILLS ARCHIVE)

and included most of Eisenstein's innovative ideas on film (see below). Eisenstein traveled to Hollywood in the early 1930s under the aegis of Paramount, but his projects were turned down. Later, he tried to do an epic film in Mexico, which was financed by the American writer Upton Sinclair—this project bogged down, too. When he returned to Russia, worse was in store. Joseph Stalin had seized power and disliked innovation; eventually, Eisenstein was forced to toe a very narrow political line. His later films are less interesting, more strained than the creative masterpieces of his early years.

POTEMKIN (1925)

Comment: This film looks at the 1905 Russian Revolution against czarist rule through two vignettes: a mutiny on the battleship *Potemkin,* and reprisals against the population of Odessa (where the ship was based) by the czarist army. To some, it's the greatest film ever made; to most, it's at least in the top ten.

Plot: Eisenstein was famous for putting together a montage of images that didn't follow a normal plot line. *Potemkin* is split into five parts—mimicking the five-act structure of classical drama. The first part, titled "Men and Maggots," builds up the reasons for the *Potemkin's* sailors' mutiny. It shows the rotten, maggot-ridden food and the lack of concern for these inhuman conditions by the officers. The next part, "Drama on the Quarterdeck," shows the actual and successful rebellion of the sailors. The third section, "An Appeal from the Dead," is a respite from the violence; the sailors parade past a dead comrade. The fourth part of the film, "The Odessa Steps," is one you should know (virtually every film class in the country covers it). In it, czarist troops fire upon citizens of Odessa on the city's great outdoor staircase. As the citizens run down the stairs, they are mowed down by advancing troops; we feel the horror as women, children, young and old die. (Years later, Woody Allen did a play on this famous sequence in *Bananas*). The fifth section, "Meeting the Squadron," builds up suspense masterfully as the battleship *Potemkin* advances to meet the rest of the fleet. Will the fleet fire on the battleship of heroic mutineers? The tension builds until viewers are relieved to see that no, it won't. The mutiny has united all the sailors of the fleet.

Meaning: This is a revolutionary film about the meaning of revolution for the little guy—the average person, represented by sailors, who wants fairness and freedom. But this is also a work of art: Eisenstein was a pioneer in film editing, and he made film sequences into startlingly powerful statements. For example, the Odessa stair sequence is split into many different parts—shots from many different positions, long shots, close-ups of faces, symmetrical shots, asymmetrical shots—all intercut so that in total the film is a montage of both the masses and individuals, emotion and action. Collectively it takes a massacre and gives the viewer the full impact, almost as if he or she were actually experiencing it. This film sequence takes longer than it would for people to

actually run on the stairs, but in subjective terms, the film is really more accurate (who doesn't remember some horrible thing seeming to happen in slow motion?). If you want to sound like a critic, you can say that the total effect of this film is like music—you feel it rather than just see it.

AKIRA KUROSAWA

(1910–)
(Japanese)

Akira Kurosawa is considered Japan's greatest director, and its most "un-Japanese" director as well—like many great artists he's less a part of a local tradition as much as he is uniquely individual. One critic called him the "most Shakespearean of directors," and in fact, his *Throne of Blood* is widely considered to be the best film adaptation of *Macbeth* ever made.

For all of his individualism, Kurosawa is possibly best known for taking different traditional forms and making them his own. One of his most notable moves: adapting elements and techniques from the traditional form of Japanese theater, No, and translating it to film. Among the best examples of this are his films *Rashomon, Living,* and *The Seven Samurai.* From Western traditions, he's not only adapted Shakespeare, but also writers Fyodor Dostoyevsky (*The Idiot*) and Maxim Gorky (*The Lower Depths*). His work is groundbreaking—not just literal remakes of famous works, but works that incorporate his unique vision.

Just as he has taken inspiration from other works, he too has become an inspiration to other filmmakers. An interesting film trivia note: Kurosawa also made an epic film in 1958 called *The Hidden Fortress*, about a strong-minded princess and a wise swordsman who protects her. George Lucas was inspired and translated much of it for his own epic *Star Wars*.

THE SEVEN SAMURAI (1954)

Comment: A classic Japanese film which was inspired in part by American Westerns; in turn it inspired later American Westerns, all the way to the spaghetti Westerns of Sergio Leone. As many people know, it was remade in the United States as the Western with an unforgettable theme song, *The Magnificent Seven*. But *The Seven Samurai* is far more than a run-of-the-mill Western. Set in sixteenth-century Japan, famous for its imagery, its great themes, and its pioneering spirit, it succeeded critically as well as popularly.

Plot: Seven Japanese warriors, samurai without a master, are hired by villagers to protect them from a band of brigands. (For those who quibble, these samurai technically should be termed *ronin*, a Japanese term for samurai who are not attached to a lord.) The film is a long (three-hour) buildup to the inevitable battle with those brigands.

Most of the film follows a very basic pattern. First the brigands threaten the village, then the villagers recruit the samurai, then the samurai spend time fortifying and preparing the village, and then, they battle the brigands. Along the way we get to know the samurai, a set of very different personalities who together form a very professional fighting group. We see their relations with the villagers, which are

somewhat strained by the inevitable differences between the two very different sets of people.

The climax of the film is the battle at the end, which takes place during a fierce rainstorm. Here the fixed formality of the film gives way to the exhilarating chaos of a battle in the water and the mud. Finally, in an epilogue, we see the villagers singing as they plant a new rice crop, while in another shot, the surviving samurai are standing at the graves of their fallen compatriots.

Meaning: The epilogue suggests the themes of the film: separation and isolation. There are three discreet groups—"good" villagers, "evil" brigands, and the samurai taking an uneasy middle ground. All are eternally apart. No one successfully crosses the boundaries of his group. Obviously for us, the samurai are the most compelling characters. They are apart from the villagers they are protecting and in some senses they are superior (or so they may feel), yet at the same time they are mere employees—rootless, without a home and family, and most important, without a society which defines their roles and morality. So they must depend upon and create their own values. This was a revolutionary (and very un-Japanese) theme, but it was very successfully transferred to the West as the idea of lone warriors living very carefully by their own rules. In this sense, it took a Japanese director to define a very Western theme.

KAGEMUSHA (THE SHADOW WARRIOR) (1980)

Comment: This is an epic masterpiece about the power of images. It explores the role media images have in creating leaders (whom do we really follow, the real leader or the TV cartoon the image makers create?); it analyzes the power of film in expounding ideas; it discusses the role of honor in morally ambiguous circumstances; and it addresses these very modern questions in a very unexpected setting: that of medieval, sixteenth-century Japan. Some compare it to Shakespeare's *Tempest;* others call it, on another level, the first truly successful costume epic. Like most of Kurosawa's films, *Kagemusha* is about virtually all the major themes of life—and death.

Plot: This is a story about one of Japan's greatest warlords, Shingen, and an ornery thief who looks strikingly like

THE SEVEN
SAMURAI
(NATIONAL FILM
ARCHIVE,
LONDON)

the great warlord. *Kagemusha* literally means the shadow warrior, and sure enough, the film is about the role of the thief as Shingen's double, his shadow. In the opening scene we see both of them together and hear how Shingen considers himself a thief as well, albeit on a much larger scale.

As you might expect, Shingen is soon killed by the enemy and now the leaders of his warring clan decide to keep the troops together by having the thief impersonate Shingen. Shingen's impetuous son is not suitable for the role of clan leader—Shingen himself had rejected him as a successor. The thief doesn't like the idea, and at first

resists doing much more than posing for the role (and playing with Shingen's grandson) but gradually, he finds the role taking control of him. In a key portion, he speaks out during a council of war and finds himself suggesting a cautious strategy that Shingen himself would have undoubtedly proposed.

Now tragedy ensues. Shingen's son finds out that the thief is an imposter and takes charge of the clan. He casts out the thief and gets involved in a disastrous battle. All the while the thief looks on, horrified at the destruction of the great clan he has come paradoxically to represent.

Meaning: Kurosawa sounds a lot like Shakespeare: The idea of life as a stage and all of us "merely players" is clearly evident—in this case the actor, the thief, becomes defined by his role. And yet the actor actually exceeds his role: The thief proves to be greater even than the clansmen he comes to represent, who ultimately reject him and lose themselves. In this, Kurosawa seems to be talking about the folly and falseness of human life and institutions; it's all a shadow game, fought by shadows for shadowy ideas and ideals.

JEAN RENOIR

(1894–1979)
(French)

Renoir was a potter, the son of the famous painter Pierre Auguste Renoir. He married his father's last model, and to please his wife, entered filmmaking and made her a star. Along the way, he made himself one of the world's great directors. His early films were not suc-

JEAN RENOIR
(NATIONAL FILM
ARCHIVE,
LONDON)

cesses; he sold his father's paintings one by one to finance his projects. ("Each sale seemed a betrayal," he said.) Then came some moderate successes, then *La Chienne* in 1931; a film about a clerk who falls in love with a prostitute. It was France's first sound film shot on location, and more important, a critical success. (Unfortunately for Renoir, the lead actress was a woman other than his wife, and because of this, she divorced him.)

A slew of critically acclaimed films followed, including *Boudu Saved from Drowning* in 1932 (it was remade many years later by Hollywood as *Down and Out in Beverly Hills*), *Grand Illusion*, and *The Rules of the Game*, a masterpiece made in 1939 about a house party, set at a time just before a war, "a world dancing on a volcano." This antiwar film was a major bomb (only later would it be recognized as great), and Renoir left France, eventually winding up in Hollywood and taking American citizenship. But he didn't quite fit in; so he went on to India where he made his first color picture, *The River,* and where he critically influenced the great Indian director Satyajit Ray. After the war, he returned to Europe.

Renoir's films are famed for their charm. Despite the realistic characters, he understands human weakness and shows it both realistically and sympathetically. His films have virtually no villains. When asked why, he said enigmatically: "Everyone has his reasons." Many of his films have a sort of cheerful melancholy, sensitive to the moods and feelings of the characters and the viewers.

GRAND ILLUSION (1937)

Comment: This is an antiwar film that could never have been made in America—it presents its message along with an exploration of the death of chivalry and aristocratic values, ideas we associate with the long-dead past. Yet when this film was made, it was scarcely twenty years since aristocratic Europe truly can be said to have died, a victim of the First World War. By watching this masterpiece (consistently voted among the ten best films ever made by virtually everybody) we get a feel for the poignancy of war, and the death of an era.

Plot: This is the ultimate prison camp movie: It revolves around the attempts of French prisoners of war to escape from the Germans. The aristocratic French Captain de Boeldieu and

his pilot, Marechal, have been shot down by the Germans. In prison, they meet Rosenthal, a rich French Jew. These main characters plot an escape, but before they can do so are transferred to an escape-proof castle run by the ramrod aristocratic German Captain von Rauffenstein (played by bull-necked Erich von Stroheim in his best role). As you can guess, the two aristocratic enemies, von Rauffenstein and de Boeldieu, find they share a common background—against which the war seems absurd. But Boeldieu recognizes the changes in the wind, and he acts as a decoy to help Rosenthal and Marechal escape. In so doing, he is mortally wounded by von Rauffenstein, who is overcome by what he has done.

Meanwhile, Marechal and Rosenthal are on the run when they are taken in by a German farm woman, who falls in love with Marechal. But they cannot stay, for the war is not yet over, and Marechal leaves with Rosenthal to return to France.

Meaning: There is a melancholic air to the film that defies description. It states its themes lyrically, effortlessly: War is hypocritical, sad, foolish. But the dying military caste that champions it, or rather lives by its rules, is to be pitied as much as admired: It has a code, the death of which, to some degree, is to be mourned. We see nobility of spirit and birth in von Rauffenstein and de Boeldieu, as well as a newer nobility in the common man Marechal, his rich friend Rosenthal (who suffers as a Jew by being an outcast in some senses), and in the German farm woman. Renoir personalizes the sadness of war in a film with no real villains except for the great villain of war itself.

LUIS BUÑUEL

(1900–1983)
(Spanish/French)

Add an artistic life in Paris in the 1920s to a Jesuit education in Spain and you get the dark laughter of Buñuel; always ready to expose the absurdity of life. "A religious education and surrealism have marked me for life," he once said. Although he was Spanish, due to censorship most of his career was spent in France.

THE DISCREET CHARM OF THE BOURGEOISIE (THE MUSEUM OF MODERN ART/FILM STILLS ARCHIVE)

His early films were exercises in total surrealism, which meant giving up the linear pattern of normal films and attempting to let the unconscious speak through dreams, fragments of thought, images, and fantasies. Sigmund Freud, that great pioneer of psychoanalysis, was fascinated by Buñuel's early efforts. With Salvador Dalí, the master of surrealistic painting, Buñuel made *Un Chien Andalou (An Andalusian Dog)*, which included a famous scene of a razor slicing an eyeball. His next film, *L'Age d'Or (The Golden Age)*, was widely acclaimed as a masterpiece. But by the 1930s, movie-

goers wanted escape, not artistic innovation, and Buñuel left directing until 1947. In 1950 he came out with *Los Olvidados* (*The Young and the Damned*), a masterpiece about slum life in Mexico. There he also made *Mexican Bus Ride*, about a bridegroom on a bus, then returned to Spain to make *Viridiana*, a 1961 masterpiece about a group of beggars who reenact the Last Supper in a house they take over. After this period, Buñuel switched his camera from the lower class to the middle and upper classes, satirizing the illusions and boredom of life among those who don't have to struggle to eat.

With Buñuel, the word that comes up frequently is juxtaposition—his films are a crazy quilt of images; he loves interruptions, clever asides, and weird images.

THE DISCREET CHARM OF THE BOURGEOISIE (1972)

Comment: This is a surrealistic comedy about a dinner that just can't get started.

Plot: Six friends want to eat together, but each time they're ready, something absurd thwarts them. The film begins with four of them arriving at the house of their friends the Sénechals, only to be told they've arrived a day early. So they go on to a local restaurant, only to find that the manager has just died (his body is in the next room). So they go on to plan another eating engagement, but each time they get close to food something else happens—ranging from the arrival of the cavalry, to a police raid, to an abortive affair (the husband arrives at an inopportune moment), to a visit at a cafe with no coffee, tea, alcohol, or anything else.

Meaning: All the interrupted meals

form the texture of the film and satirize the cacophony and false starts that plague modern life. But Buñuel doesn't stop there. First of all (as with so many European films), his film is very political: one of the six friends is the ambassador of the fictional South American dictatorship of Miranda, which to some degree represents Buñuel's native land of Spain under the totalitarian rule of General Franco. If you're a foreign film fan, you'll also find many plays on and jokes about other French films (as well as one on *The French Connection*). On another level, the film is about the pettiness of bourgeois life: the specter of death hangs over all the characters (ghosts hover in and around the abortive dinner attempts), yet the guests ignore death, blindly wrapped up in their chitchat, all the elegant accoutrements, and all the discreet power of bourgeois life.

SATYAJIT RAY

(1921–1992)
(Indian)

Ray was the world's premier humanistic director, inspired in part by the writings of the Indian Nobel novelist and poet Rabindranath Tagore. His films are famous for their naturalness, for revealing in small situations (a boy looking at a flower, a husband and wife arguing) great social and political forces.

Ray was a native of Bengal, the area in the northeast of India that includes Calcutta, the great cultural, political, and economic center. He was educated in a university there founded by

Tagore. As a boy, he loved film—he literally went to movie houses and took notes on what he saw. As a young man, he saw Vittorio De Sica's *The Bicycle Thief* while on a trip to London. He was fascinated with De Sica's use of nonprofessional actors, and vowed to do the same with his first film, *Pather Panchali,* the first of his famed Apu Trilogy. He began shooting it with friends on weekends. He was encouraged in his task by Jean Renoir, who was in India shooting *The River.*

Ray's films fall into three main periods: the first, which includes his masterpiece The Apu Trilogy, is realistic (in fact, in one film one hundred minutes of his characters' lives are matched with one hundred minutes of film); his next period, which began in the late

1960s, adds montage and is more complex—these films seem darker, as indeed the times were, with many Indians turning to Maoism, as the government became more openly corrupt. Ray surprised some Indian audiences with his open examination of Indian corruption, blaming it less on the legacy of British colonialism than on Indians themselves. His last period is more modern, with faster sequences, but as always, centering on personal human relations in a unique and humane vision.

THE APU TRILOGY (1955)

Pather Panchali (*Song of the Road* or *Lament of the Path*) (1955)

Aparajito (1957)

Apur Sansar (*The World of Apu*) (1959)

Comment: If you want to see a film about India, forget Richard Attenborough's *Gandhi* and see The Apu Trilogy. It's the story of the life of one man, born a poor Brahman (upper caste) in a Bengali village. A series of young actors play Apu, from birth until adulthood. It's all based on a two-volume novel by Bibhuti Bandapaddhay. The film's soundtrack is by famed Indian musician Ravi Shankar.

Plot: *Pather Panchali,* the first in the trilogy (and Ray's first film), looks at the life of a young boy, Apu (who is born early in the film), his mother, father, and sister, along with his old grandmother. In the next film, *Aparajito,* they have left the medieval village for the big city of Banaras; here Apu goes to school, then to the University of Calcutta. This film shows how India is both modern and corrupt—but also how people can rise above the degradation of industrial life. Finally, in *The World of Apu,* Apu gets married and has a son; but tragedy strikes when his wife dies in childbirth. Apu at first hates his young son, whom he sends to live with grandparents, but through a good friend, comes to realize the continuity and beauty of life, and is reunited with his son. The trilogy has now come full circle.

Meaning: In the film, Apu's mother, father, and wife die, yet Apu learns to love life and find himself. Apu comes to realize he is dominated by his desire for learning and love. The film stresses the continuity of life, and the power of love, and in such scenes as the reuniting of father and son, conveys the beauty of human relationships and love simply, without sentimentality.

JEAN-LUC GODARD

(1930–)
(Swiss/French)

Jean-Luc Godard is one of those directors you love—or hate; many filmgoers number themselves among the latter. Why the controversy? Because Godard is a genuinely revolutionary filmmaker in both technique and politics, one of the first so-called modernists. He's been linked with others of the French New Wave that came in the 1950s and 1960s, but unlike his compatriots François Truffaut and Claude Chabrol, he was more unorthodox. His films are often experimental: actors may talk directly to the camera, the film may change from positive to negative, pseudointerviews may be intercut with action, handheld cameras may be used along with jump cuts, often there's little continuity, and the soundtrack may turn off and on. Needless to say, this can be as much annoying as exhilarating. Yet Godard has had a profound impact on film, influencing such directors as Roman Polanski, Bertolucci, and more recently, Gus Van Sant.

His film career can be divided into three parts. The first began with his breathtaking *Breathless,* which took the film world by storm (more below); it ended with *Weekend,* about a married couple who decide to murder the wife's parents for inheritance money. During the next phase, which took place during the revolutionary 1960s, he made smaller films for a specific audience of Marxists and leftist students; these were done to stimulate discussion of revolutionary art and politics. Godard evidently thought the revolutionary fervor of the 1960s would continue; with its collapse he returned to making more mainstream films, although he still tries to keep his leftist views and ideals. *Hail, Mary* takes an unconventional look at Christianity (the angel Gabriel flies in on an airplane).

BREATHLESS (A BOUT DE SOUFFLE) (1959)

Comment: This New Wave film influenced such American films as *Bonnie and Clyde, Chinatown,* and *Drugstore Cowboy.* It was Godard's first feature film, and it was lead actor Jean Paul Belmondo's first major role. It made director and actor stars, and in many ways was one of the most influential

BREATHLESS (THE MUSEUM OF MODERN ART/FILM STILLS ARCHIVES

and modern films in recent history. François Truffaut cowrote the screenplay.

Plot: An unconventional take on a love story between a carefree French hoodlum, Michel, (played by Jean-Paul Belmondo) and an American, Patricia (played by Jean Seberg). It is a play on American gangster films; Michel has stolen a car and on the way back to Paris kills a policeman on the highway. The film follows Michel's attempt to persuade Patricia to go to Italy with him, before the police close in. Patricia alternately enjoys—and is repelled by—Michel's dangerous lifestyle. At the end, she helps him hide, then tells the police his whereabouts. They shoot him in the streets.

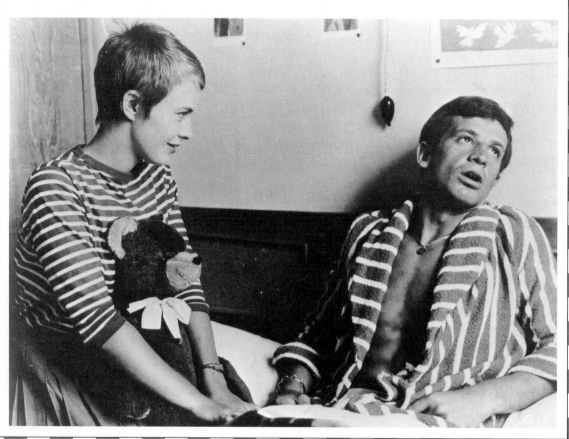

Meaning: This is one of the first films about films. Michel takes film archetypes like Humphrey Bogart to heart as defining elements of his life. It's a look at culture in ferment—the aimlessness and anomic nature of modern life—through a contrast of opposites (male/female, the French love/hate relationship with American culture), and through the hip, cynical characters.

FEDERICO FELLINI

(1920–1993)
(Italian)

Flamboyant and controversial, Fellini is famous for his semi-autobiographical films, yet his own life is mired in mist. Fellini had a habit of artistically reinventing his past.

What is known about the director's early life is that he ran away from a boarding school to a traveling circus. Although he was returned to his parents within several days, this incident made a deep impression on him, and led to his love for the entertainment professions. Fellini's big break came in 1945, when noted director Roberto Rossellini asked him to collaborate on a documentary he was making. It became the noted *Open City,* a classic of neorealistic drama. He went on to film *The White Sheik,* which bombed at the box office. Undeterred, he made the successful *The Young and the Passionate,* about his adolescent life. *La Strada* (see below) was an even greater success, and gave him an international reputation. *La Dolce Vita* was a masterpiece about the degradation of life in Rome's fast set. Some of his later films, like *Fellini Satyricon,* an imagistic quasi fantasy set in ancient Rome, were seen by many as overdone; he returned to autobiography and filmed one of his greatest films, *Amarcord,* about life in a small town in prewar Italy, examining how Italy turned to fascism.

LA STRADA (THE STREET) (1954)

Comment: Considered by many critics Fellini's greatest movie, this is what film critics call neorealism with a difference. It looks at life unflinchingly and realistically, but has an unusual, even macabre, heart.

Plot: Zampano (played by Anthony Quinn) is an aging, brutal man who has a strongman act—he travels around on a motorcycle with trailer, and performs feats of strength. He has bought a female helper-sexual concubine from a poor family. When she leaves, he goes back for a replacement and finds only the half-witted Gelsomina (played by Fellini's wife, Giulietta Masina). She is frightened, but soon cheerfully and submissively performs her duties—so much so that she in effect becomes the star of Zampano's act. They soon join a circus, but Zampano clashes with the clowns and is jailed. Upset, Gelsomina confides in a circus fool, a sympathetic man who realizes that Gelsomina actually wants to stay with Zampano. He realizes that her destiny may be intertwined with his. Unfortunately, when Zampano is released from jail, he jealously clashes with the fool, and although meaning only to beat him up, kills him. Gelsomina mourns by whimpering constantly, further enraging Zampano, who decides to abandon her. She is heartbro-

LA STRADA
(THE MUSEUM OF
MODERN
ART/FILM STILLS
ARCHIVE)

ken and soon dies from grief. Zampano continues with his act, but five years later, when he learns that Gelsomina has died, he is oddly distraught, finally sobbing his guts out at the beach. Through Gelsomina he has obtained humanity—and now he has lost her.

Meaning: *La Strada* means "the road" in Italian, and indeed, this film is a spiritual road trip about a brutal, uncaring man's journey to humanity and feeling. It's an odd and sordid love story, a look at what makes the human spirit. Although the film won the Grand Prize at Venice in 1954, it provoked controversy; the Italian government wanted to censor it for portraying undesirable and false aspects of Italian lower-class life to the world, and left-wing critics considered it a betrayal of neorealism. Fortunately, the Catholic press loved it, and a prominent Genoese, Cardinal Siri, saved the film for the world.

INGMAR BERGMAN

(1918–)
(Swedish)

A number of years back, Bergman was extraordinarily popular; today his star has fallen quite a bit with the critics and the public. Many feel that he is often too serious to the point of pomposity, dullness, or pretension. Yet Bergman at his best is great indeed: his best films, including the comedy *Smiles of a Summer Night* and his dramas *Wild Strawberries* and *Fanny and Alexander* (a magical film about two

WILD STRAWBERRIES (THE MUSEUM OF MODERN ART/FILM STILLS ARCHIVE)

years of a wealthy family, centering on the children of one of the sons) are destined to remain classics of world film. His major themes centered on the inner loneliness of individuals, particularly of women, and existential despair.

Bergman was the son of extremely strict evangelical parents; his father was a Lutheran pastor. He began working in university productions while still a student, and made his name in Sweden as theater director of the Goteborg City Theater before moving into film. Bergman achieved worldwide critical success with *The Seventh Seal*, which examines existential despair in the horror of life during plague-ridden

medieval Sweden. He continued these themes with a series of films set in modern times, including *Through a Glass Darkly, Winter Light,* and *The Silence. Scenes From a Marriage* was a six-part series that took apart married middle-class life.

WILD STRAWBERRIES (SMULTRONSTÄLLET) (1957)

Comment: This is the story of an old man who finally wakes up to life. Through flashbacks and dream sequences we see the meaning and substance of the old man's life; through the action and dialogue in the present sequences we watch the development of meaning in the man's life.

Plot: Professor Isak Borg is a seventy-six-year-old doctor (of what we don't know) on his way from his retirement home to the university in Lund to be honored on an anniversary. Sharing the ride is his daughter-in-law, who lets him realize that she considers him a cold, selfish old man. This is compounded by the dream Borg had the previous night, where he saw his lonely, friendless funeral. On the road, Borg picks up some hitchhikers: a quarreling couple and later three young hikers; ultimately it is through one of them, Sara, that Borg remembers his past love for another, which brings him back to the happiness and honesty of his youth.

Meaning: The title *Wild Strawberries* symbolizes the youthful days of Borg's life. The film is a trip to the past, through time and through the unconscious, a road trip through time that brings Borg to the true destination he's been seeking. Okay, maybe it's a bit pretentious, even obvious, but like many of Bergman's better films, it makes a good point.

FRANÇOIS TRUFFAUT

(1932–1984)
(French)

Truffaut began his career in film as a trend-setting critic who broke with the past. Writing in the influential film magazine *Cahiers du Cinéma,* he sought to define the "true men of the cinema," that is, those who rejected the excessive literary and traditional modes of the past and were freer and more spontaneous. (Included among Truffaut's true men were the Americans John Ford and Orson Welles as well as Jean Renoir.) Truffaut put his ideas into practice with *The Four Hundred Blows,* his first feature film, which he made at twenty-seven (more below), about a rebellious youth named Antoine Doinel. Truffaut followed Doinel in five films. Among them: *Love at Twenty,* in which Doinel clumsily explores sex. In the next, Doinel is lured by sexual adventure. In *Love on the Run,* Doinel writes a novel, which makes his reputation, and the novel turns out to be the record of his life as filmed by Truffaut. This blurring of fact and fiction fascinated Truffaut and is an ingredient in many of his films, as is the role of education and learning in an individual's life. Two of his best films exemplify this love: *Jules and Jim* is about two intellectuals in 1912 France arguing about literature and finding their feminine ideal; *The Wild Child* is a masterful work about the attempts of a scientist in 1798 to teach an inarticulate child, who had been abandoned as a baby in the woods years before, how to speak.

THE FOUR HUNDRED BLOWS (LES QUATRE CENT COUPS) (1959)

Comment: Truffaut's first major work, this is an unsentimental look at the problems of adolescence and adolescent rebellion—with a warm touch.

Plot: The story of a twelve-year-old schoolboy, Antoine Doinel, who lives with selfish quarrelsome parents in a poor section of Paris, and has a petty and cruel schoolteacher. He and a friend decide to skip school; later he hides out at his friend's home. They

THE FOUR HUNDRED BLOWS (THE MUSEUM OF MODERN ART / FILM STILLS ARCHIVE)

steal a typewriter, and on trying to return it, Antoine is caught and sent to a reform camp; he eventually escapes and makes his way to the sea.

Meaning: This is at least a partially autobiographical film by a then twenty-seven-year-old director. It is based on Truffaut's experiences as a child and in a reform school. It shows both the problems of adolescence and the often hypocritical world they are preparing to inhabit as adults, along with the constant human striving for freedom.

BEYOND HOLLYWOOD:
THE TWELVE MAJOR FILM-PRODUCING NATIONS

 With all of the money pouring into Hollywood, you'd think it would be the largest film producer in the world. It is, in terms of cash—but it's far from number one in terms of the actual number of films made each year.

Each year Hollywood's influence grows, and as we said before, many foreign filmmakers have a love/hate relationship with this huge center of American filmmaking. On the one hand, they may take at least some inspiration from some American images and they enjoy what we produce; on the other hand, they resent the impact of U.S. films in their native countries. Hollywood has the money to lavishly produce films which, when exported abroad, often outdraw indigenous films and other forms of the performing arts. One anthropologist in Indonesia, in love with their traditional shadow plays, was dismayed to find this art form was decaying in favor of U.S. B movies. So, quite logically, many foreign filmmakers and critics worry that Hollywood will eventually destroy their film industries and art forms and take away some vital part of their national culture.

Some countries resort to protectionism or quotas. France, for example, puts a tax on U.S. film imports and spends the money it earns on the French film industry. In 1988, South Koreans demonstrated against and boycotted U.S. films. But maybe all this worry is just temporary. For example, U.S. soap operas were the rage on

Brazilian TV until some savvy Brazilian producer put on Brazilian soaps with the same glitzy production values. Brazilians turned to the local soaps in droves: it was a lot more fun imagining the life of the rich and famous in nearby São Paulo than in far away and incomprehensible California.

Local film industries are thriving in many areas of the world. India is the world's single largest film producer (see page 424); the rest of the Asian film market combined is as large as India's and very dynamic.

As in the United States, much of the success comes from appealing to the lowest common denominator—sex and violence. In terms of popular culture, many Asian film industries began by copying common Western themes (when the softcore porn film *Emmanuelle* came out, Asian producers got into the act with *Tokyo Emmanuelle, Hong Kong Emmanuelle, Black Emmanuelle,* and *Yellow Emmannuel.* In terms of more artistic or innovative films, Asia now seems poised to become the center of great filmmaking, much like Europe was in the postwar years.

But first, back to the lowest common denominators: sex and violence. Most Asian comedy is slapstick and very popular. Indian and Philippine audiences prefer boy-meets-girl melodramas. Asia's contribution to world B movies was the kung-fu movie. The first known kung-fu movie was a silent film produced in 1920 in prerevolutionary China, *Thief in the Car.* The first talking kung-fu movie was also made in China, in 1935, but the genre really came into vogue in the early 1970s, and involved filmmakers in Hong Kong, and later Japan, Korea, Thailand, Indonesia, Taiwan, the Philippines, and the United States.

In Asia, as in the United States, great entertainment conglomerates are gobbling up smaller independent film companies. In Japan, the names to watch are Toho, Shochiku, Toei, and Nikkatsu.

Japan, like France and Italy, has a long history of great filmmaking. Besides Kurosawa, great Japanese directors include Yasujiro Ozu, who makes deceptively simple stories of ordinary life; Juzo Itami, a deflator of middle-class life, a gentle satirist on the order of Preston Sturges; and Hiroaki Yoshida, the master of "Japanimation," or the overlay of cartoons onto live-action sequences.

Recently, China's "Fifth Generation" of filmmakers, the first generation to graduate from the Peking Film Academy since the Cultural Revolution, have been making waves with

Top Film-Producing Nations— Average Number of Films Produced Annually

1. India 667
2. Japan 340
3. France 191
4. United States 190
5. Taiwan 190
6. Turkey 166
7. Philippines 156
8. Russia 148
9. Italy 139
10. Thailand 126
11. Hong Kong 124
12. Spain 96

such films as *The Horse Thief* and *Peking Opera Blues*. Hong Kong has become a critically acclaimed hotbed of action-comedy movies by directors such as Tsui Hark and John Woo (who has now come to Hollywood), termed by many critics as the best popular films today. For those interested in film, the words for many are: "Go east."

A FEW GREAT FILMS OUTSIDE THE U.S./WESTERN EUROPEAN/ JAPANESE AXIS AND ONE GREAT FILM PIONEER

The great directors and films we mentioned above are far from a definitive or inclusive list, but you probably noticed the predominance of Western directors. This is because the U.S., European, Japanese, and Indian filmmakers have had the time and the money and the paying public, so their films receive the most attention. But a host of innovative and interesting filmmakers from areas outside the mainstream of the dominant film culture are directing films destined to become world classics. Here's a brief look at some films modern critics find the most compelling.

YEELEN (BRIGHTNESS)

(1987)

DIRECTOR:
SOULEYMANE CISSE
(Mali, Africa)

Set in Mali before colonialism (and before Morocco invaded in the 1700s) this is the tale of a young man of the Bambara culture seeking *komo*, the mysteries of nature and the gods, against the wishes of his evil father. In the course of his heroic journey to knowledge, the young man learns the ancient rites and eventually fights against his father's magic. This is considered by critics one of the finest African movies and by any account a great film.

YAABA

(1989)

DIRECTOR:
IDRISSA OUEDRAOGO
(Burkina Faso, Africa)

This is a gentle film about the coming of age of a boy, Bila, and his relationship with his young female cousin Nopoko and an aged woman, Yaaba, whom villagers have cast out as a witch. It's set in a village in the outskirts of Ouagadougou, and we watch as Yaaba imparts some of her elemental wisdom to the young boy.

THE TRAVELING PLAYERS

(1975)

DIRECTOR:
THEO ANGELOPOULOS
(Greece)

According to some critics, Angelopoulos is the world's greatest unknown director, and this is one of his best. It's a look at Greek political history from 1939–52—the beginning of World War II, the Greek Civil War, and the period shortly after—accomplished

A New Film Hot Spot

 An up-and-comer in the world of international film—Latin America. Countries leading the pack in film production—Argentina and Mexico. While countries like Brazil, Colombia, and Venezuela are still primarily producing soap operas, Argentina and Mexico are turning out noteworthy films; Chile, with a young but promising film industry, appears to be on the verge of breaking out. In all, it looks like Latin American films are following in the tracks of Latin American literature, which caught on with an international audience beginning about 1967 with the publication of Gabriel García Márquez's *One Hundred Years of Solitude*. Films such as *Like Water for Chocolate* (*Como agua para chocolate*) and *A Place in the World* (*Un lugar en el mundo*) were box office successes outside of Latin America. Other films have won a great deal of attention. Two Argentine films were finalists for the 1992 foreign-language Oscar. A Mexican film, *Principio y Fin* (*Beginning and End*), directed by Arturo Ripstein, once a student of Luis Buñuel, was the winner in Spain's 1993 San Sebastian festival, where the audience prize went to an Argentine film. Other directors to keep an eye out for: Argentina's Marcelo Pineyro and Alberto Lecchi, Mexico's Guillermo del Toro and Paul Leduc.

through looking at a group of itinerant actors who spend years wandering throughout Greece performing a Greek folk tale, *Golfo the Shepherdess*. Past and present merge until the film ends at the beginning in 1939.

RED SORGHUM

(1988)

DIRECTOR: ZHANG YIMOU

(China)

Set in China in the 1920s and 1930s, this is, in the opening words of the film, "... a story about my grandma and grandpa—with, maybe, a little stretching of facts." Gong Li is a young bride-to-be who is abducted by a bandit, Jiang Wen. The tale as a whole is an unconventional epic about Chinese winemakers who fight the Japanese.

OUSMANE SEMBENE

(1923–)
(Senegal)

Another great director—Sembene, from Senegal—is one of Africa's premier pioneering filmmakers. He was the first to use African languages in his films instead of colonial English or French. He started as a writer, but sought a larger audience than his books could obtain, so he began filming his short stories or novels. His films are generally about the difficulties of life for common people in contemporary Africa and celebrate the heroics of their struggle for existence and dignity; his actors are often nonprofessionals.

HOLLYWOOD ON THE GANGES:
INDIA, THE WORLD'S LARGEST FILM INDUSTRY

 India, to some degree, is immune to all the international fears of Hollywood. It possesses a thriving film industry that produces almost seven hundred films yearly (about four times Hollywood's output), which are avidly watched by its huge audience. More than thirteen million tickets are sold daily, filling the thirteen thousand theaters. It is estimated that only about 7 percent of screen time in India is spent on foreign

POSTER OF
JUNOON,
DIRECTED BY
SHYAM BENEGAL
(NATIONAL FILM
ARCHIVE,
LONDON)

films, including Hollywood blockbusters.

One reason India has been able to withstand a cultural onslaught from Hollywood and elsewhere is the receptiveness of the industry to its audience. Indians are a diverse group—there are over sixteen different official languages, and films are made in every one, along with a host of less widespread languages. Another reason is less appealing—many Indian films are

ACADEMY CINEMA ONE
OXFORD STREET · 437 2981

presents

SHASHI KAPOOR
JENNIFER KENDAL
SHABANA AZMI
NAFISA ALI

in

A stirring romantic drama, set in the days of the Indian Mutiny

JUNOON
(A A)

URDU DIALOGUE · ENGLISH SUB-TITLES

Directed by
SHYAM BENEGAL

the equivalent of U.S. television or Hollywood, designed specifically to appeal to the lowest common denominator. The theme preferred in India is rich boy meets poor girl, usually a melodrama often with music. Even India's great directors like Satyajit Ray occasionally resort to films of this type to keep the money coming in for more artistic features.

Because of the large number of different languages spoken, there are really several film industries in India. The Hindi films, produced in the language of the north and of government, are distributed nationwide. One of the best Hindi directors is Ketan Mehta, who has innovatively combined traditional folk-art forms into some of his films; in others, he brilliantly satirizes contemporary Indian commercial films. He also isn't afraid to tackle controversial topics, as he did in *Bhavni*, about India's untouchables (people outside the caste system, the lowest of the low in the Indian social structure).

Non-Hindi films are usually produced and confined to their specific regions. In terms of impact, the Tamil films of Southern India achieve the next highest viewing. Satyajit Ray's films, which were mostly produced in Calcutta in the Bengali language, were mostly seen in Bengal and in foreign film festivals, although they are sometimes seen at odd hours like Sunday morning in Hindi areas. Interestingly, Ray's foray into Hindi language films outraged some Hindi audiences; they were so bored that in some areas they smashed theater furniture.

A final trivia note: the most watched

Yes, India tops Hollywood as the world's largest film producer, and, as you'd expect, Indian films beat out American offerings in Indian movie theaters. But when it comes to television, U.S. shows are extremely popular. Among the highest rated shows are the soap opera THE BOLD AND THE BEAUTIFUL, M*A*S*H reruns, and World Wrestling Federation matches— which are also a huge hit in Nigeria.

Small Country, Big Films

The so-called capital of black African filmmaking isn't a large city, but a small landlocked rural country in West Africa, Burkina Faso. Although it's one of the world's poorest countries, it has a national film organization, a film school, a private studio complex, and hosts a biennial African film festival. Most of the films that come out of here are dubbed "crime doesn't pay" films: they're usually set in small villages and tell the story of a person who falls into crime and then into trouble because of it. One leading director from Burkina Faso is Idrissa Ouedraogo, whose 1993 film *Samba Traore* (about a gas station robber who gets caught in the end) won a prestigious Silver Bear award in the 1993 Berlin Festival.

film in history until recently was not *Gone With the Wind*, or *Batman*, but *Mother India*. This Indian film, in continuous showing since its release in 1957, was probably seen by the most number of paying patrons. However, since the advent and increased popularity of the VCR, some U.S. films, such as *Star Wars*, are probably winners if home viewing is included . . . at least for now. But Indians have many VCRs and many new films, so the race is not yet over.

CONTENTS

MUSIC OF THE WORLD

Music rises from the human heart. When the emotions are touched, they are expressed in sounds, and when the sounds take definite forms, we have music.

 Confucius said these words thousands of years ago—and they still hold. Music is the wordless expression of the human heart and soul. It's a form of communication that speaks to levels deep inside us, touching our unconscious as well as our conscious.

It's this ability that makes music, in many ways, the language of the world. Needing no words, it needs no translation, and so crosses cultural boundaries with great ease. It crosses the boundaries of time as well—the music of yesterday is often as meaningful as that of today.

When you listen to an American rock song, chances are you're hearing a condensed history of music. Modern rock has its origins in England, which in turn borrowed from American blacks, who in turn built upon the music of their ancestors from Africa. And sometimes you'll also hear allusions to the classical past as well.

The following section looks at music from the West and the East, and the past and present. It runs through the top composers of the Western tradition and the top popular music of the rest of the world.

It's a quick examination of a cultural ambassador that knows no country or time—the melodic language of the human race.

I'LL TAKE THE FIFTH: TEN TOP WESTERN CLASSICAL COMPOSERS FROM BEETHOVEN TO BRAHMS AND BACH AGAIN

Popular music, by definition, keeps changing. What is hot today sounds hopelessly outdated tomorrow. As for traditional music, its popularity is often usurped by popular music, which, of course, well . . . keeps changing. But classical music persists—even as punk gives way to new wave, which gives way to grunge, which gives way to rave, and so on.

The problem is, unless you're a real classical fan, the composers tend to blur a little. You may know their names, but you're not quite sure what they wrote. Or you know some of the most important pieces someone wrote . . . you think.

Here, then, is a quick look at the classical composers the well-educated person needs to know—or at least be familiar with—and their most important works.

JOHANN SEBASTIAN BACH (REPRODUCED FROM THE COLLECTIONS OF THE LIBRARY OF CONGRESS)

JOHANN SEBASTIAN BACH

(1685–1750)
(German)

In his time, Bach was considered a mere organist—or perhaps not a *mere* organist, since he was the court organist at Weimar, court conductor for the prince of Anhalt-Cöthen, and finally, had a twenty-seven-year stint as cantor at the Thomasschule in Leipzig. But no one really thought of him as a composer, even though he wrote such things as six concertos for the margrave of Brandenburg (now aptly known as the *Brandenburg* Concertos), thirty "Goldberg" Variations for the prince of Anhalt-Cöthen, not to mention two hundred church cantatas. Yet it took a hundred years for Bach to be recognized as a composer—when Mendelssohn found the score of the *St. Matthew Passion* and performed it.

So for most of his adult life, Bach toiled at his day job—teaching fifty-four boys Latin and singing, composing the music for four different churches, playing the instruments at the church services, all under the unimpressed eye of the rector at Thomasschule, who didn't like Bach's music or his inability to discipline his students. (In fact, to make it more difficult for the rector to fire him, Bach got himself a sponsor in the person of the elector of Saxony and became his court composer.) Yet, in spite of the long hours and the indignities—which included living with his family in a none-too-comfortable dormitory—Bach managed to continue composing.

Now, of course, he's considered one of the greatest Western composers of all time. His music straddles the old and the new—falling between the Renaissance and the baroque period, and bearing aspects of each. Instead of following the contemporary operatic style of music, he revived and developed the hundred-year-old polyphonic style. His compositions are known for their complexity and depth. And given his post as a church organist and cantor, most of his works are deeply religious in spirit and often largely designed for church services. As some experts have said, Bach's music was composed for the glory of God—and listening to his music, from the grandiose Passions to the more simple preludes, this transcendental belief comes through.

Hit parade: the six *Brandenburg* Concertos; *The Well-Tempered Clavier*; *St. Matthew Passion*; the Mass in B Minor; *The Art of the Fugue*.

Bach didn't make big bucks off the sale of copies of his work. In fact, virtually no classical composer did. Until the nineteenth century, they got paid once for the publication of their work, then anyone could pirate it once it was published. An example of how little the value of an original score was: Bach's St. Matthew Passion was discovered when it was bought as wrapping paper in the estate sale of a dead cheesemonger.

GEORGE FRIDERIC HANDEL

(1685–1759)
(German-English)

Bach's contemporary, Handel, was many things Bach wasn't—extroverted, cosmopolitan, unmarried . . . and successful (or at least much of the time). He's the *other* major baroque composer, and the one who possibly best represents the end of the age.

Handel had his first taste of success as an operatic composer. He had studied with Italian opera composers, had some success in Italy as a composer and, while court composer to the elector of Hanover, took leaves of absence to try his hand at Italianate opera in London. But this led to a bit of trouble. Apparently, he was having such a fine time at the English court that he didn't return to Hanover as often as he should have, much to the displeasure of the elector. Then the elector became King George I of England—which made matters a bit sticky for a composer who was trying to make his mark with London society. So Handel composed the *Water Music* as a peace offering, which, apparently, worked.

Unfortunately, though, Handel's career ran aground anyway. The Italianate opera he was writing and producing didn't exactly set the English audiences on fire. And Handel ran into other problems—difficulties with performers, with rival composers and companies, and, finally, a slide into bankruptcy. To pull himself out of financial trouble, he opted for a different strategy: English oratorio. Orato-

GEORGE FRIDERIC HANDEL (REPRODUCED FROM THE COLLECTIONS OF THE LIBRARY OF CONGRESS)

powers, and in so doing, the timeless aspirations of humankind.

Hit parade: *Water Music; Saul; Israel in Egypt; Messiah; Samson; Joseph and His Brethren; Semele; Judas Maccabaeus; Solomon; Jephtha.*

WOLFGANG AMADEUS MOZART

(1756–1791)
(Austrian)

It's tough not to have heard of Mozart. He is probably the most famous child prodigy in the arts in general, and definitely one of the geniuses of music. The subject of an Oscar-winning film, his life was perfectly suited for the screen—short, colorful, sometimes comical, but ending in tragedy.

Mozart started playing the piano at age four, composing for it at age five, playing the violin soon after, and touring internationally before age six. For many people, this would be the height of their career. But for Mozart, it was just the beginning. He was exposed to different forms of music from an early age, but Italian opera was the one that gripped him—and opera remained one of his main focuses, even as he composed concertos, symphonies, and quartets. As he grew older, he held different positions, including two stints as court organist to the less-than-musical archbishop of Salzburg, but couldn't quite settle down. He finally moved to Vienna, where he reached the height of his reputation, the height of his domestic happiness—and the depths of his financial and physical existence. Here

rio, a large musical composition for soloists, chorus, and orchestra that tells a story, was cheaper and easier to produce because it didn't require scenery, costumes, or actors—and it caught on.

Perhaps one of the reasons his music captured his audiences is that it captures the spirit of England at the time. Powerful, confident, rousing, Handel's work—perhaps most notably epitomized by the "Hallelujah" Chorus from the *Messiah*—sums up the energy of a country nearing the height of its he married, had children, and continued composing music. Of his six children, only two survived; he was having trouble finding work and managed (barely) to feed his family through teaching; he grew worried about his health. He died soon after and a pauper's grave was the culmination of a short, full life marked by poverty and illness—and the production of some of the most beautiful music in the world.

For all his troubles and concerns, Mozart's music remains untouched by them. As he said in a letter to his father, ". . . music, even in the most terrible situations, must never offend the ear, but must please the hearer, or in other words, must never cease to be music." And this shows. His work is marked by a lyrical enthusiasm, a lightness. He is known for his impeccable phrasing, his rich harmonies, and his graceful melodies. Of course, there's always that famous criticism of Mozart's work: too many notes. But, as many people might counter, what wonderful notes they are.

Hit parade: *The Marriage of Figaro; Don Giovanni; Così fan tutte;* String Quintet in C Major; String Quintet in G Minor; Symphony no. 35 (*Haffner*); Symphony no. 40; Symphony no. 41 (*Jupiter*); Clarinet Quintet in A Major.

WOLFGANG AMADEUS MOZART (REPRODUCED FROM THE COLLECTIONS OF THE LIBRARY OF CONGRESS)

LUDWIG VAN BEETHOVEN

(1770–1827)
(German)

It's easy to come up with a mental image of Beethoven—tormented, in a rage at the keyboard, intense . . . and frankly, the stereotype probably isn't that far off the mark.

Beethoven was a man who marched to his own drummer. Throughout his life, he was a staunch individualist—he wouldn't wear a wig; he refused to be confined by sponsorship of a prince—and his music celebrates individual freedom and the power of human dignity. His work comes right between the classical and romantic periods—and falls into both camps. Romantic by nature, with its crashing chords and emotional questing, and classic in its control, Beethoven's music is the voice of an age in flux and the harbinger of what would follow.

He started in music at an early age. His father, reportedly a hot-tempered man with a taste for alcohol, pushed Beethoven to become a second Mozart. Because of this (or, perhaps more likely, in spite of this), Beethoven did go on to perform at an early age, appearing as a keyboardist at age eight, and moving into a position as assistant harpsichordist of the electoral orches-

LUDWIG VAN BEETHOVEN (REPRODUCED FROM THE COLLECTIONS OF THE LIBRARY OF CONGRESS)

tra at age thirteen. But he really began moving ahead later, in Vienna—where he studied with composer Franz Josef Haydn, and composers Salieri and Albrechtsberger as well. He became well known for his piano improvisations, began composing more, and started performing his own works. By 1802, he had already composed two symphonies, three concertos, and sixteen works for string quartets.

In spite of the success, life wasn't easy for Beethoven. He had started going deaf and, while his music initially shows him fighting optimistically against his affliction, he grew more depressed over it. He became unable to perform and wound up in a number of soured love affairs. While he was always considered intense, "untamed" as some said, as he aged his dark side grew more apparent. He was described as often argumentative, and, in his later years, sloppy, unclean, prone to self-delusion. But his music . . . in this area, there was no decline. If anything,

The Sounds of Silence

The true extent of Beethoven's being able to compose while deaf is amazing. Supposedly, he could compose in his head for strings, "listen" to the results, then add in brasses, again without a score, and listen again to the results. He was a very active composer—he stamped and thumped around the room while composing. So proficient was he at imagining sound that apparently he took awhile to realize he was going deaf.

the music he produced in the later years of his life is his best.

Hit parade: Symphony no. 3 (*Eroica*); the opera *Fidelio*; Piano Sonata no. 29 in B-flat Major (*Hammerklavier*); Symphonies nos. 4, 5, 6, 7, and 8; the *Diabelli* Variations; Symphony no. 9 (*Choral*).

JOHANNES BRAHMS

(1833–1897)
(German)

An ardent perfectionist, Brahms seems never to have written a false note. This could be due to incredible skill, incredible luck, or a combination of the two. Or, of course, it could be because he destroyed anything that didn't meet his tough standards. . . .

All right, probably the latter is the case. And it fits. Brahms had high standards and an even higher level of self-discipline. Worried that the romantic composers would sap German music of its vitality and make it weak and syrupy, he quashed any tendency toward romanticism in his own music and instead used logic as the basis for his composing.

His life was as strictly disciplined as his output—no youthful high jinks like Mozart, no rages like Beethoven. Born into a poor family, he earned his living at an early age playing piano in inns. He toured as a performer, began composing, and eventually was taken under the wing of established composer Robert Schumann (see page 448). Brahms never married, but, in effect, adopted a family in Schumann's, taking care of them after

JOHANNES BRAHMS (REPRODUCED FROM THE COLLECTIONS OF THE LIBRARY OF CONGRESS)

Schumann's death. His work really started catching on when he spearheaded a movement against opera composer Richard Wagner and his "modern iconoclasm." As one of the chief voices defending classicism, Brahms became more famous and his music more popular. But even at the height of his popularity, he was calculated and cautious. He didn't write his first symphony until he was in his forties—and carried it around for a while without showing it to anyone.

As you'd expect given this sort of stance, Brahms's music is often complex. He wanted his work to consistently improve, so he constantly set up new heights to scale, new problems to overcome. In fact, some music critics say that you need as much discipline to truly appreciate Brahms's music as he needed to write it. Interestingly for a composer who is possibly best known for his "Lullaby," most of his work is moody and dark. But then possibly this is fitting for someone who set himself apart—a classic composer in a romantic era.

Hit parade: Hungarian Dances; *German Requiem; Variations on a Theme by Haydn; Academic Festival Overture.*

FRÉDÉRIC CHOPIN

(1810–1849)
(Polish)

The romantic of romantics, the poet of the piano, Chopin was and is known best for his smaller works, such as preludes, mazurkas and waltzes, small gems of lyricism and the musical equivalent of miniature paintings. Even his longer pieces are actually sustained versions of smaller ones. And most are written for the piano.

Which makes sense, since the piano was his instrument. In his time, he was the hottest salon pianist in Paris, playing for small gatherings, teaching select pupils, and composing the works that would win him lifelong fame. Paris was also where he met writer George Sand (through an intro-

FRÉDÉRIC CHOPIN (REPRODUCED FROM THE COLLECTIONS OF THE LIBRARY OF CONGRESS)

duction by composer Franz Liszt) and started his famous affair with her—making the two of them one of the popular couples of the time.

But, while Chopin himself was a social being, in the center of things, his music is much the opposite. His work is usually melancholy and soulful, even in his most enthusiastic works. Known for its harmonics and chords supporting a melodic theme that is expanded throughout a piece, this is music that expresses and explores the intimate emotions of both the composer and the listener.

Hit parade: the twenty-six Preludes; fifty-one Mazurkas; the Nocturnes; the Scherzos; the Concerto in F Minor; the "Revolutionary" Etude.

FRANZ LISZT

(1811–1886)
(Hungarian)

Liszt was a composer with a goal—to produce "humanistic music" that was both religious and dramatic. Pretty lofty stuff . . . and, in many ways, an unreachable ideal.

But Liszt did try. A child prodigy who began performing piano at age nine and touring shortly after, he was first known as a virtuoso pianist. And piano remained the central force of his life. He traveled through Europe, and later settled in Paris, where he became friendly with the literati and lived with the comtesse d'Agoult and had three children (one of whom, Cosima, later married composer Richard Wagner). After a split with the comtesse, he reached the height of his popularity as a performer, but decided to quit while he was ahead. He retired to Weimar, where he became court conductor, directed the opera and concerts, and composed. But producing music wasn't his only task in later years; he was also quite a humanist—a helpful, generous man, he was friend and supporter of young composers. And in

FRANZ LISZT
(REPRODUCED
FROM THE
COLLECTIONS OF
THE LIBRARY OF
CONGRESS)

1865, he fulfilled one nonmusical dream, when he received minor orders from the Church of Rome.

But music is clearly where he made his mark. As a composer, he was an innovator—the father of symphonic poems that are logically organized but nontraditional. They usually use a musical leitmotiv (literally, leading theme) as the foundation of the piece; this sets the melodic development, and the rhythmic and harmonic, as well. This was a breakthrough in composition, and one that set the stage for later developments into the twentieth century.

Hit parade: Piano Concertos nos. 1 and 2; *Les Préludes*; *Legend of St. Elizabeth*; Hungarian Rhapsodies; *Faust*; the Dante symphony; *the Mephisto Waltz.*

PYOTR ILICH TCHAIKOVSKY

(1840–1893)
(Russian)

Tchaikovsky didn't have the happiest of lives: he apparently had a depressive nature; his marriage was a disaster; in a state of nervous collapse, he left his wife after only one month; unable to stick it out at work, he resigned from the Moscow Conservatory and retired to the country where he could write. He separated himself from the other Russian composers of the time, taking exception to their fervent nationalism and their use of Russian folk music. Because of this, he was treated like a creative outlaw—a non-Russian Russian composer, if you will. And, finally,

Чайковскій.
Tschaikowsky.

while these aren't melancholy, they're still unabashedly expressive. Maybe this is why Tchaikovsky is such a crowd pleaser.

He's the most popular Russian composer, possibly second only to Beethoven in terms of popularity among all Western classical composers. Characterized by strong melodies, lavish orchestration, and gripping rhythms, his work has a broad appeal. Even when it's depressing, it has a, well, an "in-your-face" quality that a listener can't ignore.

Hit parade: his three ballets, *Swan Lake*, *The Sleeping Beauty*, *Nutcracker*; the Fourth and Fifth Symphonies, Sixth Symphony (*Pathétique*); *1812 Overture*; the opera *Eugene Onegin*.

CLAUDE DEBUSSY

(1862–1918)
(French)

The musical equivalent of the French Impressionist painters, Debussy was an original—painting pictures with music by using new techniques and smashing the old rules.

He started more traditionally—first getting attention when he won the Prix de Rome with his cantata *L'Enfant prodigue*. At this early point in his career, he took Wagner as his musical model. But he soon moved into the experimental, innovative work that made him famous. Whether in melody, rhythm, or structure, Debussy wasn't afraid to try completely different things. Groundbreaking, yes—but irritating to some. By using chords that weren't based on traditional harmonics or ones that weren't part of the key in

while tradition has it that he died of cholera, many believe that he actually committed suicide—convinced to do so by a so-called court of honor—because of his homosexual relationship with a young aristocrat.

So it's no wonder that the bulk of his work is melancholic, gloomy, and pessimistic. Of course, there are exceptions: his ballets and works like the *1812* Overture. However, even

PYOTR ILICH
TCHAIKOVSKY
(REPRODUCED
FROM THE
COLLECTIONS OF
THE LIBRARY OF
CONGRESS)

which the music was written, his music often sounds like there is no key at all.

For all of the musical iconoclasm and brash experimentation, Debussy himself was a shy, retiring man. He wasn't given to socializing, spent much of his time with literary people instead of fellow composers and musicians, and married twice. But it was his music that truly absorbed him. Until he died of cancer, he continued push-ing the bounds of modern music, often writing for flute and harp.

Others in his time tried to produce the same effects as Debussy, but none managed to pull it off. In fact, while he inspired others to experiment and paved the way for future innovative composers, when it comes to his specific type of music—musical impressionism—he was it. To put it bluntly, musical impressionism not only was born with Debussy but died with him, too.

Hit parade: *Suite Bergamasque* (including *Clair de lune*); *Prélude à l'Après-midi d'un faune*; *La Mer*; *Feux d'artifice*; *La Cathédrale engloutie*; *Pelléas et Mélisande*; *Nocturnes*; *Children's Corner*.

CLAUDE DEBUSSY (REPRODUCED FROM THE COLLECTIONS OF THE LIBRARY OF CONGRESS)

IGOR STRAVINSKY

(1882–1971)
(Russian)

Stravinsky knew how to make a splash. Already well known for his ballet scores for *The Firebird* and *Petrushka*, he *really* made his mark with the first performance of *Le Sacre du printemps* (*The Rite of Spring*). His ballet score was such a departure from "normal" music that critics and audiences alike went crazy—calling it anything from blasphemy to an attempt to ruin music.

Why the strong initial reaction? Stravinsky took traditional music and exploded it, using distortion, competing rhythms, polytonality, even dissonance and plain old cacophony. But it wasn't pure noise, as so many contemporary critics complained. *Le Sacre du printemps* also is extremely melodic, a complex and intricate work that used instruments in fresh, new ways.

So when all is said and done, Stravinsky won out. The hubbub eventually died down; his music (while still considered shocking by many) became more accepted; and Stravinsky continued writing, and usually receiving critical and public accolades. Even flexible, he tried his hand at different musical forms and styles, even switching to neoclassicism at one point. The one unifying theme to all his work: experimentation.

Hit parade: the ballets *L'Oiseau de feu (The Firebird)*, *Petrushka*, *Le Sacre du printemps (The Rite of Spring)*, *Le Chant du Rossignol (The Song of the Nightingale)*; *Orpheus*; the opera-oratorio *Oedipus Rex*; the choral *Symphony of Psalms*; *Symphonies of Wind Instruments*; *Requiem Canticles*.

IGOR STRAVINSKY (REPRODUCED FROM THE COLLECTIONS OF THE LIBRARY OF CONGRESS)

OTHER GREAT WESTERN COMPOSERS

 While the previously mentioned composers are, arguably, the greatest or the best known, there are other Western composers who deserve mention. Here, then, is a quick rundown of the *other* great Western composers whose works still capture the human spirit in music.

Who	Period	Famous For
LEONINUS (FRENCH, LATE 12TH CENT.). Considered one of the first important composers of the West (and, in fact, one of the first whose name is still known). Composed for the Cathedral of Notre-Dame in Paris while it was still being built.	Medieval	His "Gothic motets"—compositions for two voices or parts. Technically, this means not two voices only, but two melodies. The first voice, usually sung by a chorus, was the Gregorian chant (the simple chants that were the standard form of religious music). The chant acted sort of like a bass line, consisting of long, slow notes under the piece. The second voice, usually called an organal voice and sung by a solo singer, was a melody of notes that worked against the chant.
PEROTINUS (FRENCH, D. C. 1200). Not a well-known name nowadays, but one of the most influential musician-composers of his time. He was one of the first musicians to serve in the finished Notre-Dame Cathedral and became an innovator where religious music (the prevailing music of the time) was concerned.	Medieval	No names of his work exist, but he's known for the style he developed called *discantus* or *déchant*. In this two-voice style, both voices, the chant and the organal, move at the same pace, unlike the earlier styles. But the voices usually move in contrary motion, that is, one would rise in notes, the other descend. He's also known for composing motets for three or four parts, something that wasn't standard composing practice for two hundred or more years. Finally, he also developed a style called "conductus" that sometimes wasn't based on a Gregorian chant—and sometimes wasn't even religious.

Who	Period	Famous For
GUILLAUME DE MACHAUT (FRENCH, C. 1300–1377). A true Renaissance man, he was a musician, a poet, a priest, even a diplomat (in service to King John of Bohemia). Famed for his poetry, which he set to music, he was also known for his musical innovations, called *ars nova,* or new art.	Early Renaissance	While he wrote more nonreligious than religious works, he's especially noted for his *La messe de Nostre Dame.* This piece is technically known as the first completely integrated polyphonic four-part mass. In simpler English, this means that the piece uses four parts or voices, but is unified or integrated by using the same rhythms and melodies throughout all six sections of the mass.
FRANCESCO LANDINO (ITALIAN, D. 1397). One of the most prolific Italian composers of his time, he composed more than one third of the music in the period. Blind from childhood, he played virtually every instrument around. He was also known for his poetry and was a friend of famous poet Petrarch.	Early Renaissance	Chiefly wrote nonreligious music, unlike many others in his time. He's mainly known for three types of compositions: madrigals, *ballate* (dance songs), and *cacce* (light songs dealing with realistic subjects such as hunting or fishing).
ORLANDE DE LASSUS (FLEMISH, 1532–1594). Started as a choirboy and wound up being one of the leading High Renaissance composers. Traveled extensively, first as a choirboy, then as a choir director, and lived in a number of different European countries.	High Renaissance	A wide range of his work than for any particular composition. His work embodied the Renaissance ideal—that is, he combined different styles from different countries and wound up with something new, exciting, and universal (if, by the universe, we take the contemporary meaning of European in mind). Known for everything from Italian madrigals to German lieder.

Who	Period	Famous For
GIOVANNI PIERLUIGI DA PALESTRINA (ITALIAN, C. 1525–1594). Considered the top Renaissance composer. His life was full of ups and downs. His first big break came when he was appointed as master of the Julian choir at St. Peter's Basilica in Rome by Pope Julius III, who had been bishop of Palestrina, Palestrina's hometown, and had heard Palestrina's organ playing. The pope later got him into the pontifical choir, a group that usually required passing an entrance exam and being elected by members. But then came some bad years: the next pope, Pope Paul IV, was a stickler for rules and forced Palestrina to retire. Palestrina went through a number of other church-related musical jobs, and lost his wife and three sons to epidemics. He later married a wealthy widow and wound up successfully running her furrier business. But he kept composing and working at St. Peter's, and his work continued to be heard.	High Renaissance	One of the most influential Renaissance composers; influenced many later great composers including Bach, Mozart, Wagner, Liszt, and Debussy. Known for his exceptional a cappella (voices unaccompanied by instruments) church music—motets, madrigals, hymns, and other pieces. In fact, as far as it is known, he wrote no instrumental music at all. Key elements of his compositions? Texture, subtlety, and freedom.
CLAUDIO MONTEVERDI (ITALIAN, 1567–1643). Widely credited as one of the leading innovators of his time, a time when musical styles were changing. Because of this, he's often called the last madrigalist and the first opera composer, which isn't really true, but does capture his role in between musical styles. Composed both religious and secular music and was widely noted for both, but apparently wrote no purely instrumental music.	Baroque	Operas, especially *Orfeo,* his first and considered by many the first *modern* opera; and later operas, *Il Ritorno d'Ulisse in patria* and *L'Incoronazione di Poppea.* Also known for his church music, especially *Vespro della beata Virgina.* In terms of style, he's noted for his introduction of such things as innovative harmonies, the use of tremolo (when the bow is moved back and forth quickly on a string instrument, producing a vibrato tone) and pizzicato (when a string instrument is plucked instead of bowed).

Who	Period	Famous For
HENRY PURCELL (ENGLISH, 1659–1695). The son of a court musician; his short life revolved around music. He began as a young singer in the Chapel Royal, became keeper of the king's keyboard and wind instruments, composer for the king's violins, organist of Westminster Abbey and of the Chapel Royal. He also worked writing music for the duke of York's theater, and it was in this capacity that his reputation as a composer was established. Both his "official" compositions and his other works were admired by his contemporaries, earning him recognition as the finest English composer in his time—a status he still holds.	Baroque	His opera *Dido and Aeneas,* considered by many to be the finest opera in English musical history, as well as *Dioclesian, King Arthur, The Fairy Queen, The Tempest, The Indian Queen,* songs such as "Nymphs and Shepherds," harpsichord pieces, and a set of trio sonatas for violins.
ALESSANDRO SCARLATTI (ITALIAN, 1660–1725). Considered the father of the modern Italian opera. Had a successful career from the time he wrote his first opera at age nineteen. He won the patronage of Queen Cristina of Sweden, then became musical director at the court of Naples and conductor of the conservatory, and finally founded the Neapolitan school of opera. Throughout it all, he composed music—almost 120 operas, not to mention 500 chamber cantatas, about 200 masses, 14 oratorios, and more.	Baroque	Operas above all, although he also composed oratorios, masses, etc. His most famous opera is *Tigrone.* Noted for his melodies based on the form called da capo aria (a three-part structure in which the first section is repeated after a contrasting middle portion); also known for establishing the operatic overture.

Who	Period	Famous For
ANTONIO VIVALDI (ITALIAN, 1678–1741) The composer who was largely responsible for making the solo violin the dominant instrument in musical compositions—and thus setting the stage for the sound of a modern symphony orchestra. Called the Red Priest because of his flaming red hair, he became popular in about 1712 and was known for his violin concertos as well as religious music and operas. But his reputation faded quickly after his death, and his works weren't rediscovered and played again until about the nineteenth century when J. S. Bach's transcriptions of Vivaldi's violin concertos for the keyboard resurfaced and gained in popularity.	Baroque	Violin concertos, such as the twelve concertos of *L'Estro Armonico,* as well as the program music *The Four Seasons.*
JEAN-BAPTISTE LULLY (ITALIAN-FRENCH, 1632–1687). (Also known as Giovanni Battista Lulli). Soared to success because of the combination of his musical talents, ambition, and salesmanship. Born in Florence, but moved to Paris as a boy. There, through various machinations and lobbying efforts, he was made operatic director or superintendent of music by King Louis XIV.	Baroque	Chiefly operas, including *Thésée, Atys, Isis, Armide et Renaud,* and *Acis et Galathée.* Known for using ballet as an integral part of his operas and for developing the French lyric tragedy.

Who	Period	Famous For
CHRISTOPH W. GLUCK (GERMAN, 1714–1787). One of the leading German opera composers. While he was somewhat of a success in his early years, he really hit his stride after studying Handel's work. In Paris in the 1770s, he entered into a famous competition with fellow composer Niccolò Piccinni, Gluck representing the French style of opera, Piccinni, the Italian. The entire city was split into two camps, each supporting one of the two composers. Gluck finally won with his last opera, *Iphigénie en Tauride,* and retired.	Classic	Operas, including *Orfeo ed Euridice,* which is considered one of the finest modern music dramas and probably the best operatic adaptation of the famous myth about Orpheus; *Alceste; Paride ed Elena; Iphigénie en Aulide; Orphée* (a French adaptation of *Orfeo*); and his last opera, *Iphigénie en Tauride.*
FRANZ JOSEF HAYDN (AUSTRIAN, 1732–1809) The most famous composer of his day, he was born a peasant and earned his early living playing in street orchestras. But he moved up in life, and spent most of his adult years working as musical director in the court of two Princes Esterházy in Hungary. During this period, he composed a huge number of pieces and developed the four-movement string quartet and the classical symphony (which had the sonata or first movement as a basic structural element). Even though he rarely traveled, his music did—and his international reputation grew. He was pensioned at age sixty, and finally took his first real vacation to London, where he wrote two of his most famous oratorios (the *Creation* and the *Seasons*), then settled in Vienna.	Classic	His oratorios, such as *The Creation* and the *Seasons,* not to mention a vast amount of music, including 104 symphonies, 50 concertos, 84 string quartets, and much more.

Who	Period	Famous For
FRANZ SCHUBERT (AUSTRIAN, 1797–1828). One of the great masters of music, noted especially for his role as originator of the art of the lieder, or songs. The son of a schoolmaster, he entered into music at an early age, and began writing musical compositions in his early teens. He admired Beethoven, and apparently the feeling was mutual. When a friend showed Beethoven Schubert's work, Beethoven reportedly said, "Truly he has the divine spark." Schubert's life wasn't easy, though, for all his talent. He spent many years living poor, eking out a living by teaching. But through it all he wrote music, even through a bout of syphilis. And just before his death from typhus, he continued to compose, including possibly his best-known work, the Symphony no. 9 in C Major. A huge fan of Beethoven's, he was buried near his idol's grave.	Romantic	Numerous symphonies, especially his Symphony no. 9 in C Major (*The Great*) and Symphony no. 8 in B Minor (*Unfinished*). Also noted for his songs that render famous writer Goethe's poetry to music, including "Der Erlkönig," "Wandrers Nachtlied," and "Gretchen am Spinnrade." Goethe himself apparently didn't appreciate these: Schubert sent them to him, but Goethe just sent them back without any message. Other well-known works include the song cycles *Die Schöne Mullerin, Die Winterreise,* and *Schwanengesang,* published posthumously, two string quartets (in D Minor and G major), and more than six hundred songs, including "Hark, Hark the Lark!
FELIX MENDELSSOHN (GERMAN, 1809–1847). Burst onto the scene at an early age: he was performing piano at age nine. Soon after, he had become friends with such other notable creative types as writer Goethe and composer Carl Maria von Weber, composed his first symphony, and, by age sixteen, had completed his first opera. One reason for his early proficiency? He was born into a cultured, well-to-do family who encouraged his aspirations. In fact, his most famous piece, the overture to Shakespeare's *A Midsummer Night's Dream,* was first tried out during a concert given by his family.	Romantic, but inspired by classic	The *Midsummer Night's Dream* overture, as well as symphonies and chamber music. Sometimes criticized for lacking true passion and for being overrefined and sickly sweet.

Who	Period	Famous For
ROBERT SCHUMANN (GERMAN, 1810–1856). Considered the stereotypical romantic, both in his life and his music. A sentimental, dreamy youth who started out studying law, he switched over to music (specifically piano) after hearing Rossini's operas and famous violinist Paganini's concerts. But he threw himself so fervently into the piano that he hurt his right hand by using a finger-strengthening device. In the meantime he married virtuoso pianist Clara Wieck, the daughter of his piano teacher, and began composing music instead of performing. His wife popularized his work by performing it all over Europe. But throughout his life he was plagued by mental illness, which recurred as he became more successful. He tried to commit suicide by jumping into the Rhine River, was fished out, and died a few years later in a mental institution.	Romantic	Above all his compositions for piano, such as *Carnaval, Kinderscenen,* and the Piano Concerto in A minor. Most noted are his scenes from Goethe's *Faust,* Symphony no. 1 in B-flat Major (*Spring*), Symphony no. 3 in E-flat Major (*Rhenish*), as well as numerous chamber works and songs.
GIOACCHINO ROSSINI (ITALIAN, 1792–1868). Composer of some of the most popular Italian operas, especially *The Barber of Seville.* In fact, at the height of his popularity, he visited Vienna and the crowds forgot about such masters as Beethoven, Mozart, and Schubert and hailed him as their new musical hero. But he stopped most of his composing at age thirty-seven, at the pinnacle of success and thereafter only turned out a few pieces. Some thought this was due to laziness, but others believed it was because the composer felt that his public no longer wanted to hear his type of music.	Romantic	Romantic operas, especially *Il Barbiere di Siviglia* (*The Barber of Seville*), an immediate success that gripped the musical world. Also known for his *Otello, La Gazza ladra* (*The Thieving Magpie*), *Guillaume Tell* (*William Tell*).

Who

HECTOR BERLIOZ (FRENCH, 1803–1869). Considered one of the first great orchestral specialists among composers, Berlioz is known both for his works and for his textbook on instrumentation, which is still being used in musical conservatories today. His life was filled with ups and downs—while a student at the Paris Conservatory, he became engaged to actress Harriet Smithson. But while he was in Italy after winning the Prix de Rome, he learned she had married someone else. He bought poison and pistols and planned to return, but fell in love with the Italian countryside and stayed there for a few years. When he returned to Paris, Harriet was divorced, so he married her . . . and wasn't all that happy. (One of his most famous works, the *Symphonie fantastique,* expresses both his love for and disillusionment with his wife.) Life on the professional side wasn't smooth either: His reputation soared in Russia, England, and Germany, but his major works weren't played in France. This lack of recognition in France darkened his later years, as did the deaths of his second wife and son, and a prolonged bout of ill health. Through it all, however, Berlioz continued to compose.

Period

Romantic realism

Famous For

A number of huge works, including the *Symphonie fantastique,* as well as *Roméo et Juliette,* a dramatic symphony for solo voices and chorus, the cantata *La Damnation de Faust,* and the comic opera *Béatrice et Bénédict.*

Who	Period	Famous For
GIUSEPPE VERDI (ITALIAN, 1813–1901). The musical genius whose work still dominates Italian opera. The son of an innkeeper and grocery store owner, he was largely subsidized in his music studies by local people who believed in his talent. They were right to believe in him: he wrote music throughout his life, and once he had made his mark with his second opera, *Nabucco,* in 1842, he was successful for the rest of his life. A key reason for his success and enduring popularity: his work is marked by drama, emotion, and, most important, strong characters whose motives, actions, and passions are developed through the music, not through the story line.	Romantic realism	Numerous operas, including *Rigoletto, La Traviata, Il Trovatore, Otello,* and *Falstaff.* His most famous nonopera was the requiem mass called, simply, *Requiem Mass.*
GEORGES BIZET (FRENCH, 1838–1875). Since Bizet died when he was only thirty-six, he didn't get much of a chance to make his mark. But in his short life, he was able to produce two pieces of music that are considered masterpieces, the opera *Carmen* and the incidental music he composed for a play called *L'Arlésienne* (*The Woman of Arles*).	Romantic realism	*Carmen*—an opera that is now considered a masterpiece, even the finest French opera ever written. But when it premiered in 1875, it wasn't that well received, chiefly because of some of its innovations: it included spoken words, was set in a "foreign" locale (Spain), and revolved around a less-than-genteel protagonist (a gypsy who works in a cigarette factory . . . and actually smokes!).

Who	*Period*	*Famous For*
RICHARD WAGNER (GERMAN, 1813–1883). While he considered himself the greatest composer, poet, and philosopher who ever lived, Wagner's contemporaries often didn't agree. So Wagner went through a number of ups and downs in his professional life. A number of his musical efforts flopped, he did a stint in debtors' prison, he was often vilified by critics and ostracized for his political viewpoints. But there were those who believed in his talent: Franz Liszt, who aided him financially and performed his *Lohengrin* in 1850; the King of Bavaria, who gave him financial backing for a theater in Bayreuth; and for a time philosopher Nietzsche, who initially saw Wagner as the embodiment of his Superman but then later considered him the incarnation of decadence. To this day, his work (not to mention his life and his philosophy) is alternately praised and reviled. But most recognize his contribution to opera. He restructured opera, dropping the usual recitative and aria, using instead a changing dramatic line accented with heavy use of different leitmotivs.	Romantic realism	Operas in particular, including the *Ring* cycle, *Lohengrin, Tristan and Isolde,* and *Parsifal.*

Who	Period	Famous For
MODEST PETROVICH MUSSORGSKY (RUSSIAN, 1839–1881). A truly Russian composer, Mussorgsky used the Russian language and traditions as his chief guiding forces. He felt that the Russian language was naturally melodic, so his operas evolved from traditional Russian sources. More specifically, his arias were based on the style of Russian folk songs; his recitatives, on Russian church chants. The result? Operas that were completely Russian in inspiration, subject, and sound.	Realist	*Boris Godunov,* which is often called the best Eastern European opera. When first produced, though, it wasn't all that well received. The problems? The depressing story (revolving around a czar who has killed the real heir to the throne, suffers from intense guilt, and eventually dies from fear and remorse) and the dissonance in the music. His other most notable piece: *Pictures at an Exhibition.*
ARNOLD SCHOENBERG (AUSTRIAN, 1874–1951). A music innovator who developed a new technique, the "serial" technique, also known as the "twelve-tone row." Briefly, in the old tonal system certain notes are more important: they're the stable tones of the scale. In the twelve-tone row, all tones are equally important. The composer sets up a sequence of these twelve tones, and while he can use it melodically or harmonically, invert it or use it backward, he can't change the sequence. He can't repeat any of the tones until he's used the other eleven in the sequence, and so on. It sounds complicated (and it is), but it was an innovation that revolutionized orchestral music. Schoenberg was inspired by the Expressionist artists who were his friends (in fact, he, too, painted with them). When the Nazis came to power in Germany, he formally rejoined the Jewish faith and came to the United States, where he continued composing and teaching.	Expressionism	His innovation more than any specific pieces. In fact, he never really connected with a popular audience until years after his death. This said, his best-known pieces are the unfinished *Moses und Aron,* the Violin Concerto, String Quartet no. 4, the Piano Concerto, *Ode to Napoleon, A Survivor from Warsaw, Verklärte Nacht* for string sextet.

Who	Period	Famous For
BÉLA BARTÓK (HUNGARIAN, 1881–1945). Inspired by the folk music of Hungary, Yugoslavia, and Romania, Bartók was big on ethno-musicological research and traveled from village to village collecting more than five thousand folk tunes, which he subsequently published. But he didn't use them in his own work. Instead, he took many of their elements—melodies, rhythms, and the arrangement of voices—and used them as the basis for his own unique creations.	Modern	A range of work: two violin and three piano concertos, the opera *Duke Bluebeard's Castle,* the ballets *The Wooden Prince* and *The Miraculous Mandarin,* a range of chamber music including the *Music for Strings, Percussion and Celesta,* Sonata for two pianos and percussion, and others.
PAUL HINDEMITH (GERMAN, 1895–1963). Called the greatest modern German composer. He had an interesting life: he ran away from home at age eleven because of his parent's opposition to a career in music and supported himself by playing different musical instruments in dance halls, cafés, and movie theaters. From this spotty background, he moved on to study at a top conservatory, finally becoming leader of the Frankfurt Opera Orchestra and a noted composer. But he ran into trouble when Germany became Nazi-run. His work, specifically one opera, *Mathis der Maler,* was called "objectionable to Nazi philosophy" because of its pointed comments on politics and it was banned. So Hindemith left Germany, moved to Paris, London, and eventually, to the United States, where he taught at Yale. Later he was appointed to the music faculty at Zurich University and settled in Switzerland until his death.	Modern	*Philharmonic Concerto; Mathis der Maler* (first a symphony, 1932; then an opera, 1934); the ballet *Nobilissima visione; Symphonic Metamorphoses on a Theme by Weber; Requiem for Those We Love; Die Harmonie der Welt.*

Who	Period	Famous For
SERGEY PROKOFIEV (RUSSIAN, 1891–1953). One of Russia's finest modern composers, who had the unenviable task of creating music that fit within the often rigid "requirements" of official Communist policy. But even with these strictures, Prokofiev managed to keep his integrity intact and produce many fine pieces. He left Russia in May 1918 when the political situation seemed shaky and remained in self-imposed exile for eighteen years. He finally returned to Russia (then the Soviet Union) and continued composing. But Stalinist Russia proved to be a problem for him. Although he met with success, the party central committee cited his music as "marked with formalist perversions . . . alien to the Soviet people" and his last opera, *The Story of a Real Man,* was called "unfavorable" by the Union of Composers (a Communist group that watchdogged creative musical works). It wasn't allowed to be performed until after Stalin's death— which happened to be the same day Prokofiev died.	Modern	The ballets *Romeo and Juliet* and *Cinderella;* movie scores for famed Russian filmmaker Sergei Eisenstein; operas, including *The Love of Three Oranges* and his greatest, *War and Peace;* and, of course, the children's classic, *Peter and the Wolf.*

Who	Period	Famous For
DMITRI SHOSTAKOVICH (RUSSIAN, 1906–1975). Another of Russia's great composers, and often considered the finest of the twentieth century. Initially, he wrote his music in support of Soviet ideology and principles, but as the Soviet government became more conservative, his music became more innovative. The result: official criticism of his opera *The Nose* and his *October* Symphony (Symphony no. 2 in B Major). He was forced to withdraw his second opera, *Lady Macbeth of Mtsensk,* since it was roundly reviled, criticized for being decadent, and for not upholding what was called "Soviet realism." But he regained popularity and acceptance with later works (many of which were commemorations of historical Soviet events, like the 1917 Revolution) and was even awarded a Lenin Prize for his eleventh symphony, commemorating the October Revolution of 1905.	Modern	Many symphonies in particular, including Symphony no. 7 in C Major (*Leningrad*); Symphony no. 10 in E Minor; Symphony no. 11 in G Minor (*The Year 1905*); Symphony no. 12 in D Minor.

IT'S ONLY RAGA AND ROLL, BUT I LIKE IT:
WHAT THEY'RE LISTENING TO AROUND THE WORLD

Picture this: you're sitting in the el-Fishawi Café in Old Cairo, feeling like a true world citizen. You're sipping an *ahwa turki* (Turkish coffee), the music comes on, and your mind drifts, back to . . . an MTV music countdown show you saw just before you left the States.

Quite a thud—and, unfortunately, a common one. Western music—especially rock from the United States—has taken over the airwaves (and hearts) of much of the rest of the world. No matter where you go, some form of American pop music seems to have gotten there before you.

CONJUNTO
FOLKLÓRICO
NACIONAL DE
CUBA (COURTESY
ICM ARTISTS,
LTD.)

But, lately, in a sort of Revenge of the Rest of the World, the tables have been turned. Suddenly, it's *not* all rehashes of Western disco or pop dominating the radio. And justly. Because beyond the Japanese cover versions of Janet Jackson and the Chinese black-market cassettes of vintage Bob Dylan, there's a whole world of popular music, often based on older, traditional forms, that has existed.

And it's on *our* airwaves now, in our record stores, on our concert stages. Just as the rest of the world had listened to Anglo-American music, the West has discovered the sounds of

other countries and cultures. Frankly, the music has always been there, but we weren't listening. And now we are—probably because now we can, without leaving home. It's simply become more accessible. In other words, world music, as it's colloquially called, is on a roll.

One important note: we're not talking about the kind of traditional music that has effectively died in certain countries and only gets trotted out for tourists. We're talking about ethnic music that actually lives, music that people *really* listen to. In some cases, it's traditional styles that have married rock and resulted in unique ethnic sounds at once ancient and modern. In other cases, it's traditional music being played just as it has been for years. And in still others, it's modernized traditional music, still the same roots but with a twentieth-century spin.

But the bottom line is the same: this is music that captures the spirit of different cultures.

In the following sampler of world music, we've overlooked the West, not because Europe and other Western areas don't have indigenous music, but because they've been accessible for years. Instead, we've concentrated on music from Africa, Asia, the Middle East, and Latin America.

AFRICAN

It's almost impossible to sum up African music in a few lines or, for that matter, to pick one or two styles and pretend they reflect the entire continent. That said, of course, we're going to try to do this anyway. . . .

While world music has become hot in the United States and the rest of the world, U.S. music remains a big draw overseas. A recent example: rap music has taken Bangkok and other Thai cities by storm. Thai rap stars, called dek rap (rap kids), have picked up the musical style and fashion style of U.S. rappers, complete with baggy pants, sneakers, huge T-shirts, and baseball caps worn backward. But Thai rap is a bit different from American rap. Instead of talking about social problems or life in the ghetto, Thai rap songs are big on love, specifically romances gone bad. Other areas of Southeast Asia are equally fond of rap, Malaysia and Indonesia in particular, where basic U.S. rap music backs up traditional Malay lyrics.

Highlife is one of the most famous types of African popular music—and one of the oldest. It supposedly has its roots in the late nineteenth century when disbanded West Indian and Ghanaian soldiers with nothing to do formed marching bands. They developed their own style, a multicultural mélange of American and European jazz and pop, Ga and Akan tribal rhythms, with a touch of calypso and Latin sounds. By the 1920s, highlife was the hottest music played at dances and nightclubs. In fact, it became known as highlife because the people who attended the dances where it was played were the quintessence of cosmopolitan sophistication—tails for the men, ball gowns for the women. Chiefly played by brass-dominated bands, highlife was, in effect, African swing. But there always were variations on it: sometimes it was played by a full orchestra, complete with strings and woodwinds; other times by swing bands, or small combos. And as time went on, highlife evolved away from the brass dance bands to guitar bands.

Given all these instrumental variations, there are, of course, musical variations as well. But highlife typically boils down to a fairly simple setup: one toe-tapping melody repeated again and again, with instrumental solos breaking in—sometimes taking off on the theme, other times playing something completely different. Pure highlife is still being played, and it has also spawned a number of offshoots and derivatives. Some incorporate reggae or rock. It even became "Eurodiscoized," and, in the 70s, a German form called "burgher highlife" emerged.

Kwela started in the 40s as streetcorner music—a few kids, one or two pennywhistles, a guitar, maybe a tea-chest bass, and a couple of vocalists, and you had the makings of a major music craze. Sometimes called South African jive, it was born after World War II, when South African musicians, used to a heavy diet of American jazz and pop music on the radio, adapted the sounds they had heard to their own instruments and more traditional African music and generated their own brand of dance music. It grew so popular that it was actually banned in Johannesburg for supposedly causing traffic tie-ups. Apparently performers would play by the roadside; drivers would become so caught up by the music that they would slow down or even stop and pull over to listen. But the ban didn't make any difference. *Kwela* continued growing in popularity, winding up on airwaves across the continent—in Rhodesia, Zambia, and Malawi. It spawned some stars, among them Lemmy "Special" Mabaso, Spokes Mashiyane, and Elias Lerole and his Zigzag Flutes (who had a song on the European charts in 1956).

M'bube (literally, "bombing") is another type of African music that was born in the war-torn 40s. An a cappella style sung by choruses, it won its name because the sound of the vocals supposedly sounded like airplanes zooming in to bomb the countryside. In spite of this less than melodic-sounding description, it's actually very melodic, with swooping vocals—the African answer to gospel, in some ways. It's recently caught the Western public's attention because of the group Ladysmith Black Mambazo, a South African choir used by such American stars as Paul Simon.

Other popular styles:

Juju: Traditional Yoruba music revolving around basic percussion

brought into the twentieth century by adding vocals and other instruments, initially accordions and, now, electric guitars, and often going on and on, with one song often lasting half an hour, and performances lasting all night.

Makossa: Rhythm-based dance music born in the 1950s, characterized by a heavy bass line. One of the most popular types of African music, it's also very big in Paris.

Mbaqanga: Good old rock and roll with an African twist. An electric (literally) blend of *kwela, m'bube,* rhythm and blues, and Western rock, especially hot in the 60s. It faded out somewhat in the 80s, but recently has been catching on again with comebacks by groups like Mahlathini and the Mahotella Queens.

Palm wine: Relaxing bar music, literally; born in palm-wine bars, where patrons drank, yes, palm wine. The music initially consisted of a vocalist, an acoustic guitar, and, for occasional percussion, a bottle, and still is much the same—but usually without the bottle.

Rai: Urban music that evolved out of regional folk music and Bedouin lyric poetry. It got its name from the filler phrase that singers used in their songs: *Ya rai,* loosely translated as "that's what I think." Especially known for its outspoken lyrics, often on topics that are dicey by Islamic terms—anything from the joys of drinking to female virginity—making it kind of like a cross between rap and country music.

Soukous: A catchall name for perhaps the most popular black African dance music; initially referring to just a Congolese dance, now applied to Zairean and Congolese pop; it's also sometimes called (very simply) Zairean pop. A real crowd pleaser with its fast drumming, tight harmonies, intricate guitar lines, and *animateurs*—performers who yell to the audience and dance. But it's actually very traditional: a rumba-based style with guitar melodies that often are translations of traditional *likembe* (thumb-piano) ones.

ARABIC

In many cases, it's tough to pinpoint a distinct style of Arabic popular music. Often it's an offshoot of one of the main traditional styles, but identifiable to a specific artist, not a style in and of itself, or it's modernized or Westernized folk or traditional music, or in some cases, maybe it's basically Western rock with an Arabic spin. Much of popular Arabic music clearly has its roots in the traditional. For example, oud (lute) players are often musical stars; their instrument is a traditional one, but often the lyrics they sing are modern, and so on.

That said, there are certain forms that are clear-cut:

Musiqqa sharqiyah—"Eastern music"—is the leading Arabic popular music. Even though it's technically Egyptian popular music, it's often referred to as the pan-Arab style because it spread to most of the Arab world. It's a pretty basic form if you boil it down: a vocalist singing melodramatic lyrics (usually about love), backed by an orchestra typically heavy on the strings, with other instruments ranging from guitars to saxes to Arabic instruments like the oud (lute), *riqq* (tambourine),

There's a type of Arabic music called al-ani watanya that isn't really a pop style but was extremely popular for a period of time. The time? During the Gulf War. Actually al-ani watanya are traditional Kuwaiti patriotic songs. The name literally means "national songs," and the songs are just that—popular songs about Kuwait, all very stirring, dramatic (some would say melodramatic), and hyperemotional. These songs resurged with a vengeance during the Gulf War as Kuwaitis became highly patriotic.

and *qanum* (zither). Of course, there are variations on the theme. For all of its being easily explained, *musiqqa sharqiyah* isn't necessarily straightforward. The music can incorporate any number of influences, including traditional Arabic music, folk music, etc. One other typical feature of *musiqqa sharqiyah*—it's *long*. One song can open with a purely instrumental intro that lasts up to half an hour; then it's on to the vocals, which also run on and on.

You can't talk about this style without mentioning Uum Kalthum, the (female) Elvis of Egypt. To a great degree, she single-handedly made *musiqqa sharqiyah* what it is today—*the* foremost Arab music. She popped onto the scene in the 1920s, and became the hottest musical star of the Arab world.

Although it's clearly secular, *musiqqa sharqiyah* grew out of religious and ceremonial music. In the early 1900s, most popular performers were Muslim men who would sing at weddings and the like as well as at coffee houses. But with the rise of Uum Kalthum (who was discovered singing religious texts with her father), the music grew and spread.

Other popular styles:

Iranian or Persian jazz: not jazz as we know it, but traditional Persian music wedded to Western rock. Like so much other Arabic music, it's heavy on poetic lyrics.

New wave (or Al jeel): Western rock and disco with a uniquely Egyptian flavor, especially where percussion and rhythms are concerned. Fittingly dubbed "generation" (*al jeel*) music, this is (sort of) *musiqqa sharqiyah* for the young. Like *musiqqa sharqiyah*, lyrics are romantic, often bordering on the melodramatic, but they're shorter, probably to fit the attention span of their fans.

Shaaby: Egyptian street music. The name means "music for the people," and, to a great degree, that's what it is—music for the masses. In fact, it originated in Cairo's lower-middle-class neighborhoods. One person in particular gets the credit for *shaaby*—ex-waiter Ahmed Adeweya, who ended up with a following almost as fanatical as Uum Kalthum's. Lyrics are slang-riddled, often about the seedy side of life in Cairo. Consider this the Egyptian equivalent of punk.

Tarab: The more classical form of Arabic music, but still popular, and often the basis of modern music. *Tarab* (meaning "enchantment") is noted for its vocals; done "Arab style"—that is, heavy on the ornamentation—they are sung over a background of traditional Arabic instruments, and sometimes other instruments such as the harmonica and drums. It has also spread to sub-Saharan countries where it is called *tarabu*.

INDIAN AND PAKISTANI

First, a little background: you can't discuss Indian music without a quick mention of ragas, the tune patterns of classical Indian music and, in many cases, the foundation that popular music still is built on. Actually, traditional **ragas** aren't just music. According to tradition, they can cure people of illness or perform other magical acts. Some ragas are meant to be played only at certain times of the year or at a specific time of day—play them at another time and the music could hurt

whoever is playing it or listening. So what is a raga? It's a bit difficult to explain since there really is no direct parallel in Western music. Put technically, a raga is the system of melody, meter, and structure of Indian music, as well as each of the hundreds of specific melody patterns. To put it more simply, a raga sets the parameters within which a musician can improvise a melody, its tones, pitches, phrasing, and so on. The bottom line? Without ragas, you wouldn't have most of Indian music, classical or popular.

Of course, with exposure to the West, many of the classic elements of Indian music fell by the wayside. While certain types of popular music still revolve around ragas, others are just Indian versions of Western music.

So what, really, is Indian popular music today? Simple. More often than not, it's film music. Most people, including most Indians, get their first earful of Indian music on a film sound track. It's logical, since films are such a hot commodity in India.

Ghazals are sometimes the type of music found in Indian films; they're also a popular music form in and of themselves, unconnected to film. *Ghazals* are light semiclassical songs based on the classical *ghazal* poetry, lyrical Persian love couplets. As you might expect, then, the key to modern *ghazals* is the lyrics. Even today, *ghazal* lyrics are sometimes the actual texts of ancient Persian poetry. More often than not, though, modern *ghazals* have lyrics that are easier to understand. Even if they're still based on the ancient poetry, they've been streamlined—a Cliffs Notes version, in effect.

In the past, *ghazals* were more music for the upper class. Wealthy patrons would get in-home performances. And the performers themselves were usually highly trained, from families of *ghazal* players. But slowly *ghazal*s became music for the masses and, in the process, it changed and became more accessible. The songs were cut to be shorter, and the music was simplified and added Western instruments.

Qawwali is another form of traditional music that has been modernized. Especially popular in Pakistan, *qawwali* is Muslim religious music that often has a new Western twist. *Qawwali* singing was used by the mystic Sufi branch of Islam as a form of ecstatic worship of God. In its more traditional form, it's a chorus of male vocals, with one or two leads improvising over a background of traditional instruments—usually harmoniums, *tabla*s (pairs of different-sized hand drums), and *dholak*s (bass drums)—and synchronized clapping. But it's no longer just religious, a trend that was helped when the film industry discovered it and started tossing *qawwali* into films, sometimes sung by women.

Now there's a modern form of *qawwali* that has its roots in tradition, but has spun off to meet modern times. Instead of songs about God or divine love, you're just as apt to hear about regular love, even drinking. Classical Urdu has been replaced by modern; and Western instruments and musical styles are incorporated.

Other popular forms:

Bhangra: Punjabi folk music brought into the twentieth century; but actually more rock than folk now. It started as ceremonial music, sung and danced to at such times as harvests. It has become more Westernized, and is often electrified: instead of just the traditional *dhol* and *dholak*

drums, it often uses synthesizers and the like.

Indipop: Not really a true style; just Western-style pop with Hindi lyrics. The corresponding style in Pakistan has, of course, Urdu lyrics.

Pakistani folk music (with different names depending upon the region): updated folk music is big in Pakistan, including such forms as *loake geet* (literally, "people's song," this is religious folk), *wai* (Sufi religious poetry adapted for modern audiences), Pashto folk (from the province near Afghanistan, often updated into electric folk), etc.

CHINESE

One problem with looking at Chinese popular music from mainland China: it was missing in action for quite a long time. Until recently, there wasn't much of it being written. For example, during the height of the Cultural Revolution, only about twelve major works were written, published, or performed. These were usually written by committee—by groups of musicians or composers—then often credited to an institution or organization. And they were supposed to be "models" of correct entertainment. Not the most creative atmosphere. But by the 70s, things loosened up a bit, and individuals were able to get credit for what they wrote. Still, the emphasis was on political correctness. An example: one hit song of the time was the less-than-enthralling sounding "Ode to the Red Flag." Then came the collapse of the Gang of Four (also commemorated in song, such as the top hit of 1976 according to Beijing's *People's Daily*: "Indignantly Condemn the Wang-Zhang-Jiang-Yao Gang of Four") and a (semi)return to creative freedom.

Since then, Chinese popular music has rebounded, to a degree. What's hot? A great deal of it is pop ballads generally from non-Communist Hong Kong or Taiwan, the so-called Cantopop; these are updated Cantonese folk songs, now with Western influence—Chinese versions of rock or disco. Oddly (or ironically) enough, after the Tiananmen Square massacre, the old "model" music resurged in popularity, this time in disco form. On the flip side, there has also been an increase in political protest songs.

Some other popular forms of Chinese music:

"Yellow" music: No, not a name given it by Hollywood in the 40s, but a form of music that evolved in 1930s Shanghai. Usually love songs with Chinese melodies, heavy on the (Western) strings. Vestiges of this style remain.

Revolutionary songs: Not as popular as they once were, but still part of the Chinese music scene. These emerged when the People's Liberation Army was first becoming a force to reckon with in Shanghai and elsewhere. Most were traditional folk songs updated to educate the masses, with touches of the West, particularly militaristic ones gleaned from Russian revolutionary songs, military brass bands, and even Protestant hymns. And the titles of these songs didn't mince words about their content, like the very popular "The Three Disciplines and the Eight Points of Attention." Nowadays, they're set to a rock or disco beat and are seen as hip, not revolutionary.

Traditional Chinese instrumen-

According to the BEIJING REVIEW, the hottest thing in Chinese pop isn't a musical style, but one man—Xu Peidong. He's written more than three hundred songs, scored more than a hundred TV shows, and written five operas to boot. And this one-man music movement is largely responsible for shifting public attention away from music imported into mainland China from Taiwan and Hong Kong, not to mention the West. His works usually incorporate traditional folk songs.

tals: Not pop, but still popular. Traditional Chinese music continues strong, most of it played on the traditional instruments such as flutes and stringed instruments that include the *qin* (seven-stringed zither) or *pipa* (lute).

JAPANESE

Much of Japanese popular music owes more to Western than Eastern traditions. Japanese radio and television are flooded with pop-rock, punk-rock, salsa, pseudo-disco, even the blues—in short, virtually everything you'd hear in the United States, but with Japanese lyrics. Although even that isn't always the case: many Japanese songs are sung in English, or in so-called Japlish, an often bizarre, sometimes unintentionally funny, blend.

That's not to say that all popular music is completely Western. There has been an effort to bring the Japanese element into Japanese rock. Some artists use traditional instruments in certain songs; others try to incorporate Japanese folk music. For example, Okinawan rock (from, logically, Okinawa) uses traditional instruments like the samisen (the lute used in Kabuki music), the koto (zither), wood flutes, Japanese percussion, and the like. Still, the bulk of Japanese popular music is Western.

Enka is one of the only truly Japanese forms of popular music. But it's often not all that appreciated by the young, but by older audiences—and, for that matter, it's also not attracting many new performers, so it may be a dying form. *Enka* (from *en* meaning "public speech," and *ka* meaning "song") is a blend of many elements, including samisen music, Buddhist chanting, folk music, and, yes, Western music (usually ballads dating from the 60s or earlier). The result is usually a melodramatic torch song of sorts. It's very big with businessmen at karaoke bars.

Minyo—traditional and folk music—is also still around, but, unfortunately, it's completely set in stone. What happened? The styles were standardized into one core. A *minyo* association consisting of performers and teachers was formed to teach students the music exactly as it was when formalized. No improvisations, no interpretations, nothing but the very specific old ways. As a result, this music has become not only creatively static, it's also chiefly played at ceremonies.

LATIN AMERICAN

Latin American music is about as diverse as you can get—and it makes sense. After all, Latin America consists of a large number of countries. And the different styles of music reflect the different locations and histories of these countries. Listen to the music from countries on the Atlantic-Caribbean coast and you'll hear African influences; Andean countries, and you'll hear hints of centuries-old indigenous Indian music; Mexico, the music of Andalusian Spain, and so on. Generally speaking, Latin American popular music is influenced by the conquerors, settlers, slaves, and cultures of years past, usually African, Spanish, or Por-

The language of modern pop music is English, at least for now. Recently, eleven of the top twenty hits in Japan had English titles. German rock songs averaged fifty-six English words in a tune. Reason: the originators of most pop were American or English, and the current stars grew up listening to English lyrics.

tuguese, and, in more limited cases, other European countries, such as Holland, Italy, and Germany.

Another key point about the different Latin American musical styles: more often than not, when you're listening to it, you're probably dancing, too. In other words, a large amount of Latin American popular music is also dance music like the samba, the tango, salsa, the bolero, and the list goes on and on. Here's a look at a few:

To start, there's the music associated with Rio's Carnival—*samba.* This is one of Brazil's most popular musical styles, known the world over. Its roots and sound are squarely in African traditions: driving drum beat, chanted choruses, pulsing rhythms. In fact, it is said to have originated not in Rio, as popularly thought, but in the more black city of Salvador. But this isn't the only form of samba. There are actually two general types of samba. The samba of Carnival, often referred to as *samba de enredo* (or narrative samba), is music for a crowd, written to be sung and drummed by hundreds of people at once—all members of a samba "school" performing at Carnival. It's called narrative samba because it's written around a specific historical or religious epic theme, which is echoed by the costumes of the school. And like the epics it sings about, this musical style never dies. It's an integral part of Carnival, the perfect musical form to capture the exuberance and energy of the celebration. The other general type of samba is *samba canceo* (pop or song samba). This is a much more intimate form of samba, played by small combos fronted by a sambista (singer). It has gone through a number of incarnations, from some watered-down years when it became more pop than samba, but lately there's been a back-to-the-roots movement. And samba canceo is again being sung—and listened to—for its traditional rhythms and music.

Just as with samba, many people automatically think of the **tango** just as a dance. But tango music (more specifically, *tango canción*, or "tango song") is more than just background for dancing, it's even considered Argentina's national music. It has taken several forms through the years from its roots as raunchy saloon or brothel music, when it was usually played by trios of violin, a harp or piano, and a flute, to a cleaned-up version, so-called new guard tango, played by larger bands that included accordions and double basses, to even a sort of tango fusion, which combined tango with jazz and classical. Some forms of tango have drifted quite far from its roots, but more often than not, tango retains its traditional style—dramatic, emotional, poetic, even tragic at times.

Some other popular styles:

Andean music: No catchy name for this style, it's a revival of the music of the Quechua Indians. Usually revolves around panpipes (sikus or zamponas), quena flute, and guitar (sometimes acoustic, sometimes electric, depending on the modernity of the sound). This type of music saw a resurgence in popularity in the 60s. An adulterated version of this style is *pan-Andean* music, which is kitschier, more commercial, and includes European instruments and influences along with the traditional Andean sound.

Bolero: Especially popular in Mexico and Cuba, this style has distinct Spanish roots. (In fact, it's also popular in Spain.)

Bossa nova: Another form of dance music that has faded in popularity to a

A new type of world music has been hitting the airwaves, the music of Native Americans. In addition to drumming and chanting music and powwow music, there's the more pop waila (also called chicken-scratch music), the party music of the Tohono O'odham tribe of Arizona; and even rap coming from Native American/African-American bands.

great degree from its height in the 50s and 60s, but still hangs on. A mix of jazz and song samba known for its cool sophistication.

Cumbia (or cumbiamba): Dance music with an Andean Indian-Latin-Afro beat. Traditionally played on flutes and drums; now more commonly played by full bands. Marked by a shuffling beat (probably because it originally was meant to be danced while holding a candle).

Llanera: Traditional Venezuelan music that is essentially the equivalent of American country and western since it is the music of the cowboys working on the plains (in fact, *llanera* comes from the word *llanos*, meaning "plains"). It's usually played with instruments, such as guitars, mandolins, plains harps, drums, and scrapers called *charrasca*, but there are variations. Sometimes it's played by symphony orchestras and transformed into a semiclassical sound; and sometimes electrified and updated.

Musica popular brasilera: As you'd think, Brazilian popular music (or MPB, as the in-crowd calls it), which is a blend of everything popular. Take a little samba, a little bossa nova, and add jazz, rock and pop, and you've got it. MPB ranges from the extremely experimental to the more pop-ish.

Ranchera: Mexican country and western, usually played by guitar, *bajo sexto* (acoustic bass), and sometimes accordion.

Rock nacional: Plain old rock (with touches of everything from reggae to folk) with a Latin American flavor.

THE CARIBBEAN

Where music is concerned, there's a lot of crossover between the Caribbean and Latin America, chiefly due to the paths of conquerors and slave ships. Similarly, a great deal of it is actually dance music. One of the most popular forms of Caribbean music is the **merengue.** There are actually different merengues played in different countries—a Haitian one, a range of Latin American ones—but the most famous is the style played in the Dominican Republic, earning the title of the country's national music. This is energetic music, usually played in a zippy 2/4 rhythm, marked by repeated phrases. Its instrumental mix usually includes accordions, drums (often the tambora drum), scraper, and saxophones, which periodically break into *jaleos,* or arpeggios. Styles vary, from country, or more traditional, merengue (sometimes called *ripiado,* "ripped") to more sophisticated pop merengue, which can include synthesizers, rap, and other modern touches. Haitian merengue (or, more technically, *méringue*) is a sloweddown version, heavy on the guitars and light on the accordions.

Listen to **calypso** with its infectious melodies, rhythmic beat, and clever lyrics, and you'll hear the African influence. It's a direct descendant of slave singing, a combination of spirituals, hymns, and songs that slave work teams sang as they worked. In fact, many of the key traditional elements of calypso are traceable to the times of slavery and the period just after, when they were freed. Take the lyrics, traditionally so heavy on the double entendre. Slaves used their song lyrics to

mock their masters and ex-slaves to mock the wealthy, but both had to cloak the insults under double meanings and insinuations. Sparring sections of songs, when singers trade insults or comments back and forth, stem from the singing duels different slave work gangs held, and from the days just after emancipation when bands of people would fight in the streets, but first have an insulting song duel. This is also where the braggadocio quality in performers and the traditionally extravagant calypso stage names developed—a pugnacious stance against both the elite and rival gangs. On the musical side, the steel drums probably evolved from the bamboo sticks (called "tamboo bamboo") that was the only form of percussion affordable. More recently, the spread of calypso to the United States has resulted in the addition of brass instruments (from New Orleans jazz), guitar, bass, and violin (from folk music).

And calypso is still evolving. As with so many other music styles, there are different versions that have emerged. There's traditional calypso, often almost a burlesque form, with suggestive lyrics about sex, extravagant names and costumes and other touristy trappings. There's a more stripped down and modernized calypso, less corny but also less true to its roots, with a distinct big band or rock tone to it. There's extempo calypso, an improvisatory form; Bajan calypso, a rougher, tougher form with electric bass and guitar that emerged in Barbados; watered-down pop calypso, which is usually calypso more in name only than in actual style. The variations on the theme go on and on.

Reggae has become what calypso was in the 40s and 50s: probably one of the best-known Caribbean styles, and definitely one of Jamaica's most popular exports. It emerged in the 60s, evolving out of *ska*—the Jamaicanized R&B with a syncopated beat that was the music of the Kingston ghetto—and the slower, heavier child of ska called rock steady. Reggae was an even slower, heavier version of rock steady, and it quickly caught on. One reason: in addition to a captivating rhythm, reggae is, in many ways, more than just music. It's a lifestyle and a political and social movement, probably due to its ties to Rastafarianism, the Jamaican religious movement that preaches the eventual return of Jamaican Africans to their spiritual home of Ethiopia, and so reveres the late Ethiopian emperor Haile Selassie. Early on, a large number of reggae musicians converted to Rastafarianism. And with that, Rastafarianism began having a strong impact on the music. More than the dreadlocks they wear or the ganja they smoke, the Rastafarian philosophy has greatly influenced reggae. It's brought a more African flavor to the music, especially in terms of drums. And it's lent strength to the political message of the music. To a great degree, reggae is still the music of the ghetto, so lyrics are often about the problems of ghetto life, the poverty and racism suffered by black Jamaicans.

At this point, it's vital to mention Bob Marley, perhaps the most famous reggae star of all, and one whose work captured the raw side of life in Trench Town, the Kingston ghetto in which he lived. His death in 1981 marked the end of the classic reggae years. Not that reggae died with him. Now there are offshoots of classic reggae—"lover's reggae or rock," pop reggae without the bite of classic reggae; ragga or dancehall, similar to rap with its emphasis on chanted vocals (often the only instru-

ments are drum and keyboard), sexual references, and even violent fans; and techno-reggae, known for slick production utilizing modern digital techniques. And, of course, there's still classic reggae, much as it used to be.

Other popular styles:

Rumba: Not the rhumba you may have heard, but another Cuban sound, relying mainly on drums and other percussion instruments fronted by a solo vocalist and sometimes backed by a small chorus.

Salsa: Another dance music and, in terms of popularity, it's as hot as the sauce with the same name. There's straight salsa, high-energy dance music with a strong beat; there's salsa erotica or salsa romantica (the name depends on how hot the lyrics are, but the style is similar: crooning lead vocals and slowed-down rhythms).

Soca: Calypso soul, with electric bass and guitars lending muscle and grit to the calypso beat. Born in Trinidad, soca emerged in the 70s; it's often dance and party music.

Son: The precursor to salsa and one of Cuba's leading styles, marked by a strong syncopated rhythm (played on wooden sticks or "claves"), chanted chorus, and, usually, improvised lead. Instruments and specific styles vary, ranging from violins to trumpets; from country to jazz; from stronger Hispanic influences to stronger African.

Zouk: Dance music again, this time usually high tech and high energy. Just what you'd expect from a musical style whose name means "party" in Antillean Creole slang. But there are different types of zouk, from concrete zouk (zouk-béton, the hardest and fastest version) to pop-zouk (a more saccharine, watered-down version), to zouk-love (as you'd expect, love songs).

LANGUAGES OF THE WORLD

CONTENTS

LANGUAGES OF THE WORLD

TALK TO ME!
AN INTRODUCTION
TO WORLD LANGUAGES

Languages are a window to the many diverse cultures and peoples of the world. They're a means of communication, yes, but they're more, too. As the Lebanese writer Ahmad Faris al-Shidyaq (who writes under the name Faryaq) said:

Every language in the world has something beautiful and something ugly about it, for language is nothing more than the expression of the activities, thoughts, and actions of human beings. There is naturally always something to blame and something to praise.

Language is *alive;* it's not dry grammatical rules and vocabulary lists, but a vibrant record of our thoughts, actions, ideas, and emotions. And so this section is more than a listing of languages. It's an attempt to get beneath the basics to give an idea of how people from different cultures really express themselves.

Given all the diversity of cultures in the world, it's not surprising to realize that there are so many languages in the world. Today, anywhere from three thousand to ten thousand different languages are spoken on the planet every day; the consensus number is about four thousand.

You'll never hear most of them. Many are obscure languages from the isolated jungles of the Amazon or the high mountains of New Guinea that are unfortunately dying out as settlers from the cities move in. Trumai, for example, is a language that was spoken in a remote jungle village in South America. But a flu epidemic brought in by Europeans reduced the number of speakers to ten by 1962. It's been the same story across the globe.

Most languages are spoken only by a few people—and then a few languages are spoken by most people. You can literally learn most of the world's languages and not be understood by 99.9 percent of the population. You'd be the world's foremost linguist and be able to speak to only a few thousand people. On the other hand, if you learned just three languages—English, Mandarin Chinese, and Hindi—you could speak to a majority of the world.

In the section below we describe some of the world's major languages, the major language families of the world, and some of the world's mystery tongues. And if we go into detail, it's because language is important. As the Nigerian poet Gabriel Okara said about spoken language:

What of spoken words? Spoken words are living things like cocoa-beans packed with life. And like cocoa-beans they grow and give life. . . . They will enter some insides, remain there and grow like the corn blooming on the alluvial sod at the riverside.

WHAT IS A LANGUAGE?

 Now let's loosely define what a language is and make a very important distinction:

Language is a way of combining words and sounds in a grammatical way that is understood by listeners who are fluent in the same language; it is mutually intelligible. Why bother saying that? Because it points out that languages are different from *dialects*, which are diverse forms of the *same* language that can be understood by speakers of the language (even though they sound somewhat different). Deciding what's a dialect and what isn't can get controversial. English clearly has different dialects (just ask any British person about American English), but sometimes what we call languages are really just dialects. For example, linguists recognize two languages in Scandinavia: Continental Scandinavian and Insular Scandina-

vian. The separate languages Swedish, Norwegian, and Danish are really dialects of Continental Scandinavian. But try telling a Swede he speaks Continental Scandinavian. Language is more than scientific linguistics—it's emotional, too.

All languages are probably equal: All natural languages seem to be pretty much equally complex and well developed. No, this is not being politically correct. Scientists have yet to find a truly primitive language, something we might call a "Stone Age" language with poorly developed grammar and vocabulary. Some languages are less complex in some areas, but seem to offset this with being complex in others. Early linguists were surprised to find that supposedly "primitive" Native American languages were actually quite complex, with high levels of abstraction. At least one had verbs varying much like Latin.

The Top Ten Languages in the World by Number of Speakers

		Native Speakers	Nonnative Speakers	Total
1.	Mandarin	827 million	103 million	930 million
2.	English	319	144	463
3.	Hindi	327	73	400
4.	Spanish	326	45	371
5.	Russian	172	119	291
6.	Arabic	182	32	214
7.	Bengali	184	8	192
8.	Portuguese	167	22	179
9.	Malay-Indonesian	49	103	152
10.	Japanese	125	1	126

WHAT (MOST) PEOPLE ARE SPEAKING:
THE TOP LANGUAGES OF THE WORLD BESIDES ENGLISH

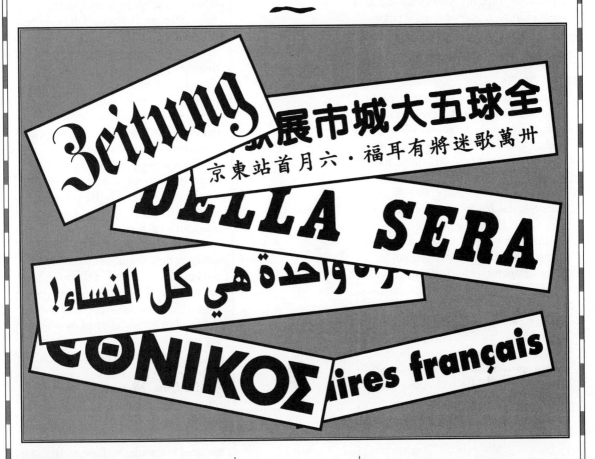

 In this section we describe the top eleven languages that are spoken in the world today. And we've added Swahili to make it a round dozen, and to include at least one language from the great Bantu African family of languages.

Many of these top languages are fairly closely related to one another. (Of course, some linguists think that all languages are related. They've linked proto-Chinese to proto–Indo-European and have thus found a rela-

tionship between English and Chinese—but that's another story.) In fact, seven of the languages listed here—French, English, German, Spanish, and Portuguese, along with Hindi and Bengali—all come from one common mother, the Indo-European family of languages.

But despite some of these common links, we're all too often separated by language. Take the international population conference held in Cairo, Egypt, in 1994. Translators had a devil of a time putting common English jargon into the other tongues. A French translator was stymied by "female empowerment." So were the Chinese translators. They needed to know what kind of power everyone was talking about—political, personal, or physical? But it was worse for the Russians. "Reproductive health" was translated into "health that reproduces itself again and again." "Family leave" translated into Russian had everyone taking a vacation after a baby was born; the Arabic translation made it sound like the husband and wife left each other. The moral: languages are windows into other cultures and despite all our human similarities, there are differences, too. Languages reveal some of the differences and similarities. Maybe another moral is that the English language is increasingly becoming cluttered with jargon—and jargon is difficult to translate because it often has no meaning.

And for a bit a trivia: the grand prize for mistranslation came from the time Americans were introducing Coke into China and came up with the bizarre slogan, "Bite the wax tadpole." Needless to say, they redid their ad campaign.

Now for the world's largest language:

CHINESE

How many speak it: 1.2 billion

Who speaks it: About one-quarter of the world's population speak Chinese. It's spoken, appropriately enough, in China, Singapore, and Taiwan, and by numerous overseas Chinese, people of Chinese origin living in Europe, Asia, and the Americas.

But before you picture 1.2 billion people talking happily among themselves, you've got to know that there are many different dialects of Chinese. And despite what we said above about dialects, Chinese dialects are so varied that they really are almost separate languages. A Chinese speaker in Hong Kong can't understand a Chinese speaker in Beijing, although if both communicated by writing rather than speech each could understand the other.

Chinese dialects are written in the same way (or almost the same) but sound very different. To give you an idea of the difference; to say "I have one," a Hong Kong speaker would say something that sounds like *'Ngo 'yau yat ko*. A Beijing speaker would say *Wo you i ge*. You can see that there are similarities, but the differences are pretty large, too. The Chinese government has tried to rectify matters by promoting an official dialect that everybody has to learn. The dialects you'll most often come across are:

Mandarin: North Mandarin is the official language of China, Taiwan, and Singapore. It's called *putonghua,* or common language, in China; *guo yu,* or national language, in Taiwan. It and a few other Mandarin dialects account for most of the Chinese spoken in northern, central, and western China, including Beijing.

Cantonese (Yueh): Spoken in southern China and Hong Kong and popular among many Singaporeans. It's very common also in New York, San Francisco, and Vancouver, B.C.

Other dialects include Hakka (Fujian), Hunan, Kan, Northern Min, Southern Min, and Wu. In all, there are more than fifty dialects.

Comments: To an a nonspeaker, Chinese looks and sounds virtually impossible and seems the most difficult language in the world. But like any other language, it has its difficult points and its easy points.

Surprisingly, the writing system is not nearly as impossible as it appears. Chinese is usually written in individual characters that each represent one sound and look like you need a Ph.D. to understand them. But take a close look and you'll see certain patterns are repeated in most characters. These are the 227 (or thereabouts) so-called radicals, the basic symbols that are combined in various ways to make up the bulk of characters. So to learn four thousand different characters, you don't really have to learn four thousand totally new symbols. For the most part, all you have to learn are new combinations. For example, there's a radical or symbol that looks something like a square. One of these symbols means "mouth" (*kou*); lump three together and you have a new word: conduct. The idea behind three mouths meaning conduct is that if you don't behave well you'll set people (mouths) talking. But the Chinese have many such explanations for their characters, and many are purely fictional.

In a great many cases, each character is not a single word. Most modern Chinese words are combinations of two or more characters and sounds. For example, the Chinese character for "big" (*da*) and the character for "small" (*xiao*) together make up the word "size" (*daxiao*). Interestingly, Chinese is one of the "purer" languages in the world. Because each character represents a sound, Chinese doesn't take in as many complete foreign words as other languages. Think how many characters it

The problems of translating texts can cause diplomatic problems or embarrassment. For example, when the United States signed agreements under Nixon and Carter with the People's Republic of China, our diplomats evidently didn't read the Chinese version of the agreement. The English versions say the United States "acknowledges" the Chinese position on the independent island of Taiwan, which is in keeping with the U.S. position that the Taiwanese should make up their own minds whether to join China or not. But the Chinese versions say that we "admit" the Chinese position—something altogether different.

would take to transliterate a word like "computerization." Instead, Chinese often coins its own words, sometimes taking one distinctive sound from the foreign. America is *Meiguo,* or "beautiful" (*mei*, the middle sound in America) "country" (*guo*). But on the other hand, particularly in recent years, it has been adding English loan words, like *a si pi lin* (aspirin), *kekou kele* (Coca-Cola), and *qiao ke li* (chocolate).

Chinese doesn't have many individual sounds, so most sounds mean many things. The sound *shi* can mean "poem," "to be loose," "damp," "find," "dung," "city," "try," or "business." But Chinese uses tones to make some of these sounds sound different. Mandarin Chinese has four tones: a rising tone (like when you're asking a question), a middle tone (goes down, then up), a high tone (stays high), and a falling tone (sort of like when you're angry and say "What!"). And when you add tones and combine sounds with other sounds, Chinese does the job of getting a point across as well as any other language.

Chinese is weak in what *we* think of as grammar. It is not an inflected language; in other words, words don't change sounds to show different meanings like in English (sink, sank, sinking). In fact, it doesn't have different tenses of verbs at all (I go, I went, I was going, etc.), although it does have a past tense marker; instead, the *context* is all important. This doesn't mean spoken Chinese is a snap to learn. There are all sorts of idiomatic expressions; word order is extremely important; and improper use of tones can result in all sorts of awkward situations. Use the wrong tone in a restaurant and you could get fried scorpion instead of fish.

HINDI

How many speak it: More than three hundred million people are native speakers of Hindi, but it's an official language of eight hundred million citizens of India. Another eighty-five million Indians and citizens of Pakistan speak the Muslim dialect/language called Urdu. Urdu has the same grammar but uses a Persian script and has many Persian and Arabic words.

Who speaks it: Many people of northern India speak Hindi as a native tongue; it's the largest single language in India. But it has a lot of competitors: English, Bengali, Marathi, Punjabi, and Tamil, to name a few of the thirty-three major languages on the subcontinent of India. India has much linguistic diversity, and sometimes wars have started over language.

Hindi has many regional dialects. In a broad sense, Hindi includes a large group of dialects all spoken in the North from Rajasthan to Bihar. One of these dialects in the West has become the formal spoken and literary language now called Hindi.

Comments: In some ways, Hindi is like the Italian of India. Like Italian, it's a changed version of an ancient language. Italian had its Latin beginnings; Hindi goes way back to Sanskrit, the language of the Aryan invaders of the Indian subcontinent that was probably spoken before 1000 B.C.E.

Let's take a few seconds to digress and explain this very important ancestor of Hindi. Sanskrit is one of the sacred languages of Hinduism, and it is still much studied in India today. It belongs to the Indo-Aryan branch of the Indo-European family. ("Aryan" is the name

these people gave themselves; Iran and very possibly Eire, or Ireland, are derived from the word.) Sanskrit itself means "polished [speech]"; the term was used to contrast it with the speech of the common people.

Sanskrit is very highly inflected: the words change a lot according to the job they do in a sentence. It has a huge vocabulary, so huge that writers in the language sometimes became enamored of it and played word games to show its flexibility. Here's an irresistible example of how an ancient epic writer produced a complete poetic stanza based on a few sounds:

dadado dudda-dud-dadi
dadado duda-di-da-doh
dud-dadam dadade dudde
dad' adada-dado 'da dah

This is not just idle babble; it means something: "The giver of gifts, the giver of grief to his foes/the bestower of purity, whose arm destroys the givers of grief,/the destroyer of demons, bestower of bounty on generous and miser alike/raised his weapon against the foe." It's obviously not the greatest poem ever written, but it gives you an idea of the tremendous flexibility and vocabulary of Sanskrit.

So regardless of what we said earlier about all languages being equal, maybe we should add that Sanskrit seems a little more equal than the rest. It is not an easy language to learn, but it is one of the most potent languages of the world with a great literature.

But we can't all be saints or grammarians, and as time passed, people began speaking a simpler form of the language, until the spoken tongue evolved into what is today known as Hindi.

Fortunately for anyone interested in learning it, Hindi is much simpler than Sanskrit grammatically. In one sense, it's like English in that it lost most of its case endings—those are endings on nouns and some other words used to indicate their proper function in a sentence. (A remaining English equivalent is the 's, as in "the man's bag.") Instead of cases, Hindi uses *post*positions, small words that are stuck onto the end of nouns and work like English *pre*positions. Verbs are simpler than in Sanskrit, too. Only the present and future indicative forms are fully conjugated. Hindi relies a lot on participles, the equivalent of the English *-ing* verb endings.

But Hindi does use a lot of Sanskrit vocabulary. And because both are members of the Indo-European family of languages, they're not really so alien as they first may seem to us. You can see the similarities with some Hindi words. The word *raj* (ruler) is clearly related to "royal" or "regal." "Death" in Hindi sounds like *mrityu,* and it doesn't take too much imagination to see its similarity to the Latin *morte* and our "mortal."

The writing system is very different. Hindi uses a simplified form of the script Sanskrit is written in. It's called Devanagari, and is a squiggly script with lines on top that you've probably seen if you have been in an Indian restaurant. It is basically an alphabet of consonants to which signs for vowels are attached above, below, or next to the basic consonant side. Hindi can be written in Persian letters as well. These are the slightly modified Arabic script brought in by the Mogal conquerors of India. In this script, Hindi is called Urdu and uses many Persian words.

SPANISH

How many speak it: Spanish is spoken as a mother tongue by more than three hundred million people, and it's the official language for about three hundred million people as well.

Who speaks it: Spanish developed in Spain, but many more people speak it outside Europe. Spanish is the official tongue of *all* of South America and Central America, except for Brazil, French Guiana, Guiana, and Belize. It's also the official tongue of Mexico, Cuba, Puerto Rico, the Dominican Republic, and various other former colonies of Spain, including the Canary Islands. It is spoken extensively in the United States.

Spanish is divided into many dialects, but they are not so different that they can't easily be understood. Some vocabulary differences can cause trouble—*tortilla* in Mexico means what we know it as, but in Spain it means "omelette"; a Spanish woman ordering a certain fruit in a Cuban restaurant instead made an obscene reference to her anatomy that puzzled her waiter.

The largest division is between Castilian, spoken in Spain, and the Spanish-American dialects that are mostly derived from Andalusian Spanish of the 1500s. In the Americas, there are of course numerous dialects, such as Mexican Spanish and Argentine Spanish.

Comments: At first Spanish seems to be easier to learn than other languages. For one thing, the spelling makes sense. Most sounds are spelled the way they sound. Even the grammar initially seems more organized and regular. This is no accident. Many years ago the Spanish Academy deliberately regularized much of the language. But after studying it for a year or two, Spanish starts looking harder. Syntax, the order of words in a sentence, can be particularly tricky.

Spanish is the largest of the Romance languages, the languages that stem from Latin, and ultimately, from the Indo-European family of languages that includes Sanskrit and Hindi. Like other Romance languages, Spanish includes many basic features that are different from English. Words have gender: in Spanish they are masculine or feminine. Every noun is either a "he" or a "she," including things like tables and chairs. The definite article "the" has different forms depending on the gender and the number of the noun. Verbs tend to follow regular conjugations with the verb ending telling who is doing what. In English, we say "I speak," "you speak"; in Spanish, they say "Hablo" and "hablas." You usually don't need the personal pronoun to explain who is speaking; the end of the verb tells you.

Most Spanish words are derived from Latin, but some come from Basque, German, and Arabic, which is not surprising since Arab-speaking Moors ruled Spain for many years. These Arabic-derived words usually have the Arabic word for "the," *al*, in front, such as *alcázar*, or "fortress."

ARABIC

How many speak it: About 186 million native speakers but many millions more speak or read Arabic as the holy language of Islam.

Who speaks it: Spoken in many countries of the Middle East and North Africa from Morocco in North Africa to Iraq in Asia. In addition, as a religious language Arabic is studied by Muslims in all Muslim lands, including Iran, Pakistan, and Indonesia, as well as in the United States.

Arabic has many dialects. The written language, *fusha,* or Modern Standard Arabic, is based on the Qur'an but is modernized; it is very similar in all Arab areas. Local dialects are simplified and changed from the standard. The main dialects include the Egyptian, which is widely understood since Egyptian movies and television are watched throughout the area; the Levantine (spoken in Syria and Lebanon); and the North African.

Comments: Arabic is the sacred language of Islam, and its importance extends far beyond the 186 million native Arabic speakers to include all who embrace Islam. In fact, most Muslims are not Arabs but a diverse group of people from non-Arab lands like Turkey, Iran, Indonesia, Pakistan, India, Indonesia . . . and the United States. Most of them speak languages totally unrelated to Arabic. But all appreciate the rhythmic, sonorous beauty of the Arabic in the Islamic holy book, the Qur'an. In a way, they have to. The Qur'an is seen as the word of God *only* when in Arabic.

But you have to *hear* the Qur'an being read by a good reciter, or at least hear a muezzin calling the faithful to prayer, to really appreciate the language. And you've got to have an open mind and suspend certain prejudices. To many Western ears, Arabic sounds too guttural, too alien, to be beautiful.

To be sure, Arabic has certain sounds that are difficult to appreciate, let alone pronounce. There's the *'ayin* letter, which looks like a backward three, for example. It makes a sound that is virtually impossible to describe. One Arabic scholar described it as "a very strong guttural produced by compression of the throat and expulsion of breath." Among other sounds, there's a glottal stop called the *hamza*. The best way to approximate this is to say "bottle" like a Cockney Englishman and leave out the *t*'s. And there's the *ghain* letter, which sounds sort of like a French *r*. There's the emphatic *kha*, which sounds like the *ch* in the Scottish "loch." Finally, there's an emphatic *d* called *daad* that is deceptive—you may think you've got it right, but it's said that virtually all non-native speakers get it wrong.

But many Westerners have mastered Arabic, and many have mastered its sister tongue, Hebrew. Both languages belong to what is called the Hamito-Semitic group of tongues, a very distinctive and historically interesting group that includes the ancient languages of Akkadian, Assyrian, Phoenician, and Aramaic.

The most important feature of virtually all Semitic languages is their root structure, which makes them in some ways easy to learn. Words are mostly based on roots of usually three consonants (sometimes two, rarely more). These three letters convey a basic meaning that is modified by sticking other consonants and vowels among them or around them.

For example, the root consonants *TLB* in Arabic refer to the act of looking for, or searching. To get different meanings, the Arabs put in different vowel sounds in different positions. So *TaLaBa* means "he searched"; but replace the middle *a* with an *i* and you

have *TaLiBa,* which means "desire." Similarly, *TaaLiB* means "student, seeker of knowledge," *maTLuuB* means "wanted." As you can see, Arabic is very flexible and able to incorporate new meanings easily. For example, *maTLuBaat* means "debts" or "liabilities" as on a corporate balance sheet. You can probably see the derivation; a debt is something that the holders are looking to see paid in full.

In another way, Arabic verbs change into different but similar meanings based on a regular pattern of verb forms. Of course, Arabic has many irregularities, usually for the most common words, which makes it more difficult to learn despite its pleasingly logical superstructure.

Arabic is written in a distinctive flowing script based on the same alphabet as ours (believe it or not) with many (but not all) letters connected together in each word, and many (but not all) letters varying depending on whether they are at the beginning, middle, or end of a sentence. Other languages such as Persian and Urdu also use this script in slightly modified form.

One interesting feature of written Arabic (and Hebrew) is that short vowel sounds are usually not written. An Arabic sentence like "Can you read this?" is in effect written like this: "Cn y rd ths?" The short vowel sounds are sometimes written in children's books and in religious writings. They are written as short lines above and below the letters.

A final note: Arabic is an easy language to rhyme, for reasons we won't go into here. And so for Arabs, poetry and rhetoric are far more important than with us.

BENGALI

How many speak it: 196 million.

Who speaks it: Bengali is spoken in Bengal province and surrounding areas in India by Hindus and in the neighboring nation of Bangladesh by Muslims.

Bengali has two main dialects: Sadhu-Bhasa, which is the literary language and has many Sanskrit words. It is nearly unintelligible to uneducated people. There's Calit-Bhasa, which is the colloquial speech. It is based on the speech of Calcutta and nearby areas.

Comments: The capital city of the Bengali literary language is Calcutta, a city you probably associate with extreme poverty. But Calcutta is also a city that publishes the most literary magazines in the world, a city where a hotel doorman is very possibly moonlighting as a contributing editor or essayist.

Bengali has always been an innovative language of literature. Though it was the first Indian language to develop modern Western literary styles of fiction and drama, Bengali also has a long history of its own. Like Hindi, it derives from Sanskrit, and it's in some senses the most "modern" of the Indian languages. It got rid of the old Indo-European gender distinctions that are the bane of French, German, and Spanish language learners, forcing them to remember if a table is male or female. It also got rid of the informal "you" form. In case you've forgotten, so did English: we no longer say "thou" and "thine." Bengali goes one further in that most of the time the plural is used with all verbs. One interesting distinction that Bengali makes is

between rational and nonrational beings. This didn't come from Sanskrit but from its own local culture.

That culture has long influenced the language and resulted in a literature that is probably the most extensive on the Indian subcontinent. The folk culture has been continuously prolific since the tenth century. From then until the present day, the Bengali people have produced countless songs, folktales, ballads, and aphorisms. Written Bengali literature began with the fourteenth-century *Vaishnava,* or song to the Hindu god Vishnu, and continued with poetry dedicated to Sakti (the manifestation of feminine energy), and included famous lyrics to Kali by Ramprased Sen that are still recited today. But Bengali language or literature can't be mentioned without talking about Rabindranath Tagore, a literary genius who wrote songs, poems, novels, and essays. Tagore brought Bengali literature to world attention by winning the Nobel Prize for Literature, something probably every striving literatus in modern Calcutta hopes to emulate.

RUSSIAN

How many speak it: 170 million native speakers; about 290 million speakers in total, many of whom learned it when their areas were under Soviet control.

Who speaks it: Citizens of Russia, as well as ethnic Russians in various newly independent states of the former Soviet Union, along with many non-Russian citizens of these states.

Comments: Russian is the largest

of a great family of Slavic languages, which includes Polish, Czech, Serb, Ukrainian, and other Eastern European tongues. Together, about three hundred million people speak Slavic languages. About half of them speak Russian, but if you speak any one of these tongues you can pretty much manage with the rest. They're fairly closely related. For example, "good evening" in Russian sounds like this: *dobry vyecher;* In Czech it's *dobry vecer;* in Serbian or Croatian it's *dobra vecer;* in Polish it's *dobry wieczor.*

Like some but not all Slavic languages, Russian uses the Cyrillic alphabet, derived from the Greek alphabet by two Greek bishops from Constantinople back in the ninth century. So it's different from ours, but there are nonetheless similarities. The letters *a, e, k, m, o,* and *t* sound approximately the same, but some can be deceptive: *p* is "r"; *b* is "v," *c* is "s." The old Soviet Union's CCCP was not pronounced as it looked to us, but as "Se, Se, Se, Ar."

Russian and other Slavic languages, along with English, German, French, etc., share a common ancestor—our mother tongue of Indo-European. But Russian is considered to be closer to the early forms of the original Indo-European. Like the original tongue (and along with Latin, etc.), Russian has a complicated case system. Verbs are simpler, but they preserve an old Indo-European distinction of aspect, which basically means whether an action was finished or unfinished, momentary or continual. In English, we use phrases like "he was writing" to say what a Russian can say with just the verb.

Russian is a beautiful language, but it can be difficult for someone learning

the language to pronounce well, particularly because of such consonant compounds like *shch, zdr, vstv,* and *vstr.* Say the colloquial greeting *zdravstvuytye* ("good day") and you'll see what we mean.

PORTUGUESE

How many speak it: There are about 170 million native speakers; about 180 million speak it as an official tongue.

Who speaks it: Portuguese is the official language of Portugal, and most important, it's the official language of its large and powerful daughter country of Brazil. In addition, it's spoken in former Portuguese colonies, including Angola, Mozambique, Cape Verde, the Azores, Madeira, and to a very slight degree in the colonial city of Macau in China.

Comments: Don't make the mistake of thinking that Portuguese is really just another form of Spanish. It's true that like other Romance languages it shares a lot of vocabulary with its Spanish sibling, together with a similar grammatical structure. But there are occasional differences even here: "to dine" is *cenar* in Spanish but *jantar* in Portuguese.

But more important, Portuguese follows certain grammatical patterns that belong to earlier forms of the Romance languages. In case you're insatiably curious about this, we'll mention that among other things it includes the future subjunctive tense and it places an object pronoun after a verb instead of before. In Spanish, to say "I speak to him" you say, in effect, "To him I speak": *le* (to him) *hablo* (I speak). In Portuguese, you say "I speak to him" as we do in English: *falo-lhe,* with *lhe* meaning "to him." Nevertheless, a Spanish speaker can read Portuguese and get by fairly easily.

Pronunciation is also different. Portuguese includes a very distinctive nasal sound, somewhat French-sounding (and certainly not heard in Spain). It's marked by a squiggly line over a vowel called a tilde, and is a derivative of the *n* sound but the "n" is gone. The best way to describe it is by example. Bread is *pão* in Portuguese, but pronounce it by holding your nose. That gives you the approximation of this sound. But it can't give you a feeling for the sounds of this often beautiful language.

MALAY-INDONESIAN

How many speak it: 155 million speakers; about 50 million native speakers.

Who speaks it: Indonesians speak Indonesian. Malaysians and Singaporeans speak Malaysian, but the languages are essentially the same.

Comments: Indonesian is a new language doing the hard job of uniting a diverse region. Indonesia is an archipelago nation in Southeast Asia that is made up of more than seventeen thousand islands, several of which are very large ones, and whose people speak two hundred or so different languages or dialects. One of these many languages is Javanese, which numbers more than sixty million native speakers (about the same as Italian) and has a long written tradition going back to the eighth century.

But to unite the people of this vast island region, Indonesian members in the colonial parliament back in 1918 decided to use Malay. Malay was the language spoken on the neighboring Malay Peninsula and nearby Java coast. It's related to most of the other languages of the area, and more important, it has a long history as a language of commerce. Malay has many Arabic words introduced by traders who came to the region in the Middle Ages bringing Islam. In fact, early Malay was written in an Arabic script called *jawi.* *Jawi* is used only in some religious texts; today Indonesian is written in Roman letters, like English.

The Indonesians made strong efforts to popularize a more developed form of this Malay language. Publishing houses issued books in the language and intellectuals argued in it. Like modern Hebrew, a new language was born out of an old one. It was called Indonesian, or Bahasa Indonesia.

Indonesian is a fun language for a beginner. It's deceptively easy to learn . . . at first. Pronunciation is easy; verb forms don't change. But after a while, difficulties arise. Indonesian is decidedly not a Western language, and it doesn't completely fit into a familiar grammatical scheme.

For example, at first glance, Indonesian verbs are wonderfully simple. They're not conjugated by number, person, or tense. To say "Bill laughs," you say "Bill *tertawa*"; to say "Bill, Bob, and Joe laughed," you say "Bill, Bob, and Joe *tertawa.*" But maybe to get back at you, verbs take many additions to make new meanings that can be confusing. For example, the root word *tinggi* means "high." Add the prefix *memper* and you have *mempertinggi,* which means "to heighten." Now stick on the suffix *kan* and you have *mempertinggikan*. Indonesian has many such prefixes and suffixes, and some of them change depending on context. But even that's not so difficult. Besides, Indonesian is a beautiful-sounding language to most English or American ears. It has no harsh sounds, and its musical quality has made some call it the "Italian of the Orient."

FRENCH

How many speak it: French is the native language for 72 million people, and an official language for 124 million people.

Who speaks it: Get ready for a long list of French speakers: French is not only the main language of France, where it is the official language and mother tongue for most people (although there are minorities who speak Basque, etc.), it is spoken in many parts of Europe and many former French colonies around the world, principally in Africa and in the Pacific. "Francophone Africa" is a common term for the former French-speaking colonies where French is still the official language. It includes much of West Africa (Senegal, Ivory Coast, Gabon, etc.) and Central Africa (Niger, Chad), as well as Zaire. In addition, French is still widely spoken in the North African states of Morocco, Algeria, and Tunisia.

In North America, French is an official language of Canada and the native tongue of most of the province of Quebec. It is also a language of French Guiana in South America, Haiti (in a distinctive form), Guadeloupe, and Martinique, as well as on the South Pacific islands of New Caledonia, Tahiti, Vanuatu, and many others.

Comments: Obviously, French is a major world language, but many French are concerned that it is losing ground to English—and they're right in many senses. It seems as if everyone is now learning English as a second language—even eighty percent of French language students choose to study it. This is hard to take for a country with a very proud linguistic tradition. More annoying to many is that French has been deluged with many new English words, resulting in a language mix called Franglais. They range from political words like *congrès, meeting,* and *vote;* cultural words like *western, bestseller,* and *brunch;* to technical and business terms like *databank, marketing,* and *software.*

Recently, the government proposed a law that would have banned many of these words and replaced them with French equivalents. "Airbag," for example, would have been replaced with *coussin gonflable de protection,* which is a mouthful. The law didn't pass.

Despite French concerns, French and English have had a long history of trading words back and forth. After all, when William the Conqueror took over England back in 1066, he brought with him his Norman language, which introduced a great many French words into English and changed it forever. In many ways, English is a double language with an older Anglo-Saxon way of saying something and a (relatively) newer French way, as in *answer* or *respond,* and *freedom* or *liberty.* Sometimes we've switched with the French—we may say *savoir faire,* while they may say *know-how.*

But now the French are concerned

that the trading has gone so far that they're losing their heritage. The French have long been concerned with the status of their language. Way back in 1635 the Académie Française was founded and charged with purifying the language and making it universal in France. Since then, the government has passed many laws regulating the use of foreign words. The Académie and its cohorts did something else with the language as well. Over the years, French syntax (word order and such) was rigidly standardized, making French the ideal diplomatic language. It's very easy to be specific in French. It's easy to write detailed treaties with few vagaries that can give rise to misunderstandings later. Until most recently, French was the major language of discourse among most nations. It still is an important means of communication in linguistically diverse countries such as in Africa, where it may serve as a lingua franca (no pun intended) among different peoples.

As you probably know, French is a Romance language. But French has some peculiarities that make it quite different from its cousins Italian and Spanish. Although other Romance languages link together sounds from one word to another, French carries this to an extreme. When you see written French, you see separate words. But when you hear it, you hear long strings that sound like one or two very long words. Some linguists compare French to North American Indian languages, which often have long words that contain many different elements strung together. In French, for example, *Je ne lui en avais pas encore parlé* (I hadn't yet spoken to him about it) is pronounced more like "jenlyuianavepazankerparlay." Just say that fast!

JAPANESE

How many speak it: 125 million speakers.

Who speaks it: Japanese is spoken primarily in Japan, though a fair number of people of Japanese origin speak it in Brazil and the United States. It is understood often in Korea and Taiwan, which were formerly colonies.

Japanese has many rural and regional dialects, but the Standard Japanese of Tokyo has become the main dialect.

Comments: Japanese writing looks somewhat like Chinese writing, and many people think that the languages are related. Guess again. In terms of grammar, Japanese is as far away from Chinese as English is.

Japanese is an agglutinating language; words are built up by sticking together units called affixes. Before you panic; it's sort of like we do when we add *dis* and *ful* to each end of "taste" to make *distasteful*. But the Japanese do it far more extensively to build complex meanings. In contrast, Chinese is an isolating language; the words stay the same no matter what.

But even if it's not like Chinese, Japanese is very, very different from English or any other Indo-European language, and many Westerners find it difficult. For example, in Japanese adjectives can show time: *shiroi* means "white"; *shirokatta*, "was white"; and *shirokute*, "being white." Saint Francis Xavier reported that Japanese must have been invented by Satan to prevent European missionaries from learning it and preaching the Christian Gospel.

Japanese can also seem maddeningly

vague to a typical Westerner. Japanese writer Sumie Mishima was not vague about this: "In the Japanese language exactness is purposely avoided."

This has led to many misunderstandings. Americans sometimes think that when a Japanese speaks of mutual understanding, he means "yes." But he really means "no." Then again, Japanese vagueness has also led to a literature that includes a great many world masterpieces.

Some of this inexactness seems to show up in the language itself. Personal pronouns aren't used that much. Verbs don't show whether they are plural or singular, they don't change whether the doer is first person (*I* or *we*), second person (*you*), or third person (*he, she, they*).

Verbs normally come at the end of the sentence or main clause. An English equivalent of a Japanese sentence might be this line from the poet Alexander Pope: "pensive poets painful vigils keep." Sometimes the object instead of the subject of the sentence is placed first. An English equivalent is Wordsworth's line: "strange fits of passion have I known." Both ways sound odd to us.

Unlike American English, Japanese is highly sensitive to status; there are complex and different ways of addressing someone close to you, someone inferior to you, someone superior to you.

It's hard to be brief about the Japanese writing system, but let's try. It's probably the most complex mélange of symbols you'll ever encounter. Here's why. For various historical reasons, the Japanese developed not one, but three different ways of writing their language—and sometimes they mix all three together:

Like many other languages, Japanese is very conscious of politeness and respect. (Unlike American English, where it is likely that your boss or teacher will say, "Just call me Bob.") In Japanese, for example, there are a number of ways of saying "you," depending on your social position:

- *anata: a standard polite "you," not used for bosses and those higher in status*

- *anta: informal, used with friends*

- *sochira: very polite, used on formal occasions*

- *kimi: used by men to other men of equal or lower position*

- *omae: colloquial, seen by some as slightly derogatory*

- *teme: impolite*

Women generally use more polite forms than men. But today, some of the status forms are changing and becoming more casual.

Kanji: selected Chinese characters, usually with a Japanese sound.

Katakana: a syllabary of forty-seven characters derived from the Chinese characters, but usually with Japanese sounds. This alphabet is used frequently in scientific literature and public documents.

Hiragana (or "simple *kana*"): a syllabary derived from a cursive form of Chinese characters and used frequently in daily life.

For all this complexity, the Japanese are not linguistic purists or snobs. They're quite happy to add foreign words and terms to their language. In fact, much of their early vocabulary comes from the Chinese, and today they've borrowed many Western terms that they usually transliterate in *kana* sounds. But then Japanese culture and language are easily able to make even the most foreign things somehow uniquely Japanese.

GERMAN

How many speak it: 120 million speakers.

Who speaks it: German is the principal and official language of Germany and Austria; it is also an official language of Switzerland (along with French and Italian), and of Luxembourg (along with French). It's spoken in certain communities in Belgium, France, and other countries, and is the most common second language of the former Yugoslavs and Turks.

There is really no standard German dialect. Germany has been divided into small separate states for so long that there are many dialects. They range from the Low German of West-phalia, which is mutually intelligible with Dutch, to the High German of Bavaria, Switzerland, and Austria. One interesting dialect of German became Yiddish, a Germanic language of the Eastern European Jews. It has several unusual features, including many many Hebrew-Aramaic words (eighteen percent) and Slavic words (sixteen percent). And it uses Hebrew letters, but has a German structure along with a wonderful way of putting things. Many words like "boychik," "mensch," and "schlemiel" have entered the English language—a roundabout reintroduction to German for American-English speakers.

Comments: Though German has a long history, we don't know much about it prior to about the fourth century when it was first written. Along with its fellow languages like English, German is part of an Indo-European group that early on distinguished itself from other Indo-European languages by what is called the High German consonant shift. For some reason, ways of pronouncing consonants changed for early Germanic speakers. For example *p* became *f; k* became *h; t* became *th.*

This changed Indo-European words into forms that are familiar to us. For example, Indo-European languages like Latin called a foot something like *ped.* But with early German during the consonant shift, *ped* lost its *p* sound for an *f* sound. After a few more evolutionary changes *ped* now sounded something like . . . "foot."

If this was the only consonant shift, German would be very easy for us. But after English split off from German, the main dialect of German made another consonant shift. In some cases *d* became *t, t* became *ss, p* became *pf,*

and so on. So in English we get *cold,* in High or Upper German they get *kalt,* with a *t.*

There are more differences as well. German has a case system that tacks on endings to nouns depending on where they stand in a sentence: it probably has the most complex inflectional system among its close relatives.

German has three genders—masculine, feminine, and neuter—which means that all nouns are either a "he," "she," or "it." The problem for learners of German is that sometimes words we think would be feminine are neuter and vice versa. American writer Mark Twain thought this was ridiculous and he satirized the German language in this sample dialogue:

Gretchen: Wilhelm, where is the turnip?
Wilhelm: She has gone to the kitchen.
Gretchen: Where is the accomplished and beautiful English maiden?
Wilhelm: It has gone to the opera.

That's not the only problem for people learning German. In some very basic forms, German word order is similar to English, which is not surprising. Subjects are usually first, and verbs are next. But there's a big hitch. The verb must always be the second element in the sentence (not counting introductory or connective words such as "and" and "but"), so German can easily start sounding difficult to English speakers, with sentences like "Yesterday read I a good book." In addition, German makes compound words without spaces or hyphens, which can initially be a problem. "Main railway station" in German is all mushed together to make *Hauptbahnhof.* That's not so bad, but now say this German

English—The International Language

Like it or not—and many people, particularly the French, don't—English is fast becoming *the* world language. Today, more than three hundred million speak it as their first tongue; another three hundred million use it as a second language; estimates are that more than a billion people in all are fluent in English, and there are more every day. According to a *Reader's Digest* survey of twelve European countries, almost seventy percent of people between age eighteen and twenty-four speak English, compared with only forty percent of people twenty-five and older. Well established on all continents, English is the official language of sixty nations and is used prominently in twenty-five more. More than sixty-six percent of the world's scientists write their papers in English (the next most popular language is German, with five to twelve percent); and more than eighty percent of world data-bases are in English. It is the main language of international conferences, medicine, diplomacy, international business, and transportation.

One of the most common forms of universal English is aviation English, a deliberately restricted form of the language used in *all* international commercial flying that was established by the International Civil Aviation Organization after World War II. It uses a limited, but often technical, English vocabulary, with special features that allow listeners to check back and make sure pilots understand. Cockpit conversations are monitored to guarantee that pilots and crew use this English correctly. Here's a brief sample of this English that is understood by pilots around the world:

"Leaving flight level three nine zero. Descending to level three one zero. BA six zero six Alpha."

It's not Shakespeare, but it makes the skies safe.

---

compound word quickly: *Einkommensteurerklärung* (income tax return).

SWAHILI

How many speak it: About 48 million speak Swahili as either their mother tongue or as a lingua franca.

Who speaks it: Swahili is the official language of Kenya and Tanzania, and is widely spoken in Uganda and Zaire.

Comments: A long time ago, probably at least five thousand years ago, a West African group of people who spoke what linguists today call a Niger-Congo language began to drift apart. One group went southeast from

Cameroon across Africa at the equator. They were called Bantu speakers, from the common word "people" in their many languages of today (Bantu, Wantu, Watu, etc.). If they hadn't done much more, these Bantu speakers would be a minor feature on this diverse continent. But around the beginning of the African Iron Age, the Bantu peoples suddenly expanded their control over most of Africa. And today their five hundred different languages are spoken from Kenya in East Africa to South Africa, where the politically important Xhosa and Zulu peoples live. So a little familiarity with Swahili can give you at least a vague idea of the languages of an enormous number of people.

Swahili, or more correctly KiSwahili, is the single most spoken language of this Bantu subgroup since it does double duty as a first language for many and a lingua franca for many more.

Swahili probably began as a Bantu language that was modified to serve as a trading language between East African coastal Bantu speakers and Arab sea traders. As a language of trade, it began to spread inland in the 1800s. Just as English includes many French words, Swahili includes many Arabic words. In fact, Swahili itself is derived from the Arabic word for coastal or coastal inhabitant: *saahilii*.

But Swahili is not related at all to Arabic grammatically. In many ways it is an agglutinating language, which means that new words or meanings are built up by adding units called affixes to the beginning, end, or middle of a word. Swahili initially takes some getting used to because the additions are usually made in front of the word instead of at the end. For example, "he saw you" in Swahili is *alikuona*, which is a word of four parts: *a* (he); *li* (past tense marker); *ku* (you); and *ona* (see). You can replace these different elements and get new words. Replace *a* with *ni* (I/me) and *li* with *ta* (future tense marker) and you get *nitakuona*, or "I will see you."

But the most interesting aspect of Swahili is its division of words into classes that take different prefixes and require different additions to their accompanying verbs or adjectives.

For example, if we add the prefix *m-*

There's a renewed effort to push the pan-African movement. The newest idea: reviving the ancient West African language N'ko ("I Say") that was used as means of cross-cultural communication. Those behind the revival, chiefly Guinean scholars working for literacy, hope to see N'ko used as a lingua franca throughout the region.

to the stem word *-tu*, we get *mtu*, or "man"; to make it plural, we take away the *m* and put in *wa* to get *watu*, or "men." Similarly, *kitu* is "thing"; *vitu* is "things"; *utu* is "manhood"; *jitu* is "huge man"; *majitu* is "huge men." Verbs and adjectives usually have to follow a certain format in agreement with the beginnings. For example, *dogo* means small. To say "a small thing," we say *kitu kidogo*. To say "the small thing is broken," we say "*kitu kidogo kimevunjika*." Of course, there are many complications and differences, but that's the basic way Swahili works.

Swahili is so far the only major competitor with the old colonial languages of French and English as a medium of communication among speakers of different languages. Naturally, as a world language English has its advantages, which is why it is the official language of many African states. Swahili, however, has its advantages as well. It is a vigorous language with its own unique African rhythms and an often interesting way of coining words. (For example, *mbenzi* is a word for "rich person," one who owns a Mercedes-Benz.) Its literature is growing from the work of James Mbotela and Shaaban Robert. Internationally prominent Kenyan writer Ngugi wa Thiong'o wrote in the preface to his last English-language book: "This is my farewell to English as a vehicle for any of my writings. From now on it is Gikuyu and Kiswahili all the way!" And today, many would agree.

A FAMILY TREE OF LANGUAGE:
A BRIEF GUIDE TO THE WORLD'S MAJOR LANGUAGE GROUPS

 Note: you'll see that a few major languages aren't mentioned in these language families. The notable omissions: Japanese and Korean. And for a good reason. These are so-called orphans, languages that appear to be unrelated to any other group. Of course, some experts disagree, saying that they *are* related to other languages, but no one is quite sure. So for the time being, Japanese and Korean remain possibly the most widely used orphan languages in the world.

EUROPE AND SOUTHERN ASIA

THE IND-EUROPEAN LANGUAGES

The main languages and how many speak them: English, 322 native speakers, 148 others; Hindi, 418 million; Spanish, 381 million; Russian, 288 million; Bengali, 196 million; Portuguese, 182 million; German, 120 million; French, 72 million native speakers.

Where they're spoken: Originally throughout Europe, much of India, Russia, now on every continent and many islands.

A few words: The family of most of the languages spoken in the Western world—from Greek to Italian, Hindi to Spanish—and the most pervasive family of them all. Theory has it that the

first Indo-European language started in southern Russia and from that home base spread over most of the world. The key reason for this diffusion wasn't that the languages were particularly easy to learn. It was simple colonialism. A seminomadic peoples who lived around 4000 B.C.E., the Indo-Europeans first started conquering certain areas, and so, too, did their descendants centuries later. As a result, English, Spanish, French, Portuguese, Hindi, and other Indo-European languages are among the most spoken in the world as a native tongue, if not as a lingua franca.

AFRICA

THE AFRO-ASIATIC LANGUAGES

The main languages and how many speak them: Arabic, over 180 million speakers (plus 33 million more as a lingua franca); Amharic (Ethiopia's official language), about 20 million; Hausa, more than 37 million (plus a few million more as a second language spoken in Niger, North Nigeria and Cameroon).

Where they're spoken: North Africa, the Middle East, the eastern horn of Africa, southwest Asia, including Saudi Arabia, Israel, Egypt, Algeria, Morocco, Ethiopia, Kenya, Ghana, Malta, etc.

A few words: A language family

with roots going way back—as far back as the seventh millennium B.C.E., according to experts. As you'd expect, given the date, many of the world's ancient languages grew out of this one ancestor. There's Egyptian, dating back to before the third millennium B.C.E.; and, almost as old, the languages spoken in Babylon and Assyria, Phoenician and Akkadian. These exist only in written form nowadays, of course. But some of these oldies are still goodies. Granted, it's been updated, but Hebrew dates back to the second millennium B.C.E.; and Aramaic, the language of Jesus Christ and his followers, is still spoken but in a modern dialect form.

THE NIGER-CONGO LANGUAGES

The main languages and how many speak them: The Bantu languages, including Swahili, about 8 million regular speakers (but nearly 40 million use it as a lingua franca), and Ruanda, 7 million; Yoruba, 20 million, Igbo, 17 million; Fulani, 13 million.

Where they're spoken: Sub-Saharan Africa, including Zimbabwe, Zambia, Ruanda, Nigeria, Ghana, Senegal, etc.

A few words: Africa as a continent has about 1,300 different languages—more than any other. And this family of languages is responsible for about a thousand of the world's languages, not to mention a few thousand more dialects. The continent also covers a lot of ground. Add to this the fact that the major languages apparently diverged and evolved in their own ways more than five thousand years ago and it's no wonder a lot of people can't understand one another if they're speaking their mother tongues. The solution? Lingua francas, of course. And this part of Africa uses a

few: Swahili in East Africa; English and French in West Africa; a number of languages like Fulani, Bambara, and Kongo used among different tribes; plus pidgin English, and other pidgins and creoles.

THE NILO-SAHARAN LANGUAGES

The main languages and how many speak them: Kanuri, 4 million speakers; Luo, 4 million; Dinka, 2 million; Nubian, 1 million; Songhai, 1 million.

Where they're spoken: In two clusters around the Nile and Chari Rivers that include Nigeria, Sudan, Uganda, Chad, and Mali.

A few words: Another large family, with more than a hundred languages, most of which are spoken by only small groups of people. One of the oldest of this group: Nubian, with writings in a modified form of Coptic dating back to the eighth century.

THE KHOISAN LANGUAGES

The main languages and how many speak them: The languages of the Khoikhoin (Hottentot) and San (Bushman) tribes, spoken by fewer than fifty thousand today.

Where they're spoken: Southern part of Africa, generally around the Kalahari Desert that includes Namibia, Botswana, and Tanzania.

A few words: The smallest African language group, but better known than you might expect chiefly because these languages use "click consonants," that is, clicks as consonants. It can be pretty complicated. Clicks can be made in a number of ways, with tongue against teeth, in the mouth or throat, plus they sometimes use other sounds made in the throat or nose at the same time. In fact, one language, !Xu, uses as many as forty-eight different clicks.

ASIA

THE ALTAIC LANGUAGES

The main languages and how many people speak them: Turkish, 58 million speakers; Azerbaijani, about 15 million; Mongol, about 6 million.

Where they're spoken: From the Balkan Peninsula to northeast Asia, including Turkey, Azerbaijan, Iran, Afghanistan, parts of China, Uzbekistan.

A few words: This language family not only covers a lot of ground geographically, it also includes about forty languages that are continually evolving. In the last century alone, many of the Altaic languages have had new words entering their vocabulary; written forms have been updated, as in the case of Turkish, which had its Arabic script replaced by Latin writing as recently as 1929; and even new languages, primarily literary ones, have developed. But there's a flip side. Of the forty languages, only a few, like Turkish, remain strong. Many others are fading. Take Manchu, for instance. Once the language of the rulers of China for more than two hundred years, now only about ten thousand people speak it.

THE AUSTRO-ASIATIC LANGUAGES

The main languages and how many speak them: Vietnamese, 64 million speakers; Khmer, 8 million; Santali, 5 million.

Where they're spoken: Southeast Asia, including Vietnam, Laos, Cambodia, and parts of Malaysia, Burma, Thailand, and India.

A few words: A family with easily

more than a hundred different languages, most of them not all that well known. In fact, one of the main languages of the group, Vietnamese, isn't even definitely a family member. The problem? Chinese was so in use in Southeast Asia that it's tough to trace the history of Vietnamese.

THE CAUCASIAN LANGUAGES

The main languages and how many people speak them: Georgian, about 4 million people (speaking different dialects); Chechen, more than 600,000 speakers; the other thirty-eight or so languages have only 400,000 speakers or less.

Where they're spoken: The area around the Caucasus Mountains, between the Black Sea and the Caspian Sea, that includes Georgia, parts of Armenia, and Azerbaijan.

A few words: The Caucasian language family has several claims to fame: at least ninety percent of its roughly five million speakers still live in the region where it evolved. With about forty distinct languages in the family, this makes the region one of the most highly concentrated language areas in the world. It also wins points on the complexity scale: one of its lesser family members, Ubykh, a language spoken by very few people nowadays, has *eighty* consonants. And it wins points on the language purity scale as well: the language Bats is spoken by three thousand or so people who live in one single village in Georgia.

THE DRAVIDIAN LANGUAGES

The main languages and how many speak them: Tamil, 69 million speakers; Kannada, 44 million; Malayalam, 35 million.

Where they're spoken: Primarily southern and eastern India, but Tamil has spread to Sri Lanka, Malaysia, Vietnam, parts of East and South Africa, and a number of islands in the Indian Ocean and South Pacific.

A few words: This is one of the only language groups *not* named after the region in which it developed and possibly for a good reason. (The name Dravidian, in fact, comes from the Sanskrit *dravida,* which refers to the Tamil language.) There's a big debate about where this language group started and even where the original speakers came from. Some scholars believe they came from the south, from lands now underwater; others say that around 4000 B.C.E., people migrated from Asia; still others hold that this group might have evolved from the same ancestor as the Uralic and Altaic families. The consensus? Most agree that the language group Dravidian came from at least as far as northern India and that this language group is both ancient and modern. There are written examples of Tamil going back to the third century B.C.E. In fact, most experts believe that Tamil is probably a lot like the ancestor language called (logically) Proto-Dravidian. And the Dravidian group includes some of the world's *newest* languages, like Pengu, Naiki, and Manda that were identified in the 1960s.

THE PALEO-SIBERIAN LANGUAGES

The main languages and how many speak them: None well known; in fact, only about 25,000 people speak any of these languages. The most common? Chukchi, with 12,000 speakers.

Where they're spoken: Northeastern Sibera.

A few words: Where once the Paleo-Siberian culture thrived, now it has dwindled and with it, the language. In fact, the Paleo-Siberian family is more like a family of orphans than anything else. The languages in this group aren't actually related to one another, but because so few people speak them, they've been lumped together for ease of classification since the nineteenth century. Even their writing system isn't one that evolved from the past. Since the 1920s, Paleo-Siberian languages have used a writing system based on the Cyrillic alphabet.

THE SINO-TIBETAN LANGUAGES

The main languages and how many speak them: Chinese (including Mandarin, Cantonese, Wu, Min, and Hakka), 1.2 billion people; Burmese, 31 million; Tibetan, roughly 5 million.

Where they're spoken: China, Taiwan, and throughout Southeast Asia (including Hong Kong, Indonesia, Malaysia, Thailand, Singapore, Vietnam), Myanmar (Burma), India, and the United States.

A few words: One of the biggies in the language family world in a number of ways. First in the sheer numbers game: Chinese (or more precisely, the different Chinese languages or dialects) is spoken by a whopping 1,200 million. Second, in the number of languages: in addition to the top three languages listed above, there are almost three hundred other languages. Add to this the fact that there are so many major dialects that virtually serve as separate languages and are sometimes even viewed this way and you wind up with a huge language family. Third, on the age scale: Sino-Tibetan languages date way back. Written literary Chinese goes back to 1500 B.C.E. Compared with this, Tibetan is a relative kid, dating back to only the eighth century, though it's still older than many other languages.

(For more on the Chinese language, see page 472)

THE TAI LANGUAGES

The main languages and how many speak them: Thai (yes, with an *h*), 49 million speakers; Lao (or Laotian), 6 million; Shan and Yuan, more than 3 million each.

Where they're spoken: Thailand, Laos, northern Vietnam, China, and parts of Myanmar (Burma), and India.

A few words: One of the more problematic language families: no one's sure just how they're related to the language groups. Some experts think they're related to the Austronesian; others with the Sino-Tibetan. And the jury is still out. One of the only clues: its written text dates back to the thirteenth century. What does this prove? No one is sure.

THE URALIC LANGUAGES

The main languages and how many speak them: Hungarian (or Magyar), Hungary's national language, spoken by about 14 million people; Finnish, 6 million; Estonian, more than 1 million.

Where they're spoken: Around the north Ural Mountains, including Siberia, portions of the former Soviet Union (around the Gulf of Riga and the Kola Peninsula), Finland, and Hungary, the lone outpost separated from the other areas in this language group.

A few words: A family of languages with an identifiable ancestor called, logically enough, Proto-Uralic, that was spoken more than seven thousand

years ago in the north Ural mountains. But this ancient family is fading out a bit, sapped by the strength of Russian and other neighboring languages. Not to mention the fact that some of the speakers themselves are fading out. For example, take the Samoyedic branch—or actually more a twig—of the language group. These are the languages of the Samoyeds, the reindeer breeders and hunters of Mongol descent living in the Arctic and Siberia, who nowadays number only about thirty thousand.

OCEANIA

THE AUSTRONESIAN (OR MALAYO-POLYNESIAN) LANGUAGES

The main languages and how many speak them: Malay-Indonesian, 155 million speakers; Javanese, 64 million; Tagalog, 53 million; Sudanese, 26 million; Malagasy, 12 million.

Where they're spoken: A huge area (granted, much of it is water), from Hawaii to New Zealand and from Madagascar to Easter Island, including Madagascar, Malaysia, Indonesia, the Philippines, New Guinea, Melanesia, Micronesia, Polynesia, New Zealand, Australia, among others.

A few words: Another enormous language family with more than two hundred million speakers and about seven hundred different languages, plus a number of pidgins and creoles. Making this even more complicated is the fact that a number of languages have not only different dialects but different names. For instance, speakers of

Dayak (spoken mainly in Borneo and Sarawak) call it seventy different names, depending on the specific dialect they speak and where they live. And in some cases, dialects have become so different from the main language, they're almost separate languages unto themselves.

THE INDO-PACIFIC LANGUAGES

The main languages and how many speak them: Enga, 125,000; most others have even fewer speakers, ranging from about 100,000 on down to only 20 or so.

Where they're spoken: Basically anywhere in Oceania where the Austronesian languages aren't spoken, chiefly in parts of New Guinea and certain islands east and west of New Guinea.

A few words: As if the Austronesian language family doesn't make languages in Oceania complicated enough, this is the *other* language group in the area—and it has *another* six hundred different languages in it. Most of these are spoken in New Guinea, making New Guinea one of the most language-dense countries in the world. But for all the different languages, a number of them are marginal, at best. In fact, some have only a few dozen speakers.

THE AMERICAS

A short note: As you'd expect, owing to colonization most of the languages in North and South America are actually European languages, and so fall into the huge Indo-European family. But

before the Europeans landed and spread their languages and cultures, there were about two thousand different indigenous languages spoken, most of them extremely diverse. Hand in hand with the high number of languages are also a high number of language families. Given this fact, we have, in most cases, combined families under regional headings.

Family Prayers: The Lord's Prayer in Twenty Indo-European Languages

Just because languages are split up into families, doesn't mean that sibling tongues sound at all alike. Case in point: here's the first line of the Lord's Prayer—"Our Father who art in heaven"—in twenty different languages, all members of the huge Indo-European family. When you take a look at them, you can sometimes see similarities. In other cases, you'd be hard-pressed to find any family resemblance at all.

English:	Our Father who art in Heaven
Welsh:	Ein Tad yr hwn wyt yn y nefoedd
German:	Unser Vater der Du bist im Himmel
Yiddish:	Undzer Voter Vos bist im himl
Dutch:	Onze Vader die in de hemelen zijt
Latin:	Pater noster qui es in caelis
French:	Notre Père qui es aux cieux
Spanish:	Padre nuestro que estas en los cielos
Portuguese:	Pai nosso que estas nos ceus
Albanian:	Ati yne qe je ne qiell
Greek:	Patera mas pou eisai stous ouranous
Lithuanian:	Teve susu kurs esi danguje
Russian:	Otce nas suscij na nebasach
Polish:	Ojcze nasz ktorys jest w niebiesiech
Bulgarian:	Otce nas kojto si na nebesata
Kurdish:	Ya bawk-i ema ka la asman-a-y
Persian:	Ei pedar-e-ma ke dar asman ast
Hindi:	He hamare svargbasi pita
Sanskrit:	Bho asmakham svargastha pita
Romany:	Dade amare kaj isien k'o devle

THE NORTH AMERICAN LANGUAGES

(actually over fifty different families)

The main languages and how many speak them: Eskimo, about 100,000; Navajo, about 120,000.

Where they're spoken: Chiefly Alaska, Canada, and pockets of the United States.

A few words: Generally, a dwindling group of languages. Once there were about three hundred different languages; now there are easily fewer than half this number. And many of these languages are just barely holding on, spoken chiefly by the elderly. For example, most of the languages in this group have fewer than a thousand speakers. One interesting note, though: one language, Navajo, has actually grown over the past decade or so.

THE PENUTIAN LANGUAGES

The main languages and how many speak them: Nahuatl (or Aztec), about a million speakers; Maya (or Yucatec) and Quiché, about 250,000; Mapuché, about 250,000.

Where they're spoken: Runs from Canada through Mexico to southwest South America, but concentrated in Mexico, the Yucatán, and Chile.

A few words: A family that bridges North and South America in that the languages belonging to it are (or were) spoken from North to South America. Among the languages included are those of the North American tribes such as the Hopi, the Comanche, and the Shoshone, as well as those of the Mayans and Aztecs. But, as you'd expect, while this group once had easily over sixty languages, it's dying out.

THE MESO-AMERICAN LANGUAGES

The main languages and how many speak them: Zapotec, Otomi, Mixtec, only about 250,000 speakers each.

Where they're spoken: Throughout Central America.

A few words: This is the only family specific to the region. Other languages in Central America actually are members of either North or South American families.

THE SOUTH AMERICAN LANGUAGES

(possibly up to a hundred different families)

The main languages and how many speak them: Quechua, 8 million; Guaraní, 4 million.

Where they're spoken: Scattered throughout the continent of South America.

A few words: One of the most diverse areas in terms of language. In the past, experts believe that about two thousand different languages were spoken in South America—and this, before the influx of European languages like Spanish, French, or Portuguese. Of course, many of these languages have died out in the face of Westernization. But many still exist, and, in fact, remain relatively strong. For example, take the two largest languages: Quechua, once the language of the Incas, has become a lingua franca throughout the South American continent; and Guaraní, a Paraguayan Indian language, has become the majority language of the country and is now mainly spoken by *non*-Indians.

THE SEARCH FOR OUR MOTHER TONGUE: TRACING ENGLISH'S FAMILY TREE

"Our Father who art in heaven" seems as far from the Sindhi *E asan-ja piu, jo asmana men ahe,* as Indiana is from India.

But both languages—English and Sindhi—are related, offsprings of a common tongue that was spoken more than five thousand years ago.

Sir William Jones, a British scholar, first hypothesized in 1786 that Sanskrit had the same source as Latin and Greek and that the Germanic and Celtic languages might also. A flurry of studies followed as philologists tried to trace back to the common source. And by the late 1800s, the mother tongue had a name, not the most melodious of names, but one nonetheless—Proto-Indo-European, or, more simply, PIE. Apparently PIE is the mother of the Indo-European languages that spread across the world, from French to Farsi, German to Gheg, Yiddish to Urdu.

Tracing its roots: No one is quite sure where exactly PIE was born. But according to the most widely accepted theory, it looks like it all might have started on the south Russian steppe around 4000 B.C.E. The people who lived there were called the Kurgans (in Russian it means "burial mound," and they were given this name because of their burial practices). The Kurgans were seminomadic and began spreading west into the Danube region of Europe and beyond. By the time the Kurgans had expanded into the Adriatic area, it appears that the language was fairly well evolved.

So what did these first talkers sit around and talk about? Based upon reconstructions of the language, we can get an interesting insight into the people who launched a hundred tongues.

Since they could talk about fish but not about the ocean or the sea, lacking words for these, it's likely that they lived near bodies of water but not the coastline. It's doubtful that they were wine drinkers, because they had no word for "grape." But they did have words for other plants, such as grain, and for farming techniques and for animals, including horses, goats, sheep, cows, pigs, and dogs. They were family-oriented, given the presence of words referring to mother, father, husband, brother. There were even a number of words meaning "in-laws." This, and a few other clues, make it look as though the wife was admitted into the husband's family, pointing to a patriarchal culture. And while they weren't literate, the Kurgans did appear to have a relatively advanced culture, with words relating to such abstract areas as law, religion, and social standing.

Reconstructing the language: PIE itself appears to be relatively advanced linguistically. It may be old, but it was far from rudimentary. Reconstructions of the language, arrived at chiefly through linguistic detective work and analysis of the early written Indo-European languages, show a language with numerous stop consonants like in modern English (*p,* *b, t, d, k, g*), but also with aspirants such as *bh, dh, gh, gwh*; only one unstopped or sibilant consonant, *s;* the schwa; and the five vowels that we know in both long and short forms. PIE had three genders (masculine, feminine, and neuter); up to eight cases (ranging from nominative to instrumental); adjectives that agreed with the noun form; and different grammatical forms of words to express changes in tense and number, usually formed by a systematic change in vowels, like the English *take/took* or *foot/feet*. Add to this the probability that the speaker used different inflections to express mood, tense, voice, number, and more. All in all, PIE probably wasn't as easy as, well, pie.

PIE spreads: But it clearly caught on. From its initial roots, PIE spread as the people who spoke it moved on, migrating across Europe and Asia, settling in areas that became Mycenean

Greece, India, even Ireland and other parts of Great Britain.

The debate still rages as to the actual home of PIE. For example, because there are no words for "palm tree" or "vine," most scholars agree that the people didn't begin their migrations in the Mediterranean area, but ended up there after wandering from North Central Europe. This is backed up by the presence of the word for "beech," a tree that's common in North Central Europe. But there's no word for "oak," another common European tree, which leads scholars to think that the original talkers started in Asia.

There's no question, however, that PIE is the mother of (some) of it all.

But what was PIE's mother?

There are *also* similarities between Proto-Indo-European and the Uralic family of languages, which, of course, means they may stem from an *older* common root. The *true* mother tongue?

MYSTERY LANGUAGES:
THE WORLD'S LAST UNDECIPHERED TONGUES

 Here's a challenge open to anyone who wants to achieve a certain kind of everlasting detective fame: decipher the last of the world's unreadable ancient writings. So far, no one has cracked the key to these forgotten tongues. Maybe you can. Outsiders did much with the ancient cuneiform writing of the ancient Babylonians, Persians, and Assyrians. The decipherer of Mayan was a (formerly) obscure Russian linguist named J. N. Knorozov who had been ignored by the nonlinguistic academic establishment in the West until the late 1980s. Here are the last tongues awaiting decipherment:

ETRUSCAN

Who spoke it: The Etruscans were an ancient people who lived in central Italy from around the seventh century B.C.E. (we think) until Rome conquered and absorbed them into the growing Roman Republic in the third century B.C.E. Though mentioned in old Roman and Greek texts, they were pretty much forgotten until 1828, when a farmer's plow unearthed a tomb on land belonging to Napoleon's brother. Soon a full-scale treasure hunt was on, persisting to this day, when tombs are still being found and robbed. There's something haunting about the Etruscans. It's what we see in their statues and tomb frescoes: men and

women as seeming equals, smiling out with mysterious half-smiles, arms and legs posed with a fluidity and grace; a world of sunlight and fishing and games and fresh air. Looking out from their tomb paintings they seem to possess the secret of joy. The writer D. H. Lawrence was fascinated by the Etruscans and concocted all sorts of half-baked theories about their lives and ideas. But what are the Etruscans *really* saying?

The challenge: We know their alphabet: it's similar to the earliest Greek one, with exceptions like the curious use of "8" as the letter *f*. We also know their language sounded odd with all sorts of clicks and hisses, and we can read a few of the more prosaic pieces about who died when, but that's about it. We don't even know if they and their language were native to Italy or from Asia as some commentators suggest. One ancient author, who heard it, described the language as "unlike any other." Most texts remaining seem to be short (and boring) tomb texts that give no clues.

But then there's a fifteen-hundred-word text found on the linen wrappings of an ancient Egyptian mummy that leaves archaeologists burning with curiosity. What does it say? The problem is that while we have the texts, we don't have much else to go on—no people still speaking the language as we do with Mayan, no bilingual text as we did with the Egyptian Rosetta stone. Even more frustrating is the fact that apparently Etruscan was spoken as late as the fourth or fifth or maybe even the sixth century C.E. Why didn't any of the very busy writers of the day record it as they did with old Latin and Greek? Or did they? There's always the hope that someone will unearth a long-forgotten medieval book in some old university library, a copy of a recopy of a late Roman papyrus. Periodically, someone tackles the mummy text one more time. And there's always the possibility that advanced computer analysis may unlock the secret. Meanwhile, others fossick about the central Italian province of Tuscany, searching for one more tomb with one more inscription, one more old text from some antique dealer, or better yet, the buried remains of some Etruscan town, where, it is fervently hoped, some bilingual text with the key to this mysterious language will be found.

PROTO-INDIAN

Who spoke it: The people of the early Indus Valley civilizations, inhabitants of Harappa and Mohenjo-Daro (see page 17), were a highly civilized and literate people who lived at the dawn of history. They may have been related to the ancient Sumerians, the supposed first inventors of writing.

The challenge: In the ruins of these great cities, archaeologists have found hundreds of seals or amulets, square or oblong plaques made of a soft stone and engraved with curious writing. There are about 200 symbols (some say 400, others say 150). Experts think some of these symbols are ideograms that represent a single idea or thing while others are phonetic and represent a sound. The symbols themselves seem to be stylized representations of things in everyday life: wheat, seeds, plowing, men, soldiers, fruit, mills. But that's about all experts are reasonably sure of. The problem is that while there are many seals with writing on them, the text in all cases is short, and in many cases no one is certain what the symbols actually mean. One expert says a certain symbol means "fruit," another says "bucket," and meanwhile, absolutely no one has any idea of the language the symbols represent. But here's a puzzling coincidence: at least some symbols, maybe about fifty, are very similar to those from the undeciphered script of Easter Island, far off in the empty central Pacific Ocean. That script is estimated to have been written almost four thousand years later than the Proto-Indian script. Experts don't think much of this similarity, pointing out that many more symbols are *not* similar while the frequency of use of those that are similar is very different in both languages, and that what is similar is coincidental. Meanwhile, the mystery of Harappa and Mohenjo-Daro continues: who the people were, how they lived, what they thought, and what their end was are still unknown.

LINEAR A

Who spoke it: The Minoans who lived on the island of Crete during the Bronze Age spoke this ancient, unknown language. Archeological evidence about the Minoans is intriguing: although it is impossible to be definitive, it *seems* that these mysterious people lived pleasant lives, and that women played a far greater role in this culture than in most others.

Their houses were wide and spacious, with courtyards for air and light. Lively, brightly colored frescoes from the royal palace at Knossos depict birds, fish, and flowers. Men apparently wore simple loincloths with aprons; women, long flounced skirts and bodices open in the front that exposed their breasts, with high collars in back. Games like boxing, wrestling, and bullbaiting were popular; numerous children's toys have been found.

The principal religion was organized around the Great Mother Goddess, whose symbol was the double-headed axe. Apparently women were very important in Minoan religion. Religious frescoes often show priestesses, sometimes holding snakes (perhaps protectors of the household?) and performing devotions to the gods.

The challenge: Excavators have found many small clay tablets inscribed with a linear writing (boxes, crosses, lines, circles, etc.). Some tablets are shaped like pages and contain four to nine lines of writing that go from left to right. Apparently, there are three general classes of symbols: syllable signs, words signs or ideograms, and other signs like a word division mark. Most tablets seem to be inventories of goods held by palace officials or farmers. But no one so far has been able to progress beyond this, except to state the certainty that the language is

not Greek or any other Indo-European language. What language it is, and what those clay tablets say, is unknown. Scientists call it Linear A. (A later language, called Linear B, was deciphered in the 1950s and was discovered to be a very early form of ancient Greek.) Besides Linear A, two even earlier forms of writing, this time in hieroglypic (picture-writing) style, remain to be deciphered; they are believed to be ancestors of Linear A.

Even more intriguing is *another* writing system found on the Phaistos Disk, which was also discovered in Crete. This is an inscribed terra-cotta tablet, circular in shape and about six inches in diameter. Each side has pictographic markings set in a spiral. Some of the symbols look slightly similar to Linear B, but they are much more pictorial and represent animals, humans, household goods, plants, and tools. Nothing like it has been found elsewhere, and the text is probably too short to give enough clues to decipher it. But archaeologists are intrigued, particularly because it appears that the individual signs were literally stamped on the disk with the aid of movable type, the earliest known example of printing in the world. Who did this? One symbol, a plumed headdress, appears several times, leading some to suggest it comes from elsewhere, since Cretans did not wear them. But from where? It is hoped that other disks with the same writing will be unearthed . . . somewhere.

POLITICAL GEOGRAPHY OF THE WORLD

CONTENTS

~

A NEWSPAPER READER'S GUIDE
TO THE KEY NATIONS OF THE WORLD

NEW NATIONS ON THE MAP

POLITICAL GEOGRAPHY OF THE WORLD

 U.S. citizens have a bad reputation in the rest of the world. We're known as snobs: we're said to know everything about our country but nothing about anywhere else. However, because of our country's size and power, others know a lot about *us*. It's surprisingly easy to strike up a conversation about American politics or football even in the middle of the Arabian desert. We, on the other hand, often don't even know where Arabia is. Here's a frightening true example of our ignorance: when a U.S. ambassadorial nominee to a Southeast Asian country was asked about South Korea, he responded: "You mean there are *two* Koreas?"

Our ignorance is more than a minor failing—like it or not, the world is getting smaller and what happens "out there" *matters*—economically, politically, and socially. New links between nations are being formed or being strengthened. The Euro-pean Community is transforming once sacrosanct boundaries in Europe, while the fall of communism is increasing communication and ties between East and West. Former enemies like Vietnam are actively courting U.S. companies and tourists, and travel anywhere in the world is becoming easier—and more necessary. Already, the U.S. economy *depends* on foreign trade and contacts; it's the same case for the rest of the world. Whether it's cultural, political, or economic, the nations of the world are becoming more interdependent than ever.

And so we've listed the major political players on the world stage along with the newest nations of the world: a few facts followed by a brief current events background so the next time you read about the latest crisis in Korea you have an idea of what's going on, and why it's important—and where *both* Koreas are.

A NEWSPAPER READER'S GUIDE TO THE KEY NATIONS OF THE WORLD

There's a great variety to the nation-states of the world. The range of differences is huge. For example, the population of Nauru, a tiny island nation in the South Pacific, couldn't fill Yankee Stadium. Only 9,460 people (give or take a few) claim Nauruan citizenship, making it smaller than Liechtenstein and San Marino, two microstates in Europe. Meanwhile, over 1 billion people claim Chinese citizenship (give or take a few million). And to carry that Nauru analogy further, Nauru covers about eight square miles, while China incorporates most of East Asia, over 3.6 million square miles.

But what matters for most people is health, happiness, and prosperity—and here Nauru jumps ahead of China, with a per-capita income more than

ten times that of China and a democratically elected government. It's one of the richest nations in the world, China is among the poorest. (In case you're wondering, the island of Nauru is literally made of phosphates, which are a high-priced export.) And obviously, nations vary considerably by culture, language, and form of government.

In this section, we've grouped the world by major regions, listed and described some of the major powers or some of the more noteworthy in these regions—the ones you'll read about in the morning news. Each nation's cities are listed in order of size of population, the most populous first. These nations are considerably larger than Nauru, but most are much smaller than China. But size isn't everything, as most Nauruans would probably agree.

AFRICA (SUB-SAHARAN)

 Africa is a continent where, most scientists agree, human-kind began its long march to civilization. Today, it is a continent in turmoil. Until fairly recently, most of Africa was under colonial domination. The great powers of Europe colonized most of the continent, starting with slave traders in the 1600s and ending with a great race for colonies from the 1880s on.

But after World War II, and particularly in the 1960s, most of the Europeans left, and most of Africa became independent. But Africa's troubles were not over. The new independent African nations were formed out of the old colonies, but the problem was that most of the old colonial boundaries were artificial, cutting across tribal lines or amalgamating many diverse peoples into one unit. The post-colonial African governments agreed not to alter boundaries, fearing the consequences of continent-wide border changes. But Africa still faces many problems. Except for some bright spots like Nelson Mandela's South Africa, many nations are ruled by dictators; many others are among the poorest nations in the world; and new bloody wars, like the recent one in Ruanda, have killed hundreds of thousands, on a scale not seen since the great European world wars.

But there is hope too. Much is riding now on Nelson Mandela, whose moderate and able rule may be able to propel South Africa into an engine for continent-wide growth and prosperity.

SOME KEY NATIONS OF SUB-SAHARAN AFRICA

KENYA

(Republic of Kenya/Jamhuri ya Kenya)

VITAL STATISTICS

Geographic facts: 224,960 square miles, about the size of France; located on the eastern coast of Africa, on the banks of the Indian Ocean; straddles the equator

Cities: Nairobi (capital), Mombasa
Population: 27 million
Languages: Swahili and English (official), Kikuyu, Luhya, Luo, Meru
Ethnic groups: Kikuyu 21%, Luhya 14%, Luo 13%, Kelenjin 11%, Kamba 11%, and others, including Europeans and Asians
Religions: Protestant 38%, Roman Catholic 28%, Muslim 6%, traditional religions 26%

After it won independence in 1963, Kenya seemed to be on the fast road to capitalist success. The great nationalist leader who led his people to independence, Jomo Kenyatta, was a realist who firmly allied his nation to the West. He made it a haven for tourists and multinational corporations and emphasized traditional virtues of hard work and a team spirit. Predictably, Nairobi developed into a modern dynamic city. Tourists filled hotel coffers.

But there were problems. Kenyatta was said by opponents to favor his fellow Kikuyu people over other Kenyans, and particularly toward the end of his rule corruption was the order of the day. Opposition was not tolerated, and the

Of the top 20 countries relying most on foreign aid (excluding military assistance), 15 are in Africa. The top 10, measuring foreign aid as a percentage of gross national product, are:

Mozambique

Tanzania

Somalia

Chad

Malawi

Lesotho

Burundi

Jordan

Mauritania

Mali

Source: ASIA WEEK

great Kenyan writer Ngugi wa Thiong'o was imprisoned for his acid commentaries on contemporary Kenyan life. Kenyatta's successor, the uncharismatic Daniel arap Moi, promised better. But the trappings of power have corrupted him as well.

Meanwhile, with the highest birthrate in the world, Kenya can't keep up the economic pace it needs to preserve its standard of living. Unlike many other African nations, it doesn't have much in the way of mineral resources. It still depends a lot on agriculture (tea, coffee, and pyrethrum). But there isn't much agricultural land, and a lot of it is being ruined by overfarming. The wild animals that have attracted many tourists are suffering from widespread poaching (apparently Kenyatta's wife was involved as well as other elite members of society). Unemployment has risen alarmingly and Nairobi crime has risen with it. The wealthy and diplomatic community put bars on their windows and hire armed guards to protect them. Kenyans hoped that a little dose of democracy would help them face up to their problems and find solutions.

They were elated when President Moi allowed the parliament to open in

Liberia: The Forgotten Civil War

Not making the headlines or nightly news is the tragic and very bloody war in Liberia, a small West African nation that is home to numerous ethnic groups, including a large contingent of former slaves from the United States. They settled there in the early 1800s and dominated the country until 1980, when the president was overthrown. A more democratic Liberia was promised but instead, in 1989, Liberian leader Samuel K. Doe was overthrown and the civil war began. More than 150,000 Liberians have died, a huge proportion in a nation of only 2 million. Today, the war is less a civil war than a free-for-all, as armed militias roam the countryside killing civilians. Although there are more international aid workers and UN peacekeepers in Liberia than anywhere else on earth, they have been unable to stop the carnage.

The War in Ruanda: The Bloodiest 100 Days Since World War II

Ruanda, a tropical landlocked state in central Africa, is the site of a bloody conflict that has resulted in the deaths of at least 750,000 people, probably more than 1 million, in the days between April and September 1994.

The problem is ethnic and centers around the two main groups in this region: the Tutsi (once known in the west as the Watusis) and the Hutu. It dates back to the fifteenth century when Tutsi cattle breeders wandered into central Africa and conquered the indigenous Hutu farmers. The Tutsi dominated the government until revolts by Hutus in 1959. From then on, Hutus, who made up about 85–90% of the population, dominated. But the real problem was that the Hutu leadership was extremist, discriminating against both Tutsis and moderate Hutus.

Some Tutsi fled into Uganda and fought to regain power. By 1990, as many as a million people had fled from the fighting and Hutu domination. But in 1993, peace seemed to be in the air. The Tutsi revolutionaries and the Hutu government signed an accord that promised a multiparty democracy, a joint Hutu-Tutsi army, and mutual tolerance.

Then came the spark that set off the bloodshed. In April 1994, the airplane carrying the Hutu presidents of Ruanda and neighboring Burundi was shot down. At first it was thought to be the work of the Tutsi rebels, but it apparently was the work of Hutu extremists. In the intervening chaos, the Tutsi rebels successfully invaded Ruanda, and the Hutu army and militia fled, in the process killing hundreds of thousands of Tutsis as well as Hutus. Three million Hutus fled to refugee camps in neighboring Zaire and Tanzania, many falling victim to malnutrition, cholera, and Hutu militiamen.

1993 with the first real opposition members since the early 1960s. That was the good news; the bad news was that he closed the parliament the next day. Kenya's future progress is no longer so assured.

(See also Jomo Kenyatta, page 611.)

NIGERIA

(Federal Republic of Nigeria)

VITAL STATISTICS

Geographic facts: 356,667 square miles, more than two times the size of California; located in West Africa; the coast is bordered by mangrove swamps, the interior includes arid semidesert

Cities: Lagos, Ibadan, Abuja (capital)

Population: 98 million

Languages: English (official), Hausa, Yoruba, Ibo, and 392 others

Ethnic groups: Hausa 21%, Yoruba 20%, Ibo 17%, Fulani 9%, about 250 other smaller groups

Religions: Muslim 50% (primarily in the north); Christian 40% (primarily in the south); other traditional religions

Nigeria is a country to watch, a power of the future, despite many severe current problems. One out of six Africans is a Nigerian. Nigeria is larger in population than any other African *or* European country except for Russia.

It also is an oil-rich OPEC nation, with leaders who want to put their oil money to work. Highways have been built, health care extended, businesses aided. Nigeria is currently under a military dictatorship, but it has a history of democratic rule and a lively, independent press and intelligentsia. Nigeria is also home to some of the world's greatest writers, such as Wole Soyinka and Chinua Achebe. It's a self-confident purveyor of African culture.

All this potential doesn't mean there aren't very severe problems. A major one is the legacy of colonialism. When the British took over the region in the 1800s, they simply cobbled together many diverse groups of people and called them Nigerians. Needless to say there are many ethnic differences. The north is primarily Muslim, home to the Hausa and Fulani peoples. The east is home to Christians (the Ibo peoples) and believers in traditional religions.

One of the biggest fears in Africa is civil war based on ethnic differences. That happened in Nigeria in 1967. The Ibos tried to secede from the Nigerian union and form the independent state of Biafra. After a bloody civil war that killed over 600,000 people, Nigeria was reunited, and the government offered remarkably generous amnesty terms to the secessionists. Many outside observers were surprised at how quickly the wounds of war healed.

But Nigeria has other major problems as well: poverty, a high crime rate, periodic secessionist movements by Islamic fundamentalists, high inflation, corruption, and the effects of lower oil prices. People are still talking about a $5 billion steel mill (the largest project in sub-Saharan Africa) that has yet to make a dime—or rather, a Nigerian naira. And tensions with neighboring Cameroon over Nigeria's claim to

The name "Africa" is apparently derived from a group of Berber nomads who lived in what is today Tunisia in North Africa. They were called the Aoruigha; they had been driven far into the desert by the Carthaginians (Phoenicians who settled the coast of North Africa around 400 B.C.E.). When the Romans conquered Carthage, they renamed their new province after them—but they pronounced it Africa.

coastal oil fields may explode. And most important, the recent dictators of the country have overturned democratic elections and arrested prominent reformers. Totalitarianism is threatening this promising country.

Yet for all its often chaotic state of affairs, Nigeria is a country on the move, with an educated and dynamic populace who are agitating for political freedom. Its people really seem to be one of the best hopes of Africa.

SOUTH AFRICA

(Republic of South Africa)

VITAL STATISTICS

Geographic facts: 472,359 square miles, about twice the size of Texas; located at the southern tip of Africa; much of land is plateau with relatively sparse rainfall; rich in minerals like gold and diamonds

Cities: Cape Town (legislative capital), Johannesburg, Durban, Pretoria (administrative capital), Bloemfontein (judicial capital)

Population: 41.2 million

Languages: English, Afrikaans, Nguni, Sotho, Xhosa, Zulu, Swazi

Ethnic groups: Black 70%, belonging to different ethnic groups; whites 16%; mixed race (called coloured) 8%; Asian, principally of Indian origin, 3%

Religions: Christian; some Hindu, Muslim, traditional religions

For most of South African history, the question of race and ethnic background has dominated life.

The land was originally sparsely inhabited by the Bushmen and Hottentots; then came a great southern movement of Bantu-speaking peoples: the Zulus, Xhosa, Swazi, and Sotho. Then from Europe came the Dutch, who settled along the coast; then the English arrived. Some of the Dutch moved inland, seizing more territory from the blacks, wresting a living from the land. By this time the Dutch were known as Boers or Afrikaners, and they were clearly here to stay. By 1948, when the Boer-dominated Nationalist Party won the election in South Africa, the population included all these people, plus Indians, people of mixed race, and other European immigrants.

Nineteen forty-eight is a watershed year because this is when apartheid—or separation of peoples along racial lines—became law. It had long been practiced unofficially, but now the mixing of races was illegal. The social structure was frozen. At the top of the pyramid were the whites, who built a modern state from the riches of the land—gold, diamonds, farming, strategic metals—and at the bottom were the diverse black peoples, who did much of the unskilled work and got a very small piece of the economic pie.

As the world moved away from racism, South Africa clung to this doctrine. New black movements, most notably the African National Congress, or ANC, were formed to combat this institutionalized racism, and the South African government responded by killing or jailing their members, including a leader named Nelson Mandela. Mandela at the time espoused communism, at least partly because no other nations seemed ready to give aid to his nationalist movement.

But by the 1980s it was becoming clear that the war between the races could not be won by the whites. West-

ern nations began paying more attention to the problems of apartheid, restricting (but not banning) trade and isolating South Africa from international forums. At this point, the ANC leadership realized that serious negotiations were possible, and were the best solution to gaining freedom. They also saw that the white-built economy should not be dismantled, but enhanced. Mandela was freed from prison, and President F. W. de Klerk, the leader of the Nationalist Party, the same party that invented apartheid, now negotiated with him to dismantle what they had set up.

Free elections were set, and in 1994, Nelson Mandela became the first black leader of South Africa. His new administration included whites as well as blacks (including de Klerk), and emphasized healing rather than separation and revenge. There were some ironies—for example, as head of state Mandela signed congratulatory

Mozambique: The Unknown War— and the Unknown Peace

For more than ten years, from 1977 to 1992, a little noticed civil war raged in Mozambique, a nation twice the size of California, located in southeastern Africa. The results were devastating: about one million dead, and a ravaged landscape and economy. At the end of the war, Mozambique was declared by the World Bank to be the world's poorest country.

But there is now some tentative good news. The two main warring groups consented to talks in 1990, and ultimately agreed to hold free elections—the first in Mozambiquen history. Despite some problems, the elections went well, with U.N. and international help in putting the democratic machinery into place.

retirement letters to members of the very security forces who had once hounded him and his people—but behind all this was a concerted effort, not so much to forget the past, but to look to the future, to build a new and stronger South Africa for all races. Apparently to Mandela, this is not mere rhetoric, but a very real part of his platform. So far he seems to be succeeding in a complex balancing game. His economic program has been moderate, recognizing the legitimate grievances of the majority poor blacks while at the same time recognizing the interests of the powerful (white) businesses and foreign investors. Most are betting—and hoping—that he succeeds. (See also Nelson Mandela, page 613.)

ZAIRE

(Republic of Zaire/République du Zaïre)

VITAL STATISTICS

Geographic facts: 905,563 square miles, about one quarter the size of the U.S.; located in tropical central Africa around the equator, much of the country is tropical rain forest, bisected by the Congo River

Cities: Kinshasa (capital), Lubumbashi

Population: 42.5 million

Languages: French (official) and a host of African languages including Kikongo, Luba, and Mongo.

Ethnic groups: Bantu peoples 80%, over 200 other tribal groups

Religions: Roman Catholic 50%, Protestant 20%, Muslim 10%, traditional religions

Somalia: Not in the News Anymore, but the Problems Continue

Somalia began to unravel in the late 1980s, long before it made the six o'clock news. And the problems continue today, now that international peacekeeping efforts have failed.

Somalia had long been a client state of one of the superpowers, but as Soviet-U.S. tensions eased, the amount of foreign aid it received dropped and local tensions increased. In 1990, the Somalia dictator Muhammad Siyad Barre was overthrown, and in 1991, the central government completely broke down. People transferred their loyalty to their local clan groupings, which began battling one another for control. Problems came to a head in 1991–1992, when a drought brought famine, the effects of which were exacerbated by some clan leaders who hindered emergency food delivery. Estimates are that more than 300,000 people died of starvation or malnutrition.

Enter the U.N. peacekeepers, who first arrived in 1992 to protect the delivery of food and to help put Somalia back on track. At the height of the U.N. presence, 30,000 troops patrolled the streets and deserts of Somalia, including more than 3,000 U.S. and Italian troops. But although food supplies were distributed more effectively, the U.N. forces couldn't control the warring clans, and by 1995, the last of the U.N. forces left. Somalia was once again left to itself, and to political and economic chaos.

Somalia is in one sense proof that the lessons of Vietnam are not fully understood. The U.N. went into Somalia without much understanding of the political dynamics of a complex conflict. Eager to help, the U.N. didn't stop to consider in detail *how* to effect such help.

If there's any silver lining in the mess, it's this: one U.N. observer said that Somalis were so weary of political infighting and so distrustful of dictatorial leaders that he guessed that Somalia was ripe for democracy. The only problem, he noted, was that for democracy to come, Somalia will need outside help. For now, that seems unlikely.

Zaire is a tragedy. It is one of the largest and potentially richest nations in Africa. But it suffers from the legacy of one of the world's most corrupt rulers: Mobutu Sese Seko.

All through the Cold War Mobutu was on the American foreign policy payroll. The U.S. gave him money (billions of dollars) and diplomatic support to keep the Soviets out. But the U.S. got more than it bargained for, since Mobutu was not only corrupt but, well . . . erratic, to put it diplomatically.

He began his rule in 1965 by trying to "Zairinize" what was then called the Congo. He changed the name of the country as well as his own name, from Joseph-Desiré Mobutu to Mobutu Sese Seko Koko Ngbenda wa za Banga, which means in the official translation: "the all powerful warrior who, because of his endurance and inflexible will to win, will go from conquest to conquest leaving fire in his wake."

He also looted the country. By some accounts he put over $3 billion in European bank accounts and French real estate, mostly châteaus in the better parts of France. It's not surprising that the take-home pay of the average citizen of Zaire fell 90% (imagine living on one tenth your income). The results were horrendous: widespread hunger, schools without textbooks, major roads

with potholes the size of trucks. To top it off, Zaire also developed a very high HIV/AIDS rate with almost no medical care.

The sad part about it is that Zaire could be rich. The jungle forests are full of hardwood trees, the land is fertile (once Zaire easily fed itself), the ground is full of strategic minerals like copper and cobalt, and the large Congo River runs through the country as a transportation artery.

It's easy to blame others, but if any people have that right, the people of Zaire do. When Westerners first conquered the Kongo, as it was then known, it became the personal possession of the Belgian king. He ruthlessly exploited the land and people, setting up forced-labor plantations that were run like slave camps. Later Zaire fell under Belgian government rule; the Belgians settled the land but didn't help the Zairians very much. At independence, there were two college graduates in the entire population.

Fortunately, the U.S. reduced its support of the dictator Mobutu when the Cold War ended. In the 1990s, Prime Minister Etienne Tshisekedi wa Mulumba called for help from overseas in toppling Mobutu. Will he succeed? Stay tuned.

MIDDLE EAST AND NORTH AFRICA

 Some of the world's earliest civilizations and greatest religions began in this region, home to Judaism, Christianity, and Islam. But in recent years, the Middle East has been in the news because of its immense oil wealth as well as some of the world's worst conflicts—the Arab-Israeli wars and the Iraqi-Iranian war. Both have hindered development in this potentially rich area of the world. Now that it seems that the Arab-Israeli conflict is dying down, hope is increasing for a rapid economic takeoff. Already, some of the oil-rich states of the Arabian Peninsula are

Damascus, the capital of Syria, is the oldest capital city in the world and is also considered the world's longest continuously inhabited city, about 4,000 years.

exploring ties with Israel, and others are beginning to divert money away from tanks and guns. Several problems are looming, however. One is that most governments in the area are far from democratic. It was easy to tell the people to forgo democracy due to the wars raging in the region—if the wars end, some of the less democratic regimes may face increased unrest. And in many areas, Islamic fundamentalists are challenging secular governments and calling for a return to tradition. Peace is not yet truly on the horizon in the Middle East.

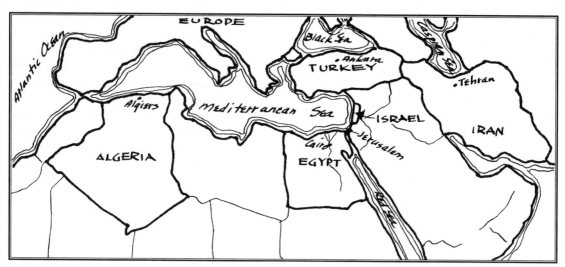

SOME KEY NATIONS OF THE MIDDLE EAST AND NORTH AFRICA

ALGERIA

(Democratic and Popular Republic of Algeria/République Algérienne Democratique et Populaire—al-Jumhiriyyah al-Jazairiyyah al-Dimuqratiya al-Shabiyyah)

VITAL STATISTICS

Geographic facts: 918,497 square miles, about one quarter the size of the U.S.; located in central North Africa along the Mediterranean Sea, the coastal plain is fertile, but behind it lies the immense and bone-dry Sahara desert

Cities: Algiers (capital), Oran
Population: 27.9 million
Languages: Arabic (official), Berber, French
Ethnic groups: Arab 75%, Berber 25%
Religion: Sunni Islam

Algeria is an oil-rich nation but don't envy it. There are too many people and not quite enough oil. Algeria's great cities are now filled with unemployed young, and its secular (and once revolutionary socialist) government is in danger of falling to Muslim fundamentalists. If and when the government falls, get ready for some major repercussions throughout the Arab world.

Algeria has almost always been on the crossroads of history. Its first inhabitants were the seminomadic Berbers. They were conquered by the Phoenicians, who founded the empire of Carthage. Then the Phoenicians were conquered by the Romans, who were in turn conquered by barbarian tribes (the Vandals, et al.), who then fell to the Arabs. Next came the Turks,

The part of the U.S. Marine hymn that goes "to the shores of Tripoli" refers to the first "war" the U.S. fought as an independent nation, from 1801 to 1805 in North Africa. The ruler of Tripoli on the North African coast (presently in Libya) had the habit of demanding protection money from the U.S.; if it was late, he attacked U.S. ships. Finally, U.S. Marines led by the U.S. consul, General William Eaton, attacked to try to depose the ruler of Tripoli. Eaton failed, but he inspired the U.S. to build a modern navy; in 1815 a U.S. squadron sailed into Algiers and negotiated a fair treaty.

then finally in 1830 the French invaded.

The French settled the land in a major way and made the country part of France (something like the way we settled the Mexican territories of Texas and California and made them states). By the 1950s, over 1 million Frenchmen were living, working, and writing in Algeria (Camus wrote his famous Existentialist books there). The native Algerians lived nowhere near as well as the French colonizers, so the native Algerians fought a bloody war for independence from the French. The future seemed bright. But the new socialist government couldn't get the economy moving, and even oil money wasn't enough to offset economic problems.

As the economy worsened, fundamentalist Islam became more popular. More and more Algerians returned to the mosques, more and more women put on the veil, more and more people felt that a return to Sharia, traditional Islamic law, would be the answer to Algeria's problems. But the government was still confident it had a majority of the people backing it.

When the government decided to hold its first multiparty free elections in 1991 they had a rude surprise. The fundamentalist Islamic Salvation Front won the first round of votes. There was no final second round; a military-backed government canceled them and banned the fundamentalist party.

Since then, the country has been racked by violence. More than 30,000 Algerians have died as the army attempts to crush its Islamic fundamentalist opponents, and the fundamentalists counter with violence of their own. The outside world has taken sides in the conflict as well—the military government has received support from the French in particular, as well as from the Spanish, German, and Italian governments, while the fundamentalists have received support from Iran and Sudan. But the bottom line is more death: foreigners and Algerians not willing to toe a strict Islamic line are periodically killed in fundamentalist terrorist shootings and the army counters with terror of its own.

(See also Muhammed Ahmed Ben Bella, page 606.)

EGYPT

(Arab Republic of Egypt/Jumhuriyyah Misr al-Arabiyyah)

VITAL STATISTICS

Geographic facts: 386,650 square miles, well over twice the size of California; over 90% of the land is arid desert, most Egyptians living in a narrow band of land along the Nile River, which divides the country, and in the Nile delta

Cities: Cairo (capital), Alexandria, Giza, Mansoura, Zagazig

Population: 60 million

Language: Arabic

Ethnic groups: Egyptian Hamito-Arab 90%, Bedouin 10%, Nubian

Religions: Sunni Muslim 90%, Coptic Christian 10%

Every 10 months, 1 million more Egyptians are born. They must somehow live in the narrow band of land along the Nile—only about the size of Maryland and Delaware combined. And it's already crowded with almost 60 million *other* Egyptians.

There's no question that Egypt has a

More than 95% of Egypt's inhabitants live no more than 12 miles from the Nile River or one of its delta distributaries. In fact, if the Aswan Dam upstream were destroyed and the Nile River Valley flooded, almost every Egyptian would be drowned within three days.

lot going for it. It is one of the world's oldest and greatest civilizations. It's the political and cultural center of the Arab world; its television programs and movies are watched by millions across the Middle East. It's a fascinating place to visit as well. Downtown Cairo is full of bazaars and medieval buildings; its cafés hold chain-smoking literary types who consider Cairo a sort of Greenwich Village for Arab writers. But Egypt is more than its past and its culture. It's also a nation with major economic and population problems: too many people, too much poverty, and too little manufacturing and farming.

Most of Egypt is desert. Yes, the land along the Nile is agriculturally rich, but there's not enough of it. And worse yet, the roads and transportation systems are often so bad it's hard getting crops to market. Israel sells tomatoes and fruits to Europe and the U.S.; much of Egypt's crops rot before they get to a major city. Many industries are still controlled by the government—and they aren't run well. And each year, Egypt's schools turn out hundreds of thousands of well-educated graduates—too many to find good jobs in the country. For a while, when the Arab states were flush with oil money, Egyptian engineers, doctors, and technicians found jobs in the rich Arab states. But now that even Saudi Arabia is tightening its belt, Egyptians have returned home looking for jobs, any jobs.

Meanwhile, Egypt's financial problems make our own budget deficit seem like nothing. It still faces a crushing debt (even though the U.S. canceled much of it, and the Europeans cut back substantially). And the government spends even more money

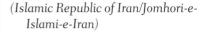

keeping the price of bread and other basic foodstuffs artificially low (a loaf of pita bread costs about a penny and a half). Why? Because most Egyptians are so poor that even a small increase means economic hardship, even starvation, and they've rioted in the streets every time the government tries to increase prices.

Egyptians often look to politics as an escape. In the 1950s, they had a hero in President Gamal Abdel Nasser, who led a revolution against the rule of the wealthy. Nasser was a socialist, but he couldn't create prosperity. Then Anwar al-Sadat took power. He promised that peace with Israel would bring unheard-of prosperity. When instead the peace was followed by economic dislocation and resultant political problems at home, Sadat was shot by Islamic fundamentalists. They argued that only Islam would bring prosperity and morality to Egypt. To advance Islam the fundamentalists have tried to reduce Western influence by destroying Egypt's vital tourist industry and foreign investment through bombings and terror. They've tried to intimidate free-thinking intellectuals into silence. So far Sadat's successor, Hosni Mubarak, has held this threat at bay.

Egyptians have a reputation for tolerance and openmindedness. But if the economy doesn't improve, look for more unrest in Egypt.

(See also Arab-Israeli Conflict, page 567; Gamal Abdel Nasser, page 614; Muhammad Anwar al-Sadat, page 615.)

IRAN

(Islamic Republic of Iran/Jomhori-e-Islami-e-Iran)

VITAL STATISTICS

Geographic facts: 636,293 square miles, about the size of Alaska; located in the eastern portion of the Middle East on the Persian Gulf; high plains and mountains in the interior, but many forested areas and oases; most of the population lives in the northern areas

Cities: Tehran (capital), Mashad, Isfahan, Tabriz, Shiraz

Population: 61.2 million

Languages: Farsi (also known as Persian, official), Turkish, Kurdish, Arabic

Ethnic groups: Persian 51%, Azerbaijani 25%, Kurdish 9%

Religions: Shiite Muslim 95%, Sunni Muslim 4%, also Zoroastrianism

Iranians often take offense when Westerners assume they're Arabs: they are not, they're Persian—with a distinct culture, a language belonging to the Indo-European family (and so distantly related to English), and for many years a separate history.

But Iran *is* a Middle Eastern nation, and much of its identity comes from Islam, specifically the Shiite sect to which virtually all Iranians belong. Iranian Shiites led by their spiritual leader Ayatollah Ruhollah Khomeini overthrew the powerful U.S.-supported government of the shah, Mohammad Reza Pahlavi, and instituted the world's first modern Islamic government. The Islamic constitution includes an elected National Assembly, and the president is elected as well, not appointed. Over the

Assembly stands a Council of Guardians—a body of senior Islamic jurists who make certain that the laws they pass meet Islamic standards; other bodies like the Assembly of Experts and the Council of Determining the Expediency of the Islamic Republic do the same thing. The Islamic-oriented government of Iran by definition does *not* allow for certain freedoms we take for granted; individual rights in the Western sense are definitely curtailed. And especially in the early years, many excesses were committed in the name of the Islamic revolution: people were executed for their beliefs or backgrounds. And today the U.S. has accused Iran of sponsoring terrorism.

And therein lies Iran's problem and challenge: can Iran's Islamic-oriented government meet the demands of a rapidly changing world? So far the jury is still out. Iran and its form of government managed to survive a devastating attack by Iraq shortly after the new government came into being. This surprised the Iraqis and virtually everyone else. But after years of war and hardship, many Iranians want something better. So far, living standards are still below what they were in the shah's day, and inflation and unemployment are high. Today there's a debate going on within Iran: should the government liberalize to a degree, let in foreign investment, and relax social rules? One side says no: its proponents want a more socialist government and strict Islamic social rules. The other side says yes. The young in particular favor liberalization along a Western model. Upcoming elections will hopefully give us a better idea of where Iranians want to go.

(See also The Islamic Revolution, page 591; Ayatollah Ruhollah Khomeini, page 611.)

ISRAEL

(State of Israel/Medinat Yisra'el)

VITAL STATISTICS

Geographic facts: 8,020 square miles, about the size of New Jersey; a fertile coastal plain along the Levant, the eastern portion of the Mediterranean; in the center is the Judean Plateau, to the south is the arid Negev desert

Cities: Jerusalem (capital, but most nations maintain embassies in Tel Aviv), Tel Aviv, Haifa

Population: 4.75 million

Languages: Hebrew and Arabic (both official), as well as English

Ethnic groups: Jewish 83%, Arab 16%

Religions: Judaism 83%, Islam 13%, Christian 2%

Despite its small size and population, Israel is almost always in the news; it is a state that has fought—and won or survived—five major wars in its brief modern history, and has always lived under an enormous threat. Now, with the historic agreements between it and the Palestine Liberation Organization (PLO), the hope is that the wars will finally be over.

Modern Israel was born in 1948, during its War of Independence. But the history of its people goes back much further than that: first to the historic claims of Jews to their ancient homeland, then to the Zionist settlements of the late 1800s and 1900s. But Jewish settlement conflicted with Arab nationalism, and has led to the wars that have plagued the region during the latter half of the twentieth century.

But Israelis don't always live in war. The nation is a dynamic democracy with a thriving culture that is now accommodating hundreds of thousands of former Soviet Jews and undergoing a political and social transformation as Sephardic (Spanish, Portuguese, and Middle Eastern) Jews move up to positions of power and to some degree mix with the Ashkenazi (Eastern European) Jews (over 20% of all Jewish marriages are now "mixed"). This is changing Israeli culture and politics, once dominated by liberal Eastern European Jews. But for most Israelis, a prime concern is working in an economy that is both modern and Levantine. It's part a crazy quilt of bureaucratic rules and regulations and part dynamic entrepreneurial economy that could be the future of a reinvigorated Middle East. Past governments have started to liberalize the economy by reducing import barriers and state subsidies and privatizing government industries. But taxation is still high, almost a third of all business activities are controlled by regulated cartels and monopolies, and unrest in the Occupied Territories has been estimated as costing about 2% of the gross national product each year, as well as exacting a psychic cost. It's hard living in a state of war with your neighbors.

But Israel has a highly educated workforce, no small advantage in today's world of value-added information technology. With the coming of a more general peace (even a "cold peace") and with the continuation of liberal government economic policies, the odds are that this nation will achieve true prosperity as well as true peace.

(See also Arab-Israeli Conflict, page 567; Menachem Begin, page 606; David Ben-Gurion, page 606; Golda Meir, page 613.)

TURKEY

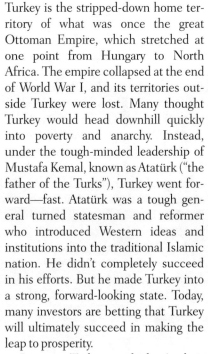

(Republic of Turkey/Türkiye Cumhuriyeti)

VITAL STATISTICS

Geographic facts: 301,381 square miles, twice the size of California; located in Asia Minor, a peninsula between the Mediterranean and Black seas, with a small portion in Europe

Cities: Istanbul, Ankara (capital), Izmir, Adana

Population: 61.8 million

Languages: Turkish (official), Kurdish, Arabic

Ethnic groups: Turkish 80%, Kurdish 18%

Religion: Sunni Muslim 98%

Turkey is the stripped-down home territory of what was once the great Ottoman Empire, which stretched at one point from Hungary to North Africa. The empire collapsed at the end of World War I, and its territories outside Turkey were lost. Many thought Turkey would head downhill quickly into poverty and anarchy. Instead, under the tough-minded leadership of Mustafa Kemal, known as Atatürk ("the father of the Turks"), Turkey went forward—fast. Atatürk was a tough general turned statesman and reformer who introduced Western ideas and institutions into the traditional Islamic nation. He didn't completely succeed in his efforts. But he made Turkey into a strong, forward-looking state. Today, many investors are betting that Turkey will ultimately succeed in making the leap to prosperity.

In a way, Turks were lucky. As their once great empire lay dying in the early

---

Saudi Arabia: Oil-Rich Ally Has Seen Better Days

Saudi Arabia is located at the epicenter of the Islamic world. The home to, and guardian of, the Muslim holy cities of Mecca and Medina it is also one of the world's largest oil exporters, and underneath the sands are huge oil reserves. In the boom years of the 1970s, as oil prices rose, Saudi Arabia spent billions to modernize itself, but more money kept coming in. Saudi Arabia tried to balance modernization with the traditional conservatism of the ruling family, the Sauds, who unified most of Arabia in the 1910s and 1920s under their rule. With so much money streaming into their coffers, the Saudi kings were literally able to buy off most opposition groups (although there have been a number of incidents of domestic unrest) and maintain their rule.

Today, however, as oil prices have dropped, Saudi Arabia is struggling under a national debt of $100 billion, and some are questioning the rich oil state's ability to keep to its old ways. Iraq still threatens in the north, militant Iran in the east, and fundamentalist Islam from within. Many of these challengers question the legitimacy of the Saud's family rule. Should the kingdom democratize itself to some degree and give its inhabitants more of a stake in defending their nation?

1900s, they lost one of the main problems that had plagued them: how to control a diverse population of Arabs, Greeks, Armenians, Jews, Bulgarians, Serbs, and Kurds, to name only a few nationalities in their polyglot empire. Only the Kurds and Greeks were left in significant numbers in present-day Turkey, and the Greeks left after a disastrous attempt to invade the fledgling state. The Armenians had left earlier in large numbers after wartime massacres.

Meanwhile Atatürk westernized Turkey. He abolished the Islamic legal system and the traditional fez and veil and changed the script from Arabic to Roman. He emphasized that Turks were culturally separate from the rest of the Muslim world (in fact they are; the Turkish language is not related to Arabic, and Turkey's nearest ethnic

cousins are the Turkic states of the former Soviet Union).

Atatürk's legacy has not really been challenged until now. In recent years, the economy has been liberalized, and Turkey has made further industrial gains. Its per capita income is low by Western European standards but high by Middle Eastern. In fact, Turkey's fondest dream is to join the European Community. Its application has not been rejected outright, but Europeans said that negotiations would have to wait a while. But, as with the rest of the Middle East, fundamentalist Islam has been gaining power. The secular government is being challenged, and poorer Turks in particular are turning to Islam. Will Atatürk's legacy remain?

(See also Cyprus, page 570; Kurd Territories, page 575.)

NORTH AMERICA

 When we say we're Americans, we mean we're U.S. citizens, and that rankles other Americans from North and South America who claim equal rights to the term. North America itself is home to three large powers that are now all linked in a giant trading bloc under the banner of NAFTA—the North American Free Trade Agreement. Hopes are that this can economically link Mexico, the U.S., and Canada and increase prosperity for all.

CANADA

VITAL STATISTICS

Geographic facts: 3,849,672 square miles; in area, the second largest country in the world; takes up most of the northern part of North America, including Arctic islands and temperate areas nearer to the U.S.

Cities: Toronto, Montreal, Vancouver, Ottawa (capital), Edmonton, Calgary, Winnipeg, Quebec

Population: 29.1 million

Languages: English and French (both official)

Ethnic groups: British Isles origin 40%, French origin 27%, other European origin 27%, indigenous Native American 1.5%

Religions: Roman Catholic 46%, Protestant 41%

In Canadian schoolbooks, Benedict Arnold is a hero. He's the man who put loyalty to the English crown first. It all depends on your point of view, and the Canadian point of view is sometimes very different from ours.

To begin with, our histories diverged many years ago. We were both colonies of Great Britain, but we rebelled back in 1775, the Canadians stayed loyal. It's hard to even establish a date for Canadian independence. Did it come in 1867, when the British North America Act established Canada as a self-governing dominion of the British Empire? Or did it really come in 1982, when the Constitution Act gave Canada its own constitution by transferring the power to make amendments from Britain? It's also easy to forget that Canada only took final form recently: the cold Atlantic province of Newfoundland only entered the Canadian federation in 1949; before that it was British.

Yet to U.S. citizens traveling to Canada it looks the same—or almost the same. Except maybe the street signs are in French along with English, and distances are marked in kilometers, not miles. The U.S. is Canada's largest trading partner, so many products on the shelves are familiar. But underneath the similarities are . . . differences.

You can see that it's neater and cleaner and safer; maybe fitting for a nation that *didn't* rebel. There's a famous story about a U.S. film com-

Arctic Ocean

Baffin Bay

Yukon

Northwest Territories

British Columbia

C A N A D A

Alberta

Hudson Bay

Newfoundland

Saskatchewan

Manitoba

Ontario

Vancouver

Quebec

Ottawa

Nova Scotia

Atlantic Ocean

Sonora

BAJA CALIFORNIA

Chihuahua

Coahuila

Nuevo Leon

Gulf of MEXICO

M E X I C O

Mexico City

Campeche

Yucatan

Quintana Roo

Pacific Ocean

NORTH AMERICA

pany shooting a tough New York crime drama in a Toronto alley. They had to bring in trash from outside. And when they returned to the alley the next day, they found that the trash was gone: it had been picked up by the sanitation workers.

Like the U.S., Canada is rich—but taxes are higher. Like the U.S., Canada is a breadbasket to the world due to its high wheat production; but unlike the U.S., warm-weather fruits are missing. Like the U.S., Canada is industrial: it manufactures cars and electronic goods, beer, and timber products. But even here there are differences. Canadian industry is dominated by a few large corporations and the government is more activist economically and socially than in the U.S. And we all know by now that Canada has long guaranteed health care to its citizens.

But Canada has its problems too. For example, for all the difficulties the U.S. has dealing with a multicultural society, we haven't faced the same crisis as Canada has with Quebec. Quebec is a former French colony (located above the New England states) that was conquered by the British in 1759–1760, and awarded to the victors by treaty in 1763. But it never assimilated with the British, nor with the rest of Canada when it joined the federation. French is still spoken and the 85% French majority in the province want to retain their culture and language. To mollify its French Canadian citizens, Canada is officially bilingual and many government jobs require fluency in both French and English.

But some Québecois want independence, or at least autonomy. In 1978 the separatist Parti Québecois under René Lévesque won provincial power, although it played down independence.

And for the next fifteen years, Canada and the French have been arguing, debating, and voting on various ways to let Quebec stay French—and inside Canada. Recently, Quebec voters shot down a call for independence but the margin was so close that the issue remains unresolved.

As for another distinct group within the Canadian federation, the Native American Inuit people won the right to a self-governing homeland in the far Canadian north. Most of the Northwest Territories—a giant land area not much smaller than California—will be called Nunavut, "Our Land." Another huge chunk of Canada will likely be next and go to another group of Native Americans.

MEXICO

(*United Mexican States/Estados Unidos Mexicanos*)

VITAL STATISTICS

Geographic facts: 761,604 square miles, three times the size of Texas; located in southern North America bordering the U.S. to the north and Guatemala and Belize in the south; widely varied terrain of mountains, desert plateaus in the north, tropical rain forest in the south

Cities: Mexico City (capital), Guadalajara, Monterrey, Puebla

Population: 92 million

Languages: Spanish, various Amerindian languages.

Ethnic groups: Mestizo (mixed Caucasian–Native American) 60%, Native American 29%, Caucasian 9%

Religions: Roman Catholic 97%, Protestant 3%

The well-known Mexican novelist Carlos Fuentes once said, "The genius of Mexico consists of preserving the values of progress without giving up the affirmation of the right to mystery, the right to amazement and endless self-discovery."

Mexico surprises almost everyone. Until recently, its politics appeared predictable. Then in early 1994, a peasant revolt erupted in the southern state of Chiapas, led by subcommandante Marcos, a charismatic masked leader who mesmerized the nation with his poetry and who reminded Mexicans of the large inequities in land ownership, particularly for the primarily Indian poor. Also in 1994, the ruling party's presidential candidate was assassinated and fingers later pointed to associates of the outgoing president.

The economy also seemed predictable until late in 1994 when the peso was suddenly devalued and Mexi-

can buying power collapsed overnight. Prices rose by 40%. While 1994 was truly a year of surprises, a watershed year, more changes are in store.

You can't understand modern Mexico without understanding the PRI, or Partido Revolucionario Institucional (Institutional Revolutionary Party), the party that governs Mexico. It's a mish-mash that includes almost everyone—right, left, and center. It's as if in the U.S. the Republicans and Democrats joined forces and ran one president every four years.

The PRI has many faults but it has managed to keep Mexico stable in a period of tremendous social change, from its founding in 1929 to the present day. It does this by coopting political opponents, giving serious challengers a stake in the system through party jobs and patronage. Every six years the political leaders of the party, led by the outgoing president, pick a successor candidate who will represent the PRI in the next election. The candidate is as good as elected.

Until recently. The last few elec-

Mexico's Heart

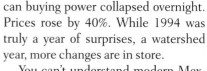 The heart of Mexico is Mexico City, the political, industrial, financial, commercial, cultural, and religious capital, and the largest city in the world, with 20 million inhabitants according to U.N. estimates. Mexico City is set high in the central highlands—the home of the great pre-Columbian cities of Teotihuacán and the Aztec capital of Tenochtitlán, on whose ruins it is built. Over 7,400 feet above sea level, surrounded by volcanoes and mountains, built in an earthquake zone, it's also one of the most polluted cities in the world: every day 11,000 tons of dust, chemicals, metals, and bacteria pour into the sky and create a horrible smog; visitors often complain of sore throats and runny eyes. Yet every year more people keep coming from the countryside, attracted by jobs and city lights. Mexico City, for all its problems, is a dynamic, lively city. Pre-Hispanic ruins still exist, as do masterpieces of colonial architecture; museums and cultural events abound and are crowded. And every Sunday, over 1.5 million people flock to Chapultepec Park, which has three lakes, a zoo, schools, an open-air theater, and, nearby, some of the great museums of the world.

tions have been close—the PRI has won with electoral victories that hover around 50%, along with charges of voter fraud. And new parties, the leftist Revolutionary Democratic Party (PRD) and the right-wing National Action Party (PAN), are gaining strength. They complain that the PRI is too complacent, that corruption is entrenched, and that freedom is stifled.

Mexico will surely change. The PRI is losing its monopoly, particularly in the governorship of Mexican states. Mexico is becoming more democratic. But quite possibly rather than evolving into a U.S.-style political system, Mexico will go a different way. Just as the PRI created a consensual style of govern-

ment, some Mexican intellectuals are calling for a new consensus to replace the old, one that will include the urban poor, the landless peasants as well as the intellectual and technocratic elite, and one that won't include the PRI.

So far, the new PRI president, Ernesto Zedillo, faces huge problems. Prices have increased, international debts are coming due, and the economic outlook is iffy. But Mexico's strengths, including an increasingly dynamic entrepreneurial class, a highly educated technocratic elite, and a highly skilled industrial workforce, predict a bright future.

(See also the Latin American "Revolution," page 584.)

SOUTH AMERICA

PERU

.Lima

Amazon R.

BRAZIL

.Brasília

.Rio de Janeiro

São Paulo

Pacific Ocean

ARGENTINA

Buenos Aires

South Atlantic Ocean

SOME KEY NATIONS OF SOUTH AMERICA

Until recently, South America was something of an economic backwater, exporting surplus raw materials to the world, but existing on the periphery in international trade and politics. The U.S. dominated its foreign affairs, and in fact some South American leaders welcomed Cuba's Fidel Castro simply as an alternative to U.S. bullying.

All this is changing now, however. South America now includes some fast-growing economic areas. Reforms in Chile, Argentina, and Brazil are revitalizing economies and societies. The old social system—where money and power was concentrated in the hands of the purest descendants of the families related to the original Spanish colonial settlers—is beginning to change. A native American Indian, for the first time in all of South America, won a national election recently in Bolivia. (Our own record in the U.S. in this regard is probably worse.) Although many areas in South America suffer from widespread poverty (shantytowns are a feature of all cities) and the drug trade in Colombia, Bolivia, and Peru has caused political unrest, the outlook for much of the continent appears hopeful.

There is talk of creating a South American Common Market and linking it to the North American NAFTA market. Most South Americans understand that with economic reform comes political reform, and greater freedom for all.

Bolivia has the dubious honor of having a government that has had the most changes. Over the last 160 years or so, the country has changed rulers more than 190 times.

ARGENTINA

(*Argentine Republic/República Argentina*)

VITAL STATISTICS

Geographic facts: 1,065,189 square miles, four times the size of Texas; located in the Southern Cone of South America, with the Andes and other mountains in the west, the very fertile pampas or plains in the central region, the wooded Gran Chaco plains in the north

Cities: Buenos Aires, Córdoba, La Matanza

Population: 34 million

Languages: Spanish (official), Italian

Ethnic groups: European origin (Spanish and Italian) 95%, native American, mestizo (mixed), Arab

Religion: Roman Catholic 92%

In the early 1900s Argentina was one of the richest nations in the world. It was wealthy from selling meat and grain grown on its rich pampas, the wide, open plains of the South American cowboys, or *gauchos*. Buenos Aires looked like a European capital. This is not really surprising since the overwhelming majority of Argentine citizens are from Spain or Italy; the few Native Americans who had inhabited the land had been wiped out or pushed out long ago.

But what goes up must come down, and by the 1920s Argentina's agricultural exports were going down in price and poverty was going up. The long happy days of prosperity were over.

Until, that is, Juan Perón came to power and it seemed for a while that the happy days were back. You can't understand Argentina unless you understand Perón, a charismatic leader with an even more charismatic wife, Eva (Evita) Perón (yes, the one who was later immortalized in a Broadway musical).

Perón was something of a Fascist who won the 1946 presidential election by promising prosperity for the workers through a state-controlled society that would provide pretty much everything to everybody. For a while Perón actually succeeded. But inevitably economic problems cropped up. And then Evita Perón (who had dispensed patronage and had come to symbolize Peronism) committed the ultimate political faux pas and died just as things were unraveling. Ultimately Juan Perón resigned and went into exile.

After some years of military dictatorships and failed democratic regimes, Argentina called Perón back one more time. But he didn't last long. This time *he* died and his new wife, Isabel, took power. But she was weak-willed and certainly no Evita, and Peronism failed once again.

Then came a period of military rule and political horrors. An increasingly repressive military regime fought an increasingly powerful guerrilla resistance. The nightmare culminated in the saga of the *desaparecidos,* or disappeared ones. These were people who were suspected of opposing the regime and were picked up by the military and secretly killed. Sometimes their children were kidnapped and adopted by childless police or military officers. But the army couldn't keep power forever. They fought a war with Great Britain over a desolate set of islands called the Malvinas (or Falklands), and when they lost that they completely lost

credibility. In 1983 a reformer, Raúl Alfonsín, was elected president. But he couldn't keep the economy going.

And then, once again, a peronista came dashing to the rescue. Carlos Saúl Menem, the handsome governor of La Rioja Province, won the election as a member of Peron's party. He promptly proceeded to violate Peron's Fascist ideas by liberalizing and privatizing the economy. Menem's economic policies bothered workers—and his social behavior shocked conservatives: he has a penchant for wining and dining beautiful models. But he seems to be succeeding in turning Argentina around. Happy days may be here again.

(See also the Latin American "Revolution," page 584; Juan Domingo Perón, page 615.)

BRAZIL

(Federative Republic of Brazil/República Federativa de Brasil)

VITAL STATISTICS

Geographic facts: 3,286,470 square miles, larger than the 48 contiguous U.S. states; located in central South America; in the north and west is the Amazon basin, a heavily wooded tropical forest and an immense and navigable river system; the northeast is poor and arid; the south-central region is the most populous and the richest agriculturally and industrially, and has half the population, most of whom are concentrated in cities along the coast

Cities: São Paulo, Rio de Janeiro, Belo Horizonte, Salvador, Brasilia (capital), Recife, Manaus

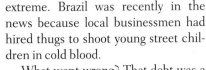

Population: 155 million
Language: Portuguese
Ethnic groups: Portuguese, African, and mulatto make the majority, also minor immigrant groups, native Americans
Religion: Roman Catholic 89%

Brazilians have a saying: "God is a Brazilian." And for these optimistic, ebullient, creative, and intelligent people, the future should seem bright. Every year some pundit or another pronounces Brazil the superpower of the future.

A few facts show why: Nearly half of South America is Brazilian territory, and nearly 40% of all South Americans are Brazilian. It is a vast land that includes the world's largest rain forest and the world's largest river (in volume), the Amazon. Its varied but mostly tropical lands are chock-full of minerals; the southern lands are agriculturally rich; the coast has great tourist potential. Besides great wildernesses it has major cities like Rio de Janeiro and São Paulo, a commercial and industrial giant of 15 million people. Brazil has a large and growing middle class, and it's turning its economy away from the heavy-handed socialist controls of the past. By any account Brazil is a major economic, military, and political world power.

Yet Brazil also has the dubious distinction of holding the world's largest foreign debt—it owes over $87 billion, some say over $100 billion. Until recently, inflation was so high that many people raced to the bank at payday to cash checks so they wouldn't lose the value of their paychecks. The school dropout rate is among the highest in the world, and the separation between the haves and the have-nots is

extreme. Brazil was recently in the news because local businessmen had hired thugs to shoot young street children in cold blood.

What went wrong? That debt was a big part of the problem. It trapped Brazil into a cycle of sending out money to pay off interest (like taking out such a high mortgage you can't afford much else), leaving little money for the home economy. Without investment, the local economy couldn't grow, employment didn't increase, and social problems got worse, not better.

There was hope for a while when Fernando Collor de Mello, a young, Kennedyesque former governor of the poor northeastern state of Alagoas, was elected president. But he was impeached for corruption and resigned. The next year a new scandal racked the Brazilian Congress and political elite. One congressman somehow managed to deposit $54 million in his bank account although his salary was only $84,000. He explained he had been very lucky—he had won 24,000 lotteries.

But recently, things have been looking better. The economy is growing again, there's a trade surplus, and investment is increasing. The northern Atlantic coast is becoming a hot tourist spot—visitors are discovering beautiful beaches, great hotels, and not too many crowds (yet). Maybe that mythical great future is finally arriving.

PERU

(Republic of Peru/República del Peru)

VITAL STATISTICS

Geographic facts: 496,222 square miles, about the size of Alaska; on the Pacific coast of South America; three basic regions: the arid coastal plain, the Andes Mountains, and the Amazon rain forest

Cities: Lima (capital), Arequipa, Callao

Population: 23 million

Languages: Spanish, Quéchua (both official), other native languages

Ethnic groups: Native American 45%, mestizo (mixed) 37%, Caucasian 15%

Religion: Roman Catholic 90%

Peru has a proud history and a future that only now seems to be improving. It was home to the Incas, one of the world's great civilizations, as well as to numerous other earlier cultures. When the Spanish conqueror Francisco Pizarro destroyed the Incan civiliza-

Central America: Out of the News, but the Problems Remain

It was hard to get through the 1980s without hearing about Central America. The isthmus connecting North America with South America was wracked with conflict. In El Salvador, a bloody civil war raged; in Nicaragua, the U.S. covertly supported rebels against the communist-oriented Sandinista government; in Guatemala, a bloody insurgency cost 100,000 lives. Honduran territory was used by insurgents and refugees in both the Nicaraguan and Salvadorean conflicts. In late 1989, the U.S. invaded Panama, which it claimed was controlled by corrupt allies of drug dealers. Only Belize, a small territory in the Yucatán, and Costa Rica, a traditionally democratic state, escaped without much political turmoil.

The reasons for the unrest were principally socioeconomic: most nations in Central America were controlled by small elites who owned most of the land and used the government to bolster their power. These elites were often supported by the U.S. who viewed them as bulwarks against communism. Despite U.S. support in Nicaragua, the elite lost control to communist-backed supporters, the Sandinistas, and the U.S. successfully supported rebels against their rule. In other nations, opposition to elite rule flared into insurrections or full-scale civil war. In El Salvador, the U.S. sought to find some sort of middle way between the elites and revolutionaries in the jungle, but for most of the 1980s, the politics were tortured and the U.S. role none too savory.

Now that the Cold War is over, Central America is no longer in the news. Peace treaties were signed in El Salvador between the leftists and the government; in Nicaragua, free elections put a moderate into power. But severe problems remain. A large percentage of the populations are still illiterate, landless, and without a say in government. This is now exacerbated by a rising crime rate, increasing ecological erosion, and destroyed roads, factories, and bridges.

On the positive side, the area's economies are slowly improving, even with (or because of) declines in U.S. aid. Due to all the international attention of the past decade, social institutions are more sophisticated, leading experts to predict a greater degree of democracy. Both left and right seem tired of armed conflict.

tion, he created a new Spanish colonial society. Its capital, Lima, became the center of a great and oppressive new empire, the seat of the Spanish viceroys of the New World, the City of the Kings.

But until recently, Peru was in dire straits. Lima still had its beautiful boulevards, but on the streets were innumerable beggars, and surrounding the city were shanty towns of shacks and hovels. Peru was besieged by terrorism, crime, and terrible poverty, the residue of a system where wealth has long been concentrated in the hands of a few. For years much of the country was controlled by the "forty-four families," a small class of rich landowners and businesspeople. Even today, the poor make up over 80% of the population and a true middle class is only gradually emerging.

Economic disparities like this create unrest. Peru was shaken in the past ten years by a shadowy and terrifying revolutionary group called the Sendero Luminoso (Shining Path), radical Maoist guerrillas trying to topple the government by terror and murder. They didn't succeed, but they managed to kill many citizens, in the process pushing the government into a repressive reliance upon the military. Recently the Sendero leader Abimael

Guzmán was captured by the government, and many hope the worst is over.

But real reforms must come to the economy. Peru is not poor when it comes to natural resources—it has oil, copper, zinc, and other minerals, agricultural and fishing industries, and some manufacturing. But mismanagement and poverty made Peru an economic basket case in the 1980s, with inflation soaring to over 3,000% and massive unemployment.

In the 1990 elections Peruvians elected Alberto Fujimori, an agronomist of Japanese immigrant parents. Two years into his administration he suspended part of the constitution in an effort to combat the senderistas. In addition, he instituted conservative economic therapy. The Chileans instituted the same therapy years before under the dictator General Augusto Pinochet. No one much liked Pinochet, but most people admit that his conservative economic policies worked. Fujimori recently won reelection despite his political clampdown. The economy is improving, the Sendero insurrection is losing steam, and for now it appears that Peru will remain stable and its economy will take off.

(See also the Latin American "Revolution," page 584.)

EUROPE

 Europe is the home to Western civilization, cross-fertilized by cultural influences from the Middle East and Africa. In the years between 1500 and 1945, Europe in effect dominated much of the world. After World War II and the emergence of the two super-powers, the U.S. and the U.S.S.R., Europe's role in world affairs diminished. For many Europeans, this was just fine. After seeing their lands devastated by war twice in the first half of the century, it was good to get away from conflict. Europeans saw their continent divided into pro-U.S. and pro-Soviet spheres. Western Europe developed rapidly from the wreckage and devastation, while Eastern Europe stagnated under Soviet domination. West Germany became an economic powerhouse, and allied itself to France in creating the European Community, a union of Western European nations. Then the Soviet empire collapsed, and suddenly the newly freed Eastern European nations sought to join the Western nations in their prosperity. Many also sought military alliances against a possible renewal of Russian stewardship.

Western Europe's response so far has been cautious. West Germany has reunited with its eastern counterpart, but for the most part, the West is watching and waiting. The eruption of a nationalist war in the newly independent nations of the former Yugoslavia brought a very slow response—a few peace-keeping forces, a lot of words,

SOME KEY NATIONS OF EUROPE

and a lot of backtracking. Western Europe is rich now—combined it is the world's largest economy—but it has its own problems of high unemployment and expensive labor. It seems afraid of conflict, and anxious to manage any changes cautiously . . . and peacefully.

FRANCE

(French Republic/République Française)

VITAL STATISTICS

Geographic facts: 220,668 square miles, four fifths the size of Texas, located in Western Europe; most of France is a wide temperate plain, with a high mountainous plateau in the center

Cities: Paris (capital), Marseilles, Lyons, Toulouse, Nice, Strasbourg

Population: 58 million

Languages: French; some minorities speak Breton, Basque, Alsatian German, and others

Ethnic groups: primarily French (a mixture of various European peoples), also 9% North African, as well as large Basque and Indochinese minorities

Religions: Roman Catholic 81%, Muslim 5%, Protestant and Jewish

In 1968 rebellious students rioted across France. They were joined in spirit by such prominent leftist intellectuals as Jean-Paul Sartre. Like students elsewhere, they were protesting the right-wing policies of government and the bourgeois values of society. The talk was of politics and the rise of left-wing ideology.

Then in 1994 another student rebellion broke out across France. This time it was over a government plan for a lower minimum wage for the young. As one student explained, "We're not revolting *against* the middle class—we just want a chance to join it."

At the risk of oversimplifying, this symbolizes the immense change that has occurred in France and the rest of

Western Europe. Today, most of the young in Europe want jobs, not enlightenment—even in France, the home of revolutions and a battleground for centuries.

France, called Gaul in its early days, has faced plenty of turmoil in its long history. Its people were famed for their fierce resistance to the invading Romans, who were led by none other than Julius Caesar. After the Romans, another famous leader stepped in: Charlemagne, who ruled a united Frankish state that covered much of Western Europe, including what is now France. But after those days of European unity, French kings faced a long history of wars with England and other states until at last they were overthrown during the bloody French Revolution of 1789. But peace didn't come: more wars did. During the years of the Napoleonic era, France fought most of Europe. It ultimately lost to a European coalition—only to face more revolutions, and in the end, not one but three German invasions: one in 1870, another in 1914, and finally, the last in 1940.

During much of this time, France couldn't seem to decide upon a form of government. It became known as a hotbed of political thought, as competing groups vied for political and intellectual power. So after World War II, many people reacted enthusiastically to General Charles de Gaulle, a right-wing leader who had led the Free French in World War II and who promised stability and a return to French grandeur.

But in the postwar years what counted for most people was the rapidly improving economy. People moved from farms into industrial cities, the standard of living rose consistently higher, and the differences between classes were reduced. This lessened the traditional power of the Communist Party, and increased the power of the moderate center parties, including that of the Socialists. Meanwhile, the rising affluence of the average French worker created vacancies at the lowest rungs of the employment ladder—and led to a rising tide of immigrant workers, particularly from the formerly French Algeria. This has now led to a backlash, as various racist groups call for the expulsion of the Arabs, and the government itself has tightened immigration policies.

These problems are not as threatening in the way of former problems. Germany is contained within the new European Union—it won't invade again. Although the economy has had problems, it is a modern producer of steel, machines, cars, and electronic equipment; France is also the largest food exporter in Western Europe, and the fourth largest economic power in the world. But unemployment is high and the government and people are worried.

The French are an unpredictable, creative nation. Intellectuals are far more important there than here; ideas count in France. So France is always a nation to watch, with a touch of very human unpredictability.

(See also Algeria, page 511; the French Revolution, page 581; Georges Clemenceau, page 607; Charles de Gaulle, page 608.)

GERMANY

(Federal Republic of Germany/Bundesrepublik Deutschland)

VITAL STATISTICS

Geographic facts: 137,838 square miles, a bit smaller than California; located in central Europe; flat in the north, hills in the center, and mountainous in the south

Cities: Berlin (capital in year 2000), Hamburg, Munich, Cologne, Frankfurt, Essen, Bonn (current seat of government)

Population: 81 million

Language: German

Ethnic groups: German 93%, Turkish and Kurds 2.5%, also Danish and Slavic minorities

Religions: Protestant 44%, Roman Catholic 37%, Muslim 2.5%

In November 1989 the Berlin Wall that divided capitalist West from communist East Berlin came tumbling down. With it, an era symbolically ended. From the period after World War II until 1990 Germany had been split into two. This was the legacy of the postwar tensions between the two superpowers. West Germany accounted for 52% of pre–World War II Germany, East Germany accounted for 22%—the rest had been taken by the Russians and Poles.

And then in October 1990, formerly communist East Germany was formally reunited with capitalist—and very prosperous—West Germany. West Germany had been the miracle story of the postwar period, quickly rebuilding ruined cities and industries to become an economic giant, the third largest economy in the world.

Much of this success was due to the U.S. Marshall Plan, an aid and development program that provided the money to get the economy going, and to German Chancellor Konrad Adenauer, who won the first postwar election promising "no experiments" to the tired German people. He structured a federal state designed to work better than the weak Weimar Republic, which had allowed Hitler to come to power.

With reunification many were assuming that the West German powerhouse would quickly absorb the East, but it hasn't turned out as easy as many had thought. East Germany was the most prosperous of the communist states, but it had paid a tremendous price: ecological degradation, inefficient industries, and poorly trained and motivated workers. The western side of the new Germany has spent billions integrating its former alter ego into itself. Now that investment is starting to pay off.

A big question of the early 1990s was whether to relocate the capital to Berlin. West Germany's capital had been Bonn, originally a quiet university town that had come to symbolize the new Germany—smaller, but more prosperous, content with economic rather than political influence. To many, the old capital Berlin symbolized the other Germany, of Hitler, Holocaust, and territorial expansion. Would a reunified Germany bring back those horrors?

Ironically, Germany has not been united for long in historical terms. Germany was supposedly founded by the legendary Prince Arminius, who defeated invading Roman legions in C.E. 9, but German tribes were not organized into a state until Charle-

magne became king of a confederation of tribes. His unified state fell apart until the first German king, Conrad of Franconia, was elected by the nobles as king of Germany in 911. With Christianity, the title of the German rulers changed to Holy Roman Emperor. But he was said to be neither holy, nor Roman, nor an emperor, since he was a secular ruler who couldn't really control all the many different and effectively independent German states, cities, duchies, and princedoms.

Finally, in the late 1800s Germany was unified under the domination of its largest state, Prussia. Its great chancellor, Otto von Bismarck, fought wars with Denmark, Austria, then France, to finally win the dream of a unified German state. But with unity came problems—for all of Europe. First Germany became embroiled in World War I, leading to the widespread European devastation. World War II was an even worse disaster; much of Europe was literally rubble with tens of millions killed. In the aftermath Germany tried to remake itself—and largely succeeded.

So what about Berlin? In 1993, Germany's parliament, the Bundestag, in a close vote decided to make Berlin the capital once more. The argument in favor is that Germany has changed much in 50 years, and has addressed its past. It seems willing to recognize that reunification will mean a new future as a member of a new integrated and peaceful Europe. The past is over, or so everyone hopes.

(See also Adolf Hitler, page 599; Helmut Kohl, page 612.)

ITALY

(Italian Republic/Repubblica Italiana)

VITAL STATISTICS

Geographic facts: 116,303 square miles; about the size of Florida and Georgia; located in southern Europe, a peninsula extending into the Mediterranean Sea; with a warm temperate climate and relatively mountainous terrain

Cities: Rome (capital), Milan, Naples, Turin, Palermo

Population: 57 million

Language: Italian

Ethnic groups: primarily Italian; some German, Slovenian, and Albanian

Religion: Roman Catholic

In many ways you'd expect Italy to be a country near collapse, and not one of the largest and most dynamic economies of the world. Every year, on average, the government falls; organized crime has plagued the south and until recently terrorism traumatized the north; there are few natural resources, strikes are frequent, and the nation was recently racked by scandal. There's an Italian saying that the Italians have rules for everything but that no one obeys them.

But despite all this—or maybe even because of it—Italy has prospered during the years since World War II. Italians admire individualism and don't expect as much from the government as other Europeans. Perhaps this forced them to become innovative economically (as well as deceptive; estimates are that 20% of the economy is underground, conducted outside of taxation and government regulation).

Today Italy is the world's sixth or seventh largest economic power (depending on who's counting). It's a major manufacturer of cars, textiles, chemicals, fashion items, and machinery. Of course there are problems, principally unemployment nationwide, underdevelopment in the south, and the always creaky system of government. Italy north of Rome is modern; in terms of development, the south, including Naples and Sicily, is far behind.

Italy is of course more than a modern power: it is also a living museum of an illustrious past: seat of the Roman Empire, which spread Latin and Greek civilization to the Western world; and the birthplace of the Renaissance and humanism, which revived ancient Greek ideas and culture.

But the past was not on people's minds in recent years, when Italy was racked by corruption that has included prime ministers, big-business barons, and politicians of the leading parties. Over 3,000 of Italy's best and brightest were accused of bribery and looting the state coffers. In reaction, Italians elected a conservative right-wing media mogul named Silvio Berlusconi as prime minister. He promised to clean up government, but was himself accused of corruption, of consorting with neo-Facists—in short, a case of the cure being worse than the disease.

The odds are that Italians will still be frustrated with government and society, no matter what. But if the future is anything like the past, Italy itself will probably—somehow—emerge more prosperous than ever.

(See also Benito Mussolini, page 614.)

UNITED KINGDOM

(United Kingdom of Great Britain and Northern Ireland)

VITAL STATISTICS

Geographic facts: 94,226 square miles, slightly smaller than Oregon. Most of the U.K. is a large island off the northwest coast of Europe; comprised of mostly rolling hills with a temperate, and wet, climate

Cities: England: London (capital), Birmingham, Leeds, Sheffield, Liverpool, Manchester; Scotland: Glasgow, Edinburgh; Wales: Cardiff; Northern Ireland: Belfast

Population: 58 million

Languages: English, Welsh, Gaelic, Scots Gaelic

Ethnic groups: English 81.5%, Scottish 9.6%, Irish 2.4%, Welsh 1.9%; in addition, West Indian and South Asian

Religions: 47% Anglican, 9% Roman Catholic, 4% Presbyterian, 2% Muslim

In the early 1900s the European island nation of Great Britain literally ruled the world—or at least a good chunk of it. Its colonies, dominions, and possessions stretched from the Rock of Gibraltar to the plains of India. Almost one quarter of the world's population owed allegiance to its sovereign, its booming economy accounted for one third of the world's exports, its powerful navy ruled the seas.

But it takes money and men to run an empire, and two world wars cost Britain millions of both. The peoples of the African and Asian colonies began demanding and winning independence, and fairly soon, Great Britain was much smaller and much poorer. Its colonies and possessions dwindled to very few (including that perennial problem of Northern Ireland), and its economic power declined to the extent that France, Germany, and Italy all boasted more powerful economies. Its political power waned as well; the U.S. Navy took over much of the job of patrolling the world's seas.

But there were benefits, at least for the average man or woman on the street. Labor governments came into power that guaranteed health care and welfare, and worked to provide jobs. Britain had once been the home of conservative laissez-faire economics, but now it became the home to the welfare state. The British people liked it that way (most of them, that is; with marginal taxes approaching 98% on unearned income, the very rich did not). But the economy couldn't do it all. Soon Britain suffered from what Europeans came to call "Englanditis"—too much government intervention stifling the economy.

The people decided they wanted a change once again. They elected Margaret Thatcher, the Iron Lady of the Conservative Party (or Tory Party, as they are also called). She was an admirer of Ronald Reagan, and, like him, she brought down taxes and inflation, crushed some powerful unions, and got the economy humming again. There have been some ups and downs since Thatcher left office, but, like the U.S., Britain has changed fundamentally. As in the U.S., corporate restructerings have increased productivity, reduced the number of well-paid jobs, and increased the number of low-paid jobs. This creates hardships, but so far it appears the only other alternative is to have high unemployment—which is what Britain's fellow European Community members across the English Channel are experiencing.

Some of the British are still leery of giving up some of their much-vaunted independence to the European Union, but more realize that Britain's future lies with her neighbors in what may one day truly become an even more powerful "United States of Europe."

(See also Northern Ireland, page 577; Winston Churchill, page 595; Margaret Thatcher, page 617.)

RUSSIA

(Russian Federation)

VITAL STATISTICS

Geographic facts: 6,592,800 square miles, the largest nation in the world, over twice the size of the U.S.; modern Russia includes about 75% of the former Soviet territories. With a varied terrain of grasslands, forests, Arctic tundra, deserts, and mountains, it also has virtually every type of climate except for tropical

Cities: Moscow (capital), St. Petersburg (formerly Leningrad), Novosibirsk, Nizhny Novgorod, Samara

Population: 148 million

Languages: Russian (official); also Ukrainian, Belorussian, Uzbek, Armenian, and others

Ethnic groups: Russian 82%, Tatar 3%, numerous small minorities as well, including Chuvash, Chechen, and Bashkir

Religions: Russian Orthodox 25%, many nonreligious, in keeping with its

The last statue of Soviet founder N. Lenin commissioned by the Communist Party was completed by tombstone maker Peter Gerasimov just as the Soviet Union collapsed. Today in Russia and other former lands there's a glut of statues of Lenin and other communists, and many have been destroyed. But some SoHo, New York, art dealers bought Gerasimov's 16-foot Lenin statue for $15,000 and moved it to the East Village in New York City, where it stands on top of an apartment building, waving at the World Trade Center, a tall symbol of capitalism.

years under communism, which officially espoused atheism

That old cold warrior Richard Nixon said it best: "Those who suggest that because of its vast problems Russia should no longer be treated as a world power ignore an unpleasant but undeniable truth: Russia is the only nation in the world that can destroy the United States. Therefore Russia remains our highest foreign policy priority."

Russia is by far the largest piece of the old Soviet Union left after the breakup in 1991. It has inherited many of the enormous problems the Soviet Union faced in its last years. But the years under communism were probably not an aberration. There is a continuity in all of Russian and Soviet history that everyone should understand if they wish to fathom the nation today.

Russia has had a long history of expansionism, of controlling its neighbors, and in turn of suffering from the depredations of outside conquerors as well as its own absolutist rulers. The suffering Russian soul, ennobled and deepened by the problems imposed by fate, is a constant theme in its literature and film.

The land was long ago settled by Slavs, an Indo-European–speaking people. Later Scandinavian Vikings came in, and then there was a cultural invasion of Orthodox Christianity, which arrived in the tenth century under the influence of Greek Byzantine culture. And then, in the traumatic thirteenth century, the Russians were conquered by the Mongols. They endured 200 years under their rule.

Finally Ivan the Great, the Grand Duke of Moscow, broke free from

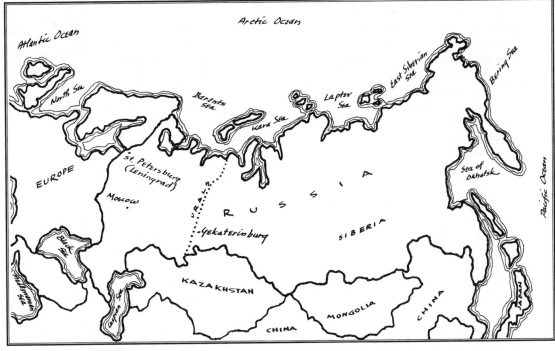

RUSSIA

Mongol domination. Under his grandson, Ivan the Terrible, absolutist rule was established; Ivan called himself the "Czar and Autocrat of All Russia"— and he meant it. Later czars continued his form of rule and expanded Russia. Peter the Great won territories in the west near the Baltic Sea. He also began Russia's long flirtation with Western ideas, ordering his subjects to dress in Western ways, and introducing Western science and architecture. Catherine the Great seized Turkish lands to the south and Polish lands to the west. But then Russia was once more traumatized—this time during the Napoleonic Wars when the French conqueror marched eastward and actually captured Moscow.

After the communist N. Lenin seized power in 1917, many of the basic Russian themes played out again, but

this time to a communist conductor. Initially Lenin gave up some territory to obtain peace with Germany. The remaining territories were set up as separate republics; in reality they were subject to central control from Moscow, just as under the czars—only more so. And the cruel excesses of Ivan the Terrible were far exceeded by Joseph Stalin, a paranoid ruler who killed tens of millions of people in the 1930s.

Then came World War II. The Germans invaded and destroyed much of the Soviet Union, ultimately causing the deaths of up to 30 million Soviet citizens. But in a heroic effort that is still remembered today, just as German troops reached the outskirts of Moscow the tide began to turn, Soviet troops counterattacked, and ultimately regained their lost territory and more—becoming the first of the Allies to reach Berlin and raising their Red flag over the German Reichstag. They didn't stop with symbolism; they also put communists in power in most of the European nations they liberated during the war. Was this imperialism? No question about it. But it was also fear of outside invaders with a penchant for Russian land.

The suffering should have ended with the end of World War II, or more correctly in 1953 with the end of the dictator Stalin. For a while things looked bright. The new premier, Nikita Khrushchev, undid some of Stalin's excesses and the economy started to improve. But Khrushchev was erratic—the type of man who would pound his shoe on a table in front of the world—and he embarrassed his fellow communists. They wound up supporting Leonid Brezhnev, a stolid and dull man who presided over the decay of the Soviet empire.

The problem was that Soviet-style communism just wasn't working. The huge factories produced shoddy goods and they couldn't produce even these well. Centralized control from Moscow economic planners created huge logistic messes. And it simply was costing too much to keep up militarily with the Americans. The Soviet invasion of Afghanistan in an attempt to keep a friendly state on its borders was perhaps the straw that broke the camel's back—the cost of war further sapped morale and drained the economy.

The last Soviet premier, Mikhail Gorbachev, thought he could solve all these problems. But instead the nation imploded. Gorbachev tried to reorganize society by granting more political and economic freedom. But this resulted in non-Russian nationalists from the territories agitating for inde-

pendence. And the economy didn't get better, it got worse. And with all the years of decay, many Communist Party members simply didn't believe in the party anymore. And so the Soviet Union ended not with a bang but a whimper. It split apart into 13 separate republics.

Under President Boris Yeltsin things haven't changed all that much despite a faster pace of reform. There are still many minorities in the new Russian borders; when one such group, the Chechens, sought independence, Yeltsin reacted by sending military forces to retake the Chechen lands. The economy is still a mess: the transition to capitalism in a people long used to having leaders make decisions for them has been difficult, much more so than in China. Organized crime now controls upward of 50% of the economy (that number comes from Russian officials). The people are unhappy. Economic reformers have had to backtrack and go much more slowly in the face of popular opposition. The communist and far-right opposition is growing.

But Russia is still a power, as Nixon said. The nuclear weapons remain, although they are no longer aimed at us. As in the past, Russia has also been seeking to once again dominate its neighboring former Soviet states. Many of them have gathered together in a loose confederation called the CIS, or the Commonwealth of Independent States—and the CIS leader is clearly Russia. Russia is also seeking, so far successfully, to keep its former Eastern European client states out of NATO, the American-European military alliance.

So is there any hope from history? Of course. For all the talk above about historical themes, let's not forget that any nation is a mass of contradictions. Russia is no exception. Russia has had absolute leaders, yes, but some historians claim that traditional rural society also had a form of democracy. Economists point out that under Nicholas II's energetic minister Count Witte, Russian capitalism hummed along admirably.

So what will the future bring? It will be difficult, but Russia still has a highly educated scientific elite, a treasure house of natural resources, and it has been a great power for generations.

Now it appears that the economy is improving. Democratic reforms appear to be taking hold. The bottom line is that Russia has always survived and somehow triumphed, despite a history of very real suffering and conflict.

(See also New Countries That Were Once Part of the Soviet Union, page 553; The Russian Revolution of 1917, page 586; Mikhail Gorbachev, page 609; Nikita Khrushchev, page 612; Vladimir Ilyich Lenin, page 612; Josef Stalin, page 616; Boris Yeltsin, page 618.)

ASIA

~

Asia is the world's largest continent, and appropriately enough, home to the world's largest nations in terms of population (India and China) and to one of the world's largest economies (Japan). For much of the twentieth century, this continent has been convulsed by political change. It was the site of fierce fighting as Japan sought to create an Asian empire. War broke out in the 1930s in China, then throughout Asia in the 1940s. In the aftermath of the Allied victory, the former colonial powers of Britain, France, and the Netherlands withdrew from the region, and a

host of new problems arose. First communism triumphed in China, and then in the northern areas of Korea and Indochina, bringing new wars to the region. Meanwhile, India became independent, but not before bloody riots divided the former British colony into two nations: Hindu India and Muslim Pakistan. The Vietnam War, the Cambodian war, and the Korean wars are covered elsewhere, but suffice to say that the past fifty years were tumultuous.

But now, most of the conflicts are over, and the Pacific Rim Asian nations have become the fastest growing

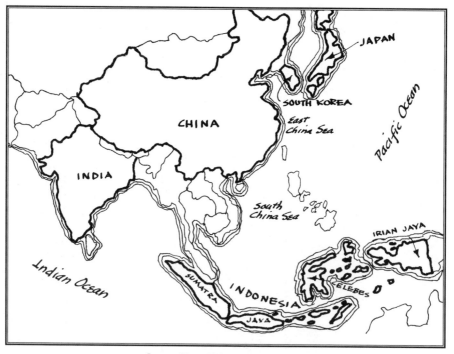

SOME KEY NATIONS OF ASIA

economies in the world. Japan has reentered its former wartime conquests as a major investor, closely followed by the U.S. and Europe. But these nations don't dominate as before. Instead, most of the countries of the region are becoming (or have become) full-fledged economic powers in their own right. The "Asian model" of development has become the talk of all other less-developed nations, as well as in the West. Estimates are that in the next twenty years, the Pacific Asian nations will be more powerful than Europe and the U.S. combined, the dominant economic powers in the world.

CHINA

(People's Republic of China/Zhonghua Renmin Gongheguo)

VITAL STATISTICS

Geographic facts: 3,696,100 square miles, slightly larger than the U.S.; takes up most of East Asia; most of the land is mountainous or desert; the eastern part is the most cultivated, and includes three great rivers: the Yangtze, Yellow, and Zhujiang

Cities: Shanghai, Beijing (capital), Tianjin, Shenyang, Wuhan, Canton

Population: 1.2 billion

Languages: Manadarin Chinese (official), many other Chinese dialects, which are virtually distinct languages; many other languages

Ethnic groups: Han Chinese 94%; minorities include Mongols, Koreans, Manchus, Tibetans, and many others

Religions: China is officially atheist, but religions include Confucian-

ism, Taoism, Buddhism, Islam, and some Christianity

"Black cat, white cat. Who cares what color as long as it catches mice?"

When Chinese leader Deng Xiaoping said these famous words in the 1960s, China was a poor country whose communist leadership was paralyzed by ideological debate. For most of them, what mattered was what kind of communist you were. Deng argued that what really counted was economic progress. Who cared if money came from capitalist ideas?—it was still money.

Not too long after Chairman Mao Zedong's death in 1976, Deng had his chance to put his pragmatic views to the test when he became the leader of China. He had his work cut out for him. Despite very real progress in reducing population growth, improving health, and raising educational standards, China was still a very backward country after years of Maoist rule.

First of all, there were agricultural problems, and in China, agricultural problems mean more than a higher price for a bag of potato chips. For example, Mao's big effort to improve the economy known as the Great Leap Forward was followed by a famine that killed 30 million people (this was pretty much a secret until recently). Even in good years crops were poor. The government had tried to organize people into communes—agricultural factories where the state, rather than the people, owned the land. But they weren't working. The best example was the commune Da Zhai. It was long shown to fellow Chinese and foreign guests as an example of collective farming in action. But the whole thing was a sham: records were faked, crops

Chinese Holidays

Whether in China or any of the U.S.'s (or world's) many Chinatowns, the Chinese celebrate various holidays, which most of us know nothing about. If you've ever wondered what's going on when the fireworks start going off, here are some of the major Chinese holidays.

New Year: Probably the single most important holiday, this is the first day of the new year in the Chinese (lunar) calendar, which dates to 104 B.C.E., and originally was primarily an agricultural festival marking the beginning of spring. In addition to the firecrackers and street celebrations, the highlight is the reunion dinner, when the extended family gets together. Parents try to keep the kids awake until midnight—if they do, they'll live longer lives. On New Year's Day, housewives visit temples to pay homage to ancestors, and the young pay their respects to the old. On the second day, there are more street celebrations, but on the third many people stay home; this is a bad day, a day of quarreling with friends. So the best strategy is to avoid everyone. And on the fourth day, most businesses reopen, but some celebrate the ninth day after new year as well.

Ching Ming Festival: This is the time when Chinese visit the tombs of their ancestors, and make offerings of cooked rice, wine, lettuce, meat, and fruits. Candles are lit, incense paper is burned, and prayers are offered. Ancestor worship brings good fortune and luck—and those neglecting it are said to suffer bad luck. So why not be on the safe side? most Chinese say.

Dragon Boat Festival: The fifth day of the fifth lunar month is the festival of dragon boat (like giant canoes with 20 people rowing them) races; all the while spectators eat traditional rice dumplings. It's a fun time, but it's based on the suicide of a hero named Qu Yuan 2,000 years ago. But that's a long, long story.

Seven Sisters Festival: Falling on the seventh day of the seventh lunar month, this is a romantic festival that celebrates the love affair of a legendary fairy and cowherd, who were sort of a Chinese Romeo and Juliet.

Moon Cake Festival: On the fifteenth day of the eighth lunar month, the original end of the autumn harvest, the Chinese celebrate the night they began their revolt against foreign Mongol rulers. Today, Chinese make gifts of moon-shaped cakes, and have moon cake parties under the moonlight, while children play with colorful lanterns, symbolic of those carried by the revolutionaries.

were brought in from outside, the "happy farmers" were more like actors than real workers. This wasn't the only example; a giant industrial record-setter had done much the same thing.

So Deng and his allies loosened political control to allow the economy to grow. This unleashed a growing amount of disrespect for the Communist Party; but Deng offered nothing to replace it and he backed down from offering real political freedom. In June 1989 students demonstrated in Tian-

anmen Square and Deng reacted strongly. The army attacked the unarmed students, killing many and arresting many more. To this day the Chinese government has harassed and imprisoned those speaking out for greater freedom from party rule.

But Deng succeeded with the economy. Recently China had the fastest economic growth rate in the world. Deng began with rural development, allowing farmers to lease land and sell their produce. Rural development proceeded rapidly and many small private businesses were set up. Meanwhile, long inefficient state industries were told to make a profit and not to expect more subsidies from the central government.

Even the government got involved in capitalist business. The People's Liberation Army manufactures weapons as well as bicycles, and exports to nations around the world. Deng also encouraged free-trade zones, first in Shenzhen, near Hong Kong, later in other areas. He allowed investors from Hong Kong and other nations into China, quickening the pace of development. Shanghai, once the bustling home of Western colonialists and later a hotbed of radical Chinese thought, is once again an economic powerhouse. And long gone are the drab Mao jackets: one of China's newest millionaires sells cosmetics; fashion is big business in China.

So Deng has offered the nation stability and economic progress at the price of political repression. And there has still been no lessening of government control over non-Chinese areas like Tibet and the Muslim northwest. But repression can't hold back a rising tide of problems. Peasants, who make up the bulk of the population, are increasingly angry at high taxation (including levies from corrupt party bosses); workers at inefficient state factories are upset with low wages; students and intellectuals want freedom of speech. Already, a nascent dissident movement has formed. They are armed with high-tech communications equipment that just might work better than guns in winning over the people.

No matter what happens, experts are betting that the Chinese economy will grow rapidly. Some say it just may become the largest economy of the

twenty-first century. But the Chinese are more concerned about the near future: what will happen in the next few years after Deng's death. Most Chinese greatly fear *luan,* or disorder—they have too much experience with its disastrous results.

(See also The Chinese Revolution, page 589; Mao Zedong, page 602; Chiang Kai-shek, page 607; Sun Yat-sen, page 617; Zhou Enlai, page 619.)

INDIA

(Republic of India/Bharat)

VITAL STATISTICS

Geographic facts: 1,266,595 square miles, one third the size of the U.S.; occupies most of Indian subcontinent; in the north are the Himalayan Mountains (the highest in the world) and the tropical Assam hills; central India includes the Ganges and Deccan plains, which are warm and very densely populated

Cities: Bombay, Calcutta, New Delhi (capital), Madras, Bangalore, Hyderabad

Population: 911 million

Languages: Hindi and English (both official) and 16 regional languages including Bengali, Telugu, Marathi, Tamil, and Urdu

Ethnic groups: heb-Aryan 72%, Dravidian 25%

Religions: Hindu 83%, Muslim 11%, Christian 2%, Sikh 2%, other native religions.

India has not ever been an easy country to understand. Perhaps it is too deep, contradictory, and diverse, and few people in the contemporary world have the time or inclination to look beyond the obvious, especially because in our country we have the greatest scope for free expression of opinion and all differences are constantly being debated.

So said Indian Prime Minister Indira Gandhi. India is more than a nation, it's a huge and complex mixture of different cultures, languages, religions, and classes. To understand India to any degree, you have to understand the great diversity that makes up this enormous nation, one of the major powers of the world, and *the* major power on the subcontinent.

India incorporates speakers of over 17 different major languages and many minor ones, in addition to English; three major religions—Hinduism, Islam, and Sikhism—and has an enormous diversity of wealth and education: hundreds of millions of Indians are poor illiterate villagers, but India also has one of the world's largest middle classes and conducts advanced scientific research in many fields. Even the periphery of India's culture or society is huge and diverse: India's census includes widely separated peoples called "tribal peoples" who range from Andaman islanders of the Indian Ocean to hill tribespeople of Assam; together, they make up a nation in themselves of over 30 million people. And the Hindu caste system, a religiously motivated separation of society into relatively rigid classes, also makes for severe divisions. The highest caste of Brahmans technically cannot deal very much with the lowest castes—this has created many social problems as well.

Managing or ruling such a diverse

Homelessness is a key problem in India. One frightening example: in Bombay, over 100,000 inhabitants pay for the right to sleep on a part of the sidewalk.

nation is clearly difficult—and doing so democratically would seem nearly impossible, yet India has managed to maintain a democratic system during the years that followed independence from Britain in 1947. Democracy has moderated many Indian differences, allowing a safety valve for tensions and allowing some issues to disappear as modernization continues. Along the way, there have been major problems, of course. Several wars and border incidents have been fought with the neighboring (Muslim) Pakistanis, and internally India has had to cope with a violent separatist movement from radical members of the Sikh religion, who want an independent or autonomous Sikh state. Indian Prime Minister Indira Gandhi was assassinated by Sikh terrorists. Meanwhile, the southern Indians, who speak Tamil languages, which are unrelated to the Indo-European languages of the dominant north, want a greater say in state affairs; one of their number from the neighboring island nation of Sri Lanka assassinated Indira Gandhi's son, Prime Minister Rajiv Gandhi, for his efforts to moderate a conflict there. But despite this unrest, democracy has continued, freedom of speech is maintained, and India has advanced considerably.

For years, India was an ally of the Soviet Union, and its economy was subject to many government controls. This was in part a legacy of the British, in part due to the popular socialist ideas of the postwar years. But more recently, controls have been lifted and India's economy has begun to take off rapidly. Small-scale industry has been emphasized, and foreign investment encouraged. In addition, India has been aided by the large numbers of ethnic Indians living abroad. They make up one of the world's wealthiest and most dynamic groups and control many powerful multinational corporations. As India liberalizes its economy, they are tying their companies' fortunes to that of their mother country, promising more prosperity for the world's second most populous nation.

(See also Kashmir, page 571; Sri Lanka, page 578; Mohandas K. Gandhi, page 597; Indira Gandhi, page 608; Jawaharlal Nehru, page 614.)

INDONESIA

(*Republic of Indonesia/Republik Indonesia*)

VITAL STATISTICS

Geographic facts: 735,268 square miles; an archipelago in Southeast Asia comprised of approximately 17,000 islands, including Sumatra to the north, Java (the most densely populated), Kalimantan (most of the island of Borneo), Sulawesi, and Irian Jaya (the western half of the island of New Guinea); the land is tropical; many of the islands are volcanic and include mountains in the interior; large rain forests once covered much of the land, but these have been cut in many places

Cities: Jakarta (capital, on Java), Surabaya and Bandung (on Java), Medan (on Sumatra), Semarang (on Java)

Population: 199 million

Languages: Bahasa Indonesia (official), Javanese, many other Austronesian languages, others on Irian Jaya

Ethnic groups: Malay (Indonesians are mostly Malay, but split into many subgroups with separate regional languages), Chinese, Irianese

Religions: Muslim 88%, Christian 9%, others, including Hindu

At first glance, Indonesia is an unlikely success story. It is the world's fourth largest nation in terms of population. Most of its people are crammed onto the island of Java, one of the most densely populated areas of the world. Since Indonesia is an archipelago made up of about 17,000 islands, as you might expect, it has a complex mixture of many different ethnic groups, although most of them are relatively closely related.

Indonesia was a Dutch colony until World War II. Perhaps Indonesians were lucky that the Dutch were fairly oppressive colonialists, because it forced them to build up a strong anti-Dutch nationalist movement, a kind of secret government.

During World War II, the Japanese invaded Indonesia and imprisoned the Dutch colonists. But they sometimes helped the Indonesian nationalists, even supporting an Indonesian militia with Indonesian officers up to battalion level. So by the time the Dutch returned after the war the Indonesians were united against them, no matter what dialect they spoke or island they were from.

After four years of war, the Dutch flag was lowered and Indonesia was independent. Now it faced a different set of problems. First there was the new president, Sukarno. He was a popular nationalist who became more dictatorial and pro-communist as his rule lengthened. The army became worried at the rise of the communists, and in a bloody period in 1965 killed thousands of them (this all became the basis of an excellent book and later movie, *The Year of Living Dangerously*). They put in their chief of staff, General Suharto, as president. After the killing was over Suharto turned the economy onto a capitalist track.

Clearly Suharto and his military cronies were no saints. Although Suharto has been reelected six times, he's really more of a dictator. He and his fellow officers control much of Indonesia's business (look at the boards of most major Indonesian corporations and you'll often find Suharto's family or his top soldiers and their families). In fact, under the doctrine *dwi fungsi* or dual function, the army is *expected* to be involved in politics, business, and society as well as in the military.

This was an unusual arrangement, but on the other hand, the economy started to boom. Rice production

soared and Indonesia became self-sufficient in 1984; oil and gas production took off (Indonesia is a very vocal member of OPEC), timber production increased, finished wood products grew as exports, then other manufactured goods. Indonesia and Japan are economically very close; that helped as well. Of course, there's a downside ecologically. Indonesia's beautiful rain forests are disappearing fast.

Indonesia is still a poor country, but it is changing and growing rapidly, and it looks as if the change will continue. There has been some political unrest and rioting and the government has clamped down harshly and fast. The saddest case is the island of Timor, where the people are fighting for independence and have been callously ignored by the world, and periodically killed by the Indonesian army.

But as modern roads and electricity extend into rural areas and job oppor-

Vietnam: On the Capitalist Path?

Vietnam was united under communist rule in 1975, after a long war in which well over 1 million Vietnamese and almost 60,000 Americans died. When the victorious North Vietnamese entered Saigon, the southern capital, it appeared as if Western influence was over for generations in this populous Southeast Asian nation of 73 million.

But Vietnam is changing. After the failure of central control of the economy, which had kept Vietnam near the bottom of the list of the world's poorest countries and that put many millions close to starvation, the government instituted *doi moi,* or reform. Land was given back to farmers, central control was loosened, banking was modernized, and the economy began to take off.

In a few short years, Vietnam has become the world's third largest rice exporter, and the economy is growing at the fast clip of 9% per year. And the U.S. is back. Chrysler and Ford are setting up new assembly plants, Motorola is selling phone systems, and U.S. consultants confidently talk of Vietnam as a boom area for U.S. business. Saigon, now Ho Chi Minh City, is bustling once more with commercial activity, and most visitors report that the political atmosphere is relaxed.

Vietnam is still communist, and conservatives in the government are still trying to slow the pace of reform. But most experts are betting that the trend toward liberalization will continue and that Vietnam will become an integrated member of the prosperous Southeast Asian bloc.

tunities for the poor open up, the odds are that Indonesia will continue to grow and prosper.

(See also Sukarno, page 616.)

JAPAN

(Nippon)

VITAL STATISTICS

Geographic facts: 145,856 square miles, slightly larger than California; Japan covers a mountainous archipelago off the northeastern coast of Asia

Cities: Tokyo (capital), Yokohama, Osaka, Nagoya, Sapporo, Kobe, Kyoto

Population: 125 million

Language: Japanese

Ethnic groups: Japanese 99.4%, Korean 0.5%

Religions: Shintoist, Buddhist

In 1853, an American naval commodore named Matthew C. Perry led a naval squadron into Japanese waters to "convince" Japan to open its borders to world trade. For 200 years, Japan had shut itself off from the world, concerned that outside influence would destroy the Japanese way of life. After naval bombardments by European and American warships in 1864, Japan realized it had to act—and fast.

The Meiji Restoration was the answer. It put governmental power back in the hands of the emperor, and out of the hands of the powerful feudal samurai class. Along with his advisors he designed a modern form of government modeled on the European. The rest is history: Japan modernized rapidly and soon became an industrial power on par with the Western powers

of Britain, Germany, and the U.S. Even its complete destruction in World War II did not hold Japan back for long. In fact, with various reforms instituted by the U.S. occupiers, by 1952 Japan was ahead of its prewar prosperity.

Today, Japan is the world's second largest economic power and a powerful exporting nation. That ironically bothers those very nations that had acted to open it up to trade so many years before.

But why was Japan so successful? Economists and pundits have debated the answers for years. One reason for its postwar growth might be that Japan followed the advice of Western technical experts and paid attention to quality control and worker input (those same experts were ignored back in the U.S. until recently). But more important, Japan has had a long history of high-quality production—even the early (and often racist) European imperialists were impressed with its capabilities. Japan also created a dedicated and very loyal workforce by developing a system of guaranteed employment in large companies. If you've got a guaranteed job, the odds are you don't want or need a strong union; and the odds are you'll cooperate with your bosses. That's just what happened in Japan. Another possible cause for success was MITI, the Ministry of International Trade and Industry. Under its aegis Japan evolved a form of government coordination of the economy, a kind of managed capitalism in which MITI and huge banks, rather than shareholders, played a dominant role in guiding corporations and supporting them while they were developing new markets or products. To (over) simplify: American firms had to pay attention to short-term profits; Japanese firms could plan for the long term.

Whatever the reasons, Japan has become a major exporting nation and has built up huge trade surpluses. This has led some Americans to complain that Japan is unfair: always ready to sell to the U.S., but not so ready to buy.

The reality is not so simple. While the U.S. is Japan's leading export market, Japan is the second largest export market for the U.S. In recent years Japan has invested heavily in U.S. businesses (buying the communications giant MCA, setting up car factories, and buying U.S. stocks). However, Japan *has* been unfair in some senses—for example, it is loath to import U.S. agricultural products like apples and rice. But for all of our talk of the Japanese threat, the U.S. has moved ahead of Japan in the key cutting-edge industries of software, communications, and biotechnology. And recently Japan has suffered a recession that is making experts rethink Japan's economic and political structure.

Changes are in the air once again in Japan and Asia. Costs are rising relentlessly in Japan, so more and more of its companies are locating manufacturing facilities overseas. Japan has invested heavily in Asia, as well as in the U.S., and increasingly in Latin America. Japan is now also reconsidering its lifetime employment idea; the cost of keeping workers on a permanent payroll is simply too high. It's finding that government planning might not be as efficient in the new world economy as America's more chaotic but highly efficient reliance on the marketplace. Like everyone else, Japan is finding that economic growth in the coming years will require even more radical changes than in the past.

SOUTH KOREA

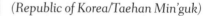

(Republic of Korea/Taehan Min'guk)

VITAL STATISTICS

Geographic facts: 38,025 square miles, about the size of Indiana; South Korea is on a peninsula it shares with North Korea; the land is mountainous

Cities: Seoul (capital), Pusan, Taegu, Inchon, Kwangju

Population: 44.5 million

Language: Korean

Ethnic group: Korean

Religions: Buddhist 47%, Protestant 38%, Roman Catholic 11%

South Korea is one of the miracle stories of Asia, rising out of the ashes of the past.

Korea suffered in the early years of the twentieth century as a Japanese protectorate; for all intents and purposes it was a colony. And just when Koreans were rejoicing at their liberation from the Japanese in 1945, political differences among Korean politicians and the superpowers split the country into a communist-dominated North and a capitalist-dominated South. Then came the devastating Korean War of 1950–1953 when the North attacked the South. Over a million people were killed or wounded, about half its industry was destroyed, roads and buildings were rubble—and each side still feared the armed might of the other.

Yet out of this mess South Korea built a modern nation and economic powerhouse. The miracle was in one sense helped by the Japanese occupiers, who had exploited the country but at the same time built factories, railroads, and cities. Koreans moved from farms to cities and towns and acquired modern skills. When the Korean War was over, Koreans had the know-how to rebuild, and better yet, they had the money. The U.S. gave more in aid to South Korea than to any other country except South Vietnam and Israel; better yet, the U.S. opened up its huge market to South Korean goods. It wasn't a one-way street: South Korea sent 300,000 troops to help the Americans in Vietnam.

The three things that make a store a success—location, location, and location—also helped Korea. Nearby Japan was a great source for exports; Korea licensed Japanese technology and then sold them components for their booming industries. Most important, Korea is known for its strong Confucian work ethic and highly civilized past. Today, Korea is an economic giant in its own right, creating and selling world-class cars, computers, ships, and steel.

Along the way, politics were pretty much shunted aside. The U.S. and Korean armies protected the border with the North; the government was authoritarian but most people were too busy making money to care. But Koreans soon wanted more. There's an Asian stereotype that Koreans are the Americans of Asia, and like Americans they began agitating for freedom. In 1987, widespread riots forced the government to lift restrictions on the press, grant direct elections rather than indirect electoral college elections, and improve human rights.

The major problem still facing the South is a legacy of the past: communist North Korea. The North is much poorer and getting even poorer but ominously has formidable military power and an unstable leader. That's a bad combination on a very volatile peninsula.

(See also Korea, page 572.)

NEW NATIONS ON THE MAP

The end of the Cold War in the late 1980s and early 1990s was a mapmaker's nightmare.

Suddenly, the Soviet empire collapsed and nations half forgotten by the West were declaring independence and remaking the maps and political boundaries of Europe and the world.

What had happened exactly?

It all began with the decay of the Soviet Union. For more than 40 years, since the end of World War II, most of the nations of Eastern Europe had been under communist rule imposed by Moscow and allied to the Soviet Union against the West. The regimes were not popular, but the option to change their leaders wasn't there. As the Soviet Union continued its long slide into economic decay, its last leader, the reformer Mikhail Gorbachev, realized that he couldn't transform the homeland while holding a

gun to the heads of the Eastern Europeans. Once he changed directions, the fall was inevitable. When Eastern European people realized that this time Soviet troops wouldn't shoot, they took to the streets and the communist governments fell like dominoes.

As the governments fell, long suppressed ethnic tensions came bubbling back. This was particularly true in Yugoslavia, a confederation of southern Slavs (which is what the name means) that wasn't even allied to the Soviets. Like Yugoslavia, many of the states in Eastern Europe were cobbled together artificially—and now many of the minorities within the various states wanted to be free.

The result was a wealth of new nations on the maps of Europe. We've listed them all. But with all the unrest in these very volatile regions, there's no guarantee that there won't be yet more new nations on the maps of the future.

NEW NATIONS OF EASTERN EUROPE

BOSNIA-HERCEGOVINA

(Republic of Bosnia and Hercegovina)

Formerly part of: Yugoslavia

Size: 19,741 square miles; about the size of New Hampshire and Vermont, but much land is occupied by Serbian aggressors

Population: 4.6 million

Ethnic groups: Muslim Slav 43%, Serbian Orthodox Christian 31%, Croat Catholic Christian 17%

What's happening: War and its aftermath consume Bosnia. The problem goes back to 1463, when the Turks conquered the area. Some of the Slavic inhabitants converted and became Muslims like their rulers. Skipping ahead a few hundred years, Bosnia later became part of communist leader Josip Broz Tito's well-run federal state of southern Slavs, called Yugoslavia. Tito forced all his southern Slavs to stick together, Christian and Muslim, Croatian and Serb. For a while it seemed that the ethnic differences among all these Balkan Peninsula Slavs would fade. But when Tito died Yugoslavia started to unravel and ethnic tensions rose dangerously high.

Bosnians voted for independence in 1992. The non-Muslims in Bosnia (called the Bosnian Serbs) weren't happy with the idea. Many of them started fighting against the government. Despite this the European

SOME NEW NATIONS OF EASTERN EUROPE

Community and the U.S. recognized Bosnia as independent.

Today there isn't too much of independent Bosnia left. Bosnian Serbs, aided by fellow Serbs from the independent state of Yugoslavia, seized much of the land and "ethnically cleansed" them of Muslim Bosnians, killing them or blowing up their houses and mosques. But in late 1995, negotiators meeting in Dayton, Ohio, under U.S. auspices reached an accord that would keep the warring factions apart, in effect splitting Bosnia into two (or three)—although the nation would technically remain united.

CROATIA

(Republic of Croatia)

Formerly part of: Yugoslavia
Size: 21,829 square miles, slightly smaller than West Virginia
Population: 4.8 million
Religions: Croatian Catholic 78%, Serbian Orthodox 12%

What's happening: Croats are a southern Slavic people who are Roman Catholic instead of Orthodox Christian like the Serbs, and write the Serbo-Croat language in Roman letters instead of Cyrillic (Russian) letters. The spoken language is virtually the same.

Despite relatively minor differences, Serbs and Croats have their share of mutual hatreds going a long way back. It was most pronounced in World War II, when a powerful Croat group declared independence and allied itself with the Nazis.

More recently, when Croatia declared independence in 1991 from Yugoslavia, Serbs and Croats started fighting again sporadically. The Serbs took Croat land and the Croats have taken some Bosnian land, but the warfare was less intense than in the Bosnian-Serb War. But in 1995, hostilities flared again as Croats regained most of the land conquered by Serbs. The Croatian coastline is world famous for its beauty; it includes the famous medieval city of Dubrovnik, partially destroyed during Serbian shelling in the war.

Eastern Europe and the former Soviet Union have become the toxic waste dumps of the West. Now that many African and South American countries no longer accept toxic waste from Western companies, these companies have turned east—where countries need cash . . . and have fewer regulations.

For example, since 1989, about 34 million tons of Western waste was headed for Russia. The biggest dumpers: the U.S., Belgium, Spain, Switzerland, and, topping the list, Germany—which was responsible for over four fifths of all the waste dumped.

CZECH REPUBLIC

Formerly part of: Czechoslovakia
Size: 30,449 square miles, the size of Maine
Population: 10.3 million
Ethnic group: Czech 94%

What's happening: The Czech Republic is the real success story of Eastern Europe. It has a long past; its two provinces of Bohemia and Moravia formed the Moravian Empire in the ninth century. For generations the capital city of Prague was a major cultural center of Europe.

Czechs and their neighbors the Slovaks are both Slavic peoples. After 1914 they were joined together to form Czechoslovakia, but good times didn't last for long. In 1939 Hitler grabbed German-speaking border areas and then conquered the entire country. After World War II, the Soviets imposed a communist government even though Czechoslovakia had a successful democratic tradition.

The Czechoslovakians were very involved in the late 1980s fight against communism in Eastern Europe. One of their leading dissidents was the playwright Václav Havel, who became president of the new noncommunist government in 1989. But the Czechs and the Slovaks decided on an amicable divorce in 1992. It wasn't surprising: although they speak almost the same language, for most of history they were separated, with the Slovaks under Hungarian rule and the Czechs under German influence. The Czechs are the westernmost of the Slavs, and their economy is becoming prosperous and efficient in the Western sense.

(See also Václav Havel, page 609.)

MACEDONIA

(Republic of Macedonia)

Formerly part of: Yugoslavia
Size: 9,928 square miles, about the size of Vermont
Population: 2 million
Ethnic groups: Macedonian Serb 68%, Albanian 20%
What's happening: Macedonia has been in the news recently for the unlikely reason of its name. The neighboring Greeks are angry because Macedonia is the ancient Greek name of this land, home to the Greek ruler Alexander the Great. It's also the name of a smaller Greek province today. The Greeks don't want another Macedonia across their border but it looks as if it's here to stay. U.S. troops were stationed there to protect against possible Serbian aggression.

Modern Macedonia is made up of land split up in the early 1900s among the various states of the region after they won a war against Turkey. Yugoslavia got a western and central chunk; this is the part that became independent Macedonia in 1991. Modern Greece got the coastal Greek part. Greeks consider themselves (and not the Slavic people living in the independent state of Macedonia) as the true inheritors of the name and culture of Alexander. They're furious that some Macedonian maps show the Greek part of Macedonia as a province of this new nation.

But Macedonia is poor and weak so the danger is really symbolic. But then again, in the violent Balkan peninsula, words have a way of leading to war.

FEDERAL REPUBLIC OF YUGOSLAVIA

(Serbia)

Formerly part of: Yugoslavia
Size: 39,449 square miles, about the size of Virginia
Population: 10.5 million
Ethnic groups: Serb 80%, Albanian 15%
What's happening: Serbia used to be very important in the Balkan peninsula. It was the greatest kingdom of the region in medieval times; after the Ottoman Turks took over they recognized it as a vassal state. Then the Europeans at the Congress of Vienna recognized Serbia as an independent state.

Maybe that's part of the problem—some Serbian leaders want it to be large and important again. The other problem is that Serbs are scattered throughout what was once Yugoslavia. They make up 12% of Croatia, 31% of Bosnia-Hercegovina, 13% of the Kosovo region in southern Yugoslavia, and 2% of other areas. After Yugoslavia fell apart in 1991, Serbia has been fighting to keep the Serbs together—under Yugoslavian/Serbian rule.

Look for the name Kosovo to pop up in the news: this is the heart of medieval Serbia but it's made up of almost 90% Albanians and Muslims. There's talk that if this area seeks independence, Albania, Turkey, and Greece could be dragged into war.

SLOVAKIA

(Republic of Slovakia)

Formerly part of: Czechoslovakia
Size: 18,932 square miles, about the size of Vermont and New Hampshire
Population: 5.3 million
Ethnic groups: Slovak 87%, Hungarian 10%
What's happening: Slovakia is the unhappier half of what was once Czechoslovakia. Slovaks wanted to separate from the Czechs because they felt they were overshadowed by them culturally, economically, and politically. The problem is this newly independent state has inherited much of the old-style Soviet heavy industry and not much of the new-style Western entrepreneurial spirit. There's not much foreign investment, and while the people are happy to be independent, they're looking for the prosperity that seemed so close just a few years back.

SLOVENIA

(Republic of Slovenia)

Formerly part of: Yugoslavia
Size: 7,819 square miles, about the size of New Jersey
Population: 2 million
Religion: Roman Catholic Slovene 91%
What's happening: Not too much is happening politically, which in this area of the world is a good thing. Slovenia is the part of the old Yugoslavia bordering Austria and Italy, and it has close ties to Western Europe even though its inhabitants are Slavic, as are the majority of former Yugoslavians. It declared independence in 1991, but it doesn't border Serbia and has avoided war.

NEW COUNTRIES THAT WERE ONCE PART OF THE SOVIET UNION

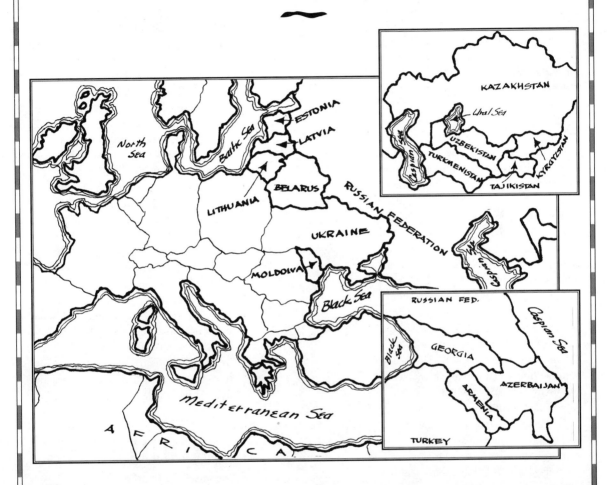

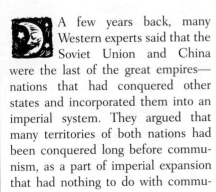

 A few years back, many Western experts said that the Soviet Union and China were the last of the great empires—nations that had conquered other states and incorporated them into an imperial system. They argued that many territories of both nations had been conquered long before communism, as a part of imperial expansion that had nothing to do with commu-

nism. The only difference, they said, was that these lands would remain forever part of China or the Soviet Union. Unlike the Western colonial powers, China and the Soviet Union would not give up their imperial conquests.

Of course, Soviet theorists argued differently. Yes, they agreed, the Soviet Union *did* include many non-Russian states, but that didn't matter because the Soviet Union was not set up as an instrument of Russian domination but as an association of states under the communist ideology. In fact, they could point to the fact that Joseph Stalin, the chairman of the Communist Party and leader of the Soviet Union from the late 1920s until 1953, was not a Russian at all, but a Georgian. Would the British Empire in the 1890s have given the prime ministership to an Indian? Surely not.

The argument was resolved by events—and the results surprised both sides. Few experts expected such a rapid dissolution of the Soviet Union and such a strong assertion of nationalism. Suddenly, nationalists from territories long presumed to be almost the heartland of the Soviet Union were clamoring for—and winning—independence. The Soviet Union was not such a strong empire after all. Experts started talking about the awesome power of nationalism as former citizens battled one another just because one was from a different ethnic group.

But now, events may be surprising experts once again. The dismal economic performance of some of the former Soviet territories is leading to talk of a reassociation with Russia. What will happen? The best guess is that some of the Slavic areas may seek a greater—but still loose—association with their Slavic Russian cousins.

ARMENIA

Size: 11,306 square miles, about the size of Maryland
Population: 3.7 million
Ethnic group: Orthodox Armenian 93%

What's happening: A long time ago, Armenia stretched from the Black Sea to the Caspian Sea, and included much of what is now Turkey. Today's Armenia is much smaller but it is a proud state. Despite tremendous odds, sandwiched between Muslim empires like those of the Ottomans and the Persians, Armenia has maintained its own distinct culture, language, and religion since Babylonian times.

Armenia is fortunate to have about 3 million fellow Armenians living outside its borders, many of whom are Americans or Europeans and can help out financially. Although Armenia is well developed economically, it is tied to the other former Soviet republics, and unrest there hurts Armenia. Recently, it has fought a bloody war with Azerbaijan over a small enclave called Nagorno-Karabakh, which lies within Azerbaijan's borders but is populated mostly by Armenians. To make matters worse, Armenia is still feeling the aftereffects of a terrible earthquake in 1988; it's one of those ironies of history that many Armenian Americans live in Los Angeles.

AZERBAIJAN

(Republic of Azerbaijan)

Size: 33,000 square miles, about the size of Maine
Population: 7.4 million
Ethnic groups: Azerbaijani Turkic 82%, Russian 6%, Armenian 6%
What's happening: Azerbaijan was settled by Turkic tribes and influenced by Persian culture. And today the Azerbaijanis reflect that mixture: they speak

a Turkic language but follow the Shiite branch of Islam, like their Iranian (Persian) neighbors. In fact, the border of Iran also contains an Azerbaijani province, which makes Iran just a little nervous that maybe the Azerbaijanis will get some ideas and try to unite with their siblings across the border.

Azerbaijan has had a tough time since independence. Although it's oil rich, it is one of the poorest areas of the old Soviet Union. Many of its problems come from the war with Armenia over the Nagorno-Karabakh enclave; if hostilities end, read about this country on the business page: it's already attracting the big oil companies.

BELARUS

(Republic of Belarus)

Size: 80,134 square miles, about the size of Utah

Population: 10.3 million

Ethnic groups: Belarussian 80%, Russian 13%

What's happening: In the old days, Belarus was called White Russia because the native dress was white; but until recently the heart of Belarus was red. Belarus is part of the old Soviet heartland—its voters chose to *stay in* the Soviet Union in a public referendum in 1991. Although they didn't get their wish, close ties to Russia have been maintained and it looks like the nations may get even closer soon. Belarus is also looking to Germany for trade and aid. Belarus is heavily industrialized and its people are well-educated but it needs raw materials from the outside to survive.

ESTONIA

(Republic of Estonia)

Size: 17,413 square miles, about the size of Vermont and New Hampshire

Population: 1.5 million

Ethnic groups: Estonian 65%, Russian 30%

What's happening: Estonians speak a language that's related to Finnish and Hungarian. They were conquered by the Russians in 1721 but have maintained a fierce independent spirit throughout the years of Russian rule. And that's the problem today: what to do with the Russians living in independent Estonia. Many Estonians want them to leave, or pass an Estonian proficiency test. Multiculturalism is not the word in this former Soviet state.

GEORGIA

(Republic of Georgia)

Size: 26,911 square miles, about the size of South Carolina

Population: 5.5 million

Ethnic groups: Georgian 70%, Armenian 8%, Russian 6%

What's happening: Georgians are an ancient people. They stem from tribes who formed part of the ancient Hittite empire. In later years they embraced Christianity and retained it while around them the world turned Islamic. They fought to keep their culture and religion under Islamic rule.

Georgia's most famous citizen was Stalin, who became the dictator of the Soviet Union. But Georgians are known as a happy, fun-loving, dynamic people, so it's unfortunate that violence has become so bad since independence. Organized crime is a major problem. Worse yet, two even smaller groups of people within this tiny land want independence. The Ossetians and Abkhazians formed their own armed separatist movements. Recently the Russians intervened to help out the Georgians. They were asked in by Georgia's second most famous citizen, their president Eduard Shevardnadze, once the Soviet Union's foreign minister.

KAZAKHSTAN

Size: 1,049,200 square miles, about twice the size of Alaska

Population: 17 million

Ethnic groups: Kazakh 40%, Russian 37%, German 6%, Ukrainian 5%

What's happening: This is the ninth largest country in the *world,* yet most people have never heard of it. It's a vast desert land, once inhabited only by Turkic Kazakh nomads, that is rich in oil, gold, magnesium, uranium, and chromium. No wonder Chevron and other American companies have jumped right in.

Politically, Kazakhstan is an oddity: the Kazakhs are a minority in their own state; and the old communists still run the country. It also still has nuclear weapons and is taking its time about giving them up. But it looks like this resource-rich country knows what it is doing: it has balanced off the Russians

with the Americans and it's positioning itself as an economic link between Russia and China.

KYRGYZSTAN

(The Kyrgyz Republic)

Size: 76,642 square miles, about the size of Idaho

Population: 4.5 million

Ethnic groups: Kyrgyz 52%, Russian 22%, Uzbek 13%

What's happening: Kyrgyzstan is a poor nation that may well be an example to follow for the rest of the area. It has its share of problems, it has a poorly educated majority, and it's still highly dependent on Russia although it resents its huge neighbor to the north.

But rather than just sitting there, the government is going all-out trying to encourage foreign investors, private enterprise, and human rights. Kyrgyzstan has a mixture of ethnic groups but instead of oppressing the minorities, the government has tried to include them. And fortunately, there are apparently large reserves of strategic minerals.

The U.S. has been impressed with all the Kyrgyz efforts to develop along Western lines and is providing technical aid. So are the Turks, who are related to these Turkic-Mongolian people.

LATVIA

(The Republic of Latvia)

Size: 24,900 square miles, about the size of West Virginia
Population: 2.5 million
Ethnic groups: Latvian 54%, Russian 33%
What's happening: Latvia was long known as the "workshop of the Baltic," and under Soviet rule it manufactured everything from motorcycles to telephone switchers; its capital and port of Riga was the main transit point for goods going west. But today, the economy is in shambles and there are ethnic problems as well. Back in 1935, 77% of the population was Latvian, but in 1989 the number was only 52%. Another 34% were Russian, the largest proportion of Russians outside of Russia. And as in Estonia and Lithuania, these Russians are not all that welcome: they'll now be required to learn the language and culture if they want to stay.

LITHUANIA

(Republic of Lithuania)

Size: 25,170 square miles, about the size of West Virginia
Population: 3.7 million
Ethnic groups: Lithuanian 80%, Russian 9%, Polish 7%
What's happening: There was once a Lithuanian empire that extended from Ukraine to Poland. Most of the world may have forgotten, but these fiercely independent people

have not. Russia won Lithuania in 1795, and after a failed revolution in 1863 they even banned the Lithuanian language. It's not surprising that Lithuania was the leader in the independence movement against the Soviet Union. Despite its independence, Lithuania is still tied economically to Russia. There are many economic problems but the future looks bright: Lithuania is a major industrial center that is also self-sufficient agriculturally. And it has a large number of ethnic relations in the U.S. and Canada who want to help out the mother country now that she's free.

MOLDOVA

(Republic of Moldova)

Size: 13,012 square miles, about twice the size of Hawaii
Population: 4.4 million
Ethnic groups: Moldovan 65%, Ukrainian 14%, Russian 13%
What's happening: Moldova is a tiny strip of land next to Romania that's causing a lot of heartache. Moldovans are not Slavs like the Russians, but Romanian like the Romanians. They speak a dialect of this language, which is related to Latin and the Romance languages. Moldova was once called Bessarabia and has a back-and-forth history: for years it was ruled alternately by Turks and Crimean Tatars; Russia got it from the Turks in 1812; lost it after World War I; and got it back after World War II.

Now that Moldova is independent, Moldovans are talking about reuniting with Romania. But even this tiny land has a minority problem. There are many ethnic Russians and Ukrainians who live in a heavily industrialized smaller strip inside Moldova. They resent Romanian influence and tried to secede from Moldova and formed the Dniester Socialist Republic. Russians supported them until the Russian government signed an agreement with the Moldovan government. But tensions are still high. And just to make things worse, a Turkic-speaking people, the Gagauzi, have decided they want independence as well. Moldova may get still smaller.

TAJIKISTAN

(Republic of Tajikistan)

Size: 54,019 square miles, about the size of Florida
Population: 5.9 million
Ethnic groups: Tajik 62%, Uzbek 23%, Russian 8%
What's happening: This is a high land of the Pamir and Alai mountain ranges, called the "Rooftop of the World." It has a forbidding climate of extreme temperatures and near-Sahara dryness: in one nine-year period only 2.3 inches of precipitation were measured. To round things off, the threat of earthquakes is constant and most buildings outside the capital are one story for this reason.

As you may expect, this area is one of the poorest areas of the old Soviet Union; and to make matters worse it has fought a horrible civil war. Russian troops called in to protect ethnic Russians living here got caught in the crossfire. And there are also border

tensions with neighboring Uzbekistan related to ancient tribal hostilities. All in all, it looks like this land will stay poor and forbidding.

TURKMENISTAN

(Republic of Turkmenistan)

Size: 188,417 square miles, about the size of Oregon and Idaho combined
Population: 4.1 million
Ethnic groups: Turkmen 72%, Russian 9%, Uzbek 9%
What's happening: A long time ago the Turkmens were a nomadic Turkic people who roamed the harsh Central Asian Kara-Kum desert or lived in the oases. They were known for their fierceness; one major occupation was kidnapping Persians or Russians and holding them for ransom.

A lot has changed since then. Under communism, the land was collectivized and the nomads were forced to settle. But then again, a lot hasn't changed—the land is still virtually empty, the economy is underdeveloped, and underneath lie many untapped oil and natural gas deposits. The government is still quasi-communist, run by corrupt cronies of the old bosses. Most of the people simply don't care about politics of any stripe. But as this nation opens up, people may wonder why all the oil wealth seems to be going in the pockets of a few.

UKRAINE

Size: 235,443 square miles, a little smaller than Texas

Population: 51.5 million

Ethnic groups: Ukrainian 73%, Russian 22%

What's happening: Ukraine was once the American Midwest of the Soviet Union: the breadbasket, the home to a third of its heavy industry, the big producer of iron ore and coal, and the home to the most advanced aspects of the military-industrial complex.

But when the independence option came as the Soviet Union was collapsing, the Ukrainians wanted out. Most of them, that is. In the west, where the Ukrainian language with its soft endings are more dominant, people are happy about looking to the new capital of Kiev instead of Moscow. But in the east, where a Russian minority and heavy industry predominate, the people are backing closer ties to Mother Russia.

Not that Ukraine *should* be part of Russia again. Ukrainian language and culture is actually more closely tied to Eastern Europe than to Russia, although Ukraine's central location has made it a crossroads for all types of Slavic (and other) peoples. Ukraine has endured Mongol, Polish, and Russian rule, and the Ukrainian cossacks (or frontiersmen) have fought hard against many conquerors. Today, the country is evolving toward democracy, one of the few former Soviet states to buck the trend to authoritarian rule.

UZBEKISTAN

(Republic of Uzbekistan)

Size: 172,700 square miles, about the size of Oklahoma and Colorado combined

Population: 22.1 million

Ethnic groups: Uzbek 70%, Russian 11%

What's happening: Uzbekistan is the home to King Cotton and it's paying the price. Under the old centrally planned economy of the Soviet Union, Uzbekistan was supposed to grow this crop to the exclusion of virtually all else. Seventy-five percent of the nation's arable land was devoted to it; and since cotton is a dirty crop requiring a lot of pesticides and fertilizer, the environment is paying the price.

Meanwhile, Islamic fundamentalism is rising—it actually never was completely suppressed during the long years of communist rule. Ethnic tensions are rising too, and Russians who once formed the area's technical class are leaving. Because Uzbekistan borders the other four Central Asian republics and because it is the most populous, stability here is important for regional reasons.

NEW NATIONS IN AFRICA AND THE MIDDLE EAST

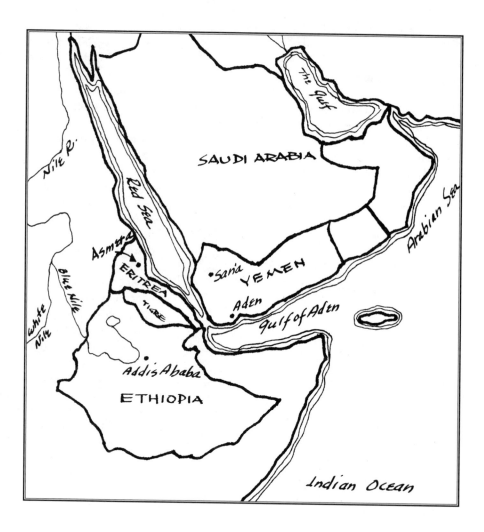

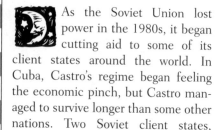

As the Soviet Union lost power in the 1980s, it began cutting aid to some of its client states around the world. In Cuba, Castro's regime began feeling the economic pinch, but Castro managed to survive longer than some other nations. Two Soviet client states,

Ethiopia and South Yemen, began dissolving. One split into two (or three, depending on the final outcome) and one joined with another state. You probably haven't heard much of either, but for the record, here are two of the world's newest political incarnations.

ERITREA

Formerly part of: Ethiopia
Size: 36,170 square miles, about the size of Indiana
Population: 3.5 million
Religions: Muslim 51%, Christian 49%

Eritrea is a small nation on the African side of the Red Sea. Until recently it didn't even exist except in the minds of its people, although it is a distinct area that for a long time was part of the Ethiopian kingdom of Askum (although the Eritreans and others in the Ethiopian empire spoke different languages). Then the Italians decided they wanted a colony, and they picked this area to attack. From 1889 to 1941 Eritrea was a colony, and Asmara looked something like a small Italian city in the desert. But then Ethiopia reclaimed its old province, and for the next 31 years Eritreans fought a bloody war of independence. Finally, in 1992, Eritrean troops along with some other revolutionary armies broke out and began winning. They reached the Ethiopian capital and toppled the government.

Eritrea declared itself independent on May 24, 1993—the world's newest Independence Day. The future looks good. So far, the government seems capable, given all the problems stemming from years of war. Apparently, a spirit of sacrifice and democracy was fostered during the years of fighting side by side in difficult conditions.

YEMEN

(Republic of Yemen)

Formerly split into: North Yemen, South Yemen; North Yemen (the Yemen Arab Republic) was frequently called Yemen, the South was called the People's Democratic Republic of Yemen
Size: 203,796 square miles, about the size of France
Population: 12.9 million
Ethnic groups: mostly Arab, some Indian

The fact that Yemen was split into two for much of the Cold War was not a major geopolitical problem. (If you're wondering, it's on the southern portion of the Arabian peninsula, a mountainous area that includes deserts, fertile land, and the Arab world's only bit of rainy tropics.)

But from 1967, when Britain relinquished its colony of Aden (a major refueling point on the way to India), South Yemen was the Arab world's only communist state. Over 300,000 people fled to capitalist North Yemen, and Soviet advisors tried to communize the South, but it was so poor that small-scale private farming and trading was all that existed. North Yemen was also poor but its leaders were more pragmatic and they managed to live off modest oil discoveries and remittances from Yemenis working in oil-rich Saudi Arabia.

Although both sides had fought wars in the past, as ideological differences waned, and as South Yemen got more and more unstable, in 1990 the two states decided to unify, making up the most populous nation on the Arabian Peninsula. In 1994, civil war broke out. Rebels in the south resented northern dominance. But the north was more powerful and sent its

army south, attacking and capturing the southern capital of Aden. Yemen is still united.

CONTENTS

POLITICS OF THE WORLD

"Politics is the science or art of government, the administration and management of public affairs." That's a dull definition for something that affects all of us, that's often exciting, often frightening, sometimes helpful, sometimes horrible.

The Chinese leader Mao Zedong had a better, more revolutionary definition: "Politics is war without bloodshed, war is politics with bloodshed." He saw politics as a great clash of interests and, typically, could never let go of the idea of fierce competition. Of course, he practiced what he preached—and millions died.

But maybe Madame de Staël, an aristocratic writer in early-nineteenth-century France, had the better, and paradoxically more modern, view: "The pursuit of politics is religion, morality, and poetry all in one." For all its problems, politics is the ultimate human pastime, the ultimate game. Politics is like baseball, it's an amalgamation of everything—which is why politicians and pundits enjoy it so much. Just watch them on a Sunday morning talk show; they *love* their sport.

But for the rest of us, politics is what we get interested in when we're not getting what we want. We tend to ignore politics until we realize our needs and desires are being ignored. Then we get *very* interested. And that leads to the major political trend in human history; the politics of inclusion.

Politics is (or should be) *inclusive;* it should give all of us a say in how we're governed. If modern world politics is anything, it is the struggle of peoples, movements, and religions to have a say in the conduct of their own affairs.

This section is based on that theme. It covers the major political systems of the twentieth century—the theories behind the political movements that have changed our times. But politics is practical, not theoretical, and so most of this section deals mostly with what really happened to change our lives. It looks at modern revolutions, beginning with the mother of them all, the French Revolution. And it looks at the great and near great politicians who made the front pages, and at the greatest world leaders of this century—and what all this means today. It also takes a look at the new international organizations that are trying (and sometimes succeeding) to keep the world together.

Finally, we look at the long-standing political problems that still frustrate world peace and harmony. These are the stories behind the newspaper or TV news you read or hear every day—a capsule look at the national, multinational, and world problems we're still hearing and talking about.

SEVEN WORLD HOT SPOTS: POLITICAL DISPUTES THAT YOU'LL PROBABLY SEE IN THE NEWS . . . AGAIN

Some world problems have a way of lingering and festering. They appear, disappear, then reappear again in the daily newspapers of the world. Usually they're based on land: who controls it, who gets to live on it.

Until recently the U.S. and the Soviet Union usually took opposing sides in these conflicts. Sometimes there were very real moral reasons for backing one side or another, but many times the reasons were said to be "geopolitical," which really meant if the Soviets were on one side, we decided to join the other—and vice versa.

All this could get pretty cynical. For one thing, almost every obscure corner of the world was declared "geopolitically strategic" at one point or another. For another, the morality could get very dicey. For example, during the 1970s we supported Ethiopia and the Soviets supported Somalia in their dispute over the Ogaden, a dry and remote desert region populated by Somali nomads but controlled by Ethiopia. Naturally, we set up military posts in our ally Ethiopia and the Soviets put in military bases in their ally Somalia, and each superpower talked of their love of and historic ties to its ally. Then local Marxists seized control in Ethiopia—and after a short while the U.S. and the Soviets calmly switched client states. The U.S. moved into the former Soviet bases in Somalia, the Soviets moved into Ethiopia, and both sides started talking about their *real* ties to their new ally.

A PALESTINIAN YOUTH SLINGS STONES AT ISRAELI BORDER POLICE (REUTERS/ BETTMANN)

Of course, once the Cold War was over, no one cared about either nation anymore, and they both degenerated into anarchy, aided by mounds of heavy weapons and automatic rifles helpfully supplied by both sides. Finally we moved in to save Somalia from itself and our legacy of arms sales—and congratulated ourselves on our humanity.

Now that the Cold War is over, the great danger that a local dispute could go nuclear with the superpowers' involvement has ended. But paradoxically, without the superpowers damping down things, there could be a *greater* possibility of large-scale regional conflict.

Below we've listed some of the longest lasting and most dangerous conflicts in the world today. This list is by no means comprehensive. (The crisis in the former Yugoslavia is covered in New Nations of Eastern Europe on page 549.) The conflicts we've chosen are international in scope rather than local, and have often resisted efforts to solve them peacefully. Please note that the politics can get very passionate. Every effort has been made to be as fair as possible to both sides.

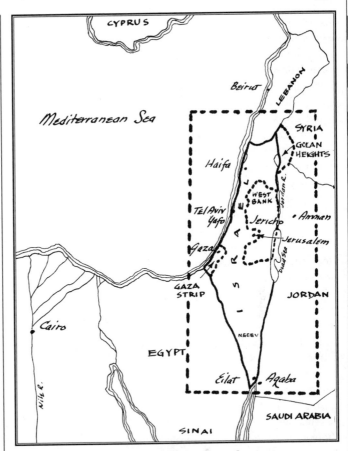

AREA OF THE ARAB-ISRAELI CONFLICT

ARAB-ISRAELI CONFLICT

Who's against whom: Israel against the Palestinians and various Arab states and groups.

What they're arguing about: Originally, over the existence of Israel, and over Jewish control of part of the land also called Palestine. Today the dispute (for most parties) is over the fate of the Palestinians living in the territories occupied by Israel during the 1967 war: the West Bank, a sizable chunk of territory sandwiched between Jordan and Israel and East Jerusalem, part of a city that both groups view as a capital city; the separate Gaza Strip, a

piece of land on the Mediterranean contiguous to Egypt, and the Golan Heights, highlands originally belonging to Syria. Certain Arab groups still want the whole area, as do certain Jewish groups.

The stakes: Very high, but going down. The U.S. and the Soviet Union used to be on opposite sides in this conflict, and the potential for superpower flare-ups was high. Now the danger is of a major regional dispute that could go nuclear, as well as the threat from continued terrorism.

Background: The history of the area is complex, and both sides have set forth detailed historical reasons

567

justifying their claim. Essentially, Palestine was the Jewish homeland in biblical times, leading to Jewish claims today. The area was later conquered by Alexander the Great, then Rome. Under Roman rule Jewish resistance flared up, and eventually the Roman emperor's son (and eventual emperor) Titus destroyed the Temple in Jerusalem and Jews were expelled. Later the area came under Byzantine rule, then was conquered by the Arabs. Most of the inhabitants became Muslim (although a sizable minority had become Christian during Roman and Byzantine times and remained so). The descendants of these people are the Palestinians of today. Except for a few brief interludes of Christian Crusader rule, the area remained under Muslim rule. It eventually fell under the Ottoman (Turkish) Empire and remained under their rule until 1917, when the British defeated the Turks during World War I and took the area.

Meanwhile, in the late 1800s the Zionist movement had formed in Europe. It advocated a return to Zion (the Hebrew word for Israel), and with its encouragement European Jews began settling in Palestine.

Palestinian nationalism began growing as well, particularly in response to the growing Jewish and European presence. In 1964 various Palestinian groups united (loosely) under the umbrella of the PLO, or Palestine Liberation Organization. For years, the Israelis did not regard the PLO as legitimate due to its participation in terrorist acts, its call for the destruction of Israel, and claim of land now occupied by Israelis. Today many fundamentalist Palestinians do not regard the PLO as legitimate due to its decision to negotiate with the Israelis.

Back to British-ruled Palestine: Zionist settlement accelerated in the 1920s and 1930s, and Arabs began rioting and agitating against it. The British decided to restrict Jewish immigration, despite the Balfour Declaration, which pledged in 1917 its support for a Jewish homeland. But in the aftermath of World War II and the murder of 6 million European Jews, Britain had problems keeping the survivors out. So they turned over the whole problem to the new U.N., which decided to partition the territory on a roughly 50-50 basis.

Conflict: Get ready for a long litany of wars, incursions, terrorist attacks, and other forms of conflict—and this is just a brief summary of *some* key dates and conflicts.

The Jews agreed to the U.N. partition plan and declared the state of Israel in 1948; the Arabs didn't agree and attacked—and lost not only the war but some more land. About 600,000 Palestinians fled by the time a U.N. cease-fire was in effect. Then, in:

1956: What had become an armed peace punctuated by border incursions was broken when Egypt announced it would nationalize the Suez Canal. Israel, Britain, and France attacked and seized the canal region. They were ordered to withdraw by the U.N. and the U.S.

1967 (the Six-Day War): Egyptian President Gamal Abdel Nasser closed the Gulf of Aqaba to the Israelis, who responded by attacking Egypt and Syria, later Jordan. They seized the Sinai Peninsula, Jerusalem, and the West Bank, as well as the Golan Heights of Syria. Another armed peace followed, with sporadic border violence and terrorism. The U.N. passed Resolution 242, which called for the "return

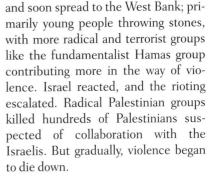

of occupied territories." The lack of the definite article "the" before "occupied territories" has led to years of dispute: the Arabs claim it means *all* the territories, the Israelis claim it means *some*.

1973 (the Yom Kippur War): Anwar al-Sadat of Egypt launched an initially successful surprise attack on Israeli forces in the Sinai; Israeli troops eventually crossed the Suez Canal and threatened Egypt; a U.S.-U.S.S.R. brokered peace ended that war.

1977: Egyptian President Sadat announced he would seek peace with Israel and traveled to Jerusalem to address the Knesset, Israel's legislative body.

1979: Under the Camp David Accords of this year peace was achieved between Egypt and Israel. Israel returned the Sinai to Egypt and Egypt granted full diplomatic recognition to Israel. A framework was devised for Palestinian autonomy, but typically for the Middle East, this crucial part of the agreement fell apart. Egypt was initially shunned by other Arab nations, but gradually returned to the fold. Peace prospects looked more possible particularly as the Soviet Union decayed and their hard-line allies like Syria started getting more interested in a peaceful solution. But at this point Israel's government wasn't too interested in or trusting of Arab overtures, and, in fact, invaded southern and central Lebanon in order to halt cross-border Palestinian attacks. This reduced the attacks, but the Israelis were caught in the quagmire of the Lebanese civil war and withdrew from most territory, retaining a "security zone" with proxy Lebanese Christian militias in charge.

1987: The intifada, or uprising, by Palestinians began in the Gaza Strip

and soon spread to the West Bank; primarily young people throwing stones, with more radical and terrorist groups like the fundamentalist Hamas group contributing more in the way of violence. Israel reacted, and the rioting escalated. Radical Palestinian groups killed hundreds of Palestinians suspected of collaboration with the Israelis. But gradually, violence began to die down.

1991: In the aftermath of the Gulf War (in which the PLO supported the losing side of Saddam Hussein), formal negotiations began between Israel and its Arab neighbors with much fanfare but little progress. Israel wouldn't meet with the PLO, but did agree to meet with Palestinian delegates attached to the Jordanian delegation.

1993: In an earth-shaking turnaround, Israel and the PLO agreed to recognize each other and discuss peace. As the negotiations continued, a formula for limited autonomy in Gaza and in the West Bank town of Jericho was worked out. A terrorist attack by a Jewish settler in the Hebron mosque initially set things back, and the intifada flared up again. And then Arabs launched several terrorist attacks against Israelis. As always in the Middle East, violence begat more violence. But after some more negotiations the PLO and Israel began talking again.

1994: The autonomous Palestinian areas of Gaza and Jericho were established, and Yasir Arafat set himself up in Gaza. But so far, autonomy has if anything increased poverty, and sporadic terrorism continues. Negotiations are continuing for the next step: Israeli withdrawal from most of the rest of the West Bank, except for areas around settlements.

1995 and beyond: Tough negotiations are still ahead. The assassination of Israeli Prime Minister Yitzhak Rabin may hinder the peace process, but the Israeli government quickly vowed to continue. Sticking points will probably be:

- East Jerusalem, which contains Jewish and Arab holy sites and which both sides claim; the Israelis formally annexed the area and don't consider it part of the West Bank but as part of unified Jerusalem and the capital of Israel. The Palestinians want it for the capital of a Palestinian state.
- How much land will ultimately revert to the Palestinians.
- What kind of entity the Palestinians will create (most are betting that a Palestinian state will ultimately be declared).
- The presence and status of Jewish settlements on the West Bank and in Gaza. These occupy a significant amount of land and are a prime source of friction.
- The spoiler role of radical Islamic groups like Hamas, a fundamentalist group with a growing following; and certain far-right Israeli groups.
- Meanwhile, negotiations will probably continue over the Golan Heights, the portion of Syria seized by the Israelis during the 1967 war.

CYPRUS

Who's against whom: Greece and Greek Cyprus against Turkey and Turkish Cyprus.

What they're arguing about:

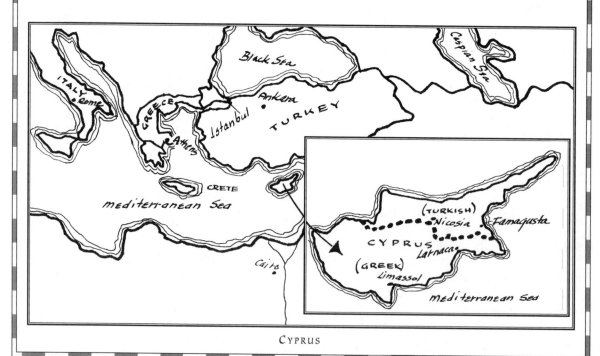

CYPRUS

Who should control Cyprus, an island nation in the Mediterranean, 50 miles south of Turkey and 180 miles from Greek territory. Cyprus is 80% Greek, 20% Turkish. Right now the Turks control 37% of the land, the Greeks the rest. Cyprus is a beautiful island and, on the Greek side, prosperous.

The stakes: Fortunately, not too high. The Greek and Turkish governments have kept an eye on their Cypriot counterparts so things won't get too much out of hand. Although Greece and Turkey are in many ways enemies, they are also fellow members of the NATO alliance.

Background: Cyprus was settled by Greeks in antiquity, but it has also been conquered by virtually everyone—Assyrians, Egyptians, Romans, Byzantine Greeks, Arabs, English (Richard I captured it in 1191), the Venetians, and then the Turks, who ruled it from 1571 until 1878, when the British took over again. But by this time a sizable Turkish population had arrived. Under the British the Greek Cypriots began agitating for *enosis,* or union, with Greece, something the Turkish Cypriots weren't too happy about, and something Turkey pressured against.

Conflict: Cyprus got independence as a new nation in 1960. The government was dominated by Greek Cypriots. Under their leader, Archbishop Makarios, Turkish Cypriot rights gradually eroded. The U.N. sent in a peace-keeping force in 1969, but the Turkish Cypriots now wanted autonomy. Then in 1974 Makarios was deposed by a pro-*enosis* group, and claims were made that Greece was about to take over the island. If they were planning to, they didn't do it in time. Instead, Turkey invaded the

island in July 1974 and by the time a cease-fire was in effect they controlled 37% of the island. Greeks were forced from their homes on the Turkish side and vice versa. After numerous back-and-forth talks on a new bicommunal state all failed, the Turkish portion declared independence in 1983 as the Turkish Republic of North Cyprus. But no one except for Turkey recognized this new state. The Greek side remains the officially recognized government of Cyprus.

Talks have continued ever since over how the island can be unified again. The Turks have offered to give up some land, the Greeks say it isn't enough. Meanwhile, the former capital, Nicosia, is a divided city like Berlin once was, and U.N. troops keep the peace.

KASHMIR

Who's against whom: India against Pakistan.

What they're arguing about: Who should control Kashmir, a mountainous province split between India and Pakistan, located near China. If the dispute ever is solved, Kashmir could be the ultimate tourist destination. Many visitors call this land of mountains and alpine valleys one of the most beautiful areas of the world.

The stakes: Very high. U.S. analysts consider this might even be a possible source of a regional nuclear war.

Background: The conflict began with a rajah (Indian ruler) of Kashmir who couldn't make up his mind. When the British left their colony of India in 1947 it was agreed that India would be divided into two separate states: a

KASHMIR

Muslim portion called Pakistan, and a predominantly Hindu portion called India. Kashmir was a province caught in the middle. It had a Hindu rajah but a majority Muslim population.

The rajah couldn't decide which side to join. While he was dithering, Muslim Pakistan encouraged fierce Pathan tribesmen to invade. The rajah asked for Indian aid; and soon a war was on. After a U.N. cease-fire Pakistan had a third of Kashmir, India controlled the other two thirds.

Conflict: The dispute has been going on ever since. India has tried to formally integrate Kashmir into itself, but each time it tries Pakistan gets angry. In the late 1980s their war got

hot in the icy heights 18,000 feet up on the Siachen Glacier.

In 1990 things got even hotter: Muslim fundamentalists supported by Pakistan fomented a revolt in Indian Kashmir; the Indian police killed 50 people and Pakistan and India threatened war. A revolt has continued ever since. About 15 people die each day and India has been accused of cracking down harshly, while Pakistan has been accused of backing violence in a dispute that should be settled peacefully. Back in 1972 the two sides had agreed to resolve the matter without violence and without third-party intervention, but obviously it hasn't worked out. The U.S. now supports the U.N. or someone else coming in diplomatically to cool down tempers and solve this issue.

India takes any suggestion of outside interference very badly. When a U.S. State Department official said that Kashmiris had a right to decide their own fate, the popular *Indian Times* called her the "goddess of Indian terrorists, secessionists and other outlaws," and suggested that a "black carpet" be rolled out instead of the traditional red when she visited India.

KOREA

Who's against whom: South Korea against North Korea.

What they're arguing about: Both have agreed that a reunified Korea is an ultimate goal, but neither wants to reunite under the governmental system of the other. Another problem is that North Korea is very poor and under a new and possibly unstable

leader. The fear is of the unknown: what will North Korea do?

The stakes: High, but going down. North Korea has been developing nuclear weapons but now has apparently agreed to stop. U.S. troops are stationed on the borders as a trip wire, China and Japan are nearby and have a stake in the conflict.

Background: Korea is the last of the countries divided into two as a result of the superpower conflicts at the end of World War II. (In case you've forgotten, the others were Vietnam, reunified under communism in 1975; Germany, reunified under capitalism in 1990; and Yemen, reunified under capitalism in 1990.)

At the end of World War II, Korea, a former Japanese protectorate, was divided into two zones, the north under Soviet administration, the south under American administration, pending reunification and independence. In 1948 a U.N. commission was sent to hold elections for a Korean government. They were denied access to North Korea, so they held them only in the U.S.-controlled south. The south became the Republic of Korea; a short while later the Soviets left the north after their protégé Kim Il Sung founded the communist Democratic People's Republic of Korea.

Conflict: In 1950 communist North Korea attacked the South (to simplify, we'll refer to each side as North or South), apparently with Soviet knowledge of the plan, but not the timing. Soon, the North had overrun most of the South, until a daring counterattack by U.S. General Douglas MacArthur, who had been authorized to lead a U.N. (mostly U.S.) force to defend the South. MacArthur pushed the North Koreans far back to

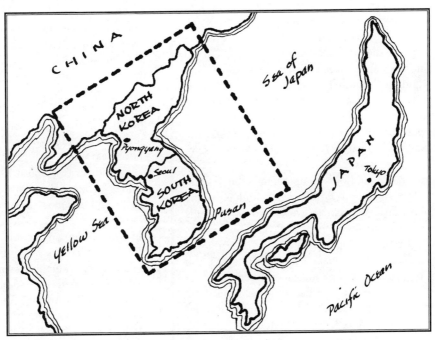

THE TWO KOREAS

the North, near the Chinese border. Then communist Chinese troops intervened, crossing the border in large numbers and pushing MacArthur back to the South. The war settled into a stalemate near the 38th parallel—this was the truce line splitting the country once more in 1953.

An armed peace followed, marked by occasional skirmishes as 39,000 U.S. troops remained on the border. In 1953 the U.S. signed a mutual defense treaty with South Korea; the Soviets and the Chinese signed similar ones with the North. Meanwhile North Korea kept up an aggressive posture, sending a team into the South in 1968

Another Korean War

About 80 years before the conflict known as the Korean War began, the U.S. was involved in *another* undeclared war with Korea—a four-day war in May 1871 summed up in a contemporary newspaper headline as "Our Little War with the Heathen."

The source of the conflict was commercial. United States businesses wanted to establish trade in Korea. One attempt—sending a merchant ship to Korea—failed, as Koreans destroyed it at sea. So in May 1871, the U.S. sent the U.S. minister to China, Frederick Low, into Korea to open the lines of communication, explain the U.S. position, and convince Korea to abandon its isolationism.

Diplomacy failed. So Low's companions—the "Asiatic Squadron": five ships and 1,500 men, commanded by Admiral John Rodgers—went to work. Two of the ships set out on a recon mission up the Han River. The Koreans had already spurned diplomacy, so a show of arms was equally unwelcome. They opened fire on the ships, the U.S. ships retaliated, and the four-day war began. At the end, about 350 Koreans were casualties; three Americans were killed and 10 wounded. And Korea remained isolationist—out of the hands of U.S. commerce.

to assassinate the president; seizing the U.S. spy boat *Pueblo* the same year (to be fair, we *were* in North Korean waters); blowing up South Korean officials on a visit to Burma in 1983; and destroying a South Korean airliner in 1987.

Throughout this period, talks between the two sides had been sporadic. In 1972, both governments agreed that reunification was a goal, but they couldn't agree on much else. Posturing, occasional gestures of good will, and violence have been the norm, kept under control until recently by the superpowers. With the fall of the Soviet Union, the North Koreans began developing a nuclear weapons program as the ultimate guarantor of independence. This set Western and South Korean teeth on edge. The U.S. and U.N. wanted to inspect North Korean nuclear facilities. Finally, in 1994, North Korea agreed to freeze its nuclear program. In return, the U.S. agreed to supply two modern nuclear reactors that can't be turned to weapons production. And talk was in the air of a North-South summit.

But the real fear is over what will happen now that the North Korean founding father and leader, Kim Il Sung, has died. His son is a bit off-base (he loves films and had his secret police kidnap two South Korean filmmakers to have them make films for him). And by most accounts North Korea is a mess—the streets are empty, old and bad-looking people have been literally forced to leave the capital since they're an embarrassment to the regime (yes, it's true), and farming and industry are collapsing. But the guns are ready.

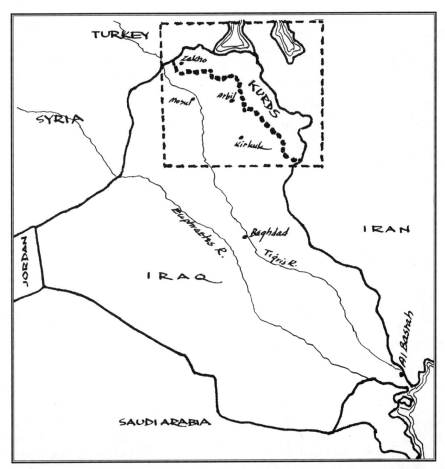

KURDISH TERRITORIES

KURD TERRITORIES IN TURKEY, IRAQ, AND IRAN

Who's against whom: Kurds, a distinct people who speak an Indo-European language related to Farsi (Persian), against Turkey, Iran, Iraq, and fellow Kurds.

What they're arguing about: Kurds want some kind of real autonomy in the countries they live in but none of the above governments wants to give it to them. In addition, various Kurdish groups are fighting over political differences.

The stakes: Regional in scope, but relatively high regional stakes since the Kurdish regions have water and oil. In human terms, the toll has been horrifying: the Iraqis have used chemical warfare against the Kurds, and all sides have resorted to violence and barbarity.

Background: Until they made the evening news during the Gulf War, the Kurds were the forgotten people of the Middle East. And odds are they're already forgotten again, despite their long-standing efforts to create a Kurdish state, or at least some autonomous regions where they can teach and learn their language and live as they want to.

The Kurds live in the mountainous regions of southeastern Turkey, northern Iraq, and northwestern Iran (Persia). Estimates are they make up 19% of the population of Turkey, 23% of Iraq, and 10% of Iran. In addition, they form an 8% minority in Syria, and smaller proportions in Armenia and Lebanon, totaling in all some 15 to 20 million people. As a point of trivia it appears that Saladin, the heroic Islamic enemy of Richard the Lionhearted, was Kurdish in origin.

For a long time, most Kurds lived under the rule of the (Turkish) Ottoman Empire and the shah of Iran, and although they periodically revolted against Ottoman rule, they also fought for them. After World War I, the losing Turks were supposed to allow the formation of an independent Kurdistan (and an independent Armenia), but their strong new leader, Kemal Atatürk, put an end to that idea and reestablished Turkish control over much of the area.

Since then, the idea of an independent Kurdistan has been a potent dream, but the political realities have instead led to the Kurds acting as proxies for the various powers in the region.

The Turks have established a large military presence in the Turkish Kurdish regions, and until recently banned the use of Kurdish in schools. They claim the Kurds are "mountain Turks" and although they've allowed Kurds to be represented in government, the Kurdish representatives are not allowed to talk about Kurdish concerns, only "mountain Turkish" concerns. Obviously, it can get absurd,

particularly since Kurdish is in no way related to Turkish. Not that Kurds have fared any better in Iran or Iraq.

Conflict: Recent Kurdish history is a sad tale of warfare, betrayal, and more warfare. During the Iraq-Iran War, each side used Kurdish proxies to fight each other, and Iraqi leader Saddam Hussein used chemical weapons against Kurds he said had betrayed him. The dead included women and children.

Just after the Gulf War (when the U.S. and allies defeated Iraq) the allies gave the Kurds a semiautonomous region in northern Iraq, and other Kurds were given safe haven in Turkey that later turned into another killing field. Hopes for an independent Kurdistan have been hampered not only by outsiders but by factionalism in Kurdish ranks. Some dialects of Kurdish are mutually unintelligible, which makes for tensions. More to the point, some Kurdish groups are very different politically. The whole area is a mess of conflicts and conflicting parties.

The radical PKK (Kurdish Workers' Party) has sponsored terrorism in Turkey; it's allied against some Iraqi Kurds who were used by the Turks to fight their more radical brethren. Then in 1995, the Turkish Army attacked Kurdish areas in Turkey and Iraq; Turkish bombers were sent in an attempt to bomb the Kurds into submission. Meanwhile, despite the atrocities, some Iraqi Kurds have been seeking a compromise with Saddam Hussein. It's not as much cynical politics as survivor politics—the Kurds are alone in a hostile Middle Eastern sea.

NORTHERN IRELAND

Who's against whom: Catholic Northern Irish against the Protestant Northern Irish; with significant involvement by Great Britain and, to a lesser extent, Ireland.

What they're arguing about: Who should control Northern Ireland: the Catholics want it joined to Ireland, the Protestants want it to remain British. Northern Ireland consists of six of the nine provinces of Irish Ulster and is part of Britain, the United Kingdom.

The stakes: Not too high for the world, and getting lower now that talks are going on. Main problem: if the talks don't succeed, terrorism could increase again.

Background: The source of the conflict concerns the place of Protestants who have settled in Ireland since the Middle Ages. In 1066 William the Conqueror conquered England and brought over his fellow Normans; in 1170–72 his predecessors took Ireland and settled Anglo-Normans there. By the time of the Reformation, England and Scotland had left the Roman Catholic Church, while Ireland remained Catholic. In 1607, 170,000 Protestants (mostly Scots) were settled by the British in Northern Ireland among the Irish Catholic minority. By 1700 the Catholics owned less than 15% of the land in Northern Ireland.

Meanwhile British rule over all of Ireland wasn't exactly exemplary: Catholics were forbidden to hold political office and were taxed to support the Anglican (English Protestant) Church in Ireland. English absentee landlords controlled most of the Irish farmlands and charged high rents to Irish tenant

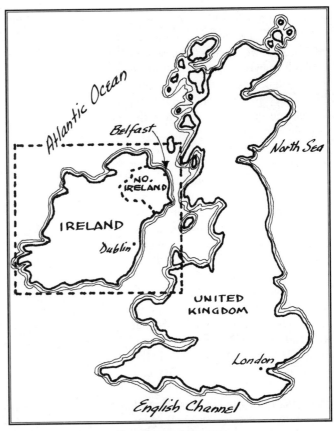

NORTHERN IRELAND

farmers (many of whom starved during the potato famine). Gradually, the British reformed their rule, but the Irish wanted self-government or independence. They established a nationalist movement called Sinn Fein, and later a radical wing called the Irish Republican Army (IRA).

In 1920, after much violence, the British Parliament agreed to grant self-government. But not to all of Ireland. It divided Ireland into two: the bulk of Ireland was declared a self-governing dominion. In 1938 Ireland became fully independent as Eire; in 1949 it left the British Commonwealth.

But meanwhile the six northern provinces of Ulster, called Northern

Ireland and inhabited by a two-thirds majority of Protestants, remained British. They were granted the right to local rule from the capital in Belfast. In the ensuing years, the Protestant-dominated government abused its powers and discriminated against the Catholic minority.

Conflict: In 1956 the IRA in Northern Ireland started a bombing campaign against Protestant rule because discrimination against Catholics was increasing. Britain intervened to improve conditions for Catholics. British troops were sent in, local government was suspended, and direct rule from London imposed.

But violence continued from both sides. The IRA split into factions, including a political IRA, a Provisional IRA, and the Irish National Liberation Army. The Protestants formed the paramilitary Ulster Defense Association. Both sides fought each other; the occupying British troops were shot at as well. By the late 1980s, 2,600 people had died.

Britain tried twice to impose self-government with power shared between Irish and Catholics but each time it failed. Meanwhile Ireland announced its opposition to the IRA, claiming that terrorism was hindering prospects for a peaceful solution. In 1985 Britain and Ireland agreed that Ireland would play a consultative role in deciding the future of Northern Ireland, but that this territory would remain within the United Kingdom. For a while it looked like this agreement might work, but various local factions from both sides in Northern Ireland denounced it.

Then, in 1994, the IRA's political wing, Sinn Fein, agreed to forgo violence and enter talks with the British and the Irish. For the first time in

years, the prospects looked good. In 1995, Gerry Adams, the Sinn Fein president, visited the U.S. to gain financial and moral support. Meanwhile, the high Catholic birthrate is switching the proportions in Northern Ireland—Catholics are now 43% of the population—and if the trend continues they'll be a majority in twenty years. It is hoped that a peaceful solution will be found that can meet the aspirations of both sides before then.

SRI LANKA

Who's against whom: A civil war on the island nation formerly called Ceylon (at the eastern tip of India) between the majority Sinhalese Sri Lankans and the 20% Tamil minority.

What they're arguing about: The Tamils are an Indian people, mostly Hindu, who want a greater amount of autonomy from the majority people on the island, the Buddhist Sinhalese.

The stakes: Not high in terms of world conflict, but pretty high regionally. Across the water from Sri Lanka are 40 million fellow Tamils who live in the Tamil Nadu state of India. India has intervened to try to bring peace: it has suffered military causalities, and then angry Tamil terrorists assassinated Indian Prime Minister Rajiv Gandhi.

Background: Sri Lanka is a tropical island that looks a lot like most conceptions of paradise—and many early travelers called it that. If you've ever seen *The Bridge on the River Kwai* you've seen Sri Lanka; it was filmed there. Recently it seems more like hell and the tourists are long gone.

As Ceylon, Sri Lanka was a part of

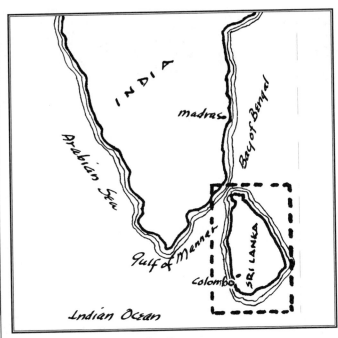

SRI LANKA

British India until 1948, and under the British the Tamil minority achieved a fair amount of power. When independence came, the Sinhalese wanted their turn, and one of the Sinhalese political parties, the Sri Lanka Freedom Party (SLFP), agitated for Sinhala as the official language and Buddhism as the official religion. This prompted the Hindu Tamils to form their own separatist party, which called for their own Tamil state in the north and east of Sri Lanka, where most Tamils live.

Conflict: Although the government offered concessions, by the 1980s the conflict was getting hotter, with Tamil terrorists, called the Tamil Tigers, killing Sinhalese and moderate Tamils, and the government responding with indiscriminate force. Over 300,000 Tamils fled to India. But soon the Tamil Tigers had gained the north and said they'd be happy with autonomy, not independence. But they wanted east Sri Lanka too. Finally a frustrated India intervened and tried to crush the Tigers, suffering a fair number of casualties. They withdrew, and then more killing erupted between the Sinhalese-dominated government and the Tigers. In 1993, the Sri Lankan president and the main opposition leader were assassinated. But more recently, the conflict seems to have died down. The Tigers and the Sri Lankan government have agreed to a truce and peace negotiations—and, so far, peace seems to be in the air.

YOU SAY YOU WANT A REVOLUTION? FIVE OF THE MOST IMPORTANT POLITICAL REVOLUTIONS IN HISTORY

 What's a revolution? You might think that's pretty obvious. You know one when you see one or read about one, like the French Revolution or the American Revolution. But to some experts at universities, think tanks, and the CIA the American revolution wasn't one at all—it wasn't violent or radical enough.

Why the concern with an exact definition? It isn't just a problem for historians, although to understand the contemporary world you have to understand revolutions. Most modern nations at this point have suffered through them. They virtually define modern history.

THE FRENCH REVOLUTION: BARRICADE ON THE BOULEVARD, PARIS (REPRODUCED FROM THE COLLECTIONS OF THE LIBRARY OF CONGRESS)

But the CIA for one would like to know what exactly a revolution is so it will be able to predict when and where the *next* one will occur. To this end they've studied hundreds of them, and they've evolved complex computer programs with thousands of variables. Experts then input all sorts of political and social data, from the average wages of factory workers to the number of religious magazines sold. Then the computer and its program go to work to decide if a revolution is imminent in any given country. It sounds better than it works—so far humans seem to be too unpredictable for computers. For all its technical firepower,

the CIA seems to have missed the Iranian revolution and the second half of the Russian revolution when communism gave up.

In the meantime, let's settle for a definition of a revolution in general, and leave the predictions and details to the experts. According to the *Dictionary of Political Thought,* a revolution is "any major transformation that occurs simultaneously on the social and political level, upsetting expectations and conformities that were sufficiently well established to define all important forms of association under the preceding order."

In other words, a revolution is an event that surprises almost every expert, upsets almost everyone else, and changes almost everything. As the revolutionary Mao Zedong said:

A revolution is not a dinner party, or writing an essay, or painting a picture, or doing embroidery; it cannot be so refined, so leisurely and gentle, so temperate, kind, courteous, restrained and magnanimous. A revolution is an insurrection, an act of violence by which one class overthrows another.

THE FRENCH REVOLUTION

(1787–1799)

Bloody and cruel, the French Revolution is a textbook case of a revolution gone wrong. Unfortunately, the pattern it followed was all too typical. Events overtook egalitarian ideas; terror and chaos reigned. By the end, almost

The origin of "right" and "left" to denote political beliefs stems from the position of factions in the French National Assembly of 1789. The (conservative) nobles sat to the right of the president of the Assembly, and to the left sat the more liberal members of the Third Estate, or commoners.

everyone breathed a sigh of relief when a short, brilliant, dictatorial general named Napoleon seized power. But the relief didn't last. His rule led to war across Europe, and at the end of it all, Napoleon was gone and a king back on the French throne. True, the revolution had produced permanent gains in terms of human and civil rights, but at a tremendous cost. It is not insignificant that for most people, the most memorable aspect of this revolution is the guillotine, a supposedly humane means of execution that claimed revolutionaries as well as aristocrats, children as well as hardened criminals.

Causes: Just detailing the causes of this revolution would fill a book. Basically, by the late 1700s France had an overly centralized system run by a weak and vacillating (but apparently well-meaning) king, Louis XVI. There were the same economic problems that fill the news today—inflation, budget deficits, and high taxes—but at a far worse level. Production was stagnant, but prices had risen. Taxes were onerous. For example, some peasants paid up to 70% of their income in taxes, while the aristocrats were completely exempt. Yet the power of the old order was such that few saw the ferment. As the famed French historian Alexis de Tocqueville said, "Never was any such event so inevitable, yet so completely unforeseen."

Events: The real catalyst for change came from the bourgeoisie, the rising class of merchants and professionals who produced the goods, paid the taxes, but didn't enjoy the same privileges as the noble elite. They wanted power, and got it when the king convened the Estates General, a sort of parliament that had last been convened over a hundred years before.

The largest group of this parliament was the so-called Third Estate, comprised of bourgeoisie and peasant commoners; they demanded a one-man, one-vote say in the Estates General, and when they didn't get it, they went to a nearby tennis court, and took the appropriately named "tennis court oath" to stay together as a new National Assembly, until an egalitarian constitution was written.

Tensions were in the air. King Louis XVI was not obdurate, but mobs in Paris were massing excitedly, looking for trouble. On July 14, 1789, they stormed the Bastille, a political prison in central Paris. Unfortunately, it was almost empty—the only prisoners freed were five bleary-eyed common criminals and two lunatics. But it was the symbolism that counted, and it ignited a conflagration of revolution across France.

Aristocratic estates were seized, government administration collapsed, nobles began to flee across the borders. A month later, the National Assembly abolished feudalism, and produced the *Declaration of the Rights of Man,* which guaranteed "liberté, égalité, fraternité." (Interestingly, this was based on the 1776 Virginia Bill of Rights penned by Thomas Jefferson.)

At just this point, things started going downhill. The Comte de Mirabeau, a sympathetic aristocrat and a moderating influence on the revolutionaries, died at just the wrong time. With his death the king's already reduced role in government collapsed. In panic, the king tried to flee France (in a giant carriage that slowly lumbered down the rutted roads, virtually advertising its royal cargo). He was captured, stripped of his powers, and soon thrown into prison.

Now that the king was out, the only authority left in France was the new constitution. But rule of law could not withstand the onslaught of several new political clubs of radicals (and some moderates), all jockeying for power. The Feuillants, the Girondins, and, most notorious, the Jacobins proclaimed a republic in 1792. Naturally, the kingdoms surrounding France did not like all these anti-monarchic doings; naturally they tried to intervene militarily to put royalists back on the throne; surprisingly, they could not succeed. French revolutionary armies were militarily successful, much more so than the mercenary armies of the aristocrats.

The Jacobin political group, led by a lawyer, Robespierre, eventually won control of the government. It ushered in the infamous Reign of Terror, immortalized in Charles Dickens's *A Tale of Two Cities.* Under the chillingly named Committee of Public Safety, the Jacobins sent thousands to their deaths, including the queen, Marie Antoinette (Louis had met the guillotine in 1792, a year earlier). Soon the terror claimed its very progenitors: Robespierre found himself condemned to death one night in the National Assembly. A few hours later he attempted suicide but managed only to blow off part of his jaw. Bandaged and bleeding, he was duly executed the next day, and with him, his party fell from power.

Radical fervor was almost spent. A new form of government, called the Directory, was now created. But it was weak and unable to resist a powerful new general, Napoleon Bonaparte, who was more devoted to law and order than rule of law, more devoted to power than to democracy. But in one area France was successful: her revolutionary armies had by now expanded

The "Body Count" of the French Revolution

Here's a horrifying breakdown of the casualties of the French Revolution tracked by British historian Sir Archibald Alison in his massive 1860 *History of Europe*. His source? Prudhomme, the republican, who broke down the deaths during the Reign of Terror in this manner:

Guillotined by sentence of the revolutionary tribunals		
Nobles	1,278	
Noblewomen	750	
Wives of laborers and artisans	1,467	
Religieuses [nuns]	350	
Priests	1,135	
Common persons, not noble	13,623	
	18,603	18,603
Women who died from illness produced by excitement and grief		3,748
Women killed in La Vendée [a war within the revolution]		15,000
Children killed in La Vendée		22,000
Men slain in La Vendée		900,000
Victims under Carrier at Nantes		32,000
of whom were:		
Children shot	500	
Children drowned	1,500	
Women shot	264	
Women drowned	500	
Priests shot	300	
Priests drowned	460	
Nobles drowned	1,400	
Artisans drowned	5,300	
Victims at Lyons		31,000
	TOTAL:	**1,022,351**

Alison notes that "in this enumeration are not comprehended the massacre at Versailles, at the Abbey, the Cannes, or other prisons, on the 2d of September, the victims of the Glacière of Avignon, those shot at Toulon and Marseilles, or the persons slain in the little town of Bedouin, of which the whole population perished. . . ."

French control into the Netherlands, Switzerland, and Italy.

Now the last phase of the revolution had begun. The weak Directory gave way to the so-called Consulate, a triumvirate of leaders actually led by a minority of one: Napoleon. He was made the First Consul (read dictator) of France, then Consul for Life, then Emperor of the French. The chaos was over, the Napoleonic Wars had begun.

Impact: This was truly the mother of revolutions in Europe, if not the world.

French revolutionary armies imposed the ideas of the revolution on the portions of Europe they conquered. Even after Napoleon was defeated and aristocratic rulers attempted to turn back the clock, the ideas did not die. In 1830 and again in 1848, many Europeans rose in revolt for many of the ideals of the revolution.

What were these ideals? Individual liberty, government under a constitution, rule of law, democracy, separation of powers, abolition or reduction of class distinctions and feudal powers . . . and finally, nationalism. Now, more than ever, people began to see themselves as part of a national, versus a local or class-defined, whole. The rise of nationalism had repercussions that have lasted today—as anyone watching the war in the former Yugoslavia is aware. In the end, then, the French Revolution helped set into motion forces that have not yet been spent. In fact, another revolutionary from the opposite side of the globe, Mao Zedong of China, informed a visiting President Nixon that it was still too soon to assess the international consequences of the French Revolution. So far, he seems to have been right.

THE LATIN AMERICAN "REVOLUTION"

Here's a revolution that doesn't quite fit our definition. It's actually more than one revolution. Then in some senses it's not a revolution at all, since the enormous political changes were not accompanied by much social change. And because it all occurred south of the border, it's an aspect of history that most

(North) Americans know absolutely nothing about, although in terms of violence, drama, and impact, it was a major event in world history.

Picture this: a vast 300-year-old empire, extending from the hot dry Mexican deserts of North America to the icy, storm-ridden tip of South America, encompassing millions of people, billions of dollars of wealth. And watch how in the short span of fifteen years, almost spontaneously, definitely haphazardly, this empire collapses.

The empire was the Spanish empire in the Americas, created out of the conquests of the sixteenth-century conquistadors, such as Cortés in Mexico and Pizarro in Peru. It included present-day Argentina, Chile, Uruguay, Paraguay, Bolivia, Peru, Ecuador, Colombia, Venezuela, most of Central America, Mexico (including Texas, Arizona, New Mexico, and California), and the Caribbean islands of Puerto Rico and Cuba. At the end, Spain would be left those last two islands—the rest would be independent states.

A successful revolution? To its main instigator, Simón Bolívar, it was not, it was a tragedy. Just before his death he wrote: "America is ungovernable. He who serves a revolution ploughs the sea."

Causes: Since the revolt against Spanish rule began in many separate areas, it is impossible to list all of the causes. But certainly the two earlier revolutions, American and French, had made their impact. They showed that revolutions could work—aristocrats and colonial powers could be defeated. More to the point, the French Revolution had unleashed Napoleon, who had seized the mother country of Spain back in Europe, leaving her American colonies to some degree afloat.

But the colonies didn't revolt, not yet. Instead, the South American colonists sought to *maintain* Spanish authority in the colonies by setting up their own loyalist, anti-Napoleonic governments. But the colonists were victims of their own success. They found they liked self-government. And they were good at it. When the British tried to invade Buenos Aires, for example, it was the self-governing colonists who beat them back—twice. (The captured British war flag resides to this day in a local museum.)

After Napoleon's defeat, there was still a chance for the reimposition of Spanish rule in the Americas, but it was destroyed by the Spanish king, Ferdinand VII, who was blind to the new aspirations for self-government sweeping his colonies. He didn't negotiate; he fought. And he lost.

Events: So what happened? A series of uncoordinated armed revolts, all culminating in the loss of empire. At the most basic level, the story of this revolution is the story of three men: Iturbide in Mexico, Bolívar in Venezuela, and San Martín in Argentina.

Let's first shift to Spanish North America, namely Mexico. Here, a poor parish priest named Father Miguel Hidalgo y Costilla made a famous speech in 1810, asking his Indian parishioners:

My children, will you be free? Will you make the effort to recover from the hated Spaniards the lands stolen from your forefathers 300 years ago?

The peasants heeded these words, and formed an army that looked like it might succeed where Moctezuma had failed. But the army soon got out of control, killing any Spaniards it came

across and degenerating into a disorderly mob. Hidalgo marched with it, increasingly discouraged by what he had unleashed. He wouldn't worry long—his peasants were defeated by Spanish loyalists and Hidalgo was captured and executed. But he had created a revolutionary momentum; shortly thereafter, another leader, Agustín de Iturbide, succeeded where Hidalgo had failed. Iturbide marched into Mexico City in 1821. The independence of Mexico was now a reality.

Back in South America, there was Simón Bolívar, born in Caracas, an intellectual at first inspired by Napoleon's revolutionary rhetoric, then disgusted by Napoleon's increasing megalomania and desire for conquest.

So Bolívar resolved to do things differently. And in the wake of the chaos created by Napoleon, he set up an independent government in the Spanish colony of Venezuela—only to see it crushed by the despotic King Ferdinand. Bolívar wasn't discouraged, however. Something of an intellectual (and incidentally, a lover of parties, dancing, and the good life), he taught himself strategy, literally by the book, and began building an army to challenge Spanish colonial rule.

Meanwhile, at the other end of the continent, there was José de San Martín, preparing another army, the "Army of the Andes," to liberate the Southern Cone of South America. San Martín was emotionally opposite the flamboyant Bolívar. He was quiet, not flashy, almost shy; and like him, his army was thoroughly professional and efficient.

Without any coordination, the two generals managed to pull off an immensely successful strategic coup—they created a huge, continent-wide pincer movement against the Spanish. San Martín's army moved over the Andes from Argentina to Chile, then, along with British and Chilean volunteers, sailed up the coast to Peru. Meanwhile, Bolívar's army moved south from Venezuela and Colombia, and from there, down toward Peru. San Martín made it first to the Peruvian capital, Lima, where he induced the Spanish viceroy to leave. The fall of the "The City of the Kings," the crown jewel of Spain's empire, was hugely symbolic, and Spain's rule was soon over throughout its former empire.

Bolívar and San Martín met in Guayaquil, the steamy coastal city of Ecuador. Unfortunately, they could not get along. Their inability to see eye-to-eye mirrored the problems of setting up a unified federal state of South America to run something along the lines of the U.S. up north. And so South America fragmented into a continent of squabbling nation-states run by the conservative elites. Bolívar died prematurely, bitter and discouraged. San Martín himself died a lonely exile in London.

Impact: These revolutions produced political independence. They literally liberated a continent (well, most of one), but much social business remained undone. The rigid class distinctions for the most part remained: the locally born criollos, of pure Spanish blood, remained on top, under them the mestizos, part Spanish, part Indian, and at the bottom of the social ladder, the Indians. For the most part, feudal wealth still ruled; political reform, land reform, social reform did not come yet. Other revolutions, such as another, later Mexican revolution and the Nicaraguan revolution, would address these problems. In many

cases, only today are issues such as Indian rights and land reform being seriously addressed. (For example, only recently did a native American achieve high office in Bolivia.)

THE RUSSIAN REVOLUTION OF 1917

This culminated in the first successful communist revolution, "ten days that shook the world." It actually began as a more liberal revolt against the autocracy of Russia's royal ruler, the czar—but by the end the liberals were out and Russia and her empire, renamed the Union of Soviet Socialist Republics, was under communist rule. As with most extreme revolutions, society was completely reorganized; feudal aristocratic rule was completely destroyed, church power was crushed, fledgling capitalism was replaced by total state control—"dictatorship of the proletariat," or more precisely, rule by a cohesive group of Communist Party members. Russia and, indeed, the world had entered a new era.

Causes: The immediate cause was the demoralization and chaos caused by World War I.

Russia had entered the war against Germany and Austria-Hungary with high hopes, but by 1917 she had paid an inordinately high price: over 5 million casualties, food shortages at home, transportation a mess, ammunition shortages on the front. The government was weak, wracked by squabbling (in the last year of the czar's rule there were four different prime ministers). After the relative failure of a major

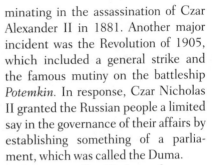

offensive, troops started deserting and coming home—ripe for rebellion.

But there were deeper causes as well. Russia was ruled by an autocratic, hereditary leader, the czar, who was unable to liberalize society sufficiently to appease the growing middle and working classes. And although at first glance it appeared that the Russian economy was modernizing rapidly, a more thorough look shows major problems. Agricultural production, which still occupied the great bulk of the people, was growing at a rate of only 2% per year—while the population was growing at a rate of 1.5%. Russia was simultaneously weak and strong, and the government resorted to coercion to redress its weakness. For example, to fuel the more rapidly growing industrial sector the government exacted very high taxes. Russians on average paid 50% more in taxes than the British, yet earned only 27% as much. Result: an increasingly disaffected populace, particularly in the cities—and a broad range of angry opposition groups, from communists to liberal democrats, who looked to republican democracies like England for inspiration.

Events: There were three main phases to the revolution: the February Revolution, the liberal phase; the October Revolution, when the Bolshevik communists seized power; and the Civil War, in which the Bolsheviks defended their government against an assortment of enemies.

But let's backtrack a minute. With all the problems we mentioned above, it would be surprising if this revolution was the first attempt against czarist rule and, in fact, it wasn't. Since the 1800s, there had been a series of revolts or actions against the czars, cul-

minating in the assassination of Czar Alexander II in 1881. Another major incident was the Revolution of 1905, which included a general strike and the famous mutiny on the battleship *Potemkin*. In response, Czar Nicholas II granted the Russian people a limited say in the governance of their affairs by establishing something of a parliament, which was called the Duma.

But it was all too little, too late, particularly now that the war was hindering any material or social progress. The czar was committed by alliances to pursue the war; after years of suffering, the bulk of the Russian people were not. In February 1917, workers' riots broke out in Petrograd (St. Petersburg); when the workers were joined by disaffected troops the end was in sight. The Duma refused to disband at the czar's orders; instead, it induced the czar to abdicate. They picked a liberal leader, Prince Lvov, to head the government but soon he was replaced by another liberal, Alexander Kerensky. So far, so good.

But now Kerensky and his cohorts made a number of strategic errors that ruined any hopes of a liberal, democratic Russia. Probably the most glaring was the decision to continue to pursue the war. And it certainly wasn't wise to allow the more radical communist Bolsheviks to be armed either. In this case, Kerensky sought to win over these dangerous allies, seeking their aid to counter a largely ineffectual threat from the army commander in chief, General Kornilov.

Now for phase two, the Bolshevik phase. The Bolsheviks were the more violently revolutionary wing of the Russian Socialist Democratic Labor Party, led by Vladimir Ulyanov, known as Lenin. Lenin was a brilliant leader who had spent most of the war in exile in Switzerland—until the Germans sent him in a sealed train to the Russian border, hoping he would do mischief to the Russian leadership and get them out of the war. It was a good gamble. After biding his time, on November 6, 1917, Lenin ordered the Red Guard (the Bolshevik paramilitaries) to seize the Winter Palace, where Kerensky's government was entrenched. (Incidentally, this is called the October Revolution even though the main action took place in November because the Russian calender at the time was the Julian, which ran 13 days behind.) Kerensky fled and his government fell. (Kerensky himself eventually wound up in New York City, where he lived until 1970.) A day later, the Bolsheviks were elected by an "All Russian Congress of Soviets" as supreme leaders.

Under the banner "Peace, Land,

Bread," Lenin won broad support—and when he didn't get it, he had no hesitation in shooting the opposition or seizing power by force. Once in power he moved quickly to transform Russian society. Factories were nationalized; the land and property of aristocrats, the Church, landed gentry, and capitalists was seized; the czar was arrested and, along with his family, shot. And peace was made with the Germans at the Treaty of Brest-Litovsk.

Phase three was the bloodiest phase of revolution—a series of battles and campaigns that devastated the Russian countryside. Arrayed against the Bolsheviks were the White Russians, that is, those loyal to the czar or to the liberals. At one point, the Allies of World War I, including a small American contingent, defended against Bolshevik rule up north in Archangel. But Lenin's enemies tended to be unfocused and uncoordinated. So although the fighting was fierce, sometimes heroic, and almost always tragic, Bolshevik rule was probably never really threatened. Under the brilliant and ruthless leadership of the commissar of war, Leon Trotsky, the Red Guard racked up victories. By 1920, the war was pretty much over.

Impact: Enormous. The success of communism galvanized much of the world. Russia's success led many to presume it was just a matter of time before the rest of the world joined them—in fact, this was just what orthodox communist theory predicted, and a great many otherwise intelligent Western intellectuals believed it. Interestingly, communist theory didn't match reality as far as Russia was concerned, since Marx had prophesied that communism would first arise in the most advanced capitalist countries

The Cult of the Leader in Communism

Communism as it has been practiced in the twentieth century can't seem to get away from dictatorial leaders who are literally almost worshipped by the people—or by the propagandists who write the newspapers. The cult of the leader was most pronounced in the Soviet Union under Stalin. The main reason was a deep-seated fear—Stalin periodically purged communist party members, which effectively meant shooting or imprisoning them. One contemporary recalls that after Stalin made a speech, the clapping lasted for what seemed to be hours—everyone was afraid to be the first to stop clapping. A poem to Stalin by Soviet poet Alexis Tolstoy shows this worship and fear at its worst:

Thou bright sun of the nations
The unsinking sun of our times
And more than the sun, for the sun has no wisdom.

Rails and Revolution

To a large degree, trains were responsible for the rise of communism in Russia. Their problems aided the collapse of the czar, and their advantages aided the communists.

First, the Japanese feared the completion of the trans-Siberian railway, which would provide an easy rail link from European Russia to the east. They attacked before it was completed in 1904 to halt Russian influence—and won, weakening the precommunist czarist government. Then, during World War I, the main lines couldn't handle supplies for the army, further weakening the government.

Finally, during the revolution itself, Lenin returned to Russia on a train and his Bolsheviks early on seized and held the main rail line, preserving an effective monopoly on internal transportation. The Red Army leader, Leon Trotsky, ran the war effort in an armored train. His train exploits were fictionalized in the book (and movie) *Dr. Zhivago*. Trains were also the principal means of transport to the communist prison camps—the gulags. Prisoners were shipped in unheated red cattle cars, foreshadowing the later Nazi use of trains for their prisoners.

like Germany. After World War I there were several abortive attempts to put Marx's predictions into practice, such as the failed Spartacist revolt in Germany. To this end, Lenin's Bolsheviks formed the Communist International (Comintern), designed to give aid to (and maintain control of) budding communists abroad. As Lenin said, "We have always known, and shall never forget, that our task is an international one, and that victory [in Russia] is only half a victory, perhaps less, until an upheaval takes place in all states, including the wealthiest and most civilized."

But it was left to Stalin, the next major Soviet leader, to truly spread communist rule.

One interesting immediate effect: Sun Yat-sen, the liberal leader of the Canton government of China, was impressed by Lenin (particularly by his abandoning of claims on China). He authorized cooperation between his Kuomintang party and the newly formed Communist Party of China. Ultimately, this led to yet another revolution that transformed another huge area of the globe.

THE CHINESE REVOLUTION

This was the *other* communist revolution. Its leader, Mao Zedong, upended traditional Marxist theory and sought revolution from the least advanced portion of society, the peasants, and argued for guerrilla warfare instead of urban insurrection. Theorists disagreed. In fact, Stalin in the Soviet Union ordered the Chinese communists to support Mao's opponents. But in the end, Mao proved his point in the most effective way possible—he won on the battlefields of China. In 1949 his armies took control of the most populous country on earth and in the same year he announced the formation of the People's Republic of China.

Causes: The story of the causes of the Chinese revolution reads like the history of China. Let's skip a few thousand years and start at the beginning of the twentieth century.

We open with a traditional China: Empress Dowager Tzu Hsi in Peking (now Beijing) and a decaying government: corrupt, repressive, and beholden to foreigners, to whom it had granted extraordinary concessions, being too weak to resist the onslaughts of imperial Britain, Germany, Japan, and France. (For example, a significant portion of the great seaport of Shanghai was controlled by the Western powers, with Western police and government.) The famous sign at a Shanghai club reading "No dogs or Chinamen allowed" was no myth and not easily overlooked by Chinese nationalists.

But even more significant, China just wasn't working: it was wracked by rampant corruption, periodic famine, and extreme poverty.

The first consequence of traditional misrule was the rise of a liberal-minded Western-educated revolutionary, Sun Yat-sen. The story of Sun is the story of the first Chinese revolution.

Eventually Sun managed to create a government in the south under the aegis of a new, representative political party, the Kuomintang (KMT). He had significant help from the newly formed Soviet Union; in terms of practical help the Western powers ignored him or hindered him. Under his eventual successor, Chiang Kai-shek, the north was unified with the south, and for all of Chiang's faults (and there were many), it seemed that China was perhaps headed for a gradual improvement.

Unfortunately, the Japanese chose this time to invade the north of China. As they fought and plundered their way down into central and southern China they destroyed any hopes for liberal democracy. Moreover, Chiang had not been able to address most of the basic problems of industrialization and agriculture. Add to this rising corruption and growing brutality, and you have the recipe for another, but more violent revolution.

Events: Let's get a little Communist Party history. Back in the mid-1930s, just after Chiang had unified China, he had felt confident enough to try to destroy the communists once and for all. The communists obliged him by ordering an urban insurrection. Chiang managed to eliminate most of them (his troops had a habit of shooting suspects in the head on crowded boulevards), but not all. Some escaped from most of the major cities and made their way to safety via the famous Long March. This was a five-thousand-mile trek across the wilds of China to the mountain fastness of Yan'an in Shaanxi province. Along the way, the man who had predicted urban insurrection wouldn't work won control of the Chinese Communist Party—Mao Zedong. And along with his principal cohorts, the diplomat Zhou Enlai and the phlegmatic peasant soldier Zhu De (Chu Teh), he bided his time and built up a substantial peasant army. Mao pursued a strategy of attrition, not direct confrontation. As he said:

If the enemy advances, we retreat.

If the enemy halts and encamps, we harass.

If the enemy seeks to avoid battle, we attack.

If the enemy retreats, we pursue.

This was brilliantly successful advice. Much of Mao's strategy was based on the ancient writings of general Sun Zi, as well as inspired by the famous Chinese novel *The Water Margin*. Unlike Mao, Chiang was a nonintellectual and pursued a more conventional strategy.

With the Japanese invasion, Mao's communists grew more powerful, as Chiang was forced to take the brunt of the Japanese attacks, while Mao pursued his effective guerrilla strategy.

But in fact, *both* sides preferred to marshal their resources for the eventual fight against the other, something that rankled the Americans no end once they got into the war.

But perhaps the Chinese on both sides were right; Japan's loss was probably inevitable once the U.S. was involved. With the American victory in 1945, it was left to the U.S. to try to convince Chiang to bide his time to defeat the communists. He didn't—and moreover, by now Mao had an army of 1 million highly committed soldiers. He controlled the countryside, Chiang's troops were holed up in the cities. After Mao took Manchuria and immense stores of weapons (aided by Russian troops), the end was near. Mao's troops swept south, across the Yangtze River. They drove Chiang's troops ever south, until the last remnants fled across the seas to the island of Formosa, where they created the Republic of China on less than 1 percent of Chinese territory. Mao was master of the mainland, the true master of China.

Impact: As with the Russian Revolution, the impact was enormous. The two largest nations of Asia were now communist. China's example was followed by other nations, including Cambodia and to some extent Vietnam (and to this day, by the Shining Path guerrillas of Peru). In China, there was much reconstruction and development; by 1952 the economy had already once again reached the levels of the 1930s. As with Lenin, Mao quickly instituted communist reforms—land was collectivized, property was nationalized, landlords were tried and in some cases killed. Literacy programs were instituted; foreign influence was drastically reduced—with the exception of the

Soviets, who were welcomed. Yet China was an immense nation. It was hard to change a traditional culture and the grinding poverty so easily. And there was much repression, many failed experiments that hindered China's economic potential, many prison camps. As Mao said to Nixon at the end of his life: "I haven't been able to change [China]. I've only been able to change a few places in the vicinity of Beijing." In one sense, it was left to a later successor, Deng Xiaoping (himself a top official for much of Mao's rule, and a man who had made the Long March), to truly transform China. But that is another chapter of Chinese history.

THE ISLAMIC REVOLUTION IN IRAN

This is the first religious revolution of the twentieth century. It overturned secular Iran, which was an oil-rich Middle Eastern Islamic nation, and a staunch American ally, ruled by Shah Reza Pahlavi. A traditional religious leader, the Ayatollah Ruhollah Khomeini, challenged the shah and overturned the conception that religion was a spent force in a rapidly modernizing world. He successfully toppled the shah's regime—and changed history.

Fundamentalists the world over have looked to the success of this revolt and have been inspired—just as secularists in the Middle East and elsewhere have shuddered. As the main instigator, Ayatollah Khomeini said: "Victory is not achieved by large populations; it is achieved by strength of faith."

Causes: The ruler of Iran, the shah, Reza Pahlavi, was a modernizing leader who wanted to make Iran a regional superpower. He inherited this goal from his father, Iran's first modern shah. The first shah was a strong-willed self-made man named Reza Khan who had seized power in 1921. In his next twenty years of rule, Reza Khan attempted to undo a thousand years of tradition and Islam by abolishing the veil and secularizing schools and courts; in effect, Westernizing Iran.

Strong fathers often have weak sons. For all the military trappings Reza Khan's son surrounded himself with, he did not have his father's force of will. He had a tendency to vacillate between liberal ideas and totalitarian methods. He brought new roads, new schools, gave women the vote, introduced profit sharing for factory workers. But it was not enough. Iran was modernizing rapidly, but tensions were increasing as well. Traditionalist peasants were flocking into the cities and finding inadequate housing in slums; the gap between the rich and the poor was increasing. And so anxious was the shah to create a modern state (he wanted to surpass France by 1993) that he brought in a large number of Westerners to modernize his army, run his oil fields, and build his factories. This angered many—Iran was always a proud nation. Most important, the shah antagonized the still-powerful Islamic clergy, who were shut out of things, and who were worried that Iran was losing its soul.

Opposition was increasing but the shah countered it with repression: his ruthless secret police force, SAVAK, was notorious. By now he had a wide range of enemies—communists and

socialists on the left, European-oriented liberals in the middle, and religious fundamentalists on the right.

But the spark that set the revolution off came from Islam, and inexorably, it was Khomeini and his supporters who set the pace of revolt.

Events: Back in 1963 the shah had summarily expelled an uncompromising ayatollah named Ruhollah Khomeini. (Incidentally, "ayatollah" is a title meaning "mirror of God." It is conferred somewhat informally on Shiite Muslim clerics who are acknowledged for their piety and scholarship.) In some ways by exiling Khomeini the shah helped create his own principal enemy; until that point Khomeini's audience was rather limited. Exile gave the ayatollah stature and prestige and he was not one to miss such an opportunity. From his home in exile, the charismatic and committed Khomeini developed into a powerful antagonist, writing and then tape-recording messages of opposition to an increasingly antagonized population.

Now for a few more sparks. In October 1977, Khomeini's son died. Although Khomeini was still in exile and the funeral was held in Iraq, services were held in many cities in Iran as well. This proved to many Iranians that Islam was still a vigorous force; despite all the shah had done, the Khomeini Islamic opposition had many supporters.

A few weeks later, in one of those ironies of history, President Jimmy Carter visited Iran and toasted the shah for creating "an island of stability" in the Middle East, blessed by the "love of his people." This visible sign of strong American support prompted the shah to try to discredit Khomeini once and for all. He authorized a letter in a

Teheran newspaper condemning Khomeini as a licentious poetry writer, a British secret agent, and a foreigner. Needless to say, the plan backfired miserably. No one believed the letter. Instead, the shah angered everybody. Riots broke out; first in the holy city of Qom, then another in the province of Azerbaijan in the north, then across the country. By September 7, 1978, the shah decided to proclaim martial law. On September 8, protesters assembled in Teheran's Jaleh Square. When they didn't disperse, government troops opened fire and hundreds were killed.

This day was immortalized as Black Friday—and it was the beginning of the end for the shah. Widespread strikes paralyzed Iran; the opposition was out in the open. Now it was the shah's supporters who were frightened. By some reports, up to 100,000 Iranian royalists fled the country in the next few months.

The shah tried to backtrack, even asking for forgiveness for the corruption that had plagued the country. But it was too late. On January 16, 1979, the shah left Iran for an "extended vacation," leaving a liberal, nationalist government in charge. He never returned, eventually dying in exile. Now it was the other exile's turn for power. On February 1, 1979, Ayatollah Khomeini returned to Iran on an Air France jet.

Four days later Khomeini appointed a new provisional government. Shortly thereafter, he sponsored a national referendum on whether an Islamic government should be established. With the approval of an overwhelming majority, he declared April 1 "the first day of a government of God."

Impact: Until the Iranian revolu-

tion, most experts in the West had pretty much discounted the force of religion. For example, despite all the unrest in Iran prior to the revolution, not one U.S. embassy official had seen fit to interview Khomeini or his supporters.

But the full impact of the revolution remains to be seen, because in many ways the Iranian revolution is not yet over. The final shape of Iranian government and society is still not yet established. The revolution itself went through several more phases, first consolidating its power, then surging abroad (at one point, the Ayatollah had declared, "We shall export our revolution to the whole world"). Iranians preached fundamentalist Islamic values in other Middle Eastern nations, particularly in Lebanon.

Throughout, the revolution has met many challenges, from internal enemies (communists have killed more than a few fundamentalist leaders, including one prime minister) as well as from abroad. As in other revolutions, thousands of opponents have died, been imprisoned, or have fled the country.

All this was exacerbated by the war with Saddam Hussein's Iraq, a traditional enemy. Sensing that Iran was weak, Saddam attacked. Initially, it was believed by most experts that the invading Iraqis would prevail in a few weeks. But once again Iran overturned conventional wisdom by surviving. Nevertheless, Iran paid a tremendous human and economic cost. After the war ended in a stalemate, Iran once more looked inward and the revolution seemed to take on a somewhat less activist stance. Iran seems to be opening up again to the world, albeit in a markedly different manner than under the shah. Yet at the same time, evidence points to Iran's support for overseas terrorism. In 1995, the U.S. declared a trade embargo against Iran for this reason.

But no matter what the specifics, the broader idea of the Iranian revolution, that is, the idea of an *Islamic* revolution, or more generally, of a *religious* revolution, has had a great impact. It has energized fundamentalist Muslims across the Islamic world. Fundamentalists have wide support in Tunisia, Algeria, Egypt, the West Bank, and have won power in Sudan. Whether or not more Irans occur remains to be seen.

MOVERS AND SHAKERS: FOUR INFLUENTIAL MODERN WORLD LEADERS (. . . FOR GOOD OR FOR EVIL)

There are many people who could have been included in this section. Space limitations dictated we choose only four. For example, we didn't include Franklin Delano Roosevelt, chiefly because he was an American president and this book focuses on the world outside of the United States. But his impact was enormous. First, he was probably responsible for preventing the collapse of the United States during the Great Depression, saving us from a great deal of political chaos and keeping us strong in time of World War II. And although he (fortunately) broke his promise to keep us out of that war, he tried his hardest to keep Britain in it, and in so doing helped save the world from Hitler.

Another man we haven't included is Joseph Stalin, who loomed over the world in the mid-twentieth century. To some, he was the vanguard of the future; to others, he was the devil incarnate. Recent revelations coming out of Russia confirm the latter view. As more and more mass graves are uncovered, the enormity of Stalin's paranoid crimes against his own people is finally coming to light. But to choose the most influential leaders, we should look to the impact on the future, and that's why we chose Mahatma Gandhi over Stalin to round out the four most influential modern world leaders. The twentieth century was a very violent century, but there were many bright spots as well. Gandhi has influenced countless thou-

sands with his nonviolent teachings. Most adherents were unknown, but some, like Václav Havel of the Czech Republic or Martin Luther King, Jr., are world famous.

WINSTON CHURCHILL

(1874–1965)

Claim to fame: Britain's greatest modern prime minister; a man who kindled British resistance to Hitler's Nazi Germany during the darkest days of World War II, when it looked as if a German victory was inevitable.

In his own words:

Victory at all costs, victory in spite of all terror, victory however long and hard the road may be; for without victory there is no survival.

We shall fight on the beaches, we shall fight on the landing grounds, we shall fight in the fields and in the streets, we shall fight in the hills, we shall never surrender.

These are not dark days: these are great days.

Life and times: With stirring words like these, Churchill galvanized a nation when invasion by the Nazis seemed

WINSTON
CHURCHILL
(PHOTO BY J.
RUSSELL, 1941;
REPRODUCED
FROM THE
COLLECTIONS OF
THE LIBRARY OF
CONGRESS)

imminent. Rhetoric rolled off his tongue easily and beautifully; he was made for a great crisis like World War II.

He was in most ways an anachronism, a man who looked backward to the greatness of a British Empire that was now declining; a man who championed virtues and ideals that had really disappeared in most of England and the world. He was a Victorian statesman—or even a medieval one—in a world of planes, bombs, independence movements, and radios.

Churchill was an aristocratic son of another British statesman, Randolph Churchill, and a famous socialite American mother, Jeanette (Jennie) Jerome. His adult life began at the

height of the British Empire; he marched with Lord Kitchener against the fundamentalist Mahdist forces in the Sudan desert. When he died most British colonies were just a memory.

His was a life filled with ups and downs. He served in high posts in the cabinet during World War I and was responsible for Britain's most disastrous campaign, the attack in the Dardanelles (in Turkey), which resulted in defeat. He was made a scapegoat for the war's general failures and resigned to serve in Europe as a front-line low-ranking officer. He rejoined the cabinet in 1917, but after the war it appeared that his career was effectively over. He was already anachronistic, widely viewed as a has-been.

But as Hitler's power grew, Churchill's supporters became more vocal. Churchill had long been outspoken against the German threat, and now more people were listening to him rather than ridiculing him. In 1940, when the weak government of Prime Minister Neville Chamberlain finally realized that its policy of appeasing Hitler had failed, Churchill entered the cabinet and then became prime minister. He ignited the British population during the days after Hitler had invaded France and controlled most of Western Europe. Maintaining a close working relationship with President Roosevelt, Churchill adroitly managed to get substantial U.S. aid well before the U.S. entered the war.

Churchill actually seemed to enjoy the challenges of the World War II years—his, and Britain's, "finest hour." After the war he was defeated for reelection, although he was elected in 1951 once more.

Influence: Churchill is probably the single person most responsible for saving Europe from Nazi rule, particularly in light of recent revelations that Hitler was ready to negotiate a peace with England—and that many in the government were anxious to go along. But not Winston Churchill.

He had many faults: among them, he never recognized Indian aspirations for independence (he called Mahatma Gandhi a half-dressed fakir); he never really understood the problems of the working class. But he understood the necessity for strength against tyranny. Toward the end of his life, as a respected elder statesman, he summed up his role in history: "It was the nation and the race dwelling all round the globe that had the lion's heart. I had the luck to be called upon to give the roar."

MOHANDAS K. GANDHI

(1869–1948)

Claim to fame: Called Mahatma (literally "Great Soul"). A pioneer of nonviolent resistance and a leader in India's independence movement; regarded as a great politician and a great moral teacher.

In his own words:

Means are not to be distinguished from ends. If violent means are used there will be bad result.

One needs to be slow to form convictions, but once formed, they must be defended against the heaviest odds.

The greatest lessons in life, if we would but stoop and humble ourselves, we

would learn not from the grown-up learned men, but from the so-called ignorant children.

Life and times: Even Gandhi's worst enemies conceded his personal honesty and integrity. Most politicians, indeed most people, present a facade to the world—Gandhi strived to present the unvarnished truth. Characteristically, his autobiography is titled *The Story of My Experiments with Truth*. Even here, he never claimed that he succeeded, just that he tried. Gandhi was no naive saint; in fact, he was probably one of the best—and slipperiest—politicians of all time. He just did it all more honestly.

He was born in Porbandar, on the Kathiawar Peninsula in British India, and initially followed the typical career path of an educated middle-class Indian: he studied law in London, dressed in a British manner, and affected educated British customs and accent. He returned to set up a lucrative law practice in Bombay. But in 1893, he moved out of this lifestyle and began moving toward a new life that was to make him and his philosophy famous. His first move: to British South Africa, where he was shocked at the illogic and absurdity of discrimination against Indians. He worked hard to change this.

Eleven years later, in 1914, he returned to India and soon became involved in the Swaraj (Home Rule) movement, which began as an attempt to win greater autonomy for India. India was then a British colony—the crown jewel of the British Empire. This struggle dominated the rest of his life.

Gandhi began leading nonviolent civil disobedience movements against British rule, and suffering arrest for his

actions. His plan was to shame the British into granting greater freedom. (He kept a sense of humor about it all. When asked by a British reporter for his views on Western civilization, he replied, "I think it would be a very good idea.")

MOHANDAS K. GANDHI (REPRODUCED FROM THE COLLECTIONS OF THE LIBRARY OF CONGRESS)

His strict pursuit of nonviolent means gradually succeeded. He won the respect of much of the world—including many of his British enemies. By the late 1930s and early 1940s, he was considered one of the leaders of the Indian independence movement and, with Jawaharlal Nehru and Mohammed Jinnah, led negotiations for eventual independence.

By the time independence was announced in 1947, Gandhi had shifted focus. He was more concerned with communal strife in India. He argued (unsuccessfully) against the partition of India into Muslim Pakistan and Hindu India, and more successfully for an end to discrimination against outcastes, untouchables and those lowest or outside of the Hindu caste system. Ultimately, his views led to his death—he was assassinated by a Hindu fanatic.

Influence: Gandhi's fight was centered on India, but his influence was worldwide. His ideas have motivated thousands of freedom fighters, including such notables as Václav Havel of the Czech Republic and Martin Luther King, Jr. In India, his moderating influence helped solidify a democratic tradition that has survived many crises. India is still the world's largest democracy.

Gandhi's ideas have been criticized by many as ultimately flawed. Nonviolence works best when it confronts a relatively enlightened oppressor such as the British—many other regimes would have simply shot him. When asked about this, Gandhi (typically) conceded this criticism and added that he would have accepted death as would (hopefully) his followers. Sooner or later, he reasoned, even the most evil regime would grow tired of killing and his methods would succeed. As you can see, Gandhi was no weakling. In fact, he once said:

Non-violence does not admit of running away from danger. . . . Between violence and cowardly flight I can only prefer violence to cowardice.

ADOLF HITLER
(REPRODUCED
FROM THE
COLLECTIONS OF
THE LIBRARY OF
CONGRESS)

ADOLF HITLER

(1889–1945)

Claim to fame: Probably the single most destructive human to have walked this planet (with Joseph Stalin a close second). Hitler launched an aggressive war that accelerated the transformation of the world, geopolitically, morally, and even scientifically.

In his own words:

Whatever goal man has reached is due to his originality plus his brutality.

Nazism and the Average Person

The evil of Nazism lay in its power to subvert normal people. As one German put it: "Each act, each occasion, is worse than the last, but only a little worse. You wait for the next and the next. You wait for one great shocking occasion, thinking that others, when such a shock comes, will join you in resisting somehow." The problem was that very few Germans did resist Hitler.

One who did, Martin Niemoller, was a pastor who changed from an ardent nationalist into a German anti-Nazi. As he said in his famous statement on behalf of activism in the face of evil:

"When the Nazis attacked the communists, I was a little uneasy, but after all, I was not a communist, so I did nothing, and then they attacked the Socialists, and I was a little uneasier, but still, I was not a Socialist, and I did nothing, and then they attacked the schools, the press, the Jews, and I was always a little uneasier, but I did nothing. And then they attacked the Church, and I was a Churchman, and I did something—but then it was too late."

The grossly impudent lie always leaves traces behind it, even after it has been nailed down. [Hitler's "big lie" theory: that one lie, repeated often enough, will be believed.]

Life and times: How to sum up the man? Hitler's able biographer, Alan Bullock, concludes:

Pity and mercy he regarded as humanitarian claptrap. . . . Everything that spoke of the human spirit and of the thousand forms by which it has flowered, from mysticism to science, was alien to him.

Yet this is a man who was unquestionably popular in his adopted country (he was born in Austria) and a man who was respected and tolerated by the leaders of the great nations of Europe for years. He represents the greatest failure of European civilization.

As a youth Hitler drifted around Austria's capital city, Vienna, at the time a center of anti-Semitism. Hitler wanted to be an artist but lacked tal-

ent: he consistently failed to get into art school. World War I was his salvation. He joined the German army and served as a corporal in the front-line trenches. A good soldier—he won the Iron Cross, First Class, an unusual honor for an enlisted man (ironically, he was recommended by a Jewish senior officer)—the war years were characteristically the happiest years of his life.

After the war, he was once more at a loss. Drifting around postwar Germany, he became a police informer. Assigned to spy on a small political party, he wound up joining and taking control. He renamed it the National Socialist German Workers' Party (NSDAP, or Nazis, for short) and transformed it into a potent force for his ambition—including a paramilitary unit of storm troopers that easily intimidated opponents through brutality.

And so began his active political career. His first move was an attempt to seize the local Bavarian government. He failed, and after a loud trial where he practiced his rhetoric and piercing stare, he was imprisoned briefly. Here

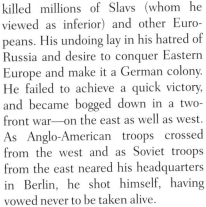

he dictated a book, *Mein Kampf* (My Struggle), which outlined his ideas: Germany had been betrayed into surrendering during World War I; Jews were behind much of Germany's problems; race was all-important; peoples of the "Aryan" (German and Nordic) race were the creators of culture with a duty to dominate and rule. Hitler's ideas were not complex—even he realized that his appeal lay in raw emotion and hate.

Hitler's influence and power came not from the power of his thought but from the despair many Germans felt after World War I, when they were (probably unfairly) made to take the blame and pay the price for having supposedly started an aggressive war in Europe. His appeal broadened considerably after 1930, when unemployment stood at over 6 million and the poor saw him as a savior who would bring employment, and many rich saw him as a palatable alternative to the rising Communist Party. By 1933 the Nazi Party had almost 1 million members.

Hitler's party dominated the German parliament, the Reichstag, but in the last election before he took power he suffered a loss. It didn't stop him. Using personal charisma to manipulate his appointment as chancellor in 1933, he then transformed German government, ultimately "legally" enshrining himself as the absolute dictator, the embodiment of Germany, the *führer*.

Hitler's role in launching World War II is covered elsewhere—suffice it to say that he was loyal to his words written in *Mein Kampf*. He created a totalitarian state, destroyed European Jewry, launched an aggressive war against German neighbors in an attempt to win *lebensraum,* or living space, for the "master race" of German "Aryans," and

killed millions of Slavs (whom he viewed as inferior) and other Europeans. His undoing lay in his hatred of Russia and desire to conquer Eastern Europe and make it a German colony. He failed to achieve a quick victory, and became bogged down in a two-front war—on the east as well as west. As Anglo-American troops crossed from the west and as Soviet troops from the east neared his headquarters in Berlin, he shot himself, having vowed never to be taken alive.

He rightly feared the consequences of the hatred he had himself created.

Influence: In his time, Hitler's influence was very large—both in Germany and the world. To many, it appeared that democracy had failed, and Hitler's Germany was seen as a model for the future. Of course, Hitler failed, but neo-Nazi movements still have some potency today and the initial success of his appeal to racism and hate has not gone unnoticed by some leaders today.

Hitler's war accelerated change in Europe and the world. To defeat Hitler, governments invested heavily in industry and research; war spending brought the world out of economic depression and hastened the development of new technologies that were used as weapons and later for peacetime purposes. National liberation movements in Asia and Africa were strengthened by the knowledge that European colonial powers were not invincible; more to the point, the principal colonial powers, Britain and France, were too weak in the postwar years to hold on to their possessions abroad. Hitler also hastened the rise of two superpowers—the U.S. and the Soviet Union. Ironically, he held both in contempt: one comprised of racially

The History of Racism

Hitler's anti-Semitism and racism had deep European roots. Anti-Semitic riots occurred in the Greco-Egyptian city of Alexandria as far back as the first century. But modern racism got its start in the nineteenth century. The French Revolution of 1789 brought many new ideas of race to the intellectual forefront; later the Comte de Gobineau wrote a history based on race. Racism was initially promulgated not so much against others, but in favor of breeding superior races. But clearly, if someone feels his race is superior, others are inferior—and Jews living in Central Europe were favorite targets. The great German historian Heinrich von Treitschke said that "Jews are our national misfortune" back in 1879. Much of this German racism was based on the rising myth of a German *volk,* or people, a romantic conception of Germany in the (supposedly) heroic Middle Ages. *Volk*-ish ideas spread to Austria, where Jörg Lanz von Liebenfels (a nom de plume of Josef Lanz) founded a new religious order based on racial purity. Fortunately, Liebenfels didn't have much of a following, which is not surprising considering the crudity of his theories; for example, he divided the human race into two: Aryans and apemen. But at least one man thought the theories reasonable: Heinrich Himmler of Hitler's notorious SS was an ardent admirer and structured the SS on similar lines. Anti-Semitism was perhaps strongest in Russia, where the Jews, as among the newest minorities, without many connections, were hated as newcomers. Czarist officers printed and circulated the *Protocols of the Elders of Zion,* a crude forgery that supposedly was an outline of Jewish plans to take over the world. Significantly, many of Hitler's anti-Semitic followers were Baltic Germans, who came from areas near Russia. Interestingly, much of German anti-Semitism was not based on Jews as a single race, but as a conglomeration of races—hence not at all "pure Aryan." The irony of it all is that Germans themselves are a conglomeration of races. The supposedly pure Prussian state, whose people formed the backbone of the German army, registered itself as a Slavic nation at the international Congress of Vienna at the turn of the nineteenth century.

inferior Slavs and the other of "mongrelized" Americans.

Hitler's worst legacy is the sense of insecurity he created. Hitler created fear: fear of Germany and fear of the brutality that lies underneath all "civilized" nations.

MAO ZEDONG

(1893–1976)

Claim to fame: Revolutionary called "The Great Helmsman" who led the Chinese people through a communist revolution and became the first chairman of the People's Republic of China. Responsible for great changes in China—greater equity, a rise in literacy and health—as well as the deaths of millions.

In his own words:

A revolution does not march a straight line. It wanders where it can . . . above all, [it] is possessed of enormous patience.

Communism is not love. Communism is a hammer which we use to crush the enemy.

The revolutionary war is a war of the masses; it can be waged only by mobilizing the masses and relying on them.

I am alone with the masses.

There may be thousands of principles in Marxism but in the final analysis they can be summed up in one sentence: Rebellion is justified.

Life and times: Mao was a classic revolutionary—before, during, and after the Chinese revolution. He never quit.

His strategic writings have been studied by such diverse groups as the leaders of the Shining Path guerrillas of Peru as well as by scholars at the U.S. National War College. Although many of his ideas are derived from Chinese classics like the ancient military strategist Sun Zi, it was Mao who made them a success. He succeeded in creating a new form of communist revolution, based on the rural peasantry, not the urban workers—and he succeeded in winning the leadership of one quarter of the world's population.

Mao was the son of a well-to-do peasant, and did not get along well with his father. To some (including his Confucian enemies in Taiwan), this fact explained his later revolutionary philosophy. Mao himself liked to ascribe it to his native province of Hunan: the Hunanese are known as great eaters of hot red peppers, which supposedly accounts for their strong personalities and political activism. There is a saying that China can only be conquered when all the Hunanese are dead.

Whatever the causes, while working as a library assistant at the University of Peking (Beijing), this young Hunanese discovered the works of Marx and Engels, and quickly became involved with the Chinese Communist Party (CCP), founding a local branch.

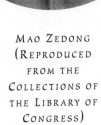

MAO ZEDONG
(REPRODUCED
FROM THE
COLLECTIONS OF
THE LIBRARY OF
CONGRESS)

Fairly early on, Mao realized the great strength inherent in popular peasant movements. He made this the central focus of his career, setting up a "people's republic" in Jiangxi in southeastern China. In 1931–1934, when the communists were attacked by the conservative nationalist leader Chiang Kai-shek's forces, he and the others were forced to undertake the now-famous two-year Long March to remote Shaanxi province in northwestern China. During this time, Mao was elected chairman of the CCP (1935).

From a new base in Yan'an, ensconced in a cave burrowed into a cliff, Mao developed his philosophy: different from other communist philosophies in its emphasis on the peasantry, on the rigorous importance of ideology, and on the necessity for reeducation of those opposed to its rule.

By this time the Japanese had invaded China and Mao directed his rural guerrillas against them as well as against his principal enemy in China, nationalist leader Chiang Kai-shek. After the war his troops took the offensive and by 1949 controlled China, renaming it the People's Republic of China. Mao now rewarded his peasant supporters, encouraging them to seize land from the landlords and farm it for themselves. These were probably the best years of Mao's rule.

But Mao was ever the revolutionary, ever the governmental innovator. In 1958, he instigated the Great Leap Forward, an attempt to push China into modernity quickly—by confiscating peasant land and instead organizing peasants into giant collectives. (He even pushed for backyard steel furnaces to drastically increase steel production.) "Setting up a people's commune is like going to heaven.... The sharp knife severs the roots of private property, opening a new historical era," he wrote.

But the Great Leap Forward was more like a trip to hell: a dismal failure that produced a famine that killed upward of 30 million people. Chinese leaders were too afraid to tell Mao of the catastrophe until it was too late (one who tried was drummed out of the party). Mao resigned the chairmanship of the party, and now a more moderate policy was pursued.

But in 1966 he once again encouraged change and revolution. The Cultural Revolution (1966–1976) was a campaign against "revisionist forces," the "counterrevolutionaries" within the nation who had to be rooted out. The result was terror and chaos, as armed students roamed the streets and government literally came to a standstill.

As the Cultural Revolution died down, Mao's second in command, Zhou Enlai, presided over reconstruction. And as his health deteriorated, Mao lost political clout. Even so, he was on hand to greet President Richard Nixon during his first visit to

Mao Zedong has become a prime engine for small-time capitalists in China. They're making a mint producing Mao memorabilia: not just reprints of his little red book, busts, or buttons, but such kitschy items as Mao tie clips, Mao key chains, Mao medals, Mao lighters, Mao calendars, even Mao T-shirts. The boom in Mao collectibles began when people, especially foreigners, started buying artifacts from the Cultural Revolution, especially buttons and badges—which were produced by the billions during that time. Then Chinese capitalists realized there was money to be made by creating their own Mao artifacts—and an industry was born.

China. Nixon praised his accomplishments, yet Mao said that he had not done much more than change the environs of Beijing. Was he being cynical, falsely modest, or wistfully aware of his failures? No one knows.

Influence: Mao's influence was tremendous. In China he transformed the lives of 1 billion people. He smashed the traditional system of landlords, he educated millions, improved health care for millions, and destroyed the lives of millions. His troops reconquered Tibet, kept all of China under the rule of a police state, and quashed free thought. During the Cultural Revolution he was almost worshipped. One excerpt from a Red Guard's diary reads:

At 1:10 pm on October 18, the most, most happy and the most, most unforgettable moment in my life, I saw Chairman Mao, the never-setting red sun.

People literally had to pay daily homage to the man. Around the world, his thought spawned other revolutions, including the still smoldering rebellion in the Andean Mountains of Peru. And although Mao was not a capitalist, perhaps the current economic revolution in China that is bringing so much prosperity could not have occurred without his strong initial efforts. On the other hand, the human costs were so high.

46 OTHER INFLUENTIAL MODERN LEADERS IN THE WORLD (A BRIEF BIOGRAPHICAL DICTIONARY)

 The great French leader Charles de Gaulle once said that "politics are too serious a matter to be left to politicians." He was probably right, even if he meant it half tongue in cheek (after all, he was a politician himself). Like it or not, politicians still dominate politics as well as the news of the world. Here's a brief dictionary of the lives and the places and the times of some of the most prominent men and women in recent history—all politicians, of course.

YASIR ARAFAT

(1929–)

Palestinian political leader, now seen by many as a moderating influence in the Mideast. Born in Jerusalem and educated at Cairo University (where he led the Palestinian Students' Union), he cofounded the Al Fatah resistance group in 1956. The Palestinian Liberation Organization—a coalition of different factions—was founded in 1964, and five years later, Al Fatah took control of the group and Arafat became PLO chairman. He increased the stature of the PLO and steered it to world acceptance (in 1974, the PLO was formally recognized by the U.N. and won diplomatic recognition from more than 100 countries). He lost influence when challenged by radicals in the PLO, and was later forced to leave his Beirut base when Israel invaded. However, he maintained control over the PLO and eventually convinced colleagues to negotiate with Israel. The negotiations are still ongoing, with Palestinian authority recognized in the Gaza Strip and portions of the West Bank. Arafat faces considerable opposition from fundamentalist radicals, but so far still maintains a tenuous authority.

HAFEZ AL-ASSAD

(1928–)

Syrian president, considered by many to be the most skillful politician in the Middle East—especially for his years of maintaining strong ties with the Soviet Union, opposing Israel, while still avoiding a complete break in relations with the United States. Assad became involved in nationalistic politics at age 16 when he joined the Ba'ath Socialist party. He graduated from the Syrian military academy, became an airman, and went for further studies in the Soviet Union. He then became general, defense minister, and air force commander when the Ba'ath party took control of Syria—and began establishing a power base. He led a bloodless coup in 1970, deposing state head Salah Jadid, and became president—a post he has held since.

As president, he opposed the Camp David treaty; has fought with Israel over control of Lebanon, has been accused of complicity with terrorists, but has denied these charges, and has interceded on behalf of Western hostages held in Lebanon.

MENACHEM BEGIN

(1913–1992)

Israeli prime minister, best known for his role fashioning the peace treaty with Egypt even though he was long a hard-liner where the Arab world was concerned. Begin was a member (and commander in chief) of Zionist resistance group Irgun Zvai Leumi, where he made a name for himself as a strong leader. He formed the rightist Herut party and later was joint chairman of the Likud party, in opposition to Golda Meir. As prime minister, he was involved in peace talks with Egyptian President Anwar al-Sadat and U.S. President Jimmy Carter, resulting in treaty and his co-winning of the Nobel Peace Prize (1978) with Sadat.

MUHAMMED AHMED BEN BELLA

(1916–)

Algerian revolutionary leader and first president of independent Algeria—who wound up out of power because he wasn't left-wing enough. Founder of

the National Liberation Front (FLN), which fought eight-year war for independence from the French, Ben Bella was then appointed president. He lost support because he wasn't enthusiastic enough about the Pan-Arab cause and was deposed in 1965 by a coup led by the further-left minister of national defense, General Houari Boumedienne.

DAVID BEN-GURION

(1886–1973)

One of the founding fathers of the State of Israel—and, to many, a human symbol of Israel. Ben-Gurion was a Zionist leader, and chairman of the Jewish Agency, which was the main institution during British rule. He announced the birth of the state of Israel in May 1948 and served as first prime minister.

FIDEL CASTRO

(1926–)

Cuban revolutionary and head of government since 1959—the bearded, army fatigue–wearing personification of communist Cuba. Castro led the successful guerrilla war against President Fulgencio Batista, and, once in power, instituted a self-described "Marxist-Leninist program" of agricultural, economic, educational, and social reforms —many of which have proved unsuccessful. Initially encouraged by the U.S.

(who wanted Batista removed), he won international prestige for quashing the U.S.-backed Bay of Pigs invasion by Cuban émigrés. On one hand, Castro developed strong ties with China and the Soviet Union; on the other, he held independent foreign policy positions, which led to his appointment as president of nonaligned countries movement in 1979. During the 1980s and 1990s, he presided over a decaying Cuban economy, and now is one of the last communist leaders in the world.

CHIANG KAI-SHEK

(1887–1975)

Chinese nationalist and president of the Republic of China. Successor to Sun Yat-sen, founder of Kuomintang party, he governed China during growing communist threat. Chiang had support of Europe and the United States, who thought he had a hold on the loyalty of his public. They were wrong—China fell to communist forces led by Zhou Enlai and Mao Zedong. Chiang withdrew with the remnants of his army to Formosa (now Taiwan), where he was reinstated as president of "Nationalist China" and never set foot on mainland China again. He was ineffective as a leader of China and hated by his U.S. liaison during World War II, the crusty General Joseph Stilwell, who called him "Peanut."

GEORGES CLEMENCEAU

(1841–1929)

French prime minister (called "The Tiger" because of his take-no-hostages debating style) who many think may have helped push the world toward World War II. Why? When he presided over the Paris Peace Conference in 1919, Clemenceau didn't disguise his hostility toward the Germans or his open displeasure with the Treaty of Versailles. Even after his resignation, he remained a political gadfly and vocal critic.

DENG XIAOPING

(1904–)

Communist Chinese political leader whose political career parallels the political changes in China. Born into a comfortable middle-class family, Deng joined the Chinese Communist Party while a student in Paris—where he also became good friends with fellow revolutionary Zhou Enlai. From then on, his life was tied to the party. He supported Mao Zedong, participated in the Long March, and quickly rose to high positions. Long associated with the right wing or more pragmatic faction of the party, he periodically suffered from this association. During the Chinese Cultural Revolution (1966–1969) he was branded a counterrevolutionary and sentenced to internal exile, but was finally rescued by his old friend and patron Zhou and reinstated as a political figure. After Zhou and Mao died, Deng became de facto leader of China. He promoted extensive economic liberalization, limited political reform, and stronger ties with the West but lost worldwide internal support when he backed the crackdown on the democratic rights movement and sanctioned the army massacre of an estimated 5,000 demonstrators in Tiananmen Square.

EAMON DE VALERA

(1882–1975)

Irish revolutionary, prime minister (for 21 years), and president. Under his leadership, Ireland broke most links with Great Britain, producing a new constitution and more. Once a member of the revolutionary Sinn Fein party, he created his own, Fianna Fáil, which opted for parliamentarian procedure over violence as a means for change.

FRANCISCO FRANCO BAHAMONDE

(1892–1975)

Spanish dictator who overthrew the republican government in a brutal civil war (1936–1939), aided by Mussolini and Hitler. Franco rewrote the constitution so he'd be ruler for life, then have the state switch back to a monarchy upon his death. He kept a tight authoritarian hand on the government until his death, allowing no reform or moderniza-

tion. His pact with the U.S.—military bases allowed in Spain for economic aid—kept him on good terms with other Western countries in spite of his decidedly undemocratic regime. After his death, his handpicked successor surprised most everyone by turning the government toward democracy.

INDIRA GANDHI

(1917–1984)

First female prime minister of India, and one of the most powerful women of the twentieth century. Daughter of Indian Prime Minister Nehru (but no relation to Mohandas Gandhi), and a consummate politician, she spent most of her life in politics—and wound up in trouble because of dubious political practices. She led India during heavy strife with Pakistan. She later was convicted of election malpractices in 1975 and reacted by declaring a state of emergency, in effect, making her dictator. When it was lifted, she lost her seat, but rebounded only 18 months later and was reelected prime minister in 1980. Assassinated by Sikh members of her bodyguard.

CHARLES DE GAULLE

(1890–1970)

French president and leader of the Free French during World War II. De Gaulle was lauded as a hero for his staunch line against the Germans; but many politicians opposed his ideas for a strong right-wing presidency. It didn't matter—he bided his time, built up his popularity, and was pushed back into power as head of the interim Government of National Safety when the revolt of French settlers in Algiers led to the fall of the Fourth Republic. Four months later, the new constitution gave the president the powers de Gaulle had earlier argued for—and shortly thereafter he was voted president of the Fifth Republic by a whopping 78% of the electorate. De Gaulle was known for his strong (but high-handed) foreign policy initiatives, including granting independence to France's African colonies. He had troubles throughout his years in office, including several assassination attempts. He won the presidency a second time but was forced to resign four years later after defeat of his proposals.

MIKHAIL GORBACHEV

(1931–)

Soviet prime minister who won a Nobel Peace Prize shortly before he lost the support of his people—and control of his country. Gorbachev oversaw beginning of Soviet loosening, but ultimately lost office due to his moderate views, which were attacked by those on both the right and left. He leaped into the international public eye through his attempts to reform and modernize Soviet Union—economically and politically—via his restructuring program of perestroika and his call for more openness, glasnost. Initially his plans met with support, but reforms reducing the power of the Communist Party started

causing dissension. Severe economic troubles turned much of the public against him, clamoring for a return to the good old days . . . or a faster move to modernize. A conservative coup pushed him from office; he was restored to power for a short time, but then lost it again when most of the Soviet republics opted for independence.

HAILE SELASSIE

(1892–1975)

Emperor of Ethiopia known for his resistance to an Italian attack in the years prior to World War II, long a U.S. ally. Haile Selassie was a prime mover in establishment of Organization of African Unity; but he ran into domestic troubles—economic problems, famine, and growing dissatisfaction. He was deposed by left-wing army officers in 1974. He is still revered by the Rastafarian religious sect (named after him; he was born Ras Tafari Makonnen).

VÁCLAV HAVEL

(1936–)

The voice of democracy in Czechoslovakia—first as a dissident playwright, then as president after the communists were ousted. Czechoslovakia's leading anti-communist dissident; his books were banned—but his works were read and performed outside of Czechoslovakia, and his international reputation grew. In spite of numerous arrests and harassments, Havel actively opposed regime. Elected president by direct popular vote after heading up nonviolent "velvet revolution" that resulted in communist overthrow.

HO CHI MINH

(1890–1969)

Vietnamese political leader and hero of his people; founder of the Socialist Republic of Vietnam. Born Nguyen Van Thanh, he changed his name to Ho Chi Minh, meaning "The Seeker After Light" or "He Who Enlightens," and was called, affectionately, Uncle Ho by his followers. A revolutionary, he founded the Communist Party and organized the guerrilla Vietminh movement against Japanese occupation of Vietnam, and later against the French colonizers of his country. He became prime minister and president of North Vietnam, and spearheaded communist resistance in South Vietnam. His last act before he died: rejecting American peace proposals of 1969.

SADDAM HUSSEIN

(1937–)

Iraqi political leader and seemingly perpetual thorn in the side of the U.S. As a student, Saddam joined the Arab Ba'ath Socialist party and became active in nationalistic movements. He was sentenced to death for his involvement in an assassination attempt on Iraqi head of state Gen. Abdul Karem Kassim (in which Saddam was wounded), escaped to Syria, then Egypt, where he found an ideological leader in President Gamal Abdel Nasser. He returned to Iraq in 1963 after Kassim fell, but was imprisoned a year later for plotting to overthrow the government. In 1966, out of jail, Saddam played a major role in the bloodless overthrow of the civilian government, which brought his Ba'ath party to power. He expanded his influence, serving first as chairman of the Revolutionary Command Council he had helped set up; then, in 1979, president. As a dictatorial president bent on furthering his own aims, he established strong ties with the Soviet Union, began waging a long war with neighboring Iran, and invaded Iraq's *other* neighbor, Kuwait—an invasion stopped by U.S. participation in the Gulf War.

ABDUL AZIZ IBN SAUD

(1880–1953)

King of Saudi Arabia, an influential Arab leader—and ruler of some of the most oil-rich territory in the world. Exiled as a child, he reclaimed his land in central Arabia (the Nejd) and more—taking over much of the land on the Red Sea coast (the Hejaz) by 1925, and so presided over a unified country renamed Saudi Arabia, which included the Islamic holy cities of Mecca and Medina. After oil was discovered in 1936, he became immensely rich and a valuable ally to the United States.

MOHAMMED ALI JINNAH

(1876–1948)

Founder of Pakistan—considered the father of his country and called "Quid-i-Azam" (Great Leader). Member of India's Viceroy Legislative Council and Indian National Congress, he became president of the Indian Muslim League. Convinced that Gandhi was only interested in Hindu interests, he made the Muslim League into a major political force and pushed for the establishment of an independent Muslim state. After riots and political turmoil, he won his state (which was much smaller than he wanted), became governor-general of Pakistan, and died 13 months later.

KENNETH DAVID KAUNDA

(1924–)

Founding president of Zambia. While Kaunda was a leading force in push for Zambian independence from London, he ran into problems as president—due to a poor economy and difficulty with militant black and white racists. His solution: suspending the democratic constitution and replacing it with one that recognized no political party but his own. One of Africa's leading statesmen, he has also served as president of the Organization of African Unity. To his credit, he voluntarily stepped down when it became apparent that his economic policies weren't working.

JOMO KENYATTA

(1890–1978)

First prime minister and president of independent Kenya. An ardent nationalist, while in voluntary exile (in England and Russia) Kenyatta was considered leader of his people. He was accused by the British of leading Mau Mau guerrilla group and he was ultimately sentenced to seven years of hard labor. Upon release, he became active in politics and eventually headed the republic. Faced with internal divisions, he emphasized Africanization of the economy to the detriment of non-indigenous settlers who had earlier seized some of the best land. Kenyatta also emphasized capitalist development; under his administration Kenya grew at a fast clip economically. He died in office.

AYATOLLAH RUHOLLAH KHOMEINI

(1900–1989)

Iranian religious and political leader of the Shiite Muslims who spearheaded the fight against the Westernized policies of the shah. Exiled in 1963 for his political beliefs, he returned to Iran in 1979 upon collapse of shah's government and essentially ruled the state. He put into effect a fundamentalist Islamic revolution, during which Iran reverted to strict Islamic practices.

NIKITA KHRUSHCHEV

(1894–1971)

Soviet premier who denounced Stalinism and the "personality cult" of Soviet politics that revered the "great leader" Stalin and led to the suppression of independent thought. Initially promoted to different government posts under Stalin, Krushchev was a poltical officer during the great fight against the Nazis at Stalingrad. After Stalin's death, he became first secretary of the party and made Nikolai Bulganin, known as the "Mayor of Moscow," premier. Eventually he ousted Bulganin and made himself prime minister. Krushchev steered a roller-coaster political course, sometimes relying on threats, other times opting for conciliatory measures. He attempted to revitalize Soviet Union, but was ousted in 1964 because of his confrontational stance toward China (considered more a threat than the U.S.) and because of his eccentricities.

HELMUT KOHL

(1930–)

West German chancellor noted most recently for his push to integrate East Germany into West Germany, a move that wound up working—so far. Kohl has been facing recent problems, though, due to weak economy, social problems of reunification, and more. He is noted for essentially centrist political stance: conservative, yet supported state intervention in the economy. Kohl has been active in supporting Germany's position within the European Community.

VLADIMIR ILYICH LENIN (ORIGINALLY ULYANOV)

(1870–1924)

Russian Marxist revolutionary and founder of the Union of Soviet Socialist Republics (U.S.S.R.). Born into a middle-class family, Lenin was educated as a lawyer, but became a fervent Marxist and was arrested and exiled for his views by the czarist Russian government. In exile, he edited a political newspaper *Iskra* (*The Spark*), and worked to build an underground political party. During World War I, he was allowed by the Germans to cross their territory back into Russia; during the October Revolution he seized power and declared the "dictatorship of the proletariat" with himself in charge. Lenin revolutionized Russian society. He fought a fierce civil war with White monarchists until triumphant in the early 1920s. Because the economy was suffering, he instituted the NEP (New Economic Policy), which allowed limited free market enterprise, in effect a step backward from communist economics. But Lenin was a pragmatist. When he died, he left a statement proposing that Josef Stalin be removed from political power, something Stalin made sure was not generally known.

NELSON MANDELA

(1918–)

South African president, African nationalist leader—and symbol of black South African fight against apartheid. As member of African National Congress (ANC), he led a campaign against South African government. Arrested for incitement in 1964, Mandela gave a famous four-hour defense speech, but was sentenced to life imprisonment. Amid international pressure, he was released from prison in 1990 (earlier efforts for his release required that he renounce violence; he refused to do so unless apartheid was ended and blacks were granted full political rights). He reentered political arena as a spokesperson for racial equality and was elected president of South Africa in the country's first free election.

GOLDA MEIR

(1898–1978)

Israeli prime minister, noted for her outspokenness. Born Golda Mabovitz in Kiev, Russia, she was raised in Milwaukee, Wisconsin, and emigrated to Palestine in 1921 with her husband, Morris Myerson. He died in 1951 and five years later she took the Hebrew name "Meir," meaning "to burn brightly." And burn brightly she did, turning into one of the most prominent Zionists and later, after Israel's statehood, one of its most well-known lead-

ers, becoming prime minister in 1969. A key problem throughout her prime ministership: conflicting views about the Arab territories occupied in 1967's Six-Day War. (Right-wingers led by Moshe Dayan wanted to colonize them; moderates wanted to return them as part of a peace settlement.) She was known for her initial diplomatic efforts to resolve the Arab-Israeli problem, which changed during the fourth Arab-Israeli war, the Yom Kippur War. She resigned in 1974, after her coalition government couldn't form cohesive policies.

MOHAMMAD REZA PAHLAVI

(1919–1980)

Shah of Iran whose social reforms and ties to the West ultimately led to his downfall. He flip-flopped between liberalism and straight autocratic authority. Reforms (such as the emancipation of women) as well as his wealth and somewhat extravagant lifestyle led to denunciations of "Western degeneracy," death threats, and, finally, the complete decline of his power. After he fled the country, Ayatollah Khomeini returned and set up a revolutionary government. He entered the U.S. for medical treatment, leaving Khomeini forces to seize the U.S. embassy, taking staffers hostage, demanding the shah's return. He eventually settled in Egypt and died there.

BENITO MUSSOLINI

(1883–1945)

Italian dictator called "Il Duce" (simply, the Leader) who hoped to establish a new Fascist Roman Empire. He first came to power in 1922 (appointed by King Victor Emmanuel III, who wanted to avoid a communist revolution), then gave himself *absolute* power in 1928. Mussolini was noted for his public works programs, economic and foreign policies (which included annexing Albania and Abyssinia) . . . as well as his ruthlessness and intolerance. He entered World War II allied with Hitler, and everything fell apart. He wound up trying to escape to Switzerland in German uniform, but was captured by Italian partisans who shot him and his mistress. Their bodies were taken to Milan, his old seat of power, for public display and vilification.

GAMAL ABDEL NASSER

(1918–1970)

President of Egypt and considered by many to be the political father of his country—the United Arab Republic. One of the leaders of the military junta that overthrew King Farouk, he was immensely popular when president, particularly for his success in getting the British to withdraw from the Suez Canal. He gained prestige among other Arab nations for the outcome of the Suez crisis when Israel invaded Sinai— and was pressured to withdraw by the

U.N. and the U.S. Although he presided over a largely undemocratic, centralized government, he was largely responsible for working to modernize Egypt, for significant land reform, and for setting Egypt as one of the leaders of the Pan-Arab movement. In his time, Nasserism, a mixture of Arab pride, socialism, and secular ideas, was a potent political movement throughout the Arab world.

JAWAHARLAL NEHRU

(1889–1964)

First prime minister of an independent India and one of the most influential leaders of India—and, in fact, of the Third World. Considered by some to be the father of Third World politics as a driving force of the nonaligned movement, which sought a path between the Soviet and American blocs, he pushed for industrialization and breakdown of traditional Hindu social practices and generally advocated gradual modernization.

KWAME NKRUMAH

(1909–1972)

First president of the republic of Ghana and considered a founding father. A Maoist who advocated extensive economic reforms, he ran into heavy political opposition. Called "the Gandhi of Africa" for his role in setting up the republic, he led a life that was far from austere. In the 1950s, he was a leader of the nonaligned movement and a key leader in the developing world. Personal extravagance as well as poorly planned public works programs drove the economy into the ground and he was ousted by the military.

JULIUS KAMBARAGE NYERERE

(1922–)

First president of independent Tanganyika, later United Republic of Tanzania, which includes the island of Zanzibar. One of the most respected and popular African leaders, he was called "Mwalimu" (Teacher) by his countrypeople. He led his country to independence as founder and leader of the Tanganyika African National Union. Nyerere was noted for his moderate politics, particularly in face of strong Marxist left wing. He hoped to institute a socialism based on rural values, but his dream was sapped by a poor economy and war against Ugandan dictator Idi Amin. He resigned the presidency in 1985, but remained leader of his party.

PAHLAVI, MOHAMMAD REZA

See Mohammad Reza Pahlavi.

JUAN DOMINGO PERÓN

(1895–1974)

Argentine president and husband of charismatic Eva (Evita) Perón, who helped secure his position. Perón was a Fascist who rose to power on the shoulders of the *descamisados* (unshirted ones), a civilian paramilitary force drawn from the lower classes, securing their support by his nationalistic, anti–American big business stance. He tried to modernize through government intervention and quashed his opponents by any means, including torture. He was deposed by the army in 1955, but his peronistas still remained a political force and he regained office in 1973 (when another man won, but stepped aside for him). He died in office, leaving the presidency to his vice president, *second* wife, Isabel.

YITZHAK RABIN

(1922–1995)

Israeli soldier and statesman, best known for his active role leading his country toward peace with the Palestinians. Born in Jerusalem, he initially followed a career in the army—fighting in the War of Independence (1948–1949) and rising through the ranks to become chief of staff of the Israeli Defense Forces. In this position, he headed the armed forces during the Six-Day War of 1967 and became a national hero. He was appointed ambassador to the U.S. from 1968 to 1973. Upon returning to Israel, he switched to national politics, becoming leader of the Labor Party and, upon Golda Meir's resignation, prime minister in 1974. During this tenure, he had several secret meetings with King Hussein of Jordan in an attempt to start peace negotiations with him. But his image was damaged due to violation of currency laws, and he resigned. He later returned to government as minister of defense in a Labor–Likkud national unity coalition and ultimately was elected prime minister again in 1992. During this period, he began actively pursuing peace negotiations with the Palestinians, culminating in a historic meeting with PLO leader Yasir Arafat on the South Lawn of the White House on September 13, 1993. While his support of peace gained him international praise, and the Nobel Peace Prize, it also met with controversy with the right-wing politicians of Israel as well as with Israeli settlers. He was assassinated by a right-wing Israeli extremist after a peace rally in late 1995.

MUHAMMAD ANWAR AL-SADAT

(1918–1981)

Egyptian president and staunch nationalist, perhaps best known for his Middle East peace initiatives. Sadat's political career was closely linked to Nasser's: was member of the conspiracy to overthrow King Farouk; vice-president under Nasser; and successor to the presidency. He ultimately broke with Nasser's politics to seek Middle

East peace—culminating in the Camp David talks with Israeli Prime Minister Menachem Begin and U.S. President Jimmy Carter and the signing of a peace treaty with Israel (the only Arab leader at the time to do so). For his efforts, he was co-winner of Nobel Peace Prize . . . and also was eventually assassinated by Muslim fundamentalists, probably more because of the failure of his internal economic policies.

JOSEF STALIN

(1879–1953)

Soviet dictator noted for his ruthless policies. His motto: "Socialism in One Country." And to this end, Stalin's leadership led to a bloodbath and the death of up to 10 million peasants either by direct execution or famine. He served under Lenin after the Bolshevik revolution of 1917, and built up power base to win leadership after Lenin's death, becoming dictator. However, his emphasis on heavy industry was probably successful, building up Soviet economic power in time to allow it to counter Hitler's invasion. He increased Soviet empire during World War II and helped start the Cold War with non-communist countries.

SUKARNO

(1901–1970)

Founding president of Indonesia and prime mover in the fight for Indonesian independence who fell due to accusations of corruption and increasing poverty. Inspired by Mohandas Gandhi, Sukarno formed Partai Nasional Indonesia, which espoused nonviolence. He became president of Indonesia—with absolute rule—after Japan surrendered at end of World War II. At first extremely popular, he lost the support of his people when his high lifestyle contrasted with extreme poverty of Indonesia and his public works programs remained uninstituted. He was deposed by General Suharto, who reversed his policies.

SUN YAT-SEN

(1866–1925)

Chinese revolutionary, considered the founding father of the Republic of China by both communists and non-communists. Founder of the Kuomintang party (Chinese National Party) and overthrower of the Manchu empire, he became first president of the republic. Sun Yat-sen advocated three principles—"Nationalism, Democracy, Socialism"—but ran into trouble with differing political factions, particularly the communists. He died of cancer still hoping to achieve unity; his widow supported Mao over Sun Yat-sen's protégé, Chiang Kai-shek, accusing him of twisting Sun's teachings. (She wound up one of three noncommunist vice-chairmen of the People's Republic and acting head of state for three years.)

MARGARET THATCHER

(1925–)

English prime minister, staunch Conservative, called the Iron Lady. Known for her unswerving positions in the face of opposition and brand of conservative politics called Thatcherism that took the Conservative Party further right. Her years in office were sometimes marked by high unemployment and economic troubles, but she reinvigorated British industry, and some economists feel that she put Britain into a better economic position than its European Community partners. Others felt she overemphasized privatization of the economy. She was a controversial leader, but most concede her competence and vigor, particularly in the Europe of her times, which seemed more geared to dull technocrats. She was reelected due to aggressive stance during the Falklands War and opposition weaknesses; later stepped down from leadership of party (which went to John Major).

JOSIP BROZ TITO

(1892–1980)

Yugoslav leader—marshal and president—who built up the Communist Party and became head of government when Yugoslavia became a republic in 1945. Tito openly defied Stalin and his policies, establishing instead a system of decentralized workers' self-government. He urged nonalignment for other socialist states, advocated a policy of "positive neutralism," and as such became a leader of the nonaligned movement and was held in high regard in Africa and Asia. His greatest accomplishment: holding together the diverse southern Slavs as one nation. His greatest failing: not providing a strong enough framework to prevent the collapse that came ten years after his death.

VO NGUYEN GIAP

(1912–)

Vietnamese military leader and mastermind behind the communist Vietnam War strategy that led to U.S. troop withdrawal. He was Ho Chi Minh's right-hand man, militarily, for years—from leading the Viet Minh army against the French to victory at Dien Bien Phu in 1954 to planning overthrow of Khmer Rouge in Cambodia in 1978 while vice-premier of Socialist Republic of Vietnam.

LECH WALESA

(1943–)

Both a labor and political leader of Poland. Walesa rose to international prominence in 1970 while an electrician at the Lenin Shipyard in Gdansk, the site of antigovernment demonstrations and a strike. Initially a trade union organizer, he became the chair of the shipyard's strike committee—a position that led to his dismissal in 1976 after he

led a major strike. He remained active in the underground labor movement, founding the free labor union Solidarnosc (Solidarity). He then became a rallying symbol for Polish laborers and drew national and international attention to his movement as he led a series of strikes in July and August of 1980. The strikes paid off—he signed an agreement with the government, winning a number of political and economic concessions. But then martial law was declared, the union was outlawed, and Walesa and other labor leaders were imprisoned. Released almost a year later, he returned to work as an electrician, and the following year won the Nobel Prize for Peace. Five years later, in 1988, he was at it again, leading another series of strikes. And they paid off again. Another historic agreement was passed, with the government relegalizing Solidarity and setting up a new government system.

BORIS YELTSIN

(1931–)

First president of Russia after the dissolution of the Soviet Union and one of the key players in the collapse of the U.S.S.R. Yeltsin became leader and president of the largest Soviet republic, Russia, in 1990. A harsh critic of Gorbachev's policies, he urged swifter restructuring. The combination of his charisma, his message, and his ability to whip up the crowds—in addition to a dismal economic climate—helped him win strong support and, ultimately, aided in the break-up of the Soviet Union. But the continuing economic

malaise in Russia under his leadership has led to growing dissent and the renewed emergence of right-wingers.

ZHOU ENLAI

(1898–1976)

First prime minister of the People's Republic of China, Mao's right-hand man, and the main envoy between the Chinese Communist Party (CCP) and the rest of the world. Zhou was one of the founding members of the party. He tended to steer a middle course politically; as such, he was largely responsible for keeping the People's Republic on track after the Great Leap Forward and the Cultural Revolution. The main Chinese leader in the 1970s, he was creator of China's "Four Modernizations" program (1975) and supervisor of détente with the U.S.—leading many people to believe he was the real leader of China, not Mao.

THE NOT SO UNITED NATIONS

Everything will be all right—you know when? When people, just people, stop thinking of the United Nations as a weird Picasso abstraction and see it as a drawing they made themselves.

—Dag Hammarskjöld,
the U.N.'s greatest secretary-general

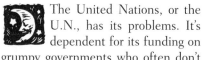 The United Nations, or the U.N., has its problems. It's dependent for its funding on grumpy governments who often don't pay, particularly when a vote goes against them (the U.S. is several hundred million dollars behind in dues). It's a lumpy bureaucracy that often serves as a dumping ground for foreign diplomats who are too obstreperous or incompetent back home. And not so long ago it had a man who served in the Nazi army as its secretary-general. It sometimes takes a political tone that can seem outlandish or unfair, and in some cases it has been powerless to act when action was needed, particularly with the tragic case of Bosnia. But as a world forum that promotes peace and cooperation, it seems to be gaining in importance, influence, and efficacy.

Under its auspices millions of starving children have been fed, the dread smallpox disease has been eliminated, and numerous projects have helped the world's poor. Its troops have restored or preserved fragile peace agreements from Zaire (the Congo) to Cyprus. It has provided a forum that has let off diplomatic steam and perhaps avoided war; it is often the only place the smaller nations can be heard.

UNITED NATIONS BUILDING (REPRODUCED FROM THE COLLECTIONS OF THE LIBRARY OF CONGRESS)

And at times it has led the fight against aggression.

Origins of the U.N.: During World War II, the nations allied against Nazi Germany referred to themselves as the United Nations; by 1942 they began laying down the bases for a formal world body to keep the peace and promote cooperation. In late spring 1945, as the war was ending, delegates from 50 nations met in San Francisco to draft the charter of the United Nations, a world assembly of nations.

The idea for such an assembly was not new: after World War I the victorious nations had set up the League of Nations, but the League had died an untimely death. It was unable to prevent war; it was unable to do much of anything, in large part because the U.S. never joined. Like the League, the new U.N. organization had a difficult task ahead. It would have to keep the peace, but it would have little power to enforce its rules. But at least this time the U.S. joined the world body.

How it's organized: The U.N. is organized something like the U.S. government in that it has a legislative branch (the General Assembly and the Security Council), a judicial branch (the International Court of Justice), and an executive branch (the Secretariat and subsidiary organizations). But there are significant differences, of course. Members of the General Assembly and the Security Council are not politicians but diplomats, appointed by the host government. And the U.N. cannot tax its members or individuals; many other powers of government are also denied it. Headquarters are in New York, but other subsidiary agencies are based in Europe, Africa, and Asia.

Here's a brief sketch of how the U.N. works, with a listing of the main organizations.

General Assembly

In effect the Congress of the U.N., but instead of individual congressmen and -women, the members are nations

of the world. Each member nation delegation gets one vote. The General Assembly meets every fall, from late September through January. State leaders and foreign ministers drop in to give their views; usually the U.S. president addresses the General Assembly once during its session. It's an important place, particularly for smaller nations, to be heard internationally. But its power is limited; it can only *discuss* or *recommend* action, and its recommendations are nonbinding on member states. It does, however, control the purse strings for U.N. programs and operations.

Security Council

Where the real power is—its decisions are theoretically binding on all member states. In reality, that power is only real if enough states with power care about its resolutions. Some decisions, like trade sanctions against a member state, are sometimes easily evaded. The Security Council consists of five permanent members—the U.S., Russia (originally the U.S.S.R.), Great Britain, France, and China (originally the Chinese nationalist government on Taiwan, later the People's Republic), plus ten other members elected by the General Assembly from among their members serving two-year terms. The Security Council is charged with investigating and discussing all issues that might lead to war or international problems (which is why you always hear it mentioned during crises) and recommends action, including collective armed action (such as occurred in Korea in 1950–1953 and in Kuwait in 1990–1991). Armed action requires seven votes, including the votes of *all* the permanent members of the Security Council who are present at the Security Council session.

International Court of Justice

Made up of 15 judges who sit in The Hague, the Netherlands, and who rule on legal disputes brought to it by member nations. Since nation-states are sovereign unto themselves, no nation is compelled to accept a finding by the court (in fact, the U.S. ignored it when the court found that it was misbehaving in Latin America), and the court can't enforce its decisions. Nevertheless, a negative ruling by the International Court does carry at least moral weight.

The Secretariat

This is the executive branch of the U.N.; it carries on the day-to-day work under the leader, or secretary-general, of the United Nations. The U.N. secretaries-general have been Trygve Lie, Dag Hammarskjöld (widely seen as a hero, he died in a plane crash trying to bring peace to the Congo), U Thant, Kurt Waldheim (considered an embarrassment due to his past membership in the Nazi army), Javier Pérez de Cuellar, and Boutros Boutros-Ghali, who has been attempting to increase U.N. power and prestige.

The U.N. also includes a number of special agencies under its aegis that carry out many vital functions. Heads of these agencies are nominated by member states of the U.N., usually with a fair amount of backroom maneuvering as nations jockey to put their diplomats in positions of influence. In most cases the functions of these agencies are obvious from the name:

UNICEF: United Nations International Children's Emergency Fund

FAO: Food and Agriculture Organization of the United Nations

UNESCO: United Nations Educational, Scientific, and Cultural Organization (This organization has been plagued by charges that its leadership is more interested in cushy jobs than in doing anything; its main function is to promote literacy and world science, and conserve the world's cultural heritage.

WHO: World Health Organization (One of the crowning achievements of the U.N., WHO promotes "the highest possible level of health" for all. It has succeeded in virtually eliminating the once-dreaded smallpox virus, and is working to eliminate other killers.)

ILO: International Labor Organization

ICAO: International Civil Aviation Organization

WMO: World Meteorological Organization

ITU: International Telecommunication Union

UPU: Universal Postal Union

IBRD: International Bank for Reconstruction and Development (This bank, headquartered in Washington, D.C., is usually called the World Bank.)

IMF: International Monetary Fund (A world agency that stabilizes currencies, provides credit, and promotes economic cooperation.)

The United Nations Universal Declaration of Human Rights

"All human beings are born free and equal in dignity and rights."

So begins the *Universal Declaration of Human Rights,* adopted unanimously by the United Nations General Assembly on December 10, 1948 (with the Soviet Union, the nations of Eastern Europe, South Africa, and Saudi Arabia abstaining). Since its passage, some newer nations have included the Declaration in their constitutions.

The Declaration is not as influential as it could be, but it is a start toward the worldwide recognition that all of us possess certain human rights. In thirty brief articles, the Declaration states the right of humans to:

- be free from any discrimination
- enjoy equality before the law
- have access to free and unhindered travel
- a nationality and the right to change a nationality
- work
- equal pay for equal work
- rest and leisure
- adequate medical care and security in the event of unemployment, sickness, or disability
- education
- "a social and international order in which the rights and freedoms set forth in this Declaration can be fully realized"

Clearly, the Declaration goes quite a bit beyond the other famous documents of liberty, such as the U.S. Bill of Rights and the French *Declaration of the Rights of Man.* It is seemingly revolutionary: some of its provisions might be denounced as "communistic" by some, or as impractical and overly idealistic by others. Yet in the face of the immense poverty, sickness, and inhumanity still bedeviling so many in the world, the Declaration stands at the very least as a worthwhile ideal.

Recently, Chinese dissidents seeking democracy in China quoted the Declaration as a justification for their demands. The Chinese government responded by arresting them. But their quest for rights and democracy continues.

YOU HAFTA KNOW ABOUT NAFTA: FIVE WORLD ACRONYMS YOU SHOULD KNOW

EC: European Community

(formerly the EEC, the European Economic Community; generally called the Common Market)

In unity there is strength. The EC is the name of the community of European nations that cooperate economically and politically. Together, the members of the EC make up an economy larger than that of the U.S. Size like that means economic and political clout.

The EEC came before (and led to) the EC. The EEC (European Economic Community) was founded in 1958 by the Treaty of Rome with the purpose of establishing a customs union, or in other words, a free trade zone within its boundaries, and to adopt a common tariff policy with all other nations. The original members included France, the Federal Republic of Germany, Italy, Belgium, the Netherlands, and Luxembourg. Great Britain, Ireland, and Denmark joined in 1973, Greece in 1981, and then Spain and Portugal in 1986.

As it became more successful economically, the EEC began evolving into a political entity as well. In 1967 the EEC set up a European Parliament, a Court of Justice, and other cooperative political institutions. The trend was toward removing not only all

economic barriers, but of many political barriers as well—allowing citizens of member nations to travel between countries without a passport, for example, with a "United States of Europe" as an ultimate goal. As the political aspect has become more important, the EEC evolved into the EC.

Many other European nations have applied to join as well, including Turkey (which controls a tiny chunk of European land—they were politely rejected). At the same time, many people within the EC have opposed political unity, but so far, the majority seem to favor the idea.

GATT: General Agreement on Tariffs and Trade

GATT is one of those subjects that bore almost everyone, which is why this very important treaty is either skipped or skimmed over in news programs. But it may be a major reason why your European car or Japanese camera doesn't cost you more. More important, GATT tries to keep world trade humming—which means jobs for everyone.

GATT is a treaty that took effect in 1948 under the aegis of the U.N. and now includes over 135 member nations. It's basically a framework of rules on trade that governments agree to abide by. It tries to make certain that trade restrictions set by governments do not discriminate among member countries; it also sets rules on international finance and the environment; and it tries (and succeeds) in getting member nations to lower tariffs—and so make trade freer and foreign goods cheaper. Most important, GATT established an international forum for trade talks (and arguments) among member nations. If the U.S. thinks Japan is being unfair, dumping cheap cars here and then not letting us sell our cars there (by tacking on customs duties or being persnickety about rules and regulations), the U.S. goes to GATT, which then holds discussions (which any interested member nation may join) and makes suggestions, including possible retaliation against nations with trade practices deemed unfair.

GATT is important because before it existed, governments had a tendency to raise tariffs, which made imports expensive and so kept a lot of foreign products out. Once one government did this, the tendency was for others to follow suit, setting a cycle of retaliatory tariffs that got higher and higher. Result: less trade, fewer jobs, maybe a depression. (Many argue that the Smoot-Hawley tariffs enacted in the U.S. deepened the Great Depression.) GATT is probably vital, although some say that all it really does is ratify the status quo.

NAFTA: North American Free Trade Agreement

The EEC was so successful that the U.S., Mexico, and Canada decided to try their own version, gradually eliminating trade barriers among the three nations. The idea is basic: if trade is freer, it's easier for *all* three economies to grow faster, and for more jobs to result. There was much opposition to this agreement in the U.S. and Canada whose citizens feared that jobs would migrate south to Mexico, where labor costs are cheaper. But the agreement passed in Congress and passed muster in Canada and Mexico. Today NAFTA is in effect.

NATO: North Atlantic Treaty Organization

NATO was founded shortly after World War II, in 1949, "to protect the principles of democracy and law" and (the real reason) to protect the member states against aggression from the Soviet Union. NATO was not at all concerned with the violation of democracy and law in Spain under General Franco, but it was very concerned with any and all moves by the Soviet Union.

NATO's basic mission was to coordinate allied military forces in the event of a Russian attack, and to intimidate the Russians from even contemplating action by holding joint exercises and basing U.S. troops in Europe. Troops under NATO remain under control of the nations supplying them. Another acronym you may see in connection with NATO is SHAPE, which stands for Supreme Headquarters of Allied Powers in Europe. It is the operational body of NATO, the nerve center where troop movements are coordinated and the Supreme Allied Commander works (if you're interested, his acronym is SCAP). SHAPE is located in Brussels.

The original member states were Belgium, Canada, Denmark, France, Great Britain, Iceland, Italy, Luxembourg, the Netherlands, Norway, Portugal, and the U.S. Greece and Turkey became members in 1952, while West Germany joined a bit later, in 1955 (and so in effect did East Germany when the two Germanies were reunified in 1990). And Spain entered in 1982. France under Charles de Gaulle took its military forces out, but didn't quit NATO itself. Currently, much of Eastern Europe wants to join NATO and integrate themselves with the Western powers—they're still afraid of Russia. So far, NATO has been wary about accepting new members, which would mean new commitments. Also, with the end of the Cold War NATO's functions are a little vague. Many are saying it needs more vigorous leadership and a more clearly defined mission. For example, it took a lot of handwringing and negotiating for NATO members to agree to intervene in the Serbian conflict should the Serbians not stop shelling the Bosnians.

Note: NATO wasn't the only defensive acronym founded to stop the Soviets, but it was the only one that lasted. For trivia enthusiasts, there was also CENTO (Central Asia Treaty Organization), which included Iraq, Iran, and Turkey, and SEATO (Southeast Asia Treaty Organization), which became superfluous after Vietnam fell to the communists. And the Soviets formed the Warsaw Pact, which was their equivalent of NATO. It fell apart with the collapse of the communist nations in Eastern Europe.

OPEC: Organization of Petroleum Exporting Countries

OPEC is a cartel, an organization of producers who got together to manipulate the price of oil on the world market. Once, it was really just another little known organization of nations that exported oil. It had little power, even though its members accounted for a high proportion of the world's oil production. Most members are Middle Eastern countries (although Venezuela, Nigeria, Indonesia, and Gabon are also members). They owned the oil that lay underneath their land, but the Seven Sisters—large Western oil companies like Mobil and Shell—controlled the actual drilling and production and made most of the decisions. But in the 1970s, the OPEC nations realized that if they stayed united they could control oil prices, and the Western powers who buy most of their oil could do little about it. How could they do this? Simple. Just decide to drill less. By the inexorable economic laws of supply and demand, less oil means higher prices per barrel, as competing states keep bidding up the price. In 1973 the Arab OPEC nations put an embargo on oil exports, partly in response to the Arab-Israeli wars and partly because they thought they were overproducing. Oil prices quadrupled and the Arabs gained much political power as well, as Western nations scrambled to "understand" their views. In recent years, OPEC's power has waned. They face many problems that most cartels ultimately face: it's often hard to keep up a united front. Some producers want to drill more oil (which lowers prices but increases revenues through greater sales); others want to keep the price high and production low. Several times each year OPEC nations meet to try to set production targets and that's where the political squabbling starts. But don't underestimate OPEC—it still controls about $150 billion of annual oil exports, over half the world's production. It still has the potential to flex its economic muscle.

MULTILATERAL ISSUES: NOT SO BORING ANYMORE

 It's a small world and it's getting smaller. Now many new issues, like the environment, have cropped up that would have been ignored a few years back. We're not talking about specific territory here, about who owns a certain piece of land. Instead, we're talking about pollution, food supplies, weapons—a grab bag of issues that affect all or at least many nations. In the Cold War days of diplomacy the negotiations over these issues were often farmed out to low-level diplomats (except for arms issues, which spawned a techno-diplomatic elite who used to eat caviar and negotiate in the great hotels of Geneva). No longer. In today's small world these issues are vitally important and *everyone's* involved.

NUCLEAR, CHEMICAL, AND BIOLOGICAL WEAPONS PROLIFERATION: The Crazy World of Bombs and Missiles

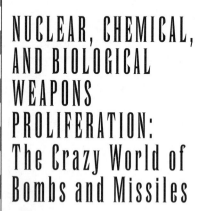

The issue: Nuclear, chemical, and biological weapons are in the arsenals of nations across the globe. No one worries much if France builds another nuclear bomb, but what about North Korea? How can the world stop the spread of dangerous weapons and reduce the chances of war?

The stakes: Extremely high. We used to worry only about nuclear war, but now we're also worried about chemical or biological terrorism by small pariah states, as well as regional nuclear wars.

Background: When the U.S. built an atomic bomb during World War II, it was in a race against scientists in Nazi Germany. Both sides were working feverishly to develop a superweapon that would decide the outcome of the war. The U.S. won the race and the war. And for a brief while it held a monopoly on nuclear weapons. But then the Soviet Union made it a nuclear club and the nuclear arms race was on.

For a long time the principal threat to the world was from the huge numbers of nuclear weapons these two superpowers stocked up and aimed at each other. Operating under a theory called Mutual Assured Destruction (MAD), both powers built up nuclear arsenals so large that it was assumed the other side wouldn't dare launch an attack because it would surely be destroyed in turn. Maybe this theory was correct, but it wasn't comforting to think that the world could be obliterated.

Meanwhile, some theorists argued that a *limited* nuclear war was at least a feasible possibility, an even less comforting thought since it raised the *probability* of nuclear war. Some small

NUCLEAR WEAPONS PROLIFERATION: ATOMIC BOMB MUSHROOM CLOUD OVER BIKINI ATOLL, 1946
(REPRODUCED FROM THE COLLECTIONS OF THE LIBRARY OF CONGRESS)

nations were listening and quietly working on their own arms programs. As the Soviets and the Americans worked on reducing their nuclear and missile arsenals through long-winded and tricky arms reduction negotiations (you may remember them by their acronyms: SALT, Strategic Arms Limitation Talks; START, Strategic Arms Reduction Talks; etc.) and as the Cold War wound down, both sides became much more worried about smaller nations getting nuclear weapons. In 1968 the Non-Proliferation Treaty (NPT) was passed. The International Atomic Energy Agency (IAEA) was charged with inspecting nuclear plants to make sure that bombs were not being built by non-nuclear powers. In 1991, the IAEA dismantled Iraq's nuclear bomb program in the aftermath

of the Gulf War. But several states, such as Israel, have not joined, and others, like North Korea, have resigned.

The problem and solutions today: So who's got nukes? The U.S. was the first to get them in 1945, followed by the Soviet Union (1949), then Great Britain (1952), then France (1960), China (1964), and India (1974). In addition, Israel is believed to have some, Pakistan might have some, and South Africa said it had built some but then dismantled them. The major worries today are:

North Korea: Recently agreed to suspend nuclear bomb program. But the military is not happy about the suspension. The danger level is still high.

Iran: Said to be following up on work

Who Has Missiles Besides the Superpowers

Country	Range (miles)	Possible Targets
Saudi Arabia	1,700	Most of the Middle East, including Israel
Israel	900	Syria, Iraq, Egypt, Lebanon, Jordan, Saudi Arabia, Iran
Czech Republic	300	Germany, much of neighboring Eastern Europe
Bulgaria	300	Turkey, Greece, Balkan states
Iran	175	Iraq, Kuwait, Azerbaijan
Syria	175	Israel, Jordan, Iraq, Iran, Turkey
Egypt	175	Libya, Sudan, Israel, Saudi Arabia
Yemen	175	Saudi Arabia, Oman
Afghanistan	175	Pakistan, Tajikistan
Pakistan	175	India
India	175	Pakistan, Nepal, Bangladesh
North Korea	175	South Korea, Russia, China
South Korea	175	North Korea
Poland	175	Germany, Belarus, Ukraine, Russia
Romania	175	Serbia, Ukraine, Hungary, Moldova
Hungary	175	Serbia, Romania, Austria
Cuba	45	U.S.

done by the shah's scientists in the 1970s, expected to have a bomb by the end of the 1990s.

Pakistan: If it has or develops some nuclear weapons, the worry is it might get involved in a small nuclear war with India, or transfer the bombs to Islamic allies in the Middle East.

New states in the Soviet Union: With the exception of Russia, these former Soviet republics have agreed to give up their weapons—but some are stalling. It's hard to give up the power that comes from owning a weapon. The problem is that this is a very volatile area; some states may get the temptation to use the weapons or threaten others. And others may sell the bombs or the technology to make them. Recently, Russia agreed to sell nuclear technology to the Iranians.

Brazil and Argentina were also said to be developing nuclear capabilities in the 1980s, but new civilian governments called off the programs.

But forget nuclear weapons for a second. Even if you have a bomb, the key is *delivering* it. And that's where missiles come in.

The frightening thing about missiles is that they're easier to build than nuclear bombs, and they can deliver cheaper and easier to make chemical and biological weapons, as well as nuclear ones. Naturally, the great powers don't favor the spread of missiles either (although they've sometimes been willing to sell the technology). The Ballistic Missile Control Regime is an agreement by which major powers are trying to halt missile proliferation, but in general it hasn't been too successful. Just so you can worry a bit, above are

Terrorism:
An Enduring International Problem

The good news is that *international* terrorist incidents appear to be declining. The latest reports indicate the number of terrorist incidents declined by 25% in 1994. Governments and citizens are less tolerant of "freedom fighters" who kill innocent civilians to make a political point; and more nations are vigorously fighting them. According to the U.S. State Department Coordinator for Counterterrorism, "There's less ambivalence in the world today that terrorism is a crime, whereas in the past there was often a tendency to look the other way, because of the political motivation of the terrorists." In addition, the fall of the Soviet Union destroyed a prime supporter of international terrorists, and the winding down of conflicts in places like South Africa and Northern Ireland has reduced the arenas for activity.

But the bad news is that international terrorism in one area, the Middle East, is increasing, as hold-out factions in the Middle East peace process resort to terror to destroy negotiations. In 1994 alone more than a hundred civilians died in the West Bank and another hundred were killed in a car bombing of a Jewish center in Buenos Aires.

Also on the rise: domestic or local terrorism. The U.S. suffered the horrors of the bombing in Oklahoma City in 1995, but many in other nations still face similar horrors within their borders, particularly in the Middle East as Muslim fundamentalists battle to overturn secular governments. In Peru, one of the last leftist terrorist movements, called the Shining Path, utilizes terror to threaten the capitalist government.

Terrorism is an intractable problem. Although governments promise even greater vigilance, it is virtually impossible to stop. But as an international *political* problem terrorism is considered by most experts to be relatively minor—casualties are low relative to wars, and terrorists rarely influence political events all that decisively. But the horror they spread is all too real.

the nations (in addition to the major powers) that own missiles. As you can see from the third column, there's a fair amount of potential for conflict.

Theoretically, according to treaty, the missiles can't be loaded with anything beyond conventional weapons. But that doesn't mean much. A 1925 treaty banned using chemical weapons in war but it didn't ban their manufacture or possession. In 1992 a new treaty banned owning, making, and using them—but that didn't stop Iraq from deploying them on Kurdish villagers during the Iraq-Iran war.

Meanwhile, although biological weapons—destructive bacteria and viruses that can kill or sicken millions—are banned, nations may conduct *research* on them. The frightening thing here is the unknown—can mistakes happen and inadvertently destroy human life on earth? How do you *limit* a biological weapon; once released will its toxins circle the globe?

The major worries here are:

Iraq, Syria, Libya: All said to have conducted bio-weapons research, all in an unstable portion of the world, all governed by ruthless leaders.

Nations of the former Soviet Union: Evidently conducted bio-weapons research during the Cold War. Will some of their technology or weapons get out to other nations? The same applies to the *U.S.*

The Cold War may be over, but the potential for destruction isn't. To repeat a cliché that governments just ignore: it's about time we all grew up and put a stop to this madness.

THE LAW OF THE SEA: Who Owns the Oceans?

The issue: Who gets the riches of the world's oceans, which make up 70% of the earth? These riches include fish and other sea life in the water, and minerals and oil under the water potentially worth a fortune.

The stakes: Not too high for now, except for local disputes like a Greek-Turkish dispute over the Aegean Sea, which may contain oil. But ultimately the problems could escalate, as technology improves and it becomes easier to extract undersea minerals.

Background: A long time ago, the major issue in international affairs was freedom of the seas. An even longer time ago, there was no such thing. Nothing prevented one nation from simply grabbing the ships of another. This could be profitable for the nation doing the grabbing, but obviously, if it sent out its own trading ships, they too risked seizure. So it really was a lose-lose situation. During the Thirty Years War of Europe (1618–1648), the concept of free navigation was worked out by the Dutch legal scholar Hugo Grotius. At the time, the Netherlands was a great sea power, and Dutch ships guaranteed that navigation would be unhindered. Later, as the British became a great sea power, they took on the job, and later they were followed to a great degree by the U.S.

All states were guaranteed freedom of the seas. And all states with a coastline could claim jurisdiction and sovereignty over waters within three nautical miles from their coasts (a nautical mile is 15% more than a regular mile).

But the desire for profit ended this harmonious state of affairs. Rich fisheries far offshore and even richer mineral beds led some states to claim exclusive economic rights 12 miles and even 200 miles off their coastlines. Other states objected, and then some responded by seizing fishing boats in their claimed offshore waters. A dispute has started.

The problem and solutions today: Trying to find a solution, 86 states met at the United Nations Conference on the Law of the Sea (UNCLOS) in 1958, but they failed to agree, except on minor issues. The problem: the U.S., Soviet Union, and Britain didn't want other nations to extend their economic zones—they were making too much money fishing in these coastal waters. Finally, a third UNCLOS conference produced an agreement that allowed a 12-mile territorial limit, a 200-mile "exclusive economic zone" where each state would control mineral and fishing rights, and a 350-mile zone (and sometimes more) with mineral rights if the continental shelf extends out that far. This put one third of the world's ocean in the hands of states with a coastline, with the U.S., Australia, Indonesia, New Zealand, Canada, Russia, Japan, Brazil, Mexico, and Chile the big winners, controlling over half.

But the U.S. and its allies didn't initially sign, principally because the treaty declared that minerals outside the zone are at least partially for the benefit of mankind. In other words, if a U.S. mining company finds manganese on the seabed far out to sea, it has to share its profits with the world. There are political problems as well.

With this huge new limit, will some nations restrict freedom of navigation?

The jury is still out. Many nations are enforcing the 200-mile exclusive economic zone limit, even though the treaty is not really in effect. And so the seas are now a little less free—and a lot more profitable for some.

THE WORLD ENVIRONMENT: Who Cleans Up the Mess—and How Can We Stop Making Such a Mess?

The issue: Increasing industrialization and population are destroying the environment. But the real problem is that this problem is no longer local: if the U.S. pollutes, some of its pollution reaches everyone else. Increasingly pollution is a global rather than a local concern. And the same extends to other environmental issues as well—they now affect all of us.

The stakes: It depends on who you talk to. Some scientists and politicians feel we're rapidly heading for ecological disaster; others feel the fears are overblown by the media. One thing is for certain: time will tell.

Background: Industrialization is causing widespread ecological degradation. Let's separate the main issues:

Global warming: Is there a slow long-term rise in earth temperature? The issue isn't about better beach weather, but about potential disaster in the form of melting ice caps and widespread flooding, changed weather patterns and crop disasters. (But it could also improve the weather for some regions.) It's caused—if it's happening—by greenhouse gases. These gases are created by burning fossil fuels in cars, electric generators, and factories. Gases such as chlorofluorocarbons (CFCs) used in refrigerators are also culpable. All these gases concentrate in the atmosphere, bounce back sunlight, and in short, act like a gaseous greenhouse for the earth by trapping heat. This is clearly a worldwide problem if the threat is real.

Air pollution: CFCs are also the culprit in the depletion of the ozone layer surrounding the earth, which lets in more ultraviolet radiation, which in turn may cause crop failures, a rise in skin cancer rates, and disrupt ecosystems. (A scary harbinger of the effects seems to be a rapid decline in the world frog population; apparently, the extra sunlight kills their eggs. Frogs aren't people, but they may be like canaries in a mine, warning of disasters to come.) The fossil fuels mentioned above are also producing air pollution in the form of smog and acid rain, which is destroying forests and human lungs. Much air pollution crosses international boundaries: half of Canada's dirty air, for example, comes from us.

Water pollution: Pesticides, sewage, industrial waste—all are poured into the water and into the world's oceans. The Mediterranean is probably the most polluted body of

water in the world (although the inland seas in the former Soviet Union win the prize for toxicity), since it is hard to control dumping from so many nations.

Loss of biodiversity, forests, and natural habitat: Who cares about the Amazon rain forest? Maybe all of us. It supports the greatest number of species per square mile in the world, and is a potential gold mine of medicinal plants and biological information. It's also beautiful and unknown—and is being cut down and burned at a very fast clip, particularly after Brazil opened more branches of the Trans-Amazon highway. Ironically, as many concerned U.S. citizens were protesting the rain forest destruction, they weren't looking too closely at the clear cutting going on in the Pacific Northwest. The problem is evident: jobs (loggers, farmers, etc.) versus the environment. Which will win? Or is there a win-win solution?

The problem and solutions today: It's one thing to talk about impending disaster, it's another thing to get the many nations of the world to do something about it. But some action has been taken.

With air pollution, the developed nations of America and Europe agreed in 1985 to limit sulfur dioxide emissions (a key cause of acid rain) with "gas scrubber" attachments to exhausts, but some nations, including the U.S., later reneged a bit, saying they had already done enough. The U.S. and Canada also agreed to study the problem of acid rain jointly and work to reduce cross-border air pollution. And in 1987 a U.N. meeting in Montreal produced an agreement to cut CFC production by half. This agreement appears to be working.

More recently, the U.N. Conference on the Environment and Development (the Earth Summit) was held in Rio de Janeiro in Brazil in 1992. More than 100 leaders from states around the world attended. Agreement has been reached for less industrialized countries to develop industries that don't pollute quite as much, and for the more industrialized nations to give technology to help reach that goal. An agreement on biodiversity (maintaining the habitats of thousands of species) was also reached. It called for nations to preserve endangered habitats like tropical rain forests; in return, developed nations agree to pay royalties for bio-products like drugs produced from plants or animals in these areas. In addition, the conference established the Sustainable Development Commission to monitor compliance with this and other provisions agreed to at the conference. One problem: the commission doesn't have enforcement powers. This is always the problem with these global issues: nations aren't willing to submit to a higher authority, so those that break the agreements rarely face penalties.

Meanwhile, other groups like the International Whaling Commission and the Inter-American Tropical Tuna Commission have produced agreements on limiting the killing of whales and dolphins. The sticking point here again is compliance: some nations such as Norway want to continue hunting whales despite international concern. As always, the real problem is the will to do something about it.

WORLD HUNGER: Why Can't We Feed Our Neighbors?

The issue: There's one way to state this issue: every *two seconds,* one child dies of malnutrition or starvation—*15 million* children every year. Roughly one out of seven of us (800 million) goes to bed hungry every night.

The stakes: Extremely high in terms of the human cost; probably not so high in terms of geopolitics. The undernourished are concentrated in the poorest parts of the Third World, that is, in Africa and some sections of southern Asia and Latin America. They don't have much clout, and they don't have much access to guns to threaten much unrest.

Background: The short-term problem is really not one of overpopulation. There is enough food and money to feed everyone on the earth today. The short-term problem is distribution, getting the food to the needy people. And before we Americans blame ourselves, much of the blame also falls on corrupt governments in the areas where people are starving. Ethiopia for years ignored warnings of impending famine (its Marxist government was too busy killing enemies and buying guns); Sudan has been very concerned about rebellion in the south and very little concerned about widespread starvation there. And very often, even with the best intentioned governments, transport is so poor that a lot of the food given as relief rots on the docks.

Although famines make the news, the real problem is rarely starvation but *malnutrition.* It weakens people and renders them susceptible to diseases like dysentery, which kills many in the Third World. About 13% of Latin Americans, 12% of Middle Easterners, 19% of Asians, and 33% of sub-Saharan Africans are chronically hungry. The problem is the worst in the Sahel, a belt of nations that extends across Africa just below the Sahara. And the problem is worse for females. Sexism is alive and well everywhere. In times of scarcity and famine, females are expected to eat less. *Eighty percent of the world's undernourished children are female,* according to estimates by the international development and relief group Oxfam.

In the long term, both starvation and malnutrition stem from underdevelopment and possibly overpopulation. Overpopulation causes economic and environmental problems, which in turn cause underdevelopment and poverty; in turn this causes malnutrition.

Believe it or not: about the only nations self-sufficient in food today are the U.S., Canada, and Australia. But this isn't a problem for most of the other nations in the world—they've earned enough money (through exports) to import the food they need (and to grow the rest). And most nations of the world (even many of the poorest) have had rising crop yields over the past ten years, which helps as well.

But in the worst areas, everything has gone wrong. In the African Sahel, for example, crop yields have decreased, while population growth has been rapid. In many other poor areas, the economy and general social trends are the prime culprits that cause malnutrition in the population.

Many developing nations have urbanized rapidly, with over half of all people living in cities. This has led many governments to subsidize food and make the price artificially low (or else face the consequences of food riots in their capitals). They import the food at high prices, absorb much of the cost, and sell it to the people cheaply. This costs money, money that instead could have been spent on development. More to the point, because food prices are low, *local* farmers have a reduced incentive to spend time and money growing crops. Instead, they may abandon the land and come to the city themselves. This produces a vicious circle—more farmers in the city, more food aid needed, less land being farmed. But even when local farmers do produce food, transportation is often so poor that food spoils before it gets to the cities. In Egypt, for example, about 45% of the tomato crop rotted by the time it got to major distribution points, according to one study.

Overpopulation also often reduces the productivity of the land that is being farmed; reduced yields lead to people devastating the countryside for firewood and food; and another vicious cycle continues.

Does food aid help? Often, sadly enough, it makes things worse. It usually keeps food prices down (since it's free) and so reduces the incentives for local farmers to produce. It often goes to cities and central distribution points, so people leave their farms in the countryside to get the food. It's often given to corrupt governments to distribute, and they may sell the food instead and use the money to buy guns. And sometimes the food aid is ridiculous: canned ham, mouthwash, hamburger mixes. In addition, these gifts along with advertising may encourage people in recipient nations to waste valuable foreign exchange money on "luxuries" that are perceived as prestigious, like baby formula and canned soda.

The problem and solutions today: So should we give up? Some experts say yes. Just help out the poorest nations with their debts, and stay out. The problem will solve itself ultimately. And they say however painful it may be, it's better in the long run.

But it's hard to accept this when faced with horrific pictures like that of a half-starved three-year-old trying to avoid a vulture waiting for her to die.

Other experts suggest we can help alleviate hunger now *and* plan for the future. The key is to be smarter than we've been in the past.

We should pay much more attention to infrastructure development; that is, we should give aid to increase local food production—seeds, implements, and animals. We should also emphasize so-called micro-loans. These are of maybe a hundred dollars or so, given directly to local farmers and entrepreneurs without big-government involvement. Even if this aid money goes to cities, it helps create small businesses, which in turn create a greater demand for farm crops. Several innovative development groups are pioneering this effort; so far it seems to be working well.

We should also encourage land reform, to get the land in the hands of the producers, not huge landowners. (And on the other hand, many add that we should encourage giant agribusinesses as well.) We should lobby governments to concentrate on rural development, not large-scale prestige development projects. And we should make sure that aid groups do their

homework. There are many stories of well-intentioned organizations "helping" by spending money on completely inappropriate projects; fish farms in vegetarian societies, for example. We should listen more. The old-style aid project sent hundreds of high-tech types from the U.S. or Europe who did almost everything. (In one case in the Sahel, over 95% of the aid budget went to pay American expert salaries, leaving 5% for the local population.) The new style is to let the locals control the project; the experts fill in with guidance or expertise when needed. The bottom line is simple: much can and should be done, but it must be done better—and smarter—than before.

ECONOMIC DEVELOPMENT: Who Gets Richer, Who Gets Poorer?

The issue: About half of the world lives in poverty, generally in the Southern Hemisphere. How can they break this grip of poverty?

The stakes: Very high in terms of human costs. And the West can be hurt politically as well: poverty breeds unrest, disease, revolution, and violence, all of which might be exported to our shores. In addition, increasing numbers of economic refugees raise a moral issue for us as well: should we accept them, and if so, which ones and how many?

On the positive side, many economists are now predicting rapid growth for many of the world's poorest areas, reducing the potential for conflict and suffering.

Background: (Note: for want of a better word, we'll call the poor nations of the world the "Third World" even though many don't like this term.)

Until the years after the European Renaissance, most nations in the world were relatively equal. No area was much richer or more powerful than any other. Food production was relatively limited and local, goods were handmade, no one area possessed a huge technological advantage over another.

Then along came the capitalist and industrial revolutions in Europe, and an increasing discrepancy in terms of wealth. Technological improvements in agriculture and industry dramatically increased wealth in Europe, by increasing productivity and quality of output. European power increased as well, in the form of ships and weapons. From the 1500s on, Europe put its power to work by colonizing most of the world. Only a few non-Western states, such as Japan, Thailand, Ethiopia, Iran, Saudi Arabia, Turkey, and Afghanistan, escaped colonization, or in the case of China, Western dominance. But did colonization cause poverty?

There's a lot of debate in this area. On the negative side, the Western colonial powers came in and stifled native peoples and their cultures, overwhelmed local elites, and established a new hierarchy. This was certainly not good for the societies they transformed. Economically, the colonial powers extracted valuable resources and built up a more modern economy—but one that was geared toward profiting the colonizer, not the colo-

The major economic movers and shakers are often minorities. Jews in Europe were among the first bankers; in Africa, the major traders were often Lebanese (West Africa) and Indians (East Africa); in Southeast Asia the major entrepreneurs are often Chinese; and in the U.S., major entrepreneurial groups include South Koreans, Indians, and Chinese. These people are often resented—and sometimes killed due to envy. The Chinese in Indonesia sometimes change their names or the names of their corporations to sound native. Idi Amin of Uganda expelled all Indians in the 1970s. Significantly, the new government of Uganda has now been inviting them back.

nized. For example, for years Britain stifled India's textile manufacturing because it feared that the lower-cost Indian textiles would put its own factories out of business.

But colonialism had some positive effects as well, in that it brought roads, railroads, technological education and ideas to the colonized areas. But even here, the technology often worked against the colonies. Railroads were often designed to bring *out* raw materials—they often didn't improve the economy or the flow of people *within* the colony. Improving sanitation and health care helped reduce infant mortality, without giving the new members of society anything productive to do. Of course, individual cases varied considerably. For a variety of reasons, for example, Indians were able to create a large educated class under colonial status who could easily build on the legacy of colonialism and ultimately defeat the British and craft an increasingly prosperous society (against tremendous odds in terms of population). On the other hand, people in the areas of Africa colonized by some nations, especially Belgium and Portugal, endured terrible exploitation. At independence, they had next to nothing except for a shattered society.

Going beyond colonization, another problem for the Third World was based on a basic law: the rich tended to get richer more easily. With huge capital surpluses, it was easier for Europeans to invest in better factories and, in turn, get even larger factories making improved goods. They could overwhelm any attempt by a Third World nation to produce manufactured goods. It was harder for the poor to make advances. So after independence many Third World nations continued doing what they had done for years—supplying the Europeans with raw materials. This created a vicious cycle of continued poverty and dependence. Another difficulty is that many Third World nations are one-crop economies; when prices drop, their economies end up near collapse. The legacy of colonialism also spawned considerable unrest, making such nations unattractive for investors to build factories in the first place.

Recently, however, the tables seemed to be turning. Economic growth rates started to increase more rapidly than in the West. It seemed easier for the poor to advance economically. But then in the 1980s, the rates started going down again, except in

Asia. In Africa, Latin America, and the Middle East, the per capita gross domestic product (GDP, a key measure of economic output) actually decreased. What happened?

The problem and solutions today: Apparently in the nations losing ground, the governments got in the way of the native productive capacity of the people. In Asia, although the governments tend to be authoritarian, they encouraged private or quasi-private production. They accepted foreign investment, built up the marketplace, and developed industries that could compete with those of the industrialized nations. For example, South Korea developed a strong steel industry (and

The Politics of the Drug Trade

Illegal drugs—marijuana, cocaine, and heroin—are an international problem the U.S. is particularly concerned with. In human terms the costs are tremendous but unmeasurable. In dollar terms, the U.S. government has estimated that drug abuse costs the U.S. about $60 billion annually in lost productivity, premature death, and drug-related crime. On the other side of the equation, estimates are that drug sales by the main suppliers in Colombia alone brought in $25 billion in profits.

Clearly, drugs are big business, and controlling drugs is difficult because of this. Most drug exports are controlled by powerful and wealthy crime syndicates that can pay for the best in protection, often controlling large tracts of land and paying off police and politicians.

The international trade in drugs mostly comes from poor nations to rich ones. The Andean nations of South America—primarily Colombia, Peru, and Bolivia—are the main suppliers of cocaine. Several Asian nations, including Pakistan and Thailand, are major suppliers of opium and heroin. And now Central Asia has become perhaps the largest supplier of opium and heroin. Opium is grown in the former Soviet republics of Kazakhstan, Kyrgyzstan, Uzbekistan, Tajikistan, and Turkmenistan, sent to Afghanistan where it is manufactured into heroin, and then sent on to Europe, Asia, and the U.S. This new trade has doubled the world's supply of opiates.

International and U.S. efforts to control the drug supply have largely failed, despite large sums of money spent, such as $12 billion in an Andean initiative against cocaine supply, because the profits are so enormous. Recently, the highly respected public prosecutor of Colombia, Gustavo de Grieff, suggested the government look into legalization. Although the Colombian government quickly disavowed his views, the incident illustrated the fundamental problem with the drug trade: as long as U.S. and other consumers demand drugs, drug dealers will find it profitable to supply them.

sent that steel to Japan and the U.S.) and made arrangements to provide electronic components for Japanese cars and goods. China decided to promote "market-socialism" and allow private farmers to grow and sell what they wanted (within boundaries) and allow private ownership of small factories and stores.

Meanwhile, the rest of the developing world was overdoing state control of industry and farming—and their people were suffering. The problem isn't as black and white as it sounds, however. Many of these socialist nations acted out of a desire to reduce poverty by sharing the wealth, capitalism seeming to encourage inequality.

The success of China and other Asian nations has now spawned similar efforts in Latin America, particularly in Brazil, Chile, and Argentina, as well as in some parts of Africa and the Middle East. So far, it seems to be working. It appears that *all* peoples have innate productive capacities. And hopefully, one day the term "developed world" will mean the entire world.

ACKNOWLEDGMENTS

A book of this scope and magnitude would have been impossible to produce without the help and support of many people. We especially would like to thank the following individuals for their assistance, useful input, hard work, and ready encouragement:

Marilyn Abraham, Becky Cabaza, Trish Todd, Aviva Goode, Gillian Speeth, Robin Rue, Beki, Mitch Kelly, Doris Farson, Harold Bannon, Phillip Mannering, Susan DuMois, Margaret Procter, Shawn Foley, Angela Vitale, Gypsy da Silva, Fred Chase, Chuck Antony, George Wen, Andrew Attaway, Rose Ann Ferrick, Fred Wiemer, Linda Roberts, Susan Johnson, and Barry Varela.

INDEX

Page numbers in *italics* refer to illustrations and maps.